France

	Red Bordeaux								
Vintage	Médoc/Graves		Pom/St–Em		Sauternes & sw		Graves & dry			
2009	7–10	♀	7–10	♀	8–10	♀	7–9	♀	8–9	♀
2008	6–9	♀	6–9	♀	6–7	♀	7–8	♀	7–8	♀
2007	5–7	♀	6–7	♀	8–9	♀	8–9	♀	6–8	♀
2006	7–8	♀	7–9	♀	8–9	♀	8–9	♀	6–8	♀
2005	9–10	♀	9–10	♀	8–10	♀	8–10	♀	8–9	♀
2004	7–8	♀	7–9	♀	5–7	♀	6–7	♀	6–8	♀
2003	5–9	♀	5–8	♀	7–8	♀	6–7	♀	6–7	♀
2002	6–8	♀	5–8	♀	7–8	♀	7–8	♀	7–8	♀
2001	6–8	♀	7–8	♀	8–10	♀	7–9	♀	6–8	♀
2000	8–10	♀	7–9	♀	6–8	♀	6–8	♀	8–10	♀
1999	5–7	♀	5–8	♀	6–9	♀	7–10	♀	6–8	♀
1998	5–8	♀	6–9	♀	5–8	♀	5–9	♀	7–9	♀
1997	5–7	♬	4–7	♬	7–9	♀	4–7	♀	7–9	♀
1996	6–8	♀	5–7	♀	7–9	♀	7–10	♀	8–10	♀
1995	7–9	♀	6–9	♀	6–8	♀	5–9	♀	6–9	♬
1994	5–8	♬	5–8	♬	4–6	♬	5–8	♀	6–9	♬
1993	4–6	♁	5–7	♬	2–5	♁	5–7	♬	6–8	♬
1992	3–5	♁	3–5	♁	3–5	♁	4–8	♬	5–7	♬
1991	3–7	♬	8–10	♬	8–10	♁	7–8	♬	7–9	♬

France continued

	Burgundy						Rhône			
Vintage	Côte d'Or red		Côte d'Or white		Chablis		Rhône (N)		Rhône (S)	
2009	7–10	♀	7–8	♀	7–8	♀	7–9	♀	7–8	♀
2008	7–9	♀	7–9	♀	7–9	♀	6–7	♀	5–7	♀
2007	7–8	♀	8–9	♀	8–9	♀	6–8	♀	7–8	♀
2006	7–8	♀	8–10	♀	8–9	♀	7–8	♀	7–9	♀
2005	7–9	♀	7–9	♀	7–9	♀	7–8	♀	6–8	♀
2004	6–7	♀	7–8	♀	7–8	♀	6–7	♀	6–7	♀
2003	6–7	♀	6–7	♬	6–7	♬	5–7	♀	6–8	♀
2002	7–8	♀	7–8	♀	7–8	♀	4–6	♀	5–5	♬
2001	6–8	♀	7–9	♬	6–8	♬	7–8	♀	7–9	♀
2000	7–8	♀	6–9	♬	7–9	♬	6–8	♀	7–9	♬
1999	7–10	♀	5–7	♬	5–8	♬	7–9	♀	6–9	♀
1998	5–8	♀	5–7	♬	7–8	♬	6–8	♀	7–9	♀
1997	5–8	♬	5–8	♬	7–9	♬	7–9	♀	5–8	♀
1996	6–8	♀	7–8	♬	5–10	♬	5–7	♬	4–6	♬

Beaujolais 09, 08, 07, 06. Crus will keep. **Mâcon–Villages** (white). Drink 09, 08, 07. **Loire** (Sweet Anjou and Touraine) best recent vintages: 09, 07, 05, 02, 97, 96, 93, 90, 89; Bourgueil, Chinon, Saumur–Champigny: 09, 06, 05, 04, 02, 00, 99. **Upper Loire** (Sancerre, Pouilly–Fumé): 09, 08, 07 **Muscadet** 09 DYA.

Hugh Johnson's Pocket Wine Book 2011

Edited and designed by Mitchell Beazley, an
imprint of Octopus Publishing Group Limited,
Endeavour House, 189 Shaftesbury Avenue,
London WC2 8JY

An Hachette Livre UK Company
www.hachettelivre.co.uk

Distributed in the USA and Canada by Octopus
Books USA: c/o Hachette Book Group USA,
237 Park Avenue, New York, NY 10017

www.octopusbooksusa.com

First edition published 1977
Revised editions published 1978, 1979, 1980,
1981, 1982, 1983, 1984, 1985, 1986, 1987, 1988,
1989, 1990, 1991, 1992, 1993, 1994, 1995,
1996, 1997, 1998, 1999, 2000, 2001, 2002
(twice), 2003, 2004, 2005, 2006 (twice), 2007,
2008, 2009, 2010

A CIP record for this book is available from
the British Library.

ISBN (UK): 978 1 845 33567 0
ISBN (US): 978 1 845 33552 6

General Editor **Margaret Rand**
Commissioning Editor **Hilary Lumsden**
Project Editor **Jo Wilson**
Proofreader **Jamie Ambrose**
Art Director **Pene Parker**
Deputy Art Director **Yasia Williams-Leedham**
Designer **Mark Kan**
Production Manager **Peter Hunt**
Printed and bound in China

Picture credits in page order

1 Alamy/Andrew Paterson; 3 Getty Images/Thomas Barwick; 4 Getty Images/4 Eyes
Photography; 6 Octopus Publishing Group/Adrian Pope; 305 courtesy Bodegas
Ysios; 306 Photolibrary/Daniel P Acevedo; 307 Iberimage/Heinz Hebeisen; 308
Fotolia/Laure SFG; 309 Photolibrary/FoodCollection; 310 Corbis/Newmann; 312
Alamy/Jordi Cami; 314 Corbis/Photolibrary; 316 Alamy/Martin Siepmann/
imagebroker; 318 right, 319 right Claes Lofgren/winepictures.com; 318 left, 319 left,
320 right Iberimage/Heinz Hebeisen; 320 left courtesy Compañía de Vinos
Telmo Rodriguez SL.

HUGH JOHNSON'S

POCKET WINE BOOK

GENERAL EDITOR
MARGARET RAND

2011

Acknowledgments

This store of detailed recommendations comes partly from my own notes and mainly from those of a great number of kind friends. Without the generous help and cooperation of innumerable winemakers, merchants and critics, I could not attempt it. I particularly want to thank the following for help with research or in the areas of their special knowledge:

Sarah Ahmed	Caroline Gilby MW	Margaret Rand
Helena Baker	Annie Kay	Daniel Rogov
Susie Barrie MW	Chandra Kurt	Ulrich Sautter
Nicolas Belfrage MW	James Lawther MW	Eleonora Scholes
Philipp Blom	Konstantinos Lazarakis MW	Stephen Skelton MW
Jim Budd	John Livingstone- Learmonth	Paul Strang
Michael Cooper		Marguerite Thomas
Terry Copeland	Campbell Mattinson	Larry Walker
Michael Edwards	Adam Montefiore	Simon Woods
Sarah Jane Evans MW	Jasper Morris MW	Philip van Zyl
Rosemary George MW	Shirley Nelson	

Contents

Hugh Johnson Agenda 2011	6
How to use this book	10
Vintage report 2009	11
A closer look at 2008	12
If you like this, try this...	13
Grape varieties	15
Wine & food	20
France	32
Châteaux of Bordeaux	84
Italy	108
Germany	140
Spain & Portugal	162
Port, Sherry & Madeira	184
Switzerland	193
Austria	198
England & Wales	206
Central & Southeast Europe	207
Hungary, Bulgaria, Slovenia, Croatia, Bosnia &	
Herzegovina, Serbia, Montenegro, Macedonia,	
The Czech Republic & Slovakia, Romania, Malta	
Greece	221
North Africa & Eastern Mediterranean	225
N Africa, Cyprus, Israel, Lebanon, Turkey	
Asia & Old Russian Empire	229
North America	231
California	232
The Pacific Northwest	248
East of the Rockies	254
The Southwest	257
Canada	259
South America	260
Chile, Argentina, Other South American wines	
Australia	269
New Zealand	283
South Africa	293
The Reinvention of Spain	305

Front endpaper: Quick-reference vintage charts

Back endpaper: A little learning/the right temperature

Agenda 2011

Crunch, recession: whatever you call it, it focuses the mind on value. The wine industry was riding high when trouble struck. Suddenly its loyal customers had different priorities. The high-rollers (there were still some) saw blue-chip wines as a good store of value and kept buying all they could get. The low-rollers (that's us) asked ourselves what we really wanted from a bottle of wine, and who was providing it for the least money.

There were some obvious excesses that soon felt the draught: the affectation of bottles weighing a kilo, for example, suddenly looked plain vulgar. The extravagance of new French barrels for everything came into question. The idea even dawned on some winemakers that customers might drink more of their wine if its alcohol didn't send them straight to sleep. These are not new topics. Straws were in the wind. Suddenly they became relevant.

What we really want, and who is providing it, remains the open question. For years we have enjoyed the advances of our relatively new suppliers, happy to think that they were putting pressure on our old ones, driving prices down and quality up.

First it was Australia and California, then South America and New Zealand, now South Africa and – who's next? We see them all at first as bargain alternatives, mainly to France. We enjoy their sunny, full-fruit flavours, but we're not very happy when they start trading up. Australia, with an odd mix of breathtaking hubris and big-company stupidity, fell in step with the supermarkets, almost giving away less and less interesting wines. Their brewers (is it jealousy?)

have strangled most of their greatest talents. Result:
an almost bankrupt industry.

California has been delighted to play for its home
crowd, sadly drifting into styles of wine no one else
wants very much. South America took a different
approach: the crowd is us – there is no vast home
market. Chilean and Argentina started with good
vineyards, most of the right grapes and no *idée fixe*.
It leaves them open – sometimes too open – to passing
fashions, but the checks and balances of a world
market have, on the whole, brought out their best
points. Hubris? There's a bit of that, but realism rules.

How have the Kiwis overtaken the Aussies? In
esteem, in price, in street cred they have stormed
ahead – even in Australia, where Kiwi Sauvignon Blanc
is now the people's choice over home-grown whites.
The climate of South Island certainly has something
to do with it: that and the Clean Green Land image.
Their full-frontal Pinot Noir seemed to have cracked
an insoluble riddle: how to get the burgundy taste
in sensible quantities. I wonder how long they can
sustain such healthy prices.

South Africa, last off the grid, has not caught up
quite as fast as you might expect – in fashion terms,
that is. In quality its top wines are level with any
from the New World. In value it has its nose ahead.

So where does that put Europe? In a very different
situation: Europe has no (or hardly any) massive
conglomerates. In France, Italy, Spain, Germany,
Austria, everywhere it is down to the individual,
the family, sometimes the cooperative, to find a level
it can sustain. Mass-marketing, if it has been tried,
has flopped. You could say that more personality,
tighter definition, is Europe's way forward.

This year, in our colour supplement at the back
of the book, we highlight Spain. Spain has changed
more, and raised its game more, than any of the "New"
wine countries in the past few years. So many of its

best wines, in fact, are without precedent that new/old comparisons are hard to make. Go to it with an open mind and you'll be amazed.

Has Italy raised its game in the same way? No, but in a very different, wholly Italian way with the emphasis on what we would probably called "heritage". The Italian starting point is always the region, its traditions, its grape varieties, its way of doing things. Then it's the family. Then it's the individual, in low gear and high revs. The results are wines you have to experience to understand. What is mainstream in Italy? Sangiovese in Tuscany, Nebbiolo in Piedmont, Pinot Grigio in the northeast, the Valpolicella/Soave axis at Verona; of course, the top-euro Cabernets of Bolgheri and the Tuscan coast. Where should we look for value? In all the gaps this pattern leaves, eg. the coastal strips, the Appenine valleys with a local grape, and creative Italians (that's all of them).

Then there's the Riesling Resurgence, in which you have to include all the aromatic white wines of Germany and Austria. Yes, Grüner Veltliner is there, too, and the more and more realistic offerings of Switzerland, Hungary, central Europe and, for that matter, Greece. If unfamiliar names are enough to put you off, you'll be missing many treats.

If more personality and tighter definition are the key, the leader, once more, is France. Compare the red burgundies of today with their equivalents of a few years ago. A different drink: sappy, vital, resonant, a higher voltage with every vintage. Look at the reds of the Rhône today, with imitators all over the world. Have you tasted the Sauvignons and Chenins from the Loire Valley lately? Have you realized Bordeaux hasn't had a duff vintage in the last ten?

Forget the thousand-a-bottle superstars that get everybody talking, and saying France is unaffordable. Set your sights at, say, the price of a good chicken per bottle. (Henri IV must have had a phrase for it.) Take half a dozen crisp notes anywhere in the world of wine these days and you'll come home licking your lips.

Readers who have been here before will know that this book doesn't do wine-by-wine judgments. No scores. The one-to-four-star code is my take on the winery, district or brand as a presence in the market. As the decoder on the front flap makes clear, four stars does not mean the world's best wine; it means "grand, prestigious, expensive" – with the inference that it might also be pretentious and not worth the money. Three stars means "well-known, highly reputed".

In other words I am telling you the reputation and standing of the wine or winery – not the actual quality of what is in a given bottle. Value for money puts the stars in red. Yes, a "prestigious, expensive" wine can also be value for money, just as a one-star "everyday-quality" one can be a bargain. You build up a picture with the information I give and the vintages cited (again, read the colour code) and you make your choice.

It will have dawned on even casual visitors to my pages that this can't be one man's work, however diligent. My collaborators, many of them friends of many years, are listed on page 4. To them and to Margaret Rand, who edits us all, I raise my glass.

The memory lingers on...
In this edition I have indicated within entries 200 or so of the wines I remember having especially (and in some cases regularly) enjoyed over the past 12 months (that is, early 2009–10). It can be no guide to the future, but with so many alternatives on offer one has to start somewhere, and fragrant memories seem the best place. Lest anyone mistake these for "The World's 200 Best Wines", let me restate my fixed position: taste is personal. I like what I like – and so should you. The wines are indicated within entries in this way: *Clos de Chênes*.

How to use this book

The top line of most entries consists of the following information:

Aglianico del Vulture Bas | r dr (s/sw sp) | ★★★ | 96' 97 98 99' 00 01' 02 (03)

(with circled numbers ❶ ❷ ❸ ❹ marking parts of the line)

❶ Wine name and the region the wine comes from.

❷ Whether it is red, rosé or white (or brown/amber), dry, sweet or
sparkling, or several of these (and which is most important):

r	red
p	rosé
w	white
br	brown
dr	dry*
sw	sweet
s/sw	semi-sweet
sp	sparkling

( ) brackets here denote a less important wine
* assume wine is dry when **dr** or **sw** are not indicated

❸ Its general standing as to quality: a necessarily rough-and-ready
guide based on its current reputation as reflected in its prices:

★	plain, everyday quality
★★	above average
★★★	well known, highly reputed
★★★★	grand, prestigious, expensive

So much is more or less objective. Additionally there is a subjective rating:

★ etc   Stars are coloured for any wine which in my experience is usually
especially good within its price range. There are good everyday wines
as well as good luxury wines. This system helps you find them.

❹ Vintage information: which of the recent vintages can be recommended; of
these, which are ready to drink this year, and which will probably improve with
keeping. Your choice for current drinking should be one of the vintage years
printed in bold type. Buy light-type years for further maturing.

00 etc   recommended years that may be currently available
96' etc   vintage regarded as particularly successful for the property
in question
97 etc   years in bold should be ready for drinking (those not in bold
will benefit from keeping)
98 etc   vintages in colour are those recommended as first choice for
drinking in 2010. (See also Bordeaux introduction, p.84.)
(02) etc   provisional rating

The German vintages work on a different principle again: see p.144.

Other abbreviations

DYA   drink the youngest available
NV   vintage not normally shown on label; in Champagne,
means a blend of several vintages for continuity
CHABLIS properties, areas or terms cross-referred within the section
Châteaux Aiguilloux type so styled within entries indicates wine
(mid '09–2010) especially enjoyed by Hugh Johnson

Vintage report 2009

It wasn't the easiest of years for people who make or sell wine. There was gloom in California and Champagne, and even worse gloom in Australia, which probably had the most to be gloomy about, particularly once the bush fires started. What we needed was a great vintage to cheer us up, to give us a reason to start buying wine again – and in some regions, nature obliged. Australia produced some terrific wines, even in Victoria and South Australia, where ten days of roasting heat caused vines to shut down. Western Australia and Tasmania escaped these extremes. Smoke taint will be a problem in some areas, but vigilant producers will keep these wines away from the market.

Things were a lot calmer in New Zealand: lovely aromas and good balance are the result. In South Africa, February heat threw some of the reds off-balance by sending the alcohol up, but this is not a universal problem. Nor is smoke taint, though it exists this year – South Africa had its own bush fires in Stellenbosch and elsewhere.

But the big news of the year was, inevitably, Bordeaux. The vintage of the century? Another vintage of the century? The hype was beginning before the wines were even in barrel, causing many potential buyers to wonder if they should hold off from the 2008s and wait. In Burgundy the same applied, with some buyers ignoring the delicious 2008s in favour of future delights. This could be to the benefit of canny shoppers later. And if they're too expensive, there's the Rhône to consider: Syrah and Mourvèdre seem to have done particularly well.

In Champagne it was a pretty scary year, with thunder, rain and hail in spring and early summer, only settling into hot sunshine in mid-August. But that was enough to produce some lovely Pinot Noir, and there will certainly be vintage wines declared.

In the Loire alcohol levels in many wines are on the high side; in Spain alcohol can be a problem, too, and the cooler areas seem to have the best balance. Acidity generally is lower than in 2008. Rías Baixas and Rueda, particularly, in the latter, Verdejo, are good bets for whites; Rioja is a good bet for reds, where the alcohol produced by a hot summer was calmed by a few days of rain in September.

The Douro Valley could have done with that: it hasn't had much rain for three years. Generally balance is good for Portuguese table wines this year, though it was certainly a hot year.

Italy seems to have produced some terrific wines: Chianti looks rich and deep and aromatic, and in Brunello, recovering from the Brunellogate scandal, colours might well be a little lighter in some quarters, following a vote by the producers to exclude all varieties other than Sangiovese from the wine. (You thought that was the law before? Quite.) In the Veneto there'll be less Amarone than in the record 2008 vintage, largely due to a ruling that limits to 50 per cent the quantity of grapes that a producer can set aside for drying. The better producers, with hillside vineyards, certainly had the quality to dry more than this in 2009; lesser producers on the plains would dry far less if quality were their objective.

In California the stars of the year are some outstanding Cabernet Sauvignons and Zinfandels: the Cabernet was the strongest survivor of the storms that hit northern California in mid-October.

And England? Best vintage ever, no less. Odd, really: at the time it felt like just a run-of-the-mill English summer. There had to be some good news.

A closer look at 2008

In France they shook their heads and said, "Another Sarkozy summer..." – the joke being that they hadn't had a decent summer since they changed president. Because it wasn't much of a year, really: cool and damp on the whole, with mildew, oidium and rot attacking the grapes. Getting all three of those in the same year is more than any grower deserves.

And yet the results are remarkably good. Again (another Sarkozy factor?) a warm September saved the harvest. In Burgundy the Pinots are delicious: pure, precise and aromatic. The whites, too, are mineral and seductive, and Chablis is classic. Some growers lost all or most of their crop, however: 2008 sorted out the ultra-careful growers from the only averagely careful. As one producer said, "If you missed one treatment, you missed everything." Biodynamicists came out of it well, provided they knew what they were doing: beginners found it a very testing year. The difference between *grands crus*, *premiers crus* and *village* wines is strongly marked this year; the quality of the terroir shows, as well as the quality of the producer.

They picked late in both Burgundy and Bordeaux – an old-fashioned vintage that stretched well into October. In Sauternes they were still picking in November; and the results were, again, surprising. Is it a great year in Bordeaux? No, but it's a very good one. The Right Bank wines are aromatic, bright and rich, the Left Bank ones, particularly from St-Julien, are pure and vibrant. But it's a year to stick to the best names. The most careful growers, here as elsewhere, had the greatest success.

The same applies in the Loire, where balance and precision are the key to the vintage. Dry Chenins are superb, but hopes of a great sweet vintage were sabotaged by October rain. Sancerre is minerally and focused, and tasting like every penny of its now rather exalted price. The reds combine richness and depth with aroma: these are surely the ideal red wines for so many occasions.

Head over to Spain and once more the picture is one of a cool summer and a late harvest. Again, this means wines with balance and aroma, and not too much alcohol – just the sort of wines that we want. As in so many spots in Europe the spring was rainy and rot was a problem; careful growers came off best.

Balance is the shape of things in Austria, too: the rain and the cool conditions were tough on the growers, but the wines have verve and zing, and seem free of the excess alcohol that can mar them when producers try too hard. Will this style return with the heat of 2009? We shall see.

In Portugal the wines are looking stylish and at ease with themselves, as though the whole year had been a picnic from beginning to end – which it never is. There will be some single-quinta port declarations up in the Douro, and in table wines across the country, balance and aroma are to the fore. In Germany the wines are light but balanced: wines in the classic mould, probably for fairly early drinking. It's not a year for late-harvest wines.

Elsewhere, it's as mixed or even more so. Ripeness could be a problem in California, and New Zealand is distinctly patchy. In Australia Hunter reds were often a washout – Tyrrells didn't bottle any 2008 reds at all – a loss of about 20,000 cases to the winery. "The skins collapsed," said Bruce Tyrrell. But the whites were good, and Western Australia had a splendid year.

If you like this, try this...

One of the greatest pleasures for a wine-lover has to be the discovery of a new style of wine. The intention of this section is to point you in the right direction if you love to try something new. It's not intended to be exhaustive, but rather a handful of ideas that will, I hope, spark off more ideas – and the rest of the book will tell you what to look for next.

If you like Viognier, try Albariño
Albariño is the name of both the grape and the aromatic white wine it produces almost exclusively in Galicia, northwest Spain. At its best, like Viognier, Albariño smells of spiced white peaches. Where it differs from its Rhône counterpart is in its tongue-tingling acidity and lightness of touch. Also unlike Viognier, which is now grown all over the world, very little of this high-quality variety is grown outside its native home and, more particularly, the tiny region of Rías Baixas. Albariño is delicious with seafood and in Spain it provides the perfect foil for local dishes like tender chunks of octopus thick with olive oil, served with paprika potatoes.

If you like Pouilly Fumé, try Assyrtiko from Santorini
The two key characteristics of a great Pouilly Fumé are intense minerality and vibrant acidity. In a fine example of Assyrtiko from Santorini you'll find exactly those qualities. Where Assyrtiko differs somewhat is in its flavour profile, which tends to be broader and richer than that of Pouilly Fumé. Think lemon tart and dried wild herbs, rather than cut grass and wet pebbles. Assyrtiko wines are also sometimes oaked, which makes them a wonderful match for rich, creamy seafood dishes that would overwhelm the delicate flavours of a fine Pouilly Fumé.

If you like New Zealand Sauvignon Blanc, try English Bacchus
In recent years the world has gone mad for the bright, punchy flavours of New Zealand Sauvignon Blanc. If you're looking for refreshing flavour and tongue-tingling acidity, along with an ability to stand up to the vibrant flavours of today's fashionable Fusion food, these wines are hard to beat. Bacchus is more floral than Sauvignon Blanc and doesn't have quite the same racy acidity, but a well-made example will have many of the same crunchy, zippy flavours that make New Zealand Sauvignon Blanc so attractively moreish.

If you like Pinot Grigio, try Grüner Veltliner
It is easy to see why Pinot Grigio has proved so popular with scores of white wine drinkers the world over. It's a risk-free option that offers a light to medium-bodied, easy-drinking white with herbal aromas, fresh acidity and no oak. And Grüner Veltliner? As well as soft, herbal flavours and lovely acidity, Grüner Veltliner wines have an engaging note of white pepper and a lifted, spicy finish.

If you like unwooded Chardonnay, try Kerner
Although Kerner tastes quite different from unwooded Chardonnay, it is a fantastic, off-beat option if you're looking for a wine to perform a similar role. Originally a German crossing of Trollinger and Riesling, today's best examples of Kerner come from Alto Adige in the far north of Italy. Here the vine produces wines that offer a food-friendly combination of tangy acidity, intense herbal flavours and layers of honeyed roundness. Richer

than good Chablis and more vibrant than a fruit-driven New World Chardonnay, a well-made Italian Kerner is a beautifully refreshing wine that is a match for a huge variety of dishes.

If you like white burgundy, try white Roussillon
It would be foolish to pretend that any white wine in the world can give the same flavour as top white burgundy. There are wines, however, that offer at least some of the same thrilling grip, intensity, focus and complexity as Burgundy's best whites. In the north of Roussillon the wild terrain yields steely, nutty white wines of incredible individuality and flair. The best Roussillon whites may not have the finesse of fine burgundy but they certainly share the same mouthfilling vibrancy and seductive appeal.

If you like Pauillac, try Cafayate Tannat, Argentina
The finest wines of Pauillac are known for their power, their velvety dark fruit and their superb tannic structure. The tightly woven tannins are what make the best wines of Pauillac so compelling for many red wine drinkers and, although it may be hard to believe the same tannic finesse can be found in the New World, Argentina is now producing some beautifully structured, European-style wines from the Tannat variety, especially those from Cafayate: they frequently display greater finesse than many Uruguayan examples and are certainly less expensive than a decent Pauillac.

If you like Hermitage, try coastal Chilean Syrah
Chile has built its reputation on red wines made from Merlot and, to some extent, Cabernet Sauvignon. Syrah was first planted less than 20 years ago, and for most people Chile is the last country they would think of when looking for a wine to rival the fabulous Syrahs of the Northern Rhône. But when planted in cool, coastal locations in Chile, Syrah can produce wines with that same captivating combination of inky dark fruit, crushed black pepper, fine-grained tannins and refreshing acidity. They usually contain a touch more new oak and alcohol than you'll find in Hermitage, but the complexity of the best examples is seriously impressive.

If you like Loire Cabernet Franc, try Mencía
The characteristics that Mencía and Loire Cabernet Franc share are fine, graphite-edged tannins and a lifted, refreshing mouthfeel. The blackberry fruit of Mencía is usually a little richer than that found in a good Bourgueil or Chinon, but the leafy note to the fruit of both varieties is compellingly similar. Mencía is newly fashionable in Spain and it is currently grown in the region of Bierzo by some top producers. What makes it so appealing in an age of heavy, overextracted reds is its ability to complement almost all red-meat dishes, thanks to its fresh acidity and fine-grained tannins.

If you like Châteauneuf-du-Pape, try South Australian Grenache
The extraordinary fame and popularity of Châteauneuf-du-Pape is undoubtedly due in large part to its broad flavours of ripe red fruit, its generous alcohol and its soft, spicy tannins. Châteauneuf-du-Pape offers a big mouthful of heart-warming, supple and easy-to-enjoy red wine. Made from one of the main varieties used in the Southern Rhône, South Australian Grenache has many of the same qualities. There's a little more fruit and less of the meaty, savoury, black pepper notes found in the best wines of Châteauneuf-du-Pape, but the fleshy warmth of both wines is similar, as is their compatibility with rustic, wintery food.

Grape varieties

I n the past two decades a radical change has come about in all except
the most long-established wine countries: the names of a handful of
grape varieties have become the ready reference to wine. In senior wine
countries, above all France and Italy, more complex traditions prevail.
All wine of old prestige is known by its origin, more or less narrowly
defined – not just the particular fruit-juice that fermented.

For the present the two notions are in rivalry. Eventually the primacy
of place over fruit will become obvious, at least for wines of quality. But for
now, for most people, grape tastes are the easy reference-point – despite
the fact that they are often confused by the added taste of oak. If grape
flavours were really all that mattered, this would be a very short book.

But of course they do matter, and a knowledge of them both guides
you to flavours you enjoy and helps comparisons between regions.
Hence the originally Californian term "varietal wine", meaning, in
principle, from one grape variety.

At least seven varieties – Cabernet Sauvignon, Pinot Noir, Riesling,
Sauvignon Blanc, Chardonnay, Gewurztraminer and Muscat – taste and
smell distinct and memorable enough to form international categories
of wine. To these you can add Merlot, Malbec, Syrah, Sémillon, Chenin
Blanc, Pinots Blanc and Gris, Sylvaner, Viognier, Nebbiolo, Sangiovese,
Tempranillo. The following are the best and/or most popular wine grapes.

Grapes for red wine

Agiorgitiko (St George) Versatile Greek (Nemea) variety with juicy damson
fruit and velvety tannins. Sufficient structure for serious ageing.

Aglianico Southern Italian, dark, deep and fashionable.

Baga Bairrada grape. Dark and tannic. Great potential but hard to grow.

Barbera Widely grown in Italy, at its best in Piedmont, giving dark, fruity, often
sharp wine. Fashionable in California and Australia; promising in Argentina.

Blaufränkisch Mostly Austrian; can be light and juicy but at best (in Burgenland)
a considerable red. LEMBERGER in Germany, KÉKFRANKOS in Hungary.

Brunello Alias for SANGIOVESE, splendid at Montalcino.

Cabernet Franc, alias Bouchet (Cab Fr) The lesser of two sorts of Cabernet grown
in Bordeaux but dominant (as "Bouchet") in St-Emilion. The Cabernet of the
Loire, making Chinon, Saumur-Champigny and rosé. Used for blending with
CAB SAUV, etc., or alone, in California, Australia and South Africa.

Cabernet Sauvignon (Cab Sauv) Grape of great character: spicy, herby, tannic,
with characteristic blackcurrant aroma. The first grape of the Médoc; also
makes most of the best California, South American, East European reds.
Vies with Shiraz in Australia. Its wine almost always needs ageing; usually
benefits from blending with eg. MERLOT, CAB FR, SYRAH, TEMPRANILLO, SANGIOVESE
etc. Makes aromatic rosé.

Cannonau GRENACHE in its Sardinian manifestation; can be very fine, potent.

Carignan In decline in France. Low-yielding old vines can be v.gd; best: Corbières.
Otherwise dull but harmless. Common in North Africa, Spain and California.

Carmenère An old Bordeaux variety that is now a star, rich and deep, in Chile.
Bordeaux is looking at it again.

Cinsault/Cinsaut A staple of southern France, v. gd if low-yielding, wine-lake
stuff if not. Makes good rosé. One of the parents of PINOTAGE.

Dolcetto Source of soft, seductive dry red in Piedmont. Now high fashion.

Gamay The Beaujolais grape: light, very fragrant wines, at their best young.

Makes even lighter wine in the Loire Valley, in central France, and in Switzerland and Savoie. Known as "Napa Gamay" in California.

Grenache, alias Garnacha, Cannonau Becoming ultra-fashionable with *terroiristes*, who admire the way it expresses its site. Also good for rosé and *vin doux naturel* – especially in the South of France, Spain and California – but also the mainstay of beefy Priorato. Old-vine versions are prized in South Australia. Usually blended with other varieties.

Grignolino Makes one of the good everyday table wines of Piedmont.

Kadarka, alias Gamza Makes healthy, sound, agreeable reds in East Europe.

Kékfrankos Hungarian BLAUFRÄNKISCH; similar lightish reds.

Lambrusco Productive grape of the lower Po valley, giving quintessentially Italian, cheerful, sweet and fizzy red.

Lemberger See BLAUFRÄNKISCH. Württemberg's red.

Malbec, alias Côt Minor in Bordeaux, major in Cahors (alias Auxerrois) and the star in Argentina. Dark, dense, tannic wine capable of real quality. High-altitude versions in Argentina are the bee's knees.

Mencía Making waves in Spain with fresh, aromatic wines.

Merlot The grape behind the great fragrant and plummy wines of Pomerol and (with CAB FR) St-Emilion, an important element in Médoc reds, soft and strong (and à la mode) in California, Washington, Chile, Australia. Lighter but often good in north Italy, Italian Switzerland, Slovenia, Argentina, South Africa, New Zealand, etc. Perhaps too adaptable for its own good: can be very dull indeed.

Montepulciano A good central-eastern Italian grape, and a Tuscan town.

Morellino Alias for SANGIOVESE in Scansano, southern Tuscany.

Mourvèdre, alias Mataro A star of southern France and Australia and, as Monastrell, Spain. Excellent dark, aromatic, tannic grape, gd for blending. Enjoying new interest in, for example, South Australia and California.

Nebbiolo, alias Spanna and Chiavennasca One of Italy's best red grapes; makes Barolo, Barbaresco, Gattinara and Valtellina. Intense, nobly fruity, perfumed wine but very tannic: improves for years.

Negroamaro Dark, pungent grape of southern Italy. Quality can be excellent.

Nerello Mascalese Characterful Sicilian grape, good acidity, good quality.

Periquita Ubiquitous in Portugal for firm-flavoured reds. Often blended with CAB SAUV and also known as Castelão.

Petit Verdot Excellent but awkward Médoc grape, now increasingly planted in Cabernet areas worldwide for extra fragrance.

Pinot Noir (Pinot N) The glory of Burgundy's Côte d'Or, with scent, flavour and texture that are unmatched anywhere. Makes light wines rarely of much distinction in Switzerland and Hungary. Improving in Germany and Austria. But now also splendid results in California's Sonoma, Carneros and Central Coast, as well as Oregon, Ontario, Yarra Valley, Adelaide Hills, Tasmania, New Zealand's South Island (Central Otego) and South Africa's Walker Bay.

Pinotage Singular South African grape (PINOT N X CINSAUT). Can be very fruity and can age interestingly, but often jammy. Good rosé.

Primitivo Southern Italian grape making big, rustic wines, now fashionable because genetically identical to ZIN.

Refosco In northeast Italy possibly a synonym for Mondeuse of Savoie. Deep, flavoursome and age-worthy wines, especially in warmer climates.

Sagrantino Italian grape found in Umbria for powerful, cherry-flavoured wines.

Sangiovese (or Sangioveto) Main red grape of Chianti and much of central Italy. Aliases include BRUNELLO and MORELLINO. Interesting in Australia.

Saperavi Makes good, sharp, very long-lived wine in Georgia, Ukraine, etc. Blends very well with CAB SAUV (eg. in Moldova).

Spätburgunder German for PINOT N. Quality is variable, seldom wildly exciting.

St-Laurent Dark, smooth and full-flavoured Austrian specialty. Also in the Pfalz.

Syrah, alias Shiraz The great Rhône red grape: tannic, purple, peppery wine that matures superbly. Important as Shiraz in Australia, and under either name in California, Washington State, South Africa, Chile and elsewhere.

Tannat Raspberry-perfumed, highly tannic force behind Madiran, Tursan and other firm reds from southwest France. Also rosé. Now the star of Uruguay.

Tempranillo Aromatic, fine Rioja grape, called Ull de Llebre in Catalonia, Cencibel in La Mancha, Tinto Fino in Ribera del Duero, Tinta Roriz in Douro, Aragonez in southern Portugal. Now Australia, too. Very fashionable; elegant in cool climates, beefy in warm. Early ripening.

Touriga Nacional Top port grape grown in the Douro Valley. Also makes full-bodied reds in south Portugal.

Zinfandel (Zin) Fruity, adaptable grape of California (though identical to PRIMITIVO) with blackcurrant-like, and sometimes metallic, flavour. Can be structured and gloriously lush, but also makes "blush" white wine.

Zweigelt Popular in Austria for aromatic, dark, supple wines.

Grapes for white wine

Airén Anonymous grape of La Mancha, Spain: fresh if made well.

Albariño The Spanish name for north Portugal's Alvarinho, making excellent fresh and fragrant wine in Galicia. Both fashionable and expensive in Spain.

Aligoté Burgundy's second-rank white grape. Crisp (often sharp) wine needs drinking in 1–3 years. Perfect for mixing with cassis (blackcurrant liqueur) to make Kir. Widely planted in East Europe, especially Russia.

Arinto White central Portuguese grape for crisp, fragrant dry whites.

Arneis Aromatic, high-priced grape, DOC in Roero, Piedmont.

Bourboulenc This and the rare Rolle make some of the Midi's best wines.

Bual Makes top-quality sweet Madeira wines, not quite so rich as Malmsey.

Chardonnay (Chard) The white grape of Burgundy and Champagne, now ubiquitous worldwide, partly because it is one of the easiest to grow and vinify. The fashion for overoaked butterscotch versions now thankfully over.

Chasselas Prolific early ripening grape with little aroma, mainly grown for eating. AKA Fendant in Switzerland (where it is supreme), Gutedel in Germany.

Chenin Blanc (Chenin Bl) Great white grape of the middle Loire (Vouvray, Layon, etc). Wine can be dry or sweet (or very sweet), but with plenty of acidity. Bulk wine in California, but increasingly serious in South Africa.

Clairette A low-acid grape, part of many southern French blends.

Colombard Slightly fruity, nicely sharp grape, makes everyday wine in South Africa, California and southwest France. Often blended.

Falanghina Ancient grape of Campanian hills revived to make excellent dense, aromatic dry whites.

Fiano High-quality grape giving peachy, spicy wine in Campania, S Italy.

Folle Blanche High acid/little flavour make this ideal for brandy. Called Gros Plant in Brittany, Picpoul in Armagnac. Also respectable in California.

Furmint A grape of great character: the trademark of Hungary, both as the principal grape in Tokáji and as vivid, vigorous table wine with an appley flavour. Called Sipon in Slovenia. Some grown in Austria.

Garganega Best grape in the Soave blend. Top wines, esp sweet ones, age well.

Gewurztraminer, alias Traminer (Gewurz) One of the most pungent grapes, spicy with aromas such as rose petals and grapefruit. Wines are often rich and soft, even when fully dry. Best in Alsace; also good in Germany (Gewürztraminer), east Europe, Australia, California, the Pacific Northwest and New Zealand.

Glera Uncharismatic new name for the Prosecco vine: Prosecco is now only a wine, no longer a grape.

Grauburgunder See PINOT GR.

Grechetto or Greco Ancient grape of central and south Italy noted for the vitality and stylishness of its wine.

Grüner Veltliner Austria's signature grape, making everything from fresh, inexpensive young wines to serious, concentrated, single-site versions. The best can age well.

Hárslevelü Other main grape of Tokáji (with FURMINT). Adds softness and body.

Kéknyelü Low-yielding, flavourful grape giving one of Hungary's best whites. Has the potential for fieriness and spice. To be watched.

Kerner Quite successful German crossing. Early ripening, flowery (but often too blatant) wine with good acidity.

Loureiro The best and most fragrant Vinho Verde variety in Portugal.

Macabeo The workhorse white grape of north Spain, widespread in Rioja (alias VIURA) and in Catalan cava country. Good quality potential.

Malvasia A family of grapes rather than a single variety, found all over Italy and Iberia. May be red, white, or pink. Usually plump, soft wine. Malvoisie in France is unrelated.

Marsanne Principal white grape (with ROUSSANNE) of the northern Rhône (eg. in Hermitage, St-Joseph, St-Péray). Also good in Australia, California, and (as Ermitage Blanc) the Valais. Soft, full wines that age very well.

Moschofilero Good, aromatic pink Greek grape. Makes white or rosé wine.

Müller-Thurgau (Müller-T) Soft, aromatic wines for drinking young. Makes good sweet wines but usually dull, often coarse, dry ones. Should have no place in top vineyards.

Muscadelle Adds aroma to white Bordeaux, esp Sauternes. In Victoria it is used (with MUSCAT, to which it is unrelated) for Rutherglen Muscat.

Muscadet, alias Melon de Bourgogne Makes light, refreshing, very dry wines with a seaside tang around Nantes in Brittany.

Muscat (Many varieties; the best is Muscat Blanc à Petits Grains.) Widely grown, easily recognized, pungent grapes, mostly made into perfumed sweet wines, often fortified (as in France's *vins doux naturels*). Superb in Australia. The third element in Tokáji Aszú. Rarely (eg. Alsace) made dry.

Palomino, alias Listán Great for sherry; of local appeal (on a hot day) for table wine.

Pedro Ximénez, alias PX Makes sweet sherry under its own name, and used in Montilla and Málaga. Also grown in Argentina, the Canaries, Australia, California and South Africa.

Petit (and Gros) Manseng The secret weapon of the French Basque country: vital for Jurançon; increasingly blended elsewhere in the southwest.

Pinot Blanc (Pinot Bl) A cousin of PINOT N, similar to but milder than CHARD: light, fresh, fruity, not aromatic, to drink young. Good for Italian *spumante*. Grown in Alsace, northern Italy, south Germany and eastern Europe. Weissburgunder in Germany.

Pinot Gris (Pinot Gr) Light and fashionable as Pinot Grigio in northern Italy, even for rosé; best in Alsace for full-bodied whites with a certain spicy style. In Germany can be alias Ruländer (sweet) or GRAUBURGUNDER (dry). Also found in Hungary, Slovenia, Canada, Oregon, New Zealand...

Pinot Noir (Pinot N) Superlative black grape used in Champagne and elsewhere (eg. California, Australia) for white, sparkling, or very pale-pink *vin gris*.

Prosecco See GLERA.

Riesling (Ries) Making its re-entrance on the world stage. Riesling stands level with CHARD as the world's best white wine grape, though diametrically opposite in style. CHARD gives full-bodied but aromatically discreet wines; Riesling offers a range from steely to voluptuous, always positively perfumed, and with more ageing potential than CHARD. Germany makes the greatest Riesling in all styles. Its popularity is being revived in South Australia, where this cool-climate grape does its best to ape CHARD. Holding the middle ground, with forceful but still steely wines, is Austria, while lovers of light and fragrant, often piercingly refreshing Rieslings have the Mosel as their exclusive playground. Also grown in Alsace (nowhere else in France), the Pacific Northwest, Ontario, California, New Zealand and South Africa.

Roussanne Rhône grape of finesse, now popping up in California and Australia. Can age well.

Sauvignon Blanc (Sauv Bl) Makes distinctive aromatic, grassy wines, pungent in New Zealand, often minerally in Sancerre, riper in Australia; good in Rueda, Austria, north Italy, Chile's Casablanca Valley and South Africa. Blended with Semillon in Bordeaux. Can be austere or buxom (or indeed nauseating).

Savagnin The grape of *vin jaune* of Savoie: related to Traminer?

Scheurebe Spicy-flavoured German RIES X SILVANER (possibly), very successful in Pfalz, especially for Auslese. Can be weedy: must be very ripe to be good.

Sémillon (Sem) Contributes the lusciousness to Sauternes and increasingly important for Graves and other dry white Bordeaux. Grassy if not fully ripe, but can make soft dry wine of great ageing potential. Superb in Australia; New Zealand and South Africa promising.

Sercial Makes the driest Madeira (where myth used to identify it with RIES).

Seyval Blanc (Seyval Bl) French-made hybrid of French and American vines. Very hardy and attractively fruity. Popular and reasonably successful in eastern States and England but dogmatically banned by EU from "quality" wines.

Silvaner, alias Sylvaner Germany's former workhorse grape, can be excellent in Franken, Rheinhessen, Pfalz. Very good (and powerful) as Johannisberg in the Valais, Switzerland.

Tocai Friulano North Italian grape with a flavour best described as "subtle". Now to be called plain Friulano.

Torrontés Strongly aromatic, MUSCAT-like Argentine specialty, usually dry.

Trebbiano Important but mediocre grape of central Italy (Orvieto, Soave, etc.). Also grown in southern France as Ugni Blanc, and Cognac as St-Emilion. Mostly thin, bland wine; needs blending (and more careful growing).

Ugni Blanc (Ugni Bl) See TREBBIANO.

Verdejo The grape of Rueda in Castile, potentially fine and long-lived.

Verdelho Great quality in Australia, and in Spain as Godello: probably Spain's best white grape. Rare but good (and medium-sweet) in Madeira.

Verdicchio Potentially good dry wine in central-eastern Italy.

Vermentino Italian, sprightly with satisfying texture and ageing capacity.

Vernaccia Name given to many unrelated grapes in Italy. Vernaccia di San Gimignano is crisp, lively; Vernaccia di Oristano is sherry-like.

Viognier Ultra-fashionable Rhône grape, finest in Condrieu, less fine but still aromatic in the Midi. Good examples from California and Australia.

Viura See MACABEO.

Welschriesling Light and fresh to sweet and rich in Austria; ubiquitous in central Europe, with aliases including Laski Rizling, Riesling Italico, Olaszriesling.

Wine & food

Food these days is becoming almost as complicated as wine. We take Japanese for granted, Chinese as staple, look to Italian for comfort and then stir the pot with this strange thing called "fusion rules". Don't try to be too clever; wine you like with food you like is safest.

Before the meal – apéritifs

The conventional apéritif wines are either sparkling (epitomized by Champagne) or fortified (epitomized by sherry in Britain, port in France, vermouth in Italy, etc.). A glass table wine before eating is an alternative.
Warning Avoid peanuts; they destroy wine flavours. Olives are too piquant for many wines; they need sherry or a Martini. Eat almonds, pistachios, cashews, or walnuts, plain crisps or cheese straws instead.

First courses

Aïoli A thirst-quencher is needed for its garlic heat. Rhône, sparkling dry white; Provence rosé, Verdicchio. And *marc* or *grappa*, too, for courage.

Antipasti Dry or medium white: Italian (Arneis, Soave, Pinot Grigio, Prosecco, Vermentino); light but gutsy red (Dolcetto, Franciacorta, young Chianti).

Artichoke vinaigrette An incisive dry white: New Zealand Sauv Bl; Côtes de Gascogne or a modern Greek; young red: Bordeaux, Côtes du Rhône.
   with hollandaise Full-bodied, slightly crisp dry white: Pouilly-Fuissé, Pfalz Spätlese, or a Carneros or Yarra Valley Chard.

Asparagus A difficult flavour for wine, being slightly bitter, so the wine needs plenty of its own. Sauv Bl echoes the flavour. Sem beats Chard, especially Australian, but Chard works well with melted butter or hollandaise. Alsace Pinot Gr, even dry Muscat is good, or Jurançon Sec.

Aubergine purée (Melitzanosalata) Crisp New World Sauv Bl, eg. from South Africa or New Zealand; or modern Greek or Sicilian dry white. Or try Bardolino red or Chiaretto. Baked aubergine dishes can need sturdier reds: Shiraz, Zin.

Avocado and tiger prawns Dry to medium or slightly sharp white: Rheingau or Pfalz Kabinett, Grüner Veltliner, Wachau Ries, Sancerre, Pinot Gr; Sonoma or Australian Chard or Sauv Bl, or a dry rosé. Or *premier cru* Chablis.
   with mozzarella and tomato Crisp but ripe white with acidity: Soave, Sancerre, Greek white.

Carpaccio, beef Seems to work well with most wines, inc reds. Top Tuscan is appropriate, but fine Chards are good. So are vintage and pink Champagnes.
   salmon Chard or Champagne.
   tuna Viognier, California Chard or New Zealand Sauv Bl.

Caviar Iced vodka. Champagne, if you must, full-bodied (eg. Bollinger, Krug).

Ceviche Australian Ries or Verdelho, New Zealand Sauv Bl.

Charcuterie/salami Young Beaujolais-Villages, Loire reds such as Saumur, New Zealand or Oregon Pinot N. Lambrusco or young Zin. Young Argentine or Italian reds. Bordeaux Blanc and light Chard like Côte Chalonnaise can work well, too.

Chorizo Fino, Austrian Ries, good white Graves, Grüner Veltliner.

Crostini Morellino di Scansano, Montepulciano d'Abruzzo, Valpolicella, or a dry Italian white such as Verdicchio or Orvieto.

Crudités Light red or rosé: Côtes du Rhône, Minervois, Chianti, Pinot N; or fino sherry. For whites: Alsace Sylvaner or Pinot Bl.

Dim sum Classically, China tea. For fun: Pinot Gr or Ries; light red (Bardolino or Loire). NV Champagne or good New World fizz.

WINE & FOOD | 21

Eggs See also SOUFFLÉS. These present difficulties: they clash with most wines and can ruin good ones. But local wine with local egg dishes is a safe bet, so ★→★★ of whatever is going. Try Pinot Bl or not too oaky Chard. As a last resort I can bring myself to drink Champagne with scrambled eggs.

    quail's eggs Blanc de blancs Champagne.

    seagull's (or gull's) eggs Mature white burgundy or vintage Champagne.

    oeufs en meurette Burgundian genius: eggs in red wine with glass of the same.

Escargots Rhône reds (Gigondas, Vacqueyras), St-Véran or Aligoté. In the Midi, very good Petits-Gris go with local white, rosé, or red. In Alsace, Pinot Bl or the dry Muscat.

Fish terrine Pfalz Ries Spätlese Trocken, Grüner Veltliner, *premier cru* Chablis, Clare Valley Ries, Sonoma Chard; or manzanilla.

Foie gras Sweet white. In Bordeaux they drink Sauternes. Others prefer a late-harvest Pinot Gr or Ries (inc New World), Vouvray, Montlouis, Jurançon Moelleux, or Gewurz. Tokáji Aszú 5 Puttonyos is a Lucullan choice. Old, dry amontillado can be sublime. With hot foie gras, mature vintage Champagne. But not on any account Chard or Sauv Bl.

Goat's cheese, warm Sancerre, Pouilly-Fumé, or New World Sauv Bl.

    chilled Chinon, Saumur-Champigny, or Provence rosé. Or strong red: Château Musar, Greek, Turkish, Australian sparkling Shiraz.

Guacamole California Chard, Sauv Blanc, dry Muscat, or NV Champagne. Or Mexican beer.

Haddock, smoked, mousse, or brandade Wonderful for showing off any stylish, full-bodied white, inc *grand cru* Chablis or Sonoma, South African or New Zealand Chard.

Ham, raw or cured See also PROSCIUTTO. Alsace Grand Cru Pinot Gr or good, crisp Italian Collio white. With Spanish *pata negra* or *jamón*, fino sherry, or tawny port. See also HAM, COOKED (Meat, poultry, game).

Herrings, raw or pickled Dutch gin (young, not aged) or Scandinavian *akvavit*, and cold beer. If wine essential, try Muscadet.

Mackerel, smoked An oily wine-destroyer. Manzanilla sherry, proper dry Vinho Verde or Schnapps, peppered or bison-grass vodka. Or good lager.

Mayonnaise Adds richness that calls for a contrasting bite in the wine. Côte Chalonnaise whites (eg. Rully) are good. Try New Zealand Sauv Bl, Verdicchio, or a Spätlese Trocken. Or Provence Rosé.

Mezze A selection of hot and cold vegetable dishes. Sparkling is a good all-purpose choice, as is rosé. Fino sherry is in its element.

Mozzarella with tomatoes, basil Fresh Italian white, eg. Soave, Alto Adige. Vermintino from the coast. Or simple Bordeaux Blanc. See also AVOCADO.

Oysters, raw NV Champagne, *premier cru* Chablis, Muscadet, white Graves, Sancerre, or Guinness. Or even light, cold Sauternes.

    cooked Puligny-Montrachet or good New World Chard.

    Champagne is good with either.

Pasta Red or white according to the sauce or trimmings:

    cream sauce Orvieto, Frascati, Alto Adige Chard.

    meat sauce Montepulciano d'Abruzzo, Salice Salentino, Merlot.

    pesto (basil) sauce Barbera, Ligurian Vermentino, New Zealand Sauv Bl, Hungarian Furmint.

    seafood sauce (eg. vongole) Verdicchio, Soave, white Rioja, Cirò, Sauv Bl.

    tomato sauce Chianti, Barbera, south Italian red, Zin, South Australian Grenache.

Pastrami Alsace Ries, young Sangiovese or Cab Fr.

Pâté

    chicken liver Calls for pungent white (Alsace Pinot Gr or Marsanne),

a smooth red like a light Pomerol, Volnay, or New Zealand Pinot N,
or even amontillado sherry. More strongly flavoured pâté (duck, etc.)
needs Châteauneuf-du-Pape, Cornas, Chianti Classico, Franciacorta,
or good white Graves.

Pipérade Navarra *rosado*, Provence or southern French rosés. Or dry
Australian Ries. For a red: Corbières.

Prawns, shrimps, or langoustines Fine dry white: burgundy, Graves, New
Zealand Chard, Washington Ries, Pfalz Ries, Australian Ries – even fine
mature Champagne. ("Cocktail sauce" kills wine, and in time, people.)

Prosciutto (also with melon, pears, or figs) Full, dry or medium white: Orvieto,
Lugana, Sauv Bl, Grüner Veltliner, Tokay Furmint, white Rioja, Australian
Sem, or Jurançon Sec.

Risotto Pinot Gr from Friuli, Gavi, youngish Sem, Dolcetto or Barbera d'Alba.
with *fungi porcini* Finest mature Barolo or Barbaresco.

Salads Any dry and appetizing white or rosé wine.
NB Vinegar in salad dressings destroys the flavour of wine. If you
want salad at a meal with fine wine, dress the salad with wine or a
little lemon juice instead of vinegar.

Salmon, smoked A dry but pungent white: fino (esp manzanilla) sherry, Alsace
Pinot Gr, *grand cru* Chablis, Pouilly-Fumé, Pfalz Ries Spätlese, vintage
Champagne. If you must have a red, try a lighter one such as Barbera.
Vodka, schnapps, or *akvavit*.

Soufflés As show dishes these deserve ★★★ wines.
cheese Red burgundy or Bordeaux, Cab Sauv (not Chilean or Australian), etc.
Or fine white burgundy.
fish Dry white: ★★★ burgundy, Bordeaux, Alsace, Chard, etc.
spinach (tougher on wine) Mâcon-Villages, St-Véran, or Valpolicella.
Champagne can also be good with all textures of soufflé.

Tapas Perfect with fino sherry, which can cope with the wide range of flavours in
both hot and cold dishes.

Tapenade Manzanilla or fino sherry, or any sharpish dry white or rosé.

Taramasalata A rustic southern white with personality; not necessarily retsina.
Fino sherry works well. Try white Rioja or a Rhône Marsanne. The bland
supermarket version submits to fine, delicate whites or Champagne.

Tortilla Rioja *crianza*, fino sherry, or white Mâcon-Villages.

Trout, smoked Sancerre; California or South African Sauv Bl. Rully or Bourgogne
Aligoté, Chablis, or Champagne. Light German Riesling Kabinett.

Vegetable terrine Not a great help to fine wine, but Chilean Chard makes a
fashionable marriage. Chenin Bl such as Vouvray a lasting one.

Whitebait Crisp dry whites, eg. Furmint, Greek, Touraine Sauv Bl, Verdicchio, fino.

Fish

Abalone Dry or medium white: Sauv Bl, Côte de Beaune *blanc*, Pinot Gr, Grüner
Veltliner. Chinese-style: vintage Champagne.

Anchovies, marinated The marinade will clash with pretty well everything. Keep
it light, white, dry and neutral.
in olive oil or salted A robust wine: red, white, or rosé – try Rioja.

Bass, sea Weissburgunder from Baden or Pfalz. Very good for any fine/delicate
white, eg. Clare dry Ries, Chablis, white Châteauneuf-du-Pape. But
strengthen the flavours of the wine according to the flavourings of the fish:
ginger, spring onions more powerful Ries; porcini top Alsace Pinot Bl.

Beurre blanc, fish with A top-notch Muscadet *sur lie*, a Sauv Bl/Sem blend,
premier cru Chablis, Vouvray, or a Rheingau Ries.

Brandade *premier cru* Chablis, Sancerre Rouge, or New Zealand Pinot N.

Brill Very delicate: hence a top fish for fine old Puligny and the like.

Cod, roast Good neutral background for fine dry/medium whites: Chablis, Meursault, Corton-Charlemagne, *cru classé* Graves, Grüner Veltliner, German Kabinett or *grosses gewächs*, or a good lightish Pinot N.

Crab Crab and Ries are part of the Creator's plan.

  Chinese, with ginger and onion German Ries Kabinett or Spätlese Halbtrocken. Tokay Furmint, Gewurz.

  cioppino Sauv Bl; but West Coast friends say Zin. Also California sparkling.

  cold, dressed Alsace, Austrian or Rhine Ries; dry Australian Ries, or Condrieu.

  softshell Chard or top-quality German Ries Spätlese.

  Thai crabcakes Pungent Sauv Bl (Loire, South Africa, Australia, New Zealand) or Ries (German Spätlese or Australian).

  with black bean sauce A big Barossa Shiraz or Syrah. Even Cognac.

  with chilli and garlic Quite powerful Ries, perhaps German *grosses gewächs*.

Curry A generic term for a multitude of flavours. Too much heat makes wine problematic: rosé is a good bet. Hot-and-sour flavours (with tamarind tomato, eg.) need acidity (perhaps Sauv Bl); mild, creamy dishes need richness of texture (dry Alsace Ries).

Eel, smoked Ries, Alsace, or Austrian, according to the other ingredients. Or fino sherry, Bourgogne Aligoté. Schnapps.

Fish and chips, *fritto misto*, **tempura** Chablis, white Bordeaux, Sauv Bl, Pinot Bl, Gavi, fino, Montilla, Koshu, tea; or NV Champagne and cava.

Fish baked in a salt crust Full-bodied white or rosé: Albariño, Sicily, Greek, Hungarian. Côtes de Lubéron or Minervois.

Fish pie (with creamy sauce) Albariño, Soave Classico, Alsace Pinot Gr or Ries, Spanish Godello.

Haddock Rich, dry whites: Meursault, California Chard, Marsanne, or Grüner Veltliner.

Hake Sauv Bl or any fresh fruity white: Pacherenc, Tursan, white Navarra.

Halibut As for TURBOT.

Herrings, fried/grilled Need a white with some acidity to cut their richness. Rully, Chablis, Bourgogne Aligoté, Greek, dry Sauv Bl. Or cider.

Kedgeree Full white, still or sparkling: Mâcon-Villages, South African Chard, Grüner Veltliner, German *grosses gewächs*, or (at breakfast) Champagne.

Kippers A good cup of tea, preferably Ceylon (milk, no sugar). Scotch? Dry oloroso sherry is surprisingly good.

Lamproie à la Bordelaise 5-yr-old St-Emilion or Fronsac. Or Douro reds with Portuguese lampreys.

Lobster, richly sauced Vintage Champagne, fine white burgundy, *cru classé* Graves, California Chard or Australian Ries, Grosses Gewächs, Pfalz Spätlese.

  cold NV Champagne, Alsace Ries, *premier cru* Chablis, Condrieu, Mosel Spätlese, or a local fizz.

Mackerel, grilled Hard or sharp white: Sauv Bl from Touraine, Gaillac, Vinho Verde, white Rioja, or English white. Or Guinness.

  with spices White with muscle: Austrian Ries, Grüner Veltliner, German *grosses gewächs*.

Monkfish Often roasted, which needs fuller rather than leaner wines. Try New Zealand Chard, New Zealand/Oregon Pinot N, or Chilean Merlot.

Mullet, red A chameleon, adaptable to good white or red, especially Pinot N.

Mullet, grey Verdicchio, Rully, or unoaked Chard.

Mussels Muscadet-sur-lie, *premier cru* Chablis, Chard.

  stuffed, with garlic See ESCARGOTS.

  with chorizo Unoaked white: Grüner Veltliner, southern French. Dry rosé.

Paella, shellfish Full-bodied white or rosé, unoaked Chard.

Perch, sandre Exquisite fish for finest wines: top white burgundy, *grand cru* Alsace Ries, or noble Mosels. Or try top Swiss Fendant or Johannisberg.

Prawns With garlic, keep the wine light, white or rosé, and dry. With spices, up to and including chilli, go for a bit more body, but not oak: dry Ries good.

Salmon, seared or grilled Pinot N is the fashionable option. Merlot or light claret not bad. Or fine white burgundy: Puligny- or Chassagne-Montrachet, Meursault, Corton-Charlemagne, *grand cru* Chablis; Grüner Veltliner, Condrieu, California, Idaho or New Zealand Chard, Rheingau Kabinett/ Spätlese, Australian Ries.

    fishcakes Call for similar (as for above), but less grand, wines.

Sardines, fresh grilled Very dry white: Vinho Verde, Muscadet, or modern Greek.

Sashimi If you are prepared to forego the wasabi, sparkling wines will go. Or Washington or Tasmanian Chard, *grand cru* Chablis, Rheingau Ries, English Seyval Bl. Otherwise, iced sake, fino sherry, or beer. Trials have matched 5-putt Tokáji with fat tuna, sea urchin and *anago* (eel).

Scallops An inherently slightly sweet dish, best with medium-dry whites.

    in cream sauces German Spätlese, Montrachet, or top Australian Chard.

    grilled or seared Hermitage Blanc, Grüner Veltliner, Entre-Deux-Mers, vintage Champagne, or Pinot N.

    with Asian seasoning New Zealand, Chenin Bl, Verdelho, Godello, Gewurz.

Shellfish Dry white with plain boiled shellfish, richer wines with richer sauces.

    with *plateaux de fruits de mer* Chablis, Muscadet, Picpoul de Pinet, Alto Adige Pinot Bl.

Skate/raie with brown butter White with some pungency (eg. Pinot Gr d'Alsace), or a clean, straightforward wine like Muscadet or Verdicchio.

Snapper Sauv Bl if cooked with oriental flavours; white Rhône or Provence rosé with Mediterranean flavours.

Sole, plaice, etc., plain, grilled, or fried Perfect with fine wines: white burgundy or its equivalent.

    with sauce According to the ingredients: sharp, dry wine for tomato sauce, fairly rich for creamy preparations.

Sushi Hot wasabi is usually hidden in every piece. German QbA Trocken wines, simple Chablis, or NV *brut* Champagne. Or, of course, sake or beer.

Swordfish Full-bodied, dry white of the country. Nothing grand.

Tagine, with couscous North African flavours need substantial whites to balance – Austrian, Rhône – or crisp, neutral whites that won't compete. Preserved lemon demands something with acidity. Go easy on the oak.

Trout, grilled or fried Delicate white wine, eg. Mosel (esp Saar or Ruwer), Alsace Pinot Bl.

Tuna, grilled or seared Generally served rare, so try a red: Cab Fr from the Loire, or Pinot N. Young Rioja is a possibility.

Turbot Serve with your best rich, dry white: Meursault or Chassagne-Montrachet, Corton-Charlemagne, mature Chablis or its California, Australian or New Zealand equivalent. Condrieu. Mature Rheingau, Mosel or Nahe Spätlese or Auslese (not Trocken).

Meat, poultry, game

Barbecues The local wine: Australian, South African, Argentina are right in spirit.

    Asian flavours (lime, coriander, etc.) Rosé, Pinot Gr, Ries.

    chilli Shiraz, Zin, Pinotage, Malbec.

    Middle Eastern (cumin, mint) Crisp, dry whites, rosé.

    oil, lemon, herbs Sauv Bl.

red wine Cab Sauv, Merlot, Malbec, Tannat.

tomato sauces Zin, Sangiovese.

Beef, boiled Red: Bordeaux (Bourgogne or Fronsac), Roussillon, Gevrey-Chambertin, or Côte-Rôtie. Medium-ranking white burgundy is good, eg. Auxey-Duresses. Or top-notch beer. Mustard softens tannic reds, horseradish kills everything – but can be worth the sacrifice.

roast An ideal partner for fine red wine of any kind. See above for mustard.

stew Sturdy red: Pomerol or St-Emilion, Hermitage, Cornas, Barbera, Shiraz, Napa Cab Sauv, Ribera del Duero, or Douro red.

Beef Stroganoff Dramatic red: Barolo, Valpolicella Amarone, Cahors, Hermitage, late-harvest Zin – even Moldovan Negru de Purkar.

Boudin blanc **(white pork sausage)** Loire Chenin Bl, esp when served with apples: dry Vouvray, Saumur, Savennières; mature red Côtes de Beaune if without.

Boudin noir **(blood sausage)** Local Sauv Bl or Chenin Bl – especially in the Loire. Or Beaujolais *cru*, especially Morgon. Or light Tempranillo.

Cabbage, stuffed Hungarian Cab Fr/Kadarka; *village* Rhônes; Salice Salentino, Primitivo and other spicy southern-Italian reds. Or Argentine Malbec.

Cajun food Fleurie, Brouilly, or New World Sauv Bl; **with gumbo** Amontillado.

Cassoulet Red from southwest France (Gaillac, Minervois, Corbières, St-Chinian, or Fitou) or Shiraz. But best of all Beaujolais *cru* or young Tempranillo.

Chicken/turkey/guinea fowl, roast Virtually any wine, including very best bottles of dry to medium white and finest old reds (especially burgundy). The meat of fowl can be adapted with sauces to match almost any fine wine (eg. *coq au vin* with red or white burgundy). Sparkling Shiraz with strong, spicy stuffing.

Chicken Kiev Alsace Ries, Collio, Chard, Bergerac *rouge*.

Chilli con carne Young red: Beaujolais, Tempranillo, Zin, Argentine Malbec.

Chinese food

    Canton or Peking style Rosé or dry to medium-dry white – Mosel Ries Kabinett or Spätlese Trocken – can be good throughout a Chinese banquet. Gewurz often suggested but rarely works (but brilliant with ginger), yet Chasselas and Pinot Gr are attractive alternatives. Dry or off-dry sparkling (especially cava) cuts the oil and matches sweetness. Eschew sweet/sour dishes but try St-Emilion ★★, New World Pinot N or Châteauneuf-du-Pape with duck. I often serve both white and red wines concurrently during Chinese meals. Champagne becomes a thirst quencher.

    Szechuan style Verdicchio, Alsace Pinot Bl or very cold beer.

Choucroute garni Alsace Pinot Bl, Pinot Gr, Ries, or beer.

Cold roast meat Generally better with full-flavoured white than red. Mosel Spätlese or Hochheimer and Côte Chalonnaise are very good, as is Beaujolais. Leftover cold beef with leftover vintage Champagne is bliss.

Confit d'oie/de canard Young, tannic red Bordeaux, California Cab Sauv and Merlot, and Priorato cut richness. Alsace Pinot Gr or Gewurz match it.

Coq au vin Red burgundy. Ideal: bottle of Chambertin in the dish, two on the table.

Duck or goose Rather rich white: Pfalz Spätlese or off-dry *grand cru* Alsace. Or mature, gamey red: Morey-St-Denis, Côte-Rôtie, Bordeaux, burgundy. With oranges or peaches, the Sauternais propose drinking Sauternes, others Monbazillac or Ries Auslese. Mature, weighty vintage Champagne is good, too, and handles red cabbage surprisingly well.

    Peking See CHINESE FOOD.

    wild duck Big-scale red: Hermitage, Bandol, California or South African Cab Sauv, Australian Shiraz – Grange if you can afford it.

    with olives Top-notch Chianti or other Tuscans.

    with pomegranate molasses Young red burgundy of good quality.

    roast breast & confit leg with Puy lentils Mid-weight red with some richness.

Frankfurters German, NY Ries, Beaujolais, light Pinot N. Or Budweiser (Budvar).

Game birds, young, plain-roasted The best red wine you can afford.

> **older birds in casseroles** Red (Gevrey-Chambertin, Pommard, Santenay, or *grand cru* St-Emilion, Napa Valley Cab Sauv or Rhône).
>
> **well-hung game** Vega Sicilia, great red Rhône, Château Musar.
>
> **cold game** Mature vintage Champagne.

Game pie, hot Red: Oregon Pinot Noir.

> **cold** Good-quality white burgundy, *cru* Beaujolais, or Champagne.

Goulash Flavoursome young red: Hungarian Kékoportó, Zin, Uruguayan Tannat, Morellino di Scansano, Mencía, young Australian Shiraz.

Grouse See GAME BIRDS – but push the boat right out.

Haggis Fruity red, eg. young claret, young Portuguese red, New World Cab Sauv or Malbec, or Châteauneuf-du-Pape. Or, of course, malt whisky.

Ham, cooked Softer red burgundies: Volnay, Savigny, Beaune; Chinon or Bourgueil; sweetish German white (Rhine Spätlese); Tokàji Furmint or Czech Frankovka; lightish Cab Sauv (eg. Chilean), or New World Pinot N. And don't forget the heaven-made match of ham and sherry. See HAM, RAW OR CURED.

Hamburger Young red: Australian Cab Sauv, Chianti, Zin, Argentine Malbec, Tempranillo. Or full-strength colas (not diet).

Hare Jugged hare calls for flavourful red: not-too-old burgundy or Bordeaux, Rhône (eg. Gigondas), Bandol, Barbaresco, Ribera del Duero, Rioja Reserva. The same for saddle, or for hare sauce with pappardelle.

Indian dishes Medium-sweet white, very cold: Orvieto *abboccato*, South African Chenin Bl, Alsace Pinot Bl, Torrontés, Indian sparkling, Cava or NV Champagne. Rosé can be a safe all-rounder. Tannin – Barolo or Barbaresco, or deep-flavoured reds such as Châteauneuf-du-Pape, Cornas, Australian Grenache or Mourvèdre, or Valpolicella Amarone – will emphasize the heat. Soft reds can be easier. Hot-and-sour flavours need acidity.

Kebabs Vigorous red: modern Greek, Corbières, Chilean Cab Sauv, Zin, or Barossa Shiraz. Sauv Bl, if lots of garlic.

Kidneys Red: St-Emilion or Fronsac, Nuits-St-Georges, Cornas, Barbaresco, Rioja, Spanish or Australian Cab Sauv, top Alentejo.

Lamb, roast One of the traditional and best partners for very good red Bordeaux – or its Cab Sauv equivalents from the New World. In Spain, the partner of the finest old Rioja and Ribera del Duero *reservas*.

> **cutlets or chops** As for roast lamb, but a little less grand.
>
> **slow-cooked roast** Flatters top reds, but needs less tannin than pink lamb.

Liver Young red: Beaujolais-Villages, St-Joseph, Médoc, Italian Merlot, Breganze Cab Sauv, Zin, Tempranillo, Portuguese Bairrada.

> **calf's** Red Rioja *crianza*, Salice Salentino *riserva*, Fleurie.

Meatballs Tangy, medium-bodied red: Mercurey, Crozes-Hermitage, Madiran, Morellino di Scansano, Langhe Nebbiolo, Zin, Cab Sauv.

> **spicy Middle-Eastern style** Simple, rustic red.

Moussaka Red or rosé: Naoussa from Greece, Sangiovese, Corbières, Côtes de Provence, Ajaccio, New Zealand Pinot N, young Zin, Tempranillo.

Mutton A stronger flavour than lamb, and not served pink. Robust but elegant red and top-notch. Mature Cab Sauv, Syrah. Some sweetness of fruit suits it.

Osso bucco Low-tannin, supple red such as Dolcetto d'Alba or Pinot N. Or dry Italian white such as Soave and Lugana.

Ox cheek, braised Superbly tender and flavoursome, this flatters the best reds: Vega Sicilia, Bordeaux. Best with substantial wines.

Oxtail Rather rich red: St-Emilion, Pomerol, Pommard, Nuits-St-Georges, Barolo, or Rioja *reserva*, Ribera del Duero, California or Coonawarra Cab Sauv, Châteauneuf-du-Pape, mid-weight Shiraz.

Paella Young Spanish wines: red, dry white, or rosé: Penedès, Somontano, Navarra, or Rioja.

Pigeon Lively reds: Savigny, Chambolle-Musigny, Crozes-Hermitage, Chianti Classico, Argentine Malbec, or California Pinot N. Or try Franken Silvaner Spätlese.

Pork, roast A good, rich, neutral background to a fairly light red or rich white. It deserves ★★ treatment – Médoc is fine. Portugal's suckling pig is eaten with Bairrada Garrafeira; Chinese is good with Pinot N.
   pork belly Slow cooked and meltingly tender, this needs a red with some acidity. Italian would be good: Dolcetto or Barbera. Or Loire red, or lightish Argentine Malbec.

Pot au feu, bollito misto, cocido Rustic red wines from the region of origin; Sangiovese di Romagna, Chusclan, Lirac, Rasteau, Portuguese Alentejo, or Yecla and Jumilla from Spain.

Quail Carmignano, Rioja *reserva*, mature claret, Pinot N.

Rabbit Lively, medium-bodied young Italian red or Aglianico del Vulture; Chiroubles, Chinon, Saumur-Champigny, or Rhône rosé.
   with prunes Bigger, richer, fruitier red.
   as ragu Medium-bodied red with acidity.

Satay Australia's McLaren Vale Shiraz, or Alsace or New Zealand Gewurz. Peanut sauce is a problem with wine.

Sauerkraut (German) Lager or Pils. (But see also CHOUCROUTE GARNI.)

Sausages See also CHARCUTERIE, FRANKFURTERS. The British banger requires a young Malbec from Argentina (a red wine, anyway), or British ale.

Shepherd's pie Rough-and-ready red seems most appropriate, eg. Sangiovese di Romagna, but either beer or dry cider is the real McCoy.

Steak
   au poivre A fairly young Rhône red or Cab Sauv.
   filet or tournedos Any red (but not old wines with Béarnaise sauce: top New World Pinot N or Californian Chard is better).
   Fiorentina (bistecca) Chianti Classico *riserva* or Brunello. The rarer the meat, the more classic the wine; the more well-done, the more you need New World, fruit-driven wines. Argentina Malbec is the perfect partner for steak Argentine style, ie. cooked to death.
   Korean *yuk whe* (the world's best steak tartare) Sake.
   tartare Vodka or light young red: Beaujolais, Bergerac, Valpolicella.
   T-bone Reds of similar bone structure: Barolo, Hermitage, Australian Cab Sauv or Shiraz.

Steak-and-kidney pie or pudding Red Rioja *reserva* or mature Bordeaux.

Stews and casseroles Burgundy such as Chambolle-Musigny or Bonnes-Mares if fairly simple; otherwise lusty, full-flavoured red: young Côtes du Rhône, Toro, Corbières, Barbera, Shiraz, Zin, etc.

Sweetbreads A grand dish, so grand wine: Rhine Ries or Franken Silvaner Spätlese, *grand cru* Alsace Pinot Gr, or Condrieu, depending on sauce.

Tagines These vary enormously, but fruity young reds are a good bet: Beaujolais, Tempranillo, Sangiovese, Merlot, Shiraz.

Tandoori chicken Ries or Sauv Bl, young red Bordeaux, or light north Italian red served cool. Also cava and NV Champagne.

Thai dishes Ginger and lemon grass call for pungent Sauv Bl (Loire, Australia, New Zealand, South Africa) or Ries (Spätlese or Australian).
   coconut milk Hunter Valley and other ripe, oaked Chards; Alsace Pinot Bl (refreshing); Gewurz or Verdelho. Of course, Prosecco or NV Champagne.

Tongue Good for any red or white of abundant character, especially Italian. Also Beaujolais, Loire reds, Tempranillo, and full, dry rosés.

Veal, roast Good for any fine old red that may have faded with age (eg. a Rioja *reserva*) or a German or Austrian Ries, Vouvray, Alsace Pinot Gr.

Venison Big-scale reds, including Mourvèdre, solo as in Bandol, or in blends. Rhône, Bordeaux or California Cab Sauv of a mature vintage; or rather rich white (Pfalz Spätlese or Alsace Pinot Gr). With a sharp berry sauce, try a German *grosses gewächs* Ries, or a New World Cab Sauv.

Vitello tonnato Full-bodied whites:Chard; light reds (eg. Valpolicella) served cool.

Wild boar Serious red: top Tuscan or Priorat.

Vegetarian dishes (see also First courses)

Baked pasta dishes *Pasticcio*, lasagne and cannelloni with elaborate vegetarian fillings and sauces: an occasion to show off a grand wine, especially finest Tuscan red, but also claret and burgundy. Also Gavi from Italy.

Beetroot A medium-weight red with some softness: Southern Rhône, Tempranillo. Or white.
and goat's cheese gratin Sauv Bl.

Cauliflower cheese Crisp, aromatic white: Sancerre, Ries Spätlese, Muscat, English Seyval Bl, Godello.

Couscous with vegetables Young red with a bite: Shiraz, Corbières, Minervois; or well-chilled rosé from Navarra or Somontano; or a robust Moroccan red.

Fennel-based dishes Sauv Bl: Pouilly-Fumé or one from New Zealand; English Seyval Bl, or young Tempranillo.

Grilled Mediterranean vegetables Brouilly, Barbera, Tempranillo, or Shiraz.

Lentil dishes Sturdy reds such as southern French, Zin, or Shiraz.
dhal, with spinach Tricky. Soft light red or rosé is best – and not top-flight.

Macaroni cheese As for CAULIFLOWER CHEESE.

Mushrooms (in most contexts) Fleshy red: Pomerol, California Merlot, Rioja Reserva, top burgundy, or Vega Sicilia. On toast, best claret. Ceps/porcini, Ribera del Duero, Barolo, Chianti Rufina, top claret: Pauillac or St-Estèphe.

Onion/leek tart Fruity, off-dry or dry white: Alsace Pinot Gr or Gewurz, Canadian or New Zealand Ries, English whites, Jurançon, Australian Ries. Or Loire red.

Peppers or aubergines (eggplant), stuffed Vigorous red wine: Nemea, Chianti, Dolcetto, Zin, Bandol, Vacqueyras.

Pumpkin/squash ravioli or risotto Full-bodied, fruity dry or off-dry white: Viognier or Marsanne, *demi-sec* Vouvray, Gavi, or South African Chenin.

Ratatouille Vigorous young red: Chianti, New Zealand Cab Sauv, Merlot, Malbec, Tempranillo; young red Bordeaux, Gigondas, or Coteaux du Languedoc.

Spanacopitta Young Greek or Italian red or white.

Spiced vegetarian dishes See INDIAN DISHES, THAI DISHES (Meat, poultry, game).

Watercress, raw This makes every wine on earth taste revolting. Soup is slightly easier, but doesn't require wine.

Wild garlic leaves, wilted Tricky: a fairly neutral white with acidity will cope best.

Desserts

Apple pie, strudel or tarts Sweet German, Austrian or Loire white, Tokáji Aszú or Canadian Icewine.

Apples, Cox's Orange Pippins Vintage port (and sweetmeal biscuits).

Bread-and-butter pudding Fine 10-yr-old Barsac, Tokáji Aszú, or Australian botrytized Sem.

Cakes and gâteaux See also Chocolate, Coffee, Ginger, Rum. Bual or Malmsey Madeira, oloroso or cream sherry.
cupcakes Prosecco presses all the right buttons.

Cheesecake Sweet white: Vouvray, Anjou, or fizz – refreshing, nothing special.

Chocolate Generally only powerful flavours can compete. Bual, California

Orange Muscat, Tokáji Aszú, Australian Liqueur Muscat, 10-yr-old tawny port; Asti for light, fluffy mousses. Experiment with rich, ripe reds: Syrah, Zin, even sparkling Shiraz. Banyuls for a weightier partnership. Médoc can match bitter black chocolate. Or a tot of good rum.

and olive oil mousse 10-yr-old tawny, or as for black chocolate, above.

Christmas pudding, mince pies Tawny port, cream sherry, or liquid Christmas pudding itself, Pedro Ximénez sherry. Asti or Banyuls.

Coffee desserts Sweet Muscat, Australia Liqueur Muscats, or Tokáji Aszú.

Creams, custards, fools, syllabubs See also CHOCOLATE, COFFEE, GINGER, and RUM. Sauternes, Loupiac, Ste-Croix-du-Mont, or Monbazillac.

Crème brûlée Sauternes or Rhine Beerenauslese, best Madeira or Tokáji Aszú. (With concealed fruit, a more modest sweet wine.)

Crêpes Suzette Sweet Champagne, Orange Muscat, or Asti.

Fruit

blackberries Vintage port.

dried fruit (and compotes) Banyuls, Rivesaltes, Maury.

flans and tarts Sauternes, Monbazillac, sweet Vouvray or Anjou.

fresh Sweet Coteaux du Layon or light, sweet Muscat.

poached, ie. apricots, pears, etc. Sweet Muscatel: try Muscat de Beaumes-de-Venise, Moscato di Pantelleria, or Spanish dessert Tarragona.

salads, orange salad A fine sweet sherry or any Muscat-based wine.

Ginger flavours Sweet Muscats, New World botrytized Ries and Sem.

Ice-cream and sorbets Fortified wine (Australian Liqueur Muscat, Banyuls); sweet Asti or sparkling Moscato. Pedro Ximénez, Amaretto liqueur with vanilla; rum with chocolate.

Lemon flavours For dishes like tarte au citron, try sweet Ries from Germany or Austria, or Tokáji Aszú; very sweet if lemon is very tart.

Meringues Recioto di Soave, Asti, or Champagne *doux*.

Mille-feuille Delicate sweet sparkling white, such as Moscato d'Asti or *demi-sec* Champagne.

Nuts Finest oloroso sherry, Madeira, vintage or tawny port (nature's match for walnuts), Tokáji Aszú, *vin santo*, or Setúbal Moscatel.

salted nut parfait Tokáj Aszú, Vin Santo.

Orange flavours Experiment with old Sauternes, Tokáji Aszú or California Orange Muscat.

Panettone Jurançon *moelleux*, late-harvest Ries, Barsac, Tokáji Aszú.

Pears in red wine A pause before the port. Or try Rivesaltes, Banyuls, or Ries Beerenauslese.

Pecan pie Orange Muscat or Liqueur Muscat.

Raspberries (no cream, little sugar) Excellent with fine reds which themselves taste of raspberries: young Juliénas, Regnié.

Rum flavours (baba, mousses, ice-cream) Muscat – from Asti to Australian Liqueur, according to weight of dish.

Salted caramel mousse/parfait Late-harvest Ries, Tokáj Aszú.

Strawberries and cream Sauternes or similar sweet Bordeaux, Vouvray *moelleux* or *vendange tardive* Jurançon.

Strawberries, wild (no cream) Serve with red Bordeaux (most exquisitely Margaux) poured over.

Summer pudding Fairly young Sauternes of a good vintage.

Sweet soufflés Sauternes or Vouvray *moelleux*. Sweet (or rich) Champagne.

Tiramisú *Vin santo*, young tawny port, Muscat de Beaumes-de-Venise, Sauternes, or Australian Liqueur Muscat.

Trifle Should be sufficiently vibrant with its internal sherry.

Zabaglione Light-gold Marsala or Australian botrytized Sem, or Asti.

Wine & cheese

The notion that wine and cheese were married in heaven is not borne out by experience. Fine red wines are slaughtered by strong cheeses; only sharp or sweet white wines survive. Principles to remember (despite exceptions): first, the harder the cheese, the more tannin the wine can have; second, the creamier the cheese is the more acidity needed in the wine. Cheese is classified by its texture and the nature of its rind, so its appearance is a guide to the type of wine to match it. Below are examples, I try to keep a glass of white wine for my cheese.

Fresh, no rind – cream cheese, crème fraîche, mozzarella Light crisp white: simple Bordeaux Blanc, Bergerac, English unoaked whites; rosé: Anjou, Rhône; very light, young, fresh red: Bordeaux, Bardolino, or Beaujolais.

Hard cheeses, waxed or oiled, often showing marks from cheesecloth – Gruyère family, Manchego and other Spanish cheeses, Parmesan, Cantal, Comté, old Gouda, Cheddar and most "traditional" English cheeses Particularly hard to generalize here; Gouda, Gruyère, some Spanish, and a few English cheeses complement fine claret or Cab Sauv and great Shiraz/Syrah wines. But strong cheeses need less refined wines, preferably local ones. Sugary, granular old Dutch red Mimolette or Beaufort are good for finest mature Bordeaux. Also for Tokáji Aszú. But try white wines, too.

Blue cheeses Roquefort can be wonderful with Sauternes, but don't extend the idea to other blues. It is the sweetness of Sauternes, especially old, that complements the saltiness. Stilton and port, preferably tawny, is a classic. Intensely flavoured old oloroso, amontillado, Madeira, Marsala, and other fortified wines go with most blues.

Natural rind (mostly goats cheese) with bluish-grey mould (the rind becomes wrinkled when mature), sometimes dusted with ash – St-Marcellin Sancerre, Valençay, light, fresh Sauv Bl, Jurançon, Savoie, Soave, Italian Chard, lightly oaked English whites.

Bloomy rind soft cheeses, pure-white rind if pasteurized, or dotted with red: Brie, Camembert, Chaource, Bougon (goats milk "Camembert") Full, dry white burgundy or Rhône if the cheese is white and immature; powerful, fruity St-Emilion, young Australian (or Rhône) Shiraz/ Syrah, or Grenache if it's mature.

Washed-rind soft cheeses, with rather sticky, orange-red rind – Langres, mature Epoisses, Maroilles, Carré de l'Est, Milleens, Munster Local reds, especially for Burgundy cheeses; vigorous Languedoc, Cahors, Côtes du Frontonnais, Corsican, southern Italian, Sicilian, Bairrada. Also powerful whites, esp Alsace Gewurz and Muscat.

Semi-soft cheeses, thickish grey-pink rind – Livarot, Pont l'Evêque, Reblochon, Tomme de Savoie, St-Nectaire Powerful white Bordeaux, Chard, Alsace Pinot Gr, dryish Ries, southern Italian and Sicilian whites, aged white Rioja, dry oloroso sherry. But the strongest of these cheeses kills most wines.

Food and finest wines

With very special bottles, the wine guides the choice of food rather than the other way around. The following are based largely on the gastronomic conventions of the wine regions producing these treasures, plus much diligent research. They should help bring out the best in your best wines.

Red wines

Red Bordeaux and other Cab Sauv-based wines (very old, light and delicate: eg. pre-1959, with exceptions such as 45).
Leg or rack of young lamb, roast with a hint of herbs (but not garlic);

entrecôte; roast partridge or grouse, sweetbreads; or cheese soufflé after the meat has been served.

Fully mature great vintages (eg. Bordeaux 59 61 82) Shoulder or saddle of lamb, roast with a touch of garlic, roast ribs, or grilled rump of beef.

Mature but still vigorous (eg. 89 90) Shoulder or saddle of lamb (inc kidneys) with rich sauce. Fillet of beef *marchand de vin* (with wine and bone-marrow). Avoid beef Wellington: pastry dulls the palate.

Merlot-based Bordeaux (Pomerol, St-Emilion) Beef as above (fillet is richest) or well-hung venison.

Côte d'Or red burgundy Consider the weight and texture, which grow lighter/more velvety with age. Also the character of the wine: Nuits is earthy, Musigny flowery, great Romanées can be exotic, Pommard renowned for its four-squareness. Roast chicken or capon is a safe standard with red burgundy; guinea-fowl for slightly stronger wines, then partridge, grouse, or woodcock for those progressively more rich and pungent. Hare and venison (*chevreuil*) are alternatives.
    great old burgundy The Burgundian formula is cheese: Epoisses (unfermented); a fine cheese but a terrible waste of fine old wines.
    vigorous younger burgundy Duck or goose roasted to minimize fat.

Great Syrahs: Hermitage, Côte-Rôtie, Grange; Vega Sicilia Beef, venison, well-hung game; bone marrow on toast; English cheese (esp best farm Cheddar) but also hard goats milk and ewes milk cheeses such as England's Berkswell and Ticklemore.

Rioja *gran reserva*, Pesquera... Richly flavoured roasts: wild boar, mutton, saddle of hare, whole suckling pig.

Barolo, Barbaresco Risotto with white truffles; pasta with game sauce (eg. *pappardelle alla lepre*); porcini mushrooms; Parmesan.

White wines

Very good Chablis, white burgundy, other top-quality Chards White fish simply grilled or *meunière*. Dover sole, turbot, halibut are best; brill, drenched in butter, can be excellent. (Sea bass is too delicate; salmon passes but does little for the finest wine.)

Supreme white burgundy (le Montrachet, Corton-Charlemagne) or equivalent Graves Roast veal, farm chicken stuffed with truffles or herbs under the skin, or sweetbreads; richly sauced white fish or scallops as above. Or lobster or wild salmon.

Condrieu, Château-Grillet, Hermitage Blanc Very light pasta scented with herbs and tiny peas or broad beans.

Grand cru **Alsace: Riesling** *Truite au bleu*, smoked salmon, or *choucroute garni*. **Pinot Gris** Roast or grilled veal. **Gewurztraminer** Cheese soufflé (Münster cheese). *Vendange tardive* Foie gras or tarte tatin.

Sauternes Simple crisp buttery biscuits (eg. *langues de chat*), white peaches, nectarines, strawberries (without cream). Not tropical fruit. Pan-seared foie gras. Experiment with blue cheeses.

Supreme Vouvray *moelleux*, etc. Buttery biscuits, apples, apple tart.

Beerenauslese/Trockenbeerenauslese Biscuits, peaches, greengages. Desserts made from rhubarb, gooseberries, quince, apples.

Tokáji Aszú (5–6 puttonyos) Foie gras recommended. Fruit desserts, cream desserts, even chocolate can be wonderful. So is the naked sip.

Great vintage port or Madeira Walnuts or pecans. A Cox's Orange Pippin and a digestive biscuit is a classic English accompaniment.

Old vintage Champagne (not *blanc de blancs*) As an apéritif, or with cold partridge, grouse, woodcock.

France

**More heavily shaded areas are the
wine-growing regions**

The following abbreviations
are used in the text:

Al	Alsace
Beauj	Beaujolais
Burg	Burgundy
B'x	Bordeaux
Champ	Champagne
Lo	Loire
Prov	Provence
Pyr	Pyrenees
N/S Rh	North/South Rhône
SW	Southwest
AC	*appellation contrôlée*
ch, chx	château(x)
dom, doms	domaine(s)

Le Havre

Caen

Brest

LOIRE

Loire

Nantes
Muscadet

Anjou-
Saumur

La Rochelle

BORDEA

Médoc
Bordeaux
Pomero
St-Emi

Graves
Ent
Deu

Sauternes
Côtes du
Marman
Buze

Tursan
Biarritz
Côtes
St-M
Madi
Jurançon

Having rivals in the New World, and indeed in neighbouring Europe,
has done France nothing but good. Twenty years ago France was
coasting on its reputation. Now each vintage shows new excitement,
more individuality. Buyers crowd to see the new Bordeaux and burgundy,
but also the Rhône and increasingly the Loire. An ambitious *vigneron* in
almost any region can make a name and a following – in the widest range
of styles on earth.

It is burgundy that has changed most, with obscure family names
catching on in the market for their small productions. It is still a risky
buy – little is guaranteed – but a lucky strike is unforgettable. And so far,
climate change has been almost all to the good. It has been said that
Burgundy hasn't had a bad vintage since 1987.

Bordeaux's run of good vintages isn't quite as long as that (the early 1990s produced some spectacular rain and frost, which took their toll) but it's long enough for the phrase "vintage of the century" to provoke a response of "Again?" So is France now as reliable a buy as, say, Australia?

Even with the effects of global warming, most of France is still a marginal climate for the vines it grows. An ill-chosen lesser wine can still remind one of just how marginal some of those vineyards are. There is still no substitute, in France or, indeed, anywhere else, for choosing your producer with care. In these days of industrial versus artisanal winemaking, the person who makes the wine is crucial. A vintage is only ever as good as the people who make and grow the wines.

France entries also cross-refer to Châteaux of Bordeaux section.

Recent vintages of the French classics

Red Bordeaux

Médoc/red Graves For some wines, bottle age is optional: for these it is indispensable. Minor châteaux from light vintages need only two or three years, but even modest wines of great years can improve for 15 or so, and the great châteaux of these years can profit from double that time.

2009 Outstanding year. Hot, dry summer and extended sunny harvest have produced powerful, structured wines.

2008 Considerably better than expected. Cab Sauv ripened in late-season sunshine. Yields down due to poor fruit set, mildew and frost in places. Prices also down, so some good value.

2007 A miserable summer with a huge attack of mildew spelled a difficult year. Easy drinking; best are structured for long ageing. Variable from one estate to the next. Be selective.

2006 Cab Sauv had difficulty ripening. Good colour and alcohol. Be selective.

2005 Perfect weather conditions throughout the year. Rich, balanced, long-ageing wines from an outstanding vintage.

2004 Mixed bag, but top wines good in a classic mould. Starting to drink.

2003 Hottest summer on record. Cab Sauv can be great (St-Estèphe, Pauillac). Atypical but rich, powerful at best (keep), unbalanced at worst (drink).

2002 Saved by a dry, sunny September. Later-ripening Cab Sauv benefited most. Some good wines if selective. Drink now–2018.

2001 A cool September and rain at vintage meant Cab Sauv had difficulty in ripening fully. Some fine, fresh wines to drink now–2015.

2000 Superb wines throughout. Start tentatively on all but the top wines.

1999 Vintage rain again diluted ripe juice; so-so wines to drink now.

1998 Good (especially Pessac-Léognan), but the Right Bank is clearly the winner this year. Drink now–2015.

1997 Uneven flowering and summer rain were a double challenge. Top wines still of interest, but the rest have faded.

1996 Cool summer, fine harvest. Good to excellent. Drink now–2020.

1995 Heatwave and drought; saved by rain. Good to excellent. Now–2015.

1994 Hopes of a supreme year; then heavy vintage rain. Drink now.

1990 A paradox: a drought year with a threat of overproduction. Its results are magnificent. To 2015.

Older fine vintages: 89 88 86 85 82 75 70 66 62 61 59 55 53 49 48 47 45 29 28.

St-Emilion/Pomerol

2009 Again, outstanding. Powerful wines (high alcohol) but seemingly balanced. Hail in St-Emilion cut production at certain estates.

2008 Similar conditions to the Médoc. Late harvest into November. Tiny yields helped quality, which is surprisingly good.

2007 Same pattern as the Médoc. Huge disparity in picking dates (up to five weeks). Extremely variable.

2006 Rain and rot at harvest. Earlier-ripening Pomerol a success but St-Emilion and satellites variable.

2005 Same conditions as the Médoc. An overall success.

2004 Merlot often better than 2003 (Pomerol). Good Cab Fr. Variable.

2003 Merlot suffered in the heat, but exceptional Cab Fr. Very mixed. Some overextraction again. Top St-Emilion on the plateau good.

2002 Problems with rot and ripeness; some overextraction. Modest to good.

2001 Less rain than Médoc during vintage. Some powerful Merlot, sometimes better than 2000. Drinking now–2015.

2000 Similar conditions to Médoc. Less kind to Merlot, but a very good vintage.
1999 Careful, lucky growers made good wines, but rain was again a problem.
1998 Earlier-ripening Merlot largely escaped the rain. Some excellent wines.
1997 Merlot suffered in the rain. Only a handful of wines still of interest.
1996 Cool, fine summer. Vintage rain. Less consistent than Médoc. Now–2015.
1995 Perhaps even better than Médoc/Graves. Now–2015.
1994 Good, especially Pomerol. Drink now.
1990 Another chance to make great wine or a lot of wine. Now–2015.
Older fine vintages: 89 88 85 82 71 70 67 66 64 61 59 53 52 49 47 45.

Red Burgundy

Côte d'Or Côte de Beaune reds generally mature sooner than bigger wines of Côte de Nuits. Earliest drinking dates are for lighter commune wines – eg. Volnay, Beaune; latest for biggest wines, eg. Chambertin, Romanée. Even the best burgundies are more attractive young than equivalent red Bordeaux.

2009 Glorious middle and late summer should make beautiful reds that will be accessible before 2005s.
2008 Fine wines from those who avoided fungal diseases oidium and mildew, disaster for others. Pick and choose carefully.
2007 Small crop of attractive, perfumed wines for the medium term.
2006 An attractive year, better in Côte de Nuits (less rain); some rot problems in Côte de Beaune but there are some gems. Start drinking.
2005 The best for a generation, potentially outstanding wines everywhere. Must be kept, however tempting.
2004 Lighter wines, some pretty, others spoiled by herbaceous flavours.
2003 Reds coped with the heat better than the whites. Muscular, rich wines. Best wines outstanding, others short and hot.
2002 Middle-weight wines of great class with an attractive point of freshness. Just starting to open.
2001 Just needed a touch more sun for excellence. Good to drink now.
2000 Gave more pleasure than expected, but drink up now.
1999 Big, ripe vintage; good colour, bags of fruit, steely tannins.
1998 Ripe fruit but dry tannins. Those in balance look good now.
1997 Time to finish up these attractive wines from a sunny year.
1996 Fine summer and vintage. Top wines must be kept. 2008–2020.
1995 Small crop, potentially fine but not yet showing its expected class.
Older fine vintages: 93 90 88 85 78 71 69 66 64 62 61 59 (all mature).

White Burgundy

Côte de Beaune White wines now rarely made for ageing as long as they used to. Top wines should still improve for up to 10 years.

2009 Fine crop of healthy grapes; definitely charming, but enough acidity to age?
2008 Small crop, ripe flavours yet high acidity.
2007 Big crop – those who picked late did very well.
2006 Plentiful crop of charming, aromatic wines. Drink now.
2005 Small but outstanding crop of dense, concentrated wines.
2004 Promising for aromatic, balanced wines. Now showing their paces.
2003 Hot vintage; all but the best are falling over fast.
2002 Stylish wines, starting to show very well.
2001 Sound but anonymous. Drink soon.
2000 A big crop of ripe, healthy grapes. Drink now.

The white wines of the Mâconnais (Pouilly-Fuissé, St-Véran, Mâcon-Villages) follow a similar pattern, but do not last as long. They are appreciated more for their freshness than their richness.

Chablis *Grand cru* Chablis of vintages with both strength and acidity can age superbly for up to ten years; *premiers crus* proportionally less.

2009 All set for gorgeous, accessible wines.

2008 A small crop of powerful, juicy wines ripened well in a sunny September.

2007 Brilliant *grands crus* and *premiers crus* where not damaged by hail. Basic Chablis more modest.

2006 An early harvest of attractive, aromatically pleasing wines. Start drinking.

2005 Small but outstanding crop of dense, concentrated wines.

2004 Difficult vintage, with mildew a problem. Not for keeping.

2003 Small crop of ripe wines, but acidity is low. Drink up.

2002 Delicious wines, in most cases ready to drink.

2001 Too much rain. Relatively weak. Drink up.

2000 A great vintage for Chablis. Start the *grands crus*, drink the rest.

Beaujolais 09 Wonderful. 08 Tough going with widespread hail. 07 Attractive but without the heart of a really great year. 06 Tricky vintage with some rot. 05 concentrated wines. 04 Light, some weak, some pretty. 03 Too much heat on the grapes, some excellent. 02 Drink up fast. 01 Very good if picked before rain.

Southwest France

2009 Promises to be best year of the decade (with question mark over v. sweet whites). Conditions mostly ideal except for local hail. Yields down again.

2008 Vintage just about saved by Indian summer. Better than 2007. Quantity down.

2007 Not quite as bad as feared. Whites fared better than reds, especially the sweets. The styles are all on the light side, with quantities down.

2006 A capricious and variable summer. Wines generally better than expected. A year to drink now. Reds will keep.

2005 Best year of the decade so far. Uniformly very good.

2004 Better-than-usual acidity suggests keeping potential. Excellent in Jurançon and Madiran. Middling elsewhere.

2003 The Ribena year. Small quantities of unbalanced wines, heavy in sweet fruit and alcohol, but often with stalky tannins. Drink up.

The Midi

2009 A cool spring, a hot, dry summer. Quality is excellent.

2008 A similar year to 2007, with a wet spring and cool weather during flowering, but sufficient sunshine to produce some elegant wines from unstressed vines. Severe hail damage in Faugères.

2007 A damp spring and a coole- than-average summer, with a fine September producing some beautifully balanced wines with some ageing potential.

2006 Fine results from the best winemakers.

2005 Beautifully balanced year, sunshine and rain at right times through region.

2004 Marked by August storms and a fine September. Wines are elegantly balanced, with lower alcohol than 2003 or 2001.

Northern Rhône

2009 Promising year. Very full Syrahs, deep and intense; will live. Sound whites.

2008 Tricky, rain-hit vintage. Growers okay if cut yields big time. Cornas decent, some fine Côte-Rôties, Hermitage; Crozes are light. Good whites – will live. Note Condrieu. Reds: eight to 12 years.

2007 The best sites, the best growers at Hermitage, Côte-Rôtie, Cornas, St-Joseph have produced very good wines, with stylish fruit, life of 18+ years. The whites are good, enough depth for the future.

2006 Big, healthy crop with wines showing plenty of clear fruit and sound stuffing. Have improved well, especially at Côte-Rôtie. Good acidity in robust whites, heady Condrieu wines.

2005 Exceptional, with wonderful Syrah, still tight flavours and long ageing potential for Hermitage, Cornas and the fullest Côte-Rôties. St-Joseph reds have very bright fruit. Whites are full – good for mid-term drinking.

2004 Mid-weight, mid-term year, with Côte-Rôtie showing well over time; best reds are from top vineyards. Superb whites.

2003 A half-sized crop. Intense sun gave cooked "southern" flavours. Best reds show genuine richness, and are coming together. 25+ yrs for best.

2002 Dodgy due to heavy rain. Stick to best growers. Drink up red St-Josephs, small-grower Côte-Rôtie. Hermitage, Cornas until 2015–18. Good whites, especially Condrieu.

2001 Reds ageing very well, now stylish, fresh. Top year at Côte-Rôtie. Often very good whites. Good value if available.

2000 Reds simpler than 1999 and 2001, less bright fruit, quite warm with a gentle richness. Some stewed flavours. Hermitage gd in parts, Cornas did well, Côte-Rôtie variable. Good Condrieu, sumptuous.

1999 Very successful. Delicious, likely to live long. More balance than the 1998s. Great heart and harmony. Ace Côte-Rôties. Sound whites.

Southern Rhône

2009 Reduced crop, hit by summer drought. Higher, later areas did well. Expect big, even enormous Châteauneuf-du-Pape reds. Low acidity means early drinking Côtes du Rhône/villages reds. Respectable whites.

2008 Severe sorting needed. Many estates suppressed prestige wines (joy). Best have some body, way better than 2002; life 15 years or so. Gigondas (altitude, later ripening) fared well. Trust top names this year. Good whites.

2007 Very good, an early drinking vintage. Abundant, sweet fruit is the vintage imprint. Grenache-only wines can lack tannin but drink sumptuously. Exceptional Châteauneuf-du-Pape from top names. Very good at Gigondas. Côtes du Rhônes are fat and good. Openly fruited, aromatic whites.

2006 Good; some very good wines. Quite rich Châteauneuf-du-Pape reds, starting to tighten. More open than the 2005s, less sweet and plush than the 2007s. Good Vacqueyras, Gigondas, best villages such as Cairanne. Drink up Lirac, Villages. Good, full whites, ideal for food.

2005 Very good. Strong, compact, still very fresh wines, especially from top sites and old vines. Will age well – 20+ years for top Châteauneufs, also long-lived Gigondas. Whites best drunk young.

2004 Good, but variable. Sinew and fresh, minerally flavours in Châteauneufs suit European palates. Gigondas not always rounded. Be patient. Good fresh whites, will age well.

2003 At last this vintage is gaining cohesion and balance. Chunky, potent wines, with jam and date/raisin flavours from the best, eg. Châteauneuf – better than Gigondas, Vacqueyras. End tannins starting to fuse. Best wines can live a long time. Go for the best names, best areas.

2002 Drink up. Nature's payback: 66cm of rain in a day. Simply fruited, early reds, acceptable whites. Gigondas did best.

2001 Excellent classic vintage. Complex reds, lots of life ahead, be patient for top areas. Cracking Châteauneufs showing well now .

2000 Tasty, open wines, led by fruit. Not a long-lived year. Go for leading names. Gigondas may edge Châteauneuf in quality. Best reds are singing now.

1999 Very good, underestimated wines from the best names. Some wines advancing quickly, others have fine, clear fruit. Châteauneuf reds have moved up a gear with age, with interesting variety. Good Gigondas, Lirac.

Champagne

2009 June storms reduced yields and caused land-falls in the Marne Valley. But a glorious August and rainless September made a harvest of sumptuous wines. Sure to be a vintage year.

2008 The Champenois used up all their superlatives for a likely to be slow-developing classic vintage that might be great – but with very high acidity which will need mastering. Better for Pinot N than for Chard.

2007 Selected wines from *grand cru* villages where top growers picked later under sunny September skies will make goodish Champagnes. Otherwise a mixed bag after a cold, wet summer.

2006 Topsy-turvy growing season but fine September: made for ripe, expressive wines, especially Pinot N. Could be underrated by some houses.

2005 Not a great year overall in Champagne: a bit hot for real class, wines lacking dash and verve. Vintage wines from Bollinger and Jacquesson.

2004 Champagnes of classic finesse and "tension". Vintage year.

2002 Undoubtedly a great, graceful year for superb Pinot N and sumptuous Chard. Best released vintage of early 21st century.

2000 Shows much more character and texture as vintage reaches its peak. Bollinger Grande Année and Jacquesson Corne Bautray look best.

1999 Ripe, showy wines, ready soon. Grandstanding Dom Pérignon. Against the odds, some exceptional Champagnes (Pol Roger, Gimmonet, Paillard).

Older fine vintages: 98 96 95 90 89 88 85 82

The Loire

2009 Generally very good, although drought in parts of Anjou-Touraine and severe hail damage in Menetou-Salon and parts of Sancerre. High alcohol may be a problem in some Sauv Bl.

2008 Small harvest, especially Muscadet – early April frost and hail in Pouilly and Sancerre. Very healthy grapes – with high acidity. Very promising reds and dry whites, sweets hit by wet Nov. Fine, dry whites and reds.

2007 Very difficult summer – mildew rife. Vintage saved by fine September and October. Producer's name crucial. Austere dry whites and exceptional Anjou sweets. Reds for early drinking.

2006 Challenging vintage in which only the conscientious succeeded. Dry whites fared well, good reds, some age-worthy. Not great for sweet whites.

2005 Excellent across the board. Buy without fear, though some reds quite tannic. The sweet wines are a mix of shrivelled grapes and noble rot.

2004 Huge crop. In general better for reds than whites. Few or no sweet wines in Vouvray/Montlouis. Anjou's whites fewer and less sweet than usual.

2003 Very hot, early vintage. Wines are big and supple, some flaccid, some not. Will they last? Jury remains out. Excellent year for sweet wines.

Alsace

2009 Hot, sunny August and warm September shaped early harvest of ripe, expressive wines. Brilliant Oct made good late-harvest wines, especially scented Ries and spicy Gewurz.

2008 A cool but dry August and good September shaped a healthy vintage of dry, crisp wines – a pleasing antidote to the unctuous style of late.

2007 As throughout France, hot spring, cold, wet summer but sunny autumn weather allowed picking of healthy, ripe grapes. Promising.

2006 Hottest recorded July followed by coolest August. Top producers such as Faller and Trimbach made subtle, fine Ries.

2005 A large crop of healthy grapes harvested after an Indian summer. Ripe and well-balanced wines of character, minerality and strength.

2004 Growers who picked early and kept yields low produced classic wines. Subtle year, especially for Ries.

2002 Better than most of France. As in Champagne, some beautiful, supple wines – lots of personality, class, complete.

2001 Well-balanced wines, good but not great.

Abel-Lepitre Discreet CHAMPAGNE house, improving under Boizel Chanoine ownership. Fine Cuvée Idéale NV, impressive Brut Vintage 04 Excellent Cuvée 134 (blend of two CHARD yrs).

Abymes Savoie w ★ DYA Hilly area nr Chambéry; light, mild Vin de Savoie AC from Jacquère grape has alpine charm. SAVOIE has many such *crus*.

Agenais SW r p w ★ DYA VDP of Lot-et-Garonne, where grapes compete with prunes. Independents, eg. DOMS Lou Gaillot and Campet, better than moderate co-ops.

Aligoté DYA Fresh, thirst-quenching secondary grape from Burgundy with own appellation at bouzeron. Base wine for apéritif crème blanc cassis (Kir).

Alliet, Philippe Lo r w ★★→★★★ 02 04 05' 06 08 (09) Top CHINON producer making concentrated CUVÉES to age. Best include barrel-aged Coteau du Noire and VIEILLES VIGNES and a recent hill v'yd L'Huisserie. A little CHINON *blanc*.

Aloxe-Corton Burg r w ★★→★★★ 96' 99' 02' 03 05' 06 06 07 08 (09)

Alquier, Jean-Michel Midi r w Leading FAUGÈRES producer. White Marsanne/ Grenache Bl VDP blend; also Sauvignon Les Pierres Blanches VDP, red CUVÉES Les Premières, Maison Jaune and age-worthy Les Bastides.

Alsace Al w (r sw sp) ★★→★★★★ 00' 02' 04 05' 06 08 09' The sheltered east slope of the Vosges Mts makes France's Rhine wines: aromatic, fruity, full-strength, mostly dry and expressive of variety. Sugar levels vary widely: dry wines now easier to find. Much sold by variety (Pinot Bl, Ries, Gewurz). Matures well (except Pinot Bl, MUSCAT) 5–10 yrs; GRAND CRU even longer. Gd quality and value CRÉMANT. Formerly feeble Pinot N improving fast. See VENDANGE TARDIVE, SELECTION DES GRAINS NOBLES.

Alsace Grand Cru w ★★★→★★★★★ 90' 95 96 97 98 99 00' 02' 04 05' 06 08 09' AC restricted to 51 (KAEFFERKOPF added in 2006) of the best-named v'yds (approx 1,600 ha, 800 in production) and four noble grapes (Ries, PINOT GR, Gewurz, MUSCAT) mainly dry, some sweet. Controversial classification now widely respected. They repay several yrs in bottle.

Amiel, Mas Midi r w sw ★★★ The pioneering MAURY DOM. Warming CÔTES DU ROUSSILLON Carérades red, white Altaïr, *vin de liqueur* Plénitude from Maccabeu. Vintage and cask-aged VDN. Prestige 15 yrs a star. STÉPHANE DERENONCOURT (B'x) consults.

Amirault, Yannick Lo r ★★→★★★ 02 03 04 05' 06 08' (09) Meticulous, first-rate producer of both BOURGUEIL and ST-NICOLAS-DE-BOURGUEIL. Top La Petite Cave and Les Quartiers in BOURGUEIL and Malagnes and La Mine in ST-NICOLAS.

Ampeau, Michel Burg ★★ Following on from his father, Robert, Michel specializes in late releases of fine old burgundy of both colours, notably MEURSAULT, PULIGNY and VOLNAY-SANTENOTS.

André, Pierre Burg ★★ Négociant at CH Corton-André, ALOXE-CORTON; 5 ha of v'yds in and around CORTON plus wide range from purchased grapes. Significant improvement since purchase by Ballande Group in 2003.

d'Angerville, Marquis Burg ★★★★ One of VOLNAY's superstar DOMS with brilliant PREMIERS CRUS Clos des Ducs (MONOPOLE), Champans and Taillepieds. Quality rising yet further of late. Biodynamic.

Anjou Lo r p w (dr sw sp) ★→★★★★ Both region and umbrella AC covering Anjou and SAUMUR. Many styles: Chenin Bl dry whites range from light quaffers to potent agers; juicy reds, inc rich Gamay; juicy Cab Fr-based Anjou *rouge*; and structured ANJOU-VILLAGES; also strong, mainly dry SAVENNIÈRES;

lightly sweet to luscious COTEAUX DU LAYON Chenin Bl; dry and sweet rosé and sparkling.

Anjou-Coteaux de la Loire Lo w sw s/sw ★★→★★★ 02 03 05' 07 (09) Small (40 ha) westernmost ANJOU AC for sweet whites from Chenin Bl; less rich but nervier than COTEAUX DU LAYON. Esp DOMS du Fresche, Musset-Roullier, CH de Putille.

Anjou-Villages Lo r ★→★★★ 02 03 05' 06 08 (09') Superior central ANJOU AC for reds (Cab Fr/Cab Sauv, but a few pure Cab Sauv). Quality tends to be high and prices reasonable, esp DOMS de Brizé, Dom Philippe, DOM CADY, Clos de Coulaine, Philippe Delesvaux, DOM les Grandes Vignes, Ogereau, CH PIERRE-BISE. Sub-AC Anjou-Villages-Brissac covers the same zone as COTEAUX DE L'AUBANCE; look for Bablut, DOM de Haute Perche, Montigilet, Richou, Rochelles, CH de Varière.

Appellation Contrôlée (AC or AOC) Government control of origin and production (not quality) of all the best French wines; about 45% of the total.

Apremont Savoie w ★★ DYA One of the best villages of SAVOIE for pale, delicate whites, mainly from Jacquère grapes, but recently inc CHARD.

Arbin Savoie r ★★ Deep-coloured, lively red from MONDEUSE grapes, rather like a gd Loire Cab Sauv. Ideal après-ski. Drink at 1–2 yrs.

Arbois Jura r p w (sp) ★★→★★★ Various gd and original light but tasty wines; specialty is VIN JAUNE. On the whole, DYA except VIN JAUNE.

Ariège SW r ★05' 06 08 (09') Rare local VDP from south of Toulouse for the adventurous. Note esp DOM des Coteaux d'Engravies. Will keep.

Arlaud Burg ★★→★★★ MOREY-ST-DENIS estate with CHARMES-CHAMBERTIN, CLOS DE LA ROCHE, etc. Fine wine at all levels in relatively easy, modern style.

l'Arlot, Dom de Burg ★★★ Leading exponent in CÔTE DE NUITS of whole-bunch fermentation. Wines pale but aromatic and full of fruit. Best v'yds ROMANÉE-ST-VIVANT and NUITS-ST-GEORGES, esp Clos de l'Arlot. Gd whites, too.

Armagnac SW The alternative to Cognac, and increasingly popular – certainly *chez moi*; tasty, rustic and peppery. Hors d'Age is fine, vintages often overpriced. New AC for young white (colourless) Armagnac. Table wines: CÔTES DE GASCOGNE, GERS, TERROIRS LANDAIS.

Armand, Comte Burg ★★★ Sole owner of exceptional Clos des Epeneaux in POMMARD, as well as other v'yds in AUXEY and VOLNAY. On top form since 1999.

Aube Southern extension of CHAMPAGNE. Now known as Côte des Bar.

Aujoux, J-M Beauj Substantial grower/merchant of BEAUJOLAIS. Swiss-owned.

Auxey-Duresses Burg r w ★★→★★★ 99' 02' 03 05' 06 07 (09) Second-rank (but v. pretty) CÔTE DE BEAUNE village: affinities with VOLNAY, MEURSAULT. Best examples (red) COMTE ARMAND, MAISON LEROY, Prunier; (white) Fichet, MAISON LEROY (Les Boutonniers).

Avize Champ One of the top Côte des Blancs villages. All CHARD.

Aÿ Champ One of the best Pinot N-growing villages of CHAMPAGNE.

Ayala Revitalized AŸ-based CHAMPAGNE house, owned by BOLLINGER. Fine Brut Nature Zéro Dosage and racy Rosé. Excellent Prestige Perle d'Ayala (**99** 02).

Bandol Prov r p (w) ★★★ 96 97 98 99 00 01 02 03 04 05 06 07 Small coastal AC; PROVENCE's finest. Long-lasting oak-aged reds mainly from Mourvèdre with Grenache and Cinsault; elegant rosé from young vines, and a splash of white from CLAIRETTE, Ugni Blanc and occasionally Sauv Bl. Stars include DOMS de la Laidière, Lafran Veyrolles, La Suffrène, TEMPIER, CH'X Pibarnon, Pradeaux, Mas de la Rouvière, La Bégude, La Bastide Blanche.

Banyuls Pyr br sw ★★→★★★ One of the most original VDNS, mainly Grenache (Banyuls GRAND CRU: over 75% Grenache, aged for 2 yrs+). Newer vintage style resembles ruby port but far better are traditional RANCIOS, aged for yrs in large casks. Think fine old tawny port. Best: DOMS du Mas Blanc (★★★), la Rectorie (★★★), Vial Magnères, Coume del Mas, la Tour Vieille.

Barrique The BORDEAUX (and Cognac) term for an oak barrel holding 225 litres.

Barrique-ageing to flavour almost any wine with oak was craze in late 1980s, with some sad results. Current oak prices should urge discretion.

Barsac B'x w sw ★★→★★★★ 83' 86' 88' 89' 90' 95 96 97' 98 99' 01' 02 03' 05' 07' (09) Neighbour of SAUTERNES with similar superb golden wines from lower-lying limestone soil; fresher, less powerful and with more finesse. Repays long ageing. Top: CLIMENS, COUTET, DOISY-DAËNE, DOISY-VÉDRINES.

Barthod, Ghislaine Burg ★★★→★★★★ Impressive range of archetypal CHAMBOLLE-MUSIGNY. Marvellous poise and delicacy, yet with depth and concentration. Nine PREMIER CRUS, such as Les Cras, Fuées and Beaux Bruns.

Barton & Guestier BORDEAUX négociant now part of massive Diageo group.

Bâtard-Montrachet Burg w ★★★★ 99' 00 02' 03 04' 05' 06' 07 08 (09) 12-ha GRAND CRU downslope from LE MONTRACHET itself. Rich, fat wines, sometimes four-square. Also worthy siblings Bienvenues-B-M and Criots B-M. Seek out: BOILLOT, BOUCHARD PÈRE & FILS, CARILLON, DROUHIN, GAGNARD, LATOUR, DOM LEFLAIVE, MOREY, Pernot, Ramonet, SAUZET.

Baudry, Dom Bernard Lo r p w ★★→★★★ 02 03 04 05 06 08 (09) Excellent CHINON across the range, from Chenin Bl-based whites to Cab Fr-based rosés and excellent CHINON CUVÉES of red, from juicy Les Granges to structured Clos Guillot and Croix Boissées.

Baudry-Dutour Lo r p w ★★→★★★ 02 03 05' 06 08 (09) A merger in 2003 of DOMS de la Perrière and de la Roncée. Now CHINON's largest producer with 120 ha, inc CHX de St Louand and latest acquisition de la Grille. Reliable quality from light, early drinking to age-worthy reds.

Baumard, Dom des Lo r, p, w, sw, sp ★★→★★★★ 02 03 04 05' 06 07' (sw) 08 (09) Leading family producer of ANJOU wine, esp Chenin Bl-based whites, inc SAVENNIÈRES (Clos St Yves, Clos du Papillon), QUARTS DE CHAUME and Clos Ste Catherine (COTEAUX DU LANGUEDOC). Makes a tangy VIN DE TABLE from Verdelho. The Loire's brave screwcap pioneer.

Béarn SW r p w ★→★★ w p DYA r 08 09 Mostly rosé from MADIRAN and JURANÇON producers. Reds also from DOM ★★ Lapeyre/Guilhémas and Béarn co-op. Whites are generally sharp.

Beaujolais r (p w) ★ DYA The most basic appellation of the huge Beaujolais region, producing five million cases a yr. Some from the hills can be excellent.

Beaujolais Primeur (or Nouveau) The Beaujolais of the new vintage, made in a hurry (often only 4–5 days' fermenting) for release at midnight on the third Wednesday in Nov. Ideally soft, pungent, fruity and tempting; too often crude, sharp, too alcoholic. More of an event than a drink.

Beaujolais-Villages r ★★ 05' 06 07 08 09' Wines from better (northern) half of BEAUJOLAIS; should be much tastier than plain BEAUJOLAIS. The ten (easily) best villages are the *crus*: FLEURIE, ST-AMOUR, JULIÉNAS, CHÉNAS, MOULIN-À-VENT, CHIROUBLES, MORGON, REGNIÉ, CÔTE DE BROUILLY, BROUILLY. Of the 30 others the best lie around Beaujeu. *Crus* cannot be released *en primeur* before 15 Dec. Best kept until spring (or considerably longer).

Beaumes-de-Venise S Rh r br (p w) ★★ 05' 06 07' 09' for reds. DYA for MUSCAT. Popular leading dessert MUSCAT, from SE CÔTES DU RHÔNE; can be honeyed or muskily aromatic, peach/apricot-flavoured (eg. DOMS Beaumalric, Bernardins, Coyeux, Durban, JABOULET, Pigeade (v.gd), VIDAL-FLEURY, co-op), gd with melon, soft cheese, chocolate. Mid-weight, bit austere reds, best ripe yrs 07 03 (CH Redortier, DOMS Cassan, de Fenouillet, Durban, St-Amant) leave for 2–3 yrs. Fresh white and rosé are CÔTES DU RHÔNE.

Beaumont des Crayères Champ Bijou Côte d'Epernay co-op making excellent Pinot Meunier-based Grande Réserve NV and v. fine Fleur de Prestige 98' 00 02 04. Exceptional CHARD-led Cuvée Nostalgie 98'. Fleur de Rosé 02 03 04.

Beaune Burg r (w) ★★★ 02' 03 05' 07 08 (09) Historic wine capital of Burgundy and home to many merchants: BOUCHARD, CHAMPY, DROUHIN, JADOT, LATOUR as well as HOSPICES DE BEAUNE. No GRAND CRU v'yds but sound PREMIERS CRUS: eg. Cras, Grèves, Teurons, Cent Vignes, Clos du Roi, Bressandes for red and an increasing amount of white, of which DROUHIN'S CLOS DES MOUCHES stands out.

Becker, Caves J Al ★→★★ An organic estate, progressively biodynamic. Stylish, well-balanced wines, inc exceptional Muscat Grand Cru Froehn.

Bellet Prov r p w ★★★ Local wine of Nice; expensive, original but little known in city. White from Rolle grape is best; unexpected ageing potential. Handful of producers: CH de Bellet, Clos St Vincent, Les Coteaux de Bellet, CH de Crémat.

Bellivière, Dom de Lo r w sw ★★→★★★ 02 03 05' 06 07 08 (09') In biodynamic conversion: precise Chenin Bl in JASNIÈRES and COTEAUX DU LOIR and revelatory Pineau d'Aunis.

Bergerac Dordogne r p w dr sw ★→ ★★★ 02 04 05' 06 08 (09') Gd-value Bordeaux lookalike (*pace* Cyrano) using same grape varieties. Top properties include ★★★ DOMS l'Ancienne Cure, Clos des Verdots, Les Hauts de Caillevel, *La Tour des Gendres*, Jonc Blanc, Les Marnières. ★★ CHX Belingard-Chayne, Clos de la Colline, les Eyssards, les Fontenelles, Grinou, de la Mallevieille, les Miaudoux, le Paradis, Pion, le Raz, Thénac. See also MONBAZILLAC, MONTRAVEL, PÉCHARMANT, ROSETTE, SAUSSIGNAC.

Bertrand, Gérard Midi r p w ★★ Ex-rugger player and now one of biggest v'yd owners in south, with 325 ha; Villemajou in CORBIÈRES *cru* Boutenac, Laville-Bertou in MINERVOIS LA LIVINIÈRE, l'Hospitalet in La Clape, l'Aigle in LIMOUX, and Vin de Pays d'Oc. Best wines: La Viala (MINERVOIS), La Forge (CORBIÈRES), l'Hospitalet (COTEAUX DU LANGUEDOC).

Besserat de Bellefon Epernay house specializing in gently sparkling CHAMPAGNES (old CRÉMANT style). Now owned by Boizel Chanoine group. Improved quality.

Beyer, Léon ★★→★★★ ALSACE specialist: v. fine, intense, dry wines often needing 10 yrs+ bottle age. Superb Ries. Comtes d'Eguisheim, but no mention on label of GRAND CRU PFERSIGBERG, its originating v'yd. Gd Gewurz.

Bichot, Maison Albert Burg ★★→★★★ Dynamic merchant and owner/distributor of LONG-DEPAQUIT (CHABLIS), Clos Frantin and more. Quality on the rise.

Billecart-Salmon Family CHAMPAGNE house makes exquisite long-lived wines, vintage CUVÉES progressively fermented in wood. Superb Clos St-Hilaire Blanc de Noirs (96' 98'), NF Billecart (98 99 00), top BLANC DE BLANCS (98' 99 00) and new BRUT 04.

Bize, Simon Burg ★★★ Patrick B has developed this fine SAVIGNY DOM over 20 yrs to include LATRICIÈRES-CHAMBERTIN, CORTON-CHARLEMAGNE and some fine inexpensive whites alongside v.gd range of Savigny PREMIERS CRUS.

Blagny Burg r w ★★→★★★ (r) 99' 02' 03' 05' 07 08 (09) Austere reds now out of fashion as growers replant with CHARD in the manner of MEURSAULT. Best v'yds: Pièce sous le Bois, Sous le Dos d'Ane. AMPEAU, Jobard, Matrot, Martelet de Cherisey best.

Blanc de blancs Any white wine made from white grapes only, esp CHAMPAGNE. An indication of style, not of quality.

Blanck, Paul & Fils ★★→★★★ Grower at Kientzheim, ALSACE, producing huge range of wines. Finest from 6 ha GRAND CRU Furstentum (Ries, Gewurz, PINOT GR) and GRAND CRU SCHLOSSBERG (Ries). Also gd Pinot Bl.

Blanc de noirs White (or slightly pink or "blush") wine from red grapes, esp CHAMPAGNE.

Blanquette de Limoux Midi w sp ★★ Gd-value creamy fizz from cooler area nr Carcassonne; claims older history than CHAMPAGNE. Basic Mauzac much improved by CHARD, Chenin Bl and, more recently, Pinot N, esp in newer AC CRÉMANT DE LIMOUX. Large co-op with Sieur d'Arques label. Also Rives-Blanques, Martinolles.

Blaye B'x r w ★→★★ 01 03 04 05' 06 08 (09) Designation for top, concentrated reds from PREMIÈRES CÔTES DE BLAYE and from 2008 for single-terroir wines in new AC CÔTES DE BORDEAUX (see box, p.89).

Boillot Burg Interconnected Burgundy growers. Look for Jean-Marc (POMMARD) ★★★ for fine oaky reds and whites, Henri (VOLNAY) ★★★ and Louis (CHAMBOLLE, married to GHISLAINE BARTHOD) ★★→★★★.

Boisset, Jean-Claude Burg New kid on block now respectable after 40 yrs. Own wines and own v'yds DOM DE LA VOUGERAIE excellent. Also owns range of other businesses, latest RODET. Projects in Canada, California, Chile, Uruguay looked after by son Jean-Charles, now married to Gina GALLO of eponymous US giant.

Boizel One of CHAMPAGNE's surest values: brilliant, aged Blanc de Blancs NV and prestige Joyau de France (95 96 98 00), Joyau Rosé (00 02'). Also Grand Vintage Brut (98 99 00 02) and Cuvée Sous Bois.

Bollinger Great individualistic CHAMPAGNE house, on a roll in recent vintages (viz. Grande Année 95' 00 02). New non-vintage rosé. Luxury wines: RD (88' 90 95 96), Vieilles Vignes Françaises (98 99) from ungrafted Pinot N vines, La Côte aux Enfants, AŸ (02'). See also LANGLOIS-CH.

Bonneau du Martray, Dom Burg r w ★★★★ (w) ★★ (r) Top source for CORTON-CHARLEMAGNE plus tiny amount of red CORTON. Expect return to longer ageing potential.

Bonnes-Mares Burg r ★★★→★★★★ 90' 91 95 96' 97 98 99' 00 02' 03 05' 06 07 08 09 GRAND CRU (15ha) between CHAMBOLLE-MUSIGNY and MOREY-ST-DENIS. Sturdy, long-lived wines, more fragrant than MUSIGNY. Best: DUJAC, Groffier, JADOT, ROUMIER, DE VOGÜÉ, VOUGERAIE.

Bonnezeaux Lo w sw ★★★→★★★★ 88 89' 90' 95' 96' 97' 02 03' 05' 07 (09) Magnificently rich, almost everlasting sweet Chenin Bl with QUARTS DE CHAUME top site in COTEAUX DU LAYON. Esp: CHX de Fesles, la Fresnaye, de Varière, DOMS les Grandes Vignes, du Petit Val (Goizil).

Bordeaux B'x r w (p) ★→★★ 01 03 05' (09) Catch-all AC for generic Bordeaux (represents nearly half the region's production). Mixed quality. Most brands are in this category.

Bordeaux Supérieur B'x r ★→★★ 00' 01 03 04 05' (09) Superior denomination to above. Higher min alcohol, lower yield and longer ageing. 75% of production bottled at the property, the reverse of AC BORDEAUX.

Borie-Manoux Admirable BORDEAUX shipper, CH-owner. CHX inc BATAILLEY, BEAU-SITE, Croix du Casse, DOM DE L'ÉGLISE, HAUT-BAGES-MONPELOU, TROTTEVIEILLE.

Bouchard Père & Fils Burg ★★→★★★★★ Huge v'yd owner – largest in CÔTE D'OR? New winery continues to improve quality. Whites esp strong in MEURSAULT and CHEVALIER-MONTRACHET. New Villa Ponciago (BEAUJOLAIS). Owned by HENRIOT.

Bouches-du-Rhône Prov r p w ★ VDP from Marseille environs. Warming reds from southern varieties, plus Cab Sauv, Syrah and Merlot.

Bourgeois, Henri Lo ★★→★★★ 02 03 05 06 07 05 06 07 08 (09) Top-quality, leading SANCERRE grower/merchant in Chavignol. Also POUILLY-FUMÉ, MENETOU-SALON, QUINCY (CH), COTEAUX DU GIENNOIS (CH), CHÂTEAUMEILLANT and VDP Petit Bourgeois. Top wines include MD de Bourgeois, La Bourgeoise (r, w), Jadis, Sancerre d'Antan. See also Clos Henri (r, w) in Marlborough, NZ.

Bourgogne Burg r w (p) ★★ (r) 05' 06 07 08 09' (w) 05 06 07 08 09' Catch-all AC, with higher standards than basic BORDEAUX. Light, often gd flavour, best at 2–4 yrs. Top growers make bargain beauties from fringes of CÔTE D'OR villages; do not despise. BEAUJOLAIS crus (except RÉGNIÉ) may be labelled Bourgogne.

Bourgogne Grand Ordinaire r (w) ★ DYA Who invented this crazy name for the most basic of Burgundy? Usually Gamay for red, CHARD, Aligoté, or occasionally Melon de Bourgogne for white.

Bourgogne Passe-Tout-Grains r (p) ★ Age 1–2 yrs. The name suggests you can put any grape in, but in fact it must be a mix of Pinot N (min 33%) and Gamay. Can be fun from CÔTE D'OR DOMS.

Bourgueil Lo r (p) ★★→★★★(★) 96' 02 03 05' 06 08 (09) Burly, full-flavoured TOURAINE reds and big, fragrant rosés based on Cab Fr. Gd vintages can age 15 yrs. Esp AMIRAULT, Audebert, DOM de la Butte, DOM de la Chevalerie, Delaunay, Druet, Lame Delisle Boucard. See ST-NICOLAS-DE-BOURGUEIL.

Bouscassé, Dom SW ★★★ 00 01 02 04 05 06 (09') ALAIN BRUMONT's palatial winery in MADIRAN, where he also makes his CH MONTUS.

Bouvet-Ladubay Lo ★→★★★ Major sparkling SAUMUR house owned by Indian company United Breweries. Best is the barrel-fermented Cuvée Trésor – both white and rosé. Also still wines mainly from ANJOU-SAUMUR. Large art centre at premises at St-Hilaire-St-Florent (SAUMUR).

Bouzereau Burg ★★→★★★ Family in MEURSAULT making gd whites at gd prices and improving reds. Jean-Baptiste, son of Michel B, and Vincent B are the two best.

Bouzeron Burg w ★★ CÔTE CHALONNAISE AC specifically for ALIGOTÉ, though they don't tell you so on the label any more. Age 1–2 yrs or more from de Villaine.

Bouzy Rouge Champ r ★★★ 90 95 96 97 99 02 Still red of famous Pinot N village. Like v. light Burgundy, but can last well in sunny vintages.

Brocard, J-M Burg ★★→★★★ One of the recent success stories of CHABLIS with a fine range of wines at all levels. Also on offer: a range of BOURGOGNE *blancs* from different soil types (Kimmeridgian, Jurassic, Portlandian).

Brouilly Beauj r ★★ 05' 06 07 08 09' Biggest of the ten *crus* of BEAUJOLAIS: fruity, round, refreshing wine, can age 3–4 yrs. CH de la Chaize is largest estate. Top growers: Michaud, DOMS de Combillaty, des Grandes Vignes, Dubost.

Brumont, Alain SW ★★★ Still the media choice in MADIRAN. Notable for modern, oaked 100% Tannat wines, eg. Le Tyre, *Ch Montus*, DOM BOUSCASSÉ. Gd-value Torus brand quicker, easier drinking. Range of VDPS, esp 100% Gros Manseng.

Brut Term for the dry classic wines of CHAMPAGNE.

Brut Ultra/Zéro Term for bone-dry wines in CHAMPAGNE back in fashion.

Bugey Savoie r p w sp ★→★★★ DYA VDQS for light sparkling, still, or half-sparkling wines from Roussette (or Altesse) and CHARD (gd). Best from Montagnieu; also Rosé de Cerdon, mainly Gamay.

Burguet, Alain Burg ★★→★★★ Compact VIGNERON for outsize GEVREY-CHAMBERTIN.

Buxy Burg w Village in AC MONTAGNY with gd co-op for CHARD and Pinot N.

Buzet SW r (p w) ★★ 06 07 08 (09) Improving co-op gd for its single properties (esp English-owned, prize-winning Mazelières). Local character from (independent) ★★★ biodynamic DOM du Pech, ★★ CHX du Frandat, Tournelles.

Cabardès Midi r (p w) ★→★★★ 01 02 03 04 05 06 07 08 BORDEAUX Cab and Merlot meet MIDI Syrah and Grenache for original blends. Best is DOM de Cabrol with Vin de l'Est, Vin d'Ouest; also Jouclary, Font Juvenal. CH Pennautier is largest.

Cabernet d'Anjou Lo p s/sw ★→★★ Traditionally sweet DEMI-SEC, often derided, rosé enjoying renaissance. Can be age-worthy. CH PIERRE-BISE; DOMS de Bablut CADY, Clau de Nell, les Grandes Vignes, Ogereau, de Sauveroy.

Cabrières Midi p (r) ★★ DYA COTEAUX du LANGUEDOC. Traditionally full-bodied rosé; also sound reds mainly from energetic village co-op. Aspiring AOP.

Cady, Dom Lo r p sw ★★→★★★ 02 03 04 05' 06 07' (sw) 08 (09) Excellent ANJOU grower of everything from dry whites and off-dry rosés to lusciously sweet COTEAUX DU LAYON and CHAUME. Sweet wines are strongest suit.

Cahors SW r ★→★★★ 98 00 01' 02 04 05' 06 (08) (09') Long-established, unfocused all-red AOC, held together by compulsory Malbec (at least 70%), capable of yielding fruity, easy wines from ★★ Maison Vigoureux Pigmentum, CH Latuc, DOM Boliva; structured, more traditional from ★★★ *Clos de Gamot* (esp Cuvée Vignes Centenaires), ★★ Coutale, Triguedina, CHX du Cayrou, la Coustarelle, Gaudou, les Ifs, DOMS de la Bérengeraie, de Cause, Paillas,

Pineraie, les Rigalets, Savarines (organic); more New World style from CH Lagrézette, ★★★ CHX du Cèdre, Lamartine, la Caminade Eugénie; better control of oak and gentler vinification from cult ★★★ DOM Cosse-Maisonneuve.

Cairanne S Rh r p w ★★→★★★ 01' 03 04' 05' 06' 07' 09' Best of the 18 CÔTES DU RHÔNE-VILLAGES: full, bristling, fruit, some flair, esp DOMS D Alary, Ameillaud, Armand, Brusset, Escaravailles, Grosset, Hautes Cances, Oratoire St-Martin, Présidente, Rabasse-Charavin, Richaud, Perrin et Fils. Food-friendly, robust whites.

Canard-Duchêne CHAMPAGNE house. Improving with ALAIN THIÉNOT. Fine Cuvée Charles VII.

Canon-Fronsac B'x r ★★→★★★ 96 98 00' 01 03 05' 06 08 (09) 260-ha enclave within FRONSAC – otherwise same wines. The best rich, full and finely structured. Try CHX Barrabaque, Cassagne Haut-Canon la Truffière, la Fleur Caillou, DU GABY, Grand-Renouil, Haut-Mazeris, Lamarche Canon Candelaire, MOULIN-PEY-LABRIE, Pavillon, Vrai Canon Bouché.

Caramany Pyr r (w) ★ Theoretically superior AC for CÔTES DU ROUSSILLON-VILLAGES.

Carillon, Louis Burg ★★★ Sensibly priced and consistently fine PULIGNY producer, esp Combettes, Perrières, Referts.

Cassis Prov w (r p) ★★ DYA Fashionable pleasure port east of Marseille with traditional reputation for dry whites based on CLAIRETTE and Marsanne. Delicious with bouillabaisse, but expensive (eg. DOM de la Ferme Blanche, Clos Ste Magdeleine, Clos d'Albizzi). Growers fighting rear-guard action with property developers. Do not confuse with the blackcurrant liqueur from Dijon.

Cathiard Burg ★★★ Brilliant VOSNE-ROMANÉE producer on top form since late 1990s. Perfumed, sensual wines are charming young but will age.

Cave Cellar, or any wine establishment.

Cave coopérative Wine-growers' co-op winery; over half of all French production. Often well-run, well-equipped, and wines gd value for money, but disappearing in the economic crisis.

Cazes, Dom Midi r p w sw ★★ Large family producer in ROUSSILLON. VDP pioneer, with Merlot and Cab Sauv, esp for brand Le Canon du Maréchal and Le Crédo, also CÔTES DU ROUSSILLON-VILLAGES and delicious aged RIVESALTES. Excellent value.

Cellier des Samsons ★ BEAUJOLAIS/MÂCONNAIS co-op at Quincié, which has 2,000 grower-members. Wines widely distributed; now owned by BOISSET.

Cérons B'x w dr sw ★★ 97' 98 99' 01' 02 03' 05' 07 (08') 60-ha neighbour of SAUTERNES. Less intense wines, eg. CHX de Cérons, CHANTEGRIVE, Grand Enclos.

Chablis Burg w ★★ →★★★ 05' 06' 07 08 09' At best magical, minerally wine from N of Burgundy, but too much anonymous CHARD now made. Usually unoaked.

Chablis Grand Cru Burg w ★★★→★★★★ 95' 96' 98 99 00' 02' 03 05' 06' 07 08 09 Small block of seven v'yds on steep slope on right bank of Serein. Needs age for minerality and individual style to develop. V'yds: Blanchots, Bougros, Clos, Grenouilles, Preuses, Valmur, Vaudésir. Clos and Vaudésir best.

Chablis Premier Cru Burg w ★★★ 99 00' 02' 03 05' 06 07 08 09 Technically second-rank but at best excellent; more typical of CHABLIS than its GRANDS CRUS. Can outclass more expensive MEURSAULT and other CÔTE DE BEAUNE. Best v'yds include Côte de Léchet, Fourchaume, Mont de Milieu, Montée de Tonnerre, Montmains, Vaillons.

Chambertin Burg r ★★★★ 88 89 90' 93 95 96' 97 98 99' 00 01 02' 03 05' 06 07 08 09 13-ha (or 28-ha inc Clos de Bèze) of Burgundy's most imperious wine; amazingly dense, sumptuous, long-lived and expensive. Not everybody up to standard, but try from BOUCHARD PÈRE & FILS, Charlopin, Damoy, DROUHIN, DOM LEROY, MORTET, PRIEUR, Rossignol-Trapet, ROUSSEAU, TRAPET.

Chambertin-Clos de Bèze Burg r ★★★★ 88 89 90' 93 95 96' 97 98 99' 00 01 02' 03 05' 06 07 08 09 May be sold under the name of neighbouring CHAMBERTIN.

Splendid wines, maybe more accessible in youth. 15 growers, inc CLAIR, Damoy, DROUHIN, Drouhin-Laroze, FAIVELEY, Groffier, JADOT, ROUSSEAU.

Chambolle-Musigny Burg r ★★★→★★★★ 90' 93 95' 96' 98 99' 01 02' 03 05' 06 07 08 09 CÔTE DE NUITS village (170 ha): fragrant, complex, but never heavy wine. Best v'yds: Amoureuses, BONNES-MARES, Charmes, Cras, Fuées, MUSIGNY. Growers to note: Amiot-Servelle, BARTHOD, Digoia-Royer, DROUHIN, Groffier, Hudelot-Baillet, JADOT, MUGNIER, RION, ROUMIER, DE VOGÜÉ.

Champagne Sparkling wines of Pinots N and Meunier and/or CHARD, and its region (34,000-ha, 145-km east of Paris); made by *méthode traditionnelle*. Bubbles from elsewhere, however gd, cannot be Champagne.

Champagne le Mesnil Top-flight co-op in greatest GRAND CRU CHARD village. Exceptional Cuvée Sublime (02') from finest sites. Real value.

Champs-Fleuris, Dom des Lo r p w sw ★★→★★★ 02 03 05' 06 07 08 (09) Go-ahead 34-ha DOM. Top-notch SAUMUR *blanc*; SAUMUR-CHAMPIGNY; fine CRÉMANT; pretty rosé; when vintage warrants, succulent COTEAUX DU SAUMUR called Cuvée Sarah.

Champy Père & Cie Burg ★★→★★★ Ancient négociant house revitalized by Meurgey family. Own DOM of 17ha now biodynamic, centred on BEAUNE v'yds. Still improving. Acquisition of DOM Laleure-Piot brings 10 ha more.

Chandon de Briailles, Dom Burg ★★★ Unfashionable but fine, light reds, esp PERNAND-VERGELESSES, Ile de Vergelesses and CORTON.

Chanson Père & Fils Burg ★→★★★ Unpushy BEAUNE-based merchant of increasing quality. Look for Clos des Fèves red and CORTON-Vergennes white.

Chapelle-Chambertin Burg r ★★★ 90' 93 95 96' 98 99' 01 02' 03 05' 07 08 09 A 5.2-ha neighbour of CHAMBERTIN. Wine more "nervous", less meaty. V.gd in cooler yrs. Top producers: Damoy, JADOT, Rossignol-Trapet, TRAPET, Tremblay.

Chapoutier N Rh ★★→★★★★ Old family grower, but mainly merchant of big-bodied red, white Rhônes; biodynamic. Note low-yield special CUVÉES, full, textured CHÂTEAUNEUF: Barbe Rac, Croix de Bois (r), Côte-Rôtie La Mordorée, HERMITAGE: L'Ermite, Le Pavillon (r), L'Ermite, Cuvée de l'Orée, Le Méal (w). Also St-Joseph Les Granits (r, w). V.gd Marsanne N Rhône whites, great with food. Gd-value *Meysonniers Crozes*. Also holdings in BANYULS, COTEAUX DU TRICASTIN, COTEAUX D'AIX-EN-PROVENCE, CÔTES DU ROUSSILLON-VILLAGES (gd DOM Bila-Haut), RIVESALTES. Also Australian joint ventures, esp DOMS Tournon and Terlato & Chapoutier, and Portuguese, in Estremadura.

Chardonnay As well as a white wine grape, also the name of a MÂCON-VILLAGES commune. Hence Mâcon-Chardonnay.

Charmes-Chambertin Burg r ★★★ 90' 93 95 96' 98 99' 01 02' 03 05' 06 07 08 09 30 ha inc neighbour MAZOYÈRES-CHAMBERTIN of mixed quality. Best has

---

Chablis

There is no better expression of the all-conquering CHARD than the full but tense, limpid but stony wines it makes on the heavy limestone soils of Chablis. Chablis terroir divides into three quality levels (four, inc PETIT CHABLIS) with great consistency. Best makers use little or no new oak to mask the precise definition of variety and terroir: Barat, Bessin*, Billaud-Simon*, BOUCHARD PÈRE & FILS, Boudin*, J-M BROCARD, J Collet*, D Dampt, R / V DAUVISSAT*, J Dauvissat, B, D et E and J Defaix, Droin, DROUHIN*, Duplessis, DURUP, FÈVRE*, Geoffroy, J-P Grossot*, LAROCHE, LONG-DEPAQUIT, DOM des Malandes, L Michel, Christian Moreau, Picq*, Pinson, RAVENEAU*, G Robin*, Servin, Tribut, Vocoret. Simple, unqualified "Chablis" may be thin; best is PREMIER or GRAND CRU. The co-op, La Chablisienne, has high standards (esp Grenouille*) and many different labels (it makes one in every three bottles). (* = outstanding)

intense, ripe, dark-cherry fruit and fragrant finish. Try Bachelet, DROUHIN, DUGAT, DUJAC, LEROY, Perrot-Minot, ROTY, ROUMIER, ROUSSEAU, VOUGERAIE.

Chassagne-Montrachet Burg r w ★★→★★★★ (w) 99 00 02' 04 05' ' 06' 07 08 09 Large village at south end of CÔTE DE BEAUNE. Soil more suited to reds, but they can be overtough. Clos St Jean best red. More planted to white now, which can be brilliant in best spots: Caillerets, La Romanée, etc. Shares GRANDS CRUS MONTRACHET and BÂTARD-M with PULIGNY, plus all of Criots-B-M. Best growers: COLIN, GAGNARD, MOREY families, CH de la Maltroye, Pillot, Niellon, Ramonet.

Château (Ch/x) Means an estate, big or small, gd or indifferent, particularly in Bordeaux (see Chx of Bordeaux). In France, *château* tends to mean, literally, castle or great house. In Burgundy, DOMAINE is the usual term.

Château d'Arlay ★→★★ Major Jura estate; 65 ha in skilful hands. Wines include v.gd VIN JAUNE, VIN DE PAILLE, Pinot N, and MACVIN.

Château de Beaucastel S Rh r w ★★★★ 78' 79 81' 83 85 86' 88 89' 90' 94' 95' 96' 97 98' 99' 00' 01' 03' 04 05' 06 07' 09' Long-time organic practices, also use of old Mourvèdre, v. old Roussanne vines set this top CHÂTEAUNEUF estate apart. Also thriving merchant business, and own GIGONDAS DOM des Tourelles (from 2008). Deep, complex wines, drink first 2 yrs or from 7–8 yrs; . Recent vintages softer. Top-grade 60% Mourvèdre Hommage à Jacques Perrin red. *Wonderful old-vine Roussanne*: keep 5–25 yrs. Excellent CÔTES DU RHÔNE Coudoulet de Beaucastel red (lives 8+ yrs). Perrin et Fils CAIRANNE, GIGONDAS, RASTEAU, VINSOBRES v. gd, great value. V.gd organic Perrin Nature CÔTES DU RHÔNE (r w). (See also Tablas Creek, California.)

Château du Cèdre SW r ★★★ 02 04 06 (08) (09') Leading exponent of modern CAHORS. Esp Le Prestige more quick-maturing than top growths. Also delicious white VDP from Viognier.

Château de la Chaize Beauj r ★★★ Magnificent recently restored CH, home to leading 98-ha BROUILLY estate.

Château-Chalon Jura w ★★★ Not a CH but AC and village. Unique dry, yellow, sherry-like wine (Savagnin grape). Develops *flor* (see "Port, Sherry & Madeira") while ageing in barrels for min 6 yrs. Ready to drink when bottled (62-cl *clavelin* bottle), but ages almost forever. A curiosity.

Château Fortia S Rh r (w) ★★ 78' 81' 90 95' 96' 97 98'99 00' 01 03' 04' 05' 06' 07' (09) 30-ha CHÂTEAUNEUF estate; owner's father, Baron Le Roy, launched France's AC system in 1920s. Traditional wines have been polished up since early 2000s. Fruit is finer, inc special Le Baron (lots of Syrah) and white.

Château Fuissé Burg w ★★→★★★ Substantial producer with some of the best terroirs of POUILLY-FUISSÉ. Esp Les Clos, Combettes. Also négociant lines.

Château-Grillet N Rh w ★★ 91' 95' 98' 00' 01' 04' 05 06' 07 08 Notable 3.6-ha terraced granite v'yd; own AC. Recent improvement. Subtle Viognier, usually needs food, but lighter style since mid-2000s. Can take 3+ yrs to open. Decant.

Châteaumeillant Lo r p ★→★★ DYA A small VDQS area (82 ha) SW of Bourges in Georges Sand country. Gamay and Pinot N for light reds, *gris* and rosés. Look for: Chaillot and especially Geoffrenet-Morval.

Château de Meursault Burg r w ★★ 61-ha estate owned by PATRIARCHE; gd v'yds and wines in BEAUNE, MEURSAULT, POMMARD, VOLNAY. Cellars open to public.

Château Mont-Redon S Rh r w ★★→★★★ 78' 85 88 89 90' 94' 95' 97' 98' 00 01' 03' 04' 05' 06' 07' Gd 100-ha CHÂTEAUNEUF estate. Fine, reserved red, best at 6+ yrs, can be v. long-lived. Fresh white can age. Sound red LIRAC (mainly Grenache).

Château Montus SW r ★★★ 00 01' 02 04 05' 06 (08) (09') ALAIN BRUMONT's flagship MADIRAN property still survives at the top of this AC despite fearsome competition. Needs long ageing and decanting.

Château la Nerthe S Rh r w ★★★ 78' 81' 89' 90' 95' 96' 97 98' 99' 00 01 03 04' 05' 06' 07' (09) V.gd 90-ha CHÂTEAUNEUF estate. Modern, sleek wines, special

Champagne growers to watch in 2011

Edmond Barnaut Bouzy. Complex, fine CHAMPAGNES mainly from Pinot N culminate in first-rate Sélection Ultra Brut Grand Cru (98 02 04) and delicious Coteaux Champenois Rosé.

Raymond Boulard Visionary Massif St-Thierry grower making v.gd multi-vintage Cuvée Petraea & superb all-CHARD Les Rachais 02'★★★★

Claude Cazals Exciting Extra-Brut Blanc de Blancs (99) and exceptional Clos Cazals (96 ★★★★99).

Richard Cheurlin One of best grower-winemakers of the Aube. Rich but balanced Carte d'Or and vintage-dated Cuvée Jeanne (02 04).

Pierre Cheval-Gatinois Aÿ. Impeccable producer of *mono-cru* CHAMPAGNES and excellent still AÿY COTEAUX CHAMPENOIS (99 02).

Collard-Picard Rising Marne Valley and Côte des Blancs DOM. Impressive Cuvée Prestige from all three CHAMPAGNE grapes, two gd vintages and part oak-fermented.

Henri Giraud Grower-merchant making exceptional Pinot-led CHAMPAGNE. Excellent Prestige Cuvée Fût de Chêne (93 95 96 98'). Getting expensive.

Benoît Lahaye Fine organic Bouzy grower: excellent Essentiel NV Brut, BL DE NOIRS and 02 vintage for long ageing.

Larmandier-Bernier Vertus; top BLANC DE BLANCS grower-maker, esp Terre de Vertus Non Dosé (03 04) and Cramant Vieilles Vignes (02 04).

V. Testulat Great-value Épernay DOM and merchant. First-rate BLANC DE NOIRS and elegant Paul Vincent Vintage (99 02).

J-L Vergnon Fine restored Le Mesnil estate making exquisite all CHARD extra-BRUT CUVÉES, esp Confidence (02' 03 05).

Veuve Fourny rising Côte des Blancs star at Vertus: ★★★★ Extra-Brut 02' and new Rougemont rosé for release in 2011/12.

CUVÉES the delicious Cadettes (r) and oaked Beauvenir (w). Younger style recently. Also run v.gd Prieuré Montézargues TAVEL, gd DOM de la Renjarde CÔTES DU RHÔNE, CH Signac CHUSCLAN.

Châteauneuf-du-Pape S Rh r (w) ★★★ 78' 81' 83 85 86 88 89' 90' 94 95' 96 98' 99' 00' 01' 03' 04' 05' 06' 07' 09' 3,230 ha nr Avignon with group of 40 DOMS for best wines (quality varies over remaining 90). Mix of up to 13 red, white varieties led by Grenache, Syrah, Mourvèdre, Counoise. Top names are strong, v. long-lived . Too many sweet fruit bombs lately. Smaller names offer gd value. Prestige wines (old vines, new oak) can be too expensive. Whites fresh, fruity, or rather sturdy, best can age 15 yrs. Top growers include: CHX DE BEAUCASTEL, FORTIA, Gardine, MONT-REDON, LA NERTHE, RAYAS, Vaudieu; DOMS de Beaurenard, Bois de Boursan, Bosquet des Papes, Les Cailloux, Chante Cigale, Charbonnière, Charvin, Cristia, Font-de-Michelle, Grand Veneur, Marcoux (fantastic VIELLES VIGNES), Pegaü, Roger Sabon, VIEUX TÉLÉGRAPHE, Henri Bonneau, Clos du Mont-Olivet, CLOS DES PAPES, Clos St-Jean, Cuvée du Vatican, P Usseglio, Vieux Donjon.

Château Pierre-Bise Lo r p w ★★ →★★★★ 02 03 04 05 06 07' (sw) 08 (09) Terroir specialist COTEAUX DU LAYON, inc Chaume, QUARTS DE CHAUME, and SAVENNIÈRES, esp Clos de Grand Beaupréau and ROCHE-AUX-MOINES. V.gd Anjou-Gamay, ANJOU-VILLAGES, and Anjou Blanc.

Château Rayas S Rh r w ★★★→★★★★ 78' 79 81' 85 86 88' 89 90' 93 94 95' 96' 98' 99 00 01 03 04' 05' 06' 07' 08 09' V. traditional 12-ha estate in CHÂTEAUNEUF. Supreme, subtle, complex reds (100% Grenache) age superbly. Traditional-style white Rayas v.gd over 15+ yrs. Gd-value second wine: *Pignan*. V.gd CH Fonsalette, CÔTES DU RHÔNE. All need decanting. Gd CH des Tours Vacqueyras.

Château Simone Prov r p w ★★→★★★ Historic estate where Winston Churchill painted Mont St-Victoire. Same family for over two centuries. Virtually synonymous with AC PALETTE nr Aix-en Provence. Warming soft reds; white repays bottle-ageing. Full-bodied rosé. Original but traditional.

Château de Villeneuve Lo r w ★★→★★★★ 96 02 03 05 06 07 08 (09) Meticulous producer. Wonderful SAUMUR *blanc* (esp barrel-fermented Les Cormiers) and SAUMUR-CHAMPIGNY (esp VIEILLES VIGNES, Grand Clos). Superb COTEAUX DE SAUMUR in 2003.

Châtillon-en-Diois Rh r p w ★ DYA Small, banal AC east of middle Rhône in pre-Alps. Only adequate, lean, mainly Gamay reds; white (some ALIGOTÉ) often made into sparkling CLAIRETTE DE DIE.

Chave, Dom Jean-Louis N Rh r w ★★★★ First-class HERMITAGE family DOM. Nine prime hillside sites. Classy, bountiful, long-lived wines, esp white (mainly Marsanne), also v.gd occasional VIN DE PAILLE. Accomplished DOM ST-JOSEPH red (bought 6+ ha DOM Florentin 2009), fruity J-L Chave brand St-Joseph Offerus, fine merchant HERMITAGE red and white.

Chavignol SANCERRE village with famous steep v'yds, Les Monts Damnés and Cul de Beaujeu. Clay-limestone soil gives full-bodied, minerally wines that age 7–10 yrs (or longer); esp from Boulay, BOURGEOIS, Cotat, DAGUENEAU and Thomas Laballe.

Chénas Beauj r ★★★ 05' 06 07 08 09 Smallest BEAUJOLAIS CRU, one of the weightiest; neighbour to MOULIN-À-VENT and JULIÉNAS. Growers: Benon, Champagnon, Charvet, CH Chèvres, DUBOEUF, Lapierre, Robin, Trichard, co-op.

Chevalier-Montrachet Burg w ★★★★ ' 92 96 97 99' 00' 01 02' 04 05' 06' 07 08 (09) Just above MONTRACHET geographically, just below in quality, though still capable of brilliant, long-lived, mineral wines. Best sectors are Les Demoiselles (JADOT, LATOUR) and La Cabotte (BOUCHARD). Other top growers: Colin-Deleger, Dancer, LEFLAIVE, Niellon, CH de Puligny.

Cheverny Lo r p w ★→★★ 05' 06 07 08 (09) Loire AC nr Chambord. Pungent, dry white from Sauv Bl and CHARD. Also Gamay, Pinot N, or Cab Sauv. Richer, rarer and more age-worthy Cour-Cheverny uses local Romorantin grape only. Sparkling uses Crémant de Loire and TOURAINE ACS. Esp Cazin, Clos Tue-Boeuf, Gendrier, Huards, Philippe Tessier; DOMS de la Desoucherie, du Moulin.

Chevillon, R Burg ★★★ Delicious, approachable NUITS-ST-GEORGES with v'yds in the best sites, esp Les St-Georges, Cailles, Vaucrains, Roncières.

Chidaine, François Lo w dr sw sp (r) ★★★ Producer of ambitious, v. pure, v. precise MONTLOUIS. In 2002 took over Clos Baudoin (formerly Prince Poniatowski), making similarly styled VOUVRAY. Concentrates on dry and DEMI-SEC styles. AC TOURAINE in Cher valley. Biodynamic producer.

Chignin Savoie w ★ DYA Light, soft white from Jacquère grapes for alpine summers. Chignin-Bergeron (with Roussanne grapes) is best and liveliest.

Chinon Lo r (p w) ★★→★★★ 89' 90' 95 96' 97 02 03 05' 06 05' 06 08 (09') Juicy, light to rich TOURAINE Cab Fr from 2,300 ha. Drink young; top vintages from top growers can age 10+ yrs. Some taut, dry Chenin Bl from 36 ha. ALLIET, BAUDRY, Baudry-Dutour; CHX de la Bonnelière, de Coulaine, DOM de la Noblaie.

Chiroubles Beauj r 05' 08 09 Gd but tiny BEAUJOLAIS CRU next to FLEURIE; fresh, fruity, silky wine for early drinking (1–3 yrs). Growers: Bouillard, Cheysson, DUBOEUF, Fourneau, Passot, Raousset, co-op.

Chorey-lès-Beaune Burg r (w) ★★ 99' 02' 03 05' 06 07 08 09 Source of inexpensive burgundy north of BEAUNE: TOLLOT BEAUT or CH de Chorey (Germain).

Chusclan S Rh r p w ★→★★ 06' 07' 09' CÔTES DU RHÔNE-VILLAGES with above-average co-op. Soft reds, lively rosés. Co-op labels include Cuvée de Marcoule, Seigneurie de Gicon. Also gd CH Signac (can age) and special CUVÉES from André Roux. Drink most young.

Clair, Bruno Burg ★★→★★★ Leading MARSANNAY estate. v.gd wines from there and GEVREY-CHAMBERTIN (esp Clos de Bèze), FIXIN, MOREY-ST-DENIS, SAVIGNY.

Clairet V. light red wine. Bordeaux Clairet is an AC. Try CHX Fontenille, Penin.

Clairette Traditional white grape of the MIDI. Its low-acid wine was a vermouth base. Improvements in winemaking produce easy-drinking glassfuls.

Clairette de Bellegarde Midi w ★ DYA AC nr Nîmes: soft, dry apéritif white from CLAIRETTE. Note Mas Carlot.

Clairette de Die Rh w dr s/sw sp ★★ NV Dry or (better) semi-sweet, jolly drinking. Traditional, sweetly fruited, MUSCAT-flavoured sparkling wine from pre-Alps in east Rhône; or straight, dry CLAIRETTE, can age 3–4 yrs. Good before Sunday lunch. Achard-Vincent, A Poulet, J-C Raspail.

Clairette du Languedoc Midi w ★ DYA A rare white AC of the MIDI. Original identity was soft and creamy; now some oak-ageing and even late-harvest and RANCIO.

Clape, la Midi r p w ★★→★★★ *Cru* of note in AC COTEAUX DU LANGUEDOC. In line for imminent AOP. Warming, spicy reds from sun-soaked hills between Narbonne and the Med. Tangy, salty whites age surprisingly well. Gd: CHX l'Hospitalet, Moyau, La Négly, Pech-Céléyran, Pech-Redon, Rouquette-sur-Mer, Ricardelle, Anglès, Mas du Soleila, Complazens.

Clape, Auguste and Pierre N Rh r (w) ★★★→★★★★ 95' 97 98' 99' 00 01' 02 03' 04' 05' 06' 07' 09' *The kings of Cornas.* Supreme 5+ ha Syrah central v'yd at CORNAS, many old vines. Full, backward reds, need 6+ yrs. Epitome of patient winemaking, always gd in lesser vintages. Gd CÔTES DU RHÔNE, ST-PÉRAY, VIN DE TABLE.

Climat Burgundian word for individually named v'yd, eg. Meursault Tesson.

Clos A term carrying some prestige, reserved for distinct (walled) v'yds, often in one ownership (esp Burgundy and ALSACE).

Clos de Gamot SW ★★★ 90' 95 96 98' 00 01 02' 04 05' 06 (08) (09') 400-yr-old CAHORS estate. Ultra-traditional, long-lived wines. Top ★★★★ Cuvée Vignes Centenaires (made best yrs only) and micro-CUVÉE ★★★★ Clos St Jean easily challenges the young Turks of this AC.

Clos des Lambrays Burg r ★★★ 90' 95 99' 00 02 03 05' 06 07 08 09 GRAND CRU v'yd (6 ha) at MOREY-ST-DENIS. A virtual monopoly of the DOM du Clos des Lambrays, in recent yrs more severe in selecting only the best grapes.

Clos des Mouches Burg r w ★★★ Splendid PREMIER CRU BEAUNE v'yd, largely owned by DROUHIN. Whites and reds, spicy and memorable – and consistent. Little-known v'yds of the same name exist in SANTENAY and MEURSAULT, too.

Clos des Papes S Rh r w ★★★★ 95 98' 99' 00' 01' 03' 04' 05' 06' 07' 08 09' Top 32-ha (18 plots) CHATEAUNEUF estate Avril family owned for centuries. Rich, complex red, more full-bodied recently (mainly Grenache, Mourvèdre, drink from 6 yrs) and *great white* (fine cuisine needed; 5–15 yrs), both reward patience.

Clos de la Roche Burg r ★★★ 90' 93' 95 96' 9899' 01 02' 03 05' 06 07 08 09 Arguably the finest GRAND CRU of MOREY-ST-DENIS, arguably with as much grace as power. Best: ARLAUD, BOUCHARD, DUJAC, LEROY, LIGNIER, PONSOT, ROUSSEAU.

Clos du Roi Burg r ★★★ The best v'yd in GRAND CRU CORTON and a PREMIER CRU v'yd in BEAUNE.

Clos Rougeard Lo r w (sw) ★★★★ 02 03 04 05' 06 07 08 (09) Small, influential DOM – benchmark SAUMUR-CHAMPIGNY fine SAUMUR *blanc*, and, when possible, luscious COTEAUX DE SAUMUR.

Clos St-Denis Burg r ★★★ 90' 93' 95 96' 98 99' 01 02' 03 05' 06 07 08 09 GRAND CRU at MOREY-ST-DENIS (6.4 ha). Splendid sturdy wine growing silky with age. Growers include: ARLAUD, Bertagna, DUJAC, and PONSOT.

Clos Ste-Hune Al w ★★★★ Greatest Ries in ALSACE (02' 04 05 09'). V. fine, initially austere; needs 5–10+ yrs ageing. A TRIMBACH wine from GRAND CRU ROSACKER.

Clos St-Jacques Burg r ★★★ 90' 93 95' 96' 98 99' 01 02' 03 05' 06 07 08 09 6.7-ha hillside PREMIER CRU in GEVREY-CHAMBERTIN with perfect southeast exposure.

Five excellent producers: CLAIR, ESMONIN, Fourrier, JADOT, ROUSSEAU; powerful, velvety reds often ranked above many GRANDS CRUS.

Clos de Tart Burg r ★★★★ 90' 96' 99' 02' 03 05' 06 07 08 09 GRAND CRU at MOREY-ST-DENIS. Now first-rate and priced accordingly.

Clos de Vougeot Burg r ★★★ 90' 93' 95 96' 98 99' 01 02' 03' 05' 06 07 08 09 A 50-ha CÔTE DE NUITS GRAND CRU with many owners. Occasionally sublime. Maturity depends on grower's philosophy, technique and position. Top growers include CH de la Tour, DROUHIN, Eugenie, FAIVELEY, GRIVOT, GROS, Hudelot-Noëllat, JADOT, LEROY, LIGER-BELAIR, MÉO-CAMUZÉT, MUGNERET, VOUGERAIE.

Coche-Dury Burg ★★★★ Superb 11.5-ha MEURSAULT DOM led by Jean-Francois Coche and son Raphaél. Exceptional whites from ALIGOTÉ to CORTON-CHARLEMAGNE and v. pretty reds, too. Hard to find.

Colin Burg ★★★ Leading CHASSAGNE-MONTRACHET and ST-AUBIN family, several members of the next generation succeeding either Marc Colin (Pierre-Yves) or Michel Colin-Deleger (Bruno, Philippe).

Collines Rhodaniennes N Rh r w ★★ Exciting Rhône VDP, striking reds v.gd value, gd growers. Also young-vine CÔTE-RÔTIE, recent v'yds at Seyssuel. Mainly red, mainly Syrah (best), also Merlot, Gamay. Some delightful Viognier (best), CHARD. Reds: Barou, Bonnefond, Chatagnier, J-M Gérin, Jamet (v.gd), Jasmin, Monier, S Ogier. Whites: Barou, Y Cuilleron, Perret (v.gd), G Vernay.

Collioure Pyr r w ★★ The table-wine twin of BANYULS, with most producers making both. Gutsy red, mainly Grenache, from precipitous terraces overlooking the Med. Also rosé and, since 2002, white, based on Grenache Blanc. Top growers: Le Clos des Paulilles, DOMS du Mas Blanc, de la Rectorie, La Tour Vieille, Vial-Magnères, Madeloc.

Comté Tolosan SW r p w ★ Mostly DYA VDP, but surprising quality from ★★★ CH de Cabidos for sweet wines from Petit Manseng grapes, ★★ DOM DE RIBONNET (Christian Gerber, south of Toulouse) for experimental use of non-indigenous grape varieties. Otherwise patchy, covering a multitude of sins from entire SW.

Condrieu N Rh w ★★★ 04' 05 07 08' 09 Big, fragrant white from home of Viognier; mainly granite slopes. Can be outstanding, but recent planting (now 125 ha; 75 growers) has made quality variable (except marvellous 2004, v.gd 2008); can have too much oak, alcohol. Best: CHAPOUTIER, Y Cuilleron, DELAS, Gangloff, GUIGAL, F Merlin, Niéro, A Perret, C Pichon, ROSTAING, G Vernay (esp supreme, long-lived Coteau de Vernon), F Villard.

Corbières Midi r (p w) ★★→★★★ 01 02 03 04 05' 06 07' 08 The biggest AC of the LANGUEDOC, with cru of Boutenac. Wild scenery dominated by Mont Tauch and Mont d'Alaric. Wines like the scenery: sun-soaked and rugged. Best estates inc CHX Aiguilloux, de Cabriac, Les Clos Perdus, Lastours, Ollieux Romanis, Les Palais, Pech-Latt, de la Voulte Gasparet, DOMS du Grand Crès, de Fontsainte, du Vieux Parc, de Villemajou, Villerouge. Co-ops: Camplong, Embrès-et-Castelmaure, Tuchan.

Cornas N Rh r ★★→★★★★ 78' 83' 85' 88' 89' 90' 91' 94' 95' 96 97' 98' 99' 00' 01' 01' 02 03 04 05' 06' 07' 08 09' One of Big 3 northern RHÔNE Syrahs. Full, mineral-tinted, needs to age 5–15 yrs. Younger growers making wines to drink earlier. Top: Allemand, Balthazar (traditional), CLAPE (benchmark), Colombo (new oak), Courbis (modern), DELAS, J & E Durand, JABOULET (St-Pierre CUVÉE), Lemenicier, V Paris Tardieu-Laurent (modern), DOM du Tunnel, Voge (oak).

Corsica (Vin de Corse) r p w ACS Ajaccio, PATRIMONIO, better crus Coteaux du Cap, intriguing Corse, Sartène and Calvi. VDP: Ile de Beauté. Light, spicy reds from Sciacarello and more structured tannic wines from Nielluccio; gd rosés; *tangy, herbal whites from* Vermentino. Top growers: Abbatucci, Antoine Arena, Clos d'Alzeto, Clos Capitoro, Gentile, Yves Leccia, Montemagni, Peraldi, Vaccelli, Saperale, Fiumicicoli, Torraccia. Wines worth the journey.

Corton Burg r (w) ★★★ 90' 95 96' 9899' 01 02' 03' 05' 06 07 08 09 160 ha classified as GRAND CRU, which only a few Corton v'yds such as CLOS DU ROI, Bressandes, Rognets actually deserve. These have weight and structure; others make appealing, softer reds. DRC involvement since 2009 will increase interest. Look for d'Ardhuy, BONNEAU DU MARTRAY, CHANDON DE BRIAILLES, Dubreuil-Fontaine, FAIVELEY, Camille Giroud, MÉO-CAMUZET, TOLLOT-BEAUT. Occasional whites, eg. HOSPICES DE BEAUNE.

Corton-Charlemagne Burg w ★★★★ 99' 00' 02' 03 04 05' 06 07 08 09 SW and W exposure of hill of Corton, plus a band round the top, all more suited to white wines. Intense minerality and great ageing potential, often insufficiently realized. Top growers: BONNEAU DU MARTRAY, COCHE-DURY, FAIVELEY, HOSPICES DE BEAUNE, JADOT, P Javillier, LATOUR, de Montille, VOUGERAIE.

Costières de Nîmes S Rh r p w ★→★★ 05 06 07' 09' Best of satellite regions nr RHÔNE, SW of CHÂTEAUNEUF. Red: gd body, spiced fruit, can age 6–8 yrs, gd value. Main names: CHX de Campuget, Grande Cassagne, Mas Neuf, Mourgues-du-Grès, Nages, d'Or et des Gueules, Roubaud, de la Tuilerie; Mas des Bressades; DOMS de la Patience, Tardieu-Laurent, du Vieux Relais. Gd, fresh rosés, best whites are Roussanne.

Coteaux d'Aix-en-Provence Prov r p w ★★→★★★ Sprawling AC from hills N of Aix and on plain around Etang de Berre. A fruit salad of grape varieties, both Bordelais and MIDI. Reds are best, esp from CHX Beaupré, Calissanne, Revelette, Vignelaure; les Bastides, la Realtière, les Béates, Bas. See also COTEAUX DES BAUX-EN-PROVENCE. Sometimes lacks real identity.

Coteaux d'Ancenis Lo r p w (sw) ★ Generally DYA VDQS (220 ha) – right bank of the Loire, east of Nantes. Chiefly for dry, DEMI-SEC and sweet Chenin Bl whites plus age-worthy Malvoisie; also light Gamay, Cab Fr and Cab Sauv reds and rosés. Esp Guindon. Applying for promotion to AC status.

Coteaux de l'Ardèche r p (w) ★→★★ Hills-and-streams area W of Rhône, plenty of gd action. New DOMS; fresh reds, some oaked; Viognier (eg. Mas de Libian, CHAPOUTIER) and Marsanne. Best from Syrah, also Gamay, Cab Sauv (Serret). Burgundian-style Chard Ardèche by LOUIS LATOUR; Grand Ardèche from mature vines, but oaked. DOMS du Colombier, J & E Durand, Favette, Flacher, Mazel, Vigier, CH de la Selve.

Coteaux de l'Aubance Lo w sw ★★→★★★★ 89' 90' 95' 96' 97' 02 03 05' 06 07' (09) Small AC for sweet whites from Chenin Bl. Nervier less sumptuous than COTEAUX DU LAYON except when SÉLECTIONS DES GRAINS NOBLES. Often gd value. Esp Bablut, Haute-Perche, Montgilet, CH Princé, Richou, Rochelles.

Coteaux des Baronnies S Rh r p w ★ DYA Rhône VDP hills nr Nyons. Syrah, Cab Sauv, Merlot, CHARD, plus traditional grapes. Early drinking reds, also Viognier. DOMS du Rieu-Frais and Rosière worth a look .

Coteaux des Baux-en-Provence Prov r p ★★→★★★ 00 01 03 04 05 06 From the bauxite outcrop of the Alpilles topped by village of Les Baux. AC in own right for red and pink. White is COTEAUX D'AIX. Best estate is Trévallon, Cab Sauv/Syrah blend, but VDP for lack of Grenache. Also Mas de la Dame, DOM Hauvette.

Coteaux de Chalosse SW r p w ★ DYA, Modest VDP from local grapes. Co-op

---

Méthode Provençale

Eh? yes, you read correctly. The Rosé Research Centre in PROVENCE is working on a local rosé sparkler, made by a method which is not frankly a million miles away from that used in CHAMPAGNE. It justifies having its own name for its method by using only concentrated grape juice to induce the second fermentation in the bottle, rather than a spoonful of sugar. They haven't yet got an appellation, but they're experimenting like mad.

dominates, now merged with Tursan. Mainly found in local restaurants and stores.

Coteaux Champenois Champ r w (p) ★★★ DYA (whites) AC for non-sparkling CHAMPAGNE. Vintages follow those for CHAMPAGNE. Not worth inflated prices.

Coteaux du Giennois Lo r p w ★ DYA Small appellation (196 ha) north of POUILLY. Scattered v'yds – Cosne to Gien. Light, potentially powerful red: unconvincing and imposed blend of Gamay and Pinot N; Sauv Bl like a junior SANCERRE. Best: Emile Balland, BOURGEOIS, Catherine & Michel Langlois, Paulat, Villargeau.

Coteaux de Glanes SW France r ★★ DYA Lively, gd-value VDP from upper Dordogne. All from eight-grower co-op. Local restaurants can't get enough of this Merlot/Gamay/Ségalin blend.

Coteaux du Languedoc Midi r p w ★★→★★★ 00 01 02 03 04 05 06 07 A sprawling AC from Narbonne to Nîmes, with various *crus* and sub-divisions. Newer names are GRÈS DE MONTPELLIER, TERRASSES DU LARZAC and PÉZENAS and Sommières from 2010. New estates galore demonstrating exciting potential of the MIDI. Will disappear as larger AC LANGUEDOC, created 2007, gradually becomes established, and CRUS will stand alone as AOP.

Coteaux du Layon Lo w sw s/sw ★★→★★★★ 89 90 95 96 97 02 03 05' 07' (09) Heart of ANJOU: sweet Chenin Bl; lush with admirable acidity, almost everlasting. New SÉLECTION DES GRAINS NOBLES. Seven villages (300 ha) can add name to AC. Top ACS: BONNEZEAUX, QUARTS DE CHAUME. Growers: Baudouin, BAUMARD, Delesvaux, des Forges, DOM les Grands Vignes, Guegniard, DOM de Juchepie, Ogereau, Papin (CH PIERRE-BISE) .

Coteaux du Loir Lo r p w dr sw ★→★★★ 02 03 04 05' 07 08 (09) Northern tributary of the Loire, Le Loir is small but dynamic region with Coteaux du Loir (80 ha) and JASNIÈRES (65 ha). Potentially fine, apple-scented Chenin Bl, Gamay, peppery Pineau d'Aunis that goes well with pungent cheeses. Top growers: Ange Vin, DOM DE BELLIVIERE, Le Briseau, Fresneau, Gigou, Les Maions Rouges, de Rycke.

Coteaux du Lyonnais Beauj r p (w) ★ DYA Junior BEAUJOLAIS. Best *en primeur*.

Coteaux de Pierrevert Prov r p w ★ Cool area producing quaffable wines from high v'yds nr Manosque. DOM la Blaque, CH Régusse, M Rousset. AC since 1998.

Coteaux du Quercy SW r ★ 02 04 05' 06 (08) (09') S of CAHORS VDQS between Cahors and Montauban. Cab Fr-based wines from ★★ DOM du Merchien, ★ DOMS de la Combarade, de Guyot, de Lafage, Lagarde. Improved and more than worthy ★ co-op.

Coteaux de Saumur Lo w sw ★★→★★★ Sweet Chenin Bl. A tradition revived since 1989 – resembles COTEAUX DU LAYON but less rich. Esp DOM DES CHAMPS FLEURIS/Retiveau-Retif, CLOS ROUGEARD, Régis Neau, Vatan.

Coteaux et Terrasses de Montauban SW r p ★→★★ DYA ★★ Led by pioneering DOM de Montels, which invented this appellation single-handed, and ★ DOM de Biarnès.

Coteaux du Tricastin S Rh r p w ★→★★ 06' 07' 09' Mid-Rhône AC, hit by bad nuclear-plant events 2008–09, Tricastin lacks spread of quality. Best: DOMS de Bonetto-Fabrol, Grangeneuve best (esp VIEILLES VIGNES), de Montine (gd white), St-Luc and CH La Décelle (inc white CÔTES DU RHÔNE).

Coteaux Varois-en-Provence Prov r p w ★→★★ 01 02 03 04 05' 06 07 08 Sandwiched between COTEAUX D'AIX and CÔTES DE PROVENCE. Gd source of warming reds and fresh rosés; deserves better reputation but lacks a leader. Try CHX Routas, la Calisse, Miraval, DOM les Alysses, du Deffends.

Coteaux du Vendômois Lo r p w ★→★★ DYA Marginal Loire AC west of Vendôme (149 ha). The most characteristic wines are VINS GRIS from Pinot d'Aunis grape, which also gives peppery notes to red blends. Whites based on Chenin Bl. Producers: Patrice Colin, DOMS du Four à Chaux, J Martellière, Montrieux, Cave du Vendôme-Villiers.

Côte de Beaune Burg r w ★★→★★★★ Used geographically: the southern half of the CÔTE D'OR. Applies as an AC only to top of hill above BEAUNE itself.

Côte de Beaune-Villages Burg r ★★ 05' 07 08 09 Red wines from the lesser villages of the southern half of the CÔTE D'OR. Rarely exciting.

Côte de Brouilly Beauj r ★★ 05' 07 08 08 09 Flanks of the hillside above BROUILLY provide one of the richest BEAUJOLAIS *cru*. Try from J-P Brun or CH Thivin.

Côte Chalonnaise Burg r w sp ★★ Mid-price, -quality v'yd area south of BEAUNE. BOUZERON, RULLY, MONTAGNY for whites; MERCUREY, GIVRY and RULLY for reds.

Côte de Nuits Burg r (w) ★★→★★★★ Northern half of CÔTE D'OR. Mostly red wine.

Côte de Nuits-Villages Burg r (w) ★★ 02' 03 05' 06 07 08 09 A junior AC for extreme N and S ends of CÔTE DE NUITS; well worth investigating for bargains. Single v'yd versions beginning to appear.

Côte d'Or *Département* name applied to the central and principal Burgundy v'yd slopes: CÔTE DE BEAUNE and CÔTE DE NUITS. Not used on labels.

Côte Roannaise Central Fr r p ★→★★ 05' 06 08 09 'Small AC (220 ha) on lower slopes of the high granite hills west of Roanne, northwest of Lyon. Silky, focused Gamay. DOMS du Fontenay, Lapandéry, des Millets, du Pavillon, Robert Sérol, Vial.

Côte-Rôtie N Rh r ★★★→★★★★★ 78' 83' 85' 88' 89' 90' 91' 94' 95' 98' 99' 00 01' 03' 04 05' 06' 07' 08 09' Finest, most Burgundian Rhône red, mainly Syrah, sprinkle of Viognier. Aromatic, complex softness, great finesse with age (esp 5–10+ yrs). Top: Barge (traditional), Bernard, Bonnefond (oak), Bonserine (GUIGAL-owned), CHAPOUTIER, Clusel-Roch (organic), DELAS, Duclaux, Gaillard (oak), J-M Gérin (oak), GUIGAL (own oaked style), Jamet (wonderful), Jasmin, Monteille, Ogier (oak), ROSTAING, J-M Stéphan (organic), VIDAL-FLEURY (La Chatillonne).

Côtes Catalanes Midi r p w ★→★★ The best VDP of ROUSSILLON, covering most of area. Exciting source of innovation and investment. Growers: Matassa, La Préceptorié Centernach, CH de Casenove, DOMS Gérard Gauby, Olivier Pithon, Padié, des Soulanes, le Soula.

Côtes d'Auvergne Central Fr r r p (w) ★→★★ Generally DYA Small VDQS (412 ha), seeking promotion to AC. Mainly Gamay, though some Pinot N and CHARD. Best reds improve 2–3 yrs. Best villages: Boudes, Chanturgue, Châteaugay, Corent, Madargues. Producers: Cave St-Verny, Jean Maupertuis.

Côtes de Bourg B'x r w ★→★★ 99 00' 01 02 03 04 05' 08 (09) AC for robust red and (v. little) white from east of the Gironde. Steady quality. Top CHX: Brûlésecaille, Bujan, Civrac, Falfas, Fougas, Grand-Maison, Guerry, Haut-Guiraud, Haut-Maco, Haut Mondésir, Macay, Mercier, Nodoz, *Roc de Cambes*, Rousset, Sociondo.

Côtes du Bruhlois SW r p (w) ★→★★ 04 05' 06 08 (09') Nr Agen. Friendly co-op working alongside independents Le Bois de Simon, CH la Bastide, Clos Pountet, DOMS Coujétou-Peyret and des Thermes. Quickly improving area.

Côtes de Castillon B'x r ★★★→★★★ 00' 01 02 03 04 05' 08 (09) Flourishing region east of ST-EMILION; similar wines. Ageing potential; much recent investment. Label changes from 2008 vintage. Top: de l'A, d'Aiguilhe, Ampélia, Cap de Faugères, La Clarière-Laithwaite, Clos l'Eglise, Clos Les Lunelles, Clos Puy Arnaud, Joanin Bécot, Poupille, Robin, Veyry, Vieux CH Champs de Mars.

Côtes de Couchois Burg ★→★★ 05' 07 08 Subdistrict of BOURGOGNE *rouge* at southern end of CÔTE D'OR v'yds. Powerful reds, on the tannic side. Best grower: Alain Hasard.

Côtes de Duras Dordogne r p w ★→★★★ 06 08 (09') BORDEAUX satellite. Top include newcomers ★★★ DOMS Chator, Mouthes-les-Bihan, Petit Malromé, and CHX Condom Perceval, also more established ★★ des Allegrets, du Grand Mayne, Lafon and Laulan. Co-op (Berticot) could do better, despite help from Bordeaux star consultant MICHEL ROLLAND.

Côtes du Forez Lo r p (sp) ★ DYA Loire AC (146 ha) near St-Etienne for Gamay reds and rosés. Les Vignerons Foréziens, also Le Clos de Chozieux, Verdier et Logel.

Côtes de Francs B'x r w ★★ 98 00' 01 03 04 05' 08 (09) Fringe BORDEAUX next to CASTILLON. Mainly red but some white: tasty and attractive. Reds can age a little. New AC from 2008 vintage (see box p.89). Top CHX: Charmes-Godard, Francs, Laclaverie, Marsau, Pelan, La Prade, PUYGUERAUD.

Côtes de Gascogne SW w (r p) ★ DYA VDP. Fashionable, popular wine-bar wines led by Plaimont co-op and Grassa family (CH de Tariquet). Also DOMS d'Arton, des Cassagnoles, Chiroules de Jöy, de Laballe, de Lauroux, de Magnaut, Millet, Papolle, Pellehaut, St Lannes Sédouprat, de San Guilhem, CH Monluc. Also from MADIRAN growers, notably BRUMONT.

Côtes du Jura r p w (sp) ★ DYA Many light tints/tastes. ARBOIS more substantial.

Côtes de Millau SW r p w DYA Norman Foster's famous viaduct gives the name to co-op's red. Six independents include ★★ DOM du Vieux Noyes.

Côtes de Montravel Dordogne w dr sw ★★ 97' 01' 03' 04 05' 06 (08) Part of BERGERAC; traditionally medium-sweet, now less common. MONTRAVEL SEC is dry, HAUT-MONTRAVEL is sweet.

Côtes de Provence Prov r p w ★→★★★ r 01 03 04 05 06 07 (p w DYA) Large AC known mainly for rosé; enjoying a huge leap in quality, thanks to investment. Satisfying reds and herbal whites. STE-VICTOIRE, Fréjus and La Londe subzones, St Tropez coming soon. Leaders include *Castel Roubine*, Commanderie de Peyrassol, DOMS Bernarde, de la Courtade, Léoube, Gavoty (superb), CH'X d'Esclans, de Selle and Clos Mireille, des Planes, Rabiéga, Richeaume, Rimauresq. See COTEAUX D'AIX, BANDOL.

Côtes du Rhône S Rh r p w ★→★★ 07' 09' Carpet of vines across 170 communes in S Rhône. Many struggling to stay afloat as recession bites. Mainly Grenache, also Syrah. Best drunk young, even as PRIMEUR. Wide quality variations, Vaucluse area best. 2008 stick to small DOMS, or seek gd 2009.

Côtes du Rhône-Villages S Rh r p w ★→★★ 04' 05' 06' 07' 09' Hearty wine from 7,700 ha, inc 18 best southern Rhône villages. Most happening area, bundle of gd wines, gd prices, keen growers, all v. drinkable. Red core is Grenache, with Syrah, Mourvèdre support. Improving whites, often with Viognier, Roussanne added to CLAIRETTE, Grenache Blanc – gd with food. See BEAUMES-DE-VENISE, CAIRANNE, CHUSCLAN, LAUDUN, RASTEAU, ST-GERVAIS, SABLET, SÉGURET. New villages from 2005: MASSIF D'UCHAUX (gd), PLAN DE DIEU (robust), PUYMÉRAS, SIGNARGUES. Gd value, quality eg. CHX Fontségune, Signac, DOMS Cabotte, Chaume-Arnaud, Deforge, Grand Moulas, Grand Veneur, Jérome, Montbayon, DOMS de Mourchon, Rabasse-Charavin, Renjarde, Romarins, Ste-Anne, St Siffrein, Saladin, Valériane, Vieux Chêne, Viret, Mas de Libian, Cave Estézargues, Cave Rasteau.

Côtes du Roussillon Pyr r p w ★→★★ 02 03 04 05' 06 07' 08 East Pyrenees AC, covers v'yds of Pyrénées-Orientales behind Perpignan. Dominated by co-ops, notably Vignerons Catalans. Warming red is best, predominantly from Carignan and Grenache.

Côtes du Roussillon-Villages Pyr r ★★ 02 03 04 05 06 07 08 28 villages form best part of region. Dominated by Vignerons Catalans. Best labels: Cazes Frères, DOMS des Chênes, la Cazenove, *Gauby* (also characterful white VDP), Piquemal, Seguela, CH de Jau, Mas Crémat.

Côtes du Roussillon des Aspres Pyr AC since 2003 for reds only. Similar to basic CÔTES DU ROUSSILLON. Rarely found outside area. Based on Grenache Noir, Carignan, Syrah and Mourvèdre.

Côtes de St-Mont SW r w p ★★ (r) 06 08 (09') (p w) DYA GERS VDQS overwhelmingly dominated by *Producteurs Plaimont*, the most successful co-op in the southwest. Gd red from DOM des Maouries. Same grapes as MADIRAN (but with more emphasis on Fer Servadou) and PACHERENC.

> **Top Côtes du Rhône producers**
> La Courançonne, Domazan, l'Estagnol, Fonsalette (superb), GrandMoulas, Haut-Musiel, Hugues, Montfaucon, St-Estève, Trignon (inc Viognier); Co-ops CAIRANNE, Chantecotes (Ste-Cécile-les-Vignes), Puyméras, Rasteau, Villedieu (esp white); Cave Estézargues, DOMS Bramadou, Charvin, Combebelle, Coudoulet de Beaucastel (classy r), Cros de la Mûre, M Dumarcher, Espigouette, Ferrand, Gourget, Gramenon (v. organic), Janasse, Jaume, Perrin, Réméjeanne, Romarins, Soumade, Vieille Julienne, Vieux Chêne; DELAS, DUBOEUF, GUIGAL, JABOULET.

Côtes du Tarn SW r p w ★ DYA VDP overlaps GAILLAC; same growers but also ★★ DOM d'en Segur, esp off-dry Sauv Bl.

Côtes de Thongue Midi r w ★★ (DYA p w) Dynamic VDP, aspiring AOP from HÉRAULT. Intriguing blends in preference to single varietals. Reds will age. DOMS Arjolle, les Chemins de Bassac, la Croix Belle, Magellan, Monplézy, des Henrys.

Côtes de Toul E France (Lorraine) r p w ★ DYA V. light wines; mainly VIN GRIS.

Côtes du Vivarais S Rh r p w ★ 07' 09' DYA 700 ha around hilly ARDÈCHE villages west of Montélimar. Improving simple CUVÉES, strong Syrah fruit; more robust, oak-aged reds. Note: Mas de Bagnols, Vignerons de Ruoms.

Coulée de Serrant Lo w dr sw (★★★) 95 96 97 98 99 02 03 04 05 07 08 (09) A 7-ha Chenin Bl v'yd at SAVENNIÈRES. High priest of biodynamics Nicolas Joly's wines now below par (fail to match the theory), but daughter Véronique taking charge. Decant two hours before drinking; don't chill. Old vintages can be sublime.

Courcel, Dom Burg ★★★ Leading POMMARD estate – top PREMIER CRU Rugiens.

Crémant In CHAMPAGNE, meant "creaming" (half-sparkling). Since 1975, an AC for quality classic-method sparkling from ALSACE, Loire, BOURGOGNE, and most recently LIMOUX – often a bargain. Term no longer used in CHAMPAGNE.

Crépy Savoie w ★★ DYA Light, soft, Swiss-style white from south shore of Lake Geneva. *Crépitant* has been coined for its faint fizz.

Crozes-Hermitage N Rh r w ★★ 03' 05 06 07 09' Syrah hill/plain v'yds (1,355 ha) either side of HERMITAGE hill. Should be fruity, early drinking (2–5 yrs). Best (simple CUVÉES) have vibrant fruit, drink early. Too many oaked-up, technical, more expensive. Gd: Belle, Y Chave, CH Curson, Darnaud, DOMS du Colombier, Combier, des Entrefaux (oak), Graillot, Hauts-Chassis, Lises, Mucyn, du Pavillon-Mercurol, de Thalabert of JABOULET, *Chapoutier*, *Delas* (Tour d'Albon, Le Clos v.gd). Drink wine early.

Cuve close Short-cut method of making sparkling wine in a tank. Sparkle dies away in glass much quicker than with *méthode traditionnelle* wine.

Cuvée Wine contained in a *cuve*, or vat. A word of many uses, inc synonym for "blend" and first-press wines (as in CHAMPAGNE); in Burgundy, interchangeable with *cru*. Often just refers to a "lot" of wine.

DRC The wine geek's shorthand for DOM DE LA ROMANÉE-CONTI.

Dagueneau, Didier Lo ★★★→★★★★ 02 03 04 05' 07 08' (09) Best producer of POUILLY-FUMÉ by far and a master of stunningly pure Sauv Bl. Died in plane crash Sept 2008. Son Benjamin now in charge – impressive start. Top CUVÉES: Pur Sang, Silex and ungrafted Asteroide. Also SANCERRE; small v'yd in CHAVIGNOL.

Dauvissat, Vincent Burg ★★★ Great CHABLIS producer using old methods for v. long-lived CHABLIS. Cousin of RAVENEAU. Best: Forest, Preuses, Les Clos.

Degré alcoolique Degrees of alcohol, ie. % by volume.

Deiss, Dom Marcel ★★★ High-profile grower at Bergheim, ALSACE. Favours blended wines from individual v'yd sites. Gewurz and Ries Schoenenbourg are his best wines. Now biodynamic.

Delamotte BRUT; BLANC DE BLANCS (99 02 04); CUVÉE Nicholas Delamotte. Fine small CHARD-dominated CHAMPAGNE house at Le Mesnil. Managed with SALON by LAURENT-PERRIER. "Library" stock of old vintages: *superb BL DE BL (85')*

Delas Frères N Rh ★→★★★ Gd quality, v. strong range N Rhône merchant with CONDRIEU, CROZES-HERMITAGE, CÔTE-RÔTIE, HERMITAGE v'yds. Top wines: CONDRIEU (Clos Boucher), Côte-Rôtie Landonne, Hermitage M de la Tourette (r, w), Les Bessards (v. fine, long life). Owned by ROEDERER.

Demi-sec Half-dry: in practice more like half-sweet (eg. of CHAMPAGNE).

Deutz Brut Classic NV; Rosé NV; Brut (00 02 04). Top-flight CHARD CUVÉE Amour de Deutz (02). One of top small CHAMPAGNE houses, ROEDERER-owned. V. dry, classic wines. *Superb Cuvée William Deutz (98 02).*

Domaine (Dom) Property, particularly in Burgundy and rural France. See under name, eg. TEMPIER, DOM.

Dom Pérignon CUVÉE 98' 00 02; rosé 98 00 02' Luxury CUVÉE OF MOËT & CHANDON, named after legendary cellarmaster who first blended CHAMPAGNE. Astonishingly consistent quality and creamy character, esp with 10–15 yrs bottle age. Late-disgorged *oenothèque* releases 95' 96' .

Dopff & Irion ★→★★ 17th-century ALSACE firm at Riquewihr, now part of PFAFFENHEIM. MUSCAT Les Amandiers, Gewurz Les Sorcières. Also gd CRÉMANT D'ALSACE.

Dopff au Moulin ★★★ Ancient top-class family wine house at Riquewihr, ALSACE. Best: Gewurz GRANDS CRUS Brand, Sporen; Ries Schoenenbourg; *Sylvaner de Riquewihr.* Pioneers of ALSACE CRÉMANT; gd CUVÉES: Bartholdi, Julien.

Dourthe, Vins & Vignobles BORDEAUX merchant; wide range and quality emphasis: gd, notably CHX BELGRAVE, LE BOSCQ, LA GARDE. Beau-Mayne, Pey La Tour, Dourthe No 1 are well-made generic BORDEAUX. Essence concentrated and modern.

Drappier, André Outstanding family run AUBE CHAMPAGNE house. Pinot-led NV, Brut Zéro, Rosé Saignée, Signature Blanc de Blancs (02 04), Millésime d'Exception (02 04), superb prestige CUVÉE Grande Sendrée (99 02 04). New unsulphured BL DES NOIRS: the Drappier family are all allergic.

Drouhin, J & Cie Burg ★★★→★★★★ Deservedly prestigious grower (61 ha) and merchant. Cellars in BEAUNE; v'yds in BEAUNE, CHABLIS, CLOS DE VOUGEOT, MUSIGNY, etc., and Oregon, USA. Best include (white) Beaune Clos des Mouches, CHABLIS LES CLOS, CORTON-CHARLEMAGNE, PULIGNY-MONTRACHET, Les Folatières, (red) GRIOTTE-CHAMBERTIN, MUSIGNY, GRANDS-ECHÉZEAUX.

Duboeuf, Georges ★★→★★★★ Most famous name of the BEAUJOLAIS, proponent of *nouveau*. Huge range of CUVÉES and *crus*, but has the lustre faded?

Duclot Bordeaux négociant; top-growth specialist. Owned by Jean-François Moueix.

Dugat Burg ★★★ Cousins Claude and Bernard (Dugat-Py) make excellent, deep-coloured GEVREY-CHAMBERTIN, respective labels. Tiny volumes, huge prices.

Dujac, Dom Burg ★★★→★★★★ MOREY-ST-DENIS grower now with exceptional range of GRANDS CRUS. Lighter colours but intense fruit, smoky, strawberry character from use of stems. Also DOM Triennes in COTEAUX VAROIS.

Dulong Bordeaux merchant. Part of Grands Chais de France.

Durup, Jean Burg ★★→★★★ One of the biggest CHABLIS growers with 152 ha. Sold under various names such as DOM de l'Eglantière and CH de Maligny.

Duval-Leroy Dynamic Côte des Blancs CHAMPAGNE house. 200 ha of family-owned v'yds source of gd Fleur de Champagne NV, fine Blanc de Chard (99 00 02), and excellent prestige Femme de Champagne (96'). New single-village/v'yd bottlings, esp Authentis Cumière (03).

Échézeaux Burg r ★★★ 90' 93 96' 97 99' 02' 99' 02' 03 05' 06 07 08 09 GRAND CRU (37.7 ha) next to CLOS DE VOUGEOT. Middling weight but can have exceptionally intricate flavours and startling persistence. Best from Arnoux, DRC, DUJAC, ENGEL (now EUGENIE), GRIVOT, Lamarche, ROUGET.

Ecu, Dom de l' Lo dr w r ★★★ 89 90 95 96 97 02 03 04 05 06 09 Guy Bossard is a superb producer of biodynamic MUSCADET (esp mineral-rich CUVÉE Granite) and Gros Plant, inc sparkling, plus excellent Cab Fr. Tiny production 2007 and 2008. Hit by tiny crop in 2007 and 2008 – estate now for sale.

Edelzwicker Al w ★ DYA Blended light white. Delicious CH d'Ittenwiller (05).

d'Eguisheim, Cave Vinicole ★★ V.gd ALSACE co-op for excellent value: fine GRANDS CRUS Hatschbourg, HENGST, Ollwiller, Spiegel. Owns Willm. Top label: WOLFBERGER. Best: Grande Réserve, Sigillé, Armorié. Gd CRÉMANT and Pinot N.

Engel, R Burg ★★★ Top grower of CLOS DE VOUGEOT, ECHÉZEAUX, GRANDS-ECHÉZEAUX and VOSNE-ROMANÉE in elegant, savoury style until tragic early death of Philippe E. Resurrected as DOM EUGÉNIE from 2006 vintage by new owner, François Pinault (CH LATOUR). Expect richer wines designed for richer people.

Entraygues et du Fel SW r p w DYA ★ Minerally, cool VDQS. Diminutive appellation almost in Massif Central. Zinging white ★★ DOM Méjannassère and Laurent Mousset's red, esp red La Pauca (would keep) and rosé.

Entre-Deux-Mers B'x w ★→★★ DYA Improved dry white BORDEAUX from between rivers Garonne and Dordogne (aka E-2-M). Only 1,500 ha. Best CHX BONNET, Castenet Greffier, Fontenille, Landereau, Marjosse, Nardique-la-Gravière, Sainte-Marie, *Tour de Mirambeau*, Toutigeac.

Esmonin, Dom Sylvie Burg ★★★ Rich, dark wines from fully ripe grapes, esp since 2000. Notable GEVREY-CHAMBERTIN VIELLES VIGNES and CLOS ST-JACQUES. Cousin Frédéric has Estournelles St-Jacques.

L'Etoile Jura w dr sp (sw) ★★ Subregion of the Jura known for stylish whites, inc VIN JAUNE, similar to CH-CHALON; gd sparkling.

Eugénie, Dom Burg The new name for the old DOM ENGEL, bought by François Pinault of CH LATOUR in 2006. Now more concentrated wines at higher prices.

Faiveley, J Burg ★★→★★★★ Family-owned growers and merchants at NUITS-ST-GEORGES. V'yds (120 ha) in CHAMBERTIN-CLOS DE BEZE, CHAMBOLLE-MUSIGNY, CORTON, MERCUREY, NUITS and recent acquisitions in MEURSAULT and PULIGNY. Look for more succulent wines under new generation (from 2007).

Faller, Théo/Dom Weinbach Al ★★→★★★★ Founded by Capuchin monks in 1612, now run by Colette Faller and two daughters. Outstanding wines now often drier, esp GRANDS CRUS SCHLOSSBERG (Ries), Furstentum (Gewurz). Wines of *great character and elegance*. Great Cuvée Sainte Catherine Sélection des Grains Noble Gewurz 02.

Faugères Midi r (p w) ★→★★ 03 04 05' 06 07 08 09' Leading LANGUEDOC *cru*. Warming, spicy reds from Syrah, Grenache, Carignan, plus Cinsault and Mourvèdre. AC in 1982 for red and 2004 for white, from Marsanne, Roussanne, Rolle. Drink DOMS Jean-Michel Alquier, Léon Barral, des Trinités, St-Antonin, Ollier-Taillefer, Mas d'Alézon.

Fessy Beauj ★★ BEAUJOLAIS merchant Henry F, now owned by LOUIS LATOUR.

Fèvre, William Burg ★★★ Star turn in CHABLIS since HENRIOT purchase in 1998. Biggest owners of GRANDS CRUS. Les Clos outstanding.

Fiefs Vendéens Lo r p w ★→★★★ Mainly DYA VDQS for easy-drinking wines from the Vendée close to Sables d'Olonne. Range of varieties: CHARD, Chenin Bl, Sauv Bl, Melon (whites), Grolleau *gris*, Cab Fr, Cab Sauv, Gamay, Negrette,

---

AOP and IGP: what's happening in France

The appellations and VDPS of France will eventually convert to Appellation d'Origine Protegée (AOP) and Indication Géographique Protegée (IGP). This means that anywhere aspiring to an appellation is likely now to become AOP rather than AOC. IGP will become more specific when the all-embracing category of Vin de Table de France finally comes on-stream: it allows wines to state their vintage and grape variety – information that was previously denied to VIN DE TABLE.

Pinot N (reds and rosés). Top CUVÉES, esp from Michon/DOM St-Nicolas, are serious and age-worthy. Also Aloha, Coirier, CH Marie du Fou.

Fitou Midi r w ★★ 02 03 04 05' 06 07' 08 Powerful red, from wild hills south of Narbonne as well as coastal v'yds. The MIDI's oldest AC for table wine, created in 1948, 11 mths' barrel-ageing and benefits from bottle age. Co-op at Tuchan a pacesetter among co-ops. Experiments with Mourvèdre. Gd estates include CH de Nouvelles, DOM Bergé-Bertrand, Lérys, Rolland.

Fixin Burg r ★★★ 99' 02' 03 05' 06 07 08 09 Worthy and undervalued northern neighbour of GEVREY-CHAMBERTIN. Sometimes splendid reds. Best v'yds: Clos de la Perrière, Clos du Chapitre, Clos Napoléon. Growers include CLAIR, FAIVELEY, Gelin, Guyard and revitalized Manoir de la Perrière.

FL, Dom Lo w r sw 95 97 02 03 04 05 06 07 This is a fusion of DOM Jo Pithon (ANJOU) and CH de Chamboreau (SAVENNIÈRES), STÉPHANE DERENONCOURT consulting. Owned by Philip Fournier of Afone telephone group. Jo Pithon no longer involved.

Fleurie Beauj r ★★★ 05' 07 08 09 The best BEAUJOLAIS *cru* for immediate pleasure. Brilliantly perfumed, silky, racy strawberry fruit. Top sites include La Madone, Les Moriers. Look for Chapelle des Bois, Chignard, Depardon, Després, DUBOEUF, Ch de Fleurie, Métras, co-op.

Floc de Gascogne SW r w Locally invented Gascon answer to PINEAU DES CHARENTES. Unfermented grape juice blended with ARMAGNAC.

Fronsac B'x r ★★→★★★ 96 98 00' 01 03 05' 06 08 (09) Underrated, hilly AC west of ST-EMILION; one of the best-value reds in BORDEAUX. Top CHX: DALEM, *la Dauphine*, Fontenil, la Grave, Haut-Carles, Mayne-Vieil, *Moulin-Haut-Laroque*, Richelieu, *la Rivière*, la Rousselle, Tour du Moulin, les Trois Croix, LA VIEILLE CURE, Villars. See also CANON-FRONSAC.

Frontignan Midi golden sw ★★ NV Small AC outside Sète for sweet, fortified MUSCAT. Experiments with late-harvest unfortified VDP wines. Quality steadily improving. Leaders: CHX la Peyrade, de Stony.

Fronton SW r p ★★ 05' 06 08 (09') Better promotion is bringing these fruity, scented wines to a wider market. No longer just the "Beaujolais de Toulouse". Watch for DOMS de Caze, Joliet, du Roc; CHX Baudare, *Bellevue-la-Forêt*, Boissel, Boujac, Cahuzac, Cransac, Plaisance.

Gagnard, Jean-Noel Burg ★★★ At the top of the Gagnard clan. Beautifully expressive GRAND CRU, PREMIER CRU and *village* wines in CHASSAGNE-MONTRACHET. Also cousins Blain-Gagnard, Fontaine-Gagnard.

Gaillac SW r p w dr sw sp ★→★★★ Fast-improving AC. Mostly DYA, except oaked reds 05' 06 08 (09'). Also sweet whites 05' 06 07 08 (09'). ★★★ PLAGEOLES, Causse-Marines, de la Ramaye, Palvié DOMS ★★ d'Arlus, Cailloutis, La Chanade, d'Escausses, Gineste, Larroque, Long Pech, Mayragues, Rotier, Salmes, Sarrabelle, CHX Bourguet, L'Enclos des Roses. Gd all-rounders ★★ DOMS de Labarthe, Mas Pignou, La Vayssette.

Garage *Vins de garage* are (usually) BORDEAUX made on a v. small scale. Rigorous winemaking, but a bottle costs much the same as a full service.

Gard, Vin de Pays du Midi ★ The Gard *département* by mouth of the Rhône is important source of sound VDP production, inc Cévenne, du Pont du Gard, SABLES DU GOLFE DU LION. Duché d'Uzès an aspiring AOP .

Gauby, Dom Gérard Midi r p w ★★★ Pioneering ROUSSILLON producer. White Vin de Pays des Côtes Catalanes Les Calcinaires; Coume Ginestre; red CÔTES DU ROUSSILLON-VILLAGES called Muntada; Les Calcinaires VIELLES VIGNES. Associated with VDP Le Soula. Dessert wine: Le Pain du Sucre: biodynamic. Son Lionel following in father's footsteps.

Gers SW r p w ★ DYA VDP indistinguishable from nearby CÔTES DE GASCOGNE.

Gevrey-Chambertin Burg r ★★★ 90' 96' 98 99' 01 02' 03 05' 06 07 08 09

Village containing the great CHAMBERTIN, its GRAND CRU cousins and many other noble v'yds eg. PREMIERS CRUS Cazetiers, Combe aux Moines, Combottes, CLOS ST-JACQUES. Growers include Bachelet, L Boillot, BURGUET, Damoy, DROUHIN, DUGAT, ESMONIN, FAIVELEY, Geantet-Pansiot, Harmand-Geoffroy, JADOT, LEROY, MORTET, Rossignol-Trapet, ROTY, ROUSSEAU, SÉRAFIN, TRAPET, Varoilles. Look for their BOURGOGNE *rouge*.

Gigondas S Rh r p ★★→★★★ 78' 89' 90' 95' 98' 99' 00' 01' 03' 04' 05' 06' 07' 08 09' Hill-and-plain 1,200-ha v'yds. Grenaches topped up with Syrah, Mourvèdre. Robust, tangy, peppery wines. Slight increase of oak, esp for US market. Genuine local character in many. Try: CH de Montmirail, St-Cosme (oak), Clos du Joncuas, P Amadieu, DOM Boissan, Bouïssière, Brusset, Cassan, Espiers, Goubert, Gour de Chaulé, Grapillon d'Or, Oustet Fauquet, les Pallières, Raspail-Ay, Roubine, St-Gayan, Santa Duc, Perrin & Fils. Rosés often too heavy.

Ginestet Go-ahead BORDEAUX négociant. Quality controls for grape suppliers. Principal brands G de Ginestet, Marquis de Chasse, Mascaron.

Girardin, Vincent Burg r w ★★→★★★ Small grower turned dynamic négociant reconverting to grower on larger scale, esp whites from MEURSAULT and PULIGNY. Modern but fine.

Givry Burg r (w) ★★ 05' 06 07 08 09 Unsung village of CÔTE CHALONNAISE, with tasty reds for medium-term ageing. JOBLOT, Clos Salomon, F Lumpp best.

Gosset Old small CHAMPAGNE house now moved to Epernay. Traditional, esp Grand Millésime (99 02). Gosset Celebris (98 99 00 02) is finest CUVÉE. V.gd Celebris Rosé (03).

Gouges, Henri Burg ★★★ Pierre and Christian G make sterling NUITS-ST-GEORGES from a range of PREMIER CRU v'yds. Try Vaucrains, Les St Georges, or Chaignots.

Grand Cru One of top Burgundy v'yds with its own AC. In ALSACE, one of the 51 top v'yds covered by ALSACE GRAND CRU AC, but more vague elsewhere. In ST-EMILION, 60% of the production is covered by the ST-EMILION GRAND CRU AC.

Grande Champagne The AC of the best area of Cognac. Nothing fizzy about it.

Grande Rue, La Burg r ★★★ 90' 95 96' 99' 00 02' 03 05' 06 07 08 09 Narrow strip of VOSNE-ROMANÉE GRAND CRU (since 1991). MONOPOLE of DOM Lamarche now starting to make fine wines again.

Grands-Echézeaux Burg r ★★★★ ' 90' 93 95 96' 97 99' 00 02' 03 05' 06 07 08 09 Superlative 8.9-ha GRAND CRU next to CLOS DE VOUGEOT. Wines not weighty but aromatic. Viz: DRC, DROUHIN, ENGEL, GROS.

Grange des Pères, Dom de la Midi r w ★★★ VDP de l'HÉRAULT. Cult estate neighbouring MAS DE DAUMAS GASSAC, created by Laurent Vaillé for first vintage 1992. Red from Syrah, Mourvèdre, Cab Sauv; white Roussanne 80% plus Marsanne, CHARD. Original wines; well worth seeking out.

Gratien, Alfred and **Gratien & Meyer** ★★→★★★ Brut NV; BRUT 97' 98' 00 02 04. Superb *prestige* CUVÉE Paradis Brut and Rosé (blend of fine yrs). Excellent quirky CHAMPAGNE house, now German-owned. Fine, v. dry, lasting barrel-fermented wine inc *The Wine Society's house Champagne*. Fine vintage CUVÉE (98). Gratien & Meyer is counterpart at SAUMUR. (Gd Cuvée Flamme.)

Graves B'x r w ★→★★ 00 01 04 05' (09) Region south of BORDEAUX city with soft, earthy red; dry white more consistent. Top CHX: ARCHAMBEAU, CHANTEGRIVE, *Clos Floridene*, Crabitey, l'Hospital, Léhoul, Respide, RESPIDE-MÉDEVILLE, St-Robert CUVÉE Poncet Deville, Venus, Vieux CH Gaubert, Villa Bel Air.

Graves de Vayres B'x r w ★ DYA Tiny AC within E-2-M zone. Mainly red.

Grès de Montpellier Midi r p w Recently recognized subzone of AC COTEAUX DU LANGUEDOC sprawling v'yds in the hills behind Montpellier, inc St-Georges d'Orques, La Méjanelle, St-Christol, St-Drézery. Try Clavel, Terre Megère, St Martin de la Garrigue, Prose, Grès St Paul.

Griotte-Chambertin Burg r ★★★★ 90' 95 96' 97 99' 00 02' 03 05' 06 07 08 09

Small GRAND CRU next to CHAMBERTIN. Less weight but brisk red fruit and ageing potential, at least from DUGAT, DROUHIN, PONSOT.

Grivot, Jean Burg ★★★→★★★★ Huge improvements at this VOSNE-ROMANÉE DOM in the past decade. Superb range topped by GRANDS CRUS CLOS DE VOUGEOT, ÉCHÉZEAUX, RICHEBOURG.

Gros, Doms Burg ★★★→★★★★ Fine family of VIGNERONS in VOSNE-ROMANÉE comprising (at least) DOMS Jean, Michel, Anne, Anne-Françoise Gros and Gros Frère & Soeur. Wines range from HAUTES CÔTES DE NUITS to RICHEBOURG.

Gros Plant du Pays Nantais Lo w ★ DYA VDQS. From Gros Plant (Folle Blanche in Cognac), best crisply citric – great with oysters but v'yds diminishing rapidly (1,400 ha). Now looking for promotion to AC. Try: DOM Basse Ville, Bâtard, Luneau-Papin, CH de la Preuille.

Guelasses, Dom. des Midi r w Pretty nasty overoaked 15-ha production happily less common than formerly.

Guffens-Heynen Burg ★★★★ Belgian MÂCON and POUILLY-FUISSÉ grower. Tiny quantity, top quality. Also négociant operation for rest of Burgundy as VERGET.

Guigal, Ets E N Rh ★★→★★★★ Illustrious grower-merchant: 31-ha CÔTE-RÔTIE, plus CONDRIEU, CROZES-HERMITAGE, HERMITAGE, ST-JOSEPH. Merchant: CONDRIEU, CÔTE-RÔTIE, CROZES-HERMITAGE, HERMITAGE, south Rhône. Owns DOM de Bonserine, VIDAL-FLEURY. Top Côte-Rôtie La Mouline, La Landonne, La Turque raised 42 mths in new oak, so not typical; all reds are consciously big in style. Standard wines: gd value, reliable, esp v.gd red, also white, rosé CÔTES DU RHÔNE. Also fat, oaky Condrieu La Doriane, sound HERMITAGE white.

Hautes-Côtes de Beaune/Nuits Burg r w ★→★★★ r 05' 06 07 08 w 05' 06' 07 08 09' ACS for the villages in the hills behind the CÔTE DE BEAUNE. Attractive, lighter reds and whites for early drinking. Best: Cornu, Devevey, Duband, DOMS Carré, GROS, Jacob, Jayer-Gilles, Mazilly. Also useful large co-op nr BEAUNE.

Haut-Médoc B'x r ★★→★★★ 95 96 98 00 01' 02 03 04 05' 06 07 08 (09) 4,600 ha. Source of gd- value, minerally, digestible wines. Some variation in soils and wines: sand and gravel in south; finer, heavier clay and gravel in north, sturdier. Five classed growths (eg. CANTEMERLE, LA LAGUNE, LA TOUR-CARNET).

Haut-Montravel Dordogne w sw ★★★ 03 05' 06 07 (08) Small sub-AC of BERGERAC managing to hold its own with MONBAZILLAC and SAUSSIGNAC. Best are CH Puy-Servain-Terrement and doms Moulin Caresse and Libarde.

Haut-Poitou Lo r w p sp ★→★★ DYA VDQS (800ha) from Cab Sauv, Cab Franc, Gamay, CHARD, Sauv Bl. Cave du Haut-Poitou is largest producer (top wine: CH La Fuye) but now some 30 individual growers, with Ampelidae top producer.

Heidsieck, Charles Brut Réserve NV; BRUT 95 96 00 02; Rosé 02 Major Reims CHAMPAGNE house. Excellent *mis en cave* concept has been discontinued – crazy! Outstanding Blanc des Millénaires (95' 02) See also PIPER-HEIDSIECK.

Heidsieck Monopole Once-illustrious CHAMPAGNE house. Fair quality. Silver Top (2002) best wine.

Hengst Wintzenheim ALSACE GRAND CRU. Excels with top Gewurz from MANN and JOSMEYER; also Pinot-Auxerrois, Chasselas and Pinot N (not GRAND CRU).

Henriot BRUT Souverain NV; Blancs de Blancs de Chard NV; Brut 95 96 98; Brut Rosé 99 02 Old family CHAMPAGNE house. Fine, fresh, creamy style. Outstanding *prestige* CUVÉE Les Enchanteleurs (88' 95 96). Also owns BOUCHARD PÈRE & FILS (since 1995) and FÈVRE.

Hérault Midi Biggest v'yd *département*: 86,200 ha and declining. Includes FAUGÈRES, ST-CHINIAN, PIC ST-LOUP, PICPOUL DE PINET, GRÈS DE MONTPELLIER, PÉZENAS, TERRASSES DU LARZAC among AC COTEAUX DU LANGUEDOC. Source of Vin de Pays de l'Hérault encompassing full quality spectrum, from pioneering and innovative to basic. Also VIN DE TABLE.

Hermitage N Rh r w ★★★→★★★★ 61' 66 78' 83' 85' 88 89' 90' 91' 94 95' 96 97'

98' 99' 00 01' 03' 04 05' 06' 07' 09' Rich, mighty Syrah from 133-ha granite-based hill, east bank of Rhône. Both red, white benefit from long ageing over 20+ yrs. Abundant, complex white (Marsanne, some Roussanne) best left for 6–7 yrs. Best: Belle, CHAPOUTIER, CHAVE, Colombier, DELAS, Desmeure (oak), Faurie (pure wines), GUIGAL, Habrard (white), JABOULET, M Sorrel, Tardieu-Laurent (oak). TAIN co-op gd (esp Gambert de Loche).

Hortus, Dom de l' Midi r p w ★★★ Pioneering producer of PIC ST-LOUP. Also Vin de Pays du Val de Montferrand. Stylish wines; reds Bergerie and oak-aged Grande Réserve.

Hospices de Beaune Burg Grand charity auction on third Sunday in Nov, revitalized since 2005 by Christie's. Individuals can now buy as well as trade. Standards should be more consistent, but excellent buys among BEAUNE CUVÉES or expensive GRANDS CRUS, eg. CLOS DE LA ROCHE, CORTON (red), BATARD-MONTRACHET (white).

Hudelot Burg ★★★ VIGNERON family in CÔTE DE NUITS. New life breathed into H-Noëllat (VOUGEOT) while H-Baillet (CHAMBOLLE) challenging hard. Former more stylish, latter more punchy.

Huet Lo ★★★→★★★★ 88 89' 90' 95' 96' 97' 02' 03' 05' 06 07 08' (09) Biodynamic estate in VOUVRAY. Noël Pinguet, Gaston Huet's son-in-law, continues to run the estate. Three single v'yds: Le Haut Lieu, Le Mont, Clos du Bourg. All great agers: look for ancient vintages such as 1919, 1924, 1947, 1959 and 1964. Also *pétillant*. A world benchmark for Chenin Bl.

Hugel & Fils ★★→★★★★ Big ALSACE house, making superb late-harvest wines. Three quality levels: Classic, Tradition, Jubilee. Opposed to GRAND CRU system.

Irancy Burg r (p) ★★ 05' 06 07 08 09 Formerly Bourgogne Irancy. Light red made near CHABLIS from Pinot N and local César. Best vintages mature well. Best: Colinot.

Irouléguy SW r p (w) ★★→★★★ 04 05' 06 (08) (09') Rosés (DYA) nearly as popular as reds in this Basque AC. Tannat-based reds are cultural match for *pelota* and rugby. Excellent co-op (also for white ★★★ Xuri d Ansa) and ★★★ Ameztra, Arretxea, Brana, Ilarria and ★★ Abotra, Bordathio, Etchegaraya and Mourguy.

Jaboulet Aîné, Paul N Rh 19th-century firm at TAIN, sold to Swiss investor early 2006, wines now international. Once leading grower of HERMITAGE (esp La Chapelle ★★★ quality variable 1990s on), CORNAS St-Pierre, CROZES Thalabert, Roure; merchant of other Rhône wines, notably CÔTES DU RHÔNE Parallèle 45, VENTOUX, VACQUEYRAS. Whites lack heart (much Roussanne), drink most young. Prices up , brands the name of the game , inc new v. expensive La Chapelle white.

Jacquart Brut NV; Brut Rosé NV (Carte Blanche and Cuvée Spéciale); BRUT 00 02 04 Co-op-based CHAMPAGNE brand; in quantity the sixth largest. Fair quality. Luxury brands: Cuvée Nominée Blanc 00 02 . Fine Mosaïque Blancs de Blancs 02 04 and Rosé 02 04. *Oenothèque* older vintages now launched.

Jacquesson Bijou Dizy CHAMPAGNE house. Superb Avize GRAND CRU 96' now relaunched as single-vineyard Champ Caïn 02 : white (90 95 96'), new *saignée* skin-contact rosé Terre Rouge (04). Corne Bautray, Dizy 02 04, and *excellent numbered NV Cuvées* 728, 729, 730, 731, 732, 733, 734.

Jadot, Louis Burg ★★→★★★★ High-performance merchant house across the board with significant v'yd holdings in CÔTE D'OR and expanding fast in MÂCON and BEAUJOLAIS; esp POUILLY FUISSÉ (DOM Ferret) and MOULIN-À-VENT (CH des Jacques, Clos du Grand Carquelin). Mineral whites as gd as structured reds.

Jasnières Lo w dr (sw) ★★→★★★★ 97 02 03 05' 06 07 08 (09) VOUVRAY-like wine (Chenin Bl), both dry and off-dry from a tiny but v. dynamic v'yd north of Tours. Top growers: L'Ange Vin, Aubert la Chapelle, DOM DE BELLIVIÈRE, le Briseau, Freseneau, Gigou, les Maisons Rouges, Ryke.

Jobard, François Burg VIGNERON family in MEURSAULT. Antoine, son of François, for long-lived Genevrières, etc. Cousin Rémi for more immediate class. Both ★★★.

Joblot ★★★ Outstanding GIVRY DOM with v. high viticultural standards. Try PREMIER CRU La Servoisine in both colours.

Joseph Perrier Improved Cuvée Royale Brut NV with lower *dosage*; Cuvée Royale Blanc de Blancs NV; Cuvée Royale Rosé NV; Brut 99 00 02 Excellent smaller CHAMPAGNE house at Chalons with gd v'yds in Marne Valley. Supple, fruity style; top *prestige* CUVÉE Joséphine 98 02.

Josmeyer ★★→★★★ ALSACE house specializing in fine, elegant, long-lived organic wines in a dry style. Superb Ries Grand Cru Hengst. Also v.gd wines from lesser varietals, esp Auxerrois. Exceptional wines in 2002 and 2009.

Juliénas Beauj r ★★★ 05' 06 07 08 09 Leading *cru* of BEAUJOLAIS: vigorous, fruity wine to keep 2–3 yrs. Growers inc CHX du Bois de la Salle, des Capitans, de Juliénas, des Vignes; DOMS Bottière, du Chapon, Monnet, Michel Tête, co-op.

Jurançon Pyr w dr sw ★→★★★ (sw) 97' 09' 03 04' 05' 06 07' (09') (dr) 03' 04' 05 06 (08') (09') Hard to find bad wine in this Pyrenean AC. Top choices would include boutique ★★★★ Jardins de Babylon (Benjamin DAGENEAU) ★★★ DOMS Bellegarde, Bordenase, Castéra, Cauhapé, Lapeyre, Larrédya, Girouilh, de Souch, Uroulat, Vignan-la-Juscle, ★★ DOMS Bru-Baché, Capdevielle, Nigri, Bellevue and Giraudel. Gd-value dry white from co-op.

Kaefferkopf Al w dr (sw) ★★★ Since 2006 the 51st GRAND CRU of ALSACE at Ammerschwihr. Permitted to make blends as well as varietal wines.

Kientzler, André ★★→★★★ Small, v. fine ALSACE grower at Ribeauvillé. V.gd Ries from GRANDS CRUS Osterberg and Geisberg and wonderfully aromatic Gewurz from GRAND CRU Kirchberg. Also v.gd Auxerrois and sweet wines.

Koehly, Christian ★★★ Front-rank ALSACE grower died tragically young in Jan 2009. Top Ries from GRAND CRU Altenberg de Bergheim and v.gd PINOT GR Grand Cru Gloeckelberg. Exceptional late-picked wines esp in 2002. Buy stock at auction.

Kreydenweiss, Marc ★★→★★★ Fine ALSACE grower: 12 ha at Andlau, esp for PINOT GR (v.gd GRAND CRU Moenchberg), Pinot Bl and Ries. Top wine: Grand Cru Kastelberg (ages 20 yrs); also fine Auxerrois Kritt Klevner and gd VENDANGE TARDIVE. One of first in ALSACE to use new oak – now older casks, too. Gd Ries/PINOT GR blend Clos du Val d'Eléon. Biodynamic. Great 2005 vintage.

Krug Grande Cuvée; Vintage 88 90 95 96 98; Rosé; Clos du Mesnil (BLANC DE BLANCS) 88 90 96 98'; Krug Collection 76 81 85 Small, supremely prestigious CHAMPAGNE house. Rich, nutty wines, oak-fermented: long ageing, superlative quality and soaring price. Great successes in 1998, a challenging year. New Clos d'Ambonnay (95' 96) for billionaires.

Kuentz-Bas ★→★★ Al Famous grower/merchant at Husseren-les-Châteaux, esp PINOT GR, Gewurz. Gd VENDANGES TARDIVES. Owned by Caves J-B Adam.

Ladoix Burg r (w) ★★ 99' 02' 03 05' 07 08 09 Village at north end of CÔTE DE BEAUNE, inc some CORTON and CORTON-CHARLEMAGNE. After yrs in shadow of ALOXE, now undergoing revival in the hands of Claude Chevalier, Michel Mallard, Sylvain Loichet. Exuberant whites of interest, too.

Ladoucette, de ★★→★★★ 03 05 06 07 08 (09) Largest individual producer of POUILLY-FUMÉ, based at CH de Nozet. Expensive luxury brand Baron de L. Sancerre Comte Lafond, La Poussie; Vouvray Marc Brédif. Owns Albert Pic (CHABLIS).

Lafarge, Michel Burg ★★★★ Top 11.5-ha VOLNAY estate run by vigorous octogenarian Michel and son Frédéric. *Clos des Chênes*, Caillerets and Clos du Château des Ducs all outstanding, along with fine BEAUNE and POMMARD.

Lafon, Dom des Comtes Burg ★★★→★★★★ Long famous for whites, MEURSAULT and MONTRACHET while red VOLNAY now outstanding. Also in Mâconnais while Dominique L has started own label in BEAUNE.

Laguiche, Marquis de Burg ★★★★ Largest owner of LE MONTRACHET. Superb DROUHIN-made wines perhaps just below the summit.

Lalande de Pomerol B'x r ★★→★★★ 95 96 98 99 00' 01' 04 05' 06 07 08 (09) Northerly neighbour of POMEROL. Wines similar, but less structured and refined. New investors and younger generation: improving quality. Top CHX: des Annereaux, BERTINEAU-ST-VINCENT, Les Cruzelles, La Fleur de Boüard, Garraud, Grand Ormeau, Jean de Gué, Haut-Chaigneau, Les Hauts Conseillants, Perron (La Fleur), La Sergue, Siaurac, TOURNEFEUILLE.

Landron (Doms) Lo w dr sp ★★→★★★ First-rate producer of organic MUSCADET DE SÈVRE-ET-MAINE with several CUVÉES, bottled by terroir, inc Amphibolite age-worthy Fief du Breil, Clos de la Carizière and good sparkling – Gros Plant/Pinot N.

Langlois-Chateau Lo ★★→★★★ A top SAUMUR sparkling (CRÉMANT only) house – BOLLINGER-owned. Also still wines, esp exceptional Saumur Blanc Vielles Vignes.

Languedoc Midi r p w General term for the MIDI and now AC enlarging COTEAUX DU LANGUEDOC to inc MINERVOIS and CORBIÈRES, and also ROUSSILLON. Rules the same as for COTEAUX DU LANGUEDOC, with 5-yr period for name-changing. The bottom of the pyramid of MIDI ACS.

Lanson Père & Fils Black Label NV; Rosé NV; BRUT 98' 02 Important improving CHAMPAGNE house now part of Boizel Chanoine group. Long-lived luxury brand: Noble Cuvée as BLANC DE BLANCS, rosé and vintage blend (98'). New single-vyd Clos Lanson (07 08).

Laroche ★★ Change of ownership in 2009 for large-scale CHABLIS grower and merchant with interests in south of France, Chile and South Africa. Majority owner now Groupe Jeanjean. Try Grand Cru Réserve de l'Obédiencerie.

Latour, Louis Burg ★★→★★★ Famous traditional family merchant making sound white wines from CÔTE D'OR v'yds (esp CORTON and CORTON-CHARLEMAGNE), Mâconnais and the ARDÈCHE (all CHARD) and less exciting reds (all Pinot) from CÔTE D'OR and Coteaux du Verdon. Now also owns Henry Fessy in Beaujolais.

Latour de France Pyr r (w) ★→★★ Theoretically superior village in CÔTES DE ROUSSILLON-VILLAGES. Esp Clos de l'Oum, Clos des Fées. Best wines usuallyVin de Pays des Côtes Catalanes.

Latricières-Chambertin Burg r ★★★ 90' 93 95 96' 99' 00 02' 03 05' 06 07 08 09 GRAND CRU neighbour of CHAMBERTIN (6.8 ha). Similar wine but lighter, eg. from BIZE, Drouhin-Laroze, FAIVELEY, LEROY, Rossignol-Trapet, TRAPET.

Laudun S Rh r p w ★→★★ 06 07' 09' Village of CÔTES DU RHÔNE-VILLAGES (west bank). Soft, clear reds (lots of Syrah), bright rosés, stylish whites. Agreeable wines from Serre de Bernon co-op. DOM Pelaquié best, esp ace white. Also CHX de Bord, Courac, Marjolet, St-Maurice, DOM Duseigneur, Prieuré St-Pierre.

Laurent-Perrier Brut NV; Rosé NV; BRUT 99 00 02 Dynamic family-owned CHAMPAGNE house at Tours-sur-Marne. Fine minerally NV; excellent luxury brands: Grand Siècle la Cuvée Lumière du Millésime (90 96), Cuvée Grand Siècle Alexandra Brut Rosé (02). But Ultra Brut fails to impress.

Lavilledieu-du-Temple SW r p w ★ DOMS du Rouch and de Gazania continue to carry the torch for this precarious VDQS.

Leflaive, Dom Burg ★★★★ Among the best white burgundy growers, at PULIGNY-MONTRACHET. Best v'yds: Bienvenues, CHEVALIER-MONTRACHET, Folatières, Pucelles and (since 1991) LE MONTRACHET. Also MÂCON from 2004. Ever-finer wines on biodynamic principles.

Leflaive, Olivier Burg ★★→★★★ High-quality négociant at PULIGNY-MONTRACHET, cousin of the above. Reliable wines, mostly white, but drink them young.

Leroy, Dom Burg ★★★★ DOM built around purchase of Noëllat in VOSNE-ROMANÉE in 1988. Extraordinary quality (and prices) from tiny biodynamic yields. Also original Leroy family holdings, DOM d'Auvenay.

Leroy, Maison Burg ★★★★ Burgundy's ultimate NÉGOCIANT-ÉLEVEUR at AUXEY-DURESSES. Sky-high standards and finest stocks of expensive old wine.

Liger-Belair Burg ★★★→★★★★ Two recently re-established DOMS of high quality. Vicomte Louis-Michel L-B makes brilliantly ethereal wines in VOSNE-ROMANÉE, while cousin Thibault makes plump red wines in NUITS-ST-GEORGES.

Lignier Burg ★→★★ Family in MOREY-ST-DENIS. Best is Hubert (eg. CLOS DE LA ROCHE), but watch Virgile L-Michelot and DOM Lucie & Auguste L.

Limoux Pyr r w ★★ AC for great-value sparkling BLANQUETTE DE LIMOUX or better *Crémant de Limoux*, also unusual *méthode ancestrale*. Oak-aged CHARD for white Limoux AC. Red AC since 2003 based on Merlot, plus Syrah, Grenache, Cabernets, Carignan. Pinot N in CRÉMANT and for VDP. Growers: DOMS de Fourn, Laurens, des Martinolles, de Mouscaillou, Rives Blanques. Sound co-op: Sieur d'Arques.

Lirac S Rh r p w ★★ 98' 01' 03 04 05' 06' 07' 09' Next to TAVEL. Fair-value red (can age 5+ yrs), helped by impetus from CHÂTEAUNEUF-DU-PAPE owners so more depth, cleaner wines. Reds lead over rosé, esp DOMS Joncier, Lafond Roc-Epine, Lorentine, Maby (Fermade), André Méjan, de la Mordorée (best), Rocalière, R Sabon, CHX Bouchassy, Manissy, Mont-Redon, St-Roch, Ségriès, Clos de Sixte. Gd whites (5 yrs).

Listrac-Médoc B'x r ★★→★★★ 95 96 98 00' 01 03 05' 06 08 (09) Neighbour of MOULIS in the southern MÉDOC. Grown-up clarets with tannic grip. Now rounded out with more Merlot. Best CHX: Cap Léon Veyrin, CLARKE, DUCLUZEAU, FONRÉAUD, FOURCAS-DUPRÉ, FOURCAS-HOSTEN, Mayne-Lalande, Reverdi.

Long-Depaquit Burg ★★★ BICHOT-owned CHABLIS DOM, inc flagship GRAND CRU brand La Moutonne.

Lorentz, Gustave ★★ ALSACE grower and merchant at Bergheim. Esp Gewurz, Ries from GRAND CRUS Altenberg de Bergheim, Kanzlerberg. Also owns Jerome Lorentz. Equally gd for top estate and volume wines.

Lot SW Important VDP often from CAHORS growers seeking wider market. Also from newly planted surrounding countryside, eg. ★★ DOMS de Sully and Belmont.

Loupiac B'x w sw ★★ 96 97' 98 99' 01' 02 03' 05' 07 (09) Across river Garonne from SAUTERNES. Lighter and fresher in style. Top Clos-Jean, LOUPIAC-GAUDIET, Mémoires, Noble, RICAUD, Les Roques.

Lubéron S Rh r p w ★→★★ 07' 09' Country wines from 2,500-ha v'yds in far SE of Rhône, can be over the top; modern methods. Syrah popular. Many new producers. Star is CH de la Canorgue. Also DOM de la Citadelle, CH Clapier, Edem, Fontvert, O Ravoire, St-Estève de Neri (improving), Tardieu-Laurent (oak), Cellier de Marrenon, Val-Joanis, LA VIEILLE FERME (w).

Lussac-St-Emilion B'x r ★★ 95 98 00' 01 03 05' (09) The lightest of the ST-EMILION satellites. Co-op the main producer. Top CHX: Barbe Blanche, Bel Air, Bellevue, Courlat, la Grenière, LUSSAC, LYONNAT, Mayne-Blanc.

Macération carbonique Traditional fermentation technique: whole bunches of unbroken grapes in a closed vat. Fermentation induced inside each grape eventually bursts it, giving vivid, fruity, mild wine, not for ageing. Esp in BEAUJOLAIS; now much used in the MIDI and elsewhere, even CHÂTEAUNEUF.

Mâcon Burg r w (p) DYA Sound, usually unremarkable reds (from Gamay), tasty dry (CHARD) whites.

Mâcon-Lugny Burg w sp (r) ★★ 07 08 09' Leading Mâconnais village. Try Les Charmes from excellent co-op or Genevrières from LATOUR.

Mâcon-Villages Burg w ★★→★★★ 06' 07 08 09' Catch-all name for better Mâconnais wines, which may also use their own names eg. MÂCON-LUGNY, La Roche Vineuse, etc. Quality individual growers emerging. Try Bonhomme, Guillot-Broux, LAFON, Maillet, Merlin, co-ops at Lugny, Prissé, Viré.

Macvin Jura w sw ★★ AC for "traditional" MARC and grape-juice apéritif.

Madiran SW r ★★→★★★ 95' 00' 01 02 04 05' (08) (09') Babies and grannies beware of these big, Tannat-based reds. Co-ops and some independents making easier, fruity wines, but most growers stick to what they know. ★★★ CHX MONTUS and BOUSCASSÉ now chased hard by Barréjat, Berthoumieu, Capmartin, Chapelle, Lenclos. Clos Basté, Crampilh, Labranche-Laffont, Laffitte-Teston and *Laplace* all need ageing.

Mähler-Besse B'x First-class Dutch négociant in BORDEAUX. Loads of old vintages. Has share in CH PALMER.

Mailly-Champagne ★★★ Top CHAMPAGNE co-op, all GRAND CRU grapes. *Prestige* CUVÉE des Echansons (98') great wine for long ageing. Real value.

Maire, Henri ★→★★ The biggest grower/merchant of Jura wines, with half of the entire AC. Some top wines, many cheerfully commercial. Fun to visit.

Malepère Midi r ★ DYA Originally Côtes de la Malepère, now plain Malepère AC near LIMOUX for reds that combine BORDEAUX and the MIDI. Fresh reds with a touch of rusticity provide original drinking. esp CH Guilhem.

Mann, Albert ★→★★★ Top growers of ALSACE at Wettolsheim: rich, elegant wines. V.gd Pinot Bl, Auxerrois and Pinot N, and gd range of GRANDS CRUS wines from SCHLOSSBERG, HENGST, Furstentum and Steingrubler.

Maranges Burg (w) ★★ 02' 03' 05' 07 08 09 CÔTE DE BEAUNE AC beyond SANTENAY (243 ha): one-third PREMIER CRU. Best: Contat-Grange, Chevrot, DROUHIN, GIRARDIN.

Marc Grape skins after pressing; the strong-smelling brandy made from them.

Marcillac SW r p ★★ DYA Best 3 yrs or so after vintage. Unmistakable violet-hued, grassy, red-fruit character from Aveyron hillside terraces. DOMS du Cros, Costes, Mioula, Vieux Porche and gd co-op.

Margaux B'x r ★★→★★★★★ 89 90' 95 96 98 00' 01 02 04 05' 06 08 (09) Largest communal AC in the southern MÉDOC, grouping v'yds from five villages. Known for its elegant, fragrant style. 21 classed growths. Top CHX: BRANE-CANTENAC, FERRIÈRE, MARGAUX, PALMER, RAUZAN-SÉGLA.

Marionnet, Henry Lo r w ★★→★★★ 05' 06 07 08' 09' Influential TOURAINE grower fascinated by grape varieties. Wines include Sauv Bl (top is Le M de Marionnet) and *Gamay*, esp the unsulphured Première Vendange, Provignage (from ungrafted Romorantin vines planted 1850) and juicy ungrafted Cot.

Marmande Dordogne r p w ★→★★★ 04 05' 06 (08) (09') Handful of good independents (★★★ DOM Elian da Ros, CH de Beaulieu, ★★ DOM Bonnet et Laborde and CH Lassolle) outclass disappointing co-op. Top CUVÉES need time.

Marne & Champagne CHAMPAGNE house, and many smaller brands, inc BESSERAT DE BELLEFON. Alfred Rothschild brand v.gd CHARD-based wines. Improving quality under BOIZEL CHANOINE ownership.

Marque déposée Trademark.

Marsannay Burg r p (w) ★★ 05' 06 07 08 09 (rosé DYA) Easy-to-drink wines of all three colours. Little of note except reds from gifted producers such as Audoin, Charlopin, CLAIR, *Pataille* and TRAPET. No PREMIERS CRUS yet, but plans afoot.

Mas, Doms Paul Midi r p w ★★ Big player in the MIDI; own estates and négociant wine, VDP and AC. Innovative marketing. Known for Arrogant Frog VDP range; also La Forge and Les Vignes de Nicole.

Mas de Daumas Gassac Midi r p w ★★★ 96 97 98 99 00 01 02 03 04 05 06 07 08 Pioneering VDP set an example of excellence in the MIDI, with Cab-based reds produced on apparently unique wind-borne glacial soil. Quality now rivalled and surpassed by many, eg. neighbouring GRANGE DES PÈRES. Wines include new super-CUVÉE Emile Peynaud, rosé Frizant, delicious, rich, *fragrant white blend to drink* at 2–3 yrs. VDP status. Intriguing sweet wine: Vin de Laurence (MUSCAT, Sercial).

Massif d'Uchaux S Rh r ★→★★ Rhône village since 2005, promising cool zone with able growers, stylish, full wines. Note: CH St Estève, DOMS La Cabotte, Chapoton, Cros de la Mûre (v.gd), de la Guicharde, Renjarde.

Mau, Yvon Négociant, part of Freixenet, owns Ch Brown (PESSAC-LÉOGNAN) and Preuillac (MÉDOC; improving).

Maury Pyr r sw ★★ NV red VIN DOUX NATUREL from ROUSSILLON. From Grenache grown on island of schist in limestone hills. Much recent improvement, esp at Mas Amiel. RANCIOS age beautifully. Also gd red table wines.

Mazis- (or Mazy-) Chambertin Burg r ★★★ 88' 90' 93 95 96' 99' 00 02' 03 05' 06 07 08 (09) GRAND CRU neighbour of CHAMBERTIN (12 ha); can be equally potent. Best from DUGAT-PY, FAIVELEY, HOSPICES DE BEAUNE, LEROY, Maume.

Mazoyères-Chambertin See CHARMES-CHAMBERTIN.

Méditerrananée, Vin de Pays de Regional VDP from southern RHÔNE/PROVENCE. Easy reds, characterful whites: Viognier. Originally Portes de la Méditerrananée.

Médoc B'x r ★★ 98 00' 02 03 04 05' 06 08 (09) AC for reds in the flatter, northern part of the MÉDOC peninsula. Gd if you're selective. Earthy, with Merlot adding flesh. Top CHX: GREYSAC, LOUDENNE, Lousteauneuf, LES ORMES-SORBET, POTENSAC, Ramafort, Rollan-de-By (HAUT-CONDISSAS), LA TOUR-DE-BY, TOUR HAUT-CAUSSAN.

Meffre, Gabriel S Rh ★★ Big merchant at GIGONDAS, bought by Boisset/Eric Brousse in 2009. For now, owns DOM Longue Toque. Recent progress, quality can vary, new focus not yet clear. Also bottles, sells small CHÂTEAUNEUF DOMS. Sound northern Rhône Laurus (new oak) range, esp CROZES-HERMITAGE, ST-JOSEPH.

Mellot, Alphonse Lo r p w ★★→★★★ 02 03 04 05 06 07 08' (09) V. fine range of SANCERRE (white and esp reds) from leading grower: La Moussière (white and red), barrel-fermented Cuvée Edmond, Génération XIX (red and white), Les Demoiselles and En Grands Champs (red). Since 2005 in Coteaux Charitois (VDP) CHARD and Pinot N.

Menetou-Salon Lo r p w ★★ 05 06 07 08 AC (450 ha) SW of SANCERRE; similar wines. Best producers: BOURGEOIS, *Clement* (DOM de Chatenoy), Jacolin, Henry Pellé, Jean-Max Roger, Teiller, Tour St-Martin. V. severely hit by hail in 2009.

Méo-Camuzet Burg ★★★★ V. fine DOM in CLOS DE VOUGEOT, NUITS-ST-GEORGES, RICHEBOURG, VOSNE-ROMANÉE. Jayer-inspired. Esp Vosne-Romanée Cros Parantoux. Now also some less expensive négociant CUVÉES.

Mercier & Cie, Champagne Brut NV, Brut Rosé NV, Demi-Sec Brut One of biggest CHAMPAGNE houses at Epernay. Controlled by MOËT & CHANDON. Sold mainly in France. Full-bodied, Pinot N-led CUVÉE Eugene Mercier.

Mercurey Burg r (w) ★★→★★★ 99' 02' 03' 05' 06 07 08 09 Leading red wine village of CÔTE CHALONNAISE. *Gd middle-rank burgundy*, inc improving whites. Try CH de Chamirey, FAIVELEY, M Juillot, Lorenzon, Raquillet, de Suremain.

Mesnil-sur-Oger, Le Champ ★★★★ One of the top Côte des Blancs villages. Structured CHARD for v. long ageing.

Méthode champenoise Traditional method of putting bubbles into CHAMPAGNE by refermenting wine in its bottle. Outside CHAMPAGNE region, makers must use terms "classic method" or "*méthode traditionnelle*".

Meursault Burg w (r) ★★★→★★★★ 99' 00' 02' 04 05' 06' 07 08 09 CÔTE DE BEAUNE village with some of world's greatest whites: savoury, dry, nutty, mellow. Best v'yds: Charmes, Genevrières, Perrières. Also: Goutte d'Or, Meursault-Blagny, Poruzots, Narvaux, Tesson, Tillets. Producers include: AMPEAU, J-M BOILLOT, *M Bouzereau*, V BOUZEREAU, Boyer-Martenot, CH DE MEURSAULT, COCHE-DURY, Ente, Fichet, Grivault, P Javillier, JOBARD, LAFON, Labille-Latour, O LEFLAIVE, LEROY, Matrot, Mikulski, P MOREY, G ROULOT. See also BLAGNY.

Midi Broad term covering Languedoc, Roussillon and even Provence. A melting-pot; quality improves with every vintage. One of France's most exciting and challenging wine regions. ACS can be intriguing blends; VDP, esp D'OC, are often varietals. Brilliant promise, rewarding drinking. But of course no guarantee.

Minervois Midi r br sw (p w) ★→★★ 02' 03 04 05' 06 07' 08 09 Hilly AC region; gd, lively reds, esp CHX Bonhomme, Coupe-Roses, la Grave, Oupia, St Jacques d'Albas, La Tour Boisée, Villerembert-Julien, Clos Centeilles, Ste Eulalie, Faiteau; co-ops La Livinière, de Peyriac, Pouzols. See ST-JEAN DE MINERVOIS.

Minervois-La Livinière Midi r (p w) ★→★★★★ Quality village, only sub-appellation or *cru* in MINERVOIS. Stricter selection and longer ageing. Best growers: Abbaye de Tholomies, Borie de Maurel, Combe Blanche, CH de Gourgazaud, Clos Centeilles, Laville-Bertrou, DOMS Maris, Ste-Eulalie, co-op La Livinière, Vipur.

Mis en bouteille au ch/dom Bottled at the CH, property, or estate. NB *dans nos caves* (in our cellars) or *dans la région de production* (in the area of production) are often used but mean little.

Moët & Chandon By far the largest CHAMPAGNE house and enlightened leader of v'yd research and development. Now owns 1,500 ha often in the best sites. Greatly improved Brut NV, recent fine run of grand vintages, esp 90 95 and an awesome 03, esp the rosé. Impressive CUVÉE DOM PERIGNON. Branches across Europe and New World.

Mommessin, J BOISSET-owned BEAUJOLAIS and MÂCON merchant, better noted for reds than whites. Family still own CLOS DE TART in MOREY-ST-DENIS.

Monbazillac Dordogne w sw ★★→★★★★★ 90' 95' 01' 03' 04 05' 06 07' (09') Popularization of foie gras and blue cheese make this sweet BERGERAC a serious challenge in quality and price to SAUTERNES. Top producers: ★★★ L'Ancienne Cure, Clos des Verdots, Tirecul-la-Gravière and La Grande Maison; ★★ CHX de Belingard-Chayne, Le Fagé, Les Hauts de Caillavel, Poulvère, Theulet. Also the co-op's *Ch de Monbazillac*.

Mondeuse Savoie r ★★ DYA SAVOIE red grape. Potentially gd, deep-coloured wine. Possibly same as Italy's Refosco. Don't miss a chance, eg. *G Berlioz*.

Monopole A v'yd that is under single ownership.

Montagne-St-Emilion B'x r ★★ 95 98 00' 01 03 05' (09) Largest and possibly best satellite of ST-EMILION (1,600 ha). Similar style of wine. Top CHX: Beauséjour, Calon, La Couronne, Croix Beauséjour, Faizeau, Haut Bonneau, Maison Blanche, Roudier, Teyssier, *Vieux Ch St-André*.

Montagny Burg w ★★ 05' 06' 07 08 09' CÔTE CHALONNAISE village. Between MÂCON and MEURSAULT, both geographically and gastronomically. Top producers: Aladame, J-M BOILLOT, Cave de Buxy, Michel, CH de la Saule.

Monthélie Burg r (w) ★★→★★★ 99' 02' 03' 05' 07 08 09 Little-known VOLNAY neighbour, sometimes almost equal. Best v'yds: Champs Fulliot, Duresses. Fragrant red, esp BOUCHARD PÈRE & FILS, COCHE-DURY, DROUHIN, Garaudet, LAFON, CH de Monthélie (Suremain).

Montille, de Burg ★★★ Hubert de Montille made long-lived VOLNAY, POMMARD. Son Etienne has expanded DOM with purchases in BEAUNE, NUITS-ST-GEORGES and potentially outstanding Vosne-Romanée Malconsorts. Etienne also runs CH de Puligny. Also Deux Montille (white wines) négociant venture with sister Alix.

Montlouis Lo w dr sw (sp) ★★→★★★ 89' 90' 95' 96' 97' 02' 03' 05' 07 08 (09) Sister AC to VOUVRAY on south side of Loire making similar range of wines from Chenin Bl. 370 ha. Currently *one of the Loire's most exciting acs*. Top growers include Berger, Chatenay, CHIDAINE, Damien Delecheneau, Deletang, Jousset, Moyer, Frantz Saumon, TAILLE-AUX-LOUPS, WEISSKOPF.

Montrachet Burg w ★★★★ 92' 93 95 96' 97 99 00' 01 02' 03 04 05' 06 07 08 09 GRAND CRU v'yd (8.01 ha) in both PULIGNY- and CHASSAGNE-MONTRACHET. Potentially the greatest white burgundy: strong, perfumed, intense, dry yet luscious. Top wines: LAFON, LAGUICHE (DROUHIN), LEFLAIVE, Ramonet, ROMANÉE-CONTI. DOM THÉNARD disappoints.

Montravel Dordogne ★★ p w dr DYA (r) 02' 04 05' 06 (08) (09') Subregion of BERGERAC with its own AC. Reds usually in modern style. Best are ★★ DOMS de

Bloy, de Krevel, CHX Jonc Blanc, Laulerie, Masburel, Masmontet, Moulin-Caresse. Separate ACS for semi-sweet CÔTES DE MONTRAVEL, sweet HAUT-MONTRAVEL.

Morey, Doms Burg ★★★ VIGNERON family in CHASSAGNE-MONTRACHET, esp Jean-Marc, Marc, Thomas, Vincent, Michel M-Coffinet. Also Pierre Morey in MEURSAULT. All better known for whites than reds.

Morey-St-Denis Burg r (w) ★★★ 90' 93 95 96' 97 98 99' 00 02' 03 05' 06 07 08 (09) Small village with four GRANDS CRUS between GEVREY-CHAMBERTIN and CHAMBOLLE-MUSIGNY. Glorious wine often overlooked. Amiot, ARLAUD, CLOS DE TART, CLOS DES LAMBRAYS, DUJAC, LIGNIER, Perrot-Minot, PONSOT, ROUMIER, Taupenot-Merme.

Morgon Beauj r ★★★ 03 05' 06 07 08 09' Firm, tannic BEAUJOLAIS *cru*, esp from Côte de Py subdistrict. Becomes meaty with age. Try Desvignes, Foillard, Gaget, Lafont, Lapierre, CH de Pizay.

Mortet, Denis ★★★ Ultra-perfectionist Denis made exceptionally powerful, deep-coloured wines in GEVREY-CHAMBERTIN until his untimely death in early 2006. Son Arnaud looks for more elegance. Try new, successful FIXIN.

Moueix, J-P et Cie Libourne-based merchant and proprietor named after legendary founder. Son Christian runs company. CHX include LA FLEUR-PÉTRUS, HOSANNA, MAGDELAINE, TROTANOY. BELAIR-MONANGE acquired in 2008. Distributes PÉTRUS. Also in California: see Dominus.

Moulin-à-Vent Beauj r ★★★99 03 05' 07 08 09' Biggest and potentially best wine of BEAUJOLAIS. Can be powerful, meaty, long-lived; can even taste like fine Rhône or burgundy. Many gd growers, esp CHX du Moulin-à-Vent, *des Jacques*, DOM des Hospices, JADOT, Janodet, Merlin.

Moulis B'x r ★★→★★★ 98 00' 01 02 03 04 05' 06 08 (09) Tiny inland AC in the south MÉDOC, with many honest, gd-value wines. Top CHX: Biston-Brillette, Branas Grand Poujeaux, Dutruch Grand Poujeaux, BRILLETTE, CHASSE-SPLEEN, MAUCAILLOU, POUJEAUX.

Mouton Cadet Biggest-selling red BORDEAUX brand. Revamped and fruitier since 2004. Also white, rosé, GRAVES AC and MÉDOC AC.

Mugneret Burg ★★★ VIGNERON family in VOSNE-ROMANÉE. Dr Georges M-Gibourg best (esp ECHÉZEAUX), also Gerard M and Dominique M.

Mugnier, J-F Burg ★★★→★★★★ Outstanding grower of CHAMBOLLE-MUSIGNY LES AMOUREUSES and MUSIGNY at CH de Chambolle. Winery rebuilt to accommodate 9-ha NUITS-ST-GEORGES Clos de la Maréchale since 2004.

Mumm, G H & Cie Cordon Rouge NV; Mumm de Cramant NV, Cordon Rouge 98 00 02 04; Rosé NV Major CHAMPAGNE grower/merchant. Owned by Pernod-Ricard. Improved quality, esp in relaunched excellent CUVÉE R Lalou 98'.

Muré, Clos St-Landelin ★★→★★★ One of ALSACE's great names; 16 ha of GRAND CRU Vorbourg, esp fine in full-bodied Ries and PINOT GR. The Pinot N Cuvée "V" (04 05), truly ripe and vinous, is the region's best. Sumptuous 09s from 2011.

Muscadet Lo w ★→★★★ DYA (but see below) Popular, gd-value, often delicious bone-dry wine from nr Nantes. Overall high quality; 2009 first normal-volume vintage since 2005. Should never be sharp, but always refreshing. Perfect with fish and seafood. Best are from zonal ACS: MUSCADET-COTEAUX DE LA LOIRE, MUSCADET CÔTES DE GRAND LIEU, MUSCADET DE SÈVRE-ET-MAINE. Choose a SUR LIE.

Muscadet-Coteaux de la Loire Lo w ★→★★ 04 05 06 07 08 09 Small MUSCADET zone E of Nantes (best SUR LIE). Esp Guindon, CH du Ponceau, Les Vignerons de la Noëlle.

Muscadet Côtes de Grand Lieu ★→★★ 04 05 06 07 08 Most recent (1995) of MUSCADET's zonal ACS and the closest to Atlantic coast. Best are SUR LIE from eg. Bâtard, Eric Chevalier, Choblet (DOM des Herbauges), Malidain.

Muscadet de Sèvre-et-Maine ★→★★★ 01 02 03 04 05 06 07 08 09 Largest and best of MUSCADET's delimited zones. Top Guy Bossard (DOM DE L'ECU),

Bernard Chereau, Bruno Cormerais, Michel Delhommeau, Douillard, Gadais, DOM de la Haute Fevrie, Joseph Landron, Luneau-Papin, Louis Métaireau, Sauvion. Wines from these properties can age beautifully – try 1986 or 1989.

Muscat Distinctively perfumed and usually sweet wine from the grape of same name, often fortified as VDN. Dry table wine in ALSACE.

Muscat de Lunel Midi golden sw ★★ NV Tiny AC based on MUSCAT, fortified, luscious and sweet. Some experimental late-harvest VDP wines. Look for DOM de Bellevue, CH du Grès St Paul.

Muscat de Mireval Midi sw ★★ NV Tiny fortified MUSCAT AC near Montpellier. A handful of producers. DOM La Capelle the best.

Muscat de Rivesaltes Midi golden sw ★★ NV Sweet, fortified MUSCAT AC wine near Perpignan. Popularity waning; Muscat Sec VDP instead; best from Cazes Frères, CH de Jau.

Musigny Burg r (w) ★★★★ 85' 88' 89' 90' 91 93 95 96' 98 99' 01 02' 03 04 05' 06 07 08 09 GRAND CRU in CHAMBOLLE-MUSIGNY (10 ha). Can be the most beautiful, if not the most powerful, of all red burgundies. Best growers: DROUHIN, JADOT, LEROY, MUGNIER, PRIEUR, ROUMIER, DE VOGÜÉ, VOUGERAIE.

Napoléon Brand name of PRIEUR family's Vertus CHAMPAGNE house now owned by British wine merchant. Seek out mature vintages 95 96.

Nature "Natural" or "unprocessed" – esp of still CHAMPAGNE.

Négociant-éleveur Merchant who "brings up" (ie. matures) the wine.

Nuits-St-Georges Burg r ★★→★★★★ 90' 93 95 96' 98 99' 01 02' 03 04 05' 06 07 08 09 Important wine town: underrated wines, typically sturdy, tannic, need time. Best v'yds: Cailles, Vaucrains, Les St Georges south of Nuits; Boudots, Murgers by VOSNE; Clos de la Maréchale, Clos St Marc in Prémeaux. Many merchants and growers include: Ambroise, L'ARLOT, J Chauvenet, R CHEVILLON, Confuron, FAIVELEY, GOUGES, GRIVOT, Lechéneaut, LEROY, LIGER-BELAIR, Machard de Gramont, Michelot, MUGNIER, *Rion*.

d'Oc (Vin de Pays d'Oc) Midi r p w ★→★★ Largest VDP, covering LANGUEDOC-ROUSSILLON with focus on varietal wines. Tremendous recent technical advances. Main producers: Jeanjean, VAL D'ORBIEU, DOMS PAUL MAS, village co-ops, plus numerous small individual growers. Encompasses both the best and the worst of the MIDI.

Orléans Lo r p w ★ DYA Recent (2006) 90-ha AC for whites (chiefly CHARD), *gris*, rosé and reds (Pinot N and esp Meunier) from small area around Orléans.

Orléans-Clery Lo r ★ DYA 30 ha separate AC for simple Cab Fr reds from same zone as AC ORLÉANS.

Pacherenc du Vic-Bilh SW Fr w dr sw ★★→★★★ Small production from most growers of MADIRAN, ranging from dry (DYA) esp CHX MONTUS and BOUSCASSÉ, ★★★ Cuvée Ericka (CH Laffitte-Teston) to sweet (ageing needed for oaked versions) from above, Berthoumieu, Capmartin, Crampilh, Labranche- Laffont.

Paillard, Bruno Brut Première Cuvée NV; Rosé Première Cuvée; Chard Réserve Privé, Brut 96' 98. New vintage Blancs de Blancs 95' 96. Superb Prestige Cuvée Nec Plus Ultra (95 96). Youngest grand CHAMPAGNE house. Fine quality. Refined, v. dry style best expressed in Blanc de Blancs Réserve Privée and Nec Plus Ultra (90' 96) only now fully mature. Bruno Paillard heads BOIZEL CHANOINE group and owns CH de Sarrin, Provence.

Palette Prov r p w ★★★ Tiny AC nr Aix-en-Provence. Full reds, fragrant rosés and intriguing whites, red CH SIMONE, now challenged by CH Henri Bonnaud.

Pasquier-Desvignes ★→★★ V. old firm of BEAUJOLAIS merchants nr BROUILLY.

Patriarche Burg ★→★★ One of the bigger Burgundy merchants. Cellars in BEAUNE; also owns CH DE MEURSAULT (61 ha), sparkling Kriter, etc.

Patrimonio Corsica r p w ★★→★★★★ AC Some of the island's best, from dramatic limestone hills in north CORSICA. Characterful reds from Nielluccio, intriguing whites, even late harvest, from Vermentino. Top growers: Antoine Arena, Clos de Bernardi, Gentile, Yves Leccia at E Croce, Pastricciola.

Pauillac B'x r ★★★→★★★★ 89' 90' 94 95' 96' 98 00' 01 02 03' 04' 05' 06 08 (09) Communal AC in the MÉDOC with three First Growths (LAFITE, LATOUR, MOUTON). Famous for its powerful, long-lived wines. Other top CHX include GRAND-PUY-LACOSTE, LYNCH-BAGES, PICHON-LONGUEVILLE and PICHON-LALANDE.

Pécharmant Dordogne r ★★→★★★ 01' 04 05' 06 (08) (09') Iron in the soil gives minerality and grip to wines from this subregion of BERGERAC. Best: DOM du Haut-Pécharmant, de l'Ancienne Cure, Les Chemins d'Orient, Clos des Côtes, CH d'Elle, Renaudie, Terre Vieille, de Tilleraie, de Tiregand. New World style from dom des Costes. Also gd BERGERAC co-op at Le Fleix.

Pernand-Vergelesses Burg r w ★★★ 99' 02' 03' 05' 06 07 08 09 Village next to ALOXE-CORTON containing part of the great CORTON-CHARLEMAGNE and CORTON v'yds. Ile des Vergelesses also first rate. Growers: CHANDON DE BRIAILLES, CHANSON, Delarche, Dubreuil-Fontaine, JADOT, LATOUR, Rapet, Rollin.

Perrier-Jouët Brut NV; Blason de France NV; Blason de France Rosé NV; Brut 98 Historic CHAMPAGNE house at Epernay, one of first to make dry CHAMPAGNE, once the smartest name of all; now best for respectable vintage wines. De luxe Belle Epoque 96 98 99 02 (Rosé 02) in a painted bottle.

Pessac-Léognan B'x r w ★★★→★★★★ 90' 95 96 98 00' 01 02 04 05' 06 08 (09) AC created in 1987 for the best part of N GRAVES, inc all the GRANDS CRUS: HAUT-BRION, LA MISSION-HAUT-BRION, PAPE-CLÉMENT, DOM DE CHEVALIER, etc. Plump, minerally reds and BORDEAUX's finest barrel-fermented dry whites.

Petit Chablis Burg w ★ DYA Fresh and easy, lighter almost-CHABLIS from outlying v'yds. La Chablisienne co-op is gd.

Pézenas Midi r p w COTEAUX DU LANGUEDOC subregion from v'yds around Molière's town. Try Prieuré de St-Jean-de-Bébian, DOMS du Conte des Floris, des Aurelles, Stella Nova, Monplézy.

Pfaffenheim ★→★★ Respectable ALSACE co-op. Style can be a little rustic.

Pfersigberg Eguisheim ALSACE GRAND CRU with two parcels; v. aromatic wines. Gewurz does v. well. Ries, esp Paul Ginglinger, BRUNO SORG and LÉON BEYER Comtes d'Eguisheim. Top grower: KUENTZ-BAS.

Philipponnat NV; Rosé NV; Brut 99 02 Cuvée 1522 00; Clos des Goisses 85' 91 95 96 98 99 Small CHAMPAGNE house known for well-structured wines and now owned by BOIZEL CHANOINE group. *Remarkable single-v'yd Clos des Goisses* and charming rosé.

Picpoul de Pinet Midi w ★→★★ COTEAUX DU LANGUEDOC *cru* and aspiring AC/AOP, exclusively from the old variety Picpoul. Best growers: AC St Martin de la Garrigue, Félines-Jourdan, co-ops Pomerols and Pinet. *Perfect with an oyster.*

Pic St-Loup Midi ★→★★★ r (p) 99 00 01 02 03 04 05 06 07 COTEAUX DU LANGUEDOC *cru*, anticipating own AC/AOP. Growers: Cazeneuve, Clos Marie, de Lancyre, Lascaux, Mas Bruguière, Mas Mortiès, DOM DE L'HORTUS, Valflaunès. Some of the LANGUEDOC's best: stylish and long-lasting.

Pineau des Charentes Strong, sweet apéritif: white grape juice and Cognac.

Pinon, François Lo w sw sp ★★★ 89 90 95 96 97 02 03 04 05 06 08 (09) Eco-friendly producer of v. pure VOUVRAY in all its expressions, inc a v.gd *pétillant*.

Pinot Gris ALSACE grape formerly called Tokay d'Alsace: full, rich white, a subtler match for foie gras than usual *moelleux*.

Piper-Heidsieck CHAMPAGNE-makers of repute at Reims. Improved Brut NV and fruit-driven Brut Rosé Sauvage; BRUT 00 02 04. V.gd CUVÉE. Sublime DEMI-SEC, rich yet balanced. Old Piper Cuvée Rare (viz. 79') still lovely, as is the 99.

To decipher codes, please refer to "Key to symbols" on the front flap of jacket, or "How to use this book" on p.10.

Pithon-Paillé Lo r w sw This is the latest venture in Jo Pithon's yo-yo career – small négociant vinifying and buying from quality growers – in partnership with Joseph Paillé. Concentrating on Chenin Bl and Cab Fr.

Plageoles, Robert and Bernard Father-and-son team promoting eccentric wines from authentic GAILLAC varieties. Ondenc yields ★★★★ Vin d'Autan (one of France's great stickies); ★★★ Prunelard, a deep, fruity red; Verdanel, a modern, dry white of unusual personality; and Mauzac, a gently sparkling Mauzac Nature.

Plan de Dieu S Rh r ★→★★ Rhône village since 2005, big, heady wines from v. stony, windswept plain next to RASTEAU. Try: CH la Courançonne, DOMS Durieu, Espigouette, Saint-Pierre, Vieux-Chêne.

Pol Roger Brut White Foil renamed Brut Réserve NV; Brut 96' 98 99 00 02; Rosé 99; Blanc de Chard 98' ★★★★ Supreme, family owned Epernay CHAMPAGNE house now with vines in AVIZE joining 85 ha of family v'yds. V. fine, floral NV, new Pure Brut (zero *dosage*) great with seafood. Sumptuous Cuvée Sir Winston Churchill (96' 98 02).

Pomerol B'x r ★★★→★★★★ 88 89' 90' 94 95 96 98' 00' 01 04 05' 06' 08 (09) Tiny 800-ha AC bordering ST-EMILION but no limestone; only clay, gravel, sand. Famed Merlot-dominated, rich, unctuous style. La Conseillante, L'ÉGLISE-CLINET, L'ÉVANGILE, LA FLEUR DE GAY, LA FLEUR-PÉTRUS, PÉTRUS, LE PIN, TROTANOY, VIEUX-CH-CERTAN.

Pommard Burg r ★★★ 90' 96' 98 99' 01 02' 03 05' 06 07 08 09 The biggest CÔTE D'OR village. Few superlative wines, but many potent, tannic ones to age 10+ yrs. Best v'yds: Epenots, Rugiens. Growers include Comte Armand, Billard-Gonnet, J-M BOILLOT, COURCEL, HOSPICES DE BEAUNE, Huber-Vedereau, LEROY, Machard de Gramont, DE MONTILLE, CH de Pommard, Pothier-Rieusset.

Pommery Brut NV; Rosé NV; BRUT 82' 98 00 02 Historic CHAMPAGNE house; brand now owned by VRANKEN. Outstanding Cuvée Louise (89' 90' 98) and supple wintertime Blanc de Noirs.

Ponsot Burg ★★→★★★★ Idiosyncratic top-quality MOREY-ST-DENIS DOM with great range of GRANDS CRUS, esp CLOS DE LA ROCHE. Extra kudos for Laurent P's fight against fraudulent bottles.

Potel, Nicolas Burg ★★→★★★ Good-value reds, but Nicolas P not involved in eponymous merchant brand since March 2009. Own BEAUNE-based DOM being rebranded DOM de Bellene.

Pouilly-Fuissé Burg w ★★→★★★★ 99' 00' 02' 04 05' 06' 07 08 09 The best white of the MÂCON region. Wide range of quality and prices available. Stylistic differences according to location. Wines from Chaintré the softest, Fuissé the most powerful, Vergisson for minerality. Top growers: Barraud, de Beauregard, Bret Bros, Ferret, CH DE FUISSE, Merlin, CH des Rontets, Saumaize, VERGET.

Pouilly-Fumé Lo w ★→★★★★ 04 05' 06 07 08 09 Frequently disappointing white from upper Loire, near SANCERRE. Best is round and full-flavoured. Must be Sauv Bl. Top CUVÉES can improve 5–6 yrs. Growers include BOURGEOIS, Cailbourdin, Chatelain, DAGUENEAU, Serge Dagueneau & Filles, CH de Favray, Edmond and André Figeat, Masson-Blondelet, Redde, CH de Tracy.

Pouilly-Loché Burg w ★★ 05' 06' 07 08 09' POUILLY-FUISSÉ's neighbour. Similar, cheaper; scarce. Try Clos des Rocs, Tripoz. Can be sold as POUILLY-VINZELLES.

Pouilly-sur-Loire Lo w ★ DYA Historic but neutral, non-aromatic wine from same v'yds as POUILLY-FUMÉ but different grape: Chasselas. Now only 33 ha in production. Best: Serge Dagueneau & Filles, Landrat-Guyollot, Michel Redde.

Pouilly-Vinzelles Burg w ★★ 05' 06' 07 08 09 Superior neighbour to POUILLY-LOCHE. Best producers: Bret Bros, Valette.

Premier Cru (1er Cru) First Growth in BORDEAUX; second rank of v'yds (after GRAND CRU) in Burgundy.

Premières Côtes de Blaye B'x r w ★→★★ oo' o1 o3 o4 o5' o6 o8 (o9) Mainly red AC east of the Gironde. Greatly improved quality. New AC designation as of 2008 (see box p.89). Best CHX: Bel Air la Royère, Gigault (Cuvée Viva), Haut-Bertinerie, Haut-Colombier, Haut-Grelot, Jonqueyres, Monconseil-Gazin, Mondésir-Gazin, Montfollet, Roland la Garde, Segonzac, des Tourtes.

Premières Côtes de Bordeaux B'x r w dr sw (p) ★→★★ 98 oo' o1 o3 o5' o8 (o9) Long, narrow, hilly zone on the right bank of the Garonne opposite the GRAVES. Renamed Côtes de Bordeaux: Cadillac from 2008 vintage (see box p.89). Medium-bodied, fresh reds. Quality extremely varied. Best: Alios de Ste-Marie, Carignan, Carsin, Clos Ste-Anne, Le Doyenné, Grand-Mouëys, Lezongars, Mont-Pérat, Plaisance, Puy Bardens, REYNON and Suau.

Prieur, Dom Jacques Burg ★★★ MEURSAULT estate with fine range of GRANDS CRUS from MONTRACHET to MUSIGNY. Look for greater interest in new post-RODET era.

Primeur "Early" wine for refreshment and uplift; esp from BEAUJOLAIS; VDP, too. Wine sold *en primeur* is still in barrel, for delivery when bottled.

Producteurs Plaimont The best-known, most exciting and successful co-op in the SW, perhaps the whole of France. They use only authentic Gascon grapes.

Propriétaire récoltant Owner-manager.

Provence See CÔTES DE PROVENCE, CASSIS, BANDOL, PALETTE, COTEAUX DES BAUX-EN-PROVENCE, BOUCHES-DU-RHÔNE, COTEAUX DE PIERREVERT, COTEAUX D'AIX-EN-PROVENCE, COTEAUX VAROIS-EN-PROVENCE, VDP DE MEDITERRANÉE.

Puisseguin St-Emilion B'x r ★★ 98 oo' o1 o3 o5' (o9) Satellite neighbour of ST-EMILION; wines firm and solid in style. Top CHX: Bel Air, Branda, Durand-Laplagne, Fongaban, Guibot la Fourvieille, DES LAURETS, La Mauriane, Soleil. Also Roc de Puisseguin from co-op.

Puligny-Montrachet Burg w (r) ★★★→★★★★ oo o2' o4 o5' o6' o7 o8 o9 Smaller neighbour of CHASSAGNE-MONTRACHET: potentially even finer, more vital and complex wine (apparent finesse can be result of overproduction). V'yds: BÂTARD-MONTRACHET, Bienvenues-Bâtard Montrachet, Caillerets, CHEVALIER-MONTRACHET, Combettes, Folatières, MONTRACHET, Pucelles. Producers: AMPEAU, J-M BOILLOT, BOUCHARD PÈRE & FILS, CARILLON, CH de Puligny, Chavy, DROUHIN, JADOT, LATOUR, DOM LEFLAIVE, O LEFLAIVE, Pernot, Sauzet.

Puyméras S Rh r w ★ Ordinary S Rhône village since 2005, high v'yds; reliable co-op, modest reds, sound whites. Try Cave la Comtadine, Puy de Maupas.

Pyrénées-Atlantiques SW DYA VDP for wines not qualifying for local ACS MADIRAN, PACHERENC DU VIC-BILH, TURSAN, or JURANÇON. Esp BRUMONT varietals.

Quarts de Chaume Lo w sw ★★★→★★★★ 89' 90' 95' 96' 97' o2 o3 o4 o5' o7 (o9) Tiny (50 ha), exposed hillside close to Layon devoted to Chenin Bl. Almost everlasting, golden wine with strong mineral undertow. Esp BAUMARD, Branchereau, Yves Guegniard, CH PIERRE-BISE, Suronde. Stunning 2007s.

Quatourze Midi r w (p) ★★ DYA Tiny *cru* of COTEAUX DE LANGUEDOC by Narbonne. Reputation kept almost single-handedly by CH Notre Dame du Quatourze.

Quincy Lo w ★→★★ Drink within 3 years. Small area (224 ha) west of Bourges in Cher Valley. SANCERRE-style Sauv Bl. Worth trying. Growers: Mardon, Portier, Jacques Rouzé, Silice de Quincy, Tatin-Wilk (DOMS Ballandors, Tremblay).

Rancio The most original, lingering and delicious style of VDN, reminiscent of tawny port, in BANYULS, MAURY, RIVESALTES, RASTEAU, wood-aged and exposed to oxygen and heat. Same flavour is a fault in table wine.

Rangen Most southerly GRAND CRU of ALSACE at Thann. 18.8 ha, extremely steep slopes, volcanic soils. Top wines: powerful Ries and PINOT GR from ZIND-HUMBRECHT and SCHOFFIT.

Rasteau S Rh r br sw (w p dr) ★★ o6 o7' o9' One of best two COTES DU RHÔNE villages

NB Vintages in colour are those you should choose first for drinking in 2011.

– big-flavoured reds, mainly Grenache, esp Beaurenard, *Cave des Vignerons* (gd), CH du Trignon, DOMS Didier Charavin, Collière (new), Escaravailles, Girasols, Gourt de Mautens (low yields), Rabasse-Charavin, Soumade, St-Gayan, Perrin & Fils (gd white, too). Grenache dessert wine VDN worth a try.

Ratafia de Champagne Sweet apéritif made in CHAMPAGNE of 67% grape juice and 33% brandy. Not unlike PINEAU DES CHARENTES.

Raveneau Burg ★★★ Great CHABLIS producer using old methods for extraordinary long-lived wines. Cousin of DAUVISSAT. Vaillons, Blanchots, Les Clos best.

Regnié Beauj r ★★ 08 09 Former BEAUJOLAIS VILLAGES turned *cru*. Sandy soil makes for lighter wines than other *crus*. Try Aucoeur, DOM des Braves, DUBOEUF, Laforest, Pechard.

Reine Pédauque, La Burg ★ Name of a barge on Canal de Bourgogne and a négociant in BEAUNE and ALOXE-CORTON, now owned by Ballande group.

Reuilly Lo w p r ★→★★★ 05' 06 07 08 09 Small AC (186 ha) west of Bourges for Sauv Bl whites plus rosés and VIN GRIS made from Pinot N and/or PINOT GR as well as reds from Pinot N. Best: Claude Lafond, DOM de Reuilly, Sorbe.

Ribonnet, Dom de SW ★★ Just south of Toulouse, Swiss-born Christian Gerber uses grape varieties from all over Europe to produce a fascinating range of VDP in all colours.

Riceys, Rosé des Champ p ★★★ DYA Minute AC in AUBE for a notable Pinot N rosé. Principal producers: *A Bonnet*, Jacques Defrance.

Richeaume, Dom Prov r ★★ Gd Cab Sauv/Syrah. Organic; a model.

Richebourg Burg r ★★★★ 90' 93' 95 96' 97 98 99' 00 01 02' 03 05' 06 07 08 09 VOSNE-ROMANÉE GRAND CRU. Powerful, perfumed, expensive wine, among the best. Growers: DRC, GRIVOT, GROS, LEROY, LIGER-BELAIR, MÉO-CAMUZET.

Rimage Modern trend for a vintage VDN. For early drinking. Think gd ruby port.

Rion, Patrice Burg ★★★ Premeaux-based DOM with excellent NUITS-ST-GEORGES holdings, esp Clos des Argillières, Clos St Marc and CHAMBOLLE.

Rivesaltes Midi r w b dr sw ★★ NV Fortified wine made nr Perpignan. A struggling but rewarding tradition. Top producers worth seeking out: DOMS CAZES, CH de Jau, Sarda-Malet, des Schistes, Vaquer. The best are delicious and original, esp old RANCIOS. See MUSCAT DE RIVESALTES.

Roche-aux-Moines, La Lo w sw ★★→★★★ 89' 90' 95' 96' 97' 99 02 03 04 05' 06 07 08 (09) A 33-ha *cru* of SAVENNIÈRES, ANJOU. Potentially powerful, intensely minerally wine; age or drink "on the fruit". Growers include: Le Clos de la Bergerie (Joly), DOM des Forges, CH PIERRE-BISE.

Rodet, Antonin Burg ★★→★★★ COTE CHALONNAISE merchant just sold (2009) to JEAN-CLAUDE BOISSET. Needs rejuvenating. Also CH de RULLY.

Roederer, Louis Brut Premier NV; Rich NV; Brut 97 99 00 02; Blanc de Blancs 97 99 00 02; Brut Rosé 99 02 Top-drawer family-owned CHAMPAGNE house with enviable 218-ha estate of top v'yds. Magnificent Cristal (can be greatest of all *prestige cuvées*, viz 88' 90' 95 02' 02) and Cristal Rosé (90' 95 96 02). New Brut Nature from 2010. Also owns DEUTZ, DELAS, CH DE PEZ, CH PICHON-LALANDE. See also California.

Rolland, Michel Ubiquitous and fashionable consultant winemaker and Merlot specialist working in BORDEAUX and worldwide, favouring super-ripe flavours.

Rolly Gassmann ★★ Distinguished ALSACE grower at Rorschwihr, esp for Auxerrois and MUSCAT from Moenchreben v'yds. Off-dry house style culminates in great rich Gewurz Cuvée Yves (00 02 05). Now biodynamic.

Romanée, La Burg r ★★★★ 96' 98 99' 00 01 02' 03 05' 06 07 08 09 GRAND CRU in VOSNE-ROMANÉE (0.8 ha). MONOPOLE of LIGER-BELAIR. Now made with flair by Vicomte Louis-Michel L-B. Older vintages distributed by BOUCHARD.

Romanée-Conti Burg r ★★★★ 71 76 78' 80 85' 88' 89' 90' 93' 95 96' 97 98 99' 00 01 02' 03 04 05' 06 07 08 09 A 1.7-ha MONOPOLE GRAND CRU in VOSNE-

ROMANÉE; 450 cases per annum. The most celebrated and expensive red wine in the world, with reserves of flavour beyond imagination.

Romanée-Conti, Dom de la (DRC) ★★★★ Grandest estate in Burgundy. Inc the whole of ROMANÉE-CONTI and LA TÂCHE, major parts of ECHÉZEAUX, GRANDS-ECHÉZEAUX, RICHEBOURG, ROMANÉE-ST-VIVANT and a tiny part of MONTRACHET. Crown-jewel prices (if you can buy them at all). Keep top vintages for decades.

Romanée-St-Vivant Burg r ★★★★ 90' 93 95 96' 99' 02' 03 05' 06 07 08 09 GRAND CRU in VOSNE-ROMANÉE (9.3 ha). Similar to ROMANÉE-CONTI but lighter and less sumptuous. Growers: ARLOT, CATHIARD, DRC, DROUHIN, Hudelot-Nöellat, LEROY.

Rosacker ALSACE GRAND CRU of 26 ha at Hunawihr. Produces best Ries in ALSACE (see CLOS STE-HUNE, SIPP-MACK).

Rosé d'Anjou Lo p ★→★★ DYA Pale, slightly sweet rosé enjoying a comeback in the hands of young VIGNERONS; look for Mark Angeli, Clau de Nell, DOMS de la Bergerie, les Grandes Vignes, des Sablonnettes.

Rosé de Loire Lo p ★→★★ DYA The driest of ANJOU's rosés. AC technically covers SAUMUR and TOURAINE, too. Best: Bablut, Ogereau, CH PIERRE-BISE, Richou.

Rosette Dordogne w s/sw ★★ DYA Pocket-sized AC said to be birthplace of BERGERAC wines. Small band of growers make *moëlleux* apéritif wines, sensational with foie gras or mushrooms. Try Clos Romain, CH Puypezat-Rosette, DOMS de la Cardinolle, de Coutancie.

Rostaing, René N Rh ★★★ CÔTE-RÔTIE 8-ha estate with top-grade plots, three wines, all v. fine, wait 4–5 yrs. Top is beautiful Côte Blonde (5% Viognier), also La Landonne (darker fruits, 15–20 yrs). Accomplished style, resembles breeding of gd burgundy, pure fruit at heart; some new oak. Shapely CONDRIEU, also LANGUEDOC DOM Puech Noble (r, w).

Roty, Joseph Burg ★★★ Small grower of classic GEVREY-CHAMBERTIN, esp CHARMES-CHAMBERTIN and MAZIS-CHAMBERTIN. Long-lived wines.

Rouget, Emmanuel Burg ★★★★ Inheritor of the legendary estate of Henri Jayer in ECHÉZEAUX, NUITS-ST-GEORGES and VOSNE-ROMANÉE. Top wine: Vosne-Romanée Cros Parantoux.

Roulot, Dom G Burg ★★★ Outstanding MEURSAULT producer; fine range of v'yd sites, esp Tessons Clos de Mon Plaisir and PREMIERS CRUS eg. Bouchères, Perrières.

Roumier, Georges Burg ★★★★ Reference DOM for BONNES-MARES and other brilliant CHAMBOLLE wines in capable hands of Christophe R. Long-lived wines but still attractive early.

Rousseau, Dom Armand Burg ★★★★ Unmatchable GEVREY-CHAMBERTIN DOM with thrilling CLOS ST-JACQUES and GRANDS CRUS. Unchanging, fragrant Pinot of extraordinary intensity.

Roussette de Savoie w ★★ DYA Tastiest fresh white from south of Lake Geneva.

Roussillon Midi Main region for VDN (eg. MAURY, RIVESALTES, BANYULS). Younger vintage wines are competing with aged RANCIO wines. See CÔTES DU ROUSSILLON (and CÔTES DU ROUSSILLON-VILLAGES), COLLIOURE, for table wines and VDP CÔTES CATALANES. Now included under AC LANGUEDOC.

Ruchottes-Chambertin Burg r ★★★★ 90' 93' 95 96' 98 99' 00 01 02' 03 05' 06 07 08 09 GRAND CRU neighbour of CHAMBERTIN. Similar splendid, lasting wine of great finesse. Top growers: MUGNERET, ROUMIER, ROUSSEAU.

Ruinart "R" de Ruinart Brut NV; Ruinart Rosé NV; "R" de Ruinart Brut (98 99). Oldest CHAMPAGNE house, owned by Moët-Hennessy. Already high standards should go higher still with talented new cellar master (since 2007). Prestige Cuvée **Dom Ruinart** is one of the two best vintage BLANC DE BLANCS in CHAMPAGNE (viz. 95 96 98). DR Rosé also v. special (88' 90').

Rully Burg r w (sp) ★★ (r) 05' 07 08 09' (w) 07 08 09'CÔTE CHALONNAISE village. Still white and red are light but tasty. *Gd value, esp white*. Growers include Delorme, Devevey, FAIVELEY, DOM de la Folie, Jacqueson, RODET.

Sables du Golfe du Lion Midi r p w ★ DYA VDP from Mediterranean coastal sand-dunes: esp Gris de Gris from Carignan, Grenache, Cinsault. Giant Listel dominates production.

Sablet S Rh r w (p) ★★ 06' 07' 09' Improving CÔTES DU RHÔNE village, sandy soils, often smooth, easy, fruited reds, esp DOMS de Boissan, Espiers, Les Goubert, Piaugier, Roubine, de Verquière. Gd full whites for apéritif or food.

St-Amour Beauj r ★★ 06 07 08 09' Northernmost *cru* of BEAUJOLAIS: light, fruity, resistible (except on 14 Feb). Growers to try: Janin, *Patissier*, Revillon.

St-Aubin Burg r w ★★★ (w) 05' 06 07 08 09' (r) 02' 03 05' 06 07 08 09' Now front-line CÔTE DE BEAUNE white-wine village, also pretty reds. Best v'yds: En Remilly, Murgers Dents de Chien. Best growers: J C Bachelet, COLIN, Lamy, Prudhon.

St-Bris Burg w ★ DYA Neighbour to CHABLIS. Unique AC for Sauv Bl in Burgundy. Fresh, lively, worth keeping from J-H Goisot.

St-Chinian Midi r ★→★★★ 01 02 03 04 05' 06 07' 08 09' Hilly area of growing reputation in COTEAUX DU LANGUEDOC. AC since 1982 for red, and for white since 2005, plus new *crus* Berlou and Roquebrun. Warm, spicy southern reds, based on Syrah, Grenache, Carignan. Gd co-ops Berlou, Roquebrun; CH de Viranel, DOMS Canet Valette, Madura, Rimbaud, Navarre.

St-Emilion B'x r ★★→★★★★ 89' 90' 94 95 96 98' 00' 01 03 04 05' 08 (09) Large, Merlot-dominated district on Bordeaux's Right Bank. ST-EMILION GRAND CRU 5,500-ha AC the top designation. Warm, full, rounded style; the best firm and long-lived. Top CHX: ANGÉLUS, AUSONE, CANON, CHEVAL BLANC, FIGEAC, MAGDELAINE, PAVIE. Also *garagistes* LA MONDOTTE and VALANDRAUD. Gd co-op.

St-Estèphe B'x r ★★→★★★★ 88' 89' 90' 93 94 95' 96' 98 00' 01 02 03 04 05' 06 08 (09) Most northerly communal AC in the MÉDOC. Solid, structured wines. Top CHX: COS D'ESTOURNEL, MONTROSE, CALON-SÉGUR. Also many gd unclassified estates eg. HAUT-MARBUZET, ORMES-DE-PEZ, DE PEZ, PHÉLAN-SÉGUR.

St-Gall BRUT NV; Extra Brut NV; Brut Blanc de Blancs NV; Brut Rosé NV; Brut Blanc de Blancs 99 00 02; Cuvée Orpale Blanc de Blancs 95 96' 98. Brand used by Union-Champagne co-op: top CHAMPAGNE growers' co-op at AVIZE. Fine-value Pierre Vaudon NV and excellent Orpale (95' 96).

St-Georges-St-Emilion B'x r ★★ 98 00' 01 03 05' (09) Tiny 200-ha ST-EMILION satellite. Usually gd quality. Best CHX: Calon, MACQUIN-ST-GEORGES, TOUR DU PAS-ST-GEORGES, Vieux Montaiguillon.

St-Gervais S Rh r (w, p) ★ 07' 09' West bank Rhône village. Decent co-op, local star is excellent, long-lived (10+ yrs) DOM Ste-Anne red (marked licorice flavours from Mourvèdre); gd Viognier. Also DOM Clavel.

St-Jean de Minervois Min w sw ★★ Fine sweet VDN MUSCAT. Much recent improvement, esp from DOM de Barroubio, Michel Sigé (St-Jean de Minervois, Clos du Gravillas), village co-op.

St-Joseph N Rh r w ★★ 90' 99' 01' 03' 05' 06' 07' 09' AC running length of N Rhône (65 km). Reds all Syrah. In south, attractive red-fruited wines around Tournon; elsewhere darker flavours, more new oak. Better, more complete wines than CROZES-HERMITAGE, esp from CHAPOUTIER (Les Granits), Gonon (top class), B Gripa, GUIGAL (Lieu-dit St-Joseph); also J-L CHAVE, Chèze, Courbis, Coursodon, Cuilleron, DELAS, J & E Durand, B Faurie, P Faury, Gaillard, N Jaboulet Perrin Frères, JABOULET, Monier-Perréol, A Perret, Vallet, F Villard. Gd food-friendly white (mainly Marsanne), esp Barge, CHAPOUTIER (Les Granits), Cuilleron, Gonon (top), B Gripa, P Faury, A Perret.

St-Julien B'x r ★★★→★★★★ 88' 89' 90' 93 94 95' 96' 98 00' 01 02 03 04 05' 06 08 (09) Mid-MÉDOC communal AC with 11 classified (1855) estates, inc three LÉOVILLES, BEYCHEVELLE, DUCRU-BEAUCAILLOU, GRUAUD-LAROSE, etc. The epitome of harmonious, fragrant and savoury red wine.

St-Nicolas-de-Bourgueil Lo r p ★→★★★ 89' 90' 95 96' 97 02' 03 05' 06 08 (09)

Companion appellation to BOURGUEIL producing identical wines from Cab Fr. Ranges from easy drinking to age-worthy. More tannic and less supple than CHINON. Try: Yannick Amirault, Cognard, Lorieux, Frédéric Mabileau-Rezé, Taluau-Foltzenlogel, Gerard Vallée.

St-Péray N Rh w sp ★★ 04' 05' 06' 07' 08' 09 White Rhône (mainly Marsanne) from only 60 ha granite hillside v'yds. Some *méthode Champenoise – worth trying*. Still white is fresh, gd flinty style, can age. Top: S Chaboud, CHAPOUTIER, CLAPE, Colombo, B Gripa (v.gd), J-L Thiers, TAIN co-op, du Tunnel, Voge (oak).

St-Pourçain Central Fr r p w ★→★★ DYA 2009 promoted to AC (600 ha). Light red and rosé from Gamay and/or Pinot N, white from Tressalier and/or CHARD (v. popular), or Sauv Bl. Growers: DOM de Bellevue, Grosbot-Barbara, Nebout, Pétillat, Ray, and gd co-op (Vignerons de St-Pourçain) with range of styles, inc drink-me-up Cuvée Ficelle.

St-Romain Burg r w ★★ (w) 05' 06 07 08 09' Crisp, *mineral whites* and clean-cut reds from vines tucked away in the back of the CÔTE DE BEAUNE. PREMIER CRU v'yds expected soon. Alain Gras best. Also Buisson, De Chassorney.

St-Sardos SW r p w VDQS nr Montauban DYA ★ Worthy co-op has only one competitor, its founder DOM de la Tucayne. Syrah-based wines worth trying.

St-Véran Burg w ★★ 05' 06 07 08 09' AC loosely surrounding POUILLY-FUISSÉ with variable results, depending on soil and producer. DUBOEUF, Deux Roches, Poncetys for value, Cordier, Corsin, Merlin for top quality.

Ste-Croix-du-Mont B'x w sw ★★ 97' 98 99' 01' 02 03' 05' 07 (08) (09) Sweet white AC facing SAUTERNES across the river Garonne. Well worth trying, esp CHX Crabitan-Bellevue, Loubens, du Mont, Pavillon, la Rame.

Ste-Victoire Prov r p ★★ New subzone of CÔTES DE PROVENCE from the southern slopes of the Montagne Ste-Victoire. Dramatic scenery goes with gd wine. Try Mas de Cadenet, Mauvan.

Salon ★★★★ The original BLANC DE BLANCS CHAMPAGNE, from LE MESNIL in the Côte des Blancs. Awesome reputation for long-lived wines – in truth, sometimes inconsistent but on song recently, viz. 90 96' 97.

Sancerre Lo w (r p) ★→★★★ 03 05' 06 07 08 09Benchmark for Sauv Bl, often more aromatic and vibrant than POUILLY-FUMÉ. Top wines can age 8+ yrs. Top growers now making remarkable reds (Pinot N). Sancerre rosé rarely worth the money. Parts badly hit by hail in 2009 . Best inc: Gérard Boulay, BOURGEOIS, Cotat, François Crochet, Lucien Crochet, André Dezat, Thomas Laballe, ALPHONSE MELLOT, Mollet, Vincent Pinard, Pascal & Nicolas Reverdy, Claude Riffault, Jean-Max Roger, Vacheron, André Vatan.

Santenay Burg r (w) ★★★ 99' 02' 03 05' 06 07 08 (09) Sturdy reds from village south of CHASSAGNE-MONTRACHET. Best v'yds: La Comme, Les Gravières, Clos de Tavannes. Top growers: GIRARDIN, Lequin-Roussot, Muzard, Vincent. Watch DOM Jessiaume

Saumur Lo r w p sp ★→★★★ 02' 03 05' 06 07 08 09 Umbrella AC for light whites plus more serious, particularly from SAUMUR-CHAMPIGNY zone; mainly easy-drinking reds, pleasant rosés, pungent CRÉMANT and SAUMUR MOUSSEUX. Saumur-Le-Puy-Notre-Dame new AC for Cab Fr reds. Producers include: BOUVET-LADUBAY, Antoine Foucault, CLOS ROUGEARD, René-Hugues Gay, Guiberteau, DOMS DES CHAMPS FLEURIS/Retiveau-Retif, Paleine, St-Just; CH DE VILLENEUVE, Cave des Vignerons de Saumur.

Saumur-Champigny Lo r ★★→★★★ 95 96' 97 02' 03 04 05' 06 07 08 (09) Popular nine-commune AC for quality Cab Fr, ages well in gd vintages. Look for Bruno Dubois, CHX de Targé, DE VILLENEUVE; Clos Cristal, CLOS ROUGEARD; DOMS CHAMPS FLEURIS, de la Cune, Filliatreau, Legrand, Nerleux, Roches Neuves, St-Just, Antoine Sanzay, Val Brun; Cave des Vignerons de Saumur-St-Cyr-en-Bourg.

Saussignac Dordogne w sw ★★→★★★ 05' 06 07' (09) Now fully sweet wines from region adjoining MONBAZILLAC, with perhaps more acidity. Best: ★★★ DOM de Richard, Lestevénie, La Maurigne, Les Miaudoux, Clos d'Yvigne, ★★ CHX Le Chabrier, Court-les-Mûts, Le Payral, Le Tap, Tourmentine.

Sauternes B'x w sw ★★→★★★★ 83' 86' 88' 89' 90' 95 96 97' 98 99' 01' 02 03' 05' 07' (09) District of five villages (inc BARSAC) that make France's best sweet wine. Strong, luscious, golden, demanding 10 yrs age. Still underpriced compared to red equivalents. Top CHX: D'YQUEM, GUIRAUD, LAFAURIE-PEYRAGUEY, RIEUSSEC, SUDUIRAUT, LA TOUR BLANCHE, etc. Dry wines cannot be sold as Sauternes.

Sauzet, Etienne Burg ★★★ Once again leading PULIGNY DOM with superb IERS CRUS (Combettes) and GRANDS CRUS (BÂTARD). Fresh, lively wines.

Savennières Lo w dr sw ★★★→★★★★ 89' 90' 93 95 96' 97' 99 02' 03 04 05' 06 07 08 (09) Small ANJOU district for pungent, extremely minerally, long-lived whites. BAUMARD, Closel, Clos de Coulaine (see CH PIERRE-BISE), CH d'Epiré, Yves Guigniard, DOM Laureau du Clos Frémur, Eric Morgat, Vincent Ogereau, Tijou. Top sites: COULÉE DE SERRANT, ROCHE-AUX-MOINES, Clos du Papillon.

Savigny-lès-Beaune Burg r (w) ★★★ 99' 02' 03 05' 07 08 09 Important village next to BEAUNE; similar mid-weight wines, should be delicious and lively; can be rustic. Top v'yds: Dominode, Guettes, Lavières, Marconnets, Vergelesses; growers include: BIZE, Camus, CHANDON DE BRIAILLES, CLAIR, Ecard, Girard, LEROY, Pavelot, TOLLOT-BEAUT.

Savoie E France r w sp ★★ DYA Alpine area with light, dry wines like some Swiss or minor Loires. APREMONT, CRÉPY and SEYSSEL are best-known whites; ROUSSETTE is more interesting. *Also gd MONDEUSE red.*

Schlossberg ALSACE GRAND CRU of 80 ha at Kientzheim famed since 15th century. Glorious Ries from FALLER.

Schlumberger, Doms ★→★★★ Vast and top-quality ALSACE DOM at Guebwiller owning approx 1% of all ALSACE v'yds. Holdings in GRANDS CRUS Kitterlé, Kessler, Saering and Spiegel. Range includes rare Ries, signature Cuvée Ernest and, latest addition, Pinot Gr Grand Cru Kessler.

Schlumberger, Robert de Lo SAUMUR sparkling; by Austrian method. Delicate.

Schoenenbourg V. rich, successful Riquewihr GRAND CRU (ALSACE): PINOT GR, Ries,

---

Southwest growers to watch in 2011

Domaine Mioula (MARCILLAC) Patrice Lescarret from GAILLAC is working wonders here.

Ch Lecusse (GAILLAC) Roses (the flower) increasingly important here.

Ch l'Enclos des Roses (GAILLAC) Formerly part of the Jean Cros v'yds, now in hands of Aurélie Balaran. Already wonderful wines.

Clos d'Un Jour (CAHORS) Architects-turned-VIGNERONS who are now the buzz-name in CAHORS.

Mas del Périé (CAHORS) Another v'yd spreading the Malbec message.

Ch La Coutelière (FRONTON) Fantastic value from this new Toulouse star.

Dom Bonnet et Laborde (MARMANDAIS) Determined newcomers joining band of top growers in this AC.

Dom Chiroulet (CÔTES DE GASCOGNE) Reds are unusually gd from this improving estate.

Dom Pichard (MADIRAN) New owners are breathing life into this once-top estate.

Clos Basté (MADIRAN) Fast challenging for a top spot in a highly competitive line-up.

Dom Guirardel (JURANÇON) Old estate that has recently leapt back to the top.

Dom du Moncaut (VIN DE PAYS DES PYRÉNÉES-ATLANTIQUES) Outside JURANÇON AC, but the whites are in the same style and v. promising.

v. fine VENDANGE TARDIVE and SÉLECTION DES GRAINS NOBLES, esp from DEISS and DOPFF AU MOULIN. Also v.gd MUSCAT.

Schoffit, Dom ★★→★★★ Eclectic Colmar ALSACE grower. Excellent VENDANGE TARDIVE Gewurz GRAND CRU RANGEN Clos St Theobald (00 05) on volcanic soil. Also rare, good Chasselas and fine Riesling Sonnenberg (06 08 09')

Schröder & Schÿler Old BORDEAUX merchant, owner of CH KIRWAN.

Sciacarello Indigenous Corsican grape variety, for original red and rosé.

Sec Literally means dry, though CHAMPAGNE so called is medium-sweet (and better at breakfast, teatime and weddings than BRUT).

Séguret R Rh w p ★★ 05' 06' 07' 09' Classic hillside village nr GIGONDAS.Quite full reds, mainly Grenache, can be peppery; clear-fruited whites. Esp CH la Courançonne, DOMS de l'Amauve, de Cabasse, J David (organic), Garancière, *Mourchon* (robust), Pourra, Soleil Romain.

Sélection des Grains Nobles Term coined by HUGEL for ALSACE equivalent to German Beerenauslese, and since 1984 subject to v. strict regulations. GRAINS NOBLES are individual grapes with "noble rot".

Sérafin Burg ★★★ Christian S has gained a cult following for his intense GEVREY-CHAMBERTIN VIEILLES VIGNES, CHARMES-CHAMBERTIN. Plenty of new wood here.

Seyssel Savoie w sp ★★ NV Delicate white, pleasant sparkling. eg. Corbonod.

Sichel & Co One of BORDEAUX's most respected merchant houses (Sirius a top brand): interests in CHX D'ANGLUDET, PALMER and in CORBIÈRES.

Signargues ★→★★ CÔTES DU RHÔNE village in four areas between Avignon and Nîmes (west bank). Light, fruity reds with low-key ageing potential. Note: la Font du Vent, CH Haut-Musiel, DOM Valériane.

Sipp, Jean & Louis ★★ ALSACE growers in Ribeauvillé (Louis also a négociant). Both make v.gd Ries Grand Cru Kirchberg. Jean's is youthful elegance; Louis's is firmer when mature. V.gd Gewurz from Louis, esp Grand Cru Osterberg.

Sipp-Mack ★★→★★★ Excellent ALSACE DOM of 20 ha at Hunnawihr. Great Ries from GRANDS CRUS ROSACKER and Osterberg; also v.gd PINOT GR.

Sorg, Bruno ★★→★★★ First-class small ALSACE grower at Eguisheim for GRANDS CRUS Florimont (Ries) and PFERSIGBERG (MUSCAT). Also v.gd Auxerrois.

Sur lie "On the lees". MUSCADET is often bottled straight from the vat, for max zest and character.

Tâche, La Burg r ★★★★ 90' 93' 95 96' 97 98 99' 00 01 02' 03 05' 06 07 08 09 A 6-ha (1,500-case) GRAND CRU of VOSNE-ROMANÉE. One of best v'yds on earth: big, perfumed, luxurious wine. See ROMANÉE-CONTI.

Taille-aux-Loups, Dom de la Lo w sw sp ★★★ 02' 03' 05' 06 07' 08' (09) Jacky Blot, former wine broker, is now one of the Loire's leading producers – with barrel-fermented MONTLOUIS and VOUVRAY, from dry to lusciously sweet; excellent Triple Zero MONTLOUIS *pétillant* and fine reds from DOM de la Butte in BOURGUEIL.

Tain, Cave de ★★ Main N Rhône co-op, 290 members, gd, mature v'yds; owns 25% of HERMITAGE. Sound red HERMITAGE , esp top oaked Gambert de Loche; modern range, esp CROZES. Marsanne whites gd value, also v.gd VIN DE PAILLE.

Taittinger Brut NV; Rosé NV; BRUT 00 02; Collection Brut 90 95 96. Once-fashionable Reims CHAMPAGNE grower and merchant sold to Crédit Agricole group 2006. Distinctive silky, flowery touch, though not always consistent, often noticeably dosed. Excellent luxury brand: Comtes de Champagne Blanc de Blancs (96' 98'), Comtes de Champagne Rosé (96 02), also gd, rich Pinot Prestige Rosé NV. New CUVÉES Nocturne and Prélude. Also excellent new single-v'yd La Marquetterie. (See also California: DOM Carneros.)

Tavel SRh p ★★ DYA Rosé in two styles: robust, gutsy, food a must; or more modern, pale, easy fruit, drink on its own. Best growers: DOM Corne-Loup, GUIGAL, Lafond Roc-Epine, Maby, DOM de la Mordorée (full), Prieuré de Montézargues, Rocalière (fine), CH de Manissy, Trinquevedel.

Tempier, Dom Prov r p w ★★★★ Once the pioneering grower of BANDOL. Wines of considerable longevity. Quality now challenged by several others.

Terrasses du Larzac Midi r p w ★★ Part of AC COTEAUX DU LANGUEDOC. Wild, hilly region from the Lac du Salagou towards Aniane. Cooler temperatures make for fresher wines. Several stars and rising stars, inc Mas de l'Ecriture, *Mas Jullien*. Aspiring AOP.

Terroirs Landais Gascony r p w ★ VDP, an appendix to the CÔTES DE GASCOGNE, a name that many growers prefer to use. DOM de Laballe is most-seen example.

Thénard, Dom Burg Major grower of the GIVRY appellation, but best known for his substantial portion (1.6 ha) of LE MONTRACHET. Should be better.

Thévenet, Jean Burg ★★★ Mâconnais purveyor of rich, some semi-botrytized, wines eg. Cuvée Levroutée at DOM de la Bongran. Also DOM Emilian Gillet.

Thézac-Perricard SW r p ★★ 05' 06 08 (09') VDP from area adjoining CAHORS. MALBEC-based but lighter style. Independent ★★ DOM de Lancement even better than gd co-op.

Thiénot, Alain Broker-turned-merchant; dynamic force for gd in CHAMPAGNE. Ever-improving quality across the range. Impressive, fairly priced Brut NV. Rosé NV Brut. Vintage Stanislas (99 00 02) and Voluminous Vigne aux Gamins (single-v'yd Avize 99 02). Top Grande Cuvée 96' 98 02. Also owns Marie Stuart and CANARD-DUCHÊNE in CHAMPAGNE, CH Ricaud in LOUPIAC.

Thomas, André & fils ★★★ V. fine ALSACE grower at Ammerschwihr attached to rigorous biological methods. An artist-craftsman in the cellar: v.gd Ries Kaefferkopf and magnificent Gewurz Vieilles Vignes (both 05).

Thorin, J Beauj ★ Major BEAUJOLAIS négociant owned by BOISSET.

Thouarsais, Vin de Lo r p w ★ DYA Light Chenin Bl (with 20% CHARD permitted), Gamay and Cab Fr from tiny (20-ha) VDQS south of SAUMUR. Esp Gigon.

Tollot-Beaut ★★★ Stylish, consistent Burgundy grower with 20 ha in CÔTE DE BEAUNE, inc v'yds at Beaune Grèves, CORTON, SAVIGNY (Les Champs Chevrey), and at its CHOREY-LÈS-BEAUNE base.

Touraine Lo r p w dr sw sp ★→★★★★★ 02' 03 04 05' 06 07 08 (09) Huge region (5,500 ha) with many ACS (eg. VOUVRAY, CHINON, BOURGUEIL) as well as umbrella AC of variable quality – zesty reds (Cab Fr, Côt, Gamay, Pinot N), pungent whites (Sauv Bl, Chenin Bl), rosés and *mousseux*. Many gd bistro wines, often gd value. Producers: CH de Petit Thouars, Clos Roussely, DOMS des Bois-Vaudons, Corbillières, Joël Delaunay, de la Garrelière (François Plouzeau), de la Presle; Clos Roche Blanche, Jacky Marteau, *MARIONNET*; Oisly & Thesée, Puzelat/Clos de Tue-Boeuf, Vincent Ricard.

Touraine-Amboise Lo r p w ★→★★ TOURAINE sub-appellation (220 ha). François Ier is tasty, food-friendly local blend (Gamay/Côt/Cab Fr). Chenin Bl for whites. Closerie de Chanteloup, Damien Delecheneau/la Grange Tiphaine, DOM des Bessons, Dutertre, Xavier Frissant, de la Gabillière.

Touraine-Azay-le-Rideau Lo ★→★★ Small TOURAINE sub-appellation (60 ha) for Chenin Bl-based dry, off-dry white and Grolleau-dominated rosé. Producers: CH de l'Aulée, Nicolas Paget and Pibaleau Père & Fils.

Touraine-Mesland Lo r p w ★→★★ TOURAINE sub-appellation (105 ha) best represented by its user-friendly red blends (Gamay/Côt/Cab Fr). Whites are mainly Chenin with a little CHARD. Ch Gaillard, Clos de la Briderie.

Touraine-Noble Joué Lo p ★→★★ DYA Ancient but recently revived rosé from three Pinots (N, Gr, Meunier) just south of Tours. Esp from ROUSSEAU and Sard. Became separate AC in 2001 and now totals 28 ha.

Trapet Burg ★★→★★★ A long-established GEVREY-CHAMBERTIN DOM now enjoying new life and sensual wines with biodynamic farming. Ditto cousins Rossignol-Trapet – slightly more austere wines.

Trévallon, Dom de Prov r w ★★★ 95 96 97 98 99 00' 01 03 04 05 06 07 08 In

Les Baux, but Vin de Pays des Bouches du Rhône fully deserving its huge reputation. Intense Cab Sauv/Syrah to age. BARRIQUE-aged white from Marsanne and Roussanne, a drop of CHARD and now Grenache Bl. Well worth seeking out.

Trimbach, F E ★★★→★★★★ Supreme growers of ALSACE Ries on limestone soils around Ribeauvillé, esp magnificent Clos Ste Hune (**02'**) and almost-as-good *Frédéric Emile* (97). Wines for great cuisine in dry, elegant style.

Tursan SW France r p w ★★→★★★ (Most DYA) Master chef Michel Guérard makes lovely ★★★ wines, most of which he sells in his restaurant complex at Eugénie-les-Bains. For authenticity, however, ★★ DOM de Perchade takes the palm. Lively ★ co-op, now twinned with COTEAUX DE CHALOSSE, is not bad, either.

Vacqueyras S Rh r (p, w) ★★ 90' 95' 98' 99' 00' 01' 03 04' 05' 06' 07' 09' Full-bodied, peppery, Grenache-based neighbour to GIGONDAS; can be heady. Lives 10+ yrs. Note: Arnoux Vieux Clocher, JABOULET, CHX de Montmirail, des Tours (v. fine), VIDAL-FLEURY; Clos des Cazaux (gd value), DOMS Amouriers, Archimbaud-Vache, Charbonnière, Couroulu (traditional), Font de Papier, Fourmone, Garrigue, Grapillon d'Or, Monardière (v.gd), Montirius (organic), Montvac, Perrin, Roucas Toumba, Sang des Cailloux (v.gd).

Val de Loire Lo r p w DYA One of France's four regional VDPS, formerly Jardin de la France. Wide range of single varietals, inc CHARD, Cab Fr, Gamay and Sauv Bl.

Valençay Lo r p w ★ AC in east TOURAINE 139 ha; light, easy-drinking sometimes rustic and sharp wines from similar range of grapes as TOURAINE, esp Sauv Bl. Clos Delorme (Minchin), Jacky Preys, Hubert & Olivier Sinson.

Val d'Orbieu, Vignerons du ★★ Association of some 200 growers and co-ops in CORBIÈRES, COTEAUX DU LANGUEDOC, MINERVOIS, ROUSSILLON, etc., marketing a sound range of MIDI AC and VDP wines. Cuvée Mythique is flagship.

Valréas S Rh r (p w) ★★ 06 07' 09' Low-profile CÔTES DU RHÔNE village with big co-op, close to black-truffle country. Mid-weight red (mainly Grenache, less full than CAIRANNE, RASTEAU) and improving white. Esp Emmanuel Bouchard, DOM des Grands Devers, CH la Décelle.

Varichon & Clerc Principal makers and shippers of SAVOIE sparkling wines.

VDQS *Vins délimite de qualité supérieure.* Due to be phased out at end of 2011.

Vendange Harvest. **Vendange tardive** Late harvest. ALSACE equivalent to German Auslese but usually higher alcohol.

Venoge, de Venerable CHAMPAGNE house now revitalized under Boizel Chanoine group management. Gd. niche blends: Cordon Bleu Extra-Brut, Vintage Blanc de Blancs (00 02), CUVÉE 20 ans and prestige CUVÉE Louis XV, a 10-yr-old BL DE NOIRS.

Ventoux S Rh r p (w) ★★ 06 07' 09' Widespread 6,000+ ha AC around Mont Ventoux between Rhône and PROVENCE for easy-to-drink red (Grenache-Syrah, café-style to deeper flavours), rosé and gd white (though oak use growing). Altitude gives welcome cool flavours for some. Best: LA VIEILLE FERME (r) owned by BEAUCASTEL, co-op Bédoin, Goult, St-Didier, DOMS Anges, Berane, Brusset, Cascavel, Champ-Long, Croix de Pins, Fondrèche, Font-Sane, Grand Jacquet, JABOULET, Martinelle, Murmurium, Pesquié (v.gd form), Pigeade, Terres de Solence, Valcombe, Verrière, VIDAL-FLEURY.

Verget Burg ★★→★★★ Jean-Marie GUFFENS' Mâconnais-based white wine merchant venture, nearly as idiosyncratic as his own DOM. Fine quality, plans for reds, too.

Veuve Clicquot Yellow Label NV; White Label Demi-Sec NV; Vintage Réserve 98' 99 02'; Rosé Reserve 95 96 98 99' 02'. Historic CHAMPAGNE house of highest standing, now owned by LVMH. Full-bodied, almost rich: one of CHAMPAGNE's surest things. Cellars at Reims. Luxury brands: La Grande Dame (90' 95'), Rich Réserve (96 99 02), La Grande Dame Rosé (95 96 02). Oak-fermented

---

NB Vintages in colour are those you should choose first for drinking in 2011.

vintages from 2010. New Cave Privée re-release of old vintages in several formats: superb 78 Rosé.

Veuve Devaux Premium CHAMPAGNE of powerful Union Auboise co-op. Excellent aged Grande Réserve NV, Oeil de Perdrix Rosé, Prestige Cuvée D (96).

Vézelay Burg r w Age 1–2 yrs. Up-and-coming subdistrict of generic BOURGOGNE. Flavoursome whites from chard, but gd local BOURGOGNE *rouge* is from Pinot and rare whites from Melon, as BOURGOGNE GRANDE ORDINAIRE.

Vidal-Fleury, J N Rh ★★ GUIGAL-owned shipper of improving Rhône wines and grower of CÔTE-RÔTIE, classy, v. elegant La Chatillonne (12% Viognier; wait min 5 yrs). Gd CÔTES DU RHÔNE Viognier, VENTOUX, MUSCAT DE BEAUMES-DE-VENISE, VACQUEYRAS.

Vieille Ferme, La S Rh r w ★→★★ V.gd brand of VENTOUX (r) and LUBÉRON (w) made by Perrin family of CH DE BEAUCASTEL. Gd value, easy drinking.

Vieilles Vignes Old vines – which should make the best wine. Eg. DE VOGÜÉ MUSIGNY VIEILLES VIGNES. But no rules about age and can be a tourist trap.

Vieux Télégraphe, Dom du S Rh r w ★★★ 78' 81' 85 88 89' 90 94' 95' 96' 97 98' 99' 00 01' 03' 04' 05' 06' 07' 09' Top name, maker of complex , long-lived red CHÂTEAUNEUF, and rich white (more *gourmand* since 1990s, excellent with food, always gd in lesser yrs). Second DOM: de la Roquète, gd fruit, reds gaining depth, fresh whites, both on the rise. Owns gd, slow-ageing, understated *Gigondas dom Les Pallières* with US importer Kermit Lynch.

Vigne or vignoble Vineyard (v'yd), vineyards (v'yds). **Vigneron** Vine-grower.

Vin doux naturel (VDN) Sweet wine fortified with wine alcohol, so the sweetness is natural, not the strength. The specialty of ROUSSILLON, based on Grenache or MUSCAT. Top wines, esp RANCIOS, can be remarkable.

Vin gris "Grey" wine is v. pale pink, made of red grapes pressed before fermentation begins – unlike rosé, which ferments briefly before pressing. "Oeil de Perdrix" means much the same; so does "blush".

Vin jaune Jura w ★★★ Specialty of ARBOIS: odd yellow wine like fino sherry. Normally ready when bottled (after at least 6 yrs). Best is CH-CHALON. See also PLAGEOLES. A halfway-house oxidized white is sold locally as *vin typé*.

Vin de paille Wine from grapes dried on straw mats, so v. sweet, like Italian *passito*. Esp in the Jura. See also CHAVE and VIN PAILLÉ DE CORRÈZE.

Vin paillé de Corrèze SW Revival of old-style VIN DE PAILLE nr Beaulieu-sur-Dordogne made today by 25 fanatical growers and small co-op. Modern grape varieties have replaced old hybrids. Eclectic apéritif enjoyed (folklore) by breast-feeding mothers. Look for the wine of Christian Tronche.

Vin de Pays (VDP) Most dynamic category in France (with over 150 regions). The zonal VDP are best – eg. CÔTES DE GASCOGNE, CÔTES DE THONGUE, Haute Vallée de l'Orb, Duché d'Uzès, among others. Enormous variety in taste and quality but never ceases to surprise. Became IGP for the 2009 vintage. .

Vinsobres S Rh r (p w) ★→★★ 05' 06' 07' 09' Breezy v'yds near Nyons. Top reds have bright fruit, helped by high v'yds and plenty of Syrah. Note: Cave la Vinsobraise, DOMS les Aussellons, Bicarelle, Chaume-Arnaud, Constant-Duquesnoy, Coriançon, Deurre (traditional), Jaume, Moulin (traditional), Perrin & Fils (v.gd value), Peysson, Puy de Maupas, CH Rouanne.

Vin de table Category of standard everyday table wine, not subject to particular regulations about grapes and origin. Can be source of unexpected delights if a talented winemaker uses this category to avoid bureaucratic hassle. Regulations about to change to include vintage and grape variety.

Viré-Clessé Burg w ★★ 05' 06' 07 08 09' AC based around two of best white villages of MÂCON. Extrovert style, though residual sugar originally forbidden. Try A Bonhomme, Bret Bros, Chaland, Clos du Chapitre, JADOT, Merlin, THÉVENET, CH de Viré and co-op.

FRANCE | Veu–Zin | 83

Visan S Rh r p w ★★ 06' 07' 09' Improving Rhône village for finely fruited, medium-depth reds, acceptable whites. Young growers moving it along. Best: DOMS Coste Chaude, Florane, Fourmente, des Grands Devers, Roche-Audran.

Vogüé, Comte Georges de Burg ★★★★ Iconic CHAMBOLLE estate inc lion's share of MUSIGNY. Heralded vintages from 1990s taking time to come round.

Volnay Burg r ★★★→★★★★ 90' 95 96' 97 98 99' 02' 03 04 05' 06 07 08 09 Village between POMMARD and MEURSAULT: often the best reds of the CÔTE DE BEAUNE; structured and silky. Best v'yds: Caillerets, Champans, Clos des Chênes, Santenots, Taillepieds, etc. Best growers: D'ANGERVILLE, J-M BOILLOT, HOSPICES DE BEAUNE, LAFARGE, LAFON, DE MONTILLE, ROSSIGNOL.

Volnay-Santenots Burg r ★★★ Best red wine v'yds of MEURSAULT sold under this name. Indistinguishable from other PREMIER CRU VOLNAY. Perhaps more body, less delicacy. Best growers: AMPEAU, HOSPICES DE BEAUNE, LAFON, LEROY, PRIEUR.

Vosne-Romanée Burg r ★★★→★★★★ 90' 93 95 96' 98 99' 01 02' 03 05' 06 07 08 (09). Village with Burgundy's grandest *crus* (ROMANÉE-CONTI, LA TÂCHE, etc). There are (or should be) no common wines in Vosne. Many gd growers, inc: Arnoux, CATHIARD, DRC, GRIVOT, GROS, Jayer, Lamarche, LATOUR, LEROY, LIGER-BELAIR, MÉO-CAMUZET, MUGNERET, RION.

Vougeot Burg r w ★★★ 90' 93 95' 96' 97 98 99' 01 02 03 05' 06 07 08 09 *Village* and PREMIER CRU wines. See CLOS DE VOUGEOT. Exceptional Clos Blanc de Vougeot, white since 12th century. HUDELOT-Noellat and VOUGERAIE best.

Vougeraie, Dom de la Burg r ★★→★★★ DOM uniting all BOISSET's v'yd holdings. Gd-value BOURGOGNE *rouge* up to fine MUSIGNY GRAND CRU.

Vouvray Lo w dr sw sp ★★→★★★★ For sweet Vouvray: 89' 90' 95' 96' 97' 03' 05' 08 (09). For dry Vouvray: 89 90 96' 97 02' 03 05' 06 07 08' (09). Important AC east of Tours: increasingly gd and reliable. DEMI-SEC is classic style, but in gd yrs *moelleux* can be intensely sweet, almost immortal. Variable dry sparkling: look out for *pétillant*. Best producers: Allias, Vincent Carême, **Champalou**, Clos Baudoin (CHIDAINE), Dhoye-Deruet (DOM de la Fontanerie), Foreau, Fouquet (DOM des Aubuisières), CH Gaudrelle, *HUET*, DOM DE LA TAILLE-AUX-LOUPS, Vigneau-Chevreau. If you find ancient vintages – such as 1921, 1924, 1947 or 1959 – don't hesitate.

Vranken Ever more powerful CHAMPAGNE group created in 1976 by Belgian marketing man. Sound quality. Leading brand: Demoiselle. Owns HEIDSIECK MONOPOLE and POMMERY.

Wolfberger Al ★★ Principal label of Eguisheim co-op. Exceptional quality for such a large-scale producer. V. important for CRÉMANT.

"Y" (pronounced "ygrec") B'x 80' 85 86 88 94 96 00 02 04 05 06 Intense, dry white wine produced at CH D'YQUEM, lately with more regularity. Most interesting with age. Dry style in 2004, otherwise in classic off-dry mould, but recently purer and fresher than in the past.

Zind Humbrecht, Dom ★★★★ ALSACE growers since 1620. Current DOM established in 1959, now vying with FALLER/DOM WEINBACH as the greatest in ALSACE: rich, powerful yet balanced wines, using v. low yields. Top wines from single v'yds **Clos St-Urbain**, Jebsal (superb PINOT GR 02') and Windsbuhl (esp Gewurz 05), and GRANDS CRUS RANGEN, HENGST, Brand, Goldert.

To decipher codes, please refer to "Key to symbols" on the front flap of jacket, or "How to use this book" on p.10.

(70% replanted) has paid off. Elegant, long-lived wines. Second label: Clos Canon. (Value.)

Canon-de-Brem Canon-Fronsac r ★★ 98 9900 01 03 04 05' RIP from 2006. Bought by Jean Halley of Carrefour supermarkets in 2000, wine now absorbed into CH DE LA DAUPHINE. Massive recent investment. Firm, pure expression.

Canon la Gaffelière St-Em r ★★★ 89' 90' 94' 95 96 98' 99 00' 01 02 03 04 05' 06 08 09 Leading 19-ha GRAND CRU CLASSÉ on the lower slopes of the *côtes*. Same ownership as CLOS DE L'ORATOIRE, LA MONDOTTE and Aiguilhe in Castillon. DERENONCOURT consults. Stylish, upfront, impressive wines with 35% Cab Fr.

Cantegril Graves r Saut w sw ★★ (r) 00 02 04 05 06 08 (w) 02 03 04 05' 06 07 Supple red, fine BARSAC-SAUTERNES from DOISY-DAËNE and CLOS FLORIDÉNE connection. Value.

Cantemerle Macau, H-Méd r ★★★ 89' 90 95 96' 98 00 01 02 03 04 05' 06 07 08 09 Large 90-ha property in south MÉDOC. Now merits its Fifth Growth status. Sandy/gravel soils give finer style. Second label: Les Allées de Cantemerle.

Cantenac-Brown Cantenac-Mar r ★★→★★★ 90' 94 95 96 98 99 00 01 02 03 04 05' 06 08 42-ha Third Growth sold in 2006 to private investor; owned since late 1980s by AXA Millésimes. Powerful, but more elegance since 2000. Can improve further. Second label: Brio du CH Cantenac Brown.

Capbern-Gasqueton St-Est r ★★ 98 00 02 03 04 05 06 08 34-ha property offering solid fare; same owner as CALON-SÉGUR.

Cap de Mourlin St-Em r ★★ 95 96 98' 99 00 01 03 04 05 06 08 Well-known 15-ha property of the Capdemourlin family, also owners of CH BALESTARD and CH Roudier, MONTAGNE-ST-EMILION. Riper and more supple than in the past.

Carbonnieux Pe-Lé r w ★★★ 95 96 98 99 00 02 04 05' 06 07 08 09 Large (90-ha), historic estate at Léognan for sterling red and white. Charismatic owner Antony Perrin died 2008; sons Eric and Philibert now in charge. The whites, 65% Sauv Bl (eg. 98 99 00 01 02 03 04 05 06 07 08 09), can age up to 10 yrs. CHX Le Pape and Le Sartre are also in the family. Second label: La Tour-Léognan.

Carles, de Fronsac r ★★ 98 99 00 01 02 03 04 05' 06 07 08 09 Haut Carles (★★★) is the top selection here with its own modern, gravity-fed cellars. Investment and aspirations of a top growth. Superb from 2006. Second label: juicy de Carles.

Carmes Haut-Brion, les Pe-Lé r ★★★ 89 90' 94 95 96 98 99 00 01 02 03 04 05' 06 07 08 09 Small (4.7-ha) neighbour of HAUT-BRION with classed-growth standards. 55% Merlot. Family-owned. DERENONCOURT consulting from 2009.

Caronne-Ste-Gemme St-Laurent, H-Méd r ★★ 98 99 00 01 02 03 04 04 05 06 08 40-ha MÉDOC estate. Classic, age-worthy but inconsistent.

Carruades de Château Lafite The second wine of Ch. Lafite is a relatively easy drinker. Its price went ballistic in 2009 thanks to Chinese contingent.

Carteau Côtes-Daugay St-Em r ★★ 98' 99 00 01 02 03 04 05 08 Consistent 13-ha GRAND CRU; full-flavoured wines maturing fairly early.

Certan-de-May Pom r ★★★ 95 96 98 00' 01' 04 05' 06 08 5-ha property on the POMEROL plateau. Great potential but inconsistent. Could do better.

Certan-Marzelle Pom Little J-P MOUEIX estate for *fragrant, light, juicy Pomerol.*

Chantegrive Graves r w ★★→★★★ 98' 99' 00 01 02 03 04 05' 06 07 08 With 87 ha, the largest estate in the AC; modern GRAVES of v.gd quality. Reds rich and finely oaked. Cuvée Caroline is top white (98' 99 00 01 02 03 04 05' 06 07 08).

Chasse-Spleen Moulis r (w) ★★★ 95 96 9899 00 01 02 03 04 05' 06 07 08 A 100-ha estate at classed-growth level. Consistently gd, often outstanding (eg. 90' 00' 05'), long-maturing wine. Second label: Ermitage de Chasse Spleen. *One of the surest things in Bordeaux*. Makes a little white, too. See also CAMENSAC and GRESSIER-GRAND-POUJEAUX.

Chauvin St-Em r ★★ 95 96 98' 99 00 0103 04 05 06 08 Steady performer; increasingly serious stuff. New v'yds purhased in 1998.

Côtes de Bordeaux
2008 launched the first vintage of the new appellation of Côtes de Bordeaux (14,000 ha). The label embraced and will eventually replace CÔTES DE CASTILLON, CÔTES DE FRANCS, PREMIÈRES CÔTES DE BLAYE and PREMIÈRES CÔTES DE BORDEAUX. Cross-blending of wines from these regions is allowed. For those wanting to maintain the identity of a single terroir, stiffer controls permit AC Côtes de Bordeaux with the suffixes Blaye, Castillon, Francs and Cadillac (for the PREMIÈRES CÔTES DE BORDEAUX). The CÔTES DE BOURG is not part of the new designation.

Cheval Blanc St-Em r ★★★★ 85' 86 88 89 90' 93 94 95 96' 97 98' 99 00' 01' 02 03 04 05' 06 07 08 09 40-ha PREMIER GRAND CRU class (a) of ST-EMILION. High percentage of Cab Fr (60%). Rich, fragrant, vigorous wines with some of the voluptuousness of neighbouring POMEROL. Delicious young; lasts a generation. For many, the first choice in BORDEAUX. Same ownership and management as YQUEM and Quinault L'Enclos (ST-EMILION). Second wine: Le Petit Cheval. Like all First Growth prices are super-high. New winery for 2011.

Chevalier, Domaine de Pe-Lé r w ★★★★ 89 90' 95 96' 98' 99' 00' 01' 02 03 04' 05' 06 07 08 09 Superb estate of 47 ha at Léognan. Impressive since 1998, the red has gained in finesse, fruit, texture. Complex, long-ageing white has remarkable consistency and develops rich flavours (89 90' 93 94 95 96' 97 98' 99 00 01 02 03 04 05' 06 07 08 09). Second wine: Esprit de Chevalier. Look out for DOM de la Solitude, PESSAC-LÉOGNAN.

Cissac Cissac-Méd r ★★ 95 96' 98 00 02 03 04 05 08 Pillar of the bourgeoisie. 50-ha MÉDOC *cru*. Firm, tannic wines that need time. More weight since 2001. Second wine: Les Reflets du CH Cissac.

Citran Avensan, H-Méd r ★★ 95 96 98 99 00 02 03 04 05' 06 08 90-ha estate owned by Villars-Merlaut (patriarch Jacques Merlaut died in 2008) family since 1996 (see CHASSE-SPLEEN, GRUAUD-LAROSE). Since 2001, ripe, supple; accessible early. Second label: Moulins de Citran.

Clarence de Haut-Brion, le Pe-Lé r ★★★ 89' 90 93 94 95 96' 98 99 00 01 02 03 04 05' 06 07 08 09 The second wine of CH HAUT-BRION, known as Bahans Haut-Brion until 2007. Gd value if you can find it. Blend changes considerably with each vintage.

Clarke Listrac r (p w) ★★ 98' 99 00 01 02 03 04 05' 06 08 09 Large (54-ha) estate. Massive (Edmond) Rothschild investment. Now v.gd Merlot-based red. Greater progress from 2000: dark fruit and fine tannins. Also a dry white: Le Merle Blanc du CH Clarke. CH Malmaison in MOULIS same connection.

Clerc Milon Pau r ★★★ 89' 90' 94 95 96' 98' 99 00 01 02 03 04 05' 06 07 08 09 Once-forgotten Fifth Growth owned by (Mouton) Rothschilds. More Merlot so a lot broader and weightier than sister ARMAILHAC.

Climens Saut w sw ★★★★ 83' 85' 86' 88' 89 90' 95 96 97' 98 99' 00 01' 02 03' 04 05' 06 07 09 A 30-ha BARSAC classed growth making some of the world's most stylish wine. Concentrated but with vibrant acidity giving balance; ageing potential guaranteed. Second label: Les Cyprès. Owned by Berenice Lurton (sister of Henri at BRANE-CANTENAC). Pricier than in the past.

Clinet Pom r ★★★★ 95 96 98' 99 00 01 02 03 05' 06 07 08 09 Made a name for intense, sumptuous wines in the 1980s. MICHEL ROLLAND consults. New winery 2004 with wooden vats. Second label: Fleur de Clinet introduced in 1997 but now a négociant brand.

To decipher codes, please refer to "Key to symbols" on front flap of jacket, or "How to use this book" on p.10.

BORDEAUX

Clos l'Eglise Pom r ★★★ 95 96 98 99 00' 01 02 03 04 05' 06 07 08 09 A 6-ha v'yd on one of the best sites in POMEROL. Rich, round and modern style since 1998. Same family owns HAUT-BERGEY and BARDE-HAUT.

Clos Floridène Graves r w ★★ (r) 99 00 01 02 03 04 05 06 08 (w) 98 99 00 01' 02 03 04' 05' 06 07 08 *A sure thing* from one of BORDEAUX's most famous white winemakers, Denis Dubourdieu. Sauv Bl/Sém from limestone allows the wine to age a lot of yrs; much improved red. See also CHX CANTEGRIL, DOISY-DAËNE and REYNON.

Clos Fourtet St-Em r ★★★ 89 90 94 95 96 98 99 00 01 02 03 04 05' 06 07 08 09 Well-placed First Growth on the plateau, cellars almost in town. New owner and investment from 2001; on stellar form. DERENONCOURT consults. Also owns POUJEAUX. Second label: DOM de Martialis.

Clos Haut-Peyraguey Saut w sw ★★H 86' 88' 89 90' 95' 96 97' 98 99 00 01' 02 03' 04 05' 06 07 09 Family DOM. 12 ha "upper" part of the original Peyraguey estate. Elegant, harmonious wines. Haut-Bommes (5 ha) same stable.

Clos des Jacobins St-Em r ★★ 95 96 98 00 01 02 03 04 05' 06 07 08 09 Classed growth with greater stature since 2000. New ownership from 2004; new creamy style. ANGÉLUS owner consults. Same family owns CH La Commanderie and FLEUR CARDINALE.

Clos du Marquis St-Jul r ★★→★★★ 98 99 00 01 02 03 04 05 06 07 08 09 The outstanding second wine of LÉOVILLE-LAS-CASES, cut from the same durable and powerful cloth but from separate v'yds to the *grand vin*.

Clos de l'Oratoire St-Em r ★★ 95 96 98 99 00' 01 03 04 05' 06 07 08 Serious performer on the northeastern slopes of ST-EMILION. Same stable as CANON-LA-GAFFELIÈRE and LA MONDOTTE, polished and reasonable value.

Clos Puy Arnaud Castillon r ★★ 00 01' 02 03 04 05' 06 08 09 Biodynamic estate at the top of this revived AC. 11 ha producing wines of depth and distinction. Owner formerly connected to PAVIE.

Clos René Pom r ★★ 95 96 98' 00' 01 04 05' 06 08 Merlot-dominated wine with a little spicy Malbec from sandy/gravel soils. Less sensuous than top POMEROL but gd value. Alias CH Moulinet-Lasserre.

Clotte, la St-Em r ★★ 95' 96 98' 99 00' 01 02 03 04 05 08 09 Tiny (4-ha) *côtes* GRAND CRU CLASSÉ: fine, perfumed, supple wines. Confidential but gd value.

Colombier-Monpelou Pau r ★★ 98 99 00' 02 03 04 05 06 24-ha PAUILLAC estate near PONTET CANET. Underperforming; light and easy style.

Conseillante, la Pom r ★★★★ 88 89 90' 94 95' 96' 98' 99 00' 01 02 03 04 05' 06' 07 08 09 Historic 12-ha property on plateau between PÉTRUS and CHEVAL BLANC. Some of the noblest and most fragrant POMEROL; almost Médocain in style; long ageing. Second wine (from 2007): Duo de Conseillante.

Corbin St-Em r ★★ 96 98 99 00' 01 02 04 05 08 Much improved 12-ha GRAND CRU CLASSÉ on sand and clay soils. Improvements in the new millennium. Round and supple with soft red fruit.

Corbin-Michotte St-Em r ★★ 95 96 98' 99 00 01 02 04 05 06 08 Competent rather than exciting classed growth located close to POMEROL. Medium-bodied, spicy wines. In same hands as CHX Calon and Cantelauze.

Cordeillan-Bages Pau r ★★ A mere 1,000 cases of savoury PAUILLAC made by the LYNCH-BAGES team. Rarely seen outside BORDEAUX. Better known for its luxury restaurant and hotel.

Cos d'Estournel St-Est r ★★★★ 88' 89' 90' 94 95 96' 98' 00 01 02 03 04 05' 06 07 08 09 89-ha Second Growth with eccentric pagoda *chai*. Most refined ST-ESTÈPHE; more Cab Sauv in blend since 2007. New state-of-the-art cellars in 2008. Pricey white from 2005. Second label: Les Pagodes de Cos (and CH MARBUZET for some markets). Same owner as super-modern Goulée (MÉDOC).

Cos-Labory St-Est r ★★ 89' 90' 94 95 96' 98' 99 00 02 03 04 05' 06 07 08 09

Inconsistent Fifth Growth neighbour of COS D'ESTOURNEL with 18 ha. Recent vintages have more depth and structure. Gd value. ANDRON-BLANQUET is sister CH.

Coufran St-Seurin-de-Cadourne, H-Méd r ★★ 95 96 98 99 00 01 02 03 04 05 06 08 76 ha Coufran and VERDIGNAN, in extreme north of the HAUT-MÉDOC, are co-owned. Coufran is mainly Merlot for supple wine. SOUDARS is another, smaller sister.

Couhins-Lurton Pe-Lé w r ★★→★★★ (w) 98′ 99 00 01 02 03 04 05 06 07 08 (r) 02 03 04 05 06 Fine, minerally, long-lived classed-growth white made from Sauv Bl. Now a supple, Merlot-based red from 2002 (17 ha). Same family as LA LOUVIÈRE and BONNET.

Couspaude, la St Em r ★★★ 95 96 98 99 00′ 01 02 03 04 05 06 08 09 Classed growth well-located on the ST-EMILION plateau. Modern style; rich and creamy with lashings of spicy oak. MICHEL ROLLAND consults.

Coutet Saut w sw ★★★ 86′ 88′ 89′ 90′ 95 96 97′ 98′ 99 01′ 02 03′ 04 05 07 Traditional rival to CLIMENS but zestier style. 38 ha in BARSAC. Consistently v. fine. Cuvée Madame is a v. rich selection in certain yrs (89 90 95).

Couvent des Jacobins St-Em r ★★ 95 96 98′ 99 00′ 01 03 04 05 06 08 10.7-ha GRAND CRU CLASSÉ vinified within the walls of ST-EMILION. Splendid cellars. Lighter, easy style. Denis Dubourdieu consults. Second label: Le Menut des Jacobins.

Crock, le St-Est r ★★ 95 96 98 99 00′ 01 02 03 04 05 06 07 08 V. fine property (30 ha) in the same family (Cuvelier) as LÉOVILLE-POYFERRÉ. Solid, fruit-packed ST-ESTÈPHE.

Croix, la Pom r ★★ 95 96 98 99 00 01 04 05 06 07 08 Well-reputed 10-ha property owned by négociant Janoueix. Appealing plummy POMEROL. Also LA CROIX-ST-GEORGES and other properties in POMEROL and ST-EMILION.

Croix du Casse, la Pom r ★★ 95 96 98 99 00′ 01′ 04 05 06 08 A 9-ha property on sandy/gravel soils in the south of POMEROL. Since 2005 owned by BORIE-MANOUX; investment and improvement from 2008.

Croix-de-Gay, la Pom r ★★★ 89 90 94′ 95 96 98 99 00′ 00′ 01′ 02 04 05 06 09 10 ha in the best part of the commune. Round, elegant style. La Fleur-de-Gay is made from the best parcels. Same family as Faizeau (MONTAGNE ST-EMILION).

Croizet-Bages Pau r ★★ 95 96′ 98 00′ 03 04 05 06 07 08 A 26-ha Fifth Growth. Same owners as RAUZAN-GASSIES. A new regime in the cellar is producing richer, more serious wines, especially from 2006.

Croque-Michotte St-Em r ★★ 95 96 98 00 01 03 04 05 08 A 14-ha estate on the POMEROL border. Standard ST-EMILION.

Cru Bourgeois See Cru Bourgeois box, p.98.

Cruzeau, de Pe-Lé r w sw ★★ (r) 95 96 98 00 01 02 04 05 06 08 (w) 00 01 02 03 04 05 06 07 08 Large 97-ha (two-thirds red) PESSAC-LÉOGNAN v'yd developed by André Lurton of LA LOUVIÈRE. Gd-value wines. Sauv Bl-dominated white.

Dalem Fronsac r ★★ 95 96′98′ 99 00 01 02 03 04 05′ 06 08 09 Was a full-blooded FRONSAC, now a feminine touch has added more charm. 15 ha: 85% Merlot.

Dassault St-Em r ★★ 95 96 98′ 99 00 01 02 03 04 05′ 06 08 09 Consistent, modern, juicy 23-ha GRAND CRU CLASSÉ. Owning family of Dassault aviation fame. Also La Fleur in ST-EMILION and ventures in Chile and Argentina.

Dauphine, de la Fronsac r ★★ 98′ 99 00 01 03 04 05 06′ 08 09 Total makeover since purchased by new owner in 2000. Renovation of CH and v'yds plus new, modern winery in 2002. Stablemate CANON-DE-BREM integrated in 2006, so look out for a more structured style. Second wine: Delphis (from 2006).

Dauzac Labarde-Mar r ★★→★★★ 89′ 90′ 94 95 96 98′ 99 00′ 01 02 04 05 07 08 A 49 ha Fifth Growth south of MARGAUX; now dense, rich, dark wines. Owned by an insurance company; managed by Christine Lurton, daughter of André, of LA LOUVIÈRE. Second wine: La Bastide Dauzac.

Derenoncourt, Stéphane Leading consultant winemaker; self-taught, focused on terroir, balance, elegance.

Desmirail Mar r ★★→★★★ 98 00' 01 02 03 04 05 06 07 08 Third Growth (30 ha) owned by Denis Lurton, brother of Henri (BRANE-CANTENAC). Fine, delicate style.

Destieux St-Em r ★★ 98 99 00' 01 03' 04 05' 06 07 08 09 Promotion to GRAND CRU CLASSÉ in 2006. 8-ha estate to the east of ST-EMILION at St-Hippolyte. New *chai* and investment since 1996. ROLLAND consults. Bold, powerful style.

Doisy-Daëne Barsac w dr sw (r) ★★★ 88' 89' 90' 95 96 97' 98' 99 01' 02 03 04 05 06 07 09 Family-owned (Dubourdieu) 17-ha estate producing a crisp, dry white and CH CANTEGRIL, but above all renowned for its notably fine, sweet BARSAC. L'Extravagant (90 96 97 01 02 03 04 05 06 07 09) is an intensely rich and expensive CUVÉE.

Doisy-Dubroca Barsac w sw ★★ 88' 89 90' 95 96 97' 99 01 03' 04 05 07 Tiny (3.4-ha) BARSAC classed growth allied to CH CLIMENS.

Doisy-Védrines Saut w sw ★★★ 88' 89' 90 95 96 97' 98 99 01' 03' 04 05 07 09 A 27-ha classed growth at BARSAC owned by Casteja family (Joanne négociant). Delicious, sturdy, rich: ages well A sure thing for many yrs.

Dôme, le St-Em r ★★★ 04 05 06 08 09 Micro-wine that used to be super-oaky but is now aimed at elegance and terroir expression (from 2004). Two-thirds old-vine Cab Fr. Owned by Jonathan Maltus, who has a string of other ST-EMILIONS (eg. CH Teyssier, Le Carré, Les Astéries), Australia's Barossa Valley (Colonial Estate) and California's Napa Valley (World's End).

Dominique, la St-Em r ★★★ 89' 90' 94 95 96 98 99 00' 01 04 05' 06 08 09 Classed growth adjacent to CHEVAL BLANC. Potential for rich, aromatic wines. Managed by owner of VALANDRAUD since 2006. To watch. Second label: St Paul de Dominique.

Ducluzeau Listrac r ★★ 95 96 00 01 03 04 05 06 08 Tiny sister property of DUCRU-BEAUCAILLOU. 10 ha, 50/50 Merlot/Cab Sauv. Round, well-balanced wines.

Ducru-Beaucaillou St-Jul r ★★★★ 82' 83' 85' 94 95' 96'98 99 00' 01 02 03 04 05' 06 07 08 09 Outstanding Second Growth, excellent form except for a patch in the late 80s; 75 ha overlooking the river. Added impetus from owner Bruno Borie from 2003. Classic cedar-scented claret suited to long ageing. See also LALANDE-BORIE. Second wine: Croix de Beaucaillou.

Duhart-Milon Rothschild Pau r ★★★ 90 94 95 96' 98 00' 01 02 03 04' 05' 06 07 08 09 Fourth Growth neighbour of LAFITE, under same management. Greater precision from 2002; increasingly fine quality. Second label: Moulin de Duhart.

Durfort-Vivens Mar r ★★★ 89' 90 94 95 96 98 99 00 02 03 04 05' 06 08 09 Second Growth owned and being improved by Gonzague Lurton, president of the MARGAUX winegrowers' association. Recent wines have structure (lots of Cab Sauv) and finesse.

Echo de Lynch-Bages Pau r ★★ 00 01 02 03 04 05 08 The second wine of LYNCH-BAGES. Until 2008 known as Haut-Bages-Averous. Tasty drinking and fairly consistent.

l'Eglise, Domaine, de Pom r ★★ 89 90 95 96 98 99 00 01 02 03 04 05' 06 07 08 09 Small property on the clay-gravel plateau: stylish, resonant wine. Denis Dubourdieu consults. Same stable as TROTTEVIEILLE and CROIX DE CASSE.

l'Eglise-Clinet Pom r ★★★ 89 90' 93' 94 95 96 98' 99 00' 01' 02 03 04 05' 06 07 08 09 6-ha estate. Top-flight POMEROL with great consistency; full, concentrated, fleshy wine. Expensive and limited quantity. Second label: La Petite Eglise.

l'Evangile Pom r ★★★★ 88' 89' 90 95 96 98' 99 00' 01 02 03 04' 05' 06 07 08

09 13 ha between PÉTRUS and CHEVAL BLANC. Deep-veined, elegant style in a POMEROL classic. Investment by owners (LAFITE) Rothschild has greatly improved quality. New cellars in 2004. Second wine: Blason de l'Evangile.

Fargues, de Saut w sw ★★★ 85' 86 88 89 90 95 96 97 98 99' 01 02 03' 04 05' 06 07 09 A 15-ha v'yd by ruined castle owned by Lur-Saluces, previous owner of YQUEM. Rich, unctuous wines, but balanced – maturing earlier than YQUEM.

Faugères St-Em r ★★ 98 99 00' 02 03 04 05 06 07 08 A 49-ha property. Dark, fleshy, modern ST-EMILION. Cuvée Péby is the garage wine. Stunning new Mario Botta-designed winery opened in 2009. Sister to Cap de Faugères in CÔTES DE CASTILLON and Chambrun in LALANDE DE POMEROL.

Faurie-de-Souchard St-Em r ★★ 95 96 98' 00 03 04 05 06 07 08 Previously underperforming CH on the *côtes*. Escaped declassification in 2006. Recent investment and greater effort from new generation. STÉPHANE DERENONCOURT consults. To watch.

de Ferrand St-Em r ★★ 95 96 98 00 01 03 04 05 Big (30-ha) St-Hippolyte estate owned by Baron Bich (Bic pens) family. Unexciting, medium-bodied wines.

Ferrande Graves r (w) ★★ 00 01 02 04 05 06 08 Major estate at Castres owned by négociant Castel: over 40 ha. Easy, enjoyable red and reasonable white wine; at their best at 1–4 yrs.

Ferrière Mar r ★★→★★★ 95 96' 98 99 00' 02 03 04 05 06 08 Tiny 8-ha third growth with a CH in MARGAUX village restored by same capable hands as LA GURGUE and HAUT-BAGES-LIBÉRAL. Dark, firm, perfumed *wines need time*.

Feytit-Clinet Pom r ★★ 90' 94 95 96 98 99 00 01 03 04 05' 06 07 08 09 Tiny 6.5-ha property. Once managed by J-P MOUEIX; back with owning Chasseuil family since 2000. Improvements since 2000. Rich, full POMEROL with ageing potential.

Fieuzal Pe-Lé r (w) ★★★ (r) 98' 00 01 06 07 08 09 (w) 98' 99 01 02 03 05 06 07 08 09 Classed growth at Léognan. Red form has dipped from the heights of the mid-1980s but improvements from 2006. White more consistent. New Irish owner from 2001. ANGÉLUS owner now consults for reds. One to watch.

Figeac St-Em r ★★★★ 95' 96 98' 99 00' 01 02 03 04 05' 06 07 08 First growth, 40-ha gravelly v'yd with unusual 70% Cab Fr and Cab Sauv. Rich but always elegant wines; deceptively long ageing. Owner Thierry Manoncourt (60+ vintages) awarded the Légion d'Honneur in 2009. Second wine: Grange Neuve de Figeac.

Filhot Saut w dr sw ★★ 90 95 96' 97' 98 99 01' 02 03' 04 05 07 09 Second-rank classed growth with splendid CH, 60-ha v'yd. Difficult young, more complex with age. Medium-sweet with a minerally finish.

Fleur Cardinale St-Em r ★★ 98 99 00 01 02 03 04 05' 06 07 08 09 18-ha property east of ST-EMILION. Gd from the 1980s but into overdrive since 2001 with new owner and *chai*. Promoted to GRAND CRU CLASSÉ in 2006. Ripe, unctuous, modern style.

Fleur-de-Gay, la Pom r ★★★ 1,000-case super-CUVÉE of CH LA CROIX DE GAY.

Fleur-Pétrus, la Pom r ★★★★ 89' 90' 94 95 96 98' 99 00' 01 02 03 04 05' 06 08 09 A 13-ha v'yd flanking PÉTRUS; same J-P MOUEIX management. Finer style than PÉTRUS or TROTANOY. Needs time. V. stylish.

Fombrauge St-Em r ★★→★★★ 95 96 98 99 00' 01 02 03 04 05 06 08 09 A Bernard Magrez wine (see PAPE CLÉMENT), so don't expect restraint. Big estate: 52 ha east of ST-EMILION. Since 1999, rich, dark, chocolatey, full-bodied wines. Magrez-Fombrauge is its GARAGE wine.

Fonbadet Pau r ★★ 95 96' 98' 00' 01 02 03 04 05 06 08 20-ha family-owned estate. Reliable, gd value and typical of PAUILLAC style. Potential to age.

Fonplégade St-Em r ★★ 95 96 98 00' 01 03 04 05 06' 07 08 09 A 19-ha GRAND CRU CLASSÉ New American owner from 2004. MICHEL ROLLAND consults. Definite progression since 2004: riper, with more elegance than in the past.

Fonréaud Listrac r ★★ 95 96 98 00' 02 03 04 05 06 08 One of the bigger (39 ha) and better LISTRACS producing savoury, mouthfilling wines. Investment since 1998. 2 ha of white: Le Cygne, barrel-fermented. See LESTAGE. Gd value.

Fonroque St-Em r ★★★ 96 98 01 03 04 05 06 08 19 ha on the plateau north of ST-EMILION. Biodynamic from 2008. Firm and a touch austere; more elegance recently. Managed by Alain Moueix (see MAZEYRES). MOULIN DU CADET sister estate.

Fontenil Fronsac r ★★ 98' 99' 00' 01' 02 03 04 05 06 08 09 Leading FRONSAC started by ROLLAND (1986). Ripe, opulent, balanced. *Garage*: Défi de Fontenil.

Forts de Latour, les Pau r ★★★ 88 89' 90' 94 95' 96' 98 99 00' 01 02 03 04' 05' 06 07 08 09 The (worthy) second wine of CH LATOUR; the authentic flavour in slightly lighter format at Second Growth price. From enlarged v'yds outside the central *Enclos*.

Fourcas-Dupré Listrac r ★★ 89' 90 95 96' 98' 99 00' 01 02 03 04 05 06 08 Well-run 46-ha estate making fairly consistent wine in tight LISTRAC style. Second label: CH Bellevue-Laffont. Complete renovation in 2000.

Fourcas-Hosten Listrac r ★★→★★★ 95' 96' 98' 00 01 02 03 05 06 08 09 A 48-ha estate with new owners (Hermès fashion connection) from 2006: investment and improvement from this date. More precision and finesse. To watch.

France, de Pe-Lé r w ★★ (r) 98 99 00 02 03 04 05 06 08 (w) 96 98 99 01' 02 03 04 05 06 07 08 Well-known northern GRAVES neighbour of CH DE FIEUZAL making consistent wines in a ripe, modern style. MICHEL ROLLAND consults.

Franc-Mayne St-Em r ★★ 90' 94 95 96 98' 99 00' 01 03 04 05 06 08 A 7.2-ha GRAND CRU CLASSÉ. New owners in 1996 and again in 2004 (sister property CH DE LUSSAC). Investment and renovation. Luxury accommodation as well. Fresh, fruity and structure style. Round but firm wines. To watch.

Gaby, du Canon-Fronsac r ★★ 00' 01' 03 04 05 06 07 08 09 Splendid south-facing slopes. New owners in 1999 and again in 2006 (Canadian). Serious wines.

Gaffelière, la St-Em r ★★★ 88' 89' 90' 94 95 96 98' 99 00' 01 03 04 05' 06 07 08 09 A 22-ha First Growth at foot of the *côtes*. Elegant, long-ageing wines. More precision and purity from 2000. DERENONCOURT consulting from 2004.

Galius St-Em r ★★ Oak-aged selection from ST-EMILION co-op, usually to a high standard. Formerly called Haut Quercus.

Garde, la Pe-Lé r w ★★ (r) 96' 98' 99 00 01' 02 04 05 06 07 08 (w) 01 02 04 05 06 07 08 Substantial property of 58 ha owned by négociant CVBG-Dourthe; reliable, supple reds. Tiny production of Sauv Bl/Sauvignon Gris-based white.

Gay, le Pom r ★★★ 95 96 98 99 00 01 03 04 05' 06 07 08 09 Fine 5.6-ha v'yd on northern edge of POMEROL. Major investment, with MICHEL ROLLAND consulting. Now v. ripe and plummy in style. Improvements from 2003. CH Montviel and La Violette same stable and AC. Owner has Cristal d'Arques glassware origins.

Gazin Pom r ★★★ 89' 90' 94' 95 96 98' 99 00' 01 03 04 05' 06 07 08 09 Large (for POMEROL) 24 ha, family-owned (of name: de Bailliencourt dit Courcol) neighbour of PÉTRUS. Now on v.gd form. Second label: L'Hospitalet de Gazin.

Gilette Saut w sw ★★★ 53 55 59 61 67 70 71 75 76 78 79 81 82 83 85 86 88 89 Extraordinary small Preignac CH stores its sumptuous wines in concrete vats for 16–20 yrs. Only about 5,000 bottles of each. Some bottle age still advisable. CH Les Justices is its sister (96 97 99 01 02 03' 05 07).

Giscours Labarde-Mar r ★★★ 88 89' 90 95 96' 98 99 00' 01 02 03 04 05' 06 07 08 09 Splendid Third Growth south of Cantenac. V.gd, vigorous wine in 1970s and now. 1980s were v. wobbly; new (Dutch) ownership from 1995 and revival since 1999. Cellar-door operation as well. Second label: La Sirène de Giscours. CH La Houringue is baby sister, DU TERTRE stablemate.

Glana, du St-Jul r ★★ 98 99 00 02 03 04 05 06 08 Large, 44-ha ST-JULIEN estate. Expansion through the acquisition of parcels of land from CH LAGRANGE. Undemanding; undramatic; value. Same owner as Bellegrave in PAUILLAC. Second wine: Pavillon du Glana.

Gloria St-Jul r ★★→★★★ 95' 96 98 99 00' 01 02 03 04 05' 06 07 08 09 A 45-ha ST-JULIEN estate with v'yds among the classed growths. Same ownership as ST-PIERRE. Supple wines with attractive fruit but can age. Second label: Peymartin.

Gomerie, la 09 St-Em 1,000 cases, 100% Merlot, *garagiste*. See BEAUSÉJOUR-BÉCOT.

Grand-Corbin-Despagne St-Em r ★★→★★★ 90' 94 95 96 98 99 00' 01 03 04 05 06 08 09 Dcmoted from GRAND CRU CLASSÉ in 1996 but reinstated in 2006. In between: investment and hard graft. Aromatic wines now with a ripcr, fuller edge. Still reasonable value. Also CH Maison Blanche, MONTAGNE ST-EMILION. Second label: Petit Corbin-Despagne.

Grand Cru Classé See ST-EMILION classification box, p.102.

Grand-Mayne St-Em r ★★★ 89' 90' 94 95 96 98 99 00' 01' 02 03 04 05' 07 08 09 Leading 16-ha GRAND CRU CLASSÉ on western *côtes*. Consistent, firm, full, savoury wines. New generation of Nony family at the helm.

Grand-Pontet St-Em r ★★★ 95' 96 98' 99 00' 01 02 03 04 05 06 08 A 14-ha estate revitalized since 1985. Generous, fruity wines. See BEAUSÉJOUR-BÉCOT.

Grand-Puy-Ducasse Pau r ★★★ 95 96' 98' 99 00 01 02 03 04 05' 06 07 08 09 Fifth Growth enlarged to 40 ha; stop-start quality. Last few vintages more consistent. Denis Dubourdieu consults. Second label: CH Artigues-Arnaud.

Grand-Puy-Lacoste Pau r ★★★ 86' 88' 89' 90' 94 95' 96' 98 99 00' 01 02 03 04 05' 06 07 08 09 50-ha Fifth Growth famous for Cab Sauv-driven PAUILLAC. Same ownership as HAUT-BATAILLEY. Recent investment. Second label: Lacoste-Borie.

Grave à Pomerol, la Pom r ★★★ 89' 90 94 95 96 98' 00 01 02 04 05 06 08 09 Verdant CH with small, first-class v'yd owned by Christian MOUEIX. V. fine POMEROL of medium richness. Formerly known as La Grave Trigant de Boisset.

Gressier-Grand-Poujeaux Moulis r ★★ 89 90 94 95 96 98 00 01 04 05 Since 2003, same owner as CHASSE-SPLEEN. 5,000 cases average. Little visibility. Solid in the past and in need of ageing.

Greysac Méd r ★★ 95 96 98 00' 02 03 04 05 06 08 Elegant 70-ha MÉDOC estate. Same management as CANTEMERLE. Fine, consistent quality and style.

Gruaud-Larose St-Jul r ★★★ 86' 88 89' 90' 95' 96' 98 99 00' 01 02 04 05' 06 07 08 09 One of the biggest, best-loved Second Growths. 82 ha. Smooth, rich, vigorous claret; ages 20+ yrs. More finesse from 2007. Second wine: Sarget de Gruaud-Larose.

Guadet St-Em ★★ 01 04 05 06 08 Known as Guadet-St-Julien until 2005. Narrowly missed demotion from GRAND CRU CLASSÉ in 2006. DERENONCOURT now consulting and some improvement.

Guiraud Saut w sw (r dr) ★★★ 88' 89' 90' 95 96' 97' 98 99 01' 02 03 04 05' 06 07 09 Top-quality classed growth. Over 100 ha. New owning consortium from 2006 includes manager, Xavier Planty, and CANON LA GAFFELIERE and DOM DE CHEVALIER connections, as well as Peugeot car family. More Sauv Bl than most.

Gurgue, la Mar r ★★ 98 00' 01 02 03 04 05' 06 08 Well-placed 10-ha property, for fine MARGAUX. Same management as HAUT-BAGES-LIBÉRAL.

Hanteillan Cissac r ★★ 00' 02 03 04 05' 06 Huge 82-ha HAUT-MÉDOC v'yd: v. fair wines, early drinking. 50% Merlot. Second wine: CH Laborde.

Haut-Bages-Libéral Pau r ★★★ 96' 98 99 00 01 02 03 04 05' 06 08 09 Lesser-known Fifth Growth of 28 ha (next to LATOUR) in same stable as LA GURGUE. Results are excellent, full of PAUILLAC vitality. Usually gd value.

Haut-Bages-Monpelou Pau r ★★ 95 96 98 99 00 03 04 05 06 08 09 A 15-ha stablemate of CH BATAILLEY on former DUHART-MILON land. Gd minor PAUILLAC.

Haut-Bailly Graves r ★★★★ 89' 90' 95 96 98' 99 00' 01 02 03 04 05' 06 07 08 09 Over 30 ha at Léognan. Since 1979 some of the best savoury, intelligently made red GRAVES. New US ownership and investment from 1998 (but same manager) have taken it to greater heights. Second label: La Parde de Haut-Bailly.

Haut-Batailley Pau r ★★★ 95 96' 98 99 00 02 03 04 05' 06 07 08 Smaller part of divided Fifth Growth BATAILLEY: 20 ha. Gentler than sister CH GRAND-PUY-LACOSTE. New cellar in 2005; more precision. Second wine: La Tour-d'Aspic.

Haut-Beauséjour St-Est r ★★ 95 98 99 00 01 03 04 05 08 09 18-ha property revitalized since 1992 by owner CHAMPAGNE house ROEDERER. See also DE PEZ.

Haut-Bergey Pe-Lé r (w) ★★ (r) 98 99 00 01 02 04 05 06 07 08 09 (w) 03 04 05 06 07 08 09 A 29-ha estate now producing a denser, more modern GRAVES with oak overlay. Also a little dry white. Completely renovated in the 1990s. Same ownership as BARDE-HAUT and CLOS L'EGLISE. Sister CH Branon.

Haut-Brion Pe-Lé r ★★★★ (r) 82' 83' 85' 86' 88' 89' 90' 93 94 95' 96' 97 98' 99 00' 01 02 03 04 05' 06 08 09 Oldest great CH of BORDEAUX and only non-MÉDOC First Growth of 1855 owned by American Dillon family since 1935. 51 ha. Deeply harmonious, never aggressive wine with endless, honeyed, earthy complexity. Consistently great since 1975. A little dry, sumptuous white: 90 93 94 95 96 98 99 00' 01 02 03 04'05' 06 07 08 09. See LE CLARENCE DE HAUT-BRION, LA MISSION-HAUT-BRION, LAVILLE-HAUT-BRION.

Haut Condissas Méd r ★★★ 99 00 01 02 03 04 05 06 07 Special CUVÉE at Bégadan. Selected parcel at CH Rollan-de-By. Rich, concentrated and oaky.

Haut-Marbuzet St-Est r ★★→★★★ 89' 90' 95 96' 98 99 00' 01 02 03 04 05' 06 07 08 Leading non-classified ST-ESTÈPHE estate. Rich, unctuous wines that age well. M Duboscq has reassembled ancient DOM de Marbuzet, (in total 71 ha). Also owns Chambert-Marbuzet, MacCarthy, Tour de Marbuzet. Haut-Marbuzet is 60% Merlot, seductive and remarkably consistent. CH Layauga-Duboscq in AC MÉDOC is new venture (2005).

Haut-Pontet St-Em r ★★ 98 00 01 03 04 05 Tiny 4.8-ha Merlot v'yd of the *côtes*. New owner (Janoueix – see next entry) from 2007.

Haut-Sarpe St-Em r ★★ 95 96 98 00' 01 04 05 06 08 21-ha GRAND CRU CLASSÉ with elegant CH and park, 70% Merlot. Same owner (Janoueix) as CH LA CROIX, POMEROL. Modern style.

Hosanna Pom r ★★★★ 99 00 01 02 03 04 05' 06 07 08 09 Formerly Certan-Guiraud until purchased and renamed by J-P MOUEIX. Only best 4.5 ha retained. First vintages confirm class. New cellar in 2008, shared with Providence. Stablemate of PÉTRUS and TROTANOY.

d'Issan Cantenac-Mar r ★★★ 95 96' 98 99 00' 01 02 03 04' 05 06 07 08 09 45-ha Third Growth v'yd with moated CH. Fragrant wines; more substance since late 90s. Owner Emmanuel Cruse is the new grand master of the Commanderie de Bontemps Confrérie. Second label: Blason d'Issan.

Kirwan Cantenac-Mar r ★★★ 89' 90' 94 95 96 98 99 00' 01 02 03 04 05' 06 07 08 09 A 35-ha Third Growth; from 1997 majority-owned by SCHRÖDER & SCHÿLER. Mature v'yds now giving classy wines. Rich style: MICHEL ROLLAND influenced until 2007. Second label: Les Charmes de Kirwan.

Labégorce Mar r ★★ 95 96 98 99 00 01 02 03 04 05' 07 08 In 2009 absorbed neighbouring LABÉGORCE-ZÉDÉ, making one 55-ha estate. Second wine to be Zédé de Labegorce. Solid, long-lived MARGAUX.

Labégorce-Zédé Mar r ★★→★★★ 95 96' 98 99 00' 01 02 03 04 05' 06 07 RIP. From 2009, part of CH LABEGORCE (see above). Old vintages classic and fragrant in style.

Lafaurie-Peyraguey Saut w sw ★★★ 82 83' 85 86' 88' 89' 90' 95 96' 97 98 99 01' 02 03' 04 05' 06 07 09 Fine 36-ha classed growth at Bommes; owners Groupe Banque Suez. One of best buys in SAUTERNES. New manager in 2006, formerly at PAPE-CLÉMENT. Second wine: La Chapelle de Lafaurie.

Lafite-Rothschild Pau r ★★★★ 82' 83 85 86' 88' 89' 90' 93 94 95 96' 97 98' 99 00' 01' 02 03' 04' 05' 06 07 08 09 First Growth of famous elusive perfume and style, but never huge weight, although more density and sleeker texture from 1996. Great vintages keep for decades; insatiable demand from China has driven up prices. Joint ventures in Chile (1988), California (1989), Portugal (1992), Argentina (1999), now the MIDI, Italy – even China. Second wine: Carruades de Lafite. 91 ha. Also owns CHX DUHART-MILON, L'ÉVANGILE, RIEUSSEC.

Lafleur Pom r ★★★★ 83 85' 86 88' 89' 90' 93 94 95 96 98' 99' 00' 01' 02 03 04' 05' 06 07 08 09 Superb 4.8-ha property. Elegant, intense wine cultivated like a garden for maturing. 50% Cab Fr. Second wine: Pensées de Lafleur.

Lafleur-Gazin Pom r ★★ 95 96 98 00 01 04 05 06 08 Small 8-ha J-P MOUEIX estate on the northeastern border of POMEROL. Lighter style of POMEROL.

Lafon-Rochet St-Est r ★★★ 88' 89' 90' 94 95 96' 98 99 00' 01 02 03' 04 05' 06 08 09 Fourth Growth neighbour of COS D'ESTOURNEL, 45 ha with distinctive yellow cellars (and label). Investment, selection and a higher percentage of Merlot have made this ST-ESTÈPHE more opulent since 1998. Gd value. Second label: Les Pèlerins de Lafon-Rochet.

Lagrange Pom r ★★ 95 96 98 00 01 04 05 06 Tiny 5-ha v'yd in the centre of POMEROL run by the ubiquitous house of J-P MOUEIX. Gd value but not in the same league as HOSANNA, LA FLEUR-PÉTRUS, LATOUR-À-POMEROL, etc.

Lagrange St-Jul r ★★ 88' 89' 90' 94 95 96 98 99 00' 01 02 03 04 05' 06 08 09 Formerly neglected Third Growth owned since 1983 by Suntory. 117 ha now in tip-top condition with wines to match. Marcel Ducasse oversaw the resurrection until retirement in 2007. Further investment planned. Dry white Les Arums de Lagrange since 1997. Second wine: Les Fiefs de Lagrange.

Lagune, la Ludon, H-Méd r ★★ 90' 95 96' 98 00' 02 03 04 05' 08 80-ha Third Growth in southern MÉDOC with sandy/gravel soils. Dipped in 1990s but on form from 2001. Fine-edged, now with added structure and depth. Owned by J-J Frey; recently acquired JABOULET AÎNÉ. Daughter Caroline the winemaker.

Lalande-Borie St-Jul r ★★ 98 00 01 02 03 04 05 06 07 08 09 A baby brother (25 ha) of the great DUCRU-BEAUCAILLOU created from part of the former v'yd of CH LAGRANGE. Gracious, easy-drinking wine.

Lamarque, de Lamarque, H-Méd r ★★ 90' 94 95 96 98 99 00' 02 03 04 05 06 08 Splendid medieval fortress in central MÉDOC with 35-ha v'yd; competent, mid-term wines. Second wine: Donjon de L.

Lamothe Bergeron H-Méd r ★★ 98' 00 02 03 04 05 Large 67-ha estate in Cussac Fort Médoc owned by a bank. Reliable if unexceptional claret.

Lanessan Cussac, H-Méd r ★★ 89' 90' 94 95 96' 98 00' 01 02 03 04 05 08 Distinguished 44-ha property just south of ST-JULIEN. Firmly structured wines that can age. Horse museum and tours.

Langoa-Barton St-Jul r ★★★ 90' 94 95' 96' 98 99 00' 01 02 03 04' 05' 06 07 08 09 Third Growth sister CH to LÉOVILLE-BARTON. Home to Anthony Barton; impeccable standards, gd value. Second wine: Réserve de Léoville-Barton.

Larcis-Ducasse St-Em r ★★★ 88' 89' 90' 94 95 96 98' 00 02 03 04 05' 06 07 08 09 Top classed-growth property of St-Laurent, eastern neighbour of ST-EMILION, on the *côtes*. Spectacular rise in quality (and price) since 2002. Same management as PAVIE-MACQUIN.

Larmande St-Em r ★★ 89' 90' 95' 96 98' 00' 01 03 04 05 07 08 09 Substantial 24-ha property owned by Le Mondiale insurance (as is SOUTARD). Replanted, re-equipped, and now making consistently solid wines. All-female winemaking and management team. Second label: CH des Templiers.

Laroque St-Em r ★★→★★★ 89 90 94 95 96 98 99 00' 01 03 04 05 06 08 27-ha classified GRAND CRU CLASSÉ, 17th-century CH. Fresh, terroir-driven wines. Cellar renovated 2007.

Larose-Trintaudon St-Laurent, H-Méd r ★★ 98 00 01 02 03 04 05 06 The biggest v'yd in the MÉDOC: 172 ha. Modern methods make reliable, fruity and charming wine to drink young. Second label: Larose St-Laurent. Special CUVÉE (from 1996) – Larose Perganson – from 33-ha parcel.

Laroze St-Em r ★★ 90' 95 96' 98' 99 00 01 05 06 07 08 09 Large v'yd (30 ha) on western *côtes*. Lighter-framed wines from sandy soils, more depth from 1998; approachable when young. New *tribaie* grape-sorting machine (v. ingenious, sorts according to specific gravity, and thus ripeness) in use. Second label: La Fleur Laroze.

Larrivet-Haut-Brion Pe-Lé r w ★★★ (r) 95 96' 98' 00 01 02 03 04 05' 06 07 08 Substantial 56-ha Léognan property with classed-growth aspirations; MICHEL ROLLAND consulting. Rich, modern red. Also Sauv Bl/Sém barrel-fermented white (99 00 01 02 04' 05 06 07 08). New barrel cellar and tasting room in 2007. Second wine: Les Demoiselles de Larrivet-Haut-Brion.

Lascombes Mar r (p) ★★★ 89' 90' 96' 98' 99 00 01 02 03 04 05' 06 07 08 09 A 97-ha Second Growth owned by US pension fund. Wines were wobbly, but real improvements from 2001. MICHEL ROLLAND consults. Winemaker previously with LAFITE-ROTHSCHILD. Modern style. Second label: Chevalier de Lascombes.

Latour Pau r ★★★★ 78' 82' 85 86 88' 89 90' 91 93 94 95' 96' 97 98 99 00' 01 02 03' 04' 05' 06 08 09 First Growth considered the grandest statement of the MÉDOC. Profound, intense, almost immortal wines in great yrs; even weaker vintages have the characteristic note of terroir and run for many yrs. Recently enlarged: 80+ ha inc 48 ha "Enclos" for the *grand vin*. Latour always needs 10 yrs to show its hand. New state-of-the-art *chai* (2003) allows more precise vinification. About 10% of the vineyard now organic. Second wine: LES FORTS DE LATOUR; *third wine: Pauillac.*

Latour-Martillac Pe-Lé r w ★★ (r) 98 00 01 02 03 04 05' 06 08 09 A 46-ha classed-growth property in Martillac. Regular quality (red and white); gd value at this level. White can age admirably (99 00 01 02 03 04 05 06 07 08 09).

Crus Bourgeois – officially revived

The new Cru Bourgeois label became official in November 2009, the decree signed by French prime minister François Fillon. Following the annulment of the 2003 classification, producers in the MÉDOC had been in a quandary as to how to revive this useful marketing designation. The answer, proposed by the winegrowers' association, Alliance des Crus Bourgeois du Médoc, is Reconnaissance Cru Bourgeois. This is not a classification but a certificate awarded on a yearly basis, administered by an independent body: Bureau Véritas. It is open to any producer in the MÉDOC, provided the AC credential has been obtained, and the wine evaluated once in bottle by blind tasting roughly two yrs after the harvest. Failure to obtain the label one year will not compromise applications for subsequent vintages.

Latour-à-Pomerol Pom r ★★★ 88' 89' 90' 94 95 96 98' 99 00' 01 02 04 05' 06 07 08 09 Top growth of 7.6 ha on POMEROL plateau under J-P MOUEIX management. Rich, well-structured wines that age. Rarely disappoints.

Laurets, des St-Em r ★★ 00 01 03 04 05 06 Major property in PUISSEGUIN-ST-EMILION and MONTAGNE-ST-EMILION, with 72 ha of v'yd evenly split on the *côtes* (40,000 cases). Owned by Benjamin de Rothschild of CH CLARKE (2003).

Laville-Haut-Brion Pe-Lé w ★★★★ 89' 90 92 93' 94 95' 96' 98 00' 01 02 03 04' 05' 06 07 08 09 Only 8,000 bottles/yr of v. best white GRAVES for long, succulent maturing, made at LA MISSION-HAUT-BRION. Great consistency. Mainly Sém. Name changes to La Mission Haut-Brion from the 2009 vintage

Léoville-Barton St-Jul r ★★★★ 88' 89' 90' 94' 95' 96' 98 99 00' 01 02 03' 04 05' 06 07 08 09 A 48-ha portion of great Second Growth Léoville v'yd in Anglo-Irish hands of the Barton family for over 180 yrs (Anthony Barton is present incumbent). Harmonious, classic claret; traditional methods, fair prices. Investment raised v. high standards to Super Second. See LANGOA-BARTON.

Léoville-las-Cases St-Jul r ★★★★ 82' 83' 85' 86' 88 89' 90' 93 94 95' 96' 97 98 99 00' 01 02 03' 04' 05' 06 07 08 09 The largest Léoville; 97 ha but the heart is the 53-ha *grand enclos*. Elegant, complex, powerful, wines, for immortality. Second wine CLOS DU MARQUIS. Laser-optical grape sorting in 2009.

Léoville-Poyferré St-Jul r ★★★ 86' 88 89' 90' 94 95 96 98 99 00' 01 02 03' 04 05' 06 07 08 09 The best part of the v'yd lies opposite the *grand enclos* of LEOVILLE-LAS-CASES. Now at Super Second level with dark, rich, spicy, long-ageing wines. ROLLAND consults at the 80-ha estate. Second label: CH Moulin-Riche.

Lestage Listrac r ★★ 95 96 98 00 02 03 04 05 06 08 A 42-ha LISTRAC estate in same hands as CH FONREAUD. Firm, slightly austere claret. Second wine: La Dame du Coeur de CH Lestage.

Lilian Ladouys St-Est r ★★ 95 96 98 00 02 03 04 05 06 07 08 09 Created in the 1980s, the v'yd now covers 45 ha with 100 parcels of vines. Firm, sometimes robust wines; recent vintages more finesse. New owner in 2008 (owner of rugby club Racing Métro 92 and, since 2009, PEDESCLAUX). Same management as Belle-Vue in HAUT-MEDOC.

Liot Barsac w sw ★★ 89' 90' 95 96 97' 98 99 01' 02 03 05 07 Consistent, fairly light, golden wines from 20 ha. Simple, easy-drinking and inexpensive.

Liversan St-Sauveur, H-Méd r ★★ 90' 95 96 98 00 02 03 04 05 07 A 47-ha estate inland from PAUILLAC. Same owner – Jean-Michel Lapalu – as PATACHE D'AUX. Quality oriented. Second wine: Les Charmes de Liversan.

Loudenne St-Yzans, Méd r ★★ 96' 98 00 01 02 03 04 05 06 Beautiful pink riverside CH owned since 2000 by Lafragette family. ROLLAND consults. Ripe, round reds. Also an oak-scented Sauv Bl white best at 2–4 yrs (00 01 02 04 05 06 07 08). Accommodation as well.

Loupiac-Gaudiet Loupiac w sw ★★ 96 97 98 99 01 02 03' 05 07 A reliable source of gd-value "almost-SAUTERNES", just across river Garonne.

Louvière, la Pe-Lé r w ★★★ (r) 98 99 00' 01 02 04 05 06 07 08 (w) 99 00 01 02 03 04' 05' 06 07 08 09 A 61-ha Léognan estate with CH classed as historical monument. Excellent white and red of classed-growth standard. New barrel cellar (2009). See also BONNET, COUHINS-LURTON, DE CRUZEAU, DE ROCHEMORIN.

Lussac, de St-Em r ★★ 99 00 03 04 05 06 07 08 One of the best estates in LUSSAC-ST-EMILION. New owners and technical methods since 2000. Same stable as FRANC-MAYNE and Vieux Maillet in POMEROL.

Lynch-Bages Pau r (w) ★★★★ 82' 85' 86' 88' 89' 90' 94 95' 96' 98 99 00' 01 02 03 04' 05' 06 07 08 09 Always popular, now a regular star. Priced higher than its Fifth Growth status. 96 ha. Rich, robust wine: deliciously dense; aspiring to greatness. See ECHO DE LYNCH-BAGES. From 1990, gd, oaky white: Blanc de Lynch-Bages. Same owners (Cazes family) as LES ORMES-DE-PEZ and Villa Bel-Air.

Lynch-Moussas Pau r ★★ 90' 95' 96' 98 00' 01 02 03 04 05' 07 08 Fifth Growth restored by director of BATAILLEY. On the up since 00: more fruit and flavour .

Lyonnat, du Lussac-St-Em r ★★ 00' 01 03 04 05 06 49-ha estate; well-distributed, reliable wine. The Rhône's Jean-Luc Colombo is the consulting oenologist.

Macquin-St-Georges St-Em r ★★ 95 96 98 99 00 01 03 04 05 06 Steady producer of delicious, not weighty, satellite ST-EMILION at ST-GEORGES.

Magdelaine St-Em r ★★★ 86 88 89'90' 94 95 96 98' 99 00 01 03 04 05 06 08 09 Leading *côtes* First Growth: 11 ha owned by J-P MOUEIX. Delicate, fine and deceptively long-lived. Denser weight in 2008.

Malartic-Lagravière Pe-Lé r (w) ★★★(r) 90' 95 96 98 99 00' 01 02 03 04' 05' 06 08 09 (w) 98 99 00 01' 02 03 04' 05' 06 07 08 09 Léognan classed growth of 53 ha (majority red). Rich, modern red wine since late 1990s; a little lush Sauv Bl white. Belgian owner (since 1997) has revolutionized the property. ROLLAND advises. CH Gazin Rocquencourt (PESSAC-LÉOGNAN) new acquisition in 2006.

Malescasse Lamarque, H-Méd r ★★ 98 00 01 02 03 04 05 06 07 08 Renovated property with 40 well-situated ha near MOULIS. Second label: La Closerie de Malescasse. Supple, inexpensive wines, accessible early.

Malescot-St-Exupéry Mar r ★★★ 90' 94 95 96 98 99 00' 01 02 03 04 05' 06 07 08 09 Third Growth of 24 ha returned to fine form in the 1990s. Now ripe, fragrant and finely structured. MICHEL ROLLAND advises.

Malle, de Saut r w dr sw ★★★ (w sw) 89' 90' 94 95 96' 97' 98 99 01' 02 03' 05 06 07 09 Beautiful Preignac CH of 50 ha. V. fine, medium-bodied SAUTERNES; also M de Malle dry white and GRAVES CH du Cardaillan.

Marbuzet St-Est r ★★ 96' 98 99 00' 01 02 03 04 05'06 Since 2007 the 7 ha have been integrated into COS-D'ESTOURNEL. Now a second label name for certain markets.

Margaux, Ch Mar r (w) ★★★★ 83' 85' 86' 88' 89' 90' 93 94 95' 96' 97 98' 99 00' 01' 02 03' 04' 05' 06 07 08 09 First Growth (91 ha); most seductive and fabulously perfumed of all in its frequent top vintages. Consistent since its purchase by André Mentzelopoulos in 1977. Now owned and run by daughter Corinne. Pavillon Rouge (**98** 99 00' 01 02 03 04' 05' 07 08) is second wine. Pavillon Blanc is best white (Sauv Bl) of MÉDOC, but expensive (00' 01' 02 03 04' 05 06 07 08).

Marojallia Mar r ★★★ 99 00' 01 02 03 04 05' 06 07 08 Micro-CH with 4.5 ha, looking for big prices for big, rich, beefy, un-MARGAUX-like wines. VALANDRAUD owner consults. Upmarket B&B as well. Second wine: Clos Margalaine.

Marquis-d'Alesme Mar r ★★ 89 90 95 98 00 01 04 05 06 07 15-ha Third Growth. Dropped "Becker" handle in 2009. Disappointing in recent yrs. Purchased by CH LABÉGORCE in 2006 and improvement in 2007. To watch.

Marquis-de-Terme Mar r ★★→★★★ 89' 90' 95 96 98 99 00' 01 02 03 04 05' 06 07 08 09 Renovated Fourth Growth of 40 ha dispersed around AC. Wobbled in the 1990s but looks better since 2000. Solid rather than elegant MARGAUX.

Martinens Mar r ★★ 96 98 99 00 02 03 04 05 30-ha in Cantenac. Light, supple.

Maucaillou Moulis r ★★ 96 98' 00' 01 02 03 04 05 06 08 A-63-ha property in MOULIS with gd standards. Clean, fresh, value wines. Second wine: No 2 de Maucaillou.

Mazeyres Pom r ★★ 96' 98' 99 00 01 04 05' 06 08 09 Consistent, if not exciting lesser POMEROL. 20 ha on sandier soils. Better since 1996. Alain Moueix, cousin of Christian of J-P MOUEIX, manages here. See FONROQUE.

Meyney St-Est r ★★→★★★ 89' 89' 90' 94 95 96 96 98 00 01 02 03 04 05' 06 08 Big (50-ha) riverside property in a superb situation next to MONTROSE. Rich, robust, well-structured wines. Second label: Prieur de Meyney.

Mission-Haut-Brion, la Pe-Lé r ★★★★ 83 85' 86 88 89' 90' 93 94 95 96' 98' 99 00' 01 02 03 04' 05' 06 07 08 09 Neighbour and long-time rival to HAUT-BRION; since 1983 in same hands. Consistently grand-scale, full-blooded, long-maturing wine; more flamboyant than HAUT-BRION (50% Merlot). 26 ha. LA TOUR HAUT-BRION v'yd integrated from 2006. Second label: La Chapelle de la Mission. White: LAVILLE-HAUT-BRION.

Monbousquet St-Em r (w) ★★★ 95 96 98 99 00' 01 02 03 04 05' 06 08 09 Substantial property on ST-EMILION's gravel plain revolutionized by new owner Gerard Pérse. Now super-rich, concentrated and voluptuous wines. Classified GRAND CRU CLASSÉ in 2006. Rare v.gd white (AC BORDEAUX) from 1998. Same ownership as PAVIE and PAVIE-DECESSE.

Monbrison Arsac-Mar r ★★→★★★ 88' 89' 90 95 96' 98 99 00 01 02 04 05' 06 08 09 13 ha on fine gravel soils. Delicate, fragrant MARGAUX.

Mondotte, la St-Em r ★★★→★★★★ 96' 97 98' 99 00' 01 02 03 04' 05' 06 07 08 09 Intense, always firm, virile *garagiste* wines from 4.3 ha on ST-EMILION's limestone plateau. Same ownership as CANON-LA-GAFFELIÈRE, CLOS DE L'ORATOIRE.

Montrose St-Est r ★★★→★★★★ 88 89' 90' 93 94 95 96' 98 99 00 01 02 03' 04' 05' 06 07 08 09 70-ha Second Growth famed for deep-coloured, forceful

> **Bordeaux's comic heroes**
> Jean-Michel CAZES of LYNCH-BAGES is one of a number of real-life Bordelais
> to appear in Japanese manga *Drops of the Gods*. The story this time is set
> in the Bordeaux marathon and involves a son having to source a number
> of ultra-rare wines in order to inherit his father's valuable cellar. In real
> life, of course, he'd have to sell them to pay the inheritance tax...

claret. Known as the LATOUR of ST-ESTÈPHE. Vintages 1979–85 (except 1982) were lighter. After 110 yrs in same family hands, change of ownership in 2006. Ex-HAUT-BRION director, Jean-Bernard Delmas, now managing. Environmentally conscious renovation. Second wine: La Dame de Montrose.

Moulin du Cadet St-Em r p ★★ 95 96 98 00 01 03 05 5-ha GRAND CRU CLASSÉ v'yd on the limestone plateau, now managed by Alain Moueix (see also MAZEYRES). Biodynamics practised. Robust wines.

Moulinet Pom r ★★ 96 98 00 01 04 05 06 08 09 One of POMEROL's bigger CHX; 18 ha on lightish soil. Denis Durantou of L'ÉGLISE-CLINET consults. Gd value.

Moulin Pey-Labrie Canon-Fronsac r ★★ 90 94 95 96 98' 99 00' 01 02 03 04 05' 06 08 09 Stylish wines, Merlot-dominated with elegance and structure.

Moulin de la Rose St-Jul r ★★ 95 96 98 00' 01' 02 03 04 05 06 Tiny 4-ha in ST-JULIEN; high standards. Same ownership as SÉGUR DE CABARAC in ST-ESTÈPHE.

Moulin-St-Georges St-Em r ★★ 96 98 99 00' 01 02 03 04 05 06 08 09 Stylish and rich wine. Classed-growth level. Same ownership as AUSONE.

Moulin-à-Vent Moulis r ★★ 95 98 00' 02 03 04 05' 06 A 25-ha MOULIS estate; reasonably regular quality. Lively, forceful wine.

Mouton Rothschild Pau r (w) ★★★★ 82' 83' 85' 86' 88' 89' 90' 93' 94 95' 96 97 98' 99 00' 01' 02 03 04' 05' 06' 07 08 09 Officially a First Growth since 1973. 85 ha (80% Cab Sauv); the most exotic and voluptuous of the PAUILLAC first growths. Attains new heights from 2004. New chief winemaker from 2003, previously at BRANAIRE-DUCRU. White Aile d'Argent from 1991. Second wine: Le Petit Mouton from 1997. See also Opus One (California) and Almaviva (Chile).

Nairac Saut w sw ★★ 88 89 90' 95' 96 97' 98 99 01' 02 03' 04 05' 07 09 Rich style of BARSAC, sometimes on the heavy side.

Nenin Pom r ★★★ 95 96 98 99 00' 01 02 03 04 05 06 07 08 09 LÉOVILLE-LAS-CASES ownership since 1997. Massive investment. New cellars. 4 ha of former Certan-Giraud acquired in 1999. Now a total of 34 ha. On an upward swing. Built to age. Gd-value second wine: Fugue de Nenin.

Olivier Graves r w ★★★ (r) 95 96 00 01 02 04' 05'06 08 09 (w) 96 97 98' 00 01 02 03 04' 05' 06 07 08 09 A 55-ha classed growth (majority red), surrounding a moated castle at Léognan. A sleeper finally being turned around. New investment and greater purity, expression and quality from 2002. Value at this level.

Ormes-de-Pez, les St-Est r ★★→★★★ 96 98 99 00' 01 02 03 04 05 06 07 08 09 Outstanding 29-ha property owned by LYNCH-BAGES. Dense, fleshy wines.

Ormes-Sorbet, les Méd r ★★ 95 96 98' 99 00' 01 02 03' 04 05 06 Long-time leader in northern MÉDOC. 21 ha at Couquèques. Elegant, gently oaked wines that age. Consistently reliable. Second label: CH de Conques.

Palmer Cantenac-Mar r ★★★★ 82 83' 85 86' 88' 89 90 93 94 95 96' 98' 99 00 01' 02 03 04' 05' 06 07 08 09 Neighbour of CH MARGAUX: a Third Growth on a par

Vintages shown in light type should be opened now only out of curiosity to gauge their future. Vintages in bold are deemed ready for drinking. Remember, though: many 1989s, 90s, 95s, and 96s have at least ten more years of development before them. Vintages marked 00' are regarded as particularly successful for property in question. Vintages in colour are first choice for 2011.

with the Super Seconds. Wine of power, delicacy and much Merlot (40%). 55 ha with Dutch, British (the SICHEL family) and French owners. New winemaker (since 2004) formerly with ORNELLAIA. Second wine: Alter Ego de Palmer.

Pape-Clément Pe-Lé r (w) ★★★→★★★★ (r) 90' 94 95 96 98' 99 00' 01 02 03 04 05 06 07 08 09 (w) 01 02 03 04 05' 07 08 09 Ancient PESSAC v'yd (35 ha) owned by Bernard Magrez; record of voluptuous, scented, long-ageing reds. 2.5 ha of elegant, barrel-fermented white. Ambitious new-wave direction, oak and potency from 2000 (grapes hand-destemmed!). Also CH Poumey at Gradignan.

Parenchère, de r (w) ★★ 00 01 02 03 04 05 06 Useful AC Ste-Foy Bordeaux and AC BORDEAUX SUPÉRIEUR from handsome CH with 65 ha. Cuvée Raphael best.

Patache d'Aux Bégadan, Méd r ★★ 98 99 00 02 03 04 05' 06 07 43-ha property in northern MÉDOC. Gd-value, largely Cab Sauv wine. See also LIVERSAN.

Pavie St-Em r ★★★★ 90' 94 95 96 98' 99 00' 01 02 03' 04 05' 06 07 08 09 Splendidly sited First Growth; 37 ha mid-slope on the *côtes*. Great track record. Bought by owner of MONBOUSQUET, along with adjacent PAVIE-DECESSE. New-wave ST-EMILION: intense, strong, mid-Atlantic; subject of heated debate.

Pavie-Decesse St-Em r ★★ 95 96 98' 99 00' 01' 02 03 04 05' 06 07 08 09 Small 3.6-ha classed growth. Even more powerful and muscular than brother above.

Pavie-Macquin St-Em r ★★★ 89' 90' 94 95 96' 98' 99 00' 01 02 03 04 05' 06 07 08 09 Surprise promotion to PREMIER GRAND CRU CLASSÉ in 2006 classification. 15-ha v'yd on the limestone plateau east of ST-EMILION. Astute management and winemaking by Nicolas Thienpont of PUYGUERAUD and DERENONCOURT consultant. Powerful, structured wines that need time in bottle.

Pedesclaux Pau r ★★ 98' 99 00 02 03 04 05 06 09 Underachieving 27-ha Fifth Growth being steadily revived and reorganized. New owner in 2009 (see LILIAN LADOUYS). Supple wines with up to 50% Merlot. Watch for change.

Petit-Village Pom r ★★★ 95 96 98' 99 00' 01 03 04 05 06 07 08 09 Top property which lagged until 2005. DERENONCOURT consulting. New cellar in 2007. 11 ha; same owner (AXA Insurance) as PICHON-LONGUEVILLE since 1989. Powerful, plummy wine. Second wine: Le Jardin de Petit-Village.

Pétrus Pom r ★★★★ 75' 76 78 79' 81 82' 83 85' 86 88' 89' 90 93' 94 95' 96 97 98' 99 00' 01 02 03 04' 05' 06 07 08 09 The (unofficial) First Growth of POMEROL: Merlot solo *in excelsis*. 11 ha of gravelly clay giving 2,500 cases of massively rich, concentrated wine, on allocation to the world's millionaires. Each vintage adds lustre. Long-time winemaker J-C Berrouet (44 vintages) retired in 2007. Son Olivier now at helm. JEAN-FRANÇOIS MOUEIX owner.

Peyrabon St-Sauveur, H-Méd r ★★ 99 00' 01 02 03 04 05 06 Serious 53-ha HAUT-MÉDOC estate owned by négociant (Millésima). Also La Fleur-Peyrabon PAUILLAC.

Pez, de St-Est r ★★→★★★★ 89 90' 94 95' 96' 98' 99 00 01 02 03 04 05' 06 07 08 09 Outstanding ST-ESTÈPHE *cru* of 26 ha. Now more Merlot and generous and reliable in style. Bought in 1995 by ROEDERER.

St-Emilion classification – a compromise until 2011

For those confused by the legal shenanigans surrounding the ST-EMILION classification, this is the official situation until the 2011 vintage. The 1996 classification has been reinstated, so those demoted in 2006 still hold their place. Those promoted in 2006 have also been allowed to keep their new ranking – gd news for BELLEFONT-BELCIER, DESTIEUX, FLEUR CARDINALE, GRAND CORBIN, GRAND-CORBIN-DESPAGNE AND MONBOUSQUET (GRANDS CRUS CLASSÉS), as well as PAVIE-MACQUIN and TROPLONG MONDOT (PREMIER GRANDS CRUS CLASSÉS). There are, therefore, 15 PREMIER GRANDS CRUS CLASSÉS and 57 GRANDS CRUS CLASSÉS. This is the state of affairs until a new classification is, in principle, announced in 2011.

Phélan-Ségur St-Est r ★★★ 89' 90' 95 96' 98 99 00' 01 02 0304 05' 06 07 08 09 Big and important estate (89 ha); rivals the last as one of ST-ESTÈPHE's best. From 1988 has built up a strong and reliable reputation.

Pibran Pau r ★★ 89' 90' 94 95 96 99 00' 01 03 04 05' 06 07 08 09 Small 17-ha property allied to PICHON-LONGUEVILLE. Classy wine with PAUILLAC drive.

Pichon-Longueville (formerly **Baron de Pichon-Longueville**) Pau r ★★★★ 86' 88' 89' 90' 93 94' 95 96 98 99 00' 01 02 03' 04 05' 06 07 08 09 Second Growth (73 ha) with revitalized powerful PAUILLAC wine for long ageing. Owners AXA Insurance. New barrel cellar (under an artificial lake) and visitor centre in 2008. Second label: Les Tourelles de Longueville.

Pichon-Longueville Comtesse de Lalande (Pichon Lalande) Pau r ★★★★ 76 78' 79' 81 82' 83 85' 86' 88' 89' 90' 94 95 96 98 99 00 01 02 03' 04 05' 06 07 08 09 Super-Second Growth neighbour to LATOUR (87 ha). Always among the v. top performers; a long-lived, Merlot-marked wine of fabulous breed, even in lesser yrs. ROEDERER owner since 2007. Tendency in coming yrs to increase Cab Sauv. Second wine: Réserve de la Comtesse. Other property: CH BERNADOTTE.

Pin, le Pom r ★★★★ 82 83 85 86 88 89 90' 94 95 96 97 98' 99 00 01 02 04' 05' 06 07 08 09 The original of the BORDEAUX cult mini-*crus* made in a cellar not much bigger than a garage (new modern version in the planning stage). A mere 500 cases of Merlot, with same family behind it as VIEUX-CH-CERTAN. Almost as rich as its drinkers, but prices well beyond PÉTRUS are ridiculous.

Pitray, de Castillon r ★★ 95 96' 98' 00' 03 04 05 06 Once the best known in CÔTES DE CASTILLON, now overshadowed by leading lights. Earthy, but value.

Plince Pom r ★★ 95 96 98' 99 00' 01 04 05 06 07 08 Lighter, supple wines from sandy soils. Easy drinking.

Pointe, la Pom r ★★→★★★ 8 95 96 98' 99 00' 01 04 05' 06 07 08 09 Prominent 25-ha estate. New owner and investment. Definite improvement. To watch.

Pontac-Monplaisir Pe-Lé r (w) ★★ 00 02 04 05' 06 07 08 16-ha property nearly lost to BORDEAUX sprawl. Attractive white; supple, so-so red.

Pontet-Canet Pau r ★★★ 86' 88 89' 90 94' 95 96' 98 99 00' 01 02' 03 04' 05' 06 07 08 09 81-ha neighbour to MOUTON-ROTHSCHILD. One of the most-improved MÉDOC estates in last ten yrs. V. PAUILLAC in style. Only entirely biodynamic classed growth; horse ploughing. Second wine: Les Hauts de Pontet-Canet.

Potensac Méd r ★★ 95 96 98 99 00' 01 02 03 04' 05' 07 08 09 Well-known 70-ha property of northern MÉDOC. Delon family of LÉOVILLE-LAS-CASES; class shows. Firm, vigorous wines for long ageing. Second wine: Chapelle de Potensac.

Pouget Mar r ★★ 89 90 94 95 96 98' 00' 02 03 04 05' 06 07 08 Obscure 11-ha Fourth Growth attached to BOYD-CANTENAC. MARGAUX style. New *chai* in 2000.

Poujeaux Moulis r ★★ 89' 90' 94' 95' 96' 98 99 00' 01 03 04 05 06 08 09 Purchased by CLOS FOURTET owner in 2007; 68 ha. With CHASSE-SPLEEN and MAUCAILLOU the high point of MOULIS. DERENONCOURT consults. Full, robust wines that age. Second label: La Salle de Poujeaux.

Premier Grand Cru Classé See ST-EMILION classification box (p.102) .

Prieuré-Lichine Cantenac-Mar r ★★★ 89' 90' 94' 95 96 98' 99 00' 01 02 03 04 05 06 07 08 09 A 70-ha Fourth Growth brought to the fore by the late Alexis Lichine. Vy'ds v. dispersed. Advised by STÉPHANE DERENONCOURT (see CANON LA GAFFELIÈRE, PAVIE-MACQUIN). Fragrant MARGAUX currently on gd form. Second wine: CH de Clairefont. A gd white Bordeaux, too.

Puygueraud Côtes de Francs r ★★ 95' 96 98 99 00 01' 02 03 ' 05' 06 Leading CH of this tiny AC. Wood-aged wines of surprising class. CHX Laclaverie and Les Charmes-Godard follow the same lines. Special Cuvée George from 2000 with Malbec in blend. Same winemaker as PAVIE-MACQUIN.

Rabaud-Promis Saut w sw ★★→★★★ 88' 89' 90 95 96 97' 98 99 01' 02 03' 05' 06 07 09 A 30-ha classed growth at Bommes. Discreet but generally v. gd.

Rahoul Graves r w ★★ (r) 95 96 98' 00' 01 02 04 05 08 40-ha v'yd at Portets; Supple, Sém-dominated white (00 01 02 04' 05 07 08); red could be better.

Ramage-la-Batisse H-Méd r ★★ 9 98 99 00' 02 03 04 05' 07 Consistent and widely distributed HAUT-MÉDOC; 65 ha at St-Sauveur, north of PAUILLAC. Second wine: CH Tourteran.

Rauzan-Gassies Mar r ★★ 90' 95 96' 98 99 00 01' 02 03 04 05' 07 08 The 30-ha Second Growth neighbour of RAUZAN-SÉGLA that has long lagged behind it. New generation making strides since 2000 but still has a long way to go.

Rauzan-Ségla Mar r ★★★★ 86' 88' 89' 90' 94' 95 96 98 99 00' 01 02 03 04' 05 07 08 09 A Second Growth (62 ha) long famous for its fragrance; owned by owners of Chanel (see CANON). A great MARGAUX name right at the top, with rebuilt CH and *chais*. Second wine: Ségla.

Raymond-Lafon Saut w sw ★★★ 85 86' 88 89' 90' 95 96' 97 98 99' 01' 02 03' 04 05 06 07 09 SAUTERNES estate (18 ha) acquired by YQUEM ex-manager and now run by his children. Rich, complex wines that age. Classed-growth quality.

Rayne Vigneau Saut w sw ★★★88' 89 90' 95 96 97 98 99 01' 02 03 05' 07 09 Large 80-ha classed growth at Bommes. Gd but less power and intensity than the top growths. Sweet wine and Rayne *sec*.

Respide Médeville Graves r w ★★ (r) 99 00' 01 02 04 05' 06 07 (w) 96' 99 00 01 02 04' 05' 07 08 One of better unclassified properties for both red and white. Same owner as GILETTE. Drink reds at 4–6 yrs; longer for the better vintages.

Reynon Premières Côtes r w ★★ 40 ha for fragrant white from Sauv Bl 0 03 04' 05' 06 07 08; also serious red (00 01 02 03 04' 05' 06 07), too. See also CLOS FLORIDÈNE. Second wine (red): CH Reynon-Peyrat. From 1996 v.gd CH Reynon Cadillac *liquoreux*, too.

Reysson Vertheuil, H-Méd r ★★ 96 00 02 03 04 05 06 08 Recently replanted 49-ha HAUT-MÉDOC estate; managed by négociant CVBG-Dourthe (see BELGRAVE, LA GARDE). Rich, modern style.

Ricaud Loupiac w sw (r dr) ★★ 96 97 99 01' 02 03' 05 07 Substantial grower of SAUTERNES-like age-worthy wine just across the river.

Rieussec Saut w sw ★★★★ 83' 85 86' 88' 89' 90' 95 96' 97' 98 99 01' 02 03' 04 05' 06 07 09 Worthy neighbour of YQUEM with 90 ha in Fargues, bought in 1985 by the (LAFITE) Rothschilds. Vinified in oak since 1996. Fabulously powerful, opulent wine. Also dry "R", now made in modern style – with less character. Second wine: Carmes de Rieussec.

Ripeau St-Em r ★★ 95 98 00' 01 04 05' 06 08 Lesser 16-ha GRAND CRU CLASSÉ on sandy soils nr CHEVAL BLANC. Lighter style. Better since 2000, but inconsistent.

Rivière, de la Fronsac r ★★ 96' 98' 99 00' 01 02 03 04 05' 06 08 09 The biggest and most impressive FRONSAC property, with a Wagnerian castle and cellars. 58 ha. Formerly big, tannic wines are now more refined. New owner in 2003, with consultant from LANGUEDOC, Claude Gros.

Rochemorin, de Pe-Lé r w ★★→★★★ (r) 95 96 98' 99 00' 01 02 04 05 06 08 (w) 00 01 02 03 04 05 06 07 08 An important restoration at Martillac by the Lurtons of LA LOUVIÈRE: 105 ha (three-quarters red) of maturing vines. New state-of-the-art winery in 2004. Fairly consistent quality and widely distributed.

Rol Valentin St-Em r ★★★ 96 98 99 00' 01' 02 03 04 05' 06 08 09 Originally garage-style and size, now 7.5 ha. Wines rich, modern but balanced.

Rouget Pom r ★★ 89' 90 95 96 98' 99 00' 01' 03 04 05' 06 07 08 09 Attractive old estate on the northern edge of POMEROL. 17 ha. New Burgundian owners. Investment. Now excellent; rich, unctuous wines. Gd value.

Royal St-Emilion Brand name of important, dynamic growers' co-op. See GALIUS.

St-André-Corbin St-Em r ★★ 98' 99 00' 01 03 04 05 A 22-ha estate in MONTAGNE- and ST-GEORGES-ST-EMILION. Supple, Merlot-dominated wine.

St-Georges St-Georges-St-Em r ★★ 89' 90' 95' 96 98' 00' 01 03 04 05' Noble

18th-century CH overlooking the ST-EMILION plateau from the hill to the north. 51 ha (25% of St-Georges AC). Gd wine sold direct to the public.

St-Pierre St-Jul r ★★★ 82' 85 89 90' 94 95' 96' 98 99 00' 01' 02 03 04 05' 06 07 08 09 Once-understated Fourth Growth (17 ha) owned by the president of BORDEAUX football club. Stylish and consistent classic ST-JULIEN. See GLORIA.

Sales, de Pom r ★★ 89' 90' 95 96 98' 00' 01' 04 05 06 08 Biggest v'yd of POMEROL (47 ha) on sandy/gravel soils, attached to grandest CH. Lightish wine; never quite poetry. Try top vintages. Second label: CH Chantalouette.

Sansonnet St-Em r ★★ 00' 01 02 03 04 05' 06 08 09 A small 6.8-ha estate ambitiously run in the new ST-EMILION style (rich, fat). DERENONCOURT consulting from 2006, and wines now a little more elegant.

Saransot-Dupré Listrac r (w) ★★ 90 95 96 98' 99 00' 01 02 03 04 05 06 Small 17-ha property with firm, fleshy wines. Lots of Merlot. Also one of LISTRAC's little band of whites (60% Sem).

Sénéjac H-Méd r (w) ★★ 96 98 99 00 01 02 03 04 05' 06 08 37-ha in southern MÉDOC owned since 1999 by the same family as TALBOT. Well-balanced wines. On form in recent yrs. Gd value. Special CUVÉE: Karolus.

Serre, la St-Em r ★★ 90 94 95 96 98' 99 00' 01 02 03 04 05 06 08 09 Small (6.5-ha) GRAND CRU CLASSÉ, on the limestone plateau. Pleasant, stylish wines; more flesh and purity of fruit since 2000.

Sigalas-Rabaud Saut w sw ★★★ 83 85 86 88 89' 90' 95' 96' 97' 98 99 01' 02 03' 04 05' 07 09 The smaller part of the former RABAUD estate: 14 ha in Bommes; same winemaking team as LAFAURIE-PEYRAGUEY. V. fragrant and lovely. Top-ranking now. Second label: Le Lieutenant de Sigalas.

Siran Labarde-Mar r ★★→★★★ 89' 90' 95 96 98 99 00' 01 02 03 04 05 06 07 08 09 A 40-ha property of passionate owner who resents lack of *classé* rank. Neighbour of DAUZAC. The wines age well and have masses of flavour.

Smith-Haut-Lafitte Pe-Lé r (w p) ★★★ (r) 90' 94 95 96 98 99 00' 01 02 03 04' 05' 06 07 08 09 (w) 96 97 98 99' 00 01 02 03 04 05 06 07 08 09 Classed growth at Martillac: 67 ha. Regularly one of the stars of PESSAC-LÉOGNAN. Former ski-champion owners have vastly improved quality. Luxurious spa-hotel-restaurant also. White is full, ripe, sappy; red generous, with GRAVES minerality. Second label: Les Hauts de Smith. Also CH Cantelys, PESSAC-LÉOGNAN.

Sociando-Mallet H-Méd r ★★★ 88' 89' 90' 94 95 96' 98' 99 00' 01' 02 03 04 05' 06 07 09 Splendid, widely followed estate at St-Seurin. Independently minded owner celebrated 40 vintages in 2009. Classed-growth quality; 85 ha. Conservative, big-boned wines to lay down for yrs. Second wine: Demoiselle de Sociando.

Soudars H-Méd r ★★ 94 95 96' 98 99 00' 01 03 04 05 06 Sister to COUFRAN and VERDIGNAN; 22 ha. Relatively traditional and regular quality.

Soutard St-Em r ★★★89' 90' 94 95 96 98' 99 00' 01 03 04 05 06 Potentially excellent 22-ha classed growth on the limestone plateau. Now owned by same insurance group as LARMANDE (2006). Plenty of investment. Finer style since 2007. Second label: Jardins du Soutard .

Suduiraut Saut w sw ★★★★ 81 82' 83 85 86 88' 89' 90' 95 96 97' 98 99' 01' 02 03' 04 05' 06 07 09 One of the best classed-growth SAUTERNES: 90 ha with renovated CH and gardens by Le Nôtre. Owner AXA Insurancehas achieved greater consistency and luscious quality. See PICHON-LONGUEVILLE. Second wine: Castelnau de Suduiraut. New dry wine, S, v. promising.

Tailhas, du Pom r ★★ 90 94 95 96' 98' 99 00 01 04 05 Modest 10-ha property near FIGEAC. POMEROL of the lighter kind. Average quality.

Taillefer Pom r ★★ 89 90 94 95' 96 98' 00' 01 02 03 04 05' 08 11-ha v'yd on the edge of POMEROL. Astutely managed by Catherine Moueix. Less power than top estates but gently harmonious. Gd value.

Talbot St-Jul r (w) ★★★ 88' 89' 90 94 95 96' 98' 99 00' 01 02 03 04 05' 08' 09

Important 102-ha Fourth Growth, for many yrs younger sister to GRUAUD-LAROSE. Wine similarly attractive: rich, *consummately charming*, *reliable* (though wobbly in 2006–07). Second label: Connétable de Talbot. White: Caillou Blanc drinks well young. SÉNÉJAC in same family ownership.

Tertre, du Arsac-Mar r ★★★ 89' 90' 94 95 96' 98' 99 00' 01 03 04' 05' 06 07 08 09 Fifth Growth (50 ha) isolated south of MARGAUX. History of undervalued fragrant (20% Cab Fr) and fruity wines. Since 1997, same owner as CH GISCOURS. New techniques and massive investment have produced a concentrated, structured wine, really humming from 2003.

Tertre Daugay St-Em r ★★ 95 96 98 99 00' 01 04 05 06 07 16-ha hilltop v'yd. Sister to LA GAFFELIÈRE. Escaped declassification from GRAND CRU CLASSÉ in 2006. Improvement from 2000. DERENONCOURT consulting from 2004.

Tertre-Rôteboeuf St-Em r ★★★★ 86 88' 89' 90' 93 94 95 96 97 98' 99 00' 01 02 03' 04 05' 06 07 08 09 A cult star (6 ha) making concentrated, dramatic, largely Merlot wine since 1983. Frightening prices. Also CÔTES DE BOURG property, Roc de Cambes of ST-EMILION classed-growth quality.

Thieuley E-2-M r p w ★★ Supplier of consistent quality red and white AC BORDEAUX; fruity CLAIRET; oak-aged red and white CUVÉES Francis Courselle. Also owns Clos Ste-Anne in PREMIÈRES CÔTES DE BORDEAUX.

Tour-Blanche, la Saut w sw (r) ★★★ 83' 85 86 88' 89' 90' 95 96 97' 98 99 01' 02 03 04 05' 06 07 Leading SAUTERNES classed growth. Back on form from 1988. Sauv Bl and Muscadelle 20% of blend. Rich and powerful. Second wine Les Charmilles de Tour-Blanche.

Tour-de-By, la Bégadan, Méd r ★★ 95 96' 98 00 01 02 03 04 05' 06 08. V. well-run 74-ha family estate in northern MÉDOC with a name for sturdy but reliable wines with a fruity note. Usually gd value.

Tour-Carnet, la St-Laurent, H-Méd r ★★ 89' 90 94' 95 96 98 99 00' 01 02 03 04' 05' 06 08 09 Fourth Growth (65 ha) with medieval moated fortress, long neglected. New ownership (see FOMBRAUGE, PAPE-CLÉMENT) and investment from 2000 have produced richer wines in more modern style. Second wine: Les Douves de Ch La Tour Carnet. Also *garage* Servitude Volontaire du Tour Carnet.

Tour Figeac, la St-Em r ★★ 89' 90' 94' 95 96' 98' 99 00' 01' 02 04 05 06 07 08 09 A 15-ha GRAND CRU CLASSÉ between FIGEAC and POMEROL. Biodynamic methods. Full, fleshy and harmonious.

Tour Haut-Brion, la Graves r ★★★ 89 90 94 95 96' 98' 99 00' 01 02 03 04' 05' RIP from 2005 for this classed growth. The 5.05-ha v'yd has now been integrated into that of LA MISSION-HAUT-BRION. Same owner.

Tour Haut-Caussan Méd r ★★ 00' 01 02 03 04 05' 06 Well-run property at Blaignan. Reliable. Gd value.

Tour-du-Haut-Moulin Cussac, H-Méd r ★★ 89' 90' 94 95 96 98 00' 02 03 04 05' 06 32-ha estate; intense, consistent, no-nonsense wines to mature.

Tour de Mons, la Soussans-Mar r ★★ 89 90' 94 95 96' 98' 99 00 01 0204 05' 06 Famous MARGAUX *cru* of 44 ha, in the same family for three centuries. A long dull patch but recent improvement. Still could do better.

Tournefeuille Lalande de Pom r ★★ 99 00' 01' 02 03 04 05 06 07 08 Well-known Néac CH. 17 ha. Reliable since 1998.

Tour-du-Pas-St-Georges St-Em r ★★ 96 98 99 00' 01 03 04 05 06 Wine from 16 ha of ST-GEORGES-ST-EMILION owned by Pascal Delbeck. Recent investment.

Tour du Pin, la St-Em r ★★ 95 96 98 00' 01 04 05 06 08 09 8 ha, formerly La Tour du Pin Figeac-Moueix but bought and renamed by CHEVAL BLANC in 2006. Unimpressive form previously, but new team turning things around. To watch.

Tour-St-Bonnet Méd r ★★ 95 96 98 99 00' 02 03 04 05 06 08 Consistently well-made potent northern MÉDOC from St-Christoly; 40 ha.

Tronquoy-Lalande St-Est r ★★ 95 96 98 99 00' 02 03 04 05 06 07 08 Same owners as MONTROSE from 2006. Lots of Merlot and Petit Verdot; 19 ha. High-coloured wines to age. Second wine: Tronquoy de Ste-Anne.

Troplong-Mondot St-Em r ★★★ 88' 89' 90' 94' 95 96' 98' 99 00' 01' 02 03 04 05' 06 07 08 09 PREMIER GRAND CRU CLASSÉ from 2006. Well-sited 22 ha on a high point of limestone plateau. *Wines of power and depth with increasing elegance.* MICHEL ROLLAND consults. Second wine: Mondot.

Trotanoy Pom r ★★★★ 85' 88 89' 90' 93 94 95 96 98' 99 00' 01 02 03 04' 05' 06 07 08 09 A JEAN-FRANÇOIS MOUEIX property since 1953. Only 7 ha; at best a glorious, fleshy, structured, perfumed wine. Wobbled a bit in the 1980s, but back on top form since 1989. Can occasionally rival PETRUS.

Trottevieille St-Em r ★★★ 89' 90 94 95 96 98 99 00' 01 02 03' 04 05' 06 07 08 09 First Growth on the limestone plateau. Dragged its feet for yrs. Same owners as BATAILLEY and DOMAINE DE L'EGLISE have raised its game since 2000. Denis Dubourdieu consults. Limited bottling of old, ungrafted Cab Fr.

Valandraud St-Em r ★★★★ 93 94 95' 96 98 99 00' 01' 02 03 04 05' 06 07 08 09 Leader among *garagiste* micro-wines fulfilling aspirations to glory. Originally super-concentrated; since 1998 greater complexity. Now a selection from 10 ha; on average 1,500 bottles. Virginie de Valndraud another selection. White Blanc de Valandraud from 2003.

Verdignan Méd r ★★ 98 99 00' 01 02 03 04 05 06 08 Substantial 60-ha HAUT-MÉDOC estate; sister to COUFRAN and SOUDARS. More Cab Sauv than COUFRAN. Gd value and ageing potential.

Vieille Cure, la Fronsac r ★★ 98 99 00' 01' 02 03 04 05 06 08 09 A 20-ha property, US-owned, leading the commune. Accessible from 4 yrs. Reliable value.

Vieux-Ch-Certan Pom r ★★★★ 82' 83' 85 86' 88' 89 90' 94 95' 96'98' 99 00' 01 02 04' 05' 06 07 08 09 Traditionally rated close to PETRUS in quality, but totally different in style (30% Cab Fr and 10% Cab Sauv); authentic with plenty of finesse. 14 ha.

Vieux Ch St-André St-Em r ★★ 00' 01 02 03 04 05 06 Small 6-ha v'yd i MONTAGNE-ST-EMILION owned by former winemaker of PÉTRUS. Regular qualit

Villegeorge Avensan, H-Méd r ★★ 95 96' 98' 99 00' 02 03 04 05 06 A 2 HAUT-MÉDOC north of MARGAUX. Sound, traditional MÉDOC style. Siste Duplessis in MOULIS and La Tour de Bessan in MARGAUX.

Vray Croix de Gay Pom r ★★ 88 89 90 95 96 98' 00' 04 05 06 08 09 (4 ha); in the best part of POMEROL. Improvements since 2005, but s in progress. Sister to CH Siaurac in LALANDE DE POMEROL. DERENONCOU

Yon-Figeac St-Em r ★★ 95 96 98 99 00' 02 03 04 05 06 24-ha restructured between 1985 and 1995. Avoided relegation fro CLASSÉ in 2006. Reasonably sound now but unexciting.

d'Yquem Saut w sw (dr) ★★★★ 76' 79 80' 81' 83' 85 86' 88' 89' 97' 98 99' 00 01' 02 03' 04 05' 06 The world's most famou 101 ha; 10,000 cases of v. strong, intense, luscious wine, kep intages improve for 15+ yrs; some live 100+ yrs in tra er centuries in the Lur-Saluces family, in 1999 cont ard Arnault of LVMH. The new management (s rd-thinking, and pushing prices sky-high unced "ygrec").

Italy

More heavily shaded areas are the
wine-growing regions

The following abbreviations
are used in the text:

Ab	Abruzzo	Sar	Sardinia
Ap	Apulia	Si	Sicily
Bas	Basilicata	T-AA	Trentino-
Cal	Calabria		Alto Adige
Cam	Campania	Tus	Tuscany
E-R	Emilia-Romagna	Umb	Umbria
F-VG	Friuli-Venezia	VdA	Valle d'Aosta
	Giulia	Ven	Veneto
Lat	Latium		
Lig	Liguria		
Lom	Lombardy	cs	*cantine sociale*
Mar	Marches	fz	*frizzante*
Pie	Piedmont	pa	*passito*

If the world came to an end, life in Italy would probably go on very much as before. A year ago there were two issues that could have had profound effects on the Italian wine scene: one was the scandal that enveloped one of Italy's most prestigious wines, Brunello di Montalcino: some growers had been accused of using grapes other than Sangiovese in their Brunello. It was dramatic. Wineries and their wines were sequestrated: big scandal. Two years on and all is calm: this is Italy. The other issue was the imposition by the EU on all member states of a new quality designation called (in Italy) *Denominazione di Origine Protetta* or DOP, and its corollary *Indicazione Geografica Protetta* (IGP), which were to take over from DOC/DOCG and IGT. Producers like those of Rufina, whose name would disappear into plain Chianti under the regulations, were prepared to go to the barricades to protect their heritage. No need. The magic date for changeover came and went, and everyone just carried on as before: DOC(G) and IGT remain the official, if now alternative, quality designations.

Italians may have escaped the potential rigours of the law, but, like everyone else, they have been struck by the world financial crisis. Even this could mean good news for consumers, however, who should be seeing some very attractive prices over the coming year or so.

Recent vintages

...days' rain in mid-September was not enough to cancel... of a hot, dry, late summer and autumn following a w... es, red and white, were healthy when picked, with... sugar levels. Quantity was average, quality very

8 A very wet spring was followed by a very dry summer, punctuated by rare and occasionally violent rain and hailstorms. Heat and drought brought mixed results with points of excellence; not necessarily for long keeping.

A rainy May followed a mild, dry winter and summery April. Summer itself as very hot and arid. Late August rains came to the rescue. Ideal vintage conditions made for a smaller-than-average but high-quality crop.

ear of balance, no temperature extremes, measured rainfall. Cool August generally good weather at vintage. Probably greatest of last 20 vintages.

successful along the coast and for those who picked early. Sangiovese quality level imaginable, from first-rate to diluted.

2004 Exceptionally promising along the coast, in Montepulciano, and in Montalcino, where five-star rating is debatable. Despite cool temperatures some elegant wines throughout.

2003 High sugar content meant uppish alcohol with green tannins for early picked grapes, or low-acid jamminess for later picked.

2001 Rightly considered as a great year for laying down top wines.

Older fine vintages: 99 97 95 90

Piedmont

2009 Quantity up, quality good to very good, especially for Nebbiolo, picked in ideal conditions during the first half of October. The ideal result? Yes, except there is already too much good wine sloshing around in the system. Expect prices to slide.

2008 As in Tuscany, a wet spring led to a dry hot summer, but not as hot as 2003. Some great Barberas; Nebbiolos perhaps too early to judge.

2007 Very short but good to excellent quality for Barolo, Barbaresco and Barbera. Fears of unbalanced wines proved unfounded, and some classic wines are beginning to work their way through.

2006 Excellent Nebbiolo and Barbera. Could yet prove to be vintage of the decade.

2005 Uneven for Barbera, with some rot from persistent rains, and for Nebbiolo, with some good wines difficult to sell in current market.

2004 Very long growing season, high level of quality for all major red grapes (Dolcetto, Barbera, Nebbiolo). Classic year for Barbaresco and Barolo.

2001 Classy and firm Nebbiolo and Barbera, developing into another classic.

Older fine vintages: 00 99 98 97 96 95 90 89 88

Amarone, Veneto & Friuli

2009 Valpolicella produced ten per cent less than normal, but fruit quality was superb and sugar levels high. Ideal drying conditions for *passito* should yield some classic wines. Good results, too, for Prosecco, Pinot Gr and other whites in the east.

2008 A textbook year in terms of temperature and rainfall leading to a vintage carried out under ideal conditions. Quantity a bit short, but classic wines of high quality.

2007 High hopes were dashed for some by vicious hailstorms at the end of August. Those not wiped out made some excellent wines, but very short crop, with steeply rising prices.

2006 Outstanding, with new record established for the grape tonnage reserved for drying, 30 per cent higher than any previous vintage.

2005 A difficult, damp harvest, but grape-drying technology saved Amarone and Recioto. Less successful for Soave and whites.

2004 Classic, less concentrated and rich than 2003.

2003 Very concentrated and sugar-rich grapes; some outstanding Amarone and Recioto wines.

2001 Classic for some, others preferred 2000.

Marches & Abruzzo

2009 A cool, wet spring caused mould , but a hot, dry summer compensated. Quantity down ten to 15 per cent for Verdicchio and Montepulciano, bu to very good, especially for whites.

2008 East of the Apennines conditions were rainier and cooler than in the and west, with a perfect end of the season. Some excellent wines.

2007 Spectacularly low crop due to heat and water shortage, leading to s dramatic price rises. But some top-quality reds.

2006 Irregular. Generally positive where hail did not fall; better than 2004 and 2005, but not as good as 2003.

2005 Wines of good ripeness and structure for those who waited to pick.

2004 Irregular. Better in Rosso Conero than Rosso Piceno in the Marches; best in Colline Teramane DOCG, Abruzzo.

2003 One of the best areas, as the Montepulciano grape stood up to the heat and drought, giving first-rate results.

Campania & Basilicata

2009 A wet winter was followed by a reasonably dry summer with temperature fluctuations resulting in healthy grapes of good sugar levels and aromatic character (whites), and with plenty of substance and concentration (reds).

2008 The south did not suffer the prolonged rains, nor the accompanying moulds, which prevailed in spring/summer in the north and centre. A dry and long summer. A classic year for Aglianico; good, too, for whites.

2007 Very low yields due to heat/drought aggravated by mildew devastation. Good quality for those who sprayed and waited for balanced grapes.

2006 Rain and problems of rot in lower-lying zones, much sun and a very long growing season in higher vineyards, with predictably superior results.

2005 Traditionally the last grapes to be picked, Aglianico had weight, complexity and character – perhaps the finest wines of all Italy in 2005.

2004 Slow and uncertain ripening for Aglianico; has exceeded expectations.

2003 Scorching and drought-stressed growing conditions, but the altitude of the vineyards worked in late-picked Aglianico's favour. Generally a success.

2001 Intense, perfumed and age-worthy wines.

Aglianico del Vulture Bas DOC r dr ★★★ oo oı' 04 05' 06 07 (08) (09) *vecchio* (old) after 3 yrs, RISERVA after 5 yrs. 100% from southern Italy's best black grape, often ripening at altitude into Nov. Top: Alovini, d'Angelo, Basilisco, Cantina del Notaio, Elena Fucci, Di Palma, PATERNOSTER, Le Querce, Tenuta del Portale, Terre degli Svevi.

Alba Major wine city of PIEDMONT, southeast of Turin, famous for truffles and chocolates, and home to PIEDMONT'S, if not Italy's, most prestigious wines: BAROLO, BARBARESCO, NEBBIOLO D'ALBA, ROERO, BARBERA D'ALBA and Dolcetto d'Alba.

Albana di Romagna E-R DOCG w dr sw s/sw (sp) ★ →★★★ DYA Italy's first white DOCG, justifiably for the sweet PASSITO version, not for the undistinguished dry styles. ZERBINA, *Fattoria Paradiso* and Giovanna Madonia make excellent versions.

Aleatico Red Muscat-flavoured grape for sweet, aromatic, often fortified wines of PUGLIA (Candido, Feudi di San Marzano), and ELBA (Acquabona). Limited amounts in TUSCANY'S Suvereto (Bulichella, Gualdo del Re, Casa Dei) and in LATIUM (Villa Caviciana, Occhipinti).

essandria, Gianfranco ★★★ Small producer of barriqued ALBA wines at Monforte d'Alba, esp Barolo San Giovanni, Barbera d'Alba Vittoria.

o See SALENTO

ini Ven ★★★ Top-quality Veronese producer; outstanding single-v'yd IGT es (La Grola, La Poja), AMARONE and RECIOTO. Also joint owner of Poggio al o in BOLGHERI and, since 2009, Poggio San Polo in MONTALCINO (TUSCANY).

o Pie ★★★ Pioneering producer of short-maceration BAROLO. Look for Arborina, Barolo Brunate, LANGHE DOC Arborina (NEBBIOLO), Larigi , La Villa, VDT L'Insieme and DOLCETTO D'ALBA.

AA DOC r p w dr sw sp ★ →★★★ Alto Adige or SÜDTIROL DOC with types of earthy reds and minerally whites of alpine freshness. Subns include VALLE ISARCO/Eisacktal, TERLANO/Terlaner, Val Venosta/

Vinschgau, ALTO ADIGE SANTA MADDALENA/ST-MAGDALENER, Bozner Leiten, Meranese di Collina/Meraner.

Ama, Castello di ★★★ One of the best and most consistent modern CHIANTI CLASSICO estates, near Gaiole. La Casuccia and Bellavista are top single-v'yd wines. Gd IGTS, CHARD and MERLOT (L'Apparita).

Amabile Semi-sweet.

Amaro Bitter. Suffix "–one" means "big", so Amarone means "big bitter".

Amarone della Valpolicella (formerly Recioto della Valpolicella Amarone) Ven DOC r ★★→★★★★ 90' 95 97 98 00 01 03' 06' 07 (08) (09) Relatively dry version of RECIOTO DELLA VALIPOLICELLA from air-dried VALPOLICELLA grapes; concentrated, fairly long-lived. (For producers see box, p.137) Older vintages are hard to come by but tend to dry out beyond 20 yrs. DOCG in the pipeline.

Anselmi, Roberto ★★★ Producer at Monteforte in SOAVE who, some yrs ago, abandoned the DOC rather than accept absurd new rules. Now sells wines under IGT brand names like Capitel Croce and Capitel Foscarino (dry) and I Capitelli PASSITO (sweet).

Antinori, Marchesi L & P ★★→★★★★ V. influential Florentine house of highest repute, owned by Piero A, now increasingly leaving management to his three daughters and oenologist Renzo Cotarella. Famous for CHIANTI CLASSICO (*Tenute Marchese Antinori* and Badia a Passignano), Umbrian (CASTELLO DELLA SALA), and PIEDMONT (PRUNOTTO) wines, but esp SUPER-TUSCANS TIGNANELLO and SOLAIA. Also estates in south Tuscan MAREMMA (Fattoria Aldobrandesca), MONTEPULCIANO (La Braccesca), MONTALCINO (Pian delle Vigne), in ASTI (for BARBERA), in FRANCIACORTA for sparkling (*Montenisa*) and in APULIA (Vigneti del Sud). V.gd DOC BOLGHERI Guado al Tasso.

Apulia Puglia. Italy's heel, historically a bulk producer, increasing in quality and value. Best DOC: BRINDISI, CASTEL DEL MONTE, MANDURIA (PRIMITIVO DI), SALICE SALENTINO. Producers: ANTINORI, Botromagno, Candido, Cantele, Cantine Paradiso, Castel di Selva, Co-op Due Palme, Conti Zecca, Coppadoro, La Corte, Li Veli, D'Alfonso del Sordo, MASSERIA MONACI, Michele Calò, RACEMI, RIVERA, Rubino, Rosa del Golfo, TAURINO, Valle dell'Asso, VALLONE.

Argiano Avant-garde BRUNELLO estate where Hans Vinding-Diers also makes controversial blend Solengo and smooth 100%-SANGIOVESE Suolo.

Argiano, Castello di, aka *Sesti* Astronomer Giuseppe Maria Sesti turns out classy biodynamic BRUNELLO and Bordeaux-influenced *Terra di Siena*.

Argiolas, Antonio ★★→★★★ Sardinian producer. High-level CANNONAU, NURAGUS, VERMENTINO, Bovale. Red IGTS Turriga (★★★) and Korem are among the best.

Arneis Pie w ★★→★★★ DYA Fine peachy/appley white from around ALBA, revived from near extinction in 1970s by GIACOSA and VIETTI. Fragrant, fruity, intense. ROERO Arneis DOCG, northwest of ALBA, is normally better than LANGHE Arneis DOC. Try: Correggia, BRUNO GIACOSA, Malvirà, Angelo Negro, PRUNOTTO, Sorilaria, VIETTI.

Asti Pie DOCG w sw sp ★→★★★ NV Piedmontese sparkler, known in past as Asti Spumante, from the Muscat grape. Producers are usually more interested in low prices than high quality, making DOCG status questionable. See also MOSCA D'ASTI, BARBERA D'ASTI. The rare top producers include BERA, CASCINA FO] CONTRATTO, Dogliotti-Caudrina, Vignaioli di Santo Stefano.

Avignonesi ★★★ Noble MONTEPULCIANO house, best known for long-aged VIN and OCCHIO DI PERNICE (★★★★), also for VINO NOBILE from high-density trained v'yds planted to the ancient *settonce* system. RISERVA Grandi A top red.

Azienda agricola/agraria An estate (large or small) making wine from ov

Azienda/casa vinicola A négociant making wine from bought-in and ov

Badia a Coltibuono ★★→★★★ Historic CHIANTI CLASSICO producer r Prinetti family. Top wine is 100% BARRIQUE-aged SANGIOVESE "San

The best Barbaresco to seek out
Cantina del Pino, Castello di Neive, Cascina Luisin, CERETTO, Cigliuti, Cortese, GAJA, Fratelli Giacosa, BRUNO GIACOSA, GRESY, Lano, Moccagatta, Montaribaldi, Ada Nada, Fiorenzo Nada, Paitin, Giorgio Pelissero, PIO CESARE, PRODUTTORI DEL BARBARESCO, PRUNOTTO, Punset, Ressia, Francesco Rinaldi, Massimo Rivetti, Rizzi, Roagna, Albino Rocca, BRUNO ROCCA, GIORGIO RIVETTI, Varaldo.

Banfi (Castello or Villa) ★★→★★★ MONTALCINO CANTINA of biggest US importer of Italian wine. Huge plantings at Montalcino, inc in-house-developed clones of SANGIOVESE; also CAB SAUV, MERLOT, SYRAH, PINOT N, CHARD, SAUV BL, PINOT GR. Poggio all'Oro and *Poggio alle Mura* are ★★★ BRUNELLOS. Summus and Excelsus are top SANT'ANTIMO reds. In PIEDMONT, also gd Banfi Brut, BRACCHETO D'ACQUI, GAVI, PINOT GR.

Barbaresco Pie DOCG r ★★→★★★★ 88 89' 90' 95 96' 97 98 99' 00 01 04 06 07 (08) (09) Classic Italian red, 100% NEBBIOLO. Like its neighbour BAROLO, combines depth of complex flavour with bright, clean tannins. Minimum 2 yrs ageing, 1 in wood; at 4 yrs becomes RISERVA.

Barbatella, Cascina La ★★★ Top producer of BARBERA D'ASTI: excellent Vigna dell'Angelo and MONFERRATO Rosso Sonvico (BARBERA/CAB SAUV).

Barbera Prolific red variety, dominant in PIEDMONT, also varietally in Lombardy and COLLI PIACENTINI and (for blends) throughout Italy, indeed the world. High acidity, low tannin and distinctive cherry fruit are defining characteristics. Capable of diverse wine-styles from BARRIQUED and serious to semi-sweet and frothy.

Barbera d'Alba Pie DOC r ★★→★★★ 01 03 04 05 06 07 08 (09) Potentially acidic red here generally smoothed by BARRIQUE ageing, but all too often playing second fiddle to NEBBIOLO. Best age up to 7 yrs. Some excellent wines, often from producers of BAROLO, BARBARESCO and ROERO.

Barbera d'Asti Pie DOC r ★★→★★★ 04 05 06 07 08 (09) The real thing, some say, from lands where BARBERA comes first. Two styles: fresh, fruity and somewhat sharp, or rounded by wood ageing.

Barbera del Monferrato Pie DOC r ★→★★ DYA Easy-drinking BARBERA from ALESSANDRIA and ASTI. Can be slightly fizzy, sometimes sweetish. Delimited area is almost identical to BARBERA D'ASTI but style simpler. Good producers include Accorneo, Valpane, Vicara.

Barco Reale Tus DOC r ★★ 05 06 07 08 (09) DOC for junior wine of CARMIGNANO.

Bardolino Ven DOC r (p) ★→★★ DYA Pale, summery, slightly bitter red from Lake Garda. Bardolino CHIARETTO: effectively rosé. Best include Buglioni, Cavalchina, Guerrieri Rizzardi, Le Fraghe, Montresor, Pantini, ZENATO, Zeni.

Barolo Pie DOCG r ★★★→★★★★ 88' 89' 90' 95 96' 97' 98' 99' 00 01' 04' 05 06' 07' (08) (09') By general consensus Italy's greatest red. 100% NEBBIOLO, named for one of eight villages southwest of ALBA. Must be aged 3 yrs before release (5 for RISERVA), 2 in wood. Ages well, developing floral (rose) and mineral (tar) notes. Mistakenly thought to be a blockbuster; finest are subtle, elegant. See boxes for top producers, divided between traditionalists (long maceration, large oak barrels) and modernists (abbreviated maceration, tendency towards ageing in BARRIQUE).

Barolo Chinato A dessert wine made from BAROLO DOCG, alcohol, sugar, herbs, spices and Peruvian bark. Producers: Cappellano, CERETTO, Giulio Cocchi.

rrique This 225-litre French oak container has been the major weapon of the internationalists in Italy and the *bête noire* of the traditionalists, who reject its moky, vanilla tones in favour of the neutrality of the Slavonian oak BOTTE.

ano ★★ Producer of gd DOCG CHIANTI RUFINA and IGT wines.

> **The best of Barbera d'Asti**
> Bava, BERA, BERSANO, Bertelli, Alfiero Boffa, BRAIDA, Cascina Castlèt,
> CHIARLO, CONTRATTO, COPPO, cs Nizza, cs Vinchio e Vaglio, Dezzani, Hastae,
> La Barbatella, La Morandina, La Tenaglia, Marchesi Alfieri, Marengo,
> Beppe Marino, Martinetti, Elio Perrone, PRUNOTTO, GIORGIO RIVETTI, BRUNO
> ROCCA, Scrimaglio, Scagliola, TERRE DA VINO and VIETTI.

Bellavista ★★★ FRANCIACORTA estate with expensive but convincing Champagne-style wines (Gran Cuvée Franciacorta is top). Also Satèn (a *crémant*-style sparkling). TERRE DI FRANCIACORTA DOC and Sebino IGT Solesine (both CAB SAUV/MERLOT blends). Owner Vittorio Moretti has expanded into Tuscan MAREMMA, VAL DI CORNIA (Petra) and MONTEREGIO.

Bera, Walter ★★→★★★ Small estate near BARBARESCO. V.gd MOSCATO D'ASTI, ASTI, BARBERA D'ASTI, BARBARESCO and LANGHE NEBBIOLO.

Berlucchi, Guido ★★ Italy's biggest producer of sparkling METODO CLASSICO.

Bersano Historic house in Nizza Monferrato, with Barbera d'Asti Generala, Barolo Badarina, most PIEDMONT DOC wines inc BARBARESCO, MOSCATO D'ASTI, ASTI SPUMANTE.

Bertani ★★→★★★ Well-known quality wines from Verona, esp traditional AMARONE and Valpolicella Valpantena Secco Bertani.

Bianco di Custoza Ven DOC w (sp) ★→★★ DYA Fresh white from Lake Garda, made from an eclectic mix of grapes inc SOAVE'S GARGANEGA and PIEDMONT'S CORTESE. Gd: Cavalchina, Le Tende, Le Vigne di San Pietro, Montresor, Zeni.

Bibi Graetz ★★ Fine reds from hills of Fiesole near Florence. Testamatta Rosso (SANGIOVESE and other Tuscan reds) and Bugia Bianco (Ansonica).

Biondi-Santi ★★★★ Octogenarian Franco Biondi-Santi continues at his Greppo estate to make BRUNELLO DI MONTALCINO in a highly traditional manner, as did his father, Tancredi, and his grandfather Ferruccio, aiming in best years at wines capable of lasting 100 yrs. The 2004 RISERVA Y (★★★★) might just do it.

Bisol Top brand of PROSECCO.

Boca Pie DOC r ★★ 99' 00 01' 03' 04' 06' 07 (08) (09') Obscure, NEBBIOLO-based red from northern PIEDMONT. Le Piane and Poderi ai Valloni (Vigneto Cristiana ★★) can be good if they can be found.

Boccadigabbia ★★★ Top Marche producer of IGT wines: SANGIOVESE (Saltapicchio), CAB SAUV (Akronte), PINOT N (Il Girone), CHARD (Montalperti). Proprietor also owns fine Villamagna estate in ROSSO PICENO DOC.

Boglietti, Enzo ★★★ Dynamic young producer of La Morra in BAROLO zone. Top modern-style BAROLOS (Arione, Case Nere) and outstanding Barbera d'Alba (Vigna dei Romani, Roscaleto).

Bolgheri Tus DOC r p w (sw) ★★→★★★★ Ultra-modish region on the Costa degli Etruschi, south of Livorno. Home of SASSICAIA (TENUTA SAN GUIDO), ORNELLAIA (FRESCOBALDI) and several wealthy bandwagonists. CAB SAUV/MERLOT/SYRAH/SANGIOVESE blends or varietals. Other top producers: CA' MARCANDA (GAJA), Caccia al Piano, Giorgio Meletti Cavallari, Campo alla Sughera, Campo al Mare, Casa di Terra, Collemassari/Grattamacco, Guado al Tasso (ANTINORI), LE MACCHIOLE, Poggio al Tesoro, MICHELE SATTA.

Bolla ★★ Historic Verona firm for SOAVE, VALPOLICELLA, AMARONE, RECIOTO. Today owned by powerful GRUPPO ITALIANO VINI.

Bonarda Lom DOC r ★★ 05 06 07 08 (09) Soft, fresh FRIZZANTE and still wines from OLTREPÒ PAVESE, actually made from Croatina grapes. Not to be confused with Piedmontese Bonarda.

Borgo del Tiglio ★★★→★★★★ FRIULI estate for one of northeast Italy's top MERLOT Rosso della Centa; also superior COLLIO CHARD, MALVASIA and Bianco.

Boscarelli, Poderi ★★★ Small estate with v.gd VINO NOBILE DI MONTEPULCIANO ﹖ barrel-aged IGT Boscarelli.

The Barolo roll of honour: the traditionalists
Anselma, Ascheri, Barale, Borgogno, Brezza, Brovia, BURLOTTO,
CAPPELLANO, Cavallotto, CIABOT BERTON, ALDO CONTERNO, GIACOMO CONTERNO,
Paolo Conterno, FONTANAFREDDA, BRUNO GIACOSA, Marcarini, BARTOLO
MASCARELLO, GIUSEPPE MASCARELLO, Massolino, Monchiero,
PIO CESARE (BAROLO), Poderi Colla, Francesco Rinaldi, Giuseppe Rinaldi,
Schiavenza, CASTELLO DI VERDUNO, VIETTI.

Botte Large barrel, anything from 6–250 hl, usually between 20–50, traditionally of Slavonian but increasingly of French oak. To traditionalists, the ideal vessel for wines in which an excess of oak aromas is undesirable.

Brachetto d'Acqui Pie DOCG r sw (sp) ★★ DYA Sweet, sparkling red with enticing Muscat scent. Elevated DOCG status is disputed by some.

Braida ★★★ The late Giacomo Bologna's estate; top BARBERA D'ASTI (Bricco dell'Uccellone, Bricco della Bigotta, Ai Suma).

Bramaterra Pie DOC r ★★ 99' 00 01' 03 04' 06' 07' (08) (09) Neighbour to GATTINARA. NEBBIOLO grapes predominate in a blend. Gd producer: Sella.

Breganze Ven DOC r w ★→★★★ (r) 99 01 02 03 04 06 07 (08) (09) Major production area for PINOT GRIGIO, also gd CAB. Top producer: MACULAN.

Brindisi Ap DOC r p ★★ 04 05 06 07 (08) (09) (r) DYA (p) Smooth NEGROAMARO-based red with MONTEPULCIANO, esp from VALLONE, Due Palme, Rubino. ROSATO can be one of Italy's best. See also ROSATO DEL SALENTO.

Brolio, Castello di ★★→★★★ Historic, once trend-setting estate now thriving in the hands, once again, of the RICASOLI family after a period of foreign-managed decline. V.gd CHIANTI CLASSICO and IGT Casalferro.

Brunelli, Gianni ★★★ Small-scale producer of elegant, refined BRUNELLO DI MONTALCINO. Owner of Siena's excellent restaurant, Le Logge. Not to be confused with others in MONTALCINO called BRUNELLI. Now run by Gianni's widow, Laura.

Brunello di Montalcino Tus DOCG r ★★★→★★★★ 85' 87 88 90' 93 95' 97' 99 00 01 03 04' (06') (07) (08), (09') With BAROLO, Italy's most celebrated red: strong, full-bodied, high-flavoured, tannic, long-lived. Four yrs' ageing; after 5 yrs RISERVA. After a rough patch (see BRUNELLOPOLI), more producers, land prices rocketing.

Brunellopoli BRUNELLO DI MONTALCINO is supposed to be 100% SANGIOVESE, but in 2008 a few high-profile producers were accused of including other grapes in the blend. The authorities have now withdrawn all accusations, and MONTALCINO holds its breath while the wine world forgets.

Burlotto, Commendatore G B ★★★ Fabio Alessandria turns out beautifully crafted and defined PIEDMONT varietals, esp Barolo Cannubi and Monvigliero, the latter's grapes being crushed by foot.

Bussola, Tommaso ★★★★ Leading producer of AMARONE and RECIOTO in VALPOLICELLA. Stunning Amarone Vigneto Alto and Recioto TB.

Caberlot Mellow, flavoury red from crossing of CAB FR and MERLOT claimed to be unique to the v'yds of Bettina Rogosky at her Il Carnasciale estate in the Arezzo hills of TUSCANY. Sold only in magnum.

Cabernet Franc Increasingly preferred to CAB SAUV by Italy's internationalists. Much of what was thought in northeast Italy to be CAB FR was actually Carmenère.

Cabernet Sauvignon Has played a key role in the renaissance of Italian red wine (eg. SASSICAIA). Particularly influential in TUSCANY as a lesser partner for SANGIOVESE. Now losing ground to indigenous blenders.

Ca' del Bosco ★★★★ Ground-breaking FRANCIACORTA estate now owned by giant PINOT producer SANTA MARGHERITA, but still run by founder Maurizio Zanella. Outstanding CLASSICO-method fizz, esp Annamaria Clementi (Italy's Dom Pérignon) and Dosage Zero; also excellent Bordeaux-style red Maurizio Zanella, Burgundy-style CHARD.

> **Best Brunello di Montalcino to buy**
> Pieri Agostina, Altesino, ARGIANO, BANFI, Baricci, BIONDI-SANTI, GIANNI
> BRUNELLI, Camigliano, La Campana, Campogiovanni, Canalicchio di
> Sopra, Caparzo, CASANOVA DI NERI, Casanuova delle Cerbaie, Casato Prime
> Donne, CASE BASSE, CASTELGIOCONDO, Cerbaiona, Il Colle, Corte Pavone,
> Costanti, EREDI FULIGNI, La Fuga, La Gerla, Lambardi, LISINI, La Magia, La
> Mannella, Le Potazzine, Marroneto, Oliveto, SIRO PACENTI, Palazzo,
> Pertimali, Ciacci Piccolomini, Pieve di Santa Restituta, La Poderina,
> POGGIO ANTICO, POGGIONE, Salvioni-Cerbaiola, Sesti, Uccelliera, Val di
> Suga, Valdicava.

Ca' dei Frati ★★★ The best producer of DOC LUGANA, also v.gd dry white blend IGT
Pratto, sweet Tre Filer and red IGT Ronchedone.

Cafaggio, Villa ★★★ V. reliable CHIANTI CLASSICO estate with excellent IGTS San
Martino (SANGIOVESE) and Cortaccio (CAB SAUV).

Caiarossa Tus **★★★** Riparbella in the northern MAREMMA is starting to attract serious
winemakers for its combination of altitude and proximity to the sea. This
international project (Dutch owner Jelgersma from Bordeaux, French
winemaker Dominique Génot with Australian background) is turning out some
v. classy reds (Pergolaia, Caiarossa) plus v. tasty Caiarossa Bianco.

Calatrasi Si **★★→★★★** Gd red/white IGT producer, esp D'Istinto range.

Ca' Marcanda BOLGHERI estate created by GAJA since 1996. Focus on international
varieties: CAB SAUV, MERLOT, CAB FR, SYRAH.

Campania Historic centre of Italy's southern mainland with capital in Naples.
Excellent grape varieties (Aglianico, Falanghina, FIANO, GRECO, Piedirosso),
volcanic soils, and cool v'yds all add up to high potential. Best DOCS are FALERNO
DEL MASSICO, FIANO D'AVELLINO, GRECO DI TUFO, ISCHIA, TAURASI, but many newer
areas now coming to the fore, such as Sannio (DOC), Beneventano (IGT). Good
producers include Caggiano, Cantina del Taburno, Caputo, Colli di Lapio,
D'Ambra, De Angelis, Benito Ferrara, FEUDI DI SAN GREGORIO, GALARDI, La
Guardiense, MASTROBERARDINO, Molettieri, MONTEVETRANO, Mustilli, Terredora di
Paolo, Trabucco and VILLA MATILDE.

Cannonau di Sardegna Sar DOC r dr (p) Cannonau, or Grenache, is the staple red
grape of Sardinia, thriving in the southeast but also varietally or blended
elsewhere, as reflected by Cannonau di Sardegna DOC. Best: ARGIOLAS, CONTINI,
Giuseppe Gabbas, Jerzu, Loi, Sedilesu.

Cantalupo, Antichi Vigneti di ★★→★★★ Top GHEMME wines, esp single-v'yd
Breclemae and Carellae.

Cantina A cellar, winery or even a wine bar.

Capannelle ★★★ V.gd producer of IGT and CHIANTI CLASSICO, plus 50:50
SANGIOVESE/MERLOT joint venture with AVIGNONESI.

Capezzana, Tenuta di ★★★ Tuscan estate of the Contini Bonacossi family. Gd BARCO
REALE, excellent CARMIGNANO (esp Villa di Capezzana, Trefiano). Also v.gd
Bordeaux-style red, Ghiaie Della Furba.

Capichera ★★★ Proclaimed, high-price producer of VERMENTINO DI GALLURA, esp
VENDEMMIA *tardiva*. Excellent red Mantèghja from Carignano grapes.

Cappellano ★★★ Teobaldo Cappellano, recently dead, was one of the "characters"
BAROLO, devoting part of his v'yd in *cru* Gabutti to ungrafted NEBBIOLO vines
Franco). Excellent BAROLOS of a highly traditional style; also BAROLO CHINATO.

Caprai ★★★→★★★★ Large, very high-quality, market-leading, experime
producer in Umbria's MONTEFALCO. Superb DOCG MONTEFALCO SAGRANTINO
Anni, v.gd DOC ROSSO DI MONTEFALCO.

Capri Cam DOC r p w **★→★★** Legendary island with widely abused na
interesting wines are from La Caprense.

Carema Pie DOC r ★★→★★★ 99 00 01 03 04' 06' 07 (08) (09) Elegant NEBBIOLO red from steep slopes on Aosta border. Best: Luigi Ferrando.

Carignano del Sulcis Sar DOC r p ★★→★★★ 01 04 06 (08) (09) Best: TERRE BRUNE and Rocca Rubia from CS DI SANTADI.

Carmignano Tus DOCG r ★★★ 90' 95 97' 99' 00 01 02 04 06 07 (08) (09) Region west of Florence. SANGIOVESE plus CAB FRANC, CAB SAUV make distinctive red. Best: Ambra, CAPEZZANA, Farnete, PIAGGIA, Le Poggiarelle, Pratesi.

Carpenè-Malvolti Historic producer of classic PROSECCO and other sparkling wines at Conegliano, Veneto. Seen everywhere in Venice.

Carricante Historically, principal grape of ETNA *bianco*, now making important return.

Cartizze Famous, frequently too expensive and too sweet, DOC PROSECCO of supposedly best subzone of Valdobbiadene.

Casanova di Neri ★★★ Modern BRUNELLO DI MONTALCINO, highly prized Cerretalto and Tenuta Nuova, plus Petradonice CAB SAUV and v.gd ROSSO DI MONTALCINO from Neri family.

Cascina Fonda ★★★ Brothers Marco and Massimo Barbero have risen to the top in MOSCATO D'ASTI DOC. VENDEMMIA *tardiva* and METODO CLASSICO ASTI SPUMANTE.

Case Basse ★★★★ Eco-geek Gianfranco Soldera claims to make the definitive BRUNELLO; many lovers of the traditional style agree. V. expensive and rare.

Castelgiocondo ★★★ FRESCOBALDI estate in MONTALCINO: v.gd BRUNELLO and IGT MERLOT Lamaïone.

Castellare ★★→★★★ CHIANTI CLASSICO producer. First-rate SANGIOVESE-based IGT I Sodi di San Niccoló and updated CHIANTI, esp RISERVA Vigna Poggiale. Also Poggio ai Merli (MERLOT) and Coniale (CAB SAUV).

Castello Castle. (See under name – eg. SALA, CASTELLO DELLA.)

Castell' in Villa ★★★ V. gd CHIANTI CLASSICO estate in Castelnuovo Berardenga.

Castel del Monte Ap DOC r p w ★→★★★ (p w) DYA 04 06 07 08 (09) (r) Dry, fresh, well-balanced wines. Gd Pietrabianca and excellent Bocca di Lupo from Vigneti del Sud (ANTINORI). V.gd Il Falcone, Puer Apuliae and Cappellaccio from RIVERA, Le More from Santa Lucia. Interesting new reds from Cocevola, Giancarlo Ceci.

Castelluccio ★★→★★★ Quality SANGIOVESE DI ROMAGNA. IGT Ronco dei Ciliegi and Ronco delle Ginestre. Massicone is an excellent SANGIOVESE/CAB SAUV blend.

Cataratto Sicilian white grape with as yet unrealized high potential.

Caudrina-Dogliotti Romano ★★★ Top MOSCATO D'ASTI: La Galeisa and Caudrina.

Cavalleri ★★→★★★ V.gd reliable FRANCIACORTA producer, esp sparkling. Also TERRE DI FRANCIACORTA.

Cavicchioli E-R ★→★★ Large producer of LAMBRUSCO and other sparkling wines: Lambrusco di Sorbara Vigna del Cristo is best. Also TERRE DI FRANCIACORTA.

Ca' Viola Pie Play-on-words name of home base of influential consultant Beppe Caviola. Classy DOLCETTO and BARBERA-based wines.

Ca' Vit (Cantina Viticoltori) Group of co-ops near Trento. Massive production, best being sparkling Graal.

Cecchi Tus ★→★★ Bottler, producer; La Gavina, Spargolo, CHIANTI CLASSICO RISERVA.

Cerasuolo Ab DOC p ★ The ROSATO version of MONTEPULCIANO D'ABRUZZO.

Cerasuolo di Vittoria Si DOCG r ★★ 01 03 04 05 06 07 (08) (09) Aromatic red from Frappato and NERO D'AVOLA grapes; try PLANETA, Valle dell'Acate and Cos.

Ceretto ★★→★★★ Highly visible grower of BARBARESCO (Bricco Asili), BAROLO (Bricco Rocche, Brunate, Prapò), LANGHE ROSSO Monsordo and ARNEIS. Also v.gd METODO CLASSICO SPUMANTE La Bernardina.

Cerro, Fattoria del ★★★ Estate owned by insurance giants SAI, making v. gd DOCG VINO NOBILE DI MONTEPULCIANO (esp *cru* Antica Chiusina), red IGTS Manero (SANGIOVESE) and Poggio Golo (MERLOT). Also owns La Poderina (BRUNELLO DI MONTALCINO), Colpetrone (MONTEFALCO SAGRANTINO) and the 1,000-ha northern MAREMMA estate of Monterufoli.

Chardonnay Thrived in northern Italy since the 19th century, esp in the northeast (TRENTINO-ALTO ADIGE, FRIULI-VENEZIA GIULIA). More recently it has been behind high-quality wines from TUSCANY (ISOLE E OLENA Collezione de Marchi), Umbria (CASTELLO DELLA SALA's Cervaro) and as far south as SICILY (PLANETA).

Chianti Tus DOCG r ★→★★★ Local wine of Florence and Siena. At best fresh, fruity, tangy. Of the subdistricts, RUFINA (★★→★★★), Colli Fiorentini (★→★★★), Montespertoli can make CLASSICO-style RISERVAS. Montalbano, Colli Senesi, Aretini, Pisani: lighter wines.

Chianti Classico Tus DOCG r ★★ →★★★★ 97' 99 01 04' 06' 07' (08) (09') The historic zone was allowed to add CLASSICO to its name when the CHIANTI area was extended to most of central Tuscany in the early 20th century. Covering all or part of nine communes, the land is hilly and rocky with altitudes between 250–500 m. Chianti Classico must consist of 80–100% SANGIOVESE, with an optional 20% of "other grapes" (usually CAB SAUV or MERLOT), which causes clashes between modernists and traditionalists.

Chiaretto Rosé (the word means "claret") produced esp around Lake Garda. See BARDOLINO, RIVIERA DEL GARDA BRESCIANO.

Chiarlo, Michele ★★ →★★★ Gd PIEDMONT producer (BAROLOS Cerequio and Cannubi, BARBERA D'ASTI, LANGHE and MONFERRATO ROSSO). Also BARBARESCO.

Ciabot Berton ★★★ Small La Morra grower; classy BAROLOS at modest prices.

Ciliegiolo Grape native to Tuscan MAREMMA, traditionally a blender but increasingly used varietally to great effect by Rascioni e Cecconello and Sassotondo.

Cinque Terre Lig DOC w dr sw ★★ Dry white from obscure grapes grown in steep, rocky tourist paradise on Riviera coast. Sweet version is called SCIACCHETRÀ (Burance, Arrigoni).

Cirò Cal DOC r (p w) ★→★★★ Strong red from Gaglioppo grapes; light, fruity white (DYA). Best: Caparra, Ippolito, LIBRANDI (Duca San Felice ★★★), San Francesco (Donna Madda, Ronco dei Quattroventi), Santa Venere.

Classico Term for wines from a restricted area within the limits of a DOC. By implication, and often in practice, the best of the district. METODO CLASSICO, when applied to sparkling wines, denotes the Champagne method of bottle-fermentation with disgorgement.

Clerico, Domenico ★★★ Established modernist BAROLO producer, esp *crus* Percristina and Ciabot Mentin Ginestra. Also NEBBIOLO/BARBERA blend Arte.

Coffele ★★★ Grower with some of the finest v'yds in SOAVE CLASSICO, making steely, minerally wines of classic concept. Try *cru* Cà Visco.

Colli Hills (from singular Colle). Occurs in many wine names.

Colli Bolognesi E-R DOC r w ★★ DOC name for rarely seen varietal wines, excluding those from the otherwise ubiquitous SANGIOVESE and TREBBIANO. TERRE ROSSE, the pioneer, now joined by Bonzara (★★→★★★) and others.

Colli Euganei Ven DOC r w dr s/sw (sp) ★→★★★ DYA DOC southwest of Padua for seven wines. Adequate red, white and sparkling are pleasant. Best producers: Ca' Lustra, La Montecchia, Speaia, VIGNALTA.

Colli Orientali del Friuli F-VG DOC r w dr sw ★★ →★★★★ Hills east of Udine. Zone similar to COLLIO but less experimental. Top producers include Meroi Davino, Miani, Moschioni, LIVIO FELLUGA, Rosa Bosco, Ronco del Gnemiz. Sweet wines from VERDUZZO or PICOLIT grapes can be amazing (Cos, Dri).

Colli Piacentini E-R DOC r p w ★→★★ DYA DOC inc traditional GUTTURNIO and Monterosso Val d'Arda among 11 varieties, French and local, grown south of Piacenza. Gd fizzy MALVASIA. Most wines FRIZZANTE. Good producers: Montessissa, Mossi, Romagnoli, Solenghi, La Stoppa, Torre Fornello, La Tosa.

Colli del Trasimeno Um DOC r w ★→★★★ (r) 01' 03 04 05 06' 07' (08) (09) Lively white wines from nr Perugia, but now more important reds as well. Best: Duca della Corgna, La Fiorita, Pieve del Vescovo, Poggio Bertaio.

Colline Novaresi Pie DOC r w ★→★★ DYA New DOC for old region in Novara province. Seven different wines: *bianco*, ROSSO, NEBBIOLO, BONARDA, Vespolina, Croatina, BARBERA. Includes declassified BOCA, FARA, GHEMME, SIZZANO.

Collio F-VG DOC r w ★★→★★★★ Important quality zone on border with Slovenia. Esp known for complex, sometimes deliberately oxidized whites, which may be vinified on skins in earthenware vessels/amphoras in ground. Some excellent, some shocking blends from various French, German and Slavic grapes. Numerous gd-to-excellent producers include BORGO DEL TIGLIO, La Castellada, Castello di Spessa, MARCO FELLUGA, Fiegl, GRAVNER, Renato Keber, LIVON, Aldo Polencic, Primosic, Princic, Russiz Superiore, SCHIOPETTO, Tercic, Terpin, Venica & Venica, VILLA RUSSIZ, Zuani.

Colterenzio CS (or Schreckbichl) T-AA ★★→★★★ Pioneering quality leader among ALTO ADIGE co-ops. Look for: Cornell line of selections; Lafoa CAB SAUV and SAUV BL; Cornelius red and white blends.

Col d'Orcia ★★★ Third-largest and top-quality MONTALCINO estate owned by Francesco Marone Cinzano. Best wine: BRUNELLO RISERVA Poggio al Vento.

Conterno, Aldo ★★★★ Legendary grower of BAROLO at Monforte d'Alba. V. gd CHARD Bussiadoro, BARBERA D'ALBA Conca Tre Pile. Best BAROLOS are made traditionally: *Gran Bussia*, Cicala, Colonello. Langhe Favot is a modern BARRIQUE-aged version of NEBBIOLO.

Conterno, Giacomo ★★★★ Iconic grower of super-traditional BAROLO at Monforte d'Alba, Giacomo's grandson Roberto now carrying on father Giovanni's work. Two BAROLOS: Cascina Francia and Monfortino, long-macerated to age for yrs.

Conterno-Fantino ★★★ Two families joined to produce excellent modern-style BAROLO Sori Ginestra and Vigna del Gris at Monforte d'Alba. Also NEBBIOLO/BARBERA blend Monprà.

Contini, Attilio ★→★★★ Famous Sardinian producer of sherry-like, flor-affected VERNACCIA DI ORISTANO; best is vintage blend Antico Gregori. Also gd CANNONAU.

Contratto ★★ At Canelli (owned by GRAPPA-producing family Bocchino); produces v.gd BARBERA D'ASTI, BAROLO, SPUMANTE, ASTI (De Miranda), MOSCATO D'ASTI.

Contucci ★★→★★★ Millennial producer of traditional-style VINO NOBILE, a sight of whose cellar at TUSCANY's MONTEPULCIANO *vaut le détour*.

Copertino Ap DOC r (p) ★★ 01 04 06 07 (08) (09) Savoury, age-worthy, strong red of NEGROAMARO from the heel of Italy. MASSERIA MONACI's Eloquenzia is widely available.

Coppo ★★ →★★★ Ambitious producers of BARBERA D'ASTI (Pomorosso), CHARD.

Cordero di Montezemolo-Monfalletto ★★ →★★★ Historic maker of gd BAROLO, also making fine BARBERA D'ALBA and CHARD.

Corini Small UMBRIAN producer: intriguing, innovative blend of SANGIOVESE/MONTEPULCIANO/MERLOT called Frabusco; also PINOT N Camerti.

Cortese di Gavi See GAVI. (Cortese is the grape.)

Cortona Tuscan DOC contiguous to MONTEPULCIANO's VINO NOBILE. Various red and white grapes, best results so far from AVIGNONESI's Desiderio, a Bordeaux blend, and first-rate SYRAH from Luigi d'Alessandro, Il Castagno, La Braccesca.

Corzano & Paterno, Fattoria di ★★★ Dynamic CHIANTI Colli Fiorentini estate. V.gd RISERVA, red IGT Corzano, and outstanding VIN SANTO.

CS, Cantina Sociale Cooperative winery.

Curtefranca See TERRE DI FRANCIACORTA.

Dal Forno, Romano ★★★★ V. high-quality VALPOLICELLA, AMARONE and RECIOTO grower whose perfectionism is the more remarkable for the fact that his v'yds are outside the CLASSICO zone.

D'Angelo ★★★ Long-established maker of finely crafted, traditional-style AGLIANICO DEL VULTURE. Seek esp RISERVA Vigna Caselle and *cru* Donato d'Angelo.

Di Majo Norante ★★→★★★ Lone star of Molise, south of Abruzzo, with v.gd Biferno

ROSSO, Ramitello, Don Luigi Molise Rosso Riserva and Molise Aglianico Contado, white blend Falanghina-GRECO Biblos and MOSCATO PASSITO Apianae.

DOC/DOCG Quality wine designation: see box, p.123.

Dolcetto ★→★★★ PIEDMONT's earliest-ripening red grape, for v. attractive everyday wines: dry (despite the name), fruity, fresh, with deep purple colour.

Donnafugata Si r w ★★→★★★ Well-crafted Sicilian wines of Contessa Entellina DOC: top reds are Mille e Una Notte and Tancredi; top whites Chiaranda and Vigna di Gabri. Also v. fine MOSCATO PASSITO DI PANTELLERIA Ben Rye.

Duca di Salaparuta Si ★★ Vini Corvo. Popular SICILIAN wines. Sound dry reds; pleasant soft whites. Duca Enrico (★★→★★★) was one of SICILY's pioneeering ambitious reds. Valguarnera is premium oak-aged white.

Elba Tus r w (sp) ★→★★ DYA The island's white, based on Ansonica and TREBBIANO, is v. drinkable with fish. Dry reds are based on SANGIOVESE. Good sweet white (MOSCATO) and red (ALEATICO). Top producers: Acquabona and Sapereta.

Enoteca Wine library; also wine shop or restaurant with extensive wine list. There is a national *enoteca* at the *fortezza* in Siena.

Est! Est!! Est!!! Lat DOC w dr s/sw ★ DYA Unextraordinary white from Montefiascone, north of Rome. Trades on the improbable origin of its name. Best is FALESCO.

Etna Si DOC r p w ★★ (r) 00 01 04 05 06 07 (08) (09) Wine from volcanic slopes and often considerable altitude. Once widely planted, Etna v'yds went into steep decline during the 20th century, but new investment has brought a flurry of planting and excellent wines, not dissimilar to fine burgundy, though based on NERELLO MASCALESE (r) and CARRICANTE (w). Gd producers: Benanti, Il Cantante, De Grazia, Passopisciaro, Russo, Villagrande Bonaccorsi Cambria, Nicosia.

Falchini ★★→★★★ Producer of gd DOCG VERNACCIA DI SAN GIMIGNANO, esp fresh, light Vigna a Solatio and complex, BARRIQUED Ab Vinea Doni. Giacomo Tachis is behind excellent reds: Bordeaux blend IGT Campora and SANGIOVESE-based Paretaio.

Falerno del Massico Cam DOC r w ★★ (r) 00' 01' 03 04 06 07 (08) (09) Falernum was the best-known wine of ancient times, probably sweet white. Today elegant red from AGLIANICO, fruity dry white from Falanghina. V.gd producer: VILLA MATILDE. Others: Amore Perrotta, Felicia, Moio, Trabucco.

Falesco ★★→★★★ Estate of Cotarella brothers, v.gd MERLOT Montiano and CAB SAUV Marciliano (both ★★★). Gd red IGT Vitiano and DOC EST! EST!! EST!!!

Fara Pie DOC r ★★ 97' 99' 01' 04' 06 07' (08) (09) Gd NEBBIOLO from Novara, north PIEDMONT; worth ageing; esp from Dessilani.

Farnese Ab ★★ Gd-quality supplier of the Abruzzi's favourites, esp MONTEPULCIANO D'ABRUZZO, Colline Teramane, RISERVA Opis.

Farnetella, Castello di ★★ Estate near MONTEPULCIANO where Giuseppe Mazzocolin of FELSINA makes gd SAUV BL and CHIANTI Colli Senesi. Also v.gd PINOT N Nero di Nubi and red blend Poggio Granoni.

Faro Si DOC r ★★★ 00 01' 04' 05 06' 07' (08) (09) Full-bodied but elegant red from NERELLO MASCALESE and Nerello Cappuccio grown in the hills behind SICILY's Messina. Palari, the major producer, administered the kiss of life when extinction seemed likely.

Fazi-Battaglia ★★ Well-known producer of VERDICCHIO, best known for amphora-bottle Titulus (2.8m bottles). Also Massaccio, Le Moie, San Sisto. Owns Fassati (VINO NOBILE DI MONTEPULCIANO).

Felluga, Livio ★★★ Consistently fine COLLI ORIENTALI DEL FRIULI wines, esp PINOT BL Illivio, *Pinot Gr*, SAUV BL, TOCAI, PICOLIT and MERLOT/REFOSCO blend Sosso.

Felluga, Marco ★★→★★★ The brother of Livio owns a négociant house bearing his name, plus Russiz Superiore in COLLIO DOC, Castello di Buttrio in COLLI ORIENTALI DOC. Marco's daughter Patrizia is now owner of ZUANI estate in COLLIO.

Felsina ★★★ CHIANTI CLASSICO estate; famous for BARRIQUE-aged RISERVA Rancia, IGT

ITALY

Who makes really good Chianti Classico?

AMA, ANTINORI, BADIA A COLTIBUONO, Bibbiano, Le Boncie, Il Borghetto, Bossi, BROLIO, Cacchiano, CAFAGGIO, CAPANNELLE, Capraia, Carobbio, Casa Emma, Casafrassi, Casale dello Sparviero, Casaloste, Casa Sola, CASTELLARE, CASTELL'IN VILLA, Le Cinciole, Collelungo, Colombaio di Cencio, Le Corti, Mannucci Droandi, FELSINA, Le Filigare, FONTERUTOLI, FONTODI, ISOLE E OLENA, Lilliano, Il Molino di Grace, MONSANTO, Monte Bernardi, Monteraponi, NITTARDI, NOZZOLE, PALAZZINO, PANERETTA, Panzanello, Petroio-Lenzi, Poggerino, Poggiolino, Poggiopiano, Poggio al Sole, Poggio Bonelli, Querceto, QUERCIABELLA, RAMPOLLA, RIECINE, Rocca di Castagnoli, Rocca di Montegrossi, RUFFINO, San Fabiano Calcinaia, SAN FELICE, Savignola Paolina, Selvole, Vecchie Terre di Montefili, VERRAZZANO, Vicchiomaggio, VIGNAMAGGIO, Villa Mangiacane, Villa La Rosa, Viticcio, VOLPAIA.

Fontalloro, both 100% SANGIOVESE. CHIANTI CLASSICO and RISERVA also v.gd, as are IGT CHARD I Sistri and CAB SAUV Maestro Raro.

Ferrari T-AA ★★ →★★★ TRENTO-based maker of best METODO CLASSICO wines outside of FRANCIACORTA. Giuli Ferrari is top *cru*.

Feudi di San Gregorio ★★★ →★★★★ Top CAMPANIA producer, with DOCG TAURASI, DOCG FIANO, *Falanghina*, GRECO DI TUFO. Red IGT Serpico and Patrimo (MERLOT), white IGT Campanaro. Also has estates in Basilicata and APULIA.

Fiano di Avellino Cam DOCG w ★★ →★★★ DYA Fiano is rapidly becoming the best native white grape of south Italy, planted successfully in Molise, Puglia, Calabria and SICILY as well as in CAMPANIA, its birthplace. Fiano di Avellino can have intense aromas of hazelnuts, honey. Best producers: Caggiano, Caputo, Colli di Lapio, Benito Ferrara, FEUDI DI SAN GREGORIO, Grotta del Sole, LA GUARDIENSE, MASTROBERARDINO, San Paolo, Vesevo, Villa Raiano.

Fiorita, la Lamborghini family property near Lake Trasimeno in Umbria, with touchstone SANGIOVESE/MERLOT blend Campoleone.

Florio Historic quality producer of MARSALA. Best wine: Marsala Vergine Secco Baglio Florio. Best name: Terre Arse.

Folonari Ambrogio Folonari and son Giovanni split off from RUFFINO to create their own house. They continue to make Cabreo (a CHARD and a SANGIOVESE/CAB SAUV), wines of NOZZOLE (inc top CAB SAUV Pareto), BRUNELLO DI MONTALCINO La Fuga, VINO NOBILE DI MONTEPULCIANO Gracciano Svetoni, plus from BOLGHERI, MONTECUCCO and COLLI ORIENTALI DEL FRIULI.

Fontana Candida ★★ One of the biggest producers of FRASCATI. Single-v'yd Santa Teresa stands out. See also GRUPPO ITALIANO VINI.

Fontanafredda ★★ →★★★ Large-scale producer of PIEDMONT wines on former royal estates, inc BAROLO Serralunga (150,000 bottles) and BAROLO *crus* La Delizia and La Villa, also ALBA DOCS and sparklers dry and sweet.

Fonterutoli ★★★ Historic CHIANTI CLASSICO estate of the Mazzei family at Castellina with space-age new CANTINA. Notable are *Castello di Fonterutoli* (dark, oaky CHIANTI), IGT Siepi (SANGIOVESE/MERLOT). Mazzei also owns Tenuta di Belguardo in MAREMMA, gd MORELLINO DI SCANSANO and IGT wines.

Fonti, le ★★ →★★★ V.gd CHIANTI CLASSICO house in Poggibonsi; look for RISERVA and IGT Vito Arturo (SANGIOVESE).

Fontodi ★★★ →★★★★ Outstanding CHIANTI CLASSICO estate at Panzano making RISERVA Vigna del Sorbo (SANGIOVESE and 10% CAB SAUV) and 100% SANGIOVESE IGT Flaccianello. Case Via PINOT N and SYRAH are among the best of those varietals in TUSCANY.

Foradori ★★★ Elizabetta Foradori makes *v. gd* TEROLDEGO ROTALIANO DOC and excellent Teroldego IGT Granato, white IGT Myrto. Also interesting wines from Ampeleia estate in Tuscan MAREMMA, esp IGT Kepos from various southern Rhône varieties not inc SYRAH.

Forte, Podere Pasquale Forte's Val d'Orcia estate, just south of MONTALCINO, puts cutting-edge technology at the service of ambitious SANGIOVESE (Petrucci) and CAB SAUV/MERLOT/Petit Verdot (Guardia Vigna) wines, all Orcia DOC.

Forteto della Luja ★★★ Enterprising producer of MOSCATO and BRACHETTO (both sweet sparkling) in PIEDMONT's Loazzolo.

Fossi, Enrico ★★★ High-level small estate in Signa, west of Florence, v.gd SANGIOVESE, CAB SAUV, SYRAH, Malbec, Gamay and CHARD.

Franciacorta Lom DOCG w sp (p) ★★→★★★★ Italy's major production zone for top-quality Champagne-style wines. Best producers: Barone Pizzini, BELLAVISTA, CA' DEL BOSCO, Castellino, CAVALLERI, Gatti, UBERTI, Villa. Also v.gd: Contadi Gastaldi, Monte Rossa, Il Mosnel, Ricci Curbastri. For still white and red, see TERRE DI FRANCIACORTA.

Frascati Lat DOC w dr sw s/sw (sp) ★→★★ DYA Best-known wine of Roman hills: should be limpid, golden, tasting of whole grapes. Most is disappointingly neutral today: look for Castel de Paolis, Conte Zandotti, Villa Simone, or Santa Teresa from FONTANA CANDIDA. The sweet version is known as Cannellino.

Freisa Pie DOC r dr sw s/sw fz (sp) ★★ DYA fz Usually light, frivolous, often FRIZZANTE red, tasting of raspberries and roses; sometimes serious, almost BAROLO-like. Either way, gd with salami. Look for Brezza, Cigliuti, CLERICO, ALDO CONTERNO, COPPO, Franco Martinetti, GIUSEPPE MASCARELLO, Parusso, Pecchenino, Pelissero, Sebaste, Trinchero, VAJRA, Vigneti Massa and VOERZIO.

Frescobaldi ★★→★★★★ Ancient noble family, leading CHIANTI RUFINA pioneer at NIPOZZANO estate (look for Montesodi ★★★), also BRUNELLO from CASTELGIOCONDO estate in MONTALCINO. Sole owners of LUCE estate in MONTALCINO and ORNELLAIA in BOLGHERI. V'yds also in MAREMMA, Montespertoli and COLLIO.

Friulano ★→★★ Aka Sauvignonasse or Sauvignon Vert, this is the new name for TOCAI, which may no longer be mentioned on labels due to pressure from the Hungarians. Makes fresh, pungent, subtly floral white in COLLIO, ISONZO and COLLI ORIENTALI. Good producers include BORGO DEL TIGLIO, LIVIO FELLUGA, LIS NERIS, Pierpaolo Pecorari, Ronco del Gelso, Ronco del Gnemiz, Russiz Superiore, SCHIOPETTO, LE VIGNE DI ZAMO, VILLA RUSSIZ.

Friuli-Venezia Giulia The northeast region on the Slovenian border. Several DOCS, inc ISONZO, COLLIO and COLLI ORIENTALI. Good reds, but considered the home of Italy's most adventurous whites.

Frizzante (fz) Semi-sparkling, eg. MOSCATO D'ASTI and most PROSECCO.

Fuligni ★★★ V.gd producer of BRUNELLO and ROSSO DI MONTALCINO.

Gaja ★★★★ Old family firm at BARBARESCO under direction of Angelo Gaja. High quality, even higher price. BARBARESCO is the only Piedmontese DOCG remaining after Gaja down-classed *crus* Sorì Tildin, Sorì San Lorenzo and Costa Russi as well as Barolo Sperss to LANGHE DOC so that he could blend small proportions of BARBERA in with NEBBIOLO. CHARD (Gaia e Rey), CAB SAUV Darmagi. Acquisitions elsewhere in Italy: Marengo-Marenda estate (BAROLO), commercial Gromis label; Pieve di Santa Restituta in MONTALCINO; CA' MARCANDA in BOLGHERI.

Galardi ★★★→★★★★ Producer of Terra di Lavoro, a v. gd blend of AGLIANICO and Piedirosso, in north CAMPANIA near FALERNO DEL MASSICO DOC.

Gancia Once-famous ASTI house also producing dry sparkling, today living mainly on past glory.

Garda Ven DOC r p w ★→★★ DYA (w p) 04 05 06 07 (08) (09) (r) Catch-all DOC for generally early drinking wines of various colours from provinces of Verona in Veneto, Brescia and Mantua in Lombardy. Gd are Cavalchina, Zeni.

Garganega Principal white grape of SOAVE and Gambellara.

Garofoli ★★→★★★ One of quality leaders in the Marches (near Ancona). Notable

> **What do the initials mean?**
> **Denominazione di Origine Controllata (DOC)**
> Controlled Denomination of Origin, cf. AC in France.
> **Denominazione di Origine Controllata e Garantita (DOCG)**
> "G" = "Guaranteed". Italy's highest quality designation.
> **Indicazione Geografica Tipica (IGT)**
> "Geographic Indication of Type". Broader and more vague than DOC, cf.
> VIN DE PAYS in France.
> **Denominazione di Origine Protetta/Indicazione Geografica Protetta (DOP/IGP)**
> "P" = "Protected". The EU seems to want these designations to take over
> from DOC(G)/IGT in the long term.

stylein Verdicchio Podium, Macrina and Serra Fiorese. ROSSO CONERO Piancarda and v.gd Grosso Agontano.

Gattinara Pie DOCG r ★★★ 89'90' 95 96' 97' 98 99' 00 01' 03 04' 05 06 07' (08) (09) Potentially fine NEBBIOLO-based red, considered the best from north PIEDMONT, though that's not saying a lot. Best: Travaglini (RISERVA), Antoniolo (single-v'yd wines). Others: Bianchi, Nervi, Torraccia del Piantavigna.

Gavi Pie DOCG w ★→★★★ DYA At (rare) best, subtle dry white of Cortese grapes. LA SCOLCA is best-known, gd from BANFI (esp Vigna Regale), Castellari Bergaglio, Franco Martinetti, Toledana, Villa Sparina. Broglia, Cascina degli Ulivi, Castello di Tassarolo, CHIARLO, La Giustiniana, Podere Saulino are also fair.

Ghemme Pie DOCG r ★★89' 90' 95 96' 97' 98 99' 00 01' 03 04 05 06 07' (08) (09) Neighbour of GATTINARA, not considered as gd, but sometimes better. Stars: Antichi Vigneti di Cantalupo, Ioppa, Rovellotti and Torraccia del Piantavigna.

Giacosa, Bruno ★★→★★★★ Considered Italy's greatest winemaker by some, this brooding genius suffered a stroke in 2006, but goes on working, crafting outstanding traditional-style BARBARESCOS (Asili, Santo Stefano) and BAROLOS (Falletto, Rocche di Falletto). Top wines were not sold from 2006 vintage despite quality of the vintage. Also makes a range of fine reds (DOLCETTO, NEBBIOLO, BARBERA), whites (ARNEIS) and an amazing METODO CLASSICO Brut.

Grappa Pungent and potent spirit made from grape pomace (skins, etc., after pressing), can be anything from disgusting to inspirational.

Grasso, Elio ★★★ V.gd BAROLO (look for Runcot, Gavarini, Casa Maté), full, barrel-aged BARBERA D'ALBA Vigna Martina, DOLCETTO D'ALBA and CHARD Educato.

Grave del Friuli F-VG DOC r w ★→★★ (r) 03 04 06 07 08 (09) Largest DOC of FRIULI-VENEZIA GIULIA, mostly on plains, giving forth important volumes of underwhelming wines. Exceptions from Borgo Magredo, Di Lenardo, Plozner, Ronco Cliona, Villa Chiopris, San Simone.

Gravner, Josko ★★★ Controversial COLLIO producer, believing in maceration on skins and long wood-ageing for whites. His wines are either loved for their complexity or hated for being oxidized. Expensive and hard to find.

Grechetto Umbrian white grape (Pulcinculo in TUSCANY); more flavour than TREBBIANO, often used in blends or solo in ORVIETO and other parts of Umbria. Look for Barberani, Bigi, CAPRAI, Cardeto, Colli Amerini, FALESCO, Palazzone.

Greco Various white "Grecos" (of Greek origin?) exist in southern Italy, not necessarily related, eg. GRECO DI TUFO is different from Greco of CIRÒ. Also Greco Nero.

Greco di Tufo Cam DOCG w (sp) ★★→★★★ DYA One of the best whites from the south: fruity, slightly wild in flavour and age-worthy. V.gd examples from Caggiano, Caputo, Benito Ferrara, FEUDI DI SAN GREGORIO, LA GUARDIENSE, Macchialupa, MASTROBERARDINO (Nova Serra and Vignadangelo), Vesevo, Villa Raiano.

Gresy, Marchesi di (Cisa Asinari) ★★★ Consistent, sometimes inspired producer of traditional-style BARBARESCO (*crus* Gaiun and Camp Gros). Also v.gd SAUV BL, CHARD, MOSCATO D'ASTI, BARBERA D'ASTI.

Grevepesa CHIANTI CLASSICO co-op – quality slowly rising.

Grignolino Pie DOC r ★ DYA lively light red of PIEDMONT. Verduno is the classic (BURLOTTO, CASTELLO DI VERDUNO); also D'ASTI (BRAIDA, Marchesi Incisa della Rocchetta); del Monferrato Casalese (Accornero, Bricco Mondalino, La Tenaglia).

Gruppo Italiano Vini (GIV) Complex of co-ops and wineries, biggest v'yd holders in Italy; estates inc Bigi, BOLLA, Ca'Bianca, Conti Serristori, FOLONARI, FONTANA CANDIDA, LAMBERTI, Macchiavelli, MELINI, Negri, Santi, Vignaioli di San Floriano. Has also expanded into south: SICILY and Basilicata.

Guardiense, la ★★ Large CAMPANIAN co-op turning out better-than-average whites and reds at lower-than-average prices. Riccardo Cotarella is technical director.

Guerrieri-Gonzaga See SAN LEONARDO.

Gutturnio dei Colli Piacentini E-R DOC r dr ★→★★ DYA BARBERA/BONARDA blend from the hills of Piacenza. Producers: Castelli del Duca, La Stoppa, La Tosa.

Haas, Franz ★★★ ALTO ADIGE producer; v.gd PINOT N, LAGREIN and IGT blends.

Hofstätter ★★★ ALTO ADIGE producer of top PINOT N. Look for Barthenau Vigna Sant'Urbano, LAGREIN, CAB SAUV/Petit Verdot, Gewurz.

Ischia Cam DOC w (r) ★→★★ Top producer D'Ambra: DOC red Dedicato a Mario D'Ambra, IGT red Tenuta Montecorvo, IGT white Tenuta Frassitelli and Piellero. Also gd: Il Giardino Mediterraneo, Pietratorcia.

Indicazione Geograpifca Tipica (IGT) See box, p.123.

Insolia Sicilian white grape with untapped potential; in TUSCANY, Ansonica.

Isole e Olena ★★★ →★★★★ Top CHIANTI CLASSICO estate run by astute Paolo de Marchi, with fine red IGT Cepparello. V.gd VIN SANTO, CAB SAUV, CHARD and L'Eremo SYRAH. See also LESSONA.

Isonzo F-VG DOC r w ★★★ (r) This gravelly plain of Friuli Isonzo is a multi-DOC area covering numerous red and white varietals and blends, but the stars are mostly white, scented and structured, like VIE DI ROMANS' Flors di Uis, or LIS NERIS' Fiore de Campo. Also good: Borgo Conventi, Pierpaolo Pecorari, Ronco del Gelso.

Jermann, Silvio ★★ →★★★ Famous estate with v'yds in COLLIO and ISONZO: top white blend Vintage Tunina, oak-aged blend Capo Martino and CHARD "Were dreams, now it is just wine" (yes, really).

Kante, Edi ★★→★★★★ Leading light of CARSO; fine DOC CHARD, SAUV BL, MALVASIA; gd red Terrano.

Lacrima di Morro d'Alba DYA Curiously named Muscatty light red from a small commune in the Marches, no connection with ALBA or La Morra in PIEDMONT. Gd producers: Mancinelli, MONTE SCHIAVO.

Lacryma (or Lacrima) Christi del Vesuvio Cam r p w dr (sw fz) ★→★★ DOC Vesuvio wines based on Coda di Volpe (w) and Piedirosso (r). Caputo, De Angelis, Grotta del Sole and MASTROBERARDINO produce uninspired wines.

Lageder, Alois ★★→★★★★ Top ALTO ADIGE producer. Most exciting wines are single-v'yd varietals: *Sauv Bl Lehenhof*, PINOT GR Benefizium Porer, CHARD Lowengang, Gewurz Am Sand, PINOT N Krafuss, LAGREIN Lindenberg, CAB SAUV Cor Römigberg. Also owns Cason Hirschprunn for v.gd IGT blends.

Lago di Corbara Umb r ★★ 03 04' 05 06' 07' 08 (09) Relatively recently created DOC to include quality reds of the ORVIETO area. Best from Barberani (Villa Monticelli) and Decugnano dei Barbi (Il).

Lagrein AA DOC r p ★★→★★★ 99 00' 01 03 04' 05 06' 07' (08) Deep-hued ALTO-ADIGE varietal with slightly bitter finish, rich, plummy fruit (r), with bright, minerally tones (p). Best growing zone: Gries, suburb of Bolzano. Best producers: Colterenzio co-op, Gojer, Gries co-op, HAAS, HOFSTÄTTER, LAGEDER, Laimburg, Josephus Mayr, Thomas Mayr, MURI GRIES, NALS MARGREID, Niedermayr, NIEDRIST, St-Magdalena, TERLANO co-op, TIEFENBRUNNER.

Lamberti ★★ Large producer of SOAVE, VALPOLICELLA, BARDOLINO, etc, at Lazise on the eastern shore of Lake Garda. Owned by GIV.

Lambrusco E-R DOC (or not) r p dr s/sw ★–★★ DYA Once extremely popular fizzy red, mainly in industrial, semi-sweet, non-DOC version. Best is SECCO, traditional with second fermentation in bottle (with sediment). DOCS: L Grasparossa di Castelvetro, L Salamino di Santa Croce, L di Sorbara. Best: Bellei, Caprari, Casali, CAVICCHIOLI, Graziano, Lini Oreste, Medici Ermete (esp Concerto), Rinaldo Rinaldini, Venturini Baldini.

Langhe The hills of central PIEDMONT, home of BAROLO, BARBARESCO, etc. DOC name for six Piedmontese varietals plus blends *bianco* and ROSSO. Those wishing to blend other grapes with their NEBBIOLO (or BAROLO or BARBARESCO), such as GAJA, can do so at up to 15% under "Langhe Nebbiolo".

Latisana F-VG DOC r w ★–★★ (r) DOC for 13 varietal wines from 80 km northeast of Venice. Best wine is FRIULANO (ex-TOCAI). Try wines of Grandi e Gabana.

Lessona Pie DOC r ★★ 99 01' 04 06 07 (08) (09) Dry, claret-like wine from Vercelli province. NEBBIOLO, Vespolina, BONARDA grapes. Best producer: Sella, plus new estate of Paolo de Marchi of ISOLE E OLENA, Sperino.

Librandi ★★★ Top Calabria producer pioneering research into Calabrian varieties. V.gd red CIRÒ (*Riserva Duca San Felice* is ★★★), IGT Gravello (CAB SAUV/ Gagliopppo blend), Magno Megonio (r) from Magliocco grape and IGT Efeso (w) from Mantonico grape. Other local varietals in experimental phase.

Liguria The Italian riviera is rocky, but viticulture is rewarding: most wines sell to sun-struck tourists at fat profits. Main grapes: VERMENTINO (w) and DOLCETTO (r), but don't miss CINQUE TERRE'S SCIACCHETTRÀ or red Ormeasco di Pornassio.

Lisini ★★★–★★★★ Historic estate for some of the finest and longest-lasting BRUNELLO, esp RISERVA Ugolaia.

Lis Neris ★★★ Top ISONZO estate for gd white wines, esp PINOT GR, CHARD (Jurosa), SAUV BL (Picol), FRIULANO (Fiore di Campo), plus blends Confini and Lis. Also v.gd Lis Neris Rosso (MERLOT/CAB SAUV) and sweet white Tal Luc (VERDUZZO/RIES).

Livon ★★–★★★ Substantial COLLIO producer, also some COLLI ORIENTALI wines like VERDUZZO. Expanded into the CHIANTI CLASSICO and MONTEFALCO DOCGS.

Loacker ★★–★★★ Biodynamic (and homeopathic) producer of ALTO ADIGE wines, installed in TUSCANY and making fine BRUNELLO and ROSSO DI MONTALCINO under the Corte Pavone label, plus good MORELLINO DI SCANSANO Valdifalco.

Locorotondo Ap DOC w (sp) ★ DYA Thirst-quenching dry white from APULIA'S Verdeca and Bianco d'Alessano varieties, much quaffed *in situ* by vacationing *trulli*-seekers, little sought back home.

Luce ★★★ Joint venture launched in 1998, now solely FRESCOBALDI, having bought out partner Mondavi. SANGIOVESE/MERLOT blend.

Lugana Lom and Ven DOC w (sp) ★–★★ DYA whites of southern Lake Garda, main grape Trebbiano di Lugana (or Trebbiano di Soave = Verdicchio). Dry, sappy and flavourful. Best: CA' DEI FRATI, ZENATO, Zeni.

The Maremma: beside the seaside

Names to look for in the Maremma (for IGT): Ampeleia, Belguardo, La Carletta, Casina, Col di Bacche, Fattoria di Magliano, Lhosa, La Marietta, Marsiliana, Monteti, MORIS FARMS, Montebelli, La Parrina, Poderi di Ghiaccioforte, Poggio Argentiera, Poggio Foco, Poggio al Lupo, Poggio Paoli, Poggio Verrano, Rascioni e Cecconello, Rocca di Frasinello, San Matteo, Sassotondo, La Selva, Solomaremma, Suveraia.

For Morellino di Scansano: Belguardo, La Carletta, Fattoria di Magliano, Mantellasi, Masi di Mandorlaia, MORIS FARMS, Podere 414, Poderi di Ghiaccioforte, Poggio Argentiera, Poggio al Lupo, Poggio Paoli, Le Pupille, Roccapesta, San Matteo, La Selva, Cantina di Scansano, Terre di Talamo and Vignaioli del Morellino di Scansano.

Lungarotti ★★ →★★★ Leading producer of TORGIANO, with cellars, hotel and museum near Perugia. Star wine DOCG RISERVA Rubesco. Gd IGT Sangiorgio (SANGIOVESE/ CAB SAUV), Aurente (CHARD), Giubilante. Gd MONTEFALCO SAGRANTINO. See TORGIANO.

Macchiole, le ★★★ →★★★★ Eugenio Campolmi's widow, Cinzia, continues his fine work with CAB FR (Paleo Rosso) and MERLOT (Messorio), as well as SYRAH (Scrio).

Maculan Ven ★★★ Excellent CAB SAUV (Fratta, Ferrata), CHARD (Ferrata), MERLOT (Marchesante) and Torcolato (esp RISERVA Acininobili).

Malvasia Ancient grape of Greek origin planted so widely for so long that various sub-varieties often bear little resemblance to one another: can be white or red, sparkling or still, strong or mild, sweet or dry, aromatic or neutral. Best is probably sweet *Malvasia delle Lipari*, from islands off SICILY.

Manduria (Primitivo di) Ap DOC r s/sw ★★ →★★★ Dark red, naturally strong, rarely sweet from near Taranto. Best include Casale Bevagna, Feudi di San Marzano, Ginafranco Fino, Pozzopalo, RACEMI.

Marchesi di Barolo ★★ Important ALBA house: BAROLO (esp Cannubi and Sarmassa), BARBARESCO, DOLCETTO D'ALBA, BARBERA, FREISA D'ASTI and GAVI.

Maremma Southern coastal area of TUSCANY, esp province of Grosseto. DOCS include MONTEREGIO, MORELLINO DI SCANSANO, PARRINA, Pitigliano, SOVANA (Grosseto). Attracting interest and investment for potential demonstrated by wines. Maremma Toscana IGT now increasingly used by top producers, rather than DOCS which tend to diminish perceived value.

Marsala DOC w sw SICILY's once famous fortified wine (★ →★★★), invented by Woodhouse Bros from Liverpool in 1773. An excellent apéritif, but used mostly in inferior versions for zabaglione. Dry ("virgin"), sometimes made by the *solera* system, must be 5 yrs old. Top: FLORIO, Pellegrino, Rallo. See also VECCHIO SAMPERI.

Marzemino Trentino T-AA DOC r ★ →★★ 04 05 06 07 (08) Pleasant local red. Fruity and slightly bitter. Esp from Bossi Fedrigotti, CA' VIT, De Tarczal, Gaierhof, Letrari, Longariva, Simoncelli, E Spagnolli, Vallarom.

Mascarello The name of two top producers of BAROLO: Bartolo Mascarello, of BAROLO (deceased), whose daughter Maria Theresa continues her father's highly traditional path; and Giuseppe Mascarello, of Manchiero, whose son Mauro makes superior, traditional-style BAROLO from the famous Monprivato v'yd in Castiglione Falletto.

Masi ★★ →★★★ Exponent/researcher of VALPOLICELLA, AMARONE, RECIOTO, SOAVE, etc., inc fine Rosso Veronese Campo Fiorin and AMARONE-style wines from Friuli and Argentina. V.gd barrel-aged red IGT Toar, from Corvina and Oseleta, also Osar (Oseleta). Top AMARONES Mazzano and Campolongo di Torbe.

Massa, la ★★★ Highly rated producer of top Tuscan reds IGTS La Massa and Giorgio Primo, no longer CHIANTI CLASSICO.

Masseria Monaci ★★ Estate of Severino Garofano, for decades the oenologist behind the continuing rise of quality wine in PUGLIA's Salento. Characterful NEGROAMARO (Eloquenzia, Simpotica), superb late-picked Le Braci, also Uva di Troia (Sine Pari) and AGLIANICO (Sine Die).

Mastroberardino ★★ →★★★ Historic producer of mountainous Avellino province in CAMPANIA, quality torch-bearer for Italy's south during dark yrs of mid-20th century. Top *Taurasi* (look for Historia Naturalis and Radici), also FIANO DI AVELLINO More Maiorum and GRECO DI TUFO Nova Serra.

Melini ★★ Long-established producers of CHIANTI CLASSICO at Poggibonsi. Gd quality/price; look for single-v'yd CHIANTI CLASSICO Selvanella and RISERVAS La Selvanella and Masovecchio.

Merlot Red grape grown today throughout Italy, used varietally and to blend with SANGIOVESE *et al*. Many Merlot DOCS, esp in the northeast, where grape is traditional, but quality is generally better from TUSCANY.

Metodo classico or tradizionale Mandatory terms to identify classic-method sparkling wines. "Metodo Champenois" banned since 1994.

Mezzacorona ★★ TRENTINO co-op with gd DOC TEROLDEGO, METODO CLASSICO Rotari, situated in the commune of Mezzocorona (spot the difference).

Italy's finest whites

Italy has traditionally been known for her red wines, but whites are coming along apace, and like the reds, they are excitingly different because they come from grape varieties exclusive to their zone. Examples of excellence to seek out: PIEDMONT – ARNEIS (GIACOSA), Favorita (Malvirà); Veneto – GARGANEGA (SOAVE PIEROPAN) and PROSECCO (Nino Franco); FRIULI – FRIULANO (BORGO DEL TIGLIO) and RIBOLLA (Tercic); Marche/ABRUZZO – VERDICCHIO (Bucci), PECORINO (Contesa); SARDINIA – VERMENTINO (Capichera); Liguria – VERMENTINO (Lambruschi); CAMPANIA – Falanghina (Falerno Villa Matilde), GRECO (Molettieri) and FIANO (MASTROBERARDINO); SICILY – INZOLIA (Feudi Principi di Butera), Grillo (Santa Anastasia) and Carricante (ETNA Bianco Benanti).

Molino ★★★ Talented producer of elegant ALBA wines at La Morra; look for BAROLOS Gancia and Conca, BARBERA Gattere and DOLCETTO.

Monferrato Pie DOC r p w sw ★→★★★ Hills between river Po and Apennines, bringing forth wines of mostly everyday-drinking style rather than of serious intent.

Monica di Sardegna Sar DOC r ★→★★ DYA The mainstay of Sardinian light, dry red.

Monsanto ★★★ Esteemed CHIANTI CLASSICO estate, esp for Il Poggio (first single-v'yd CHIANTI CLASSICO) and IGTS Fabrizio Bianchi (SANGIOVESE) and Nemo (CAB SAUV).

Montalcino Small town in province of Siena (TUSCANY), famous for concentrated, expensive BRUNELLO and more approachable, better-value ROSSO DI MONTALCINO.

Montecarlo Tus DOC r w ★★ DYA (w) White, increasingly red, wine area near Lucca, TUSCANY. Producers: Buonamico (red IGTS Cercatoja Rosso, Fortino), Carmignani (v.gd red IGT For Duke), red IGTS of La Torre, Montechiari, Fattoria del Teso.

Montecucco Tuscan DOC between MONTALCINO and MORELLINO DI SCANSANO. Look for CASTELLO DI POTENTINO (Sacromonte), also Begnardi, Ciacci Piccolomini, Colli Massari, Fattoria di Montecucco, Villa Patrizia. Much investment by the likes of FOLONARI, MASI, Pertimali, RIECINE, Talenti.

Montefalco Sagrantino Umb DOCG r dr (sw) ★★★→★★★★ Super-tannic, long-lasting SECCO wines, plus sweet PASSITO red from Sagrantino grapes. Gd from Adanti, Alzatura, Antonelli San Marco, Paolo Bea, Benincasa, CAPRAI, Colpetrone, Madonna Alta, Scacciadiavoli, Tabarrini, Terre de' Trinci.

Montellori, Fattoria di ★★→★★★ Tuscan producer making CHIANTI, all-SANGIOVESE IGT Dicatum, CAB SAUV/MERLOT blend Salamartano, white IGT Sant'Amato (SAUV BL), and METODO CLASSICO SPUMANTE.

Montepulciano An important red grape of east-central Italy. Also the name of a famous Tuscan town. The two are unrelated.

Montepulciano, Vino Nobile di See VINO NOBILE DI MONTEPULCIANO.

Montepulciano d'Abruzzo Ab DOC r p ★→★★★ 03' 04' 05 06' 07' 08 (09) (r) Highly popular, deep-coloured, full-flavoured red and zesty, savoury pink (CERASUOLO) of generally excellent value from Adriatic coast. Production dominated by co-ops, gd ones inc Casal Thaulero, Citra, Miglianico, Roxan, Tollo. Gd to excellent privates: Barone Cornacchia Contesa, Illuminati, Marramiero, Masciarelli, Orlandi Contucci Ponno, Pasetti, Pepe, La Valentina, Valentini, Zaccagnini.

Monteregio DOC near Massa Marittima in MAREMMA, high-level SANGIOVESE and CAB SAUV wines from Campo Bargello, MORIS FARMS, Tenuta del Fontino. Big-name investors (ANTINORI, BELLAVISTA, Eric de Rothschild, ZONIN) have flocked in.

Monte Schiavo ★★→★★★ Medium-large producer of gd to outstanding VERDICCHIO (esp Le Giuncare) and MONTEPULCIANO-based reds in the Marches. Also owns or part-owns estates in Abruzzo, APULIA and SICILY.

Montescudaio Tus DOC r w ★★ DOC between Pisa and Livorno; the best are SANGIOVESE or SANGIOVESE/CAB SAUV blends. Try Merlini, Poggio Gagliardo, La Regola, Sorbaiano.

Montevertine ★★★★ Radda estate. Non-DOCG but classic CHIANTI-style wines. IGT Le Pergole Torte a fine, pioneering example of pure, long-ageing SANGIOVESE.

Montevetrano ★★★ Small CAMPANIA producer; superb IGT Montevetrano (CAB SAUV, MERLOT, AGLIANICO).

Morellino di Scansano Tus DOC r ★→★★★ 03' 04' 05 06' 07' (08) (09) Local SANGIOVESE of the MAREMMA, the south Tuscan coast. Cherry-red, should be lively and tasty, young or matured; many have been overoaked. (See box, p.125.)

Moris Farms ★★★ V.gd producer in MONTEREGIO and MORELLINO DI SCANSANO, respectively to north and south of Grosseto; look for RISERVA and IGT Avvoltore, a rich SANGIOVESE/CAB SAUV/SYRAH blend.

Moscadello di Montalcino Tus DOC w sw (sp) ★★ DYA Revived traditional wine of MONTALCINO, once better known than BRUNELLO. Sweet fizz and sweet to high-octane MOSCATO PASSITO. Best: BANFI, COL D'ORCIA, La Poderina.

Moscato Family of fragrant fruity grapes, which include Moscato Bianco/di Canelli (used in ASTI and MONTALCINO), Moscato Giallo (TRENTINO-ALTO-ADIGE, Ven, etc.) and Moscato d'Alessandria (SICILY, Pantelleria), making a diverse range of wines: sparkling or still, light or full-bodied, but always sweet.

Moscato d'Asti Pie DOCG w sw sp ★★→★★★ DYA Similar to DOCG ASTI, but usually better grapes; lower alcohol, sweeter, fruitier, often from small producers. Best DOCG MOSCATO: L'Armangia, BERA, BRAIDA, Ca'd'Gal, CASCINA FONDA, Cascina Pian d'Oro, Caudrina, Il Falchetto, Forteto della Luja, DI GRESY, Icardi, Isolabella, Manfredi/Patrizi, Marino, La Morandina, Marco Negri, Elio Perrone, Rivetti, Saracco, Scagliola, VAJRA, Vietti, Vignaioli di Sante Stefano,

Müller-Thurgau Variety of some interest in T-AA and FRIULI. Top producers: LAGEDER, Lavis, POJER & SANDRI, Zeni. TIEFENBRUNNER'S Feldmarschall from 1000-m high v'yd in ALTO ADIGE is possibly the best dry M-T in the world.

Murana, Salvatore Si ★★★ V.gd MOSCATO and PASSITO DI PANTELLERIA.

Muri Gries ★★ V.gd producer of ALTO ADIGE DOC, specialists in LAGREIN.

Nals Margreid ★★→★★★ Small but quality-oriented ALTO ADIGE co-op making mountain-fresh whites (esp PINOT BIANCO Sirmian).

Nebbiolo The best red grape of PIEDMONT, possibly of Italy, used in BAROLO, BARBARESCO and other wines of the northwest (eg. Lombardy's VALTELLINA), though so far unsuccessful elsewhere in the wine world.

Nebbiolo d'Alba Pie DOC r dr ★★→★★★ 01' 04' 06 07 (08) (09) Two styles: full and complex, similar to BAROLO/BARBARESCO; and light, fruity and fragrant. Top examples of former from PIO CESARE, GIACOSA, G MASCARELLO, FONTANAFREDDA PRUNOTTO, SANDRONE. See also ROERO.

Negroamaro APULIAN "black bitter" red grape with potential for both high quality or high volume. See ALEZIO, BRINDISI, COPERTINO and SALICE SALENTINO.

Nerello Mascalese Medium-coloured, characterful Sicilian red grape, once widespread in northeast SICILY, recently rediscovered by the excellent Palari in Messina (FARO DOC) and growers on the upper slopes of ETNA.

Nero d'Avola Dark-red grape of SE SICILY now used throughout the island at quality levels from sublime to industrial.

Niedrist, Ignaz ★★★ Small, gifted producer of white and red ALTO ADIGE wines (esp LAGREIN, PINOT N, PINOT BL, RIES).

Nipozzano, Castello di ★★★ FRESCOBALDI estate in RUFINA east of Florence making excellent CHIANTI Montesodi.

Nittardi ★★→★★★ Reliable source of high-quality, modern-style CHIANTI

CLASSICO produced by oenologist Carlo Ferrini with German proprietor Peter Femfert.

Nozzole ★★→★★★ Famous estate owned by Ambrogio and Giovanni FOLONARI, in heart of CHIANTI CLASSICO, north of Greve.

Nuragus di Cagliari Sar DOC w ★★ DYA Lively Sardinian wine from Nuragus grape.

Oasi degli Angeli Benchmark all-MONTEPULCIANO wines from small producer in southern Marches; lush and mouthfilling.

Occhio di Pernice A type of VIN SANTO made predominantly from black grapes, mainly SANGIOVESE. AVIGNONESI's is definitive.

Oddero ★★→★★★ Well-known La Morra estate for gd-value BAROLO (look for Mondoca di Bussia, Rocche di Castiglione and Vigna Rionda).

Oltrepò Pavese Lom DOC r w dr sw sp ★→★★★ 14 wines from Pavia province, most named after grapes. Sometimes v.gd PINOT N and SPUMANTE. Gd growers: Anteo, Barbacarlo, Casa Re, Castello di Cigognola, CS Casteggio, Le Fracce, Frecciarossa, Monsupello, Mazzolino, Ruiz de Cardenas, Travaglino, Vercesi del Castellazzo, La Versa co-op.

Ornellaia Tus ★★★★ 95 97 98' 99 00 01 03 04' 05 06' 07'(08) (09) Famous estate near BOLGHERI founded by Lodovico ANTINORI, who sold to FRESCOBALDI/Mondavi consortium, now owned solely by FRESCOBALDI. Estate has many prestigious wines: excellent BOLGHERI DOC Ornellaia, superb IGT Masseto (MERLOT), v.gd BOLGHERI DOC Le Serre Nuove and IGT Le Volte.

Orvieto Umb DOC w dr sw s/sw ★→★★★ DYA The classic Umbrian white, from the ancient spiritual centre of the Etruscans. Wines comparable to Vouvray from tufaceous soil. SECCO version is most popular today, AMABILE is more traditional. Sweet versions from noble rot (*muffa nobile*) grapes can be superb, eg. Barberani's Calcaia. Other gd producers Bigi, Cardeto, CASTELLO DELLA SALA, Decugnano dei Barbi, La Carraia, Palazzone,

Pacenti, Siro ★★★ Hand-crafted, barriqued BRUNELLO and ROSSO DI MONTALCINO.

Pagani de Marchi Small, high-quality producer north of BOLGHERI. Impressive IGT varietal wines from CAB SAUV, SANGIOVESE and, in particular, MERLOT.

Palazzino, Podere Il ★★★ Small Gaiole estate with admirable CHIANTI CLASSICO.

Paneretta, Castello della ★★→★★★ Fine CHIANTI CLASSICO, IGTS Quatrocentenario and Terrine.

Pantelleria Island off the Sicilian coast noted for MOSCATO, particularly intense, super-sweet PASSITO. Watch: Abraxas, Colosi, De Bartoli, DONNAFUGATA, MURANA.

Parrina, La Tus DOC r w ★★ Large estate near Argentario peninsula in southern MAREMMA making Parrina Bianco from TREBBIANO/CHARD and Parrina Rosso from SANGIOVESE and French grapes.

Pasqua, Fratelli ★→★★ Massive producer and bottler of Verona wines: VALPOLICELLA, AMARONE, SOAVE. Also BARDOLINO and RECIOTO.

Passito (pa) Strong, mostly sweet wine from grapes dried on the vine, on trays under the sun, or indoors on trays or hanging vertically. Best known are VIN SANTO (TUSCANY) and AMARONE/RECIOTO (Veneto).

Paternoster ★★→★★★ Top AGLIANICO DEL VULTURE, esp Don Anselmo.

Pecorino Ab IGT Colli Pescaresi w ★★→★★★ Not a cheese but alluring dry white from a recently near-extinct variety. Gd producers Contesa, Franco Pasetti.

The "grey" list – the best Pinot Grigio DOCs

DOCS ALTO ALDIGE (San Michele Appiano, CALDARO, LAGEDER, NALS MARGREID, Termeno), COLLIO (Renato Keber, LIVON, Aldo Polencic, Russiz Superiore, SCHIOPETTO, Tercic, Terpin, Venica, VILLA RUSSIZ), COLLI ORIENTALI (Livio FELLUGA) and ISONZO (Borgo San Daniele, LIS NERIS, Masut da Rive, Pierpaolo Pecorari, Ronco del Gelso, VIE DI ROMANS).

Petit Verdot This Bordelais vine has begun to catch on in Italy, esp among internationalists. Casale del Giglio in Latium makes an interesting varietal.

Piaggia Outstanding producer of CARMIGNANO RISERVA, IGT Il Sasso and superb CAB FR Poggio dei Colli.

Piave Ven DOC r w ★→★★ (r) 04 05 06 07 08 (09) (w) Volume-producing DOC on plains northwest of Venice for red and white wines named after their grapes. CAB SAUV, MERLOT and Raboso reds can all age. Gd examples from Duca di Castelanza, Loredan Gasparini, Molon, Villa Sandi.

Picolit F-VG DOC w sw s/sw ★★→★★★ 01 03 04 05 06 07 08 (09) Delicate sweet wine from COLLI ORIENTALI DEL FRIULI, but with an exaggerated reputation. As France's Jurançon. Ages up to 6 yrs, but v. overpriced. Best from LIVIO FELLUGA, Meroi, Perusini, Specogna, VILLA RUSSIZ, Vinae dell'Abbazia. Apparently not related to black Picolit Neri, grown in GRAVE DEL FRIULI around Spilimbergo.

Piedmont (Piemonte) With TUSCANY, the most important Italian region for top-quality wine. Turin is the capital, ASTI and ALBA the wine centres. See BARBARESCO, BARBERA, BAROLO, DOLCETTO, GRIGNOLINO, MOSCATO, ROERO, etc.

Piemonte Pie DOC r w (sp) ★→★★ All-PIEDMONT blanket DOC inc BARBERA, BONARDA, BRACHETTO, Cortese, GRIGNOLINO, CHARD, SPUMANTE, MOSCATO.

Pieropan ★★★ The great name in SOAVE, to the regret of some, has been moving the house style from lean/mineral to broad/silky, esp as regards La Rocca and Calvarino.

Pieve di Santa Restituta ★★★ GAJA estate for a Piedmontese interpretation of BRUNELLO DI MONTALCINO.

Pinocchio Pine wine famous for its nose: longer in stressful years.

Pinot Bianco (Pinot Bl) Potentially excellent grape making many DOC wines in the northeast, esp from high sites in ALTO ADIGE ★★★. Best ALTO ADIGE growers include Colterenzio, HOFSTÄTTER, LAGEDER, NALS MARGREID, NIEDRIST, TERLANO, Termeno. Gd COLLIO ★★→★★★ producers include Renato Keber, Aldo Polencic, Russiz Superiore, SCHIOPETTO, VILLA RUSSIZ. Best from COLLI ORIENTALI ★★→★★★ La Viarte, Zamò & Zamò. From ISONZO try Masut da Rive.

Pinot Grigio World-popular varietal white of medium-low acidity and broadly appealing fruit. Has given birth to countless copycats, not to say fraudulent versions. *Caveat emptor*. The real thing can be excellent, usually dry (unlike Alsace's residual sugar Pinot Gr), full-bodied and velvety; and not cheap.

Pinot Nero (Pinot N) Planted in much of northeast Italy. DOC status and some quality in Lombardy (CA' DEL BOSCO's Pinero) and in ALTO ADIGE (co-ops of Caldaro, COLTERENZIO and NALS MARGREID, HAAS, Haderburg, HOFSTÄTTER, LAGEDER, Laimburg, NIEDERMAYR, San Michele Appiano, Termeno) and in OLTREPÒ PAVESE (Frecciarossa, Ruiz de Cardenas). Not bad in FRIULI (LE DUE TERRE, Masut da Riva); gets worse as you head south.

Pio Cesare ★★→★★★ Long-established ALBA producer, offers BAROLO and BARBARESCO in both modern (BARRIQUE) and traditional (large cask- aged) versions. Probably the best NEBBIOLO D'ALBA.

Planeta ★★→★★★ Top SICILIAN estate: Segreta *bianco* blend, Segreta ROSSO; outstanding CHARD, CAB SAUV, FIANO, MERLOT, NERO D'AVOLA (Santa Cecilia).

Podere Small Tuscan farm, once part of a big estate.

Poggio Means "hill" in Tuscan dialect. "POGGIONE" means "big hill".

Poggio Antico ★★★ Admirably consistent, top-level BRUNELLO DI MONTALCINO.

Poggione, Tenuta Il ★★★ V. reliable estate for BRUNELLO considering large volume; also ROSSO DI MONTALCINO.

Pojer & Sandri ★★→★★★ Gd TRENTINO producers, red and white wines, SPUMANTE.

Poliziano ★★★ MONTEPULCIANO estate. Federico Carletti makes superior VINO NOBILE (esp Asinone) and gd IGT Le Stanze (CAB SAUV/MERLOT).

Pomino Tus DOC r w ★★★ (r) 01 03 04 06 07 (08) (09) Fine red and white blends (esp Il Benefizio). Virtually a FRESCOBALDI exclusivity.

Prà ★★★ Excellent SOAVE CLASSICO producer, esp *cru* Monte Grande and new Staforte, 6 mths in steel tanks on lees with mechanical *bâtonnage*.

Potentino, Castello di ★★ English eccentric Charlotte Horton takes on the might of what she calls "Mort-alcino" at this medieval redoubt on the slopes of TUSCANY's eerie Monte Amiata. V.gd SANGIOVESE Sacromonte; better Piropo.

Produttori del Barbaresco ★★→★★★ Co-op and one of DOCG's most reliable producers. Often v.gd single-v'yd wines (Asili, Montefico, Montestefano).

Prosecco A recent change in the law means this name may no longer apply to a grape variety but only to wine derived from the "Glera" (new name) grape in specified DOC/DOCG zones of the Veneto and FRIULI-VENEZIA GIULIA. The purpose is to stop Piedmontese, Aussies and Californians from using the name in no matter what fizz.

Prosecco di Conegliano-Valdobbiadene Ven DOC w s/sw sp fz (dr) **★★** DYA Now DOCG-status light sparkler consumed as apéritif in all bars in Venice and throughout Italy. Off-dry is normal, truly dry (brut) is rare. Sweetest are called Superiore di Cartizze. CARPENÈ-MALVOLTI best-known; also Adami, BISOL, Bortolin, Canevel, Case Bianche, Col Salice, Le Colture, Col Vetoraz, Nino Franco, Gregoletto, La Riva dei Frati, Ruggeri, Zardetto.

Prunotto, Alfredo ★★★→★★★★ Traditional ALBA company modernized by ANTINORI in 1990s, and run by Piero's daughter Albiera. V.gd BARBARESCO (Bric Turot), BAROLO (Bussia), NEBBIOLO (Occhetti), BARBERA D'ALBA (Pian Romauldo), BARBERA D'ASTI (Costamiole) and MONFERRATO ROSSO (Mompertone, BARBERA/SYRAH blend).

Puglia See APULIA.

Le Pupille ★★★ Top producer of MORELLINO DI SCANSANO (look for Poggio Valente), excellent IGT blend Saffredi (CAB SAUV/MERLOT/Alicante).

Querciabella ★★★★ Top CHIANTI CLASSICO estate with IGT *crus* Camartina (SANGIOVESE/CAB SAUV) and barrel-fermented white Batàr. Recent purchases in Radda and MAREMMA have increased production of CHIANTI CLASSICO and added Mongrana (SANGIOVESE and CAB SAUV and MERLOT) to the portfolio.

Quintarelli, Giuseppe ★★★★ No spitting allowed at the winery of this arch-traditionalist, artisanal producer of VALPOLICELLA, RECIOTO and AMARONE. No wonder, considering the high prices.

Racemi ★★ AKA Accademia dei Racemi. Manduria-based group incorporating a number of SALENTO properties, inc Pervini, Sinfarosa, Felline, Anarkos.

Rampolla, Castello dei ★★★→★★★★ Fine estate in Panzano in CHIANTI CLASSICO, notable CAB SAUV-based IGT wines Sammarco and Alceo.

Recioto di Soave Ven DOCG w sw (sp) **★★★→★★★★** 01 04 05 07 (08) (09) SOAVE made from selected half-dried grapes: sweet, fruity, slightly almondy; sweetness is cut by high acidity. Outstanding from ANSELMI, COFFELE, Gini, PIEROPAN, Tamellini, often v.gd from Ca' Rugate, PASQUA, PRÀ, Suavia, Trabuchi.

Recioto della Valpolicella Ven DOC r s/sw (sp) **★★★→★★★★** Potentially stunning, rich, cherry-chocolaty red from grapes dried on trays up to 6 mths.

Refosco (dal Peduncolo Rosso) r **★★→★★★** 01 03 04 05 06 07 (08) 08 (09) Dark, gutsy red sometimes gd for ageing. Best from COLLI ORIENTALI DOC, Moschioni, Le Vigne di Zamo, Volpi Pasini: gd from LIVIO FELLUGA, Miani and from Dorigo, Ronchi di Manzano, Venica, Ca' Bolani and Denis Montanara in Aquileia DOC.

Regaleali See TASCA D'ALMERITA.

Ribolla Colli Orientali del Friuli and Collio, F-VG DOC w **★→★★** DYA Acidic but characterful northeastern white. The best comes from COLLIO. Top estates: II Carpino, La Castellada, Damijan, Fliegl, GRAVNER, Primosic, Radikon, Tercic.

Ricasoli Historic Tuscan family, 19th-century proposers of CHIANTI blend, whose CHIANTI CLASSICO is named after the medieval castle of BROLIO. Related Ricasolis own Castello di Cacchiano and Rocca di Montegrossi.

Riecine Tus r ★★★ First-class v. small CHIANTI CLASSICO estate at Gaiole, created by its late English owner, John Dunkley. Also fine IGT SANGIOVESE La Gioia.

Riesling (Ries) The great German is of v. little interest today in Italy, with the possible exception of one or two producers in ALTO ADIGE (HOFSTÄTTER, NIEDRIST) and in FRIULI-VENEZIA GIULIA (Ronco del Gelso, VIE DI ROMANS).

Ripasso VALPOLICELLA re-fermented on RECIOTO or AMARONE grape skins to make a complex longer-lived wine. V.gd from BUSSOLA, Castellani, DAL FORNO, QUINTARELLI, ZENATO. MASI's IGT Campo Fiorin claimed to be first and entitled to exclusivity of the title. Others say it's traditional and the name is generic.

Riserva Wine aged for a statutory period, usually in casks or barrels.

Rivera ★★ Reliable winemakers at Andria in APULIA. ★★★ CASTEL DEL MONTE Il Falcone RISERVA; v.gd Cappellaccio; Vigna al Monte; Puer Apuliae.

Rivetti, Giorgio (La Spinetta) ★★★ Fine MOSCATO D'ASTI, excellent BARBERA, interesting IGT Pin, series of super-concentrated, oaky BARBARESCOS. Now owner of v'yds both in the BAROLO and the CHIANTI Colli Pisane DOCGS. Early vintages of BAROLO along lines of BARBARESCO.

Rocca, Bruno ★★★ Admirable modern-style BARBARESCO (Rabajà) and other ALBA wines, also v. fine BARBERA D'ASTI.

Rocche dei Manzoni ★★★ Modernist estate at Monforte d'Alba. Oaky BAROLO (esp Vigna d'la Roul, Cappella di Stefano, Pianpolvere), *Bricco Manzoni* (pioneer BARBERA/NEBBIOLO blend), Quatr Nas (LANGHE).

Roero Pie DOCG r ★★ 96 97' 98' 99' 00 01' 03 04' 05 06' 07' (08') (09) Potentially serious, occasionally BAROLO-level NEBBIOLOS from the LANGHE hills across the Tanaro from ALBA. Best: Almondo, Buganza, Ca' Rossa, Cascina Chicco, Correggia, Funtanin, Malvirà, Monchiero-Carbone, Morra, Pace, Pioiero, Taliano, Val di Prete. See also ARNEIS.

Ronco Term for a hillside v'yd in northeast Italy, esp FRIULI-VENEZIA GIULIA.

Rosato Rosé; also CHIARETTO, esp around Lake Garda; and CERASUOLO, from Abruzzo; and Kretzer, from ALTO ADIGE.

Rosato del Salento Ap p ★★ DYA From near BRINDISI. Sturdy NEGROAMARO-based wine from a zone that has specialized in rosé. See COPERTINO, SALICE SALENTO.

Rosso Conero Mar DOCG r ★★→★★★ 01' 03' 04 05 06' 07' (08) (09) Some of Italy's best MONTEPULCIANO (the grape, that is): GAROFOLI's Grosso Agontano, Moroder's Dorico, MONTE SCHIAVO's Adeodato, TERRE CORTESI MONCARO's Nerone and Vigneti del Parco, Le Terrazze's Sassi Neri and Visions of J. Also gd: Casato, FAZI-BATTAGLIA, Lanari, Leopardi Dittajuti, Malacari, Marchetti, Piantate Lunghe, Poggio Morelli, UMANI RONCHI.

Rosso di Montalcino Tus DOC r ★★→★★★ 04' 05 06' 07' (08) (09) DOC for younger wines from BRUNELLO grapes, from younger or lesser v'yd sites.

Rosso di Montefalco Umb DOC r ★★→★★★ 99' 00' 01' 03 04' 05 06' 07' (08) (09) SANGIOVESE/Sagrantino blend, often with a splash of softening MERLOT. For producers, see MONTEFALCO SAGRANTINO.

Rosso di Montepulciano Tus DOC r ★★ 03 04 05 06 07 (08) (09) Junior version of VINO NOBILE DI MONTEPULCIANO, growers similar. Seen much less than ROSSO DI MONTALCINO, probably because of confusion with MONTEPULCIANO D'ABRUZZO, with which it has nothing in common.

Rosso Piceno Mar DOC r 04 05 06 07 (08) (09) Gluggable MONTEPULCIANO/ SANGIOVESE blend from southern half of Marches, SUPERIORE from restricted classic zone near Ascoli, much improved in recent yrs and v.gd value. Best: Aurora, BOCCADIGABBIA, Bucci, Fonte della Luna, Montecappone, MONTE SCHIAVO, Saladini Pilastri, TERRE CORTESI MONCARO, Velenosi Ercole, Villamagna.

Ruffino ★→★★★ Famous CHIANTI merchant at Pontassieve, east of Florence. Best are RISERVA Ducale Oro and Santedame. Oaky IGT CHARD Solatia, SANGIOVESE/ CAB SAUV Modus. Owns Lodola Nuova in MONTEPULCIANO for VINO NOBILE DI

MONTEPULCIANO and Greppone Mazzi in MONTALCINO for BRUNELLO DI MONTEPULCIANO. Excellent MERLOT/Colorino blend Romitorio di Santedame. Also owns Borgo Conventi estate in FRIULI-VENEZIA GIULIA.

Rúfina ★★★ Important subregion of CHIANTI. Best wines from Basciano, CASTELLO DI NIPOZZANO (FRESCOBALDI), Castello del Trebbio, Colognole, Frascole, Lavacchio, SELVAPIANA, Tenuta Bossi, Travignoli. Villa di Vetrice/Grati do old vintages, sometimes aged 20 yrs+ in oak barrels or concrete vats.

Sala, Castello della ★★→★★★ ANTINORI estate at ORVIETO. Campogrande is the regular white. Top wine is a splendid *Cervaro della Sala*, oak-aged CHARD/Grechetto. Muffato della Sala was a pioneering example of an Italian botrytis-influenced dessert wine. PINOT N also creditable.

Salento Southernmost section of the APULIAN peninsula: flat, between two seas, covered with old vines and ancient olive trees. Several NEGROAMARO-based DOCS inc SALICE SALENTINO, COPERTINO, BRINDISI, Alezio, Leverano. IGT Salento, covering 19 grapes red and white, is catching on.

Salice Salentino Ap DOC r ★★→★★★ 03 04 06 07 (08) (09) Smooth red from Puglia's southern tip, made from NEGROAMARO and MALVASIA NERA grapes and redolent of plums. RISERVA after 2 yrs. Top makers: Apollonio, Candido, Castello Monaci, Due Palme, Resya, Tornavento, TAURINO, Valle dell'Asso, VALLONE.

Sandrone, Luciano ★★★ Exponent of modern-style ALBA wines with deep, concentrated BAROLO Cannubi Boschi and Le Vigne, DOLCETTO, BARBERA D'ALBA and NEBBIOLO D'ALBA.

San Felice ★★ Large CHIANTI CLASSICO resort/estate. Fine RISERVA Poggio Rosso. Pugnitello, made from a Tuscan grape recovered from near-extinction, a fascinating addition. Also red IGT Vigorello (the v. first SUPER TUSCAN, from 1968) and BRUNELLO DI MONTALCINO Campogiovanni.

San Gimignano Tuscan town famous for its towers and dry white VERNACCIA, often overpriced and overvalued but occasionally convincing as a wine if not as a *vin de terroir*. Some gd red wines, too. Producers include Casale Falchini, Cesani, Guicciardini Strozza, Montenidoli, Mormoraia, Il Palagione, Panizzi, Podere del Paradiso, Pietrafitta, Pietrasereno, La Rampa di Fugnano.

Sangiovese (Sangioveto) Principal red grape of west-central Italy with a reputation of being v. difficult to get right, but sublime and long-lasting when it is. Currently the subject of enormous research and experimentation, new clones are yielding more reliable fruit. Dominant in CHIANTI, VINO NOBILE, BRUNELLO DI MONTALCINO, MORELLINO DI SCANSANO and various fine IGT offerings. Also in Umbria generally (eg. MONTEFALCO ROSSO and TORGIANO RISERVA) and across the Apennines in Romagna and the Marches. Not so clever in the warmer, lower-altitude v'yds of the Tuscan coast, nor in other parts of Italy despite its near ubiquity.

Sangiovese di Romagna Mar DOC r ★★→★★★ Often well-made and v.gd value from La Berta, Berti, Calonga, Ca' Lunga, Cesari, Drei Donà, Paradiso, San Patrignano, Tre Monti, Trere (E-R DOC), Zerbina; IGT Ronco delle Ginestre, Ronco dei Ciliegi from CASTELLUCCIO.

San Giusto a Rentennano ★★★→★★★★ V. fine CHIANTI CLASSICO producers (★★★). V.gd but v. rare VIN SANTO called Vin San Giusto. Top, long-lasting SANGIOVESE IGT Percarlo (★★★★).

San Guido, Tenuta See SASSICAIA.

San Leonardo ★★★ Superb estate in TRENTINO, run by Marchese Carlo Guerrieri Gonzaga, ex SASSICAIA. Top wine, Bordeaux blend San Leonardo, is sometimes called the "SASSICAIA of the north". Also v. promising MERLOT Villa Gresti.

San Michele Appiano Top ALTO ADIGE co-op,esp for whites. Look for PINOT BIANCO Schulthauser and Sanct Valentin (★★★) selections: CHARD, PINOT GR, SAUV BL, CAB SAUV, PINOT N, Gewurz.

Santadi ★★★ Consistently fine wines from Sardinian co-op, esp DOC CARIGNANO DEL

SULCIS Grotta Rossa, Rocca Rubia, TERRE BRUNE and IGT Baie Rosse (CARIGNANO), *Vermentino Villa Solais*, Villa di Chiesa (VERMENTINO/CHARD).

Santa Maddalena (or St-Magdalener) T-AA DOC r ★→★★ DYA Mussolini proclaimed this one of Italy's best wines, but it is far from that – v. light (from SCHIAVA grape, laced with LAGREIN), fades quickly. Not generally to Anglo-Saxon taste. Acceptable producers include: St-Magdalena (Huck am Bach), Gojer, Josephus Mayr, Georg Ramoser, Hans Rottensteiner (Premstallerhof), Heinrich Rottensteiner.

Santa Margherita Large Veneto (Portogruaro) merchants, famous for decent but overpriced PINOT GR. Also owns: Torresella (Veneto), Kettmeir (ALTO ADIGE), Lamole di Lamole and Vistarenni (TUSCANY) and CA' DEL BOSCO (Lombardy).

Sant'Antimo Tus DOC r w sw ★★→★★★ Catch-all DOC for (almost) everything in MONTALCINO zone that isn't BRUNELLO DOCG or ROSSO DOC. Sant'Antimo is a Romanesque abbey.

Sardinia (Sardegna) The Med's second-biggest island produces much decent and some v.gd wines, eg. Turriga from ARGIOLAS, Arbeskia and Dule from Gabbas, VERMENTINO of CAPICHERA, CANNONAU RISERVAS of Jerzu and Loi, VERMENTINO and CANNONAU from Dettori and the amazing *flor*-affected VERNACCIA of CONTINI. Best DOCS: Vermentino di Gallura (eg. Canayli from Cantina Gallura) and CARIGNANO DEL SULCIS (TERRE BRUNE and Rocca Rubia from SANTADI).

Sartarelli ★★★ One of top VERDICCHIO DEI CASTELLI DI JESI producers (Tralivio); outstanding, rare Verdicchio Vendemmia Tardiva (Contrada Balciana).

Sassicaia Tus r ★★★★ 85' 88' 90' 95' 97 98' 99 01' 03 04' 05 06 07' (08) (09) A CAB (SAUV and FR) made on First-Growth lines by Marchese Incisa della Rocchetta at TENUTA San Guido in BOLGHERI, Sassicaia has today been fully accepted by the international market as one of the world's top prestige and investment wines, up there with the likes of Latour, Pétrus and Grange. Some may think it a shame that a CAB should be regarded as Italy's finest, but overall, Sassicaia's effect on the image of BOLGHERI, of the Tuscan coast, of SUPER-TUSCANS and high-quality Italian wines generally has been extremely positive.

Satta, Michele ★★★ Virtually the only BOLGHERI grower to succeed with 100% SANGIOVESE (Cavaliere). Also BOLGHERI DOC red blends Piastraia and SUPERIORE I Castagni.

Sauvignon Blanc Vinified varietally throughout the northeast and elsewhere in Italy, generally for blending. V. successful in ALTO ADIGE and FRIULI-VG. Try Voglar from Peter Dipoli (ALTO ADIGE) and Piere from VIE DI ROMANS (FRIULI-VG).

Scavino, Paolo ★★★ Successful modern-style BAROLO producer. Sought-after single-v'yd wines: Rocche dell'Annunziata, Bric del Fiasc, Cannubi and Carobric. Also oak-aged BARBERA and LANGHE Corale.

Schiava High-yielding red grape of ALTO ADIGE, used for light reds such as Lago di Caldaro, SANTA MADDALENA, etc. Known locally as Vernatsch.

Schiopetto, Mario ★★★→★★★★ Legendary late COLLIO pioneer with spacious modern winery. V.gd DOC SAUV BL, *Pinot Bl*, TOCAI, IGT blend Blanc de Rosis, etc. Recent offerings include wines from COLLI ORIENTALI v'yds.

Sciacchetrà See CINQUETERRE.

Scolca. la ★★ Famous GAVI estate for gd GAVI and SPUMANTE.

Secco Dry.

Sella & Mosca ★★ Major Sardinian grower and merchant with v. pleasant white Torbato and light, fruity VERMENTINO Cala Viola (DYA). Gd Alghero DOC Marchese di Villamarina (CAB SAUV) and Tanca Farrà (CANNONAU/CAB SAUV). Also interesting port-like Anghelu Ruju.

Selvapiana ★★★ Top CHIANTI RUFINA estate. Best wines are RISERVA Bucerchiale and IGT Fornace. Also, under the Petrognano label, some fine red DOC POMINO, the DOC's only significant producer apart from FRESCOBALDI.

Settesoli, CS ★→★★ Huge, quality-conscious Sicilian co-op with nearly 7,000 ha, run by PLANETA family and giving SICILY a good name with v. well-made varietals (**Nero d'Avola**, SYRAH, MERLOT, CAB SAUV, CHARD, Grecanico, Viognier and blends.) at v. modest prices. Look for brand Mandrarossa.

Sforzato See VALTELLINA.

Sicily The Med's largest island has been hailed for its creative approach to winemaking, using both native grapes (NERO D'AVOLA, NERELLO MASCALESE, Frappato, Inzolia, Grecanico, Grillo) and international varieties. Wisely, the IGT Sicilia is widely used, avoiding obscure DOCs like Contea di Sclafani and Contessa Entellina. To seek out: Benanti, Ceusi, Colosi, Cos, Cusumano, De Bartoli, DONNAFUGATA, DUCA DI SALAPARUTA, Fazio, Firriato, Foraci, Gulfi-Ramada, Miceli, Morgante, MURANA, Pellegrino, PLANETA, Rapitalà, Sallier de la Tour, Santa Anastasia, SETTESOLI, SIV, Spadafora, TASCA D'ALMERITA, Tenuta dell'Abate.

Sizzano Pie DOC r ★★ 99 01' 03 04 06 07 (08) (09) Elegant but hard-to-find red from the province of Novara; mostly NEBBIOLO. Ages up to 10 yrs. Esp: Bianchi, Dessilani.

Soave Ven DOC w (sw) ★→★★★ 04 06 08, 09 Famous, still underrated Veronese. From the CLASSICO zone can be intense, mineral, v. fine and quite long-lived. When labelled SUPERIORE is DOCG, but best CLASSICO producers shun the "honour", stick to DOC. Sweet RECIOTO can be superb. Best: Cantina del Castello, La Cappuccina, Ca' Rugate, Cecilia Beretta, COFFELE, Dama del Rovere, Fattori, Gini, Guerrieri-Rizzardi, Inama, Montetondo, PIEROPAN, Portinari, PRÀ, Sartori, Suavia, Tamellini, TEDESCHI.

Solaia Tus r ★★★★ 85' 90' 95' 97' 99' 01' 04 06 07' (08) (09) V. fine Bordeaux-style IGT of CAB SAUV and a little SANGIOVESE from ANTINORI; first made in 1978.

Sorì Term for a high south-, southeast-, or southwest-oriented site in PIEDMONT.

Sovana MAREMMA DOC; inland near Pitigliano. Look for SANGIOVESE, Ciliegiolo from Tenuta Roccaccia, Pitigliano, Ripa, Sassotondo, Malbec from ANTINORI.

Spanna Local name for NEBBIOLO in a variety of north PIEDMONT zones (BOCA, BRAMATERRA, FARA, GATTINARA, GHEMME, LESSONA, SIZZANO).

Spumante Sparkling. What used to be called Asti Spumante is now just ASTI.

Südtirol The local name of German-speaking ALTO ADIGE.

Superiore Wine with more ageing than normal DOC and 0.5–1% more alcohol. May indicate a restricted production zone, eg. ROSSO PICENO Superiore.

Super Tuscan Unofficial term coined in 1980s for innovative wines from TUSCANY, often involving pure SANGIOVESE or international varieties, BARRIQUES, heavy bottles and elevated prices. Now losing ground to top DOCGs like BRUNELLO and CHIANTI CLASSICO.

Syrah The Rhône's great grape has become popular in TUSCANY and SICILY, mainly as a blender. Il Bosco from d'Alessandro or Case Vie from FONTODI are gd examples.

Tasca d'Almerita ★★★ Historic SICILIAN producer owned by noble family in Palermo province. Gd IGT red, white and ROSATO REGALEALI; v.gd NERO D'AVOLA **Rosso del Conte**; impressive CHARD and CAB SAUV.

Taurasi Cam DOCG r ★★★ 95 97' 98 99 00 01' 03' 04' 05 06 07' (08) CAMPANIA's historic and most celebrated red, one of Italy's outstanding wines, though not easy to appreciate. RISERVA after 4 yrs. V.gd from Caggiano, Caputo, Colli di Lapio, FEUDI DI SAN GREGORIO, MASTROBERARDINO, Molettieri, Terredora di Paulo, Vesevo and Villa Raiano.

Taurino, Cosimo ★★★ Best-known producer of Salento-APULIA when Cosimo was alive, v.gd SALICE SALENTINO, VDT Notarpanoro, and IGT Patriglione Rosso.

Tedeschi, Fratelli ★★→★★★ Long-established producer of VALPOLICELLA, AMARONE, RECIOTO. Gd IGT Capitel San Rocco red.

Tenuta Farm or estate. (See under name – eg. SAN GUIDO, TENUTA.)

Terlano T-AA w ★★→★★★ DYA ALTO ADIGE Terlano DOC applies to one white blend and eight white varietals, esp PINOT BL and SAUV BL. Best: CS Terlano (Pinot Bl Vorberg, capable of remarkable ageing), LAGEDER, NIEDERMAYR, NIEDRIST.

Teroldego Rotaliano T-AA DOC r p ★★→★★★ Attractive blackberry-scented red; slightly bitter aftertaste; can age v. well. Esp *Foradori*'s. Also gd from Dorigati, Endrizzi, MEZZACORONA'S RISERVA Nos, Zeni.

Terre Cortesi Moncaro Mar ★★★ Marches co-op, now making wines that compete with the best of the region at remarkably low prices: gd VERDICCHIO DEI CASTELLI DI JESI (Le Vele), ROSSO CONERO, RISERVA (Nerone) and ROSSO PICENO SUPERIORE (Campo delle Mura).

Terre di Franciacorta Lom DOC r w ★★★ 03 04 06 07 08 (09) So named to distinguish table wines from sparkling FRANCIACORTA. The red is an unusual blend of CAB SAUV, BARBERA, NEBBIOLO, MERLOT. Less adventurous whites from CHARD, PINOT GR. Alternative name: Curtefranca. Best producers: see FRANCIACORTA.

Terre Rosse ★★ Small estate near Bologna. Its CAB SAUV, CHARD, PINOT BL, RIES, even Viognier, were once trail-blazing wines for the region.

Terre da Vino ★→★★★ Association of 27 PIEDMONT co-ops and private estates, inc most local DOCS. Best: BARBARESCO La Casa in Collina, BAROLO Podere Parussi, BARBERA D'ASTI La Luna e I Falò.

Terriccio, Castello del ★★★ Large estate south of Livorno: excellent, v. expensive Bordeaux-style IGT Lupicaia, v.gd IGT Tassinaia. Impressive new IGT Terriccio, an unusual blend of mainly Rhône grapes.

Tiefenbrunner ★★→★★★ Medium-sized grower-négociant situated at a quaint Teutonic castle (Turmhof) in southern ALTO ADIGE village of Entiklar. Christof T has taken over from octogenarian father Herbert (winemaker since 1943) producing a wide range of mtn-fresh white and well-defined red varietals, French, Germanic and local, esp 1,000-m high Feldmarschall (see MULLER-THURGAU) and Linticlarus range CHARD/LAGREIN/PINOT N.

Tignanello Tus r ★★★★ 95 97' 98 **99**' **00 01**' 03 04' 06' 07' (08) (09) SANGIOVESE/CAB SAUV blend, BARRIQUE-aged, the wine that put SUPER TUSCANS on the map, created by ANTINORI in the early 1970s.

Tocai See FRIULANO.

Torgiano Umb DOC r p w (sp) ★★ and **Torgiano, Rosso Riserva** Umb DOCG r ★★→★★★ 97 **99 00**' **01**' 03 04 06 07' 08 (09) Gd to excellent CHIANTI-style red from Umbria, dominated by LUNGAROTTI'S Rubesco. Vigna Monticchio Rubesco Riserva outstanding in vintages such as 1975, 1979, 1985; keeps many yrs.

Traminer Aromatico T-AA DOC w ★★→★★★ DYA (German: Gewurz) Pungent white with all the aromatics of the Alsatian versions minus the residual sugar. Best from its birthplace Tramin (Italian: Termeno), notably CS Termeno and HOFSTÄTTER. Other gd producers include esp Caldaro, Colterenzio, Prima & Nuova, SAN MICHELE APPIANO, TERLANO plus Abbazia di Novacella, HAAS, Kuenhof, LAGEDER, Laimberg, NALS MARGREID, Niedermayr.

Trebbiano Principal white grape of TUSCANY, found all over Italy in many different guises. Rarely rises above the plebian except in TUSCANY'S VIN SANTO. Some gd dry whites under DOCS Romagna or Abruzzo. Trebbiano di Soave or di Lugana, aka VERDICCHIO, is only distantly related.

Trebbiano d'Abruzzo Ab DOC w ★→★★ DYA Gentle, neutral white grape of gd acidity from Pescara. That of VALENTINI is considered excellent, other gd versions from Contesa, Masciarelli, Nicodemi, La Valentina and Valori.

Trentino T-AA DOC r w dr sw ★→★★★ DOC for 20 wines, most named after grapes. Best: CHARD, PINOT BL, MARZEMINO, TEROLDEGO. Provincial capital is Trento.

Triacca ★★→★★★ V.gd producer of VALTELLINA; also owns estates in TUSCANY (CHIANTI CLASSICO: La Madonnina; MONTEPULCIANO: Santavenere).

Trinoro, Tenuta di ★★★ Individualist Tuscan red wine estate in DOC Val d'Orcia between MONTEPULCIANO and MONTALCINO. Early vintages of Bordeaux blend

Trinoro caused great excitement, then the price shot up. Le Cupole adds LAZIO's Cesanese and Puglia's Uva di Troia to the Bordeaux mix. Andrea Franchetti also has v'yds on Mt Etna.

Tua Rita ★★→★★★★ The first producer to establish Suvereto as the new BOLGHERI in the 1990s. Producer of possibly Italy's greatest MERLOT in Redigaffi, also outstanding Bordeaux blend Giusto di Notri. See VAL DI CORNIA.

Tuscany (Toscana) Italy's central wine region, includes DOCS CHIANTI, MONTALCINO, MONTEPULCIANO, etc., regional IGT TOSCANA, and – of course – SUPER TUSCAN.

Uberti ★★→★★★ Producer of DOCG FRANCIACORTA. V.gd TERRE DI FRANCIACORTA.

Umani Ronchi ★★→★★★ Leading Marches merchant and grower, esp for VERDICCHIO (Casal di Serra, Plenio), ROSSO CONERO Cumaro, white IGT Le Busche, red IGT Pelago.

Vajra, G D ★★★ V.gd consistent BAROLO producer, esp for BARBERA, BAROLO, DOLCETTO, LANGHE, etc. Also a serious still FREISA.

Val di Cornia Tus DOC r p w ★★→★★ 97 98 99' 00 01' 03 04' 05 06' 07 08 (09) DOC south of BOLGHERI, province of Livorno. SANGIOVESE, CAB SAUV, MERLOT, SYRAH and MONTEPULCIANO. Look for: Ambrosini, Jacopo Banti, Bulichella, Gualdo del Re, Incontri, Montepeloso, Petra, Russo, San Michele, Tenuta Casa Dei, Terricciola, TUA RITA.

Valdadige T-AA DOC r w dr s/sw ★ Name for the simple wines of the valley of the ALTO ADIGE – in German, Etschtaler.

Valentini, Edoardo ★★★ Son continues the tradition of long-macerating, non-filtered, non-fined, hand-bottled MONTEPULCIANO and TREBBIANO D'ABRUZZO.

Valle d'Aosta (VdA) DOC r p w ★★ Regional DOC for some 25 Alpine wines, geographically or varietally named, inc Premetta, Fumin, Blanc de Morgex et de La Salle, Chambave, Nus Malvoisie, Arnad Montjovet, Torrette, Donnas, and Enfer d'Arvier. Tiny production, wines rarely seen abroad.

Valle Isarco Eisacktal, T-AA DOC w ★★ DYA ALTO ADIGE Valle Isarco DOC is applicable to seven varietal wines made northeast of Bolzano. Gd Gewurz, MÜLLER-THURGAU, RIES and Silvaner. Top producers: Abbazia di Novacella, Eisacktaler, Kuenhof.

Vallone, Agricole ★★→★★★ Large-scale private v'yd-holder in APULIA's Salento peninsula, excellent gd-value BRINDISI ROSSO/ROSATO Vigna Flaminio, best-known for its AMARONE-like semi-dried-grape wine Graticciaia.

Valpolicella Ven DOC r ★→★★★★ 00 01 03 04 05 06 07 08 (09) (SUPERIORE) Complex denomination inc everything from light quaffers through stronger SUPERIORES to AMARONES and RECIOTOS of ancient lineage. Bitter cherry the common flavour characteristic. Best tend to come from CLASSICO subzone.

Valtellina Lom DOC r ★→★★★ DOC for tannic but elegant wines: mainly from Chiavennasca (NEBBIOLO) in northern Alpine Sondrio province. V.gd SUPERIORE DOCG from Grumello, Inferno, Sassella, Valgella v'yds. Best: Caven Camuna, Conti Sertoli-Salis, Fay, Nera, Nino Negri, Plozza, Rainoldi, TRIACCA. *Sforzato* is the most concentrated type of Valtellina; similar to AMARONE.

Valpolicella: the list

Whether it's AMARONE, RECIOTO or plain VALPOLICELLA, these producers are good to superb: Accordini, Serego Alighieri, ALLEGRINI, Baltieri, Begali, BERTANI, BOLLA, Boscaini, BRUNELLI, BUSSOLA, Ca' la Bianca, Campagnola, Ca' Rugate, Castellani, Cesari, Corteforte, Corte Sant Alda, CS Negrar, CS Valpantena, CS VALPOLICELLA, Valentina Cubi, DAL FORNO, Farina, Aleardo FERRARI, Guerrieri-Rizzardi, I Saltari, MASI, Mazzi, Nicolis, PASQUA, QUINTARELLI, Roccolo Grassi, Le ragose, Le salette, Sant'Alda, Sant'Antonio, Sartori, Speri, Tarrelli, TEDESCHI, Tommasi, Trabucchi, Vaona, Venturini, Villa Bellini, Villa Monteleone, VIVIANI, ZENATO, Zeni. Interesting IGTS: BUSSOLA's L'Errante, MASI's Toar and Osar, ALLEGRINI's La Grola, La Poja, Palazzo della Torre, Zyme's Harlequin, Oz.

Vecchio Samperi Si ★★★ Virgin-like VDT from famous MARSALA estate. Best is barrel-aged Ventennale, a blend of young and v. old vintages. Owner Marco de Bartoli also makes top DOC MARSALAS and outstanding PASSITO Bukkuram at his winery on the island of Pantelleria.

Vendemmia Harvest or vintage.

Venegazzu ★★→★★★ Iconic Bordeaux blend from eastern Veneto producer Loredan Gasparini. Even more prestigious is the *cru* Capo di Stato (being originally created to be served at the table of the president of the Italian Republic).

Verdicchio dei Castelli di Jesi Mar DOC w (sp) ★★→★★★ DYA Versatile white from near Ancona, can be light and quaffable, or sparkling, or structured, complex and long-lived (esp RISERVA, min 2 yrs old). Also CLASSICO. Best from: Accadia, Bonci-Vallerosa, Brunori, Bucci, Casalfarneto, Cimarelli, Colonnara, Coroncino, FAZI-BATTAGLIA, Fonte della Luna, GAROFOLI, Laila, Lucangeli Aymerich di Laconi, Mancinelli, Montecappone, MONTE SCHIAVO, Santa Barbara, SARTARELLI, TERRE CORTESI MONCARO, UMANI RONCHI.

Verdicchio di Matelica Mar DOC w (sp) ★★→★★★ DYA Similar to above, smaller, less-known, longer lasting. Esp Barone Pizzini, Belisario, Bisci, La Monacesca, Pagliano Tre, San Biagio.

Verduno Pie DOC r ★★ DYA Pale red with spicy perfume, from Pelaverga grape. Gd producers: BURLOTTO, Alessandria and CASTELLO DI VERDUNO.

Verduno, Castello di Pie ★★★ Husband/wife team Franco Bianco, with v'yds in Neive, and Gabriella Burlotto, with v'yds in Verduno, turn out v.gd Barbaresco Rabaja and Barolo Monvigliero with the help of winemaker Mario Andrion.

Verduzzo Colli Orientali del Friuli, F-VG DOC w dr sw s/sw ★★→★★★ Full-bodied white from indigenous variety. Ramandolo is well-regarded subzone for sweet wine. Top: Dario Coos, Dorigo, Giov Dri, Meroi. Superb LIS NERIS sweet VDT Tal Luc.

Vermentino Lig w ★★ DYA Best seafood white of Riviera, esp Pietra Ligure, San Remo. DOC is Riviera Ligure di Ponente. Esp gd: Lambruschi, Lupi. Also TUSCANY/Umbria coast: ANTINORI, Barberani, San Giusto a Rentennano, SATTA.

Vermentino di Gallura Sar DOCG w ★★→★★★ DYA *Best dry white of Sardinia*, stronger and more intensely flavoured than DOC Vermentino di Sardegna. Esp from CAPICHERA, CS di Gallura, CS del Vermentino, Depperu.

Vernaccia di Oristano Sar DOC w dr (sw fz) ★→★★★ 90' 93' 97' 00' 01 04 06 07 (08) (09) Sardinian *flor*-affected wine, like light sherry, a touch bitter, full-bodied. SUPERIORE 15.5% alcohol, 3 yrs of age. Top: CONTINI.

Vernaccia di San Gimignano See SAN GIMIGNANO.

Verrazzano, Castello di ★★ Gd CHIANTI CLASSICO estate near Greve.

Vie di Romans ★★★→★★★★ Gianfranco Gallo has built up his father's ISONZO estate to top FRIULI status. Excellent ISONZO CHARD, PINOT GR Dessimis, SAUV BL Piere and Vieris (oaked), MALVASIA/RIES/TOCAI blend called Flors di Uis.

Vietti ★★★ Exemplary producer of characterful PIEDMONT wines, inc BAROLO, BARBARESCO Masseria, BARBERA D'ALBA Carati and D'ASTI La Crena at Castiglione Falletto in BAROLO region.

Vigna (or vigneto) A single v'yd, generally indicating superior quality.

Vignalta ★★ Top producer in COLLI EUGANEI near Padova (Veneto); v.gd COLLI EUGANEI CAB SAUV RISERVA and MERLOT/CAB SAUV blend Gemola.

Vignamaggio ★★→★★★ Historic, beautiful and v.gd CHIANTI CLASSICO estate near Greve. Leonardo da Vinci is said to have painted the Mona Lisa here.

Vigne di Zamò, le ★★★ First-class FRIULI estate. PINOT BL, TOCAI, Pignolo, CAB SAUV, MERLOT and Picolit from v'yds in three areas of COLLI ORIENTALI DEL FRIULI DOC.

Villa Matilde ★★★ Top CAMPANIA producer of FALERNO ROSSO (Vigna Camararato) and *bianco* (Vigna Caracci), PASSITO Eleusi.

Villa Russiz ★★★ Impressive white DOC COLLIO Goriziano: v.gd SAUV BL and MERLOT (esp "de la Tour" selections), PINOT BL, PINOT GR, TOCAI, CHARD.

Vino Nobile di Montepulciano Tus DOCG r ★★ →★★★95' 97' 98 99' 00 01' 03 04' 05 06' 07' (08) (09) Historic SANGIOVESE (here called Prugnolo Gentile) from the town (as distinct from ABRUZZO's grape) MONTEPULCIANO, often tough with drying tannins, but complex and long-lasting from best producers: AVIGNONESI, Bindella, BOSCARELLI, La Braccesca, La Calonica, Canneto, Le Casalte, CONTUCCI, Dei, Fattoria del Cerro, Gracciano della Seta, Gracciano Svetoni, Icario, Nottola, Palazzo Vecchio, POLIZIANO, Romeo, Salcheto, Trerose, Valdipiatta, Villa Sant'Anna. RISERVA after 3 yrs. Well-priced relative to BRUNELLO.

Vin Santo or Vinsanto, Vin(o) Santo Term for certain strong, sweet wines made from PASSITO grapes, usually TREBBIANO, MALVASIA and/or SANGIOVESE in TUSCANY ("Vin Santo"), Nosiola in TRENTINO ("Vino Santo"). Tuscan versions can be extremely variable, anything from quasi-dry and sherry-like to sweet and v. rich. May spend 3–10 unracked yrs in small barrels called *caratelli*. AVIGNONESI's is mythic; plus CAPEZZANA, CORZANO & PATERNO, Fattoria del Cerro, FELSINA, Frascole, ISOLE E OLENA, Rocca di Montegrossi, San Gervasio, San Giusto a Rentennano, SELVAPIANA, Villa Sant'Anna, Villa di Vetrice. See also OCCHIO DI PERNICE.

Vivaldi-Arunda ★★ →★★★ Winemaker Josef Reiterer makes top ALTO ADIGE sparkling wines. Best: Extra Brut Riserva, Cuvée Marianna.

Viviani ★★★ Claudio Viviani is among the best of the new-wave producers who are transforming VALPOLICELLA. Outstanding AMARONE Tulipano Nero.

Voerzio, Roberto ★★★ →★★★★ BAROLO modernist. Top, v. expensive single-v'yd BAROLOS: Brunate, Cerequio, Rocche dell'Annunziata-Torriglione, Sarmassa, Serra; *impressive Barbera d'Alba*.

Volpaia, Castello di ★★ →★★★ V.gd CHIANTI CLASSICO estate at Radda. SUPER TUSCANS Coltassala (SANGIOVESE/Mammolo), Balifico (SANGIOVESE/CAB SAUV).

Zenato Ven ★★ V. reliable for GARDA wines, VALPOLICELLA, SOAVE, AMARONE, LUGANA.

Zerbina, Fattoria ★★★ Leader in Romagna; best sweet ALBANA DOCG (Scacco Matto), v.gd SANGIOVESE (Pietramora); BARRIQUE-aged IGT Marzieno.

Zibibbo Si ★★ sw dr Local PANTELLERIA name for Muscat of Alexandria. Best from: MURANA, De Bartoli.

Zonin ★ →★★ One of Italy's biggest private estates, based at Gambellara. DOC and DOCG VALPOLICELLA. Also in ASTI, APULIA, CHIANTI CLASSICO, SAN GIMIGNANO, FRIULI, SICILY and Virginia (USA).

Zuani ★★★ Small COLLIO estate owned by Patrizia, daughter of MARCO FELLUGA. Superior white blends Z. Zuani (oaked) and Z. Vigne.

Germany

The following abbreviations are used in the text:

Bad	Baden
Frank	Franken
M-M	Mittelmosel
M-S-R	Mosel-Saar-Ruwer
Na	Nahe
Pfz	Pfalz
Rhg	Rheingau
Rhh	Rheinhessen
Würt	Württemberg

More heavily shaded areas are the wine-growing regions

Other countries may be viewing climate change with alarm, but for the Riesling growers of the Mosel and Rhine, so far the news is all good.

Great wine is made at the margin – that is, the climatic margin. The greatest, riskiest, most complex wines are made where those grapes will only just ripen comfortably. But in Germany, right up to the late 1980s, conditions were often just a bit too cold for that. Catastrophic vintages were not uncommon. It was even legal for growers to add water to dilute Riesling's fierce acidity.

Warmer years have brought a succession of good vintages to Germany, making German Riesling one of the most reliable, best-value fine wines around. Acidity has fallen, too. A warmer climate is, so far, making Riesling a perfect fit in the Mosel and Rhine.

The danger, however, is not a rise in temperature; it's a more variable climate. Wine-growers adapt viticulture to expected weather, and they can't change quickly. If summers are cool and wet, you plant cover crops between rows of vines to take up excess water; if summers are hot and dry, you won't do that because cover crops will compete for water with vines. So you need to be able to second-guess the weather and be able to adapt.

Meanwhile, styles in Germany continue to evolve. For some years now the word *halbtrocken*, or half-dry, on a label has been the kiss of death. Now, suddenly, it's becoming respectable and even desirable. At the more hand-crafted end of the wine spectrum, *halbtrocken* is becoming associated with chancy wild-yeast fermentations which, free of the predictability of commercial yeasts, stop working when they feel like it. The resulting wine may be bone-dry, or it may have some residual sugar – in other words, it may be *halbtrocken*. It would be nice to think that German growers, with some of the climatic risk removed from their lives (and only some), are injecting risk elsewhere. And why not? Wine-growers are like that.

What Germany's quality wine-growers need, above all, is a change in their government's attitude to quality itself. Ever since new wine laws in 1971 dismissed the idea that some vineyards are inherently better than others, their industry has been struggling. Now the same government is planning a motorway and bridge (160 metres high!) through and over the most sensitive part of the Mosel. 'There are 240 kms of vineyard,' they say. 'Why bother about 12 of them?' Because they are some of the best. But don't expect a minister to understand that.

Recent vintages

Mosel-Saar-Ruwer

Mosels (including Saar and Ruwer wines) are so attractive young that their keeping qualities are not often enough explored. But well-made Ries wines of Kabinett class gain from at least five years in bottle and often much more: Spätlese from five to 20, and Auslese and Beerenauslese anything from ten to 30 years. As a rule, in poor years the Saar and Ruwer make sharp, lean wines, but in good years, which are becoming increasingly common, they can surpass the whole world for elegance and thrilling, steely "breeding".

2009 Uneven flowering caused a small crop (20 per cent below average). In terms of quality, a promising vintage. Excellent ripening conditions (dry and sunny September, cool and sunny October) brought plenty of Spätlesen and Auslesen. Not much botrytis, though.

2008 Early flowering, but a classic cool summer with rain and sun. Cool September temperatures slowed down ripeness and kept acidity high. Wet October made harvesting difficult; meticulous selection was necessary. Not a vintage for Auslesen and higher Prädikat wines, but Kabinetts and Spätlesen can be fine and elegant.

2007 A warm, cloudy summer and rainy August, but a fine September ripened grapes fully for an early October harvest. Very early flowering: growing season exceptionally long. Good quality with high acidity levels in beautiful Kabinetts – good quantity, too. Some botrytis at the end of harvest.

2006 A cool, wet August and more poor weather during the autumn dampened expectations. The best growers achieved very high ripeness and vibrant acidity, but ruthless selection means that quantities are low.

2005 Superb warm autumn weather from late September through to November brought grapes to very high ripeness levels, but with far better acidity than, say, 2003. Exceptional, especially in the Saar.

2004 A humid summer led growers to fear the worst, but the vintage was saved by a glorious autumn. A fine year to start drinking.

2003 Hot weather brought high ripeness levels but rather low acidity. Ironically, some great sites suffered from drought, while less-esteemed cooler sites often fared better. Despite some sensational Trockenbeerenauslesen, considerable variation in quality.

2002 It is a small miracle how the Ries grapes survived one of the wettest harvests on record to give ripe, succulent, lively wines (mostly Kabinett and Spätlese), attractive drunk young or mature.

2001 Golden October resulted in the best Mosel Riesling since 1990. Saar and Ruwer less exciting but still perfect balance. Lots of Spätlesen and Auslesen.

2000 Ries stood up to harvest rain here better than most other places. Dominated by good Qualitätswein bestimmter Anbaugebiete (QbA) and Kabinett. Auslesen rarer, but exciting.

1999 Excellent in Saar and Ruwer, lots of Auslesen; generally only good in the Mosel due to high yields. Best drank well young and will age.

1998 Ries grapes came through a rainy autumn to give astonishingly good results in the Middle Mosel; the Saar and Ruwer were less lucky, with mostly QbA. Plenty of Eiswein.

1997 A generous vintage of consistently fruity, elegant wines from the entire region. Marvellous Auslesen in the Saar and Ruwer.

1996 Variable, with fine Spätlesen and Auslesen, but only from top sites. Many excellent Eisweins.

1995 Excellent vintage, mainly of Spätlesen and Auslesen of firm structure and long ageing potential.

1994 Another good vintage, with unexceptional QbA and Kabinett, but many Auslesen and botrytis wines.

1993 Small, excellent vintage: lots of Auslesen/botrytis; near perfect harmony. Now wonderful to drink.

1990 Superb vintage, though small. Known for its powerful and still-elegant acidity – a cellar must-have for Ries lovers.

Fine older vintages: 89 88 76 71 69 64 59 53 49 45 37 34 21.

Rheinhessen, Nahe, Pfalz, Rheingau

Even the best wines can be drunk with pleasure when young, but Kabinett, Spätlese and Auslese Ries gain enormously in character by keeping for longer. Rheingau wines tend to be longest-lived, improving for 15 years or more, but best wines from the Nahe and Pfalz can last as long. Rheinhessen wines usually mature sooner, and dry Franken and Baden wines are generally best at three to six years.

2009 A year of ups and downs. Early flowering, wet summer. But mildew infections dried in late July, when dry weather took over. Sunny conditions in September and October brought high degrees of maturity and surprisingly low acidity levels. For the first time since 2003, authorities allowed acidification. Excellent wines, especially. dry.

2008 Difficult vintage: good quantity, uneven quality. Wet summer favoured mildew. Rainy September and October made it difficult to choose the picking dates. Some good late-harvest wines – but only where botrytis was under control. The Rheingau seems to have done quite well. Very welcome: alcohol levels are down to around 12 per cent in dry wines.

2007 Those who waited to pick until October had ripe grapes with cool nights conserving good acidity levels. Very good for Spätburgunder (Pinot N) and other reds as well as Ries. Dry wines seem to be maturing faster than expected.

2006 A nightmare: heavy October rains and atypical high October temperatures destroyed a promising crop. Top estates managed small quantities of quite good middle-weight wines. Most should be drunk now.

2005 The summer was warm, but rain kept drought at bay. A very fine autumn led to high ripeness levels, accompanied by excellent acidity and extract. A superb year.

2004 After an indifferent summer, a fine autumn delivered ripe, healthy grapes throughout the Rhein lands. A larger-than-average crop, so there could be some dilution, though not at top estates.

2003 Very hot weather led to rich wines in the Rheingau; many lack acidity. The Pfalz produced superb Ries. Red wines fared well everywhere.

2002 Few challenge the best from 2001, but very good for both classic-style Kabinett/Spätlese and for dry. Excellent Pinot N.

2001 Though more erratic than in the Mosel, here, too, this was often an exciting vintage for both dry and classic styles; excellent balance.

2000 The farther south, the more difficult was the harvest, the Pfalz catching the worst of harvest rain. However, all regions have islands of excellence.

1999 Quality was average where yields were high, but for top growers, an excellent vintage of rich, aromatic wines with lots of charm.

1998 Excellent: rich, balanced wines, many good Spätlesen and Auslesen with excellent ageing potential. Rain affected much of Baden and Franken. But a great Eiswein year.

1997 Very clean, ripe grapes gave excellent QbA, Kabinett, Spätlese in dry and classic styles. Little botrytis, so Auslesen and higher are rare.

1996 An excellent vintage, particularly in the Pfalz and the Rheingau, with many fine Spätlesen. Great Eiswein.

1995 Rather variable, but some excellent Spätlesen and Auslesen maturing well – like the 1990s. Weak in the Pfalz due to harvest rain.

1994 Good vintage, mostly Qualitätswein mit Prädikat, with abundant fruit and firm structure. Some superb sweet wines.

1993 A small vintage of very good to excellent quality. Spätlesen and Auslesen now at their peak.

Fine older vintages: 90 83 76 71 69 67 64 59 53 49 45 37 34 21.

Achkarren Bad (r) w ★★→★★★ Village on the KAISERSTUHL, known esp for GRAUBURGUNDER. ERSTE LAGE v'yd: Schlossberg. Wines generally best drunk during first 5 yrs. Gd wines: DR. HEGER, Michel, SCHWARZER ADLER and co-op.

Adelmann, Weingut Graf ★★→★★★★ Estate based at the idyllic Schaubeck castle in WÜRTTEMBERG. The specialties are subtle red blends (notably Vignette), RIES (look for ERSTE LAGE Süßmund), and the rare Muskattrollinger.

Ahr ★★→★★★ 97 99 03 04 05 06 07 08 09 South of Bonn. Mineral, elegant SPÄTBURGUNDER and FRÜHBURGUNDER, previously renowned for their lightness. Global warming boosts ripeness on the valley's slate soils: now the wines regularly exceed 14° – unfortunately. Best producers: Adeneuer, DEUTZERHOF, Kreuzberg, MEYER-NÄKEL, Nelles, STODDEN.

Aldinger, Weingut Gerhard ★★★ One of WÜRTTEMBERG'S leading estates: dense LEMBERGER and SPÄTBURGUNDER, complex Sauv Bl. Gd RIES, too.

Amtliche Prüfungsnummer (APNr) Official test number, showing up on every label of a quality wine. Useful for discerning different lots of AUSLESE a producer has made from the same v'yd.

Assmannshausen Rhg r ★→★★★ 93 95 96 97 98 99 00 01 02 03 04 05 07 08 09 Craggy RHEINGAU village known specifically for its cassis-scented, age-worthy SPÄTBURGUNDERS from slate soils. ERSTE LAGE v'yd: Höllenberg. Growers include KESSELER, Robert König, WEINGUT KRONE and the state domain.

Auslese Wines from selective harvest of super-ripe bunches, in many yrs affected by noble rot (*Edelfäule*) and correspondingly unctuous in flavour. Dry Auslesen are usually too alcoholic and clumsy for me.

Ayl M-S-R (Saar) w ★★★ 90 93 95 96 97 99 00 01 02 03 04 05 07 (08) All Ayl v'yds are known since 1971 by the name of its historically best site: Kupp. Such are German wine laws. Growers include BISCHÖFLICHE WEINGÜTER, *Lauer*.

Bacharach w (r) ★→★★★ 96 97 01 02 03 04 05 07 08 09 Main wine town of MITTELRHEIN. Racy, austere RIES, some v. fine. Classified as ERSTE LAGE: Hahn, Posten, Wolfshöhle. Growers include BASTIAN, JOST, RATZENBERGER.

Baden Bad Huge southwest area of scattered v'yds best known for the Pinots, and pockets of RIES, usually dry. Best areas: KAISERSTUHL, ORTENAU. Pinot N now more balanced, graceful than of yore.

Badische Bergstrasse Small district of north BADEN, surrounding the city of Heidelberg. Gd RIES and SPÄTBURGUNDER. Best producer: Seeger.

Badischer Winzerkeller Germany's (and Europe's) biggest co-op, absorbing the entire crop of 38 other co-ops to produce almost half of BADEN'S wine: dependably unambitious.

Bassermann-Jordan ★★★ 90 96 97 99 01 03 04 05 07 08 09 MITTELHAARDT estate, under new ownership since 2003, with 50 ha of outstanding v'yds in DEIDESHEIM, FORST, RUPPERTSBERG, etc. Winemaker Ulrich Mell excels at producing *majestic dry Ries* and lavish sweet wines, too.

Bastian, Weingut Friedrich ★★ 6 ha BACHARACH estate. Racy, austere RIES with MOSEL-like delicacy, esp from the Posten v'yd (ERSTE LAGE).

Becker, Friedrich ★★★ Renowned estate in the municipality of SCHWEIGEN (southern PFALZ), 18 ha, specializing in refined, barrel-aged SPÄTBURGUNDER. Some of Becker's v'yds actually lie across the state border, in Alsace.

Becker, J B ★★→★★★ The best estate at WALLUF specializing in old-fashioned, cask-aged (and long-lived) dry RIES and SPÄTBURGUNDER.

Beerenauslese (BA) Luscious sweet wine from exceptionally ripe, individually selected berries concentrated by noble rot. Rare, expensive.

Bercher ★★★ KAISERSTUHL estate; 25 ha at Burkheim, yielding consistently excellent GRAUBURGUNDER, CHARD and SPÄTBURGUNDER.

Bergdolt, Weingut ★★★ South of Neustadt in the PFALZ, this 24-ha estate produces v. fine WEISSBURGUNDER, as well as gd RIES and SPÄTBURGUNDER.

Bernkastel M-M-W w ★→★★★★ 83 88 89 90 93 94 95 97 99 01 02 03 04 05 06 07 08 09 The senior wine town of the MITTELMOSEL; the epitome of RIES. ERSTE LAGE: Doctor (sometimes overpriced), Lay. Top growers include Kerpen, LOOSEN, PAULY-BERGWEILER, PRÜM, Studert-Prüm, THANISCH (both estates), WEGELER.

German vintage notation

The vintage notes after entries in the German section are given in a different form from those elsewhere in the book. Two styles of vintage are indicated:

Bold type (eg. **99**) indicates classic, ripe vintages with a high proportion of SPÄTLESEN and AUSLESEN; or, in the case of red wines, gd phenolic ripeness and must weights.

Normal type (eg. 98) indicates a successful but not outstanding vintage.

German white wines, esp RIES, have high acidity and keep well, and they display pure fruit qualities because they are unoaked. Thus they can be drunk young for their intense fruitiness, or kept for a decade or two to develop more aromatic subtlety and finesse. This means there is no one ideal moment to drink them, so no vintages are specifically recommended for drinking now.

Germany's quality levels

The official range of qualities and styles in ascending order is:

1 **Deutscher Tafelwein:** sweetish light wine of no specified character. Will now disappear from the market.

2 **Landwein:** dryish Tafelwein with some regional style.

3 **Qualitätswein:** dry or sweetish wine with sugar added before fermentation to increase its strength, but tested for quality and with distinct local and grape character. Don't despair.

4 **Kabinett:** dry or dryish natural (unsugared) wine of distinct personality and distinguishing lightness. Can occasionally be sublime.

5 **Spätlese:** stronger, often sweeter than Kabinett. Full-bodied. Today most top SPÄTLESEN are *trocken* or completely dry.

6 **Auslese:** sweeter, sometimes stronger than SPÄTLESE, often with honey-like flavours, intense and long-lived. Occasionally dry and weighty.

7 **Beerenauslese:** v. sweet, sometimes strong, intense. Can be superb.

8 **Eiswein:** from naturally frozen grapes of BA or TBA quality: concentrated, sharpish and v. sweet. Some examples are extreme, unharmonious.

9 **Trockenbeerenauslese (TBA):** intensely sweet and aromatic; alcohol slight. Extraordinary and everlasting.

Bernkastel (Bereich) Avoid. Includes all the MITTELMOSEL. Wide area of deplorably dim quality and superficial, flowery character. Mostly MÜLLER-THURGAU.

Bischöfliche Weingüter M-S-R ★★ Famous, though seriously underperforming estate located at TRIER, uniting cathedral's v'yds with those of three other charities, the Friedrich-Wilhelm-Gymnasium, the Bischöfliches Priesterseminar and the Bischöfliches Konvikt. Owns 130 ha of top v'yds, esp in SAAR and RUWER. Management changes in 2007 and 2010 make it difficult to predict what direction the estate will take.

Bocksbeutel Inconvenient flask-shaped bottle used in FRANKEN and north BADEN.

Bodensee Idyllic district of south BADEN, on Lake Constance. Dry wines are best drunk young. RIES-like MÜLLER-THURGAU a specialty. Top village: Meersburg.

Boppard ★→★★★ 90 97 01 02 03 04 05 07 08 09 Important wine town of MITTELRHEIN with best sites all in amphitheatre of vines called Bopparder Hamm (ERSTE LAGE). Growers: Toni Lorenz, Matthias Müller, August Perll, WEINGART. Unbeatable value for money.

Brauneberg M-M w ★★★★ 88 89 90 93 94 95 96 97 98 99 01 02 03 04 05 06 07 08 09 Top M-S-R village near BERNKASTEL (304 ha): excellent full-flavoured RIES. ERSTE LAGE v'yds Juffer, Juffer-Sonnenuhr. Growers: F HAAG, W HAAG, PAULINSHOF, RICHTER, SCHLOSS LIESER, THANISCH.

Breuer, Weingut Georg ★★★→★★★★ Family estate in RÜDESHEIM (24 ha) and RAUENTHAL (7.2 ha), giving superb dry RIES. V. fine SEKT, too. Pioneering winemaker Bernhard Breuer died suddenly in 2004; now his daughter Theresa is in charge.

Buhl, Reichsrat von ★★★ Historic PFALZ estate, 60 ha (DEIDESHEIM, FORST, RUPPERTSBERG). Bought in 2005 by businessman Achim Niederberger, who also owns BASSERMANN-JORDAN and DR. DEINHARD/VON WINNING. Crisp, minerally whites, esp SILVANER RIES, from outstanding v'yd sites in and around WÜRZBURG. Superb monopoly ERSTE LAGE Stein-Harfe. Look eg. for the rich and spicy 2008 Stein-Harfe SILVANER AUSLESE. 80% dry wines.

Bürgerspital zum Heiligen Geist ★★→★★★★ Ancient charitable estate. 110 ha.

Bürklin-Wolf, Dr. ★★★→★★★★ Dynamic PFALZ family estate. 85 ha in FORST, DEIDESHEIM, RUPPERTSBERG and WACHENHEIM, inc many ERSTE LAGE sites. The full-bodied *dry wines from these are truly individual.* Now biodynamic.

Busch, Weingut Clemens M-S-R ★★→★★★ Since 1985 Busch has demonstrated the excellence of steep but obscure Pündericher Marienburg in lower MOSEL. Both dry and notably sweet RIES. Organic.

Castell'sches Fürstlich Domänenamt ★→★★★ Historic 65-ha estate in FRANKEN. SILVANER, RIES, RIESLANER, dry and sweet, and a growing reputation for red wines. Superb monopoly v'yd *Casteller Schlossberg*.

Chardonnay Grown throughout Germany; over 1,120 ha. Only the best convince, eg. BERCHER, BERGDOLT, HUBER, JOHNER, REBHOLZ, DR. WEHRHEIM, WITTMANN.

Christmann ★★★ 16-ha estate in Gimmeldingen (PFALZ) making rich, dry RIES and SPÄTBURGUNDER from ERSTE LAGE v'yds, notably Königsbacher Idig. Biodynamic farming. Young Steffen Christmann is new president of the VDP.

Christoffel, J J ★★★ Tiny domain in ÜRZIG. Classic, elegant RIES. Since 2001 leased to Robert Eymael of MÖNCHHOF.

New EU terminology

Germany's part in the new EU classification will involve, firstly, abolishing the term *Tafelwein* in favour of plain *Wein*, and secondly, changing LANDWEIN to "ggA" – *geschützte geographische Angabe* or "Protected Geographical Indication". QUALITÄTSWEIN and QUALITÄTSWEIN MIT PRÄDIKAT will be replaced by "gU": *geschützte Ursprungsbezeichnung*, or Protected Designation of Origin. The existing terms – SPÄTLESE, AUSLESE and so on – will be tacked on to gU where appropriate; the rules for these styles won't change. The old designations will continue until the end of 2011, except for that of *Tafelwein*, which won't be used after December 2010.

Clüsserath, Ansgar ★★→★★★ 5-ha family estate with remarkably age-worthy, dry RIES from TRITTENHEIMER Apotheke: delicate and mineral without being tart.

Clüsserath-Weiler, Weingut ★★★ Classic RIES from top TRITTENHEIMER Apotheke and the rare Fährfels v'yd. Steadily improving quality.

Crusius ★★→★★★ 17-ha family estate at TRAISEN, NAHE. Vivid and age-worthy RIES *from Bastei and Rotenfels of Traisen* and SCHLOSSBÖCKELHEIM.

Dautel, Weingut Ernst ★★★ A reliable source of WÜRTTEMBERG's red specialties, esp LEMBERGER. 12 ha.

Deidesheim Pfz w (r) ★★→★★★★ 90 96 97 99 01 02 04 05 07 08 09 Largest top-quality village of the PFALZ (405 ha). Richly flavoured, lively wines. ERSTE LAGE v'yds: Grainhübel, Hohenmorgen, Kalkofen, Kieselberg, Langenmorgen, Paradiesgarten. Top growers: BASSERMANN-JORDAN, Biffar, BUHL, BÜRKLIN-WOLF, CHRISTMANN, DEINHARD, MOSBACHER, VON WINNING.

Deinhard, Dr. ★★★ Fine 35-ha estate owned by Achim Niederberger (see BASSERMANN-JORDAN and BUHL), and since 2008, a brand of the newly established VON WINNING estate.

Deutzerhof, Weingut ★★→★★★ 10-ha AHR estate producing concentrated, barrique-aged SPÄTBURGUNDER. Fine quality, alarming prices.

Diel, Schlossgut ★★★ Fashionable 22-ha NAHE estate; pioneered ageing GRAUBURGUNDER and WEISSBURGUNDER in barriques. Its traditional RIES is often exquisite. Also serious SEKT.

Dönnhoff, Weingut Hermann ★★★★ 90 94 95 96 97 98 99 00 01 02 03 04 05 06 07 08 09 20-ha leading NAHE estate with magnificent RIES at all quality levels from NIEDERHAUSEN, Oberhausen, SCHLOSSBÖCKELHEIM. Dazzling EISWEIN.

Dornfelder Red grape making deep-coloured, usually rustic wines. Plantings have doubled since 2000 to an astonishing 8,100 ha.

Duijn, Jacob ★★→★★★ Former sommelier/wine merchant, now BADEN wine-grower specializing in spicy, tannic SPÄTBURGUNDER from steeply sloping granite v'yds in the Bühler Valley, ORTENAU. 10 ha.

Durbach Baden w (r) ★★→★★★ 01 02 03 04 05 07 Village with 314 ha of v'yds, of which Plauelrain is ERSTE LAGE. Top growers: LAIBLE, H Männle, Schloss Staufenberg. KLINGELBERGER (RIES) is the outstanding variety.

Egon Müller zu Scharzhof ★★★★ 59 71 76 83 85 88 89 90 93 94 95 96 97 98 99 00 01 02 03 04 05 06 07 08 09 Top SAAR estate of 8 ha at WILTINGEN, the v'yds rising steeply behind the Müllers' manor house. Its rich and racy SCHARZHOFBERGER RIES in AUSLESEN vintages is among the world's greatest wines, sublime, honeyed, immortal; best are given gold capsules. *Kabinetts* are feather-light but keep 5+ years. Gallais is a second 4-ha estate in WILTINGER Braune Kupp; gd quality, but the site is less exceptional.

Einzellage Individual v'yd site. Not to be confused with GROSSLAGE.

Eiswein Made from frozen grapes with the ice (ie. water content) discarded, producing v. concentrated wine in flavour, acidity and sugar – of BA ripeness or more. Alcohol content can be as low as 5.5%. V. expensive. Outstanding Eiswein vintages were 1998, 2002 and 2004.

Ellwanger, Weingut ★★→★★★ Jürgen Ellwanger pioneered oak-aged red wines in WÜRTTEMBERG. Today aided by his sons, who continue to turn out sappy but structured LEMBERGER, SPÄTBURGUNDER and Zweigelt.

Emrich-Schönleber ★★★→★★★★ Located in NAHE village of Monzingen. 16 ha, known for classical, precise and reliable RIES. Werner Schönleber has a knack for both dry and botrytised sweet.

Erden M-M w ★★★ 88 89 90 93 95 96 97 98 99 01 02 03 04 05 06 07 08 09 Village adjoining ÜRZIG: noble, full-flavoured, vigorous wine (more herbal and mineral than the wines of nearby BERNKASTEL and WEHLEN but equally long-living). Classified as ERSTE LAGE: Prälat, Treppchen. Growers include J J CHRISTOFFEL, Erbes, LOOSEN, Lotz, Meulenhof, MÖNCHHOF, Peter Nicolay, WEINS-PRÜM.

Erste Lage V'yd site of exceptional quality, classified according to criteria set up by influential wine-growers' association VERBAND DEUTSCHER PRÄDIKATS UND QUALITÄTSWEINGÜTER (VDP). On labels, *Erste Lage* sites are marked with a grape logo with a "1" next to it. A producer's best dry wine from an *Erste Lage* site is called GROSSES GEWÄCHS or ERSTES GEWÄCHS. Off-dry or sweet wines from *Erste Lage* v'yds display the logo, but are not called GROSSES or ERSTES GEWÄCHS.

Erstes Gewächs Translates as "first growth". Applies only to RHEINGAU v'yds. See ERSTE LAGE.

Erzeugerabfüllung Bottled by producer. Being replaced by GUTSABFÜLLUNG, but only by estates. Co-ops will continue with *Erzeugerabfüllung*.

Escherndorf Frank w ★★→★★★ 93 97 00 01 02 03 04 05 06 07 08 09 Important wine village, ERSTE LAGE steep slope: Lump. Best for SILVANER and RIES. Growers include Michael Fröhlich, JULIUSSPITAL, H SAUER, Rainer Sauer, Egon Schäffer.

Feinherb Imprecisely defined traditional term for wines with around 10–20 g of sugar per litre. Favoured by some as a more flexible alternative to HALBTROCKEN. Used on label by, among others, Kerpen, VON KESSELSTATT, M MOLITOR.

Forst Pfz w ★★→★★★★ 90 96 97 99 01 02 03 04 05 07 08 09 MITTELHAARDT village with over 200 ha of best v'yds. Ripe, richly fragrant, full-bodied but subtle wines. ERSTE LAGE v'yds: Jesuitengarten, Kirchenstück, Freundstück, Pechstein, Ungeheuer. Top growers include: Acham-Magin, BASSERMANN-JORDAN, BÜRKLIN-WOLF, DR. DEINHARD/VON WINNING, MOSBACHER, WOLF.

Franken Franconia region of distinctive dry wines, esp SILVANER, mostly bottled in round-bellied flasks (BOCKSBEUTEL). The centre is WÜRZBURG. *Bereich* names: MAINDREIECK, MAINVIERECK, STEIGERWALD. Top producers include: BÜRGERSPITAL, Castell, FÜRST, JULIUSSPITAL, LÖWENSTEIN, RUCK, H SAUER, STAATLICHER HOFKELLER, STÖRRLEIN, WIRSCHING, etc.

Franzen, Weingut Reinhold ★→★★ From Europe's steepest v'yd, Bremmer Calmont, Franzen makes reliable, sometimes exciting dry RIES and EISWEIN.

Frühburgunder An ancient mutation of Pinot N, found mostly in the AHR but also in FRANKEN and WÜRTTEMBERG, where it is confusingly known as Clevner. Lower acidity and thus more approachable than Pinot N.

Fuder Traditional RIES cask with sizes from 500 to 1,500 litres depending on the region. Unlike a barrique, a *Fuder* is used for many years. Traditionalists use the cask for fermentation, giving individuality to each *Fuder's* wine.

Fürst ★★★→★★★★★ 18-ha estate in Bürgstadt making some of the best wines in FRANKEN, particularly Burgundian SPÄTBURGUNDER (arguably Germany's finest), full-flavoured RIES, and oak-aged WEISSBURGUNDER.

Gallais, Le See EGON MÜLLER ZU SCHARZHOF.

Beware of Bereich and Grosslage

Bereich means district within an *Anbaugebiet* (region). *Bereich* on a label should be treated as a flashing red light. The wine is a blend from arbitrary sites within that district. Do not buy. The same holds for wines with a GROSSLAGE name, though these are more difficult to identify. Who could guess if "Forster Mariengarten" is an EINZELLAGE or a GROSSLAGE?

Gewürztraminer (or Traminer) Highly aromatic grape, specialty of Alsace, also impressive in Germany, esp in PFALZ, BADEN, SACHSEN.

Graach M-M w ★★★ 88 89 90 93 94 95 96 97 98 99 01 03 04 05 07 08 09 Small village between BERNKASTEL and WEHLEN. ERSTE LAGE v'yds: Domprobst, Himmelreich, Josefshof. Top growers include: Kees-Kieren, von KESSELSTATT, LOOSEN, M MOLITOR, J J PRÜM, S A PRÜM, SCHAEFER, SELBACH-OSTER, WEINS-PRÜM. All currently threatened by proposed *Autobahn*.

Grans-Fassian ★★★ Fine MOSEL estate at Leiwen. V'yds there and in TRITTENHEIM and PIESPORT. EISWEIN a specialty. 10 ha.

Grauburgunder (or Grauer Burgunder) Both synonyms of RULÄNDER or Pinot Gr: grape giving soft, full-bodied wine. Best in BADEN (esp KAISERSTUHL) and south PFALZ. 4,480 ha planted.

Grosser Ring Group of top (VDP) MOSEL-SAAR-RUWER estates, whose annual Sept auction at Trier sometimes sets world-record prices.

Grosses Gewächs Translates as "great/top growth". This is the top dry wine from a VDP-classified ERSTE LAGE v'yd, except in the RHEINGAU, which has its own ERSTES GEWÄCHS classification.

Grosslage A collection of secondary v'yds with seemingly similar character – but no indication of quality.

Gunderloch ★★★→★★★★★ 93 96 97 99 01 02 03 04 05 07 08 At this NACKENHEIM estate Fritz Hasselbach makes some of the finest RIES on the entire Rhine, esp at AUSLESE level and above. Also owns Balbach estate in NIERSTEIN.

Gutedel German name for the ancient Chasselas grape, grown in south BADEN (MARKGRÄFLERLAND). Fresh, but neutral white wines.

Gutsabfüllung Estate-bottled. Term for genuinely estate-bottled wines.

Haag, **Weingut Fritz** M-S-R ★★★★ 88 89 90 94 95 96 97 98 99 01 02 03 04 05 06 07 08 09 BRAUNEBERG's top estate, run for decades by MITTELMOSEL veteran Wilhelm Haag and now by his son Oliver. MOSEL RIES of crystalline purity for long ageing. Haag's other son, Thomas, runs SCHLOSS LIESER estate.

Haag, Weingut Willi M-S-R ★★ 6 ha BRAUNEBERG estate. Old-style RIES, AUSLESEN.

Haart, Reinhold ★★★★ Best estate in PIESPORT and Wintrich. Refined, aromatic wines capable of long ageing. Minerally and racy copybook MOSEL RIES.

Haidle, Karl ★★→★★★★ 19-ha family estate in Stetten, WÜRTTEMBERG, specializing in graceful RIES from high-altitude Pulvermächer v'yd ERSTE LAGE.

Halbtrocken Medium-dry (literally semi-dry), with 9–18 g of unfermented sugar per litre. Popular category, often better balanced than TROCKEN. See FEINHERB.

Hattenheim Rhg w ★★→★★★★ 90 93 95 97 99 01 02 03 04 05 07 08 09 Well-known 202-ha wine town, though not all producers achieve full potential. ERSTE LAGE v'yds are Mannberg, Nussbrunnen, Pfaffenberg, Schützenhaus, Wisselbrunnen and, most famously, STEINBERG. Estates include Barth, Knyphausen, Lang, LANGWERTH VON SIMMERN, RESS, SCHLOSS SCHÖNBORN, STAATSWEINGUT.

Heger, Dr. ★★★ Leading estate of KAISERSTUHL in BADEN with v.gd dry WEISSBURGUNDER, GRAUBURGUNDER, SILVANER and burgundy-inspired Spätburgunder reds. Less emphasis on RIES and Muscat, which can also be v.gd. Wines from rented v'yds released under Weinhaus Joachim Heger label. Magnificent 2008 Winklerberg Grauburgunder Grosses Gewächs.

Hessische Bergstrasse w (r) ★★→★★★ 90 93 95 96 97 98 99 01 02 03 04 05 07 (08) Small wine region (436 ha), north of Heidelberg. Pleasant RIES from STAATSWEINGÜTER, Simon-Bürkle and Stadt Bensheim.

Heyl zu Herrnsheim ★★ Leading NIERSTEIN estate, bought in 2006 by Detlev Meyer. 12 ha. Now part of the ST-ANTONY estate under same ownership. GROSSES GEWÄCHS from monopoly site Brudersberg can be excellent, but most entry-level wines are disappointing.

Heymann-Löwenstein ★★★ Estate in Lower MOSEL near Koblenz with most consistent dry RIES in MOSEL-SAAR-RUWER and some remarkable AUSLESEN and TBA. Löwenstein has inspired other WINNINGEN growers to adopt his style.

Hochheim Rhg w ★★→★★★★ 90 93 95 96 97 98 99 01 02 03 04 05 07 08 09 242-ha wine town 24-km east of main RHEINGAU area, once thought of as best on Rhine. Rich and distinctly earthy RIES from ERSTE LAGE v'yds: Domdechaney, Hölle, Kirchenstück. Growers include Himmel, Königin-Victoriaberg, KÜNSTLER, SCHLOSS SCHÖNBORN, STAATSWEINGUT, Werner.

Hock Traditional English term for Rhine wine, derived from HOCHHEIM.

Hoensbroech, Weingut Reichsgraf zu ★★ Top KRAICHGAU estate. The best wine is dry WEISSBURGUNDER from Michelfelder Himmelberg.

Hohenlohe-Oehringen, Weingut Fürst zu ★★ Noble 17-ha estate in Oehringen, WÜRTTEMBERG. Bone-dry RIES and structured LEMBERGER.

Hövel, Weingut von ★★→★★★Fine SAAR estate at OBEREMMEL (Hütte is 4.8-ha monopoly) and in SCHARZHOFBERG. In some vintages erractic quality.

Huber, Bernhard ★★★ Leading estate of Breisgau area of BADEN, with powerful long-lived SPÄTBURGUNDER, MUSKATELLER and burgundian-style WEISSBURGUNDER, CHARD.

Ihringen Bad r w ★→★★★ 97 99 01 02 03 04 05) 07 08 09 Justly celebrated village of the KAISERSTUHL, BADEN. SILVANER stronghold, but better known for its prestigious SPÄTBURGUNDER and GRAUBURGUNDER. The superb Winklerberg v'yd is made up of steep terraces on shallow volcanic soils. Stupidly the law permits wines from a loess plateau to be sold under the same name. Top growers: DR. HEGER, Konstanzer, Pix, Stigler.

Iphofen Frank w ★★→★★★ 93 97 99 00 01 03 04 05 06 07 08 09 Village in FRANKEN's Steigerwald area, renowned for RIES, SILVANER, RIESLANER. First Class v'yds: Julius-Echter-Berg, Kronsberg. Growers include JULIUSSPITAL, RUCK, WIRSCHING, Zehntkeller.

Jahrgang Year – as in "vintage".

Remember that vintage information for German wines is given in a different form from the ready/not ready distinction applying to other countries. See the explanation at the bottom of p.144.

Johannisberg Rhg w ★★→★★★★ 89 90 93 95 96 97 99 01 04 05 07 08 09
A classic RHEINGAU village with superlative long-lived RIES. ERSTE LAGE v'yds:
Hölle, Klaus, SCHLOSS JOHANNISBERG. GROSSLAGE (avoid!): Erntebringer. Top
growers: JOHANNISHOF, SCHLOSS JOHANNISBERG, Hessen.

Johannishof ★★★ JOHANNISBERG family estate RIES that are often the best from the
great JOHANNISBERG v'yds. Excellent RÜDESHEIM wines, too.

Johner, Karl-Heinz ★★→★★★★ 17-ha BADEN estate at Bischoffingen, long
specializing in New World-style SPÄTBURGUNDER and oak-aged WEISSBURGUNDER,
CHARD, GRAUBURGUNDER.

Josefshof ERSTE LAGEV'yd at GRAACH, the sole property of KESSELSTATT.

Jost, Toni ★★★ Leading estate of the MITTELRHEIN: 14 ha, mainly RIES, in BACHARACH
(sharply mineral wines). Since 2009, the excellent ERSTE LAGE Hahn is a
monopoly of Jost's. He also runs a second estate at WALLUF in the RHEINGAU.

Juliusspital ★★★ Ancient WÜRZBURG religious charity with 170 ha of top FRANKEN
v'yds. Consistently gd quality. Look for its *dry Silvaners* (they age well) and RIES
and its top white blend called BT.

Kabinett See "Germany's quality levels" box on p.145.

Kaiserstuhl Outstanding BADEN district, with notably warm climate and volcanic
soil. Villages inc: ACHKARREN, Burkheim, IHRINGEN, Jechtingen, Oberrotweil.
Renowned for Pinot varieties, w and r, and some surprising RIES and Muscat.

Kanzem M-S-R (Saar) w ★★★ 93 94 95 96 97 99 01 02 03 04 05 06 07 08 09
Small neighbour of WILTINGEN. ERSTE LAGE v'yd: Altenberg. Growers include
BISCHÖFLICHE WEINGÜTER, OTHEGRAVEN, Vereinigte Hospitien.

Karlsmühle ★★★ Small estate with two Lorenzhöfer monopoly sites making
classic RUWER RIES. Consistently excellent quality.

Karthäuserhof ★★★★ 89 90 93 95 97 99 01 03 04 05 06 07 08 09 Outstanding
RUWER estate of 19 ha at Eitelsbach with monopoly v'yd Karthäuserhofberg.
Easily recognized by bottles with only a neck label. Admired if austere TROCKEN
wines (made less austere by a run of warm yrs), but magnificent AUSLESEN.

Kasel M-S-R (Ruwer) w ★★→★★★★ 90 93 99 01 03 04 05 06 07 08 09 Stunning
flowery RIES. ERSTE LAGE v'yds: Kehrnagel, Nies'chen. Top growers: Beulwitz,
BISCHÖFLICHE WEINGÜTER, KARLSMÜHLE, KESSELSTATT.

Keller, Weingut ★★★★ Deep in unfashionable southern RHEINHESSEN, the Kellers
show what can be achieved with scrupulous site selection. Superlative,
crystalline GROSSES GEWÄCHS RIES from Dalsheimer Hubacker and expensive
RIES blend from different v'yds called G-Max. Astonishing TBA and SPÄTBURGUNDER.

Kesseler, Weingut August Rhg ★★★ 21-ha estate making fine SPÄTBURGUNDER reds
in ASSMANNSHAUSEN and RÜDESHEIM. Also v'gd classic-style RIES.

Kesselstatt, von ★★★ The largest private MOSEL estate, 650 yrs old. Run for two
decades by the quality-obsessed Annegret Reh-Gartner. Some 38 ha through
MOSEL-SAAR-RUWER producing aromatic, generously fruity MOSELS. Consistently
high-quality wines from JOSEFSHOF monopoly v'yd, PIESPORTER Goldtröpfchen,
KASEL (age-worthy, dry KABINETT) and SCHARZHOFBERG.

Kesten M-M w ★→★★★ 93 94 97 98 99 01 03 04 05 06 07 08 09 Neighbour of
BRAUNEBERG. Best wines (from Paulinshofberg v'yd) similar. Top growers:
Bastgen, Kees-Kieren, PAULINSHOF.

Kiedrich Rhg w ★★→★★★★ 93 95 97 99 01 02 03 04 05 07 08 09 RHEINGAU
village linked inseparably to WEIL'S outstanding RIES from Gräfenberg v'yd.
Other gd growers include Hessen, Knyphausen.

Klingelberger ORTENAU (BADEN) term for RIES, esp at DURBACH.

Kloster Eberbach Rhg Glorious 12th-century Cistercian abbey in HATTENHEIM
forest. Monks planted STEINBERG, Germany's Clos de Vougeot. Now the label of
the STAATSWEINGÜTER with a string of great v'yds in ASSMANNSHAUSEN, RÜDESHEIM,
RAUENTHAL, etc. Coasting for years, now up for it with a brand new winery.

> **Germany's white future**
>
> RIES is on the up; MÜLLER-THURGAU continues to slide. That's the message from the latest planting figures from Germany, showing that RIES is up to 21.9% of the total vineyard. MÜLLER-THURGAU lost 103 ha last year – not much, but still going the right way. The only other major varieties on the increase are Pinots Gr and Bl; even Pinot N dropped a little.

Knebel, Weingut ★★★ WINNINGEN is the top wine village of the lower MOSEL and Knebel showed how its sites could produce remarkable RIES in all styles. The founder died tragically in 2004; the estate continues to maintain high quality.

Knipser, Weingut ★★★→★★★★ Leading family estate in PFALZ, and one of the most serious and reliable in all Germany, 40 ha. Brothers Werner and Volker specialize in barrique-aged SPÄTBURGUNDER and other reds such as St-Laurent, Syrah and Cuvée X (a Bordeaux blend). Dry RIES can be exceptional.

Koehler-Ruprecht ★★→★★★★ 93 97 99 01 02 03 04 05 07 08 09 Outstanding Kallstadt grower. Bernd Philippi's winemaking is entirely traditional, delivering v. long-lived, dry RIES from Kallstadter Saumagen. Outstanding SPÄTBURGUNDER and gd barrique-aged Pinot varieties under the Philippi label.

Kraichgau Small BADEN district southeast of Heidelberg. Top growers: Burg Ravensburg, HOENSBROECH, Hummel.

Krone, Weingut Rhg ★★→★★★ 4-ha estate in ASSMANNSHAUSEN, with some of the best and oldest v'yds in the ERSTE LAGE Höllenberg. Famous for richly perfumed, full-bodied and ageable SPÄTBURGUNDER. Now run by WEGELER, and considerable investments are underway.

Kröv M-M w ★→★★★ 93 99 01 03 04 05 06 07 08 09 Popular tourist resort famous for its GROSSLAGE name: Nacktarsch, or "bare bottom". Be v. careful. Best growers: Martin Müllen, Staffelter Hof.

Kruger-Rumpf, Weingut ★★→★★★ Most important estate of Münster, NAHE, with charming RIES and well-crafted SPÄTBURGUNDER.

Kühn, Weingut Peter Jakob ★★★ Excellent RHEINGAU estate in OESTRICH. Kühn's obsessive v'yd management (now biodynamic) pays dividends in a full range of classic wines.

Kuhn, Philipp ★★★ Talented and reliable producer in Laumersheim, PFALZ. Dry RIES are rich and harmonious, even at QBA level. Barrel-aged SPÄTBURGUNDER combine succulence, power and complexity.

Künstler, Franz Rhg ★★★ 25-ha estate in HOCHHEIM run by the uncompromising Gunter Künstler. Produces superb dry RIES esp from ERSTE LAGE v'yds Hölle and Kirchenstück; also excellent AUSLESE.

Laible, Weingut Andreas ★★★ 7-ha DURBACH estate. Limpid, often crystalline dry RIES from Plauelrain v'yd as well as SCHEUREBE and GEWÜRZ. Andreas Sr now joined by son Andreas Jr. Younger brother Alexander founded an estate of his own – with wines that deserve to be followed.

Landwein See "Germany's quality levels" box on p.145.

Langwerth von Simmern, Weingut ★★→★★★ Famous Eltville family estate. Top v'yds: Baiken, Mannberg, MARCOBRUNN. After disappointing quality during the 1990s, back on form since 2001.

Lauer, Weingut Peter ★★→★★★The SAAR village of AYL lacked conscientious growers, until in the early 2000s Florian Lauer began exploring its subtleties with a range of v.gd parcel selections.

Leitz, J ★★★ Fine RÜDESHEIM family estate for rich but elegant dry and sweet RIES. Since 1999, Johannes Leitz has gone from strength to strength.

Leiwen M-M w ★★→★★★ 93 97 98 99 00 01 02 03 04 05 07 08 09 ERSTE LAGE: Laurentiuslay. Village between TRITTENHEIM and TRIER. GRANS-FASSIAN, CARL

LOEWEN, Rosch, SANKT URBANS-HOF have put these once overlooked v'yds firmly on the map.

Lemberger Red grape variety imported to Germany and Austria in the 18th century from Hungary, where it is known as Kékfrankos. Deep-coloured, moderately tannic wines; a specialty from WÜRTTEMBERG.

Liebfrauenstift-Kirchenstück A walled-in 13.5-ha v'yd in city of Worms producing aromatic (though rarely spectacular) RIES. Producers: Gutzler, Schembs.

Lieser M-M w ★★ 97 01 02 03 04 05 07 Once-neglected v'yds between BERNKASTEL and BRAUNEBERG. Best v'yd: Niederberg-Helden. Top grower: SCHLOSS LIESER.

Loewen, Carl ★★→★★★ Enterprising grower of LEIWEN on MOSEL making ravishing AUSLESE from town's classified ERSTE LAGE Laurentiuslay site, and from Thörnicher Ritsch, a v'yd Loewen rescued from obscurity.

Loosen, Weingut Dr. M-M ★★→★★★★ 93 95 96 97 99 01 02 03 04 05 06 07 08 09 Dynamic 18-ha estate in BERNKASTEL, ERDEN, GRAACH, ÜRZIG, WEHLEN. Deep, intense, classic RIES from old vines in some of the MITTELMOSEL's greatest v'yds. *Reliable Dr. L Ries*, from bought-in grapes. Also leases WOLF in the PFALZ since 1996. Joint-venture RIES from 1999 Washington State with Ch Ste Michelle.

Lorch Rhg w (r) ★→★★ 90 97 99 01 02 03 04 05 07 Extreme west of RHEINGAU. Some fine MITTELRHEIN-like RIES. Best growers: Fricke, von Kanitz, KESSELER, Ottes.

Löwenstein, Fürst ★★★ Top 30-ha FRANKEN estate. Tangy, savoury SILVANER and mineral RIES from historic *Homburger Kallmuth*, v. dramatic slope with 12 km of stone walls in the v'yd. Also owns a 22-ha RHEINGAU estate in Hallgarten.

Lützkendorf, Weingut ★→★★ Leading SAALE-UNSTRUT estate, 9 ha. Best are usually the elegant, bone-dry SILVANER and WEISSBURGUNDER.

Maindreieck District name for central FRANKEN, inc WÜRZBURG.

Mainviereck District name for western FRANKEN. Best-known are the SPÄTBURGUNDER v'yds of Bürgstadt and Klingenberg.

Marcobrunn Historic RHEINGAU v'yd in Erbach; potentially one of Germany's v. best. Contemporary wines scarcely match this v'yd's past fame.

Markgräflerland District south of Freiburg, BADEN. Typical GUTEDEL wine can be refreshing when drunk v. young.

Maximin Grünhaus M-S-R (Ruwer) w ★★★★ 88 89 90 93 96 97 98 99 01 03 05 07 08 09 Supreme RUWER estate of 31 ha at Mertesdorf. Wines, dry and sweet, that are miracles of delicacy, subtlety and longevity. Greatest wines come from Abtsberg v'yd, but Herrenberg can be almost as fine.

Meyer-Näkel, Weingut ★★★★ AHR estate; 15 ha. Fine SPÄTBURGUNDERS in Dernau, Walporzheim and Bad Neuenahr exemplify modern, oak-aged (but nevertheless minerally) AHR Valley reds.

Mittelhaardt The north central and best part of the PFALZ, inc DEIDESHEIM, FORST, RUPPERTSBERG, WACHENHEIM, largely planted with RIES.

Mittelmosel M-M The central and best part of the MOSEL, inc BERNKASTEL, PIESPORT, WEHLEN, etc. Its top sites are (or should be) entirely RIES.

Mittelrhein Northern and dramatically scenic Rhine area popular with tourists. BACHARACH and BOPPARD are the most important villages of this 465-ha region. Delicate yet steely RIES, underrated and underpriced. Many gd sites lie fallow.

Molitor, Markus M-M ★★★ With 38 ha of outstanding v'yds throughout the MOSEL and SAAR, Molitor has, since 1995, become a major player in the region. Magisterial sweet RIES, and acclaimed (if earthy) SPÄTBURGUNDER.

Mönchhof, Weingut M-M ★★ From his manor house hotel in ÜRZIG, Robert

Remember that vintage information for German wines is given in a different form from the ready/not ready distinction applying to other countries. See the explanation at the bottom of p.144.

It's all the co-op

Faced with a row of wines from co-ops? The best ones are in the south.
Reliable co-ops include Mayschoss-Altenahr (AHR), Bischoffingen,
DURBACH, Ehrenstetten, Hagenau, Königschaffhausen, Oberkirch,
Sasbach (BADEN), Sommerach (FRANKEN), Vier Jahreszeiten (PFALZ), Bad
Cannstatt, Fellbach, Grantschen, Collegium Wirtemberg Weingärtner
Rotenberg & Uhlbach, Weinmanufaktur Untertürkheim (WÜRTTEMBERG).

Eymael makes fruity, stylish RIES from ÜRZIG and ERDEN. Erdener Prälat usually
the best wine. Also leases J J CHRISTOFFEL estate.

Mosbacher, Weingut Pfz ★★★ Fine 15-ha estate for some of best GROSSES GEWÄCHS
RIES of FORST. Going from strength to strength. Decent Sauv Bl.

Moselland, Winzergenossenschaft Huge MOSEL-SAAR-RUWER co-op, at BERNKASTEL,
inc Saar-Winzerverein at WILTINGEN, and, since 2000, a major NAHE co-op, too.
Its 3,290 members, with a collective 2,400 ha, produce 25% of MOSEL-SAAR-
RUWER wines (inc classic-method SEKT). Little is above average.

Mosel-Saar-Ruwer M-S-R 8,980-ha region between TRIER and Koblenz; inc
MITTELMOSEL, RUWER and SAAR. 58% RIES. From 2007 wines from the three regions
can be labelled only as Mosel. (We tend to use the French spelling Moselle.)

Müller-Catoir, Weingut Pfz ★★→★★★★ 90 93 96 97 98 99 01 02 03 04 05 07 08
09 Since the 1970s, this outstanding Neustadt estate has bucked conventional
wisdom, focusing on non-interventionist winemaking. But the footsteps of
retired director Hans Günter Schwarz are big, and the new team is struggling
to catch up with the estate's previous fame.

Müller-Thurgau Fruity, early ripening, usually low-acid grape; most common in
PFALZ, RHEINHESSEN, NAHE, BADEN and FRANKEN; was 21% of German v'yds in
1998, but 14% today. Easy-to-drink wines, nothing more.

Muskateller Ancient aromatic white grape with crisp acidity. A rarity in the PFALZ,
BADEN and WÜRTTEMBERG, where it is mostly made dry.

Nackenheim Rhh w ★→★★★★ 93 96 97 01 03 04 05 06 07 08 09 NIERSTEIN
neighbour also with top Rhine terroir; similar best wines (esp ERSTE LAGE
Rothenberg). Top growers: GUNDERLOCH, Kühling-Gillot.

Nahe Na Tributary of the Rhine and a high-quality wine region with 4,135 ha.
Balanced, fresh, clean, but full-bodied, even minerally wines; RIES best. EISWEIN
a growing specialty.

Neckar The river with many of WÜRTTEMBERG's finest v'yds, mainly between
Stuttgart and Heilbronn.

Neipperg, Graf von ★★→★★★ Noble estate in Schwaigern, WÜRTTEMBERG: elegant
dry RIES and robust LEMBERGER. MUSKATELLER up to BA quality a specialty. A scion
of the family, Count Stephan von Neipperg, makes wine at Ch Canon
la Gaffelière in St-Emilion.

Niederhausen Na w ★★→★★★★ 93 95 96 97 98 99 01 02 03 04 05 07 08 09
Neighbour of SCHLOSSBÖCKELHEIM. Graceful, powerful RIES. ERSTE LAGE
v'yds: Hermannsberg, Hermannshöhle. Growers: CRUSIUS, DÖNNHOFF,
Gutsverwaltung Niederhausen-Schlossböckelheim, Mathern.

Nierstein Rhh w ★→★★★★ 93 96 97 98 99 01 03 04 05 07 08 09 526 ha.
Famous but treacherous village name. Beware GROSSLAGE Gutes Domtal: a
supermarket deception. Superb ERSTE LAGE v'yds: Brudersberg, Hipping,
Oelberg, Orbel, Pettenthal. Ripe, aromatic, elegant wines, dry and sweet. Try
Gehring, Guntrum, HEYL ZU HERRNSHEIM, Kühling-Gillot, ST-ANTONY, Strub.

Obermosel (Bereich) District name for the upper MOSEL above TRIER. Wines from
the Elbling grape, generally uninspiring unless v. young.

Ockfen M-S-R (Saar) w ★★→★★★ 90 93 95 96 97 98 99 01 02 03 04 05 07

Superb fragrant wines from ERSTE LAGE v'yd: Bockstein. Growers: Dr. Fischer, Weinhof Herrenberg, OTHEGRAVEN, SANKT URBANS-HOF, WAGNER, ZILLIKEN.

Oechsle Scale for sugar content of grape juice.

Oestrich Rhg w ★★→★★★ 90 97 99 01 02 03 04 05 07 Big village; variable, but some splendid RIES. ERSTE LAGE v'yds: Doosberg, Lenchen. Top growers: August Eser, PETER JAKOB KÜHN, Querbach, SPREITZER, WEGELER.

Oppenheim Rhh w ★→★★★ 93 96 97 98 01 03 04 05 07 08 09 Town south of NIERSTEIN; spectacular 13th-century church. ERSTE LAGE Kreuz and Sackträger. Growers include: Heyden, Kühling-Gillot, Manz. The younger generation is starting to realize the full potential of these sites.

Ortenau District around and south of Baden-Baden. Gd KLINGELBERGER (RIES) and SPÄTBURGUNDER, mainly from granite soils. Top villages: DURBACH, Neuweier, Waldulm.

Othegraven, Weingut von ★★→★★★ This KANZEM, SAAR estate was mediocre until in 1999 Dr. Heidi Kegel inherited the estate, with its superb Altenberg v'yds, and restored its reputation. Look esp for Altenberg old-vines SPÄTLESE.

Palatinate English for PFALZ.

Paulinshof, Weingut M-M ★★ 8-ha estate, once monastic, in KESTEN and BRAUNEBERG. Unusually for the MITTELMOSEL, the Jüngling family specializes in TROCKEN and HALBTROCKEN wines, as well as fine AUSLESEN.

Pauly-Bergweiler, Dr. ★★★ Fine BERNKASTEL estate. V'yds there and in WEHLEN, but wines sold under the Peter Nicolay label from ÜRZIG and ERDEN are usually best. EISWEIN and TBA can be sensational.

Pfalz Pfz Usually balmy 23,400-ha v'yd region south of RHEINHESSEN. The MITTELHAARDT area is the source of full-bodied, often dry RIES. The more southerly SÜDLICHE WEINSTRASSE is better suited to the Pinot varieties, white and red. Biggest RIES area after MOSEL-SAAR-RUWER.

Piesport M-M w ★→★★★★ 90 93 94 96 97 99 00 01 02 03 04 05 06 07 08 09 Tiny village with famous vine amphitheatre: at best glorious, rich, aromatic RIES. Great First Class v'yds: Goldtröpfchen, Domherr. Treppchen far inferior. GROSSLAGE: Michelsberg (mainly MÜLLER-THURGAU; avoid). Esp gd are GRANS-FASSIAN, Joh Haart, R HAART, Kurt Hain, KESSELSTATT, SANKT URBANS-HOF.

Portugieser Second-rate red wine grape, mostly grown in RHEINHESSEN and PFALZ, now often used for WEISSHERBST. 4,550 ha in production.

Prädikat Special attributes or qualities. See QMP.

Prüm, J J ★★★★ 71 76 83 88 89 90 94 95 96 97 99 01 02 03 04 05 06 07 08 09 Superlative and legendary 20-ha MOSEL estate in BERNKASTEL, GRAACH, WEHLEN. Delicate but long-lived wines with astonishing finesse, esp in WEHLENER SONNENUHR. Long lees ageing makes the wines hard to taste when young, but they reward patience. Gd vintages keep 30 yrs.

Prüm, S A ★★→★★★ 89 90 97 99 01 02 03 04 05 07 If WEHLEN neighbour J J PRÜM is resolutely traditional, Raimond Prüm works in a more popular style. Sound, if sometimes inconsistent, wines from WEHLEN and GRAACH.

Qualitätswein bestimmter Anbaugebiete (QbA) The middle quality of German wine, with sugar added before fermentation (as in French *chaptalization*), but controlled as to areas, grapes, etc. Its new name: g U (see p.146) is little improvement.

Qualitätswein mit Prädikat (QmP) Top category, for all wines ripe enough not to need sugaring (KABINETT to TBA).

Randersacker Frank w ★★→★★★ 97 99 01 02 03 04 05 06 07 08 09 Leading village just south of WÜRZBURG known for distinctive dry wine, esp SILVANER. ERSTE LAGE v'yds: Pfülben, Sonnenstuhl, Teufelskeller. Top growers include:

Words within entries marked like this *Alter Ego de Palmer* indicate wines especially enjoyed by Hugh Johnson over the past 12 months (mid 09–10).

BÜRGERSPITAL, JULIUSSPITAL, STAATLICHER HOFKELLER, SCHMITT'S KINDER, STÖRRLEIN, Trockene Schmitts.

Ratzenberger ★★ Estate making racy dry and off-dry RIES in BACHARACH; best from ERSTE LAGE v'yds: Posten and Steeger St-Jost. Gd SEKT, too.

Rauenthal Rhg w ★★★→★★★★ 93 97 98 99 01 02 03 04 05 07 Supreme village on inland slopes: spicy, complex Riesling. ERSTE LAGE v'yds: Baiken, Gehrn, Nonnenberg, Rothenberg, Wülfen. Top growers: BREUER, KLOSTER EBERBACH, LANGWERTH VON SIMMERN.

Rebholz Pfz ★★★→★★★★ Top SÜDLICHE WEINSTRASSE estate for decades, maintaining extraordinary consistency. Makes some of the best dry MUSKATELLER, GEWÜRZ, CHARD (Burgundian-style) and SPÄTBURGUNDER in PFALZ. Outstanding GROSSES GEWÄCHS RIES.

Regent New dark-red grape suited for organic farming and enjoying considerable success in southern wine regions. 2,180 ha are now planted. Plum-flavoured, tannic wines of little complexity.

Ress, Balthasar ★★ 42-ha RHEINGAU estate based in HATTENHEIM. Gd estate Ries, and basic Von Unserm label, red and white, can offer gd value.

Restsüsse Unfermented grape sugar remaining in (or in cheap wines added to) wine to give it sweetness. Can range from 3 g per litre in a TROCKEN wine to 300 in a TBA.

Rheingau Rhg Best v'yd region of Rhine, west of Wiesbaden. 3,097 ha. Classic, substantial but subtle RIES, yet on the whole recently eclipsed by brilliance elsewhere and hampered by some underperforming, if grand, estates. Controversially, one-third of the region is classified since 2000 as ERSTES GEWÄCHS, subject to regulations that differ from those created by the VDP for GROSSES GEWÄCHS.

Rheinhessen Vast region (26,330 ha) between Mainz and Worms, bordered by river NAHE to the west. Much dross, but includes top RIES from NACKENHEIM, NIERSTEIN, OPPENHEIM, etc. Remarkable spurt in quality in south of region from growers such as KELLER and WITTMANN.

Richter, Weingut Max Ferd ★★→★★★ Top MITTELMOSEL estate, at Mülheim. Fine RIES made from top sites like BRAUNEBERGER Juffer-Sonnenuhr, GRAACHER Domprobst, Mülheim (Helenenkloster), WEHLENER SONNENUHR. Produces superb EISWEIN from Helenenkloster almost every yr. Wines from purchased grapes carry a slightly different label.

Rieslaner Cross between SILVANER and RIES; known for low yields and difficult ripening. Makes fine AUSLESEN in FRANKEN, where most is grown.

Riesling The best German grape: fragrant, fruity, racy, long-lived. Only CHARD can compete as the world's best white grape.

Ruck, Weingut Johann ★★→★★★ Reliable and spicy SILVANER and RIES from IPHOFEN in FRANKEN'S STEIGERWALD district. Traditional in style.

Rüdesheim Rhg w ★★→★★★★ 89 90 93 96 97 98 99 01 02 03 04 05 07) 08 09 Rhine resort with outstanding ERSTE LAGE v'yds; the three best (Roseneck, Rottland and Schlossberg) are called Rüdesheimer Berg. Full-bodied wines, fine-flavoured, often remarkable in off yrs. Many of the top RHEINGAU estates own some Rüdesheim v'yds. Best growers: BREUER, JOHANNISHOF, KESSELER, LEITZ, RESS, SCHLOSS SCHÖNBORN, STAATSWEINGÜTER.

Ruländer (Pinot Gr) Now more commonly known as GRAUBURGUNDER.

Ruppertsberg Pfz w ★★→★★★ 97 99 01 02 03 04 05 07 Southern village of MITTELHAARDT. Powerful RIES from ERSTE LAGE sites Gaisböhl, Reiterpfad, Spiess. Growers include: BASSERMANN-JORDAN, Biffar, BUHL, BÜRKLIN-WOLF, CHRISTMANN, DR. DEINHARD.

Ruwer 89 90 93 97 99 01 02 03 04 05 07 08 09 Tributary of MOSEL near TRIER. V. fine, delicate but highly aromatic and remarkably long-lived RIES both sweet and dry. A string of warm summers has helped ripeness. Best growers: Beulwitz, KARLSMÜHLE, KARTHÄUSERHOF, KESSELSTATT, MAXIMIN GRÜNHAUS.

Saale-Unstrut 03 05 07 09 Climatically challenging region of 660 ha around confluence of these two rivers at Naumburg, near Leipzig. The terraced v'yds of WEISSBURGUNDER, SILVANER, GEWÜRZ, RIES and SPÄTBURGUNDER have Cistercian origins. Quality leaders: Böhme, Born, Gussek, Kloster Pforta, LÜTZKENDORF, Pawis.

Saar 89 90 93 94 95 96 97 98 99 01 02 03 04 05 07 08 09 Hill-lined tributary of the MOSEL south of RUWER. Climate differs considerably from MITTELMOSEL: v'yds are 50 to 100 m higher in altitude. The most brilliant, austere, steely RIES of all. Villages include AYL, KANZEM, OCKFEN, SAARBURG, Serrig, WILTINGEN (SCHARZHOFBERG). Many fine estates here, often at the top of their game.

Saarburg Small town in the SAAR valley, Rausch v'yd is one of the best of the region. Best growers: WAGNER, ZILLIKEN.

Sachsen 03 04 05 07) 08 09 A region of 441 ha in the Elbe Valley around Dresden and Meissen. MÜLLER-THURGAU still dominates, but WEISSBURGUNDER, GRAUBURGUNDER, TRAMINER and RIES give dry wines with real character. Best growers: Vincenz Richter, SCHLOSS PROSCHWITZ, Schloss Wackerbarth, Martin Schwarz, Zimmerling.

St-Antony, Weingut ★★ 28-ha NIERSTEIN estate with exceptional v'yd portfolio. Quality was uneven in recent yrs, but new owner (same as HEYL ZU HERRNSHEIM) seems to be turning things around.

Salm, Prinz zu Owner of Schloss Wallhausen in NAHE and Villa Sachsen in RHEINHESSEN. Until 2006 president of VDP, which implemented the v'yd classification system against some stern opposition.

Salwey, Weingut ★★★ Leading BADEN estate at Oberrotweil, esp for RIES, WEISSBURGUNDER and RULÄNDER. SPÄTBURGUNDER can be v.gd, too, and fruit schnapps are an intriguing sideline.

Sankt Urbans-Hof ★★★ New star based in LEIWEN, PIESPORT and OCKFEN. Limpid RIES of impeccable purity and raciness from 33 ha. Stunning 2008 collection.

Sauer, Horst ★★★ ESCHERNDORFER Lump is one of FRANKEN's top sites; Sauer is the finest exponent of its SILVANER and RIES. Notable dry wines and sensational TBA.

Schaefer, **Willi** ★★★ The finest grower of GRAACH (but only 4 ha). Classic pure MOSEL RIES.

Schäfer-Fröhlich, Weingut ★★★ Increasingly brilliant RIES, dry and nobly sweet, from this 12-ha estate in Bockenau, NAHE.

Scharzhofberg M-S-R (Saar) w ★★★★ 71 83 88 89 90 93 94 95 96 97 98 99 01 02 03 04 05 06 07) 08 09 Superlative SAAR v'yd: austerely beautiful wines, the perfection of RIES, best in AUSLESEN. Top estates: BISCHÖFLICHE WEINGÜTER, EGON MÜLLER, von HÖVEL, VON KESSELSTATT, VAN VOLXEM.

Scheurebe Grapefruit-scented grape of high quality (and RIES parentage), esp used in PFALZ. Excellent for botrytis wine (BA, TBA).

Schlossböckelheim Na w ★★→★★★★ 90 96 97 98 99 01 02 03 04 05 07 Village with top NAHE v'yds, inc First Class Felsenberg, In den Felsen, Königsfels, Kupfergrube. Firm yet delicate wine that ages well. Top growers: *Crusius*, DÖNNHOFF, Gutsverwaltung Niederhausen-Schlossböckelheim, SCHÄFER-FRÖHLICH.

Schloss Johannisberg Rhg w ★★→★★★ 90 94 95 96 97 98 99 01 02 03 04 05 07 08 09 Famous RHEINGAU estate of 35 ha, 100% RIES, owned by Henkell. Until recently, high prices reflected reputation more than quality. Since 2005, improved v'yd management under new director, Christian Witte. The 2007 wines are promising.

Schloss Lieser ★★★ 9-ha estate owned by Thomas Haag, from FRITZ HAAG estate, making pure, racy RIES from underrated Niederberg Helden v'yd in LIESER.

Schloss Neuweier ★★★ Leading producer of dry RIES in BADEN, from the volcanic soils of Mauerberg and Schlossberg v'yds near Baden-Baden. Particularly successful in 2008 and 2009: mineral RIES with vibrant acidity, eg. Schlossberg *alte Reben* (old vines) or Mauerberg GROSSES GEWÄCHS.

Schloss Proschwitz ★★ A resurrected princely estate at Meissen in SACHSEN, which leads former East Germany in quality, esp with dry WEISSBURGUNDER and GRAUBURGUNDER. A great success!

Schloss Reinhartshausen Rhg ★★→★★★ Famous estate, 80 ha in Erbach, HATTENHEIM, KIEDRICH, etc. Originally property of Prussian royal family, now in competent private hands.

Schloss Saarstein, Weingut ★→★★★ 90 93 97 99 01 03 04 05 07 08 09 Steep but chilly v'yds in Serrig need warm yrs to succeed but can deliver steely, minerally and long-lived AUSLESE and EISWEIN.

Schloss Schönborn ★★★ Widespread 50-ha RHEINGAU estate with superb sites, based at HATTENHEIM. Full-flavoured wines, variable, but excellent when at their best. The Schönborn family also owns a large wine estate in FRANKEN.

Schloss Vaux ★★→★★★ Superior SEKT manufacturer, specializing in bottle-fermented RIES and SPÄTBURGUNDER from top RHEINGAU sites (eg. STEINBERG or ASSMANNSHÄUSER Höllenberg). The company does not own v'yds itself, but purchases wine from leading estates (mainly from VDP members).

Schloss Vollrads Rhg w ★★90 01 03 04 05 07 08 09 One of the greatest historic RHEINGAU estates, owned by a bank since the sudden death of owner Erwein Count Matuschka in 1997. RIES in a popular and accessible style, but the estate's full potential has yet to be rediscovered.

Schmitt's Kinder ★★→★★★ Uncompromising TROCKEN wines from RANDERSACKER's best v'yds. 18 ha. Textbook FRANKEN SILVANER and RIES. Gd barrel-aged SPÄTBURGUNDER and sweet SCHEUREBE, too.

Schnaitmann, Weingut ★★→★★★ Although this new WÜRTTEMBERG star makes gd RIES and Sauv Bl, its reputation rests on a complex range of full-bodied red wines from a range of varieties. Best: Simonroth R Spätburgunder.

Schneider, Cornelia and Reinhold ★★→★★★ 7-ha family estate in Endingen, KAISERSTUHL. Age-worthy SPÄTBURGUNDER; old-fashioned, opulent RULÄNDER.

Schoppenwein Café (or bar) wine, ie. wine by the glass.

Schwarzer Adler, Weingut ★★→★★★ Fritz Keller makes top BADEN GRAU-, WEISS-, and SPÄTBURGUNDER on 55 ha at Oberbergen, KAISERSTUHL. A firm opponent of residual sugar in Pinot. Selection "A" signifies the top barrique wines.

Schwarzriesling This grape, with 2,390 ha, is none other than the Pinot Meunier of northern France. In WÜRTTEMBERG a light-bodied red.

Schwegler, Albrecht ★★★ Small WÜRTTEMBERG estate known for unusual yet tasteful red blends such as Granat (Merlot, Zweigelt, LEMBERGER and other varieties). 2 ha only, but worth looking for.

Schweigen Pfz r w ★★ 97 99 01 02 03 04 05 07 08 09 Southern PFALZ village. Best growers: FRIEDRICH BECKER, Bernhart, Jülg.

Sekt German sparkling wine v. variable in quality. Bottle fermentation is not mandatory; cheap examples may be produced in a pressure tank. Reputable wine-growers' labels are certainly a gd choice, but even at this level, sekt is sometimes only a by-product. Estates that are sekt specialists include Raumland, SCHLOSS VAUX, Wilhelmshof.

Selbach-Oster ★★★ Scrupulous 20-ha ZELTINGEN estate among MITTELMOSEL leaders. Also makes wine from purchased grapes: estate bottlings are best.

Silvaner Third-most-planted German white grape variety with 5,260 ha and thus

Remember that vintage information for German wines is given in a different form from the ready/not ready distinction applying to other countries. See the explanation at the bottom of p.144.

GERMANY

5% of the surface. Best examples in FRANKEN, where Silvaner's lovely floral flavours and its bone-dry minerally taste reach perfection. Worth looking for as well in RHEINHESSEN and KAISERSTUHL (esp IHRINGEN).

Sonnenuhr Sundial. Name of several v'yds, esp First Class sites at WEHLEN and ZELTINGEN.

Spätburgunder (Pinot Noir) The best red wine grape in Germany – esp in AHR, BADEN and WÜRTTEMBERG, and increasingly PFALZ – steadily improving quality, but most still underflavoured or overoaked. The best are convincing (eg. FÜRST, HUBER, KNIPSER, MAYER-NÄKEL, etc.). Allegedly, Charles the Fat first brought Pinot N from Burgundy to the shores of Lake Constance (BODENSEE) in 884.

Spätlese Late harvest. One better (riper, with more alcohol, more substance and usually more sweetness) than KABINETT. Gd examples age at least 7 yrs, often longer. TROCKEN Spätlesen, often similar in style to GROSSES GEWÄCHS, can be v. fine with food.

Spreitzer, Weingut ★★★ Andreas and Bernd Spreitzer produce RHEINGAU RIES from 17 ha, mainly in OESTRICH. Deliciously racy wines.

Staatlicher Hofkeller ★★ The Bavarian state domain. 120 ha of the finest FRANKEN v'yds with spectacular cellars under the great baroque Residenz at WÜRZBURG. Quality sound but rarely exciting.

Staatsweingut (or Staatliche Weinbaudomäne) The state wine estates or domains. Some have been privatized in recent yrs.

Steigerwald District in eastern FRANKEN. V'yds lie at considerable altitude but bring powerful SILVANER and RIES. Look for: Castell, RUCK, Weltner, WIRSCHING.

Steinberg Rhg w ★★★ 90 95 96 97 99 01 02 03 04 05 07 08 09 Famous 32-ha HATTENHEIM walled v'yd, planted by Cistercian monks 700 yrs ago. A monopoly of KLOSTER EBERBACH. Disappointing for yrs but now one to watch.

Steinwein Wine from WÜRZBURG's best v'yd, Stein. Goethe's favourite, too.

Stodden, Weingut Jean ★★★ A new star in the AHR. Burgundy enthusiast Gerhard Stodden crafts richly oaky SPÄTBURGUNDER. First-rate since 1999, but v. pricey.

Störrlein, Weingut ★★→★★★ Sterling dry, expressive SILVANER and RIES from RANDERSACKER in FRANKEN; fine GROSSES GEWÄCHS from Sonnenstuhl v'yd.

Südliche Weinstrasse District name for south PFALZ. Quality has improved tremendously in past 25 yrs. See FRIEDRICH BECKER, BERGDOLT, REBHOLZ, SCHWEIGEN, DR. WEHRHEIM.

Tauberfranken Underrated district of northeast BADEN: FRANKEN-style wines from limestone soils, bone-dry and distinctly cool-climate in style.

Thanisch, Weingut Dr. ★★→★★★ BERNKASTEL estate, inc part of the Doctor v'yd. This famous estate was divided in the 1980s, but the two confusingly share the same name: Erben Müller-Burggraef identifies one; Erben Thanisch the other. Similar in quality but the latter sometimes has the edge.

Traisen Na w ★★★ 90 93 95 96 97 98 99 01 02 03 04 05 07 08 09 Small village inc ERSTE LAGE v'yds Bastei and Rotenfels, capable of making RIES of concentration and class. Top grower: CRUSIUS.

Traminer See GEWÜRZTRAMINER.

Trier M-S-R w ★★→★★★ Great wine city of Roman origin, on MOSEL, between RUWER and SAAR. Big charitable estates have cellars here among Roman ruins.

Trittenheim M-M w ★★★ 90 93 95 96 97 99 01 03 04 05 07 08 09 Attractive south MITTELMOSEL light wines. Best plots in ERSTE LAGE v'yd Apotheke deserve that classification, although the site contains, since 1974, a lot of second-rate, flat land. Growers include ANSGAR CLÜSSERATH, Ernst Clüsserath, CLÜSSERATH-WEILER, GRANS-FASSIAN, Milz.

Trocken Dry. Trocken wines have a max 9 g unfermented sugar per litre. Quality has increased dramatically since the 1980s, when most were tart, even sour. Most dependable in PFALZ and all points south.

Trockenbeerenauslese (TBA) Sweetest, most expensive category of German wine, extremely rare, with concentrated honey flavour. Made from selected shrivelled grapes affected by noble rot (botrytis).

Trollinger Pale red grape variety of WÜRTTEMBERG; identical with south Tyrol's Vernatsch; mostly overcropped but locally v. popular.

Ürzig M-M w ★★★★ 90 93 94 95 96 97 98 99 01 02 03 04 05 06 07 08 09 Village on red sandstone and red slate, famous for firm, full, spicy wine unlike other MOSELS. ERSTE LAGE v'yd: Würzgarten. Growers include Berres, CHRISTOFFEL, LOOSEN, MÖNCHHOF, PAULY-BERGWEILER (Peter Nicolay), WEINS-PRÜM. Threatened by an *Autobahn* bridge 160 metres high.

Van Volxem, Weingut ★★→★★★ SAAR estate revived by brewery heir Roman Niewodniczanski since 1999. V. low yields from top sites result in ultra-ripe dry (or slightly off-dry) RIES. Atypical but impressive.

VdP, Verband Deutscher Prädikats und Qualitätsweingüter Pace-making association of premium growers. Look for its eagle insignia on wine labels, and for the ERSTE LAGE logo on wines from classified v'yds. President: Steffen CHRISTMANN.

Vollenweider, Weingut ★★★ Daniel Vollenweider from Switzerland has, since 2000, revived the Wolfer Goldgrube v'yd near Traben-Trarbach. Excellent RIES, but v. small quantities.

Wachenheim Pfz w ★★★→★★★★ 90 96 97 98 99 01 02 03 04 05 07 340 ha, inc exceptional RIES. First Class v'yds: Belz, Gerümpel, Goldbächel, Rechbächel, etc. Top growers: Biffar, BÜRKLIN-WOLF, Karl Schäfer, WOLF.

Wagner, Dr. ★★ 9-ha estate with v'yds in SAARBURG and OCKFEN. Traditional methods: all wines ferment and age in FUDER casks.

Wagner-Stempel, Weingut ★★★ 16-ha estate, 50% RIES, in RHEINHESSEN near NAHE border in obscure Siefersheim. Recent yrs have provided excellent wines, great in 2005 and 2007, both GROSSES GEWÄCHS and nobly sweet.

Walluf Rhg w ★★★ 90 96 97 98 99 01 02 03 04 05 07 08 09 Neighbour of Eltville. Underrated wines. ERSTE LAGE v'yd: Walkenberg. Growers include BECKER, JOST.

Wegeler ★★→★★★ Important family estates in OESTRICH, MITTELHARDT and BERNKASTEL. The Wegelers owned the merchant house of DEINHARD until 1997. Estate wines remain of high quality.

Wehlen M-M w ★★★→★★★★ 89 90 93 94 95 96 97 99 01 02 03 04 05 07 08 09 BERNKASTEL neighbour with equally fine, somewhat richer wine. ERSTE LAGE: SONNENUHR. Top growers are: Kerpen, LOOSEN, M MOLITOR, J J PRÜM, S A PRÜM, RICHTER, Studert-Prüm, SELBACH-OSTER, WEGELER, WEINS-PRÜM. Vineyards threatened by *Autobahn* project.

Wehrheim, Weingut Dr. ★★★ In warm SÜDLICHE WEINSTRASSE Pinot varieties and CHARD as well as RIES ripen fully. Both whites and reds are v. successful here.

Weil, Weingut Robert ★★★★ 90 94 96 97 99 01 02 03 04 05 07 08 09 Outstanding estate in KIEDRICH; owned since 1988 by Suntory of Japan. Superb EISWEIN, TBA, BA; standard wines also v.gd. Recently another ERSTE LAGE besides famous Gräfenberg was approved: Turmberg, 3.7 ha. Look for the brilliant, dense Turmberg SPÄTLESE 2008, and you'll understand why.

Weingart, Weingut ★★★ Outstanding MITTELRHEIN estate, with 11 ha in BOPPARD. Superb value, and particularly remarkable in 2008.

Weingut Wine estate.

Weins-Prüm, Dr. ★★★ Small estate; based at WEHLEN. 4 ha of superb v'yds in MITTELMOSEL. Scrupulous winemaking from owner Bert Selbach, who favours a taut, minerally style.

Words within entries marked like this *Alter Ego de Palmer* indicate wines especially enjoyed by Hugh Johnson over the past 12 months (mid 09–10).

Weissburgunder (Pinot Bl) Increasingly popular for TROCKEN wines that exhibit more burgundian raciness than German CHARD. Best from southern PFALZ and from BADEN. Some leading producers are now turning back to traditional larger oak casks instead of barriques. Also much used for SEKT.

Weissherbst Pale pink wine, sometimes botrytis-affected and occasionally even BA, made from a single variety, often SPÄTBURGUNDER.

Wiltingen M-S-R (Saar) w ★★→★★★★ 90 93 95 96 97 99 01 03 04 05 06 07 08 09 Heartland of the SAAR. 320 ha. Beautifully subtle, austere wine. Famous SCHARZHOFBERG is the best of a trio of ERSTE LAGE sites that also includes Braune Kupp and Gottesfuss. Top growers: BISCHÖFLICHE WEINGÜTER, EGON MÜLLER, KESSELSTATT, VAN VOLXEM.

Winning, von Newly established DEIDESHEIM estate, incorporating old DR DEINHARD estate. The von Winning label is only used for top wines from DR DEINHARD v'yds. The first vintage was 2008 – and a success: RIES of great purity and terroir expression, slightly influenced by a 10–20% oak fermentation. A label to watch.

Winningen M-S-R w ★★→★★★ Lower MOSEL town near Koblenz: excellent dry RIES and TBA. ERSTE LAGE v'yds: Röttgen, Uhlen. Top growers: HEYMANN-LÖWENSTEIN, KNEBEL, Richard Richter.

Wirsching, Hans ★★★ Estate in IPHOFEN, FRANKEN. Dry RIES and *Silvaner*, powerful and long-lived. 72 ha above all in ERSTE LAGE v'yds: Julius-Echter-Berg, Kronsberg.

Wittmann, Weingut ★★★ Since 1999 Philipp Wittmann has propelled this 25-ha organic estate to the top ranks in RHEINHESSEN. Crystal-clear, mineral, dry RIES from QBA to GROSSES GEWÄCHS RIES and magnificent TBA.

Wöhrwag, Weingut ★★→★★★ Just outside Stuttgart, this 20-ha WÜRTTEMBERG estate produces succulent reds and often brilliant RIES, esp EISWEIN.

Wolf J L ★★→★★★ Estate in WACHENHEIM leased long-term by Ernst LOOSEN of BERNKASTEL. Dry PFALZ RIES with a MOSEL-like finesse. Sound and consistent rather than dazzling.

Württemberg Wurt Vast area in the south, 11,520 ha, little known outside Germany. Local consumption absorbs most of the production; maybe that's why the region has been distinctly underperforming for a long time. But ambitions now rising, esp with concentrated, fruit-driven reds (esp LEMBERGER, Samtrot, SPÄTBURGUNDER). Further experiments include Sauv Bl or dark new crossings bred by the Weinsberg research station. RIES (mostly TROCKEN) tends to be rustic, although the Remstal area close to Stuttgart can have refinement.

Würzburg Frank ★★→★★★★ 93 97 98 99 01 02 03 04 05 06 07 (08) 08 09 Great baroque city on the Main, centre of FRANKEN wine: fine, full-bodied, dry RIES and esp SILVANER. ERSTE LAGE v'yds: Innere Leiste, Stein, Stein-Harfe. Growers: BÜRGERSPITAL, JULIUSSPITAL, STAATLICHER HOFKELLER, Weingut am Stein.

Zehnthof, Weingut ★★ Wide-ranging wines, notably SILVANER and Pinot varieties, from Luckert family's 12-ha estate in Sulzfeld, FRANKEN.

Zell M-S-R w ★→★★★ 93 97 99 01 02 03 04 05 07 08 09 Best-known lower MOSEL village, esp for awful GROSSLAGE: Schwarze Katz (Black Cat). RIES on steep slate gives aromatic wines. Top growers: S Fischer, Kallfelz.

Zeltingen M-M w ★★→★★★★ 90 93 95 96 97 98 99 01 02 03 04 05 06 07 08 09 Top but sometimes underrated MOSEL village near WEHLEN. Lively crisp RIES. ERSTE LAGE v'yd: SONNENUHR. Top growers: M MOLITOR, J J PRÜM, Schömann, SELBACH-OSTER.

Remember that vintage information for German wines is given in a different form from the ready/not ready distinction applying to other countries. See the explanation at the bottom of p.144.

A cool 14th

Schleswig-Holstein, best known until now for being the subject of the eponymous Question, is now Germany's newest wine region. It's right up on the Danish border, flat, framed by the North and Baltic seas, and full of sheep and cows, but there are 10 ha of vines, planted with Brussels' approval. Even the island of Sylt has vines. The first harvest is approaching…

Ziereisen, Weingut ★★ Carpenter and ex-co-op member Hans-Peter Ziereisen turned winemaker some yrs ago. A full palette from BADEN: dry Pinot whites, mineral Gutedel Steingrüble and Syrah. But best are the SPÄTBURGUNDERS from various small v'yd plots with dialect names: Schulen, Tschuppen, Rhini.

Zilliken, Forstmeister Geltz ★★★→★★★★ Former estate of Prussian royal forester with 11 ha at SAARBURG and OCKFEN, SAAR. Produces intensely minerally *Ries from* SAARBURG *Rausch*, inc superb AUSLESE and EISWEIN with excellent ageing potential.

Luxembourg

Being a small country squeezed between France and Germany can have its advantages: wine and food has taken the best (and occasionally the worst) from both. The wines show a beguiling purity of fruit, and are mostly light, mostly white and mostly dry. The MOSEL turns into the Moselle, the vineyards are steep and the notion of terroir well established. The varieties to look for are RIES, Auxerrois, Pinots Bl and Gr and GEWÜRZ; you might, however, have to dig through a lot of Rivaner (MÜLLER-THURGAU) and ELBLING to find them. There's a lot of sparkling Crémant de Luxembourg made, but also table wines grown on slate, chalk or clay, which beautifully reflect their site.

Prices are low because Luxembourg has little international reputation and must compete with both its neighbours, both of whom are close enough for the weekly shop. It's important to look for good producers, though, because regulations on yields are generous and only the most demanding growers are stricter with themselves than they have to be.

Look for Alice Hartmann (great RIES), *crémant* from Caves St-Martin, Mathis Bastian, Schumacher-Knepper, Sunnen-Hoffmann, Gloden, Cep d'Or, Bernard Massard, Domain Clos Mon Vieux Moulin, Mme. Aly Duhr, Charles Decker, and the big Vinsmoselle co-op. The bubbly can be good value.

Spain & Portugal

More heavily shaded areas are the
wine-growing regions

The following abbreviations are used in the text:

Alen	Alentejo
Bair	Bairrada
Bul	Bullas
Cos del S	Costers del Segre
El B	El Bierzo
Emp	Empordà-Costa Brava/Ampurdán
La M	La Mancha
Lis	Lisboa
Mont-M	Montilla-Moriles
Nav	Navarra
Pen	Penedès
Pri	Priorat/Priorato
Rib del D	Ribera del Duero
Rib del G	Ribera del Guadiana
R Ala	Rioja Alavesa
R Alt	Rioja Alta
RB	Rioja Baja
Set	Setúbal
Som	Somontano
U-R	Utiel-Requena
Res	*reserva*

Portugal is seeing an influx of foreign winemakers; Spain is rediscovering its heritage. Both are positive developments.

Spain and Portugal are viticulturally very different, not least because Portugal has kept a wealth of indigenous vine varieties, whereas Spain is having to hunt for its vinous heritage (see this year's supplement on p.305). The search is resulting in a flurry of fledgling production zones and wineries, many of them temples to hand-made winemaking. These Spanish innovators are home-grown. Their tastes tend toward French oak, if they can afford it, and to the power of Garnacha, the crunchiness of Mencía and the dense texture of Monastrell.

Portugal, however, has become a magnet for the international winemaking elite: Bordeaux's Bruno Prats and Jean-Michel Cazes are in the Douro; Bordelais François Lurton is making Vinho Verde, as is one of the Douro's leading winemakers, Dirk Niepoort. In Lisboa, the new name for Estremadura, Rhône star Michel Chapoutier is blending Syrah and Touriga Nacional in collaboration with Monte d'Oiro. Neighbouring *vinho regional* Ribatejo, rechristened Tejo, is getting a much-needed injection of glamour in the shape of newcomer Vale d'Algares' winery, where cutting-edge design and gadgetry have drawn comparisons with a James Bond villain's hideaway.

Port, sherry and Madeira have a separate chapter on p.184.

SPAIN

Recent vintages

Rioja

2009 A hot summer suggested raisined grapes and a repeat of 2003, but was rescued by mid-September rain, followed by sun. Extremely promising, especially in Rioja Alta and Baja.

2008 Wines in the classic style. The best are fresh and aromatic, a little lower in alcohol.

2007 A small crop. Satisfactory but not exceptional.

2006 Wines are fragrant, fresh and early maturing.

2005 Officially rated as "exceptional", but official ratings don't go below "average". Wines are full-bodied with immediate charm.

2004 Now recognized as an outstanding vintage.

2003 Top wines are sublime; however, most have proved short-lived and are already past their prime, given the hot summer.

2002 A cross between 1999 and 2000. The best are still delicious; the run-of-the-mill have already peaked.

2001 An exceptional year. Many wines to drink now. The best still have some years ahead.

2000 Huge harvest; wines distinctly bland, with little real flavour or definition.

1999 A difficult harvest; its light but very graceful wines have mainly peaked.

Ribera del Duero

2009 The very hot summer risked hot, baked fruit but the early autumn rains helped, and top producers should have very high-quality wines.

2008 A risk of rot was followed by a cool summer, and frosts in September. Selection was essential for quality.

2007 The most disastrous vintage for a decade. A damp spring was followed by a cool, sunless summer.

2006 A vintage that is still showing well; best will benefit from further ageing.

2005 Those who picked too early have green, unbalanced wines. Very good only for the true professionals.

2004 Parallels promise of Rioja. Good-quality wines and a plentiful harvest.

2003 The best wines are of good colour, glycerine and alcohol but low in acidity. The poor ones are baked.

2002 A large harvest of moderate quality.

2001 Medium-sized harvest of excellent quality; wines fulfilling their promise.

2000 Some bodegas made spectacular wines. Drink now.

1999 Very good, but fading.

Navarra

2009 A generous vintage and good quality despite the hot summer. Garnacha flourished. Likely to be a vintage to enjoy relatively young.

2008 As elsewhere a wet spring and a very late harvest. The slow ripening, however, suggests elegance if selection was careful.

2007 Surprisingly good for the best sites. At best very aromatic, well-balanced fruit, which will produce good wines that will age well.

2006 Young wines good. Only true professionals will produce wines of ageing potential.

2005 Exceptional vintage resulting in wines of deep colour, full flavours and sweet, powerful tannins.

2004 Good, intense wines for those who picked late and selectively.

2003 As in 2002, only the best and most professional producers obtained decent results. The best are already mature.

2002 The best are good, but drink now.

2001 An excellent year, with big, ripe, balanced wines that still retain intensity.

2000 Best wines are big and fleshy. Drink now.

Penedès

2009 A fresh year even given the hot weather, and a high-quality vintage. In Priorat the outcome is more mixed, as a result of successive heat spikes affecting the crop.

2008 Heavy spring rains presaged rot for many producers, and uneven fruit set. A good vintage for the better producers.

2007 A textbook year led to the vintage being qualified as "excellent" and considered one of the best in the past 50 years.

2006 Very good acidity and alcohol levels. The vintage is officially "excellent".

2005 The hardest drought of the past 50 yearst, but thanks to cold summer nights quality was excellent for reds and whites.

2004 A memorable year for red wines.

2003 Rains in August then cool nights and sunny days in September resulted in a great vintage.

2002 Despite summer rains, a good September delivered good quality.

2001 Frosts reduced the yield but warm summer produced very good wines.

2000 Perfect ripening of the grapes gave well-balanced wines. Very good.

Aalto, Bodegas y Viñedos Rib del D r ★★→★★★ 00 01 02 03 04' Glamorous estate typical of high-level new investment in RIBERA DEL DUERO. Partner Mariano Garcia was winemaker at VEGA SICILIA. Two powerful reds with dense, plummy fruit, big tannins, liquorice and oak. Top wine is PS.

Abadía Retuerta Castilla y León r ★★★ 04 05 06 One of Spain's top non-DO wineries. Next door to RIBERA DEL DUERO: making a range of consistently reliable, savoury reds from Tempranillo, Cab Sauv, Merlot and Syrah. Round, fruity Rivola; spicier, more austere Selección Especial; pure Tempranillo Pago Negralada; and elegant, minerally Syrah Pago la Garduña.

Albariño High-quality aromatic white grape of GALICIA. See PALACIO DE FEFIÑANES, PAZO DE SEÑORANS, RÍAS BAIXAS. Raimat's new Albariño, Viña 24 from COSTERS DEL SEGRE, proves its potential in different terroir.

Albet i Noya Pen r p w sp ★★→★★★ 01 03 04 05 06 07 Spain's most famous organic producer. Wide portfolio with gd CAVA.

Alicante r w sw ★→★★★★ 04 05 06 07 08 Alicante is looking up, building a reputation for Monastrell reds plus sweet wines. Quality is still variable; reds better than whites (Monastrell, Syrah, Cab, GARNACHA and Merlot; also Petit Verdot and Pinot N). Some outstanding sweet Moscatels; historic FONDILLON. Best producers: GUTIÉRREZ DE LA VEGA, Enrique Mendoza, Bernabé Navarro, El Sequé, Sierra Salinas.

Alión Rib del D r ★★★ 01 02 03 04 05 VEGA SICILIA'S second BODEGA makes modern, structured, damson/blackberry 100% Tinto Fino (Tempranillo) with sumptuous French oak. Alión needs a min of 5 yrs' ageing.

Allende, Finca R Alt r w ★★★→★★★★ 01 04' 05 Behind the doors of Miguel Ángel de Gregorio's BODEGA in Briones lies serious commitment to single-v'yd Tempranillo. *Tinto is floral, spicy*; Calvario from one v'yd is impressively bold and balanced; Aurus is sumptuous with creamy French oak. Fine, oak-influenced Rioja Blanco 07.

Artadi Bodegas y Viñedos R Ala r (p w) ★★★→★★★★ 04' 05 06 Outstanding modern RIOJA: complex, toasty, Viñas del Gaín; taut, powerful single-v'yd El Pisón; spicy, elegant Pagos Viejos. Owners of El Sequé in ALICANTE and Artazu in NAVARRA.

Baigorri, Bodegas R Ala r (p w) ★★★ 04 05 Spectacular winery producing pricey new-wave RIOJA with primary black fruits, bold tannins and upbeat oak. Best: buzzy CRIANZA, lush RESERVA, more expressive Baigorri de Garage.

Barón de Ley RB r p w ★→★★ 05 06 07 BODEGA winning recognition for its 7 Viñas, an impressive blend of Tempranillo, GRACIANO, GARNACHA, Mazuelo, Viura and "others".

Báscula, La Wine brand started by South African winemaker Bruce Jack and UK MW Ed Adams to identify interesting wines from all over Spain. Typical of the interest in Spain shown by winemakers abroad.

Berberana, Bodegas See BODEGAS UNIDAS.

Bierzo r w ★→★★★ 03 04 05 06 V. fashionable DO north of León showing potential for the indigenous black Mencía (aromatic with steely tannin), plus white

Godello. Top wineries: Bodegas Peique, Bodegas Pittacum, Dominio de Tares. Descendientes de J Palacios, biodynamic producer, led by nephew of ÁLVARO PALACIOS, impresses with French-oaked Mencías – Moncerbal, *Pétalos del Bierzo* and Villa de Corullón.

Binissalem r w ★★ 05 06 07 08 Tiny but best-known MALLORCA DO northeast of Palma. Two-thirds red production, mainly Mantonegro. Look out for Macía Batle, Biniagual.

Bodega Spanish term for (i) a wineshop; (ii) a concern occupied in the making, blending and/or shipping of wine; and (iii) a cellar.

Briones Small Riojan hilltop town near Haro, peppered with underground cellars. Home to FINCA ALLENDE and one of the most comprehensive wine museums in the world, El Museo de la Cultura de Vino.

Bullas ★→★★ 04 05 06 07 08 Small, high (400–800 m), dry Murcia DO trying hard in an excessively Mediterranean climate. Best: Chaveo from Bodega Monastrell.

Calatayud ★→★★★ 05 06 07 08 Improving mountainous Aragón DO specializing in brooding GARNACHA, often from old vines, sometimes blended with Syrah. Best: Bodegas Ateca (see JORGE ORDOÑEZ), Bodegas y Viñedos el Jalón.

Campo de Borja ★→★★★ 06 07 08 Aragón DO making excellent, great-value DYA modern, juicy GARNACHAS and Tempranillos, eg. *Bodegas Aragonesas*. For more complexity, try Tres Picos Garnacha (05) from Bodegas Borsao. Top wine Alto Moncayo's Aquilón.

Canary Islands (Islas Canarias) r w p ★→★★ Has an astonishing nine DOS. Quality is mixed; occasionally stunning dessert Malvasías and Moscatels. Many native varieties (white Listán and Marmajuelo, black Negramoll and Vijariego). Be adventurous.

Cariñena ★→★★ 03 04 05 06 07 Solid, workmanlike Aragón DO. The two leading producers are Bodegas Añadas and Bodegas Victoria.

Castell del Remei Cos del S r p w ★★→★★★ 03 05 06 07 Picturesque restored 18th-century estate. Gd white blends; v.gd vanilla-tinged, sour-red-cherry-flavoured Gotim Bru and the marvellous, minerally 1780.

Castilla-La Mancha, Vino de la Tierra In 1999, 600,000 ha here were granted VDT status. Until recently a catch-all grouping of great inconsistency; now some smaller DOS are declaring themselves, just as in Castilla y León.

Castillo Perelada, Vinos y Caves del Emp r p w sp res ★→★★★ 04 05 06 07 08 Large range of still wines and CAVA, inc fresh DYA Sauv Bl and three opulent, old-style, top reds.

Castillo de Ygay R Alt r w ★★★★ (r) 64 70 89 91 94 96 97 98 99 01 Legendary, long-lived top wines from MARQUÉS DE MURRIETA, esp GRAN RESERVA Especial.

Catalunya 04 05 06 07 Vast new (2004) DO covering the whole Catalan area. Confusion arises, as this now includes wines from more than 200 well-known producers using grapes from outside their own strictly local DO. Top names include some of the biggest: ALBET I NOYA, FREIXENET, JEAN LÉON and TORRES.

Cava Spain's traditional-method fizz is made mainly in PENEDÈS – but not exclusively; most is produced in or around San Sadurní de Noya. Dominated by FREIXENET and CODORNÍU. Quality is often higher, with a price tag to match, from smaller producers such as Agustí Torelló, Castell Sant Antoni, CASTILLA DE PERELADA, GRAMONA, JUVÉ & CAMPS, MARQUÉS DE MONISTROL, Mestres, PARXET, Raimat, Recaredo, Signat and Sumarroca. Cava is best drunk young, though local taste often favours those with major bottle-age.

Cérvoles, Celler Cos del S r w ★★→★★★ 03 04 05 06 07 High mountainous estate just north of PRIORAT making concentrated reds from Cab Sauv/Tempranillo/GARNACHA and powerful, creamy, lemon-tinged, barrel-fermented Blanc.

Chacolí/Txakoli País Vasco w (r) ★★ DYA Split into three DOS: Àlava, Guetaria and Vizcaya. All produce fragrant DYA but often quirkily sharp, *pétillant* whites, locally poured into tumblers from a height. The historic Chueca family-owned Txomin Etxaniz rounds off the aggression of the primary Hondarrabi Zuri (white) with 15% of low-alcohol Hondarrabi Beltza. Other top name: Ameztoi.

Chivite, Bodegas Julián Nav r w dr sw res (p) ★★→★★★ 03 04 05 06 07 08 Biggest, most historic and best-known NAVARRA BODEGA, with 1,600 ha of vines. Popular range Gran Feudo, esp ROSADO and new Edición Rosado Sobre Lias (*sur lie*). High spots of pricier Colección 125 range are serious Burgundian Chard in modern style, elegant botrytis Moscatel and top-of-range Pago de Arínzano, still finding its feet. Promising Verdejo Baluarate, from RUEDA, first vintage 2008. Also owns Viña Salceda in Rioja (v.gd Conde de la Salceda).

Cigales r p (w) ★→★★★ Small, high-altitude DO north of Valladolid. Produces both commercial, DYA reds, and more complex old-vine Tempranillo. Two outstanding producers each make a single wine: the lush, voluptuous César Príncipe; and more restrained, old-school Traslanzas (02 03).

Clos Mogador Pri r ★★★→★★★★ 01 02 03 04 05 06 07 René Barbier continues to rank as one of PRIORAT'S pioneers, a godfather to the younger generations

---

Mencía – a work in progress

Spain's most fashionable red grape is Mencía, revived by the Young Turks working in BIERZO. It can be powerfully crisp and crunchy, with a good wedge of tannin to boot. But frankly, it's not always fun to drink. Will 2011 be the year they learn to tame their grapes?

---

of winemakers. Simpler second wine Manyetes is gd but Clos Mogador is breathtaking and usually gd for a decade. Also exceptionally interesting is the spicy, fragrant, honeyed and complex GARNACHA *blanca*/Viognier/Marsanne/Macabeo/Pinot N Clos Nelin white.

Codorníu Pen w sp ★★→★★★ One of the two largest CAVA firms, owned by the Raventós family. Has always been at odds with arch-rival FREIXENET, favouring non-indigenous varieties, esp Chard. Best offerings: gd vintage, Reina Maria Cristina, the v. dry Non Plus Ultra, and pale, smoky Pinot N. Also owns the gradually improving Raimat in COSTERS DEL SEGRE, as well as the once-great but now slumbering Bilbainas in RIOJA.

Compañía Vinícola del Norte de España (CVNE) R Alt r w dr (p) ★→★★★ Famous RIOJA BODEGA; former benchmark, now again improving. Top quality are elegant Imperial and supple Viña Real. See also CONTINO.

Conca de Barberà w (r p) 04 05 06 07 08 Small Catalan DO once purely a feeder of quality fruit to large enterprises, now has some excellent wineries, inc the biodynamic Escoda-Sanahuja. Top TORRES wines Grans Muralles and Milmanda both produced in this DO.

Condado de Haza Rib del D r ★★→★★★ 03 04 05 Pure, oak-aged Tinto Fino. Second wine of Alejandro Fernández's PESQUERA.

Consejo Regulador Organization for the control, promotion and defence of a DO.

Contino, Viñedos del R Ala r res ★★★★ 04 05 First single-v'yd of RIOJA (1973) and a subsidiary of CVNE, makes exceptional long-lasting reds with scrupulous attention. Gd balsamic GRACIANO (a fine example of the variety), RESERVA and impressive Viña del Olivo.

Costers del Segre r w p sp ★★→★★★ 03 04 05 06 07 08 Smallish area around city of Lleida (Lérida) of which little is heard, though it has some excellent producers. Initially known purely for the modern, fruity wines and vivacious CAVA of CODORNÍU-owned Raimat. Top producers: CASTELL DEL REMEI, CÉRVOLES, TOMÁS CUSINÉ and Vinya l'Hereu de Seró.

Criado y embotellado por... Spanish for "Grown and bottled by...".

Crianza Literally "nursing"; the ageing of wine. New or unaged wine is *sin crianza* or JOVEN. Reds labelled *crianza* must be at least 2 yrs old (with 1 yr in oak, in some areas 6 mths) and must not be released before the 3rd yr. See RESERVA.

Cusiné, Tomás Cos del S r ★★★ 04 05 06 The former motor of CASTELL DEL REMEI and CELLER CÉRVOLES on his own since 2003. Two wines: modern, upbeat Vilosell (Tempranillo/Cab/Merlot/Grenache/Syrah) and oakier, intense Geol.

Denominación de Origen (DO) Official wine region.

Denominación de Origen Calificada (DOCa) Classification for wines of the highest quality; so far only RIOJA (since 1991) and PRIORAT (DOQ – the Catalan equivalent – since 2002) benefit.

Dominio de Valdepusa r w ★★★ 04 05 06 Enterprising UC Davis graduate Carlos Falcó was the first Spaniard to cultivate Syrah and Petit Verdot, and introduce drip irrigation and a scientific approach to v'yd management on his estate near Toledo in VINOS DE MADRID DO. Still innovating, still entrepreneurial. His varietals, which also include Cab, are savoury, worthwhile and v. concentrated – try the v. approachable Summa blend. Top wine Emeritus is excellent, if pricey.

Empordà-Ampurdán r p w ★→★★ 04 05 06 07 08 Small, fashionable DO near French border, not far from the celebrated El Bulli restaurant. Best wineries are CASTILLO PERELADA, Celler Marti Fabra and Pere Guardiola; the curious will be tempted by the playful and experimental Espelt, growing any number of varieties, though with variable results. Stick to the reds.

Enate Som r p w res ★★★ 04 05 06 07 08 Leading producer in SOMONTANO with gd DYA Gewurz and barrel-fermented Chard, gd if somewhat overpowering Syrah, but round, satisfyingly balanced, mature Cab/Merlot Especial Reserva.

Espumoso Sparkling (but see CAVA).

Finca Farm or estate (See under name – eg. ALLENDE, FINCA.)

Fondillón Traditional Alicante wine, made from ripe Monastrell grapes matured in oak for long periods. Made in small quantities by eg. GUTIÉRREZ DE LA VEGA.

Freixenet, Cavas Pen w sp ★★→★★★ Huge CAVA firm owned by the Ferrer family. Arch-rival of similarly enormous CODORNÍU. Best known for frosted black-bottled Cordón Negro and standard Carta Nevada. Strongly supported by advertising. Dull still wines – Ash Tree Estate. Also controls Castellblanch, Conde de Caralt and Segura Viudas.

Galicia Rainy northwestern corner of Spain producing some of Spain's best whites (see RÍAS BAIXAS, MONTERREI, RIBEIRO and VALDEORRAS).

Garnacha Traditional workhorse vine now being revived. Seekers of old-vine versions include Raúl Pérez. Rising regions inc VINOS DE MADRID, CALATAYUD.

Generoso Apéritif or dessert wine rich in alcohol.

Graciano One of the traditional grapes in RIOJA. Now popular as single-varietal, though hard to grow.

Gramona Pen r w dr sw sp res ★★→★★★ Substantial family firm making impressive range of wines based on serious research. Gd DYA Gewurz, spicy Xarel-lo-dominated Celler Batlle, sweet wines, inc Icewines and impressive Chard/Sauv Bl Gra a Gra Blanco Dulce. Top CAVAS Imperial Gran Reserva, III Lustros.

Gran Reserva (GR) See RESERVA.

Gutiérrez de la Vega, Bodegas Alicante r w res ★→★★★ 02 05 06 Small estate founded by opera-loving former general in 1978. Expanding range all branded Casta Diva, with excellent, fragrant sweet whites made from Moscatel. Best are Cosecha Miel and Monte Diva. Historic Monastrell sweet red, FONDILLÓN.

Hacienda Monasterio, Bodegas Rib del D r res ★★→★★★ 06 Peter Sisseck's involvement since 1990 has resulted in excellent Tinto Fino/Cab/Merlot blends. Currently a delicious, expressively fruity *tinto*, approachable CRIANZA and elegantly round, complex RESERVA.

Haro Spiritual and historic centre of the RIOJA Alta. Though growing, still infinitely more charming and intimate than commercial capital Logroño; home to lópez de heredia, MUGA, BODEGAS LA RIOJA ALTA, among others.

Huerta de Albalá VDT Cadiz r ★★→★★★ 06 Ambitious new (2006) estate in foothills of Sierra de Grazalema, blending Syrah, Merlot, Cab Sauv and local Tintilla de Rota. V. promising, small-production Taberner No. 1 with dense fruit and expressive French oak; gd Taberner. Barba Azul is introductory label.

Inurrieta, Bodega Nav r p w res ★★→★★★ 04 05 06 07 High-tech estate near Falces. Gd French-oaked Norte Cab/Merlot and lively DYA Mediodía Rosado. Top wine: Altos de Inurrieta. Promising production of GRACIANO and experiments with other varieties not yet permitted by DO.

Jaro, Bodegas y Viñedos del Rib del D r res ★→★★★ 04 05 06 07 Founded in 2000 by a member of the Osborne (sherry) family. Best: intense, minerally Chafandín, seriously expensive, opulent, black-fruit-scented Sed de Caná.

Joven (vino) Young, unoaked wine. Also see CRIANZA.

Jumilla r (p w) ★→★★★ 04 05 06 Arid, apparently unpromising DO in mountains N of Murcia, now discovered by ambitious modern winemakers. Best-known for dark, fragrant Monastrell. Also gd Tempranillo, Merlot, Cab, Syrah, Petit Verdot. Wines do not generally age. Gd producers: Agapito Rico, Casa Castillo, Casa de la Ermita, influential Juan Gil, Luzón, Valle del Carche, El Nido, Silvano Garcia.

Juvé & Camps Pen w sp ★★★ 04 05 Family firm making top-quality CAVA from free-run juice. Reserva de la Familia is the stalwart, with top-end GRAN RESERVA and Milesimé Chard Gran Reserva.

León, Jean Pen r w res ★★★ 99 03 04 05 06 07 Small firm; TORRES-owned since 1995. Gd, oaky Chards, expressive Merlot and high-priced super-*cuvée* Zemis.

López de Heredia R Alt r w dr sw res (p) ★★→★★★★ 81 85 87 88 89 95 96 98 99 01 02 Picturesque, old-established family BODEGA in HARO that still ferments everything in wood and oak-ages in old casks. Medium-intense Bosconia and lighter, ripe *Tondonia*. Fascinating *rosado* is always released with 10 yrs of age. Don't miss the whites, also with a decade of ageing.

Madrid, Vinos de r p w ★→★★ Altitude, temperature extremes, old GARNACHA vines – all contribute to growing quality of Vinos de Madrid DO, formerly bulk wine producer. Go-ahead names include Bernabeleva, working with Raúl Pérez making interesting Burgundian and top GARNACHA Viña Bonita. Also Marañones, Gosálbez-Ortí run by a former Iberia pilot, Jeromín, Divo, Viñedoes de San Martín (part of ENATE group) and El Regajal.

Málaga Once-famous DO now all but vanished in the face of rocketing real-estate values. One large, super-commercial firm remains – with wide range of styles: Málaga Virgen. Winemaking has been revived here by former Young Turk TELMO RODRÍGUEZ with a clear, subtle, sweet white *Molino Real Moscatel*, and more recently by JORGE ORDOÑEZ's portfolio of sweet Muscats.

Mallorca Contrary to appearances, with the celebrities and their floating gin palaces, Mallorca is v. serious about winemaking. Plenty of interest in Anima Negra, tiny Sa Vinya de Can Servera, Hereus de Ribas, *Son Bordils*. Also 4 Kilos, Biniagual. Reds are a blend of traditional varieties (Mantonegro, Callet, Fogoneu) plus Cab, Syrah and Merlot. Whites (esp Chard) are improving fast. See also BINISSALEM, PLÁ I LLEVANT.

La Mancha r p w ★→★★ The largest wine-growing region in Spain. The area has long been striving to improve its reds, which are mainly Cencibel-based (Tempranillo). Best producer is undoubtedly Finca Antigua, succeeding with international varieties: Syrah, Merlot, Cab Sauv and Petit Verdot.

Marqués de Cáceres, Bodegas R Alt r p w res ★★★ 01 04 05 06 07 08 Gd, reliable, commercial RIOJAS made by modern French methods.

Marqués de Griñón RIOJA brand owned by BERBERANA. No longer any connection with the Marqués – see DOMINIO DE VALDEPUESA.

Marqués de Monistrol, Bodegas Pen r p dr sw sp res ★→★★ Old BODEGA now owned by BODEGAS UNIDAS. Gd, reliable CAVA; but once-lively, modern PENEDÈS reds no longer so lively.

Marqués de Murrieta R Alt r p w res ★★★→★★★★ 98 02 03 04 05 06 Historic BODEGA at Ygay near Logroño, growing all its own grapes and making intense RESERVA reds. Most famous for its magnificent CASTILLO DE YGAY. Best value is the dense, flavoursome RESERVA with excellent acid balance; most striking is the intense, modern red Dalmau. Capellania is the complex, textured white.

Marqués de Riscal R Ala & Rueda r w dr (p) ★★★ 01 02 03 04 05 06 07 Don't be put off by the exhibitionist hotel by Frank Gehry of Guggenheim Bilbao fame. Quality continues to improve. Gd light reds and powerful black Barón de Chirel Reserva made with some Cab Sauv. A pioneer in RUEDA (since 1972) making fragrant DYA Sauv Bl and vibrant, lively Verdejo/Viura blend.

Mas Gil Pri r ★★★→★★★★ 04 05 06 Small estate in Calonge, Gerona, making fresh, spicy, herbal Viognier/Roussanne/Marsanne Clos d'Agón Blanc and delicious, modern, deeply flavoured Cab/Syrah/Merlot/Cab Fr Clos d'Agón Negre as well as lesser-seen Clos Valmaña duo.

Mas Martinet Pri r ★★★→★★★★ 01 02 03 04 05 Boutique PRIORAT pioneer, producer of excellent Clos Martinet. Second wine: Martinet Bru.

Mauro, Bodegas r 01 03 04 05 06 New-wave BODEGA in Tudela del Duero making serious, reliable non-DO/VDT reds. Mauro now with a touch of Syrah; best is pricey, Old-World-meets-New, complex Vendimia Seleccionada though top *cuvée* is actually the powerful Terreus (03). Sister winery: Maurodos in TORO.

Monterrei w ★→★★★ DYA Small but growing DO in Ourense, south-central GALICIA, making interesting, full-flavoured aromatic whites from Treixadura, Godello and Doña Blanca, showing there is more to Galicia than ALBARIÑO. Best is Gargalo.

Montilla-Moriles w sw ★→★★★ Medium-sized DO in south Córdoba once best known for fino styles but now concentrating on dark, unctuous, often bittersweet dessert wines made from PX (Pedro Ximénez). Until recently TORO ALBALÁ was virtually the only player, but Alvear and Pérez Barquero are now also serious.

Montsant r ★→★★★ 04 05 06 PRIORAT's closest neighbour is building its own reputation, with lower prices. Fine GARNACHA *blanca*, esp from Acústic. Cariñena and Garnacha deliver dense, balsamic, minerally reds: Celler de Capçanes, Celler el Masroig, Celler Can Blau, Etim, Joan d'Anguera and Mas Perinet all offer impressive, individual wines.

Muga, Bodegas R Alt r res (w sp) ★★★→★★★★ 98 00 01 03 04 05 Family firm in HARO, known for some of RIOJA's most spectacular and balanced reds. Gd barrel-fermented DYA Viura reminiscent of burgundy; gd dry, salmon-coloured *rosado*; reds finely crafted and highly aromatic. Best are wonderfully fragrant GRAN RESERVA Prado Enea; warm, full and long-lasting *Torre Muga*; expressive and complex Aro; and dense, rich, structured, full-flavoured Selección Especial.

Navarra r p (w) ★★→★★★ 01 02 03 04 05 06 07 08 Extensive DO east of RIOJA. Once known for ROSADO, most of its BODEGAS now produce v.gd mid-priced Tempranillo/Cab Sauv blends that are often livelier than those of its more illustrious neighbour Rioja – despite often higher yields. Up-and-coming names include Garcia Burgos, Pago de Larrainzar, Tandem. Navarra is at last trying to improve its *rosados* and regain lost ground. Best producers: Alzaña, Artazu, JULIÁN CHIVITE, INURRIETA, Nekeas, OCHOA, Otazu, Pago de Cirsus, Sarría.

Ochoa Nav r w p sw ★→★★ Much-improved family business with close ties to growth of NAVARRA DO. Gd Tempranillo, excellent *rosado* and sweet Moscatel.

Ordoñez, Jorge US-based Spaniard, importing top Spanish wines. Investor in Spanish v'yds, specializing in reinvigorating forgotten regions. See CALATAYUD.

Otazu, Bodegas Nav r New DO PAGO estate, with a blend of Tempranillo, Merlot and Cab Sauv.

Pago A v'yd or area of limited size. Term now has legal status. See VINOS DE PAGO.

Pago de Carraovejas Rib del D r res ★★★ 01 03 04 05 06 07 Founded in 1988, quality still excellent and still unable to satisfy demand. Top wine v.gd Cuesta de las Liebres.

Pago, Vinos de Category that confers DO status to six individual estates – four in CASTILLA-LA MANCHA: Dehesa del Carrizal, DOMINIO DE VALDEPUSA, Manuel Manzeneque's Finca Elez and the Sánchez Militerno family's Pago Guijoso; two in NAVARRA: Prado Irache and Pago de Arinzano. Anomalous because many distinguished estates, obvious Vinos de Pago, do not have the legal status, inc L'Ermita, PINGUS, Calvario (FINCA ALLENDE), Viña del Olivo and TORRES properties.

Palacio de Fefiñanes Rías Baixas w dr ★★★★ DYA Oldest BODEGA of RÍAS BAIXAS – first bottled wine in 1927. Standard *cuvée* remains one of the finest, most delicate pure ALBARIÑOS. Two superior styles: creamy but light-of-touch barrel-fermented version 1583 (the yr the winery was founded); and a super-fragrant, pricey, lees-aged, mandarin-orange-scented III.

Palacios, Álvaro Pri r ★★→★★★★ 00 01' 03 04 05 06 Continues to charm and surprise. Exceptional, individual wines from distinctive *llicorella* (slate) soils, from GARNACHA mainly. Les Terrasses can be drunk soonest; Finca Dofí has a dark undertone of Cab Sauv, Syrah, Merlot, Cariñena. L'Ermita is dense; needs time to develop.

Palacios, Rafael Vald w ★★★ 05 06 07 08 Small estate producing exceptional wine from old Godello vines in the Bibei Valley. Rafael – ÁLVARO PALACIOS' younger brother – is devoted to white wines. Two distinct styles, both DYA: As Sortes is intense, toasty, with striking citric and white-peach elements as well as high acidity, a v. fine expression of Godello; Louro do Bolo.

Palacios Remondo, Bodegas Rías Baixas r w ★★→★★★ 04 05 06 07 08 Proving that his skills are not just in PRIORAT, ÁLVARO PALACIOS has revved up his family winery (founded 1945). Interesting DYA oaked white Plácet (07) with citric, peach and fennel characters; and in red, super-fruity, unoaked La Vendimia; organic, smoky, red-fruit flavoured La Montesa; and big, mulberry-flavoured, GARNACHA-dominated Propiedad.

Parxet Alella p w sp ★★→★★★ DYA Small CAVA producer valiantly competing with real-estate agents from Barcelona. Zesty styles include Cuvée 21, excellent Brut Nature, fragrant Titiana Pinot N and expensive dessert version Cuvée Dessert. Best known for refreshing, off-dry Pansa Blanca and still white Marqués de Alella. Concentrated Tionio is from outpost in RIBERA DEL DUERO.

Pazo de Señorans Rías Baixas w dr ★★★ DYA Exceptionally fragrant wines from a BODEGA considered a benchmark of the DO.

Penedès r w sp ★→★★★ 98 99 00 01 02 03 04 05 06 07 08 Demarcated region west of Barcelona best known for CAVA, and TORRES has had trouble establishing an identity. Styles range from light, citric whites to highly oaked reds. Other gd producers include: ALBET I NOYA, Can Ràfols dels Caus, GRAMONA, JEAN LEÓN.

Pesquera Rib del D r ★★★ 94 95 04 05 06 Alejandro Fernández was the creative force behind modern RIBERA DEL DUERO and is still a benchmark. Satisfying CRIANZA and excellent, mature, well-seasoned Janus for those who can afford the price tag. See also CONDADO DE HAZA.

Pingus, Dominio de Rib del D r ★★★★ 01 03 04 05 Peter Sisseck's star continues to shine brightly in RIBERA DEL DUERO. Production at Pingus may be tiny but there's plenty of demand for biodynamic Pingus, with its intense, opulent black fruit, fresh herbal overtones and subtle interlaced oak and tannins; second label *Flor de Pingus* is more floral fruit. Ψ: psi – whose name is taken from the Greek letter – is the latest project.

Plá i Llevant r w dr ★→★★★ 04 05 06 07 11 wineries comprise this tiny DO in MALLORCA. Aromatic whites and intense, spicy reds. Best: Toni Gelabert, Jaime Mesquida, Miguel Oliver and Vins Can Majoral.

Priorat/Priorato r br w ★★→★★★★ 01 04 05 06 07 Isolated enclave renowned for *llicorella* (slate) soils and terraced v'yds. Moribund production revived by René Barbier and others. The pioneers – CLOS MOGADOR, MAS MARTINET, ÁLVARO PALACIOS – remain consistently gd, showing characteristic minerally purity. Recent temptation to create overextracted, overconcentrated wines at last abandoned in favour of better balance. Investors continue to flock in to buy up tiny v'yds. Other top names include Val-Llach, Cims de Porrera, Clos Erasmus, Clos de l'Obac, Clos Nelin, Clos i Terrasses. New names include Ferrer-Bobet, Torres and Dits del Terra, the project of South African Eben Sadie.

Remírez de Ganuza, Bodegas Fernando R Ala r w dr res ★★→★★★ 02 03 04 05 Boutique winery making somewhat austere Tempranillo-based wines.

Remelluri, La Granja R Ala r w dr res ★★★ 99 03 Small mountainous estate making pedigree RIOJA reds from its own 105 ha. Best is the *delicate, graceful Reserva*; other wines increasingly old-fashioned, though DYA white made from six different varieties remains as intriguing as it was originally.

Reserva Gd-quality wine matured for long periods. Red *reservas* must spend at least 1 yr in cask and 2 yrs in bottle; *gran reservas*, 2 yrs in cask and 3 yrs in bottle. Thereafter, many continue to mature for yrs. Many producers now eschew RESERVA/CRIANZA regulations, preferring clear vintage declaration.

Rías Baixas w ★★→★★★★ DYA GALICIAN DO increasing in global reputation and production. Founded on the ALBARIÑO variety, in five subzones: Val do Salnés, O Rosal, Condado do Tea, Soutomaior and Ribera do Ulla. Quality and style inconsistent but the best are outstanding: Adegas Galegas, As Laxas, Castro Baroña, Fillaboa, Coto de Xiabre, Gerardo Méndez, new kid on the block Viña Nora, PALACIO DE FEFIÑANES, Pazo de Barrantes, Quinta do Lobelle, Santiago Ruíz, Terras Gauda, La Val and Valdamor.

Ribeiro r w ★→★★★ DYA GALICIAN DO in western Ourense. Whites are low in alcohol and acidity, made from Treixadura, Torrontés, Godello, Loureiro, Lado. Top producers VIÑA MEÍN, Lagar do Merens. Also specialty sweet wine style, Tostado.

Ribera del Duero Rib del D ★★→★★★★ 01 02 03 04 05 06 07 08 Fashionable, still-expanding DO east of Valladolid with almost 250 wineries. Tinto Fino (Tempranillo) holds sway. Some Cab and Merlot. A handful of outstanding wineries but fame of VEGA SICILIA still dominates, and there is much confusion of styles and quality is inconsistent. The big worry is the plan for new motorway right across the middle. Best producers: AALTO, ALIÓN, Astrales, CONDADO DE HAZA, HACIENDA MONASTERIO, Pago de los Capellanes, PAGO DE CARRAOVEJAS, Pérez Pascuas Hermanos, PESQUERA, PINGUS, VALBUENA. See also VDT ABADÍA RETUERTA and MAURO. Others to look for: Balbás, Bohórquez, Dehesa de los Canónigos, O Fournier, Hermanos Sastre, Tinio (see PARXET) and Vallebueno.

Rioja r p w sp ★→★★★★ 64 70 75 78 81 82 85 89 91 92 94 95 96 98 99 00 01 02 03 04 05 06 07 08' A few wineries, notably LA RIOJA ALTA and LÓPEZ DE HEREDIA, continue to make exceptional, old-fashioned styles; there are the pedigree traditionalists such as CONTINO, MARQUÉS DE MURRIETA, MUGA, Marqués de Vargas, PALACIOS REMONDO, and REMELLURI and San Vicente; others, such as FINCA ALLENDE, ARTADI, BAIGORRI, RODA, Señorío de San Vicente and Tobia are producing more energetic styles. There are also many brands: the vigorous but basic Viña Pomal of formerly revered Bilbaínas, top-seller Campo Viejo, the now-reviving CVNE, the smooth reds of Faustino, the ever-reliable MARQUÉS DE CÁCERES and VALDEMAR. There are lots of very reliable, consistent producers who simply make gd wine, such as the v. drinkable Luis Cañas. Rioja whites are looking up at last. Producers now permitted to replace dull Viura with Chard, Sauv Bl and Verdejo.

Rioja Alta, Bodegas La R Alt r w dr res (p sw) ★★★ 81 95 97 00 01' 02 Discover traditional RIOJA. Delicate, mature, in three RESERVA styles. Alberdi is light and cedary with overtones of tobacco and redcurrants; Ardanza riper, a touch spicier but still v. elegant; the excellent, tangy, vanilla-edged Gran Reserva 904 and the fine, multilayered Gran Reserva 890, aged 6 yrs in oak. Also owns RÍAS BAIXAS Lagar de Cervera.

Roda, Bodegas R Alt r ★★★★ 00 01' 03 04' 05' 06 07 Ambitious young BODEGA with impressive cellar making serious modern RESERVA reds from low-yield Tempranillo, backed by strong R&D. Three wines: Roda, Roda I and Cirsión.

Rueda br w ★★→★★★ DYA Small but ever-growing DO south of Valladolid with Spain's most modern, crisp DYA whites, made from indigenous Verdejo, Sauv Bl, Viura and blends thereof. Barrel-fermented versions remain fashionable though less appealing. Best: Alvarez y Diez, *Belondrade*, MARQUÉS DE RISCAL, Naia, Ossian, José Pariente, Palacio de Bornos, Javier Sanz, SITIOS DE BODEGA, Veracruz and Vinos Sanz.

Sandoval, Finca Manchuela ★★★ 02 03 05 06 Victor de la Serna is on form: his Finca Sandoval (Syrah/Monastrell/Bobal) a wine of impressive balance, dark fruits, soft tannins, herbal notes and gd acid; second wine Salia (Syrah/GARNACHA/Bobal) altogether simpler and half the price.

Sitios de Bodega ★★→★★★ Fifth-generation winemaker Ricardo Sanz and siblings left father Antonio Sanz's Palacio de Bornos to set up their own winery in 2005. Excellent DYA RUEDA whites (Con Class and Palacio de Ménade). Associated BODEGAS Terna, from its base in La Seca, produces interesting, high-quality reds from other regions, inc Spain's first sweet Tempranillo: La Dolce Tita VDT.

Somontano ★★→★★★ 04 05 06 07 08 Cool-climate DO in Pyrenean foothills east of Zaragoza that has failed so far to fulfil expectations. Whites should be more expressive and reds are often overextracted, overoaked, without sufficient maturity of fruit or any binding regional character. Much of the problem is reliance on international varietals, which reduces regionality. Opt for Merlot, Gewurz, or Chard. Best producers: ENATE, VIÑAS DEL VERO, recently acquired by González-Byass (see Port, Sherry & Madeira); interesting newcomers inc the space-age BODEGAS Irius and Laus.

Tares, Dominio de El B r w ★★★ 04 05 06 Up-and-coming producer whose dark, spicy, purple-scented *Bembibre and Cepas Viejas* proves what can be done with Mencía. Sister winery VDT Dominio dos Tares makes a range of wines from the interesting black Prieto Picudo variety: the simple Estay, more muscular Leione and big, spicy Cumal.

Telmo Rodríguez, Compañía de Vinos r w ★★→★★★ Enthusiastic seeker of old vines, winemaker Telmo Rodríguez now sources and makes a wide range of excellent DO wines from all over Spain, inc MÁLAGA (Molina Real Moscatels), RIOJA (Lanzaga and Matallana), RUEDA (Basa), TORO (Dehesa Gago, Gago and Pago la Jara) and *Valdeorras* (DYA Gaba do Xil Godello).

Toro r ★→★★★ 03 04 05 06 07 08 Unstoppably fashionable DO in Zamora province, west of Valladolid. Forty wineries now do their best with the local Tinta de Toro (acclimatized Tempranillo). Some continue to be rustic and overalcoholic but others are boldly expressive. Try Maurodos – with fresh, black-fruit scented Prima and glorious old-vine San Román, as well as VEGA

SICILIA-owned Pintia. Also recommended: Domaine Magrez Espagne, Pago la Jara from TELMO RODRÍGUEZ, Quinta de la Quietud and Sobreño.

Toro Albalá Mont-M ★★→★★★ Antonio Sánchez is known for his eccentric wine museum and his remarkable old PXs (Pedro Ximénez). Labelled Don PX and made from sun-dried grapes, barrique-aged for a minimum of 25 yrs. Black, replete with flavours of molasses, treacle, figs, they age indefinitely. Current vintage is 1979, yet the 1910 was only recently released. Look out for unaged amber-coloured DYA Dulce de Pasas, tasting of liquid raisins and apricots.

Torres, Miguel Pen r p w dr s/sw res ★★→★★★★ 01 02 03 04 05 06 07 08 Spain's best-known family wine firm, with properties in Chile and California, continues to reinvent and renew itself. It makes some of the best from commercial to single-vy'd: ever-reliable DYA CATALUNYA Viña Sol and grapey Viña Esmeralda and PENEDÈS Sauv Bl/Parellada *Fransola*. Best reds include: classic Catalunya Gran Sangre de Toro; fine Penedès Cabernet Mas la Plana; balanced, old-style Reserva Real (06). Its CONCA DE BARBERÀ duo (*Milmanda* – one of Spain's finest Chards – and Grans Muralles multiblend) is stunning, and JEAN LEÓN has v.gd offerings, too. The range continues to expand with a workmanlike offering from RIBERA DEL DUERO (Celeste) and RIOJA (Ibéricos), gd PRIORAT (Salmos). The indefatigable Miguel Torres (father) speaks of retirement, and both son and daughter work in the business. He will be a hard act to follow.

Unidas, Bodegas Umbrella organization controlling MARQUÉS DE MONISTROL, and the BERBERANA brand, as well as workmanlike RIOJA Marqués de la Concordia and Durius from RIBERA DEL DUERO. Controls MARQUÉS DE GRIÑÓN Rioja brand.

Utiel-Requena U-R r p (w) ★→★★ Satellite region of VALENCIA starting to forge its own identity by virtue of excellent Bobal variety but hampered by its size (more than 40,000 ha), which has made it primarily a feeder for the industrial requirements of nearby VALENCIA. Promising wines from Vicente Gandía, Alvares Nölting.

Valbuena Rib del D r ★★★★ 99 00 01 02 03 04 Made with the same grapes (Tinto Fino, Cab, Merlot, Malbec and a touch of Albillo) as VEGA SICILIA but sold when just 5 yrs old. Best at about 10 yrs; some prefer it to its elder brother. For a more modern take, see ALIÓN.

Valdemar, Bodegas R Ala r p w res ★→★★★ 01 02 03 06 07 08 The Martínez-Bujanda family, from its base in Oyón, has been making wines since 1890 and continues to offer a wide choice of *reliable Rioja* styles on all levels.

Valdeorras w r ★→★★★ DYA GALICIAN DO in northwest Ourense fighting off its co-op-inspired image by virtue of its DYA Godello: a highly aromatic and nationally fashionable variety, also grown in nearby BIERZO. Best producers: Adegas A Coroa, RAFAEL PALACIOS, A Tapada and TELMO RODRÍGUEZ.

Valdepeñas La M r (w) ★→★★ 01 02 04 05 06 07 08 Big DO near Andalucían border. V.gd-value lookalike RIOJA reds, made primarily from Cencibel grape. One producer shines: Félix Solís; *Viña Albali* brand offers real value.

Valencia r w ★ 00 01 03 04 05 06 07 08 Big exporter of table wine. Primary source of sweet budget Spanish Moscatel. Most reliable producer: Murviedro.

Spanish fizz sees red

Spain's answer to sparkling Shiraz is called La Pamelita. It's from Lobban Wines, and – remember this, now – is not CAVA. It can only be mere Vino Espumoso de Calidad because it's the wrong colour: from this yr it will be made from Shiraz grown in CALATAYUD. The winemaker is Scottish-born Pamela Lobban whose time in the Australian wine trade inspired the choice.

Vega Sicilia Rib del D r res ★★★★ 60 62 68 70 81 87 89 90 91 94 95 96 98 99 Spain's most prestigious historic BODEGA. Winemaking distinguished by meticulous hard work. Wines are deep in colour, with an aromatic cedarwood nose, intense and complex in flavour, finishing long. Único is aged for 6 yrs in oak; RESERVA Especial spends up to 10 yrs in barrel, then declared as NV. See also VALBUENA, ALIÓN, Pintia in TORO and Oremus Tokáji (Hungary).

Vendimia Vintage.

Viña Literally, a v'yd.

Viña Meín Ribeiro ★★★ Small estate, in a gradually emerging DO, making two DYA exceptional whites of same name: one in steel and one barrel-fermented; both from some seven local varieties.

Viñas del Vero Som r p w res ★★→★★★★ 03 04 05 06 07 08 Improving winery, acquired by González-Byass (see Sherry). Top wines are Blecua and Secastilla.

Vino de la Tierra (VDT) Table wine of superior quality made in a demarcated region without DO. Covering immense geographical possibilities, this category includes many prestigious producers who are non-DO by choice in order to be freer of often inflexible regulation and produce the varieties they want.

Vivanco, Dinastia ★ R Alt Major family-run commercial BODEGA in BRIONES. Wine museum is worth the detour.

PORTUGAL

Recent vintages

2009 A good year overall. Bairrada and Lisboa forecast excellent quality. Heat spikes in the Douro, Tejo and Alentejo, made for full-bodied wines with high alcohol .

2008 Almost uniformly excellent; Bairrada and Alentejo particularly promising. Low yields, a long ripening period and ideal harvest conditions produced great fruit intensity, balance and aroma.

2007 Aromatic whites and well-balanced reds with round tannins.

2006 Forward reds with soft, ripe fruit and whites with less acidity than usual.

2005 Powerful reds; the Douro's finely balanced reds shine.

2004 A cool summer but glorious September and October. Well-balanced reds.

2003 Hot summer produced soft, ripe, early maturing wines, especially in the south. Best Bairrada for a decade.

Adega A cellar or winery.

Alenquer Lis r w ★★→★★★ 03' 04 05 06 07 08 09' Sheltered DOC making gd reds just north of Lisbon. Estate wines from PANCAS and MONTE D'OIRO lead the field.

Alentejo r (w) ★→★★★★★ 01 02 03 04' 05 06 07 08' 09 Huge, southerly DOC divided into subregions with own DOCS: Borba, Redondo, Reguengos, PORTALEGRE, Evora, Granja-Amareleja, Vidigueira and Moura. VINHO REGIONAL Alentejano preferred by many top estates. A reliably dry climate makes rich, ripe reds: key international varieties include Syrah, Alicante Bouschet and recently Petit Verdot. Gd whites from Antão Vaz, blended with ARINTO, Verdelho and Roupeiro. Established players CARMO, CARTUXA, CORTES DE CIMA, ESPORÃO, HERDADE DE MOUCHÃO, MOURO, JOÃO PORTUGAL RAMOS and ZAMBUJEIRO have potency and style. Of the new guard, HERDADES DA MALHADINHA NOVA, dos Grous and Dona Maria impress. Names to watch include Herdades São Miguel, do Rocim and Paco de Camoes, Terrenus, Fita Preta and QUINTA do Centro. Best co-ops are at Borba, Redondo and Reguengos.

Algarve r w ★→★★ Southern coast DOCS include Lagos, Tavira, Lagoa and Portimão. Crooner Cliff Richard's Adega do Cantor and Quinta do Morgado are at the vanguard of a shift from quaffers to quality wine. Names to watch: Monte da Casteleja and Quinta do Frances.

Aliança, Caves Bair r w sp res ★★→★★★★ Large firm with four estates in BAIRRADA, inc QUINTA das Baceladas making gd reds and classic-method sparkling. Also interests in BEIRAS (Casa d'Aguiar), ALENTEJO (Quinta da Terrugem), DÃO (Quinta da Garrida) and the DOURO (Quatro Ventos).

Alorna, Quinta de Tejo r w ★→★★ DYA Appealingly zippy, ARINTO-driven whites, creamy rosé and gd reds from indigenous and international varieties.

Alvarinho With LOUREIRO, best white grape in VINHO VERDE, making fragrant, attractive wines. Becoming popular elsewhere to add lift to blends. Known as Albariño in neighbouring Galicia.

Ameal, Quinta do w sp sw ★★★ DYA One of best VINHOS VERDES, made by ANSELMO MENDES. 100% LOUREIRO; Escolha is oaked. New sweet wine in 2007.

Aragonez Successful red grape (Spain's Tempranillo) in ALENTEJO for varietal wines. See TINTA RORIZ.

Arinto White grape. Makes v.gd, aromatic, citrus-driven wines in BUCELAS, and features countrywide, often adding welcome zip to blends, esp in ALENTEJO.

Aveleda, Quinta da w ★→★★ DYA Reliable estate-grown VINHO VERDE made by the Guedes family, whose portfolio includes acclaimed brands *Casal García* (VINHO VERDE), Charamba (DOURO) and Follies (VINHO VERDE and BAIRRADA) with national and international varieties.

Azevedo, Quinta do w ★★ DYA Superior LOUREIRO-led VINHO VERDE from SOGRAPE.

Bacalhoa, Quinta da Set r res ★★★ 01 02 03 04 05 06 Estate near SETÚBAL. Elegant, mid-weight Cab Sauv/Merlot blend made by BACALHOA VINHOS. Fleshier Palaçio de Bacalhoa has more Merlot. Gd new white Bordeaux blend with ALVARINHO.

Bacalhoa Vinhos Set/Est/Alen r w sw sp ★★→★★★★ Owned by the Berardo Group, which owns QUINTA DO CARMO and has significant holdings in CAVES ALIANÇA and SOGRAPE. Broad but accomplished range, inc BACALHOA, JP, Serras de Azeitão, Só, Catarina, Cova da Ursa and traditional Setúbal Moscatel (SETÚBAL/PENÍNSULA DE SETÚBAL), Loridos (Estremadura) and TINTO DA ANFORA (ALENTEJO).

Bairrada Bair r sp p w ★→★★★★★ 98 99 00 01 03' 04 05' 06 07 08' 09' Central Atlantic-influenced DOC famous for austere, age-worthy reds made from the Baga grape, also sparkling wines. New regulations allowing for different varieties have paved the way for more approachable wines, and whites are on the up. Leading Baga specialists include CASA DE SAIMA, CAVES SÃO JOÃO, LUÍS PATO, Quinta de Foz de Arouce and Sidónia de Sousa. Leading modernists include CAMPOLARGO and Quinta do Encontro. Rising star: Quinta das Bágeiras.

Barca Velha Douro r res ★★★★ 81 82 85 91' 95' 99 00 Portugal's most famous red was created in 1952 by FERREIRA. It is made only in exceptional years in v. limited quantities. Intense, complex with a deep bouquet, it forged the DOURO's reputation for stellar wines. Distinguished, traditional style (aged several yrs before release). Second wine known as *Reserva Ferreirinha*.

Beira Interior ★ Isolated DOC near Spain's border. Huge potential from old and elevated v'yds; QUINTAS do Cardo, dos Currais and Oscar Almeida impress.

Beiras ★→★★ VINHO REGIONAL covering DÃO, BAIRRADA and granite ranges of central Portugal. Used by innovative producers such as LUÍS and FILIPA PATO.

Branco White.

Brejoeira, Palácio da w ★★ DYA Prestigious ALVARINHO VINHO VERDE; increasing competition from estates around Monção and Melgaço.

Bright, Peter ★★ Portugal-based Australian flying-winemaker, founder of Bright Brothers, pioneer of innovatively packaged modern brands. New project is Terras de Alter and Fado in ALENTEJO. See also FIUZA & BRIGHT.

Bucelas Lis w ★★ DYA Tiny DOC north of Lisbon focused on ARINTO whites (known as "Lisbon Hock" in 19th-century England). QUINTAS da Romeira and da Murta make tangy, racy wines.

Cabriz, Quinta de Dão r w ★★→★★★ 03 04 05 06 07 Owned by DÃO SUL; modern, fruity and fresh with good Dão character. Well-priced wines.

Cadaval, Casa Tejo r w ★★ 05' 06 07 Gd varietal reds, esp TRINCADEIRA, Pinot N, Cab Sauv and Merlot. Gd-value Padre Pedro and showy red RESERVA, Marquêsa de Cadaval.

Campolargo Bair r w 05 06 07 08 Large estate, until 2004 sold grapes to ALIANÇA. Interesting reds from Baga, Cab Sauv, Petit Verdot and Pinot N. Early days but Bordeaux varietals promising, esp Diga Petit Verdot.

Carcavelos Lis br sw ★★★ Minute DOC west of Lisbon. Hen's-teeth sweet apéritif or dessert wines average 19% alcohol and resemble honeyed MADEIRA.

Carmo, Quinta do Alen r w res ★★→★★★ 01 03 04' 05 06 50 ha once co-owned by Rothschilds (Lafite), now 100% owned by BACALHOA VINHOS. Fresh white and polished reds with Cab Sauv have Bordeaux restraint. Second wine: Dom Martinho.

Cartuxa, Adega da Alen r w sp ★★→★★★★ The move from 17th-century cellars to a state-of-the-art winery in 2007 has doubled production and upped quality, too. Famous flagship Pera Manca red (95 97 98 01 03 05' 07) is big but pricey; white impressive, too. Also Foral de Evora and new Scala Coeli red from non-local grapes.

Carvalhais, Quinta dos Dão r p w sp ★★★ (r) 01 03 04 05 06 (w) DYA SOGRAPE's principal DÃO brand: eponymous single-estate wines include flagship Unico, also volume Duque de Viseu *marque* from estate and bought-in grapes. Forward wines.

Casal Branco, Quinta de Tejo r w ★★ Large family estate. Gd entry-level wines blend local CASTELÃO and FERNÃO PIRES with others. Old-vine, local fruit struts pedigree in Falcoaria range, esp RESERVA red (03 04' 05' 07).

Casal García w ★★ DYA Big-selling off-dry VINHO VERDE, made at AVELEDA.

Castelão Planted throughout south Portugal, esp in PENÍNSULA DE SETÚBAL. Nicknamed PERIQUITA. Firm-flavoured, raspberryish reds develop a figgish, tar-like quality.

Chocapalha, Quinta de Est r p w ★★→★★★ (r) 03 04 05 06 07' Fine, modern estate. TOURIGA NACIONAL and TINTA RORIZ underpin rich reds, Cab Sauv is sinewy. New ARINTO and ARINTO-driven unoaked whites join fine oaked Chard/native white blend.

Chryseia Douro r ★★★→★★★★ 01' 03' 04 05' 06 07 V. successful partnership of Bordeaux's Bruno Prats and SYMINGTON FAMILY ESTATES; dense yet elegant from port varieties now sourced from dedicated v'yds at QUINTAS de Perdiz and DE RORIZ, Chryseia's new home. V.gd second wine: *Post Scriptum* (04 05' 06 07).

Churchill Estates Douro r p Gd reds from port shipper Churchill, esp single-estate QUINTA da Gricha (03 04 05 06 07). New RESERVA, GRANDE RESERVA and single-varietal TOURIGA NACIONAL in 2007.

Colares r w ★★ Tiny DOC west of Lisbon. Coastal sandy soils account for its heritage of ungrafted Ramisco (red) and Malvasia (white) vines, giving tannic reds and oxidative whites. Biggest producer is Adega Regional de Colares (a co-op). Rising stars: newcomers Fundação Oriente and Stanley Ho are making well-structured but more contemporary styles.

Consumo (vinho) Ordinary (wine).

Cortes de Cima Alen r w ★★★ (r) 03 04 05 06 07 (w) DYA Southerly estate near Vidigueira owned by Danish family. Produces heady, fruit-driven reds from ARAGONEZ, TRINCADEIRA, TOURIGA NACIONAL, Syrah (inc flagship Incognito) and new Petit Verdot. Second label: Chaminé.

Côtto, Quinta do Douro r res ★★→★★★ (r) 99 01 03 05 06 07 Pioneer of DOURO table wines and screwcaps. Flagship is *Grande Escolha* (95 00 01 07).

Crasto, Quinta do Douro r w ★★→★★★★ (r) 01' 02 03' 04 05' 06 07' (w) DYA Excellent lush varietal wines (TOURIGA NACIONAL, TINTA RORIZ) and blends; RESERVA is v.gd value for money. Two superb single-v'yd wines are made only in top vintages from low-yielding old vines: Vinha da Ponte (98 00' 01 03 04 07') and María Theresa (00' 03' 05' 06 07) Also port. Xisto is joint-venture red with Jean-Michel Cazes from Bordeaux. Fruit from substantial new v'yds in Upper DOURO and DOURO Superior now coming on stream.

Dão r w ★★→★★★ 00' 01 02 03' 04 05 06 07' Established DOC in central Portugal. Once dominated by co-ops; investment by quality-focused producers, large and small, has improved consistency and calibre. Look for: SOGRAPE (CARVALHAIS), DÃO SUL and QUINTAS MAIAS, PELLADA, ROQUES and SAES. Rising stars: Vinha Paz, Quinta da Bica, Quinta da Falorca and Casa da Mouraz (organic). Structured, elegant reds and substantial, dry whites come into own with food.

Dão Sul Dão r w ★★→★★★★ Dynamic DÃO-based venture. Impressive range with international appeal, inc QUINTA CABRIZ, CASA DE SANTAR and Quinta dos Grilos (Dão), Sá de Baixo and das Tecedeiras (DOURO), do Encontro (BAIRRADA), do Gradil (LISBOA) and Herdade Monte da Cal (ALENTEJO). Innovative multi-regional Portuguese and cross-border blends: Homenagen (with LUÍS PATO); Four Cs; Dourat (DOURO TOURIGA NACIONAL/Spanish GARNACHA) and Pião (Dão TOURIGA NACIONAL/Italian Nebbiolo).

DFJ Vinhos r w ★→★★★ DYA Huge range, mostly volume brands for export from Tejo and LISBOA, inc Pink Elephant rosé, Segada (r w), Manta Preta (r) and Bela Fonte. Premium label Grand'Arte also sourced from the DOURO, DÃO and ALENTEJO.

Denominacão de Origem Controlada (DOC) Demarcated wine region controlled by a regional commission. See also VINHO REGIONAL.

Doce (vinho) Sweet (wine).

Douro r w ★★→★★★★ 00' 01 02 03' 04' 05' 06 07' Famous for port and now world-class sumptuous, powerful red wines, the best with a sinewy, mineral core, and surprisingly fine whites of burgundian depth and complexity. Look for BARCA VELHA, CHRYSEIA, CRASTO, NIEPOORT, POIERA, VALE DONA MARIA, VALE MEÃO and WINE & SOUL. Names to watch: Conceito, Quinta da Romaneira, João Brito e Cunha, Zimbro. VINHO REGIONAL is Duriense.

Duas Quintas Douro ★★★ r 01 02 03' 04 05 06 07' w DYA Gd red from port shipper Ramos Pinto. V.gd RESERVA and outstanding but expensive Especial.

Esporão, Herdade do Alen w r sw ★★→★★★ 03 04 05 06 07' Quality-driven big estate (600 ha with new organic trial of 80 ha). Monte Velho, Alandra and Vinha da Defesa brands showcase ALENTEJO's ripe fruit. Quatro Castas, single-varietal range, Esporão RESERVAS, v.gd Private Selection (r w), GARRAFEIRA and flagship Torre do Esporão offer depth and complexity. Recently acquired Quinta das Murças in the DOURO – 2008 is first trial vintage.

Espumante Sparkling.

Falua Tejo r p w DYA JOÃO PORTUGAL RAMOS' state-of-the-art venture. Gd entry-level Tagus Creek range of indigenous and international blends, plus more upmarket Tãmara and Conde de Vimioso.

Fernão Pires White grape making aromatic, ripe-flavoured, slightly spicy whites in Tejo. (Known as María Gomes in BAIRRADA.)

Ferreira Douro r ★→★★★★ SOGRAPE-owned port shipper making gd to v.gd DOURO wines under Casa Ferreirinha labels: Esteva, Vinha Grande, Quinta de Leda, RESERVA Especial Ferreirinha and BARCA VELHA.

Fiuza & Bright Tejo r w ★★ DYA Joint venture between PETER BRIGHT and the Fiuza family. Gd, inexpensive Chard, Merlot, Cab Sauv and Portuguese varietals.

Fonseca, José María da Lis r p w dr sw sp res ★★→★★★ Historic family-owned estate. Pioneer of SETÚBAL fortified Moscatel and volume branded wines such as LANCERS and PERIQUITA. Colecção Privada label continues tradition for innovation, esp unique Moscatel Roxo rosé. Other brands: Montado, Terras Altas (DÃO), Quinta de Camarate, Pasmados, Vinya, Privada Domingos Soares Franco and flagships FSF, Domini/Domini Plus (DOURO) and Hexagon.

Gaivosa, Quinta de Douro r w ★★★→★★★★ 01 03 04 05' 06 07 Leading estate near Régua. Characterful, concentrated old-vine red varietals (v.gd TOURIGA NACIONAL) and blends from different terroir, inc Abandonado, Quinta das Caldas, Vinha de Lordelo, RESERVA Pessoal, Vale da Raposa. Gd white: Branco da Gaivosa.

Garrafeira Label term: merchant's "private reserve", aged for min of 2 yrs in cask and one in bottle, often much longer.

Gazela w ★★ DYA Reliable VINHO VERDE made at Barcelos by SOGRAPE.

Generoso Apéritif or dessert wine rich in alcohol.

Lagoalva, Quinta da Ribatejo r w ★★ 02 03 05' 06 07 Go-ahead Tejo estate; gd use of Portuguese (esp Alfrocheiro) and international varieties (esp Syrah). Second label: Monte da Casta.

Lancers p w sp ★ Semi-sweet (semi-sparkling) rosé, widely shipped to the US by JOSÉ MARÍA DA FONSECA. Rosé Free is alcohol-free.

Lavadores de Feitoria Douro r w 18 small quality-conscious estates blending fruit from across the three DOURO regions. Principal labels: Meruge, Três Bagos.

Lisboa VINHO REGIONAL on west coast, formerly known as Estremadura. Gd-value wines from local estates and co-ops. Ambitious premium wines: CHOCAPALHA, MONTE D'OIRO, Arruda, BUCELAS, CARCAVELOS, COLARES, Encostas d'Aire, Obidos, Torres Vedras.

Loureiro Best VINHO VERDE grape variety after ALVARINHO: crisp, fragrant whites.

Madeira br dr sw ★★→★★★★ Portugal's Atlantic island: makes unfortified reds and whites (Terras Madeirenses VINHO REGIONAL and Madeirense DOC), mostly for the local market; whites from Verdelho on the up. See Port, Sherry & Madeira for famous fortified dessert and apéritif wines.

Maias, Quinta das Dão ★★ (r) 01 03 04 05' 06 07 (w) DYA Sister of QUINTA ROQUES. Benchmark Jaen and DÃO's only Verdelho; Flor das Maias (2005; 2007) is showy TOURIGA NACIONAL-dominated blend.

Malhadinha Nova, Herdade da Alen r p w sw ★★★ 03' 04 05 06 07' Young vines but mature, quality-focused approach: v.gd big, spicy reds and rich, oak-aged white from ALENTEJO's deep south. Flagship is Marias da Malhadinha. New Petit Manseng sweetie.

Mateus Rosé p sp (w) ★ World's bestselling, medium-dry, lightly carbonated rosé table wine from SOGRAPE. Original is Portuguese but international versions hail from France (Shiraz) and Spain (Tempranillo).

Mendes, Anselmo w sp ★★→★★★★ Acclaimed progressive VINHO VERDE winemaker and consultant for, among others, QUINTA DO AMEAL. Eponymous wines focus almost exclusively on ALVARINHO and include Contacto, Muros Antigos and Muros de Melgaço.

Messias r w ★→★★★ Large BAIRRADA-based firm; interests in DOURO (inc port). Old-school reds best.

Minho River between north Portugal and Spain, and VINHO REGIONAL. A number of leading VINHO VERDE producers prefer to use VR Minho.

Monte d'Oiro, Quinta do Lis r w ★★★→★★★★ 01 03 04' 05 06' José Bento dos Santos' flagships are outstanding, increasingly elegant Rhône-style Syrah/Viognier reds and Madrigal, Viognier. Gd second wine: Lybra. Chapoutier (see France) consults on winemaking and biodynamics and is new joint-venture partner for exciting Bento & Chapoutier Ex Aequo Syrah/TOURIGA NACIONAL (06 07).

Mouchão, Herdade de Alen r r es ★★★ 99 00 01 03' 05' Leading traditional estate. Intense, fragrant wines realize full potential of the Alicante Bouschet grape. *Flagship Tonel 3–4*, exceptional yrs only, has great complexity and persistence. Ponte das Canas (05, 06), recent premium release, blends Alicante Bouschet with TOURIGAS NACIONAL and Franca and Shiraz; Dom Rafael gd value.

Mouro, Quinta do Alen r ★★★→★★★★ 98 99 00 04' 05' Fabulous structured, terroir-driven reds, mostly ALENTEJO grapes. Dry-farmed, low yields, concentrated, supple wines. Flagship Mouro Gold made in exceptional yrs (99, 00, 02 05). O Mouro made with NIEPOORT.

Murganheira, Caves ★ Largest producer of ESPUMANTE. Now owns RAPOSEIRA.

Niepoort Douro r w p ★★★→★★★★ Family port shipper making exceptional, exciting DOURO wines. Core range is aromatic Tiara (w), Vertente (r), Redoma (r p w, inc w Reserve) 01 03 04' 05' 06' 07', Robustus (r) 04 05, sinewy Batuta (r) 01' 03 04 05' 07 and sumptuous Charme (r) 02 04 05' 06 07'. Drink Me is approachable red, Projectos is experimental range and also collaborates with PELLADA (Dado/Doda), SOALHEIRO (Girasol and Primeiras Vinhas) and MOURO (O Mouro).

Noval, Quinta do Douro r ★★★ Leading AXA-owned port house. Made first super-premium unfortified reds, Quinta do Noval and Cedro, in 2004. Innovative Syrah blend Cedro shows the French variety's affinity for the DOURO, as does new 100% Syrah called Labrador – after the winemaker's dog.

Palmela Península de Setúbal r w ★→★★★ CASTELÃO-focused DOC (see PEGOS CLAROS). Can be long-lived.

Pancas, Quinta de Lis r w res ★★→★★★★ (r) 01 03 05' 07 (w) DYA Prestigious estate near ALENQUER. Owner since 2006, Companhia das Quintas has overhauled range. Flagship is Grande Escolha followed by RESERVA range: TOURIGA NACIONAL and Cabernet Sauvignon and Selecção do Enólogo.

Passadouro, Quinta do Douro r w Superb RESERVA comes from single parcel of older vines (03 04' 05' 06 07'). Recently acquired v'yds to boost wine and port; new white and entry label "Passa" red.

Pato, Filipa Beiras r w sp sw LUÍS PATO's dynamic daughter produces exciting eponymous and new Vinhos Doidos labels featuring grapes from BAIRRADA and DÃO, inc Ensaios, FLP (dessert wine made with father), "3b" fizz, "Lokal" (red) and Bossa and Nossa (white).

Pato, Luís Bair r w sp sw ★★→★★★★ 95' 97 99 00 01' 03' 04 05' 06 07 *Exquisite single-v'yd Baga*: Vinhas Barrio, Pan, Barrosa and flagship Quinta do Ribeirinho Pé Franco (ungrafted vines). New Baga sweet wine. Quinta do Ribeirinho 1st Choice is a Baga/TOURIGA NACIONAL blend. João Pato, early-drinking TOURIGA NACIONAL, now joined by single-v'yd TOURIGA from Vinha Formal. Shows equal flair with whites (Vinhas Formal and Velhas) and sparkling wines. Uses BEIRAS classification, though recently persuaded to reuse DOC BAIRRADA but only for Vinha Formal ESPUMANTE.

Pegões, Adega de Península de Setúbal r w p sp sw ★→★★★ Portugal's most dynamic co-op, based in up-and-coming PENÍNSULA DE SETÚBAL, thrives under winemaker and consultant Jaime Quendera. Gd range from top to bottom, inc varietals and blends made from Portuguese and international varieties. V.gd Colheita Seleccionada red and white offer exceptional value for money.

Pegos Claros r 01 03 04 05' Benchmark PALMELA CASTELÃO, foot-trodden and aged min 3 yrs before release.

Pellada, Quinta de Dão r w 04 05' 06 07' Owned with SAES by leading DÃO light Alvaro de Castro. Intense, not dense, reds, inc flagship Pape (TOURIGA NACIONAL from Passarela v'yd with Pellada Baga) and Carrocel (100% TOURIGA). Primus is old-vine, textured white.

Península de Setúbal Up-and-coming VINHO REGIONAL covering sandy plains around Sado Estuary, formerly known as Terras do Sado. Established producers include ADEGO DE PEGÕES, BACALHOA VINHOS and Casa Ermelinda Freitas (QUINTA da Mimosa and Leo d'Honor). Names to watch: Herdades da Comporta and Portocarro, Mala Tojo, Soberanas and QUINTAS de Catralvos and Alcube.

Periquita The nickname for the CASTELÃO grape and successful brand name and trademark of JOSÉ MARÍA DA FONSECA. Periquita Classico is original 100% Castelão; red, RESERVA (and rosé and white) feature other varieties.

Poeira, Quinta do Douro r w ★★★★ (02 03' 04' 05' 06 07') Elegant flagship red from north-facing slopes from Jorge Moreira, QUINTA DE LA ROSA's winemaker. Second wine: Pó de Poeira red and unique ALVARINHO/Gouveio blend. Now joined by CS, a blend of Cab Sauv and DOURO varieties.

Ponte de Lima, Cooperativa de r w sp ★ Impressive top-tier "Seleccionado" VINHO VERDE, inc bone-dry red.

Portal, Quinta do Douro r p w sw ★★★ 00' 01 03 04 05' 06 07 New plantings and winery reaping dividends at former Sandeman estate; satisfying red wines, inc Grande Reserva and flagship Auru. Exciting new sweet wine.

Portalegre Alen r w ★→★★★ Northernmost subregion with own DOC has strikingly different terroir from the rest of ALENTEJO. Elevated with twice as much rainfall and granite soils, its wines are fresh and structured. Go-ahead local co-op but names to watch are Altas Quintas, where Paulo Laureano (HERDADE DE MOUCHÃO's winemaker) consults; Terrenus, owned by consultant winemaker Rui Reguinga; and Quinta do Centro.

Quinta Estate (see under name, eg. PORTAL, QUINTA DO).

Ramos, João Portugal Alen r w DYA Well-made ALENTEJO range from Loios and Vila Santa to premium single-varietal range and blends: QUINTA da Viçosa and v.gd Marqués de Borba Reserva (03 05). Promising new DOURO joint venture: Duorum.

Raposeira Douro w sp ★★ Well-known fizz with native varieties and Chard made by classic method at Lamego.

Real Companhia Velha Douro r p w sw ★★→★★★ r 00' 01' 02 03 04 05 06 Historic port company with extensive premium table wine v'yds across the DOURO, inc Chard, Sauv Bl, Semillon and now ALVARINHO. Brands: flagship Evel Grande Reserva, Porca de Murça, Quinta dos Aciprestes, Quinta de Cidro, Grantom and sweet Granjó from Semillon.

Roques, Quinta dos Dão r w ★★→★★★ (r) 01 03' 04 05 06 07' V.gd estate for age-worthy reds, esp flagship GARRAFEIRA blend and white Encruzado. Varietal wines from TOURIGA NATIONAL, TINTA RORIZ, Tinta Cão and Alfrocheiro Preto. Gd-value entry-level Correio label.

Roriz, Quinta de Douro r ★★★ 02 03' 04 05' 06 One of the great QUINTAS of the DOURO. Fine reds (and vintage port). Now owned by SYMINGTON FAMILY ESTATES and new base for CHRYSEIA. Second wine: Prazo de Roriz.

Rosa, Quinta de la Douro r p w ★★★ 04 05' 06 07' Firm, rich estate reds, esp RESERVA and Quinta das Bandeiras-sourced Passagem (in partnership with winemaker Jorge Moreira) from warmer DOURO Superior.

Rosado Rosé.

Saes, Quinta de Dão r w ★★★→★★★★ 01 02 03 04 05 06' 07' Alvaro Castro's other v'yd (see PELLADA), producing equally characterful and elegant wines, inc Dado/Doda – see NIEPOORT.

Saima, Casa de Bair r p sp (w DYA) ★★★ (r) 01 02 03' 04 05' 06 Small, traditional estate; big, tannic reds (esp GARRAFEIRAS 90' 91 95' 97' 01) and *fresh whites*.

Santar, Casa de Dão r ★★★ 01 02 03 04 Well-established estate now linked to DÃO SUL making welcome comeback. Structured reds; for Encruzado whites, Burgundian approach paying dividends.

Santos Lima, Casa Est r p w ★★ Family-owned ALENQUER company with export focus. Diverse range reflects extensive v'yds, inc QUINTAS da Boavista/das Setencostas and do Espírito Santo. CSL is key brand.

São João, Caves Bair r w sp ★★→★★★ (r sp) 95 97 00 01 03 (w) DYA Small, traditional firm for v.gd old-fashioned wines. Reds can age for decades. BAIRRADA: *Frei João*, Poço do Lobo. DÃO: Porta dos Cavaleiros.

Seco Dry.

Setúbal Set br sw (r w dr) ★★★ Tiny DOC south of the river Tagus. Fortified dessert wines made predominantly from the Moscatel (Muscat) grape, inc rare red Moscatel Roxo. Main producers: JOSÉ MARIA DA FONSECA and BACALHOA VINHOS.

Sezim, Casa de w ★★ DYA Beautiful estate making v.gd VINHO VERDE.

Soalheiro, Quinta de w sp ★★★ 00 02' 03 06 07' 08' ALVARINHO specialist making revelatory VINHO VERDE, inc old-vine Primeiras Vinhas (with NIEPOORT), barrel-fermented RESERVA and ESPUMANTE. Warm Melgaço location 50-km inland brings structure, concentration and texture.

Sogrape ★→★★★★ Portugal's largest wine concern, making VINHO VERDE (AZEVEDO, GAZELA, Morgadio da Torre), DÃO (CARVALHAIS), ALENTEJO (Herdade do Peso), MATEUS ROSÉ, and owner of FERREIRA, Sandeman, Offley port and BARCA VELHA in the DOURO. Approachable multi-regional brands Grão Vasco, Pena de Pato and Callabriga from VINHO VERDE, DOURO, DÃO, ALENTEJO. Also making wine in Spain, Argentina, New Zealand and Chile.

Sousa, José de Alen r res ★★→★★★ 03 04 05 06 Small ALENTEJO firm acquired by JOSÉ MARÍA DA FONSECA; wines now slightly lighter in style but flagship Mayor is solid, foot-trodden red fermented in clay amphoras and aged in oak.

Symington Family Estates Douro ★★→★★★★ Family-run port shipper and the DOURO's largest v'yd owner. Since 2000 producing serious table wines, inc CHRYSEIA with Bruno Prats, with whom it has just acquired QUINTA DE RORIZ. whose wines it has made for some time. Well-made brand Altano now includes white and organic red. Newer releases from famous port houses include Dow Val du Bomfim, Quinta do Vesúvio and Pombal do Vesúvio.

Tejo r w Engine room of gd-value wines from CASTELÃO, TRINCADEIRA, FERNÃO PIRES raising its game with switch to poorer soils and introduction of red varieties, TOURIGA NACIONAL, TINTA RORIZ and international grapes: Cab Sauv, Syrah, Pinot N, Chard and Sauv Bl. Gd results already at, eg. QUINTA DA LAGOALVA, Pinhal da Torre and FALUA. Rising star: VALE D'ALGARES. Subregions: Almeirim, Cartaxo, Coruche, Chamusca, Tomar, Santarem. VINHO REGIONAL Tejo.

Teodósio, Caves Dom Tejo r w ★→★★ Large Tejo producer. Brands include Serradayres and Casaleiro; top wines from Quinta de São João Batista. Also making wine in DÃO and PALMELA.

Tinta Roriz Major port grape (alias Tempranillo) making v.gd DOURO wines. Known as ARAGONEZ in ALENTEJO.

Tinto Red.

Tinto da Anfora Alen r ★★→★★★ 03 04 05' 06 07 Reliable red from BACALHOA VINHOS. Impressively rich Grande Escolha.

Touriga Nacional Top red grape used for port and DOURO table wines; now increasingly elsewhere, esp DÃO, ALENTEJO and LISBOA.

Trás-os-Montes DOC with subregions Chaves, Valpaços and Planalto Mirandês. Reds and whites from international grape varieties grown in the DOURO. VINHO REGIONAL Transmontano.

Trincadeira V.gd red grape in ALENTEJO for spicy wines. Known as Tinta Amarela in the DOURO.

Vale d'Algares Tejo r w p ★★→★★★ No-expense-spared project focusing on super-premium international and Portuguese varieties. Lead wine is an ambitiously priced but promising Viognier, which grape is blended with ALVARINHO for its 2nd-tier Selection White. Guarda Rios is the junior brand. A name to watch.

Vale Dona Maria, Quinta do Douro r w p ★★★→★★★★ 01' 02 03' 04' 05' 06 07'
Cristiano van Zeller's highly regarded QUINTA. *V.gd plush yet elegant reds*, inc CV,
Casa de Casal de Loivos and new VZ white. Also gd port.

Vale Meão, Quinta do Douro r ★★★→★★★★ 01' 03 04' 05 06 07' Once the source
of BARCA VELHA. Impressively structured wines typified by high percentage of
TOURIGA NACIONAL and warm, easterly location. V.gd second wine: Meandro.
New v'yd at 350 m holds exciting prospects.

Vallado Douro r w ★★★ (r) 03' 04 05' 06 07 (w) DYA Family owned DOURO estate
going from strength to strength with new winery doubling capacity and new
DOURO Superior v'yd to be planted 2011. V.gd-value sweet-fruited single-
varietals and minerally, well-structured blends, esp RESERVE; new old-vine red
Adelaide (05 07) raises bar.

Vidigueira Alen r w ★→★★★ Hot ALENTEJO DOC. Best producer: *Cortes de Cima*.
On the up, respected consultant Paulo Laureano's eponymous wines.

Vinho Regional Larger provincial wine regions, with same status as French Vin
de Pays: Acores, Alentejano, ALGARVE, BEIRAS, Duriense, LISBOA, MINHO, Tejo,
Terras Madeirenses, Terras do Sado, Transmontano. More leeway for
experimentation than DOC. See also DOC.

Vinho Verde r w ★→★★★ DOC between river DOURO and north frontier, for "green
wines", made from high-acidity grapes. Large brands such as GAZELA, Gatão
and CASAL GARCÍA usually varietal blend with added carbon dioxide – DYA. Best
have natural spritz, if any, and are single-QUINTA, single-varietal age-worthy
wines. Look out for ALVARINHO from Monção and Melgaço (eg. Adega de Monçâo
and QUINTA DE SOALHEIRO) and LOUREIRO (eg. QUINTA DO AMEAL or Afros) from
Lima. Try the reds.

Wine & Soul Douro r w (r Pintas) 02 03' 04' 05' 06 07' (w Guru) 05 06' 07 08'
Rich, imposing wines (and port) from renowned winemaking couple Sandra
Tavares and Jorge Serôdio Borges. Second wine: Pintas Character (r). New
flagship single-v'yd Manuela in 2009 follows acquisition of prized old-vine
QUINTA.

Zambujeiro Alen r ★★★ 99 00 01' 02 03 04' 05' Swiss-owned, quality-focused
estate producing powerfully structured blends from dry-farmed Portuguese
varieties. Gd second wine: Terra do Zambujeiro.

PORTUGAL

Port, Sherry & Madeira

These great classic fortified wines are having to justify their place in the world. We drink less of them than we used to: vintage port declarations, even of vintages as good as 2007, are smaller in quantity than they used to be when traditional customers could be relied upon to decant a bottle after dinner. Sherry is finding a niche with food, thanks to the popularity of tapas bars, and is discovering that we have an appetite for the very best (not surprising, given how underpriced even the greatest sherries are). Madeira is still awaiting its revival, which is good news for its aficionados, who can still pick up a century-old rarity for the price of a good young red Bordeaux. As for the 2007 vintage ports, this is the widest declaration ever, with 91 wines declared, including newcomers Niepoort Pisca and Quinta do Vesuvio Capela. The wines are intense and unusually elegant – perfect for drinking young. Sacrilege? By no means. Young vintage port, until it retreats into its shell at four or five years of age, is one of the most delicious wines around.

Recent port vintages

2008 Single-quinta year. Low-yielding, powerful wines.

2007 Classic year, widely declared. Late but mild, dry vintage produced deep-coloured, rich but well-balanced wines. Taylor's and Vesuvio are stars.

2006 A difficult year, yielding only a handful of single-quinta wines. Stars: Vesuvio, Roriz, Barros Quinta Galeira.

2005 Single-quinta year. Stars: Niepoort, Taylor de Vargellas, Dow da Senhora da Ribeira – iron fist in velvet glove.

2004 Also a single-quinta year. Stars: Pintas, Taylor de Vargellas Vinha Velha, Quinta de la Rosa – balanced, elegant wines.

2003 Classic vintage year. Hot, dry summer. Powerfully ripe, concentrated wines, universally declared. Drink from 2015/2020.

2001 Another single-quinta year. Stars: Noval Nacional, Fonseca do Panascal, do Vale Meão – wet year; relatively forward wines.

2000 Classic year. A very fine vintage, universally declared. Rich, well-balanced wines for the long term. Drink from 2015.

1999 Single-quinta year. Stars: Vesuvio, Taylor de Terra Feita, do Infantado – smallest vintage for decades; powerful.

1998 Single-quinta year. Stars: Dow da Senhora da Ribeira, Graham dos Malvedos, Cockburn dos Canais – bullish, firm wines.

1997 Classic year. Fine, potentially long-lasting wines with tannic backbone. Most shippers declared. Drink 2012 onward.

1996 Single-quinta year. Stars: Graham dos Malvedos, Warre da Cavadinha, Taylor de Vargellas – power and finesse.

1994 Classic year. Outstanding vintage with ripe, fleshy fruit disguising underlying structure at the outset. Universal declaration. Drink 2010–2030.

1992 Classic year. Favoured by a few (especially Taylor and Fonseca) over 1991. Richer, more concentrated, a better year than 1991. Drink now–2025.

1991 Classic year. Favoured by most shippers (especially Symington Family Estates with Dow, Graham and Warre) over 1992; classic, firm but a little lean in style. Drink now–2020.

1987 Classic year. Dense wines for drinking over the medium term, but only a handful of shippers declared. Drink now–2015.

1985 Classic year. Universal declaration, which looked good at the outset but has thrown up some disappointments in bottle. Now–2020 for best wines.

Almacenista Stockholder who cellars sherries but does not sell them on the open market. Historically such wines were used to boost the major producers' wines. A dying breed, partially revived in recent yrs. Also still important to manzanilla. Wines can be superb. LUSTAU offers a wide Almacenista range.

Alvaro Domecq ★★→★★★★ One of the new-wave sherry bodegas. Created by DOMECQ family members to re-establish DOMECQ name in JEREZ after corporate takeovers. Based on SOLERAS of Pilar Aranda, said to be the oldest bodega in JEREZ. Excellent 1730 label wines, inc Palo Cortado, Oloroso. Gd Fino La Janda. One of the best sherry vinegars in town.

Alvear Mont-M ★★→★★★★ Largest producer of v.gd sherry-like apéritif and sweet wines in MONTILLA, esp Solera 1927.

Andresen ★★→★★★ Family-owned port house making gd 20-yr-old TAWNY and grand old COLHEITAS (**1900**', **75**, **82**, **91**, **97**); first to register a white port with age indication (10-yr-old; new 20-yr-old).

Barbadillo, Antonio ★→★★★★ The former bishop's palace in SANLÚCAR is appropriate for the largest producer in town. Reliquia wines are exceptional, esp the palo cortado and oloroso. Solear manzanilla is a local favourite at *feria* time but also seek out Príncipe Amontillado, Obispo Gascón Palo Cortado, Cuco Dry Oloroso, Eva Cream. Look for manzanilla EN RAMA, with seasonal *sacas*. Pioneered palomino fino as a light table wine.

Barbeito Dynamic producer of finely honed Madeiras with no added caramel. Pioneers of robotic LAGARE for Madeira, single-cask COLHEITAS, 20-yr-old and 30-yr-old MALVASIA and VERDELHO/BUAL blend (vb). Bright, citrus COLHEITAS (Malvasia 2000, Boal 2001) and stylish FRASQUEIRA (Boal 1982, Verdelho 1981). At the top of its game.

Barros Almeida Large port house with several brands (inc Feist, Feuerheerd, KOPKE) owned by Sogevinus: excellent 20-yr-old TAWNY and COLHEITAS (**78' 96'**); VINTAGE PORTS on the up. Sogevinus sold Quinta Dona Matilde back to Barros family, 2009.

Barros e Sousa Traditional Madeira producer. Tiny output of 100% CANTEIRO-aged wines, inc rare vintages, gd 10-yr-old and unusual 5-yr-old Listrao blend. Watch out for Bastardo Old Reserve and Terrantez **1979**.

Blandy Best-known name of the MADEIRA WINE COMPANY, thanks to popular 3-yr-old Duke ranges. Impressive inventory of aged wines yielding fine old vintages (eg. Bual 1920, 1964, Verdelho **1968** and Sercial **1966**). Recent innovations include COLHEITAS (Malmsey 1990, 2001, Bual 1993, Single Harvest 1977) and Alvada, a moreish blend of BUAL and MALVASIA.

Borges, HM Family company. V.gd 10-yr-olds, stylish COLHEITAS (Verdelho, Boal and Sercial 1995, Malmsey 1998) and vintages, esp Sercial **1977**, **1979**, Bual 1977.

Burmester Small port house owned by Sogevinus and behind innovative fruity and forward Gilbert's G-Porto label. Best-known for fine, soft, sweet 20- and 40-yr-old TAWNY and COLHEITAS (1955', 1989); vintage improving (07').

Cálem Established Sogevinus-owned port house. Velhotes is the main brand; gd LBV. Fine reputation for COLHEITAS (90 **94**) and v.gd VINTAGE PORTS in **66**' and **70'**; returning to form (03' 05 07).

Canteiro Method of naturally cask-ageing the finest Madeira in warehouses known as lodges. Creates subtler, more complex wines than ESTUFAGEM.

Churchill 82 85 91 94 97 00 03 Independent, family-owned port shipper founded in 1981. Expansion programme focused on Tourigas Nacional and Franca is bringing more elegance to ports and wines. V.gd traditional LBV. Quinta da Gricha is the single-QUINTA port (99 00 01 03' 04 05' 06 07). Benchmark aged WHITE PORT and new 10-yr-old white.

Sherry styles

Manzanilla Fashionably pale, dry sherry with a fresh green-apple character; a popular, unchallenging introduction to the flavours of sherry. Matured (though not necessarily grown) in the humid, maritime conditions of SANLÚCAR DE BARRAMEDA where the FLOR grows more thickly, and the wine is said to acquire a salty tang. Drink cold and fresh. Deteriorates rapidly once opened. Eg. HEREDEROS DE ARGÜESO San León.

Manzanilla Pasada manzanilla aged longer than most; v. dry, complex. Eg. HIDALGO LA GITANA's single-v'yd Manzanilla Pasada Pastrana.

Fino Dry sherry, a little weightier than manzanilla. Min age of 3 yrs (as Manzanilla). Eg. GONZÁLEZ BYASS Tío Pepe. Serve as for Manzanilla.

Amontillado A fino in which the layer of protective yeast FLOR has died, allowing the wine to oxidize, creating more powerful complexity. Naturally dry. Eg. VALDESPINO Tío Diego. Commercial styles may be sweetened.

Oloroso Not aged under FLOR. Heavier and less brilliant when young but matures to a nutty intensity and pungency. Naturally dry. Also sweetened with PX and sold as an oloroso *dulce*/sweet oloroso. Eg. DOMECQ Río Viejo (dry), LUSTAU Old East India (sweet).

Palo Cortado V. fashionable. Traditionally, a wine that had lost its FLOR and become between amontillado and oloroso. Today, often blended to create the style. Often difficult to identify with certainty, though some suggest it has a keynote "lactic" or "bitter butter" note. Dry, rich, complex – worth looking for. Eg. BARBADILLO Reliquia and GUTIÉRREZ COLOSÍA.

Cream A blended sherry sweetened with grape must, PX, and/or MOSCATEL for an inexpensive, medium-sweet style. Unashamedly commercial. Eg. HARVEY's Bristol Cream, CROFT Pale Cream. Tailor-made for British market.

Pedro Ximénez (PX) Raisined sweet, dark sherry from partly sun-dried PX grapes (grapes mainly sourced from MONTILLA; wine is made in JEREZ DO). Concentrated, unctuous, decadent, a bargain. Perfect to sip with ice cream. Overall, the world's sweetest wine. Eg. REY FERNANDO DE CASTILLA Antique, EMILIO HIDALGO Santa Ana 1861, VALDESPINO Toneles.

Moscatel As with PX grape, though rarely reaches PX's level of richness. Eg. LUSTAU Emilín. Unlike Màlaga's Moscatels, Chipiona's not fermented.

VOS/VORS A relatively new category of vintage-dated sherries to showcase some of the treasures of the JEREZ bodegas. A great buy: exceptional quality and maturity at relatively low prices. Wines assessed by carbon dating to be more than 20 yrs old are called VOS (Very Old Sherry/Vinum Optimum Signatum); those over 30 yrs old are VORS (Very Old Rare Sherry/Vinum Optimum Rare Signatum). Also 12-yr-old and 15-yr-old examples. Applies only to amontillado, oloroso, palo cortado, PX. Eg. VOS HIDALGO Jerez Cortado Wellington; VORS DOMECQ 51-1a Amontillado.

Añada "Vintage" Sherry with a declared vintage. Runs counter to tradition of the vintage-blended SOLERA. Formerly private bottlings now winning public accolades. Eg. LUSTAU Sweet Oloroso Añada 1990.

Cockburn Owned by the US Fortune Brands, though SYMINGTON FAMILY ESTATES bought its assets in 2006. Popular Special Reserve Ruby. New-look 50cl bottles for white and age-dated TAWNY encourage experimentation. Dry house style for VINTAGE PORTS: 63 67 70 75 83' 91 94 97 00 03' 07'. Gd Touriga Nacional-dominated single-QUINTA wines from Quinta dos Canais (98 01' 05' 06 07).

Colheita Vintage-dated port or Madeira of a single yr, cask-aged at least 7 yrs for port and 5 yrs for Madeira. Bottling date shown on the label.

Cossart Gordon Top-quality label of the MADEIRA WINE COMPANY; drier style than

BLANDY. Best known for the Good Company brand. Also 5-yr-old RESERVES, COLHEITAS (Sercial 1988, *Bual 1995 and 1997*, Malvasia 1995 and 1998), old vintages (1977 Terrantez, 1908, 1961 BUAL).

Croft Now part of Fladgate, which reintroduced foot-treading for the much-improved 2003 VINTAGE PORT. Vintages: 60' 63' 66 70 75 77 82 85 91 94 00 03' 07. Lighter Quinta da Roêda. Indulgence, Triple Crown and Distinction: most popular brands. "Pink", a pioneering ROSÉ PORT, prompted change of rules to allow rosés; served chilled or on ice.

Croft Jerez Sherries designed for the British drinker; sweet Original Pale Cream and drier Particular. Owned by GONZÁLEZ BYASS.

Crusted Style of port usually blended from several vintages, bottled young and aged so it throws a deposit, or "crust", and needs decanting.

Delaforce Port shipper now owned by Real Companhia Velha, though Fladgate still produces the ports. Curious and Ancient 20-yr-old Tawny and COLHEITAS (64 79 88) are jewels; VINTAGE PORTS are improving: 63 66 70' 75 77 82 85 92' 94 00 03. Single-QUINTA wines from Quinta da Corte. ★★

Delgado, Zuleta ★★ Old (1774) SANLÚCAR firm. Makers of one of the classic manzanilla pasadas: La Goya.

Dios Baco ★→★★ Family-owned JEREZ bodega. V.gd Imperial VORS Palo Cortado.

Domecq ★★→★★★★ Formerly great name in sherry, latterly tossed about in the corporate brand sales that penetrated even the cathedral-like silence of the bodegas of JEREZ. Now owned by OSBORNE. An exceptional range: the excellent La Ina Fino, Río Viejo Oloroso. Outstanding collection of VORS: Amontillado 51-1a, *Sibarita Oloroso*, Capuchino Palo Cortado, Venerable PX.

Douro Rising in Spain as the Duero, the river Douro flows through port country, lending its name to the region, which is divided into the Cima (Upper) Corgo and Douro Superior, home of the best ports, and the Baixo Corgo.

Dow Brand name of port house Silva & Cosens. Belongs to SYMINGTON FAMILY ESTATES; drier style than other producers in group (GOULD CAMPBELL, GRAHAM, QUARLES HARRIS, QUINTA DE RORIZ, SMITH WOODHOUSE, QUINTA DO VESÚVIO, WARRE). V.gd range, inc CRUSTED, 20- and 30-yr-old TAWNIES, single-QUINTAS Bomfim and, since 1998, Quinta da Senhora da Ribeira; vintage: 63 66 70 72 75 77 80 83 85' 91 94 97 00' 03 07'.

Emilio Hildago ★★→★★★★ Exceptional JEREZ bodega making exquisite Privilegio Palo Cortado 1860 and v.gd Santa Ana PX 1861.

En rama Sherry bottled from the butt without filtration or cold stabilization. As a result, it needs to be sold and drunk quickly, so it is not popular with many wine shops. Prized by aficionados for its purity. BARBADILLO has bottlings labelled by the season: Saca de Primavera ("Spring Extraction"), etc.

Equipo Navazos ★★★★ Impressive project by a group of sherry fans bottling individual butts from top bodegas. Has rapidly built a reputation for the highest quality, and attention to detail in giving the origin and bottling date. Eg. La Bota de Palo Cortado Bota Punta No. 17 PC.

Estufagem Bulk process of slowly heating, then cooling, cheaper Madeiras to attain characteristic scorched-earth tang; less subtle than CANTEIRO process.

Ferreira Leading Portuguese-owned shipper belonging to Sogrape. Bestselling brand in Portugal. Well-structured, rich, spicy RESERVE (Don Antónia), 10- and 20-yr-old TAWNIES, Quinta do Porto and *Duque de Bragança*. Early maturing vintages: 66 70 75 77 78 80 82 83 85 87 90 91 94 95' 97 00 03 07'.

Flor Spanish word for "flower": refers to the layer of *Saccharomyces* yeasts that grow atop fino/manzanilla sherry in barrel, keeping oxygen at bay and changing the wine's flavour, making it aromatic and pungent.

Fonseca Guimaraens Port shipper; belongs to Fladgate. Bin 27 and organic Terra Prima RESERVE RUBIES and sumptuous yet structured vintages (the latter now only estate grapes) among best: Fonseca 63' 66' 70 75 77' 80 83 85' 92 94' 97 00' 03' 07. Impressive, earlier-maturing Fonseca Guimaraens and single-QUINTA Panascal made when no classic declaration.

Frasqueira The official name for "vintage" Madeira from a single yr. Exceptionally intense wines bottled after at least 20 yrs in wood. Date of bottling compulsory; the longer in cask, the more concentrated and complex.

Garvey ★→★★ One of the great old names of JEREZ, though less impressive today. San Patricio Fino is still a classic; also Tío Guillermo Amontillado, Ochavico Oloroso and age-dated 1780 line. Owned by Nueva Rumasa, the holding company of the RUIZ-MATEOS family.

Gaspar Florido ★★ Small, quality SANLÚCAR bodega with gd manzanilla.

Gonzalez Byass ★→★★★★ One of JEREZ's few remaining family businesses, González Byass has one of the best finos: *Tío Pepe*. Range also includes Viña AB AMONTILLADO, Elegante Fino, 1847 sweet oloroso. Exceptional VORS age-dated Del Duque Amontillado, Matúsalem Oloroso, Apóstoles Palo Cortado and the outstanding, ultra-rich Noé PX. Extensive collection of vintages, and one of the few bodegas to sell vintage sherries. Look out for new EN RAMA bottlings. Extensive interests in brandy (Soberano, Lepanto); table wines include Finca Moncloa (Tierra de Cádiz), Altozano (Tierra de Castilla), Vilarnau (cava), Beronia (Rioja) and latest acquisition, Viñas del Vero (Somontano).

Gould Campbell Port shipper belonging to SYMINGTON FAMILY ESTATES. Gd-value, full-bodied VINTAGE PORTS 70 77' 80 83 85' 91 94 97 00 03' 07.

Gracia Hermanos ★ Mont-M Firm within the same group as PÉREZ BARQUERO and Compañia Vinícola del Sur making gd-quality MONTILLAS. Esp Tauromaquia Amontillado and PX.

Graham One of port's greatest names, belonging to SYMINGTON FAMILY ESTATES. V.gd range from Six Grapes RESERVE RUBY, LBV and TAWNY (RESERVE) to excellent yr-aged TAWNIES and some of richest, sweetest VINTAGE PORTS 63 66 70' 75 77' 80 83' 85' 91' 94 97 00' 03' 07'. V.gd single-QUINTA vintage: dos Malvedos.

Gran Cruz The single biggest port brand. Mostly light, inexpensive TAWNIES. New ROSÉ PORT. A new multimedia visitor centre is planned in Gaia.

Grupo Estévez Family business with extensive interests in JEREZ and SANLÚCAR. See LA GUITA, MARQUÉS DEL REAL TESORO, VALDESPINO.

Guita, La ★→★★★ *Esp fine* manzanilla, produced by Hijos de Rainero Pérez Marín in SANLÚCAR, which also owns Gil Luque label. Both brands acquired by GRUPO ESTÉVEZ, owner of VALDESPINO, among others.

Gutiérrez Colosía ★→★★★ Family-owned and run former ALMACENISTA on the Guadalete R. in EL PUERTO DE SANTA MARÍA. Excellent old palo cortado.

Harvey's ★→★★★ Major sherry producer, tossed about in the corporate storms. Now resides with Beam Global. Famed for Bristol Cream (medium-sweet), the icon of creams; the VOS and VORS wines reveal the top quality of its old SOLERAS.

Henriques, Justino Largest Madeira shipper belonging, along with GRAN CRUZ ports, to Martiniquaise. Gd 10-yr-old, fruity, forward Tinta Negra Mole Colheita (1995, 1996), Terrantez Old Reserve NV, Vintage eg. 1934 Verdelho, 1978 Terrantez.

Henriques & Henriques Independent Madeira shipper and, unusually, v'yd owner. Rich, well-structured wines. Outstanding 10- and 15-yr-olds; v. fine RESERVES, vintage and SOLERA wines, inc Sercial 1964, Terrantez 1976, Malvasia 1954, Bual 1954, 1980, Century Malmsey-Solera 1900. Innovative extra-dry apéritif Monte Seco, v.gd "Single Harvest" COLHEITAS: Tinta Negra Mole 1998 and Boal 2000.

Herederos de Argüeso ★★→★★★ Manzanilla specialist in SANLÚCAR with v.gd *San León and San León Reserva*, and youthful Las Medallas; and the desirable VOS Amontillado Viejo.

Hidalgo, La Gitana ★★★→★★★★ Old (1792) family sherry firm in SANLÚCAR fronted by the indefatigable Javier Hidalgo, with flagship *Manzanilla La*

Gitana. The intense and savoury single-v'yd aged Pastrana Manzanilla Pasada is in impressive contrast to today's fashion for ultra-pale youthful manzanilla. Also fine oloroso, lovely palo cortado and treacly PX.

Jerez de la Frontera Centre of sherry industry, between Cádiz and Seville. "Sherry" is a corruption of the name, pronounced "hereth". In French, Xérès.

Jordões, Casal dos Organic port producers: decent LBV and vintage wines.

Kopke The oldest port house, founded in 1638. Now belongs to BARROS ALMEIDA. Mostly early maturing, fair-quality vintage wines, but some v.gd (83 85 87 89 91 94 97 00 03 04 05' 07); v.fine 40-yr-old TAWNY and COLHEITAS (66 80' 87 89).

Krohn Port shipper; gd 20- and 30-yr-old TAWNY and excellent COLHEITAS (61' 64 68 78 82 83' 91), some dating back to 1800s.

Lagar Shallow granite "paddling pool" in which port and now Madeira (see BARBEITO) is trodden by foot – or, these days, increasingly by robot.

LBV (Late Bottled Vintage) Port from a single year kept in wood for twice as long as VINTAGE PORT (about 5 yrs) so ready to drink on release; much larger volumes, robustly fruity but much less powerful and complex than vintage. No need to decant, except for unfiltered wines that can age for 10 yrs or more and are worth seeking out (CHURCHILL, FERREIRA, NIEPOORT, QUINTA DO NOVAL, SMITH WOODHOUSE, WARRE).

Leacock Volume label of the MADEIRA WINE COMPANY; sweeter house style. Main brand is St John, popular in Scandinavia. Older vintages include 1927, 1963 Sercial, 1914 Bual and Solera 1808 and 1860.

Lustau ★★→★★★★ Based in JEREZ, this sherry house continues to gather awards for its *extensive range of good wines*. Pioneering shipper of excellent ALMACENISTA sherries, inc Manzanilla Amontillado Jurado, Palo Cortado Vides. Other v.gd sherries include East India Solera, Moscatel Emilín. Latest top-quality release is sweet oloroso Añada 1990. Owned by the Caballero group.

Madeira Wine Company Formed in 1913 by two firms as the Madeira Wine Association, subsequently to include all 26 British Madeira firms, though today focused on BLANDY, COSSART GORDON, LEACOCK and MILES. Now run by a partnership of the BLANDY family and SYMINGTON FAMILY ESTATES. Though cellared together, wines preserve individual house styles; BLANDY and COSSART GORDON lead the pack. All except basic wines CANTEIRO-aged.

Malmsey (or Malvasia) The sweetest and richest of traditional Madeira grape varieties; dark-amber and honeyed, yet with Madeira's unique sharp tang.

Marqués del Real Tesoro ★ Fine Tío Mateo FINO. Part of GRUPO ESTÉVEZ.

Martinez Gassiot Port firm now owned by SYMINGTON FAMILY ESTATES, known esp for excellent rich and pungent Director 20-yr-old Tawny. Gd-value, age-worthy vintages in drier, traditional style: 63 67 70 75 82 85 87 91 94 97 00 03 07.

Miles Madeira shipper, part of the MADEIRA WINE COMPANY. Mostly basic wines in lighter style for export; niche premium range for home market.

Montecristo Mont-M Brand of popular MONTILLAS by Compañía Vinícola del Sur.

Montilla-Moriles Mont-M DO near Córdoba. Once known simply for its cheaper versions of sherry styles, Montilla owes its growing reputation to the quality of its sun-dried super-sweet PX grapes. Top producers: ALVEAR, GRACIA HERMANOS, PÉREZ BARQUERO, BODEGAS TORO ALBALÁ. Important source for PX for use in DO JEREZ, to make up for shortfall.

Niepoort ★★★ Small family-run port house; sensational table wines. Consistently fine vintage (63 66 70' 75 77 78 80 82 83 87 91 92 94 97 00' 03 05' 07), inc unique *garrafeira* (aged in demijohns), Broadbent, new single-v'yd Pisca and Secundum, designed for earlier drinking. Exceptional TAWNIES and COLHEITAS. Benchmark Dry White joined by new 10-yr-old white.

Noval, Quinta do French-owned (AXA) historic port house. Intensely fruity, structured, elegant VINTAGE PORT; around 2.5 ha of ungrafted vines make small quantity of Nacional – extraordinarily dark, full, velvety, slow-maturing, though not always made in classic declared yrs (eg. 62' 80 82 85 87). Also v.gd age-dated TAWNY and gd COLHEITAS. Vintages: 62 63 66 67 70 75 78 82 85 87 91 94' 95 97' 00' 03' 04 07'. Second vintage label: Silval. Also v.gd LBV.

Offley Brand name belonging to Sogrape. Gd, accessible, fruity range, inc Duke of Oporto volume label, Baron de Forrester age-dated TAWNY and Boa Vista Vintage: 63 66 67 70 72 75 77 80 82 83 85 87 89 94 95 97 00' 03 07. New ROSÉ PORT.

Osborne ★→★★★★ EL PUERTO DE SANTA MARÍA wine business with extensive interests in sherry, tables wines and quality port. Its instantly recognizable bull logo dots the Spanish countryside. Sherries include Fino Quinta, Coquinero Fino Amontillado. Produces table wines in Tierra de Cádiz, VDT Castilla, Rioja, Rueda and Ribera del Duero. Also port: declared VINTAGE PORTS in 95 97 00' 03' 07. (Fladgate making ports since 2005). Owned by the Caballero group, which now also owns DOMECQ.

Paternina, Federico ★★→★★★★ Marcos Eguizabal from Rioja, owner of the historic Banda Azul producer, acquired the sherry firm Díez-Mérito, retaining three VORS wines for his Paternina label, the excellent and unique *Fino Imperial*, Victoria Regina Oloroso and Vieja Solera PX.

Pereira d'Oliveira Vinhos Family-owned Madeira company. Gd basic range, COLHEITAS (Boal 1983, 1988, Malvasia 1987, Terrantez 1988) and substantial stock of fine old vintages (labelled RESERVA) bottled on demand from cask dating back to 1850 (1937, 1971 Sercial, 1966 Verdelho, 1908 and 1968 Bual).

Pérez Barquero ★★→★★★ Mont-M One of the producers leading the resurgence of MONTILLA PX. Fine Gran Barquero Fino, Amontillado and Oloroso; v. fine La Cañada PX.

Pilar Plá/El Maestro Sierra ★→★★★ Owned by JEREZ's grandest dame Pilar Plá. Wines individual but inconsistent; gd fino and some gd-value at medium ages, esp amontillado.

Poças Family-run Portuguese port firm; v.gd TAWNIES and COLHEITAS (67' 86 94). Gd LBV and recent vintages (97 00' 03 04 05' 07). Single-QUINTA from Quinta de Santa Bárbara. Gd table wines, too.

Portal, Quinta do Family-owned port firm, also making v.gd wine. Ex-SANDEMAN v'yds in Pinhão produce gd LBV and VINTAGE PORT; also specializes in v.gd fortified Moscatel, both VINTAGE and NV.

Puerto de Santa María, El The former port of sherry, one of the three towns forming the "Sherry Triangle". Production now in serious decline; remaining bodegas include former ALMACENISTA, GUTIÉRREZ COLOSÍA, OSBORNE and TERRY.

Quarles Harris One of the oldest port houses, since 1680, now owned by SYMINGTON FAMILY ESTATES. Mellow, well-balanced vintages, often v.gd value: 63 66 70 75 77 80 83 85 91 94 97 00' 03 07.

Quevedo New port brand courting a 30-something audience via social media, inc a blog, Twitter and interactive bottle labels. The untraditional approach extends to a ROSÉ PORT and talk of single-varietal ports, not yet legal; not an insurmountable problem.

Quinta Portuguese for "estate", traditionally denotes VINTAGE PORTS from shipper's single v'yds; declared in gd but not exceptional yrs. An increasing number make port from top vintages. Rising stars include Passadouro, Romaneira, Tedo, Whytingham's Vale Meão, Wine & Soul's Pintas.

Ramos Pinto Dynamic port house owned by Champagne house Louis Roederer; gd wines, too. Outstanding single-QUINTA (de Ervamoira) and TAWNIES (de Ervamoira and do Bom Retiro). Rich, sweet, generally early-maturing vintages. Exceptional celebratory 100-yr-old tawny in 2009.

Reserve/Reserva Premium ports, mostly reserve RUBY but some reserve TAWNY, bottled without a vintage date or age indication but better than basic style.

Rey Fernando de Castilla ★★→★★★★ Small bodega with good sherries and brandies. Excellent Antique amontillado, oloroso and PX, which qualify as age-dated, though not so labelled; fino less impressive.

Roriz, Quinta de Historic estate bought by SYMINGTON FAMILY ESTATES in 2009. Good ports: 99 00' 01 02 03' 04 05 06 07.

Rosa, Quinta de la V.gd single-QUINTA port from the Bergqvist family also making gd wines using traditional methods. Look for 94 95 00 03' 04 05' 07 vintages.

Rosé port Officially recognized in 2009, prompted by CROFT's pioneering Pink. "Pink" now trademarked by Croft, which recommends serving it chilled, on ice or in a cocktail.

Royal Oporto Real Companhia Velha's main port brand. Gd TAWNIES, COLHEITAS (53' 77) and recent VINTAGE PORTS, foot-trodden since 1997. New ROSÉ PORT.

Rozès Port shipper owned by Champagne house Vranken alongside São Pedro das Aguias. Popular in France. DOURO Superior single-QUINTA do Grifo, acquired 2004, shows promise. New ROSÉ PORT.

Ruby Youngest, cheapest port style: simple, sweet, red; best labelled RESERVE.

Ruiz-Mateos, Zoilo Influential family business in JEREZ. Original holding company Rumasa had its JEREZ bodegas expropriated by the state in 1983. Relaunched Nueva ("new") Rumasa now owns GARVEY. Latest acquisitions include v'yds and wines of SANDEMAN, VALDIVIA and a bodega in SANLÚCAR.

Sanchez Romate ★★→★★★ Family firm in JEREZ since 1781. Best-known in Spanish-speaking world, esp for brandy Cardenal Mendoza. Gd sherry: oloroso La Sacristía de Romate, PX Duquesa, fine, nutty amontillado NPU.

Sandeman Jerez ★→★★★ Founder George Sandeman set up twin establishments in Oporto and JEREZ in 1790. Gd sherries include Royal Esmeralda VOS Amontillado and *Royal Ambrosante VOS* Oloroso and PX. V'yds, stocks, bodega now owned by Nueva Rumasa.

Sandeman Port Lightest of SOGRAPE brands with gd aged TAWNIES, esp 20-yr-old. Vintage elegant but until recently patchy; new winery at Quinta do Seixo has produced the goods in 2007 (63 66 70 75 77 94 97 00 03 07'). Second label: seductive Vau Vintage (97' 99 00).

Sanlúcar de Barrameda One of the three towns of the "Sherry Triangle" at the mouth of the Guadalquivír. Strong maritime influence encourages FLOR growth, creating distinct manzanilla character.

Santa Eufemia, Quinta de Family port estate with v.gd old TAWNIES. Stunning 10-, 20- and 30-yr-old aged WHITE PORTS in 50cl bottles.

Sercial Madeira grape for the driest of the island's wines – supreme apéritif.

Silva, C da Port shipper. Mostly inexpensive RUBIES and TAWNIES, but gd aged TAWNIES and COLHEITAS (1952) under Dalva label.

Smith Woodhouse Port firm founded in 1784. Now firmly focused on limited-production high-quality port: good unfiltered LBV and some v. fine vintages: 63 66 70 75 77' 80 83 85 91 94 97 00' 03 07. Occasional single-estate wines from QUINTA da Madelena.

Solera System used in ageing sherry and, less commonly now, Madeira. Consists of topping up progressively more mature barrels with slightly younger wine up of same sort from next stage, or *criadera*. The object is continuity in final wine, maintaining vigour of FLOR in fino and manzanilla soleras.

Symington Family Estates ★★→★★★★ Long-established, forward-looking family-run port shippers and partner in the MADEIRA WINE COMPANY. Easily the DOURO's largest vineyard owner with 25 QUINTAS. Spectacular portfolio includes DOW, GOULD CAMPBELL, GRAHAM, MARTINEZ GASSIOT, QUARLES HARRIS, QUINTA DE RORIZ, SMITH WOODHOUSE, VÉSUVIO and WARRE; for table wine, Altano, CHRYSEIA, DOW and VÉSUVIO marques. In 2009 acclaimed senior winemaker Peter "The Nose" Symington retired after 45 vintages.

Tawny Style of port that implies ageing in wood (hence tawny in colour), though many basic tawnies are little more than attenuated RUBIES. Look for wines with an indication of age: 10-, 20-, 30-, 40-yr-old or RESERVE.

Taylor, Fladgate & Yeatman (Taylor's) ★★→★★★★ One of the best-known port shippers, highly rated for rich, long-lived VINTAGE PORTS (63 66 70 75 77' 80 83 85 92' 94 97 00' 03' 07'). Member of the Fladgate Partnership alongside CROFT and FONSECA GUIMARAENS. V.gd range, inc RESERVE, LBV and aged TAWNIES. QUINTAS Vargellas and Terra Feita produce impressive single-QUINTA VINTAGE PORT, esp rare Vargellas Vinha Velha (95, 97, 00, 04 07') from 70-plus-yr-old vines.

Terry, S A ★→★★ Sherry bodega dominating the entrance to EL PUERTO DE SANTA MARÍA; part of Beam Brands.

Toro Albalá, Bodegas Mont-M One of the top MONTILLA producers; v. fine Don PX.

Tradición ★★★ One of the new wave of sherry bodegas focusing exclusively upon small quantities of VOS and VORS; no fino made. Consistently gd amontillado, palo cortado and oloroso, from an art-filled cellar in back streets of JEREZ.

Valdespino ★→★★★★★ Famous JEREZ bodega producing *Inocente Fino* from the esteemed Macharnudo v'yd. Notably Inocente is fermented in American oak not stainless steel, and is aged longer than usual in a SOLERA that has ten stages, or *criaderas*. Tío Diego is terrific dry amontillado; also vibrant, youthful SOLERA 1842 Oloroso VOS; remarkable, aged Toneles Moscatel.

Valdivia ★★→★★★ One of newer sherry bodegas. V.gd 15-yr-old Sacromonte Amontillado and Oloroso. The bodega, owned by the RUIZ-MATEOS family until 1983, was bought back by its holding company in 2008.

Vale D Maria, Quinta do Gd-value, beautifully elegant, forward single-QUINTA VINTAGE PORT (00 01 02 03 05 07) and gd unfiltered LBV.

Vallegre Portuguese family owned port house. Vista Alegre until 1998, renamed after both its top QUINTAS, Vista Alegre and Valle Longo. V.gd unfiltered LBV.

Ventozelo, Quinta de Huge, beautifully situated estate recently acquired by Real Companhia Velha. Gd-value single-QUINTA VINTAGE PORTS.

Verdelho Traditional Madeira grape for medium-dry wines; pungent but without the austerity of SERCIAL. Increasing in popularity for table wines.

Vesúvio, Quinta do 19th-century estate restored to former glory by SYMINGTON FAMILY ESTATES, which has doubled v'yd area. VINTAGE PORT: 91 92 94 95' 96' 97 98 99 00' 01 03' 04 05' 06 07'. Exceptional 2007 vintage sees new vintage port Capela, and first table wine.

Vila Nova de Gaia City on the south side of the river DOURO from Oporto, where major port shippers traditionally mature their wines in lodges.

Vintage port Classic vintages are the best wines declared in exceptional yrs by shippers between 1 Jan and 30 Sept in the second yr after vintage. Bottled without filtration after 2 yrs in wood, the wine matures v. slowly in bottle throwing a crust or deposit – always decant. Modern vintages broachable earlier but best will last more than 50 yrs. Single-QUINTA vintage ports also drinking earlier. As for the old stuff, in 2009, 1,000 bottles of 200-yr-old port salvaged off the coast of Brazil were pronounced suitable for consumption.

Warre Oldest of British port shippers (since 1670); owned by SYMINGTON FAMILY ESTATES since 1905. Fine, elegant, long-maturing vintage wines, gd RESERVE, vintage character (Warrior), excellent unfiltered, bottle-matured LBV, 10- and 20-yr-old TAWNY Otima. Single-QUINTA VINTAGE from Quinta da Cavadinha. Vintages: 63 66 70' 75 77' 80 83 85 91 94 97 00' 03 07'.

White port Port made with white grapes, occasionally sweet (*lagrima*) but mostly off-dry apéritif styles (driest labelled Dry), with tonic and fresh mint. Since 2006, age-designated 10-, 20-, 30-, or 40-yr-old styles are raising the bar.

Williams & Humbert ★→★★★★★ Traditional sherry bodega. Dry Sack (amontillado) is bestseller. V.gd old wines: *Dos Cortados PC*, Solera Especial VOS PC.

Switzerland

More heavily shaded areas are the wine-growing regions

Swiss wine is worth investigating. All over Europe, growers are experimenting with old indigenous varieties, and Switzerland has some superb ones: Heida, Humagne *blanche*, Petite Arvine, Cornalin and Humagne *rouge*. On those mountain slopes, Chasselas, Switzerland's core vine, develops a subtle minerality undreamt of anywhere else. It also reflects its terroir, so styles vary. There are the new varieties being tried, such as Mara, Cabernet Dorsa, or Solaris. Mara is red, dense and soft, and suited to warmish spots in the south; Cabernet Dorsa is Cabernet Sauvignon x Dornfelder – frost-resistant and quite complex; Solaris is exotic-tasting white.

Recent vintages

2009 One of the best of recent years.

2008 Difficult year with lots of rain. Quality okay but not tops.

2007 Reds are less opulent than 2006. Whites are superb.

2006 Very promising and being compared to 2005.

2005 Low in quantity but high in quality.

Aargau 06 07 08 Swiss-German canton (393 ha) for fragrant Müller-Thurgau, fruity BLAUBURGUNDER. Best producer: WEINGUT ZUM STERNEN.

Aigle Vaud r w ★★ →★★★ Well-known for elegant whites and supple reds.

Aligoté White grape becoming more popular in the GENEVA area.

Amigne Traditional VALAIS white grape, esp of VÉTROZ. Total planted: 39 ha. Full-bodied, tasty, often sweet. Best: ANDRÉ FONTANNAZ ★★ 06 07' 08 or JEAN-RENÉ GERMANIER. Quality rating based on residual sugar (RS): one bee means 0–8 g/l RS, two bees mean 9–25g/l RS, three bees mean over 25 g/l RS.

AOC Compulsory since Jan 1, 2008, for all regions; each region has different rules.

Arvine Old VALAIS white grape (also Petite Arvine): dry and sweet, elegant, long-lasting wines with salty finish. 138 ha planted. Producers: CHAPPAZ, Benoît Dorsaz, SIMON MAYE & FILS, ROUVINEZ VINS, PROVINS.

Auvernier Neuchâtel r p w ★★→★★★ Old wine village on Lake NEUCHÂTEL and biggest wine-growing commune of the canton.

Bachtobel, Schlossgut ★★★→★★★★ 04 05 06' 07' V. fine estate in Weinfelden run by Hans-Ulrich Kellring until his death in 2008. V.gd PINOT N, RIES and Sauv Bl.

Badoux, Henri Aigle w ★★ Big producer of commercial wines. Try AIGLE les Murailles (classic lizard label) and Yvorne Petit Vignoble. New release: Red Lizard Wine.

Basel Second-largest Swiss town and canton. Best producers: Jauslin Weine, Weingut Fibl, Domaine Nussbaumer und Buess Weinbau.

Bern Capital and canton. V'yds in west (BIELERSEE: CHASSELAS, PINOT N, white SPÉCIALITÉS) and east (Thunersee: BLAUBURGUNDER, Müller-Thurgau); 262 ha.

Bielersee r p w ★→★★★ 06 07 08 Wine region on northern shore of the Bielersee (dry, light CHASSELAS, PINOT N and SPÉCIALITÉS such as Viognier, Sauv Bl and Malbec). Best producers: Wonderful PINOT N (esp Der Mattmann), Martin Hubacher, Lukas Hasler.

Blauburgunder German name for PINOT N; aka Clevner. Rosé to heavily oaked reds. Switzerland's main red variety. Limited editions are the trend: Pure from SALGESCH, Pinot R(h)ein from Maienfeld or Tête de Cru Staatskellerei from ZÜRICH.

Blauburgunderland Successful promotion body for the wines of SCHAFFHAUSEN.

Bovard, Louis Lavaux w ★★★ Classical interpretation of CHASSELAS. Family business for ten generations.

Bündner Herrschaft Grisons r p w ★★→★★★ Best German-Swiss region includes top villages: Fläsch, Jenins, Maienfeld, Malans. BLAUBURGUNDER ripens esp well due to warm Föhn wind, cask-aged v.gd. Also Chard, Müller-Thurgau, COMPLETER. Best: GANTENBEIN ★★★, Davaz ★★, FROMM ★★★ 05' 06 07' 08. Switzerland's best BLAUBURGUNDER is from here.

Chablais Vaud r w ★★→★★★★ Wine region on right bank of Rhône and upper end of Lake GENEVA, includes villages AIGLE, Bex, Ollon, Villeneuve, YVORNE.

Champagne The Swiss village continues to fight against the French wine-growing area that forbids everybody to use the name "Champagne" on the label. Since 2004 the Swiss wine-growers have been forbidden to use their village name.

Chanton, Josef-Marie and Mario ★★★ *Terrific Valais* spécialités: HEIDA, LAFNETSCHA, Himbertscha, Hibou, Resi, Gwäss.

Chappaz ★★★ Marie-Thérèse Chappaz of FULLY is the queen of sweet wine. Outstanding PETITE ARVINE Grain Noble.

Chasselas (Gutedel in Germany) Main white variety. Neutral flavour, takes on local character: elegant (GENEVA); refined, full (VAUD); exotic, racy (VALAIS); *pétillant* (lakes Bienne, NEUCHÂTEL, Murtensee). Only east of BASEL. FENDANT in VALAIS. Makes almost a third of Swiss wines but increasingly replaced. Best: Blaise Duboux, Philippe Gex, Raymont PACCOT, PROVINS. Producers tend to avoid malolactic fermentation, conserving acidity, and now use oak barrels.

Château Maison Blanche Yvorne w ★★ Best in the area, making one CHASSELAS.

Cicero Weinbau Zizers w r ★★★ Thomas Mattmann represents the new generation in the GRISONS. Wonderful PINOT N (esp Der Mattmann) and Sauv Bl.

Completer Native white grape, mostly used in GRISONS, making aromatic wines with high acidity. ("Complet" was a monk's final daily prayer, or "nightcap".) Best: Adolf Boner, Malans ★★, VOLG WEINKELLEREIEN.

Cornalin ★★→★★★ 05' 06 07 08 Local VALAIS SPÉCIALITÉ that has become more popular since production increased; dark, spicy, v. strong red. Best: JEAN-RENÉ GERMANIER (★★), Denis MERCIER, PROVINS. Oldest living vine in Switzerland is a Cornalin plant in Leuk, VALAIS, from 1798 (www.vitisantiqua1798.ch).

Côte, la Vaud r p w ★→★★★ Largest VAUD wine area between LAUSANNE and GENEVA.

Traditional whites with elegant finesse; fruity, harmonious reds. Esp from MONT-SUR-ROLLE, Vinzel, Luins, FÉCHY, MORGES, etc.

Cruchon, Henri Echichens w r ★★★ Biodynamic producer. Wonderful CHASSELAS, Sauv Bl, GAMARET and GAMAY.

Dézaley Vaud w (r) ★★→★★★ Celebrated LAVAUX v'yd on slopes above Lake GENEVA. Potent CHASSELAS, develops esp after ageing.

Dôle Valais r ★★→★★★ Appellation for PINOT N, often blended with GAMAY and other reds from the VALAIS: full, supple, often v.gd. Lightly pink Dôle Blanche is pressed straight after harvest. Try SIMON MAYE ET FILS.

Domaine la Colombe Féchy w ★★★★ Family company; one of the best producers of resh, elegant, minerally CHASSELAS; also try Réserve Pinot Gr.

Domaine Les Hutins Dardagny w r ★★★ Interesting Sauv Bl, GAMAY, Cab Sauv, PINOT N.

Epesses Vaud w (r) ★→★★★ 06 07' 08 LAVAUX AOC: supple, full-bodied whites.

Ermitage Alias Marsanne; a VALAIS SPÉCIALITÉ. Concentrated, full-bodied dry white, sometimes with residual sugar. Best: Dom Cornulus, Philippoz Frères.

Favré, Rene Valais w r ★★★ Based in St. Pierre de Clages. Esp PETITE ARVINE, PINOT N.

Féchy Vaud w →★★★ Famous appellation of LA CÔTE, esp elegant whites. DYA.

Federweisser German-Swiss name for white wine from BLAUBURGUNDER.

Fendant Valais w ★→★★★ VALAIS appellation for CHASSELAS. The ideal wine for Swiss cheese dishes such as fondue or raclette. PROVINS, Les Fils de Charles Favre, Antoine & Christophe Bétrisey, MAURICE ZUFFEREY.

Flétri/Mi-flétri Late-harvested grapes for sweet/slightly sweet wine.

Fontannaz, André Vétroz w ★★★ Nobody understands the AMIGNE DE VÉTROZ grape better.

Fribourg Smallest French-Swiss wine canton (115 ha, near Jura).

Fromm ★★★ 04 05' 06 07' Malans grower. Sold his second estate in New Zealand and focuses on outstanding BLAUBURGUNDER and Chard wines in GRISONS.

Fully Valais r w ★★→★★★ Village near Martigny: excellent ERMITAGE and GAMAY. Best producer: Marie-Thérèse CHAPPAZ ★★→★★★ 06 07' 08.

Gamaret Red. Resistant variety created in 1970; GAMAY x Reichensteiner.

Gamay Beaujolais grape; abounds in French cantons. Mainly thin wine used in blends (SALVAGNIN, DÔLE) and also more and more as a single variety. Try: Le Satyre Gamay from Noémie & Noé Graff.

Gantenbein, Daniel & Martha 05' 06 07 08 Most famous growers in GRISONS. Top PINOT N from DRC clones (Burgundy), RIES with clones from Loosen (Mosel).

Garanoir Grape: twin of GAMARET. Found all over Switzerland, except in TICINO.

Geneva Capital, and French-Swiss wine canton; 3rd-largest (1,297 ha). Key areas: Mandement, Entre Arve et Rhône, Entre Arve et Lac. Mostly CHASSELAS, GAMAY. Also GAMARET, Chard, PINOT N, Muscat and gd ALIGOTÉ. Best: Jean-Michel NOVELLE ★★★; interesting: Jacques Tatasciere, Domaine de la Rochette ★★.

Germanier, Jean-René VÉTROZ winemaker; Cayas (100% Syrah) ★★★ 01 02 03' 04 05' 06; Mitis (sweet) ★★★ 01' 02 03 04 05' 06. Also a pure CORNALIN 05' 06 and the PINOT N Clos du Four ★★★. Look out for new GAMAY Grand Cru.

Glacier, Vin du (Gletscherwein) Fabled oxidized, wooded white from rare Rèze grape of Val d'Anniviers. Almost impossible to find on sale. Keep looking.

Grain Noble ConfidenCiel Quality label for top Swiss sweet wines.

Grillette Domaine Cressier w r ★★★Try Viognier, Sauv Bl (new single-v'yd wines).

Grisons (Graubünden) Mtn canton, mainly German/Swiss (BÜNDNER HERRSCHAFT, Churer Rheintal; esp BLAUBURGUNDER), part S of Alps (Misox, esp MERLOT). PINOT N king. Best: Davaz, FROMM, GANTENBEIN, von Tscharner, Peter Wegelin.

Grünenfelder, Irene Jenins r ★★★ Only three wines but they're outstanding.

Heida (Païen) Old VALAIS white grape (Jura's Savagnin) for country wine of upper VALAIS (VISPERTERMINEN v'yds at 1,000+ m). Full-bodied wine with high acidity.

Best: JOSEF-MARIE CHANTON ★★ 06 07' 08. Try Heida from PROVINS, Imesch Vins, St Jodernkellerei, ROUVINEZ VINS.

HuberVini Ticino r ★★★ 05' 06 07' MERLOT Montagna Magica is superb and inspiring for other growers in TICINO.

Humagne Strong native white grape (VALAIS SPÉCIALITÉ), older than CHASSELAS. Humagne *rouge* is not related to it but also common in the VALAIS. Esp from Chamoson, Leytron, Martigny.

Johannisberg Synonym for Sylvaner in the VALAIS.

Lafnetscha Indigenous grape variety, apparently the result of an alliance between COMPLETER and HUMAGNE Blanche.

Lausanne Capital of VAUD. No longer with v'yds in town area, but long-time owner of classics: Abbaye de Mont, Château Rochefort (LA CÔTE); Clos des Moines, Clos des Abbayes, Domaine de Burignon (LAVAUX).

Lavaux Vaud w (r) ★→★★★ Now a UNESCO world heritage site: v'yd terraces stretch 30 km along the south-facing north shore of Lake GENEVA from Château de Chillon to the eastern outskirts of LAUSANNE. Main grape: CHASSELAS. Wines named for the villages: Lutry, ST-SAPHORIN, Ollon, EPESSES and more.

Mathier, Adrian Salgesch w r ★★★★ Interesting PINOT N and Marsanne.

Mauler ★★→★★★ V.gd name for sparkling in NEUCHÂTEL, esp Cuvée Exellence.

Maye, Simon et Fils w r ★★★ VALAIS producer in St. Pierre de Clages; interesting FENDANT, Païen, PINOT N and Syrah.

Mercier ★★★ 01 02 03' 04 05' 06 07 Growers in SIERRE with outstanding CORNALIN.

Merlot Brought to the TICINO in 1907 by the scientist Alderige Fantuzzi (after phylloxera): soft to v. powerful wines. Also used with Cab Sauv. Best: Castello Luigi, Conte di Luna, Werner Stucky, Luigi ZANINI, Tenimento dell'Ör.

Mont-sur-Rolle Vaud w (r) ★★ DYA Important appellation within LA CÔTE.

Morges Vaud r p w ★→★★ DYA Largest LA CÔTE/VAUD AOC: CHASSELAS, fruity reds.

Neuchâtel City and canton; 600 ha from Lake Neuchâtel to BIELERSEE. CHASSELAS: fragrant, lively (*sur lie*, sparkling). Gd OEIL DE PERDRIX, PINOT GR, Chard. Try: Château Souaillon.

Non Filtré SPÉCIALITÉ available in springtime from NEUCHÂTEL, from CHASSELAS.

Nostrano Word meaning "ours", applied to red wine of TICINO, made from native and Italian grapes (Bondola, Freisa, Bonarda, etc.).

Novelle ★★★→★★★★ 05' 06 07 GENEVA-based. V.gd Sauv Bl, Petit Manseng, GAMAY.

Oeil de Perdrix PINOT N rosé. DYA esp NEUCHÂTEL'S; name can be used anywhere.

Paccot ★★★ 06 07' 08 FÉCHY. Look here for excellent CHASSELAS, esp Le Brez.

Petite Arvine See ARVINE.

Pinot Blanc (Weissburgunder) Booming variety producing full-bodied, elegant wines. Best: Bad Osterfingen 07' 08.

Pinot Gris (Malvoisie) Dry, residually sweet whites. V. fine late-harvest in VALAIS.

Pinot Noir (Blauburgunder) See BLAUBURGUNDER Try: GANTENBEIN; Davaz (Fläsch); Kesselring (Ottoberg); Pircher (Eglisau); Baumann (Oberhallau); Meier (Kloster Sion); Christian Obrecht (Jenins) ★★★ 05' 06 07' 08.

Provins Biggest co-op in the VALAIS with a large range. Outstanding for Maître de Chais and Crus des Domaines labels, and interesting Les Titans range.

Rahm, Weinkellereien Hallau w r ★★ Big producer of commercial wines.

Räuschling Old white ZÜRICH grape; discreet fruit and elegant acidity. Try: Hermann SCHWARZENBACH, Meilen.

Riesling (Petit Rhin) Mainly in the VALAIS. Try Kesselring (Ottoberg) 07 08.

Riesling-Sylvaner Old name for Müller-Thurgau. Some elegant wines with flowery aroma and some acidity. Best producers: Daniel Marugg, Andrea Davaz, Baumann (Oberhallau) ★★ 07' 08.

Roh, Serge Vétroz w ★★★ Leading VALAIS producer with excellent FENDANT, PETITE ARVINE. Grand Cru de Vétroz range especially worth seeking out.

Rouvinez Vins Sierre w r ★★★ Try Château Lichten, CORNALIN from Montibeux, La Trémaille. Also owns Caves Orsta.

St-Gallen Eastern wine canton (218 ha). Esp for BLAUBURGUNDER, Müller-Thurgau, SPÉCIALITÉS. Try: Weingut Schmidheiny, Weingut Gonzen.

St-Saphorin Vaud w (r) ★★→★★★ 07' 08 Famous LAVAUX AOC for fine light whites.

Salgesch Important wine village in the upper VALAIS. Try ADRIAN MATHIER, Cave du Rhodan or Caves Fernand Cina.

Salvagnin Vaud r ★→★★ 07' 08 GAMAY and/or PINOT N appellation.

Schaffhausen German-Swiss canton/wine town on the Rhine. BLAUBURGUNDER; also Müller-Thurgau and SPÉCIALITÉS. Best: Baumann, Bad Osterfingen ★★. The latest trend is reds and whites with plenty of residual sugar.

Schenk Europe-wide wine giant, founded and based in Rolle (VAUD). Owns firms in France (Burgundy and Bordeaux), Germany, Italy and Spain.

Schwarzenbach Weinbau Meilen w ★★★ Dry, crisp whites, RÄUSCHLING, Kerner, RIES x Sylvaner. New: Räuschling R3 2008, from three old Räuschling clones.

Sierre Valais r w ★★→★★★ Sunny resort and famous wine town. Known for FENDANT, PINOT N, ERMITAGE, Malvoisie. V.gd DÔLE. Visit Château de Villa – wine museum and *vinotheque* with largest VALAIS wine collection.

Sion Valais r w ★★→★★★ Capital/wine centre of VALAIS. Esp FENDANT de Sion.

Spécialités (Spezialitäten) Wines of unusual grapes: vanishing local Gwäss, Himbertscha, Roter Eyholzer, Bondola, etc., ARVINE and AMIGNE, or modish Chenin Bl, Sauv Bl, Cab Sauv, Syrah. Of 47 VALAIS varieties, 43 are SPÉCIALITÉS. New varieties: Solaris, Vidal, Johanitter or Cabernet Dorsat found in north.

Sternen, Weingut zum Würenlingen r ★★★ V. interesting interpretation of PINOT N. Try Kloster Sion PINOT N.

Thurgau German-Swiss canton beside Lake Bodensee (265 ha). Wines from Thur Valley: south shore of the Untersee. Typical: BLAUBURGUNDER, also gd Müller-Thurgau. SPÉCIALITÉS include Kerner, PINOT GR, Regent. Best producer: Hans Ulrich Kesselring, died in 2008.

Ticino Italian-speaking southern Switzerland (with Misox), growing mainly MERLOT (gd from mountainous Sopraceneri region) and SPÉCIALITÉS. Try Cab Sauv (oaked Bordeaux style), Sauv Bl, Sem, Chard, MERLOT white and rosé (1,065 ha). Best producers: Guido Brivio, Daniel Huber, Adriano Kaufmann, Werner Stucky, Luigi ZANINI, Christian Zündel. All ★★★ 05' 06 07' 08.

Valais (Wallis) Rhône Valley from German-speaking upper Valais to French lower Valais. Largest most varied and exciting wine canton (30% of Swiss wine). Wide range: 47 grape varieties, plus many SPÉCIALITÉS; FLÉTRI/MI-FLÉTRI wines.

Vaud (Waadt) French Switzerland's 2nd-largest wine canton; stronghold of CHABLAIS, LA CÔTE, LAVAUX, Bonvillars, Côtes de l'Orbe, VULLY, CHASSELAS.

Vétroz Valais r w ★★→★★★ Top village near SION, esp famous for AMIGNE.

Vevey-Montreux Vaud r w ★★ Up-and-coming appellation of LAVAUX. Famous wine festival held about every 30 yrs.

Visperterminen Valais w (r) ★→★★ Upper VALAIS v'yds, esp for SPÉCIALITÉS. The highest v'yds in Europe (at 1,000+ m). Try Stoffel Weine.

Volg Weinkellereien Winterthur w r ★★→★★★ Co-op that focuses on local terroirs and SPÉCIALITÉS. Try COMPLETER or different PINOT N.

Vully Vaud w (r) ★→★★ Refreshing white from Lake Murten/FRIBOURG area.

Yvorne Vaud (r) ★★ 04 05 Top CHABLAIS AOC for strong, fragrant wines.

Zanini ★★★→★★★★ 05' 06 07' Top TICINO name with focus on MERLOT. Tops are Castello Luigi and Vinattieri Ticinesi.

Zufferey, Maurice Sierre r ★★★ Try Syrah, HUMAGNE *rouge*, CORNALIN.

Zundel ★★★ 05' 06 07' A grower to remember for top TICINO MERLOT.

Zürich Capital of largest canton. BLAUBURGUNDER mostly; esp Müller-Thurgau, RÄUSCHLING, Kerner (613 ha). Try Ladolt, SCHWARZENBACH, Zweifel Weine.

SWITZERLAND

Austria

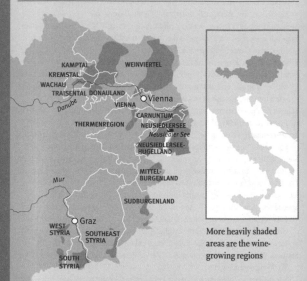

More heavily shaded areas are the wine-growing regions

Austria is undergoing something of a rethink at the moment, as growers move away from New-World-inspired oak and alcohol and back to a more traditionally Austrian approach of lightness, elegance and balance. But nothing is wasted: the years of making bigger, richer wines have resulted in greater ripeness and concentration, which are now being allied to minerality and delicacy. Grüner Veltliner and Riesling go from strength to strength, while reds, especially Blaufränkisch, are a gift to a world increasingly seeking freshness and controlled alcohol.

Recent vintages

2009 A year full of ups and downs: hot early summer, July hailstorms in Vienna, cool spells, a wet September and, finally, good weather in late October and November, when meticulous growers could harvest superb grapes. Very good for those who dared to wait.

2008 Outstanding results in the hands of the most careful producers and the coolest year since 2004. Protracted cool and rainy spells in October and November made harvesting very difficult in lower Austria and in the Burgenland; in the southern regions, the autumn was more clement.

2007 Good in Styria and, in Burgenland, for Blaufränkisch, Zweigelt and Pinot N. Excellent yields in Vienna, better for Grüner Veltliner than for Ries.

2006 A great year. Well-rounded and complex wines with great ageing potential.

2005 Elegant at its best, particularly in lower Austria, but with great discrepancies in quality. Not outstanding for reds.

2004 Cool. Grüner Veltliner and Ries fared well, especially in Wachau. Burgenland reds ripened nicely, and there was plentiful botrytis for dessert wines.

2003 A hot, dry summer, a powerful year. Very good for Grüner Veltliner whites and Burgenland reds, especially Blaufränkisch and Zweigelt. Little botrytis.

2002 Difficult for reds. Some elegant whites, excellent dessert wines. Drink now.

Achs, Paul r (w) ★★★ Outstanding GOLS estate, esp reds: PANNOBILE blends, Ungerberg, BLAUFRÄNKISCH and Pinot N. Biodynamic producer (see below).

Allram w ★ Increasingly gd KAMPTAL estate, esp for RIES and GRÜNER VELTLINER.

Alzinger w ★★★★ 99 00 01 02 03 04 05 06 07 08 Leading WACHAU estate: highly expressive RIES and GRÜNER VELTLINER.

Angerer, Kurt ★ Maverick KAMPTAL producer of powerful GRÜNER VELTLINER and RIES.

Ausbruch PRÄDIKAT wine with sugar levels between Beerenauslese and Trockenbeerenauslese. Traditionally produced in RUST.

Ausg'steckt ("hung out") HEURIGEN are not open all yr; when they are, a green bush is hung above their doors.

Bayer r w ★★ Well-made reds from bought-in grapes, often v. elegant.

Beck, Judith r w ★★ Rising biodynamic NEUSIEDLERSEE winemaker. Well-crafted reds, esp gd Pinot N and ST LAURENT.

Biodynamism A growing trend, inc P ACHS, J BECK, Fritsch, Geyerhof, GRAF HARDEGG, HIRSCH, F LOIMER, Meinklang, Sepp & Maria Muster, NIKOLAIHOF, B OTT, J NITTNAUS, PITTNAUER, F WENINGER.

Blauburger Austrian red grape variety. A cross between BLAUER PORTUGIESER and BLAUFRÄNKISCH. Simple wines.

Blauer Burgunder (Pinot N) Some fine Pinot N is now being made by Austrian producers in BURGENLAND, KAMPTAL, THERMENREGION (from growers: P ACHS, J BECK, W BRÜNDLMAYER, F LOIMER, PITTNAUER, J & R PÖCKL, C PREISINGER, PRIELER, SCHLOSS GOBELSBURG, SCHLOSS HALBTURN, F WENINGER, F WIENINGER).

Blauer Portugieser Light, fruity wines to drink slightly chilled when young.

Blauer Zweigelt BLAUFRÄNKISCH/ST LAURENT cross. Mostly for appealingly velvety wines; also a gd cuvée partner. Top producers: Grassl, G HEINRICH, J NITTNAUS, PITTNAUER, J & R PÖCKL, Scheibelhofer, SCHWARZ, WINKLER-HERMADEN.

Blaufränkisch Lemberger in Germany, Kékfrankos in Hungary. Probably Austria's top potential red grape variety, widely planted in MITTELBURGENLAND: medium-bodied, peppery acidity, a characteristic salty note, berry aromas and eucalyptus. Often blended with Cab Sauv or ZWEIGELT. Best: P ACHS, GESELLMANN, J HEINRICH, IGLER, KOLLWENTZ-RÖMERHOF, KRUTZLER, MORIC, J NITTNAUS, PRIELER, Schiefer, E TRIEBAUMER, F WENINGER.

Bouvier Indigenous aromatic grape, esp gd for Beerenauslese and Trockenbeerenauslese.

Brandl, Günter w ★★ Small but consistently *fine Kamptal estate* known esp for RIES and GRÜNER VELTLINER Novemberlese.

Braunstein, Birgit r w Rising NEUSIEDLERSEE-HÜGELLAND estate: cuvée Oxhoft.

Bründlmayer, Willi r w sw sp ★★★★ 98 99 00 01 02 03 04 05 06 07 Leading Langenlois-KAMPTAL estate. Innovator making world-class RIES, GRÜNER VELTLINER. Also Austria's best sparkling méthode champenoise.

Burgenland Province and wine region (14,500 ha) in the east bordering Hungary. Warm climate, esp around shallow LAKE NEUSIEDL. Ideal conditions for reds and esp botrytis wines near NEUSIEDLERSEE. Four areas: MITTELBURGENLAND, NEUSIEDLERSEE, NEUSIEDLERSEE-HÜGELLAND, SÜDBURGENLAND.

Buschenschank A wine tavern, often a HEURIGE country cousin.

Carnuntum r w Dynamic region southeast of VIENNA now showing gd reds. Best: Glatzer, Grassl, G Markowitsch, Netzl, PITTNAUER.

Chardonnay Best when vinified with little oak, particularly in STYRIA and BURGENLAND. Known in STYRIA as MORILLON: strong fruit, lively acidity. Esp w BRÜNDLMAYER, GROSS, KOLLWENTZ-RÖMERHOF, F LOIMER, Malat, E & W POLZ, W SATTLER, STIEGELMAR, M TEMENT, VELICH, F WIENINGER.

Christ r w Reliable VIENNA producer, particularly for GEMISCHTER SATZ.

Deutschkreutz r (w) MITTELBURGENLAND red wine area, esp for BLAUFRÄNKISCH.

Districtus Austriae Controllatus (DAC) Austria's first appellation system,

AUSTRIA

introduced in 2003. Similar to France's AC and Italy's DOC. Current DACs: KAMPTAL, KREMSTAL, LEITHABERG, MITTELBURGENLAND, TRAISENTAL, WEINVIERTEL.

Donabaum, Johann w ★★ Talented WACHAU grower with fine RIES and GRÜNER VELTLINER, esp Ries Offenberg.

Ehmoser w Small individualist WAGRAM producer, gd GRÜNER VELTLINER Aurum.

Eichinger Consistent KAMPTAL producer, GRÜNER VELTLINER, RIES. Heiligenstein.

Esterhazy ★★ Princely house at Eisenstadt back in the business with a new winery and v. promising wines, esp BLAUFRÄNKISCH.

Federspiel Medium level of the VINEA WACHAU categories, roughly corresponding to Kabinett. Fruity, elegant, dry wines.

Feiler-Artinger Burgenland r w sw ★★★★ 95 00 01 02 03 04 05 06 07 08 Outstanding RUST estate with top AUSBRUCH dessert wines *often v.gd value for money* and red blends. Beautiful baroque house, too.

Forstreiter w ★ Consistent KREMSTAL producer, particularly gd RIES.

Furmint Rare white variety cultivated in and around RUST. Usually sweet, but dry wines undergoing renaissance: H SCHRÖCK.

Gemischter Satz Blend of (mostly white) grape varietals planted in one v'yd and vinified together. Traditional method that spreads risk; back in fashion in VIENNA.

Gesellmann r w ★★ Consistent and often fine MITTELBURGENLAND producer focusing on BLAUFRÄNKISCH and red *cuvées*: Opus Eximium.

Gols r w dr sw Wine commune on north shore of LAKE NEUSIEDL in BURGENLAND. Top producers: P ACHS, J BECK, GSELLMANN, G HEINRICH, A & H Nittnaus, PITTNAUER, C PREISINGER, Renner, STIEGELMAR.

Graf Hardegg r w Large WEINVIERTEL producer. Viognier, Syrah, Pinot N and RIES.

Gross w ★★★★ 00 01 02 03 04 05 06 07 Outstanding and perfectionist south STYRIAN producer. Esp CHARD, Sauv Bl and Pinot Bl.

Grüner Veltliner Austria's flagship white grape covering 37% of v'yds. Remarkably diverse: from simple, peppery everyday wines to others of great complexity and ageing potential. Best: ALZINGER, W BRÜNDLMAYER, F HIRTZBERGER, HÖGL, M Huber, E KNOLL, Laurenz V, F LOIMER, MANTLERHOF, NEUMAYER, NIGL, NIKOLAIHOF, B OTT, PFAFFL, FX PICHLER, F PRAGER, SCHMELZ, Sommer.

Gsellmann, Hans r w sw ★ Formerly Gsellmann & Gsellmann, in GOLS.

Gumpoldskirchen r w dr sw Famous HEURIGE village south of VIENNA, centre of THERMENREGION. Signature white varieties: ZIERFANDLER and ROTGIPFLER grapes. Best producers: Biegler, Spaetrot, ZIERER.

Heinrich, Gernot r w dr sw ★★★ 99 01 02 03 04 05 06 07 08 Perfectionist GOLS estate, member of the PANNOBILE group. Outstanding single-v'yd red wines.

Heinrich, Johann r w dr sw ★★★ 97 98 99 00 01 02 03 04 05 06 08 Leading MITTELBURGENLAND producer. V.gd BLAUFRÄNKISCH Goldberg Reserve. Excellent *cuvée* Cupido.

Heurige Wine of the most recent harvest, called "new wine" for one yr. **Heurigen** are wine taverns in which growers-cum-patrons serve their own wine with simple local food – a Viennese institution.

Hiedler w sw ★★★ Leading KAMPTAL producer. V.gd RIES Maximum.

Hirsch w ★★★ Searching organic KAMPTAL producer. Esp Heiligenstein, Lamm and Gaisberg v'yds. Also Austria's screwcap pioneer.

Hirtzberger, Franz w ★★★★ 99 00 01 02 03 04 05 06 07 08 Top WACHAU producer with 20 ha at SPITZ AN DER DONAU. *Highly expressive, minerally RIES* and GRÜNER VELTLINER, esp from the Honivogl and Singerriedel v'yds.

Högl ★ w sw Individualist WACHAU producer; often fine RIES and GRÜNER VELTLINER.

Horitschon MITTELBURGENLAND region for reds: IBY, F WENINGER.

Igler ★ r Consistent grower of red wines in MITTELBURGENLAND: Ab Ericio, Vulcano.

Illmitz w dr sw (r) SEEWINKEL region famous for Beeren- and Trockenbeeren-auslesen. Best from Angerhof, Martin Haider, KRACHER, Helmut Lang, Opitz.

Jamek, Josef w WACHAU estate with restaurant. Not typical WACHAU style: often some residual sugar.

Johanneshof Reinisch r w sw Large, consistent THERMENREGION estate; some v.gd whites.

Jurtschitsch/Sonnhof w (r) dr (sw) ★★ 02 03 04 05 06 07 Large KAMPTAL estate: v. reliable whites (RIES, GRÜNER VELTLINER, CHARD).

Kamptal r w Wine region, along river Kamp north of WACHAU. Top v'yds: Heiligenstein, Käferberg, Lanum. Best: K ANGERER, G BRANDL, W BRÜNDLMAYER, Ehn, EICHINGER, HIEDLER, HIRSCH, JURTSCHITSCH, F LOIMER, G RABL, SCHLOSS GOBELSBURG, STEININGER. Kamptal is now DAC (from 2008) for GRÜNER VELTLINER and RIES.

Kattus Producer of traditional sekt in VIENNA.

Kerschbaum r ★★★ 03 05 06 07 MITTELBURGENLAND BLAUFRÄNKISCH specialist, individualist and often fascinating.

Klosterneuburg r w Main wine town of Donauland. Rich in tradition, with a wine college founded in 1860. Best producers: Stift Klosterneuburg, Zimmermann.

KMW Abbreviation for Klosterneuburger Mostwaage ("must level"), the unit used in Austria to measure the sugar content in grape juice.

Knoll, Emmerich w ★★★★ 97 98 99 00 01 02 03 04 05 06 07 08 Outstanding traditional estate in Loiben, WACHAU. *Delicate Ries, complex Grüner Veltliner.*

Kollwentz-Römerhof r w dr (sw) ★★★★ 99 01 02 03 04 05 06 07 08 Pioneering producer near Eisenstadt: Sauv Bl, CHARD, Eiswein. Also renowned for *fine reds: Steinzeiler.*

Kracher w dr (r sw) ★★★★ 95 98 99 00 01 02 03 04 05 06 07 08 Top-class ILLMITZ producer specializing in botrytized PRÄDIKATS (dessert); barrique-aged (Nouvelle Vague), others in steel (Zwischen den Seen); gd reds since 1997. Since Alois Kracher's death in 2007, the estate has been led by his son Gerhard.

Kremstal w (r) Wine region esp for GRÜNER VELTLINER and RIES. Top: Buchegger, Malat, S MOSER, NIGL, SALOMON-UNDHOF, Stagård, WEINGUT STADT KREMS.

Krutzler r ★★★ South BURGENLAND producer of outstanding BLAUFRÄNKISCH, esp Perwolff.

Lackner-Tinnacher ★ Fine SÜD-OSTSTEIERMARK estate known for elegant MORILLON and MUSKATELLER.

Leithaberg V'yd hill on the northern shore of LAKE NEUSIEDL; also a lively group of producers seeking to refine regional styles. Now a DAC.

Leitner r w sw Rising NEUSIEDLERSEE growers belonging to the PANNOBILE group. Gd Ungerberg and PANNOBILE *cuvées.*

Loimer, Fred w ★★★ Thoughtful and ambitious KAMPTAL producer with 31-ha estate, 50% GRÜNER VELTLINER; also RIES, CHARD, Pinot Gr, v.gd Pinot N. Leading exponent of biodynamic winemaking.

Mantlerhof w ★★ KREMSTAL producer with a well-considered, traditional approach. Gd Roter Veltliner.

Mayer am Pfarrplatz w Viennese producer and HEURIGE now in new ownership, with marked improvement in the wines.

Minkowitsch w Traditional WEINVIERTEL producer, interesting Gewürztraminer.

Mittelburgenland r dr (w sw) Wine region on Hungarian border concentrating on BLAUFRÄNKISCH (also DAC) and increasingly fine. Producers: BAYER, Gager, GESELLMANN, J HEINRICH, IBY, IGLER, KERSCHBAUM, Wellanschitz, F WENINGER.

Moric ★★★ Outstanding red, terroir-oriented BLAUFRÄNKISCH wine made by Roland VELICH from old vines in the MITTELBURGENLAND. Stylistically a beacon.

Morillon Name given in STYRIA to CHARD.

Moser, Lenz Austria's largest producer, based in Krems.

NB Vintages in colour are those you should choose first for drinking in 2011.

Moser, Sepp r w sw KREMSTAL grower of consistent RIES, GRÜNER VELTLINER.

Muhr-van der Niepoort w r Start-up winery in the CARNUNTUM region. Yes, Niepoort as in port. Well-judged reds.

Müller, Domaine Individualist west STYRIAN producer with international outlook, esp Sauv Bl and CHARD.

Muskateller Rare, aromatic grape for v. fragrant, dry whites, esp in STYRIA. Top: GROSS, F HIRTZBERGER, LACKNER-TINNACHER, FX PICHLER, E & W POLZ, W SATTLER.

Muskat-Ottonel Grape for fragrant, often dry whites, interesting PRÄDIKATS.

Neuburger Indigenous white grape that has long been neglected; mainly in the WACHAU (elegant, flowery), THERMENREGION (mellow, ample-bodied) and north BURGENLAND (strong, full). Best from J BECK, DOMÄNE WACHAU, F HIRTZBERGER.

Neumayer w ★★★ Top TRAISENTAL estate making powerful, focused, dry GRÜNER VELTLINER and RIES.

Neumeister w ★★★ Leading southeast STYRIAN producer, esp Sauv Bl and CHARD.

Neusiedlersee (Lake Neusiedl) V. shallow BURGENLAND lake on Hungarian border. Warmth and autumn mists encourage botrytis. See next entry.

Neusiedlersee r w dr sw Wine region north and east of NEUSIEDLERSEE. Best: P ACHS, J BECK, G HEINRICH, KRACHER, J NITTNAUS, J & R PÖCKL, STIEGELMAR, J UMATHUM, VELICH.

Neusiedlersee-Hügelland r w dr sw Wine region west of LAKE NEUSIEDL based around Oggau, RUST and Mörbisch on the lake shores, and Eisenstadt in the Leitha foothills. Best producers: B BRAUNSTEIN, FEILER-ARTINGER, Kloster am Spitz, KOLLWENTZ-RÖMERHOF, PRIELER, Schandl, H SCHRÖCK, Schuller, Sommer, E TRIEBAUMER, WENZEL.

Niederösterreich (Lower Austria) Northeastern region with 58% of Austria's v'yds: CARNUNTUM, Donauland, KAMPTAL, KREMSTAL, THERMENREGION, TRAISENTAL, WACHAU, WEINVIERTEL.

Nigl w ★★★★ 01 02 03 04 05 06 07 08 The best in KREMSTAL, making sophisticated dry whites with remarkable mineral character from Senftenberg v'yd.

Nikolaihof w ★★★★ 95 01 02 03 04 05 06 07 08 Built on Roman foundations, this impeccable WACHAU estate has pioneered BIODYNAMISM in Austria. Outstanding RIES from Steiner Hund v'yd.

Nittnaus, John r w sw ★★★ Searching organic NEUSIEDLERSEE winemaker. Esp elegant and age-worthy reds: Comondor.

Ott, Bernhard w ★★–★★★ GRÜNER VELTLINER specialist from Donauland. Fass 4; also Der Ott and Rosenberg.

Pannobile Association of youngish and ambitious NEUSIEDLERSEE growers centred on GOLS and aiming to create great wine with regional character. Current members are: P ACHS, J BECK, HANS GSELLMANN, G HEINRICH, LEITNER, J NITTNAUS, PITTNAUER, C PREISINGER, Renner.

Pfaffl r w ★★★ 05 06 07 08 WEINVIERTEL estate near VIENNA, in Stetten. Known for dry GRÜNER VELTLINER (Goldjoch) and RIES (Terrassen Sonnleiten), it also makes surprisingly gd reds.

Pichler, Franz Xavier w ★★★★ 99 00 01 02 03 04 05 06 07 08 WACHAU producer; one of Austria's best. Intense and *iconic Ries*; GRÜNER VELTLINER (esp Kellerberg).

Pichler, Rudi w ★★–★★★ Fine WACHAU producer of powerful, expressive RIES and GRÜNER VELTLINER.

Pittnauer r w ★ Consistent NEUSIEDLERSEE producer of v.gd ST LAURENT.

Pöckl, Josef & René r (sw) ★★ Father-and-son team in NEUSIEDLERSEE (Mönchhof). Well-made reds, esp Admiral, Rêve de Jeunesse and Rosso e Nero.

Polz, Erich & Walter w ★★ 01 02 03 04 05 06 07 08 V.gd large south STYRIAN (Weinstrasse) growers; esp Hochgrassnitzberg: Sauv Bl, CHARD, Grauburgunder, WEISSBURGUNDER.

Prädikat, Prädikatswein German-inspired system of classifying wine by the sugar content of the juice, from Spätlese upwards (Spätlese, Auslese, Eiswein,

STROHWEIN, Beerenauslese, AUSBRUCH and Trockenbeerenauslese). See Germany.

Prager, Franz w ★★★★ 95 99 00 01 02 03 04 05 06 07 08 Pioneer, together with JOSEF JAMEK, of top-quality WACHAU dry whites. RIES and *Grüner Veltliner of impeccable elegance* and mineral structure: Wachstum Bodenstein.

Preisinger, Claus Ambitious young winemaker with stylish reds, esp Pinot N.

Prieler w r ★★★ Consistently fine NEUSIEDLERSEE-HÜGELLAND producer. Esp gd BLAUFRÄNKISCH Goldberg.

Proidl, Erwin ★★ Highly individual KREMSTAL grower making interesting, age-worthy RIES and GRÜNER VELTLINER.

Rabl, Günter ★ KAMPTAL grower long overshadowed by more famous colleagues. V.gd GRÜNER VELTLINER.

Riesling On its own, this always means Rhine RIES. WELSCHRIESLING is unrelated. In Austria this is one of the greatest varieties, particularly in KAMPTAL, KREMSTAL and WACHAU. Top growers: ALZINGER, W BRÜNDLMAYER, F HIRTZBERGER, HÖGL, E KNOLL, NIGL, NIKOLAIHOF, PFAFFL, FX PICHLER, F PRAGER, SALOMON-UNDHOF.

Rotgipfler Fragrant indigenous grape of THERMENREGION. With ZIERFANDLER, makes lively *cuvée*. Esp Biegler, Spaetrot, STADLMANN, ZIERER.

Rust r w dr sw Historic town on the shores of LAKE NEUSIEDL, beautiful 17th-century houses testifying to centuries of wine production/trade, esp in Ruster AUSBRUCH. Top: FEILER-ARTINGER, Giefing, Schandl, H SCHRÖCK, E TRIEBAUMER, WENZEL.

St Laurent Indigenous red variety with brambly, tarry and smoky aromas and gd tannic structure. Esp from J BECK, Fischer, JOHANNESHOF REINISCH, PITTNAUER, Hannes SCHUSTER, J UMATHUM.

Salomon-Undhof w ★★★ V.gd Krems producer: RIES, WEISSBURGUNDER, Traminer. The owner also produces wine in Australia.

Sattler, Willi w ★★★ 01 02 03 04 05 06 07 Top south STYRIA grower. Esp for Sauv Bl, MORILLON, often grown on v. steep v'yds.

Schilcher Rosé wine from indigenous Blauer Wildbacher grapes (sharp, dry, high acidity). A local taste, or at least an acquired one. Specialty of west STYRIA. Try: Klug, Lukas, Reiterer, Strohmeier.

Schloss Gobelsburg ★★★→★★★★ 01 02 03 04 05 06 07 Renowned KAMPTAL estate run by Michael Moosbrugger. Excellent dry RIES and GRÜNER VELTLINER. Also RIES and GRÜNER VELTLINER Tradition, and fine Pinot N.

Grü-V

GRÜNER VELTLINER is the ideal introduction to Austrian wine for anyone who has yet to take the plunge. Yes, it is responsible for many of the country's greatest whites, but it's good at every level – even a half-litre mug served in a buzzy HEURIGE is likely to be a good drink. Don't be afraid to try whatever GRÜNER VELTLINER comes your way: inexpensive ones from generously cropped vines can still give a good taste of the grape.

Schloss Halbturn r w sw ★★ Recently revitalized estate creating ever-better wines with German and French winemakers. Esp *cuvée* Imperial, also Pinot N.

Schlumberger Largest sparkling winemaker in Austria (VIENNA). Also on the Loire.

Schmelz w ★★★ Fine, often underestimated WACHAU producer, esp outstanding RIES. Dürnsteiner Freiheit.

Schröck, Heidi r w sw ★★★ Wines of great purity and focus from a thoughtful grower. V.gd AUSBRUCH. Also v.gd dry FURMINT. See Hungary.

Schuster r w NEUSIEDLERSEE-HÜGELLAND producer. ST LAURENT.

Schwarz r sw Small but classy NEUSIEDLERSEE producer specializing in ZWEIGELT and STROHWEIN.

Seewinkel ("lake corner") Name given to the part of NEUSIEDLERSEE, inc Apetlon, ILLMITZ and Podersdorf. Ideal conditions for botrytis.

Smaragd Highest category of VINEA WACHAU, similar to dry Spätlese.

Spätrot-Rotgipfler Typical blend of THERMENREGION. Aromatic and weighty wines, often with orange-peel aromas.

Spitz an der Donau w Cool WACHAU microclimate, esp from Singerriedel v'yd. Top growers are: J DONABAUM, F HIRTZBERGER, HÖGL, Lagler.

Stadlmann r w sw THERMENREGION producer specializing in opulent ZIERFANDLER-ROTGIPFLER wines.

Steinfeder VINEA WACHAU category for light, fragrant, dry wines.

Steininger r w sp ★★ KAMPTAL grower with a range of outstanding single-varietal sparkling wines, as well as still ones.

Stiegelmar (Juris-Stiegelmar) r w dr sw ★★ Well-regarded GOLS grower. CHARD, Sauv Bl. Reds: ST LAURENT.

Strohwein Sweet wine made from grapes air-dried on straw matting.

Styria (Steiermark) Southernmost wine region of Austria. Some gd dry whites, esp Sauv Bl and CHARD, called MORILLON in Styria. Also fragrant MUSKATELLER. Includes SÜDSTEIERMARK, SÜD-OSTSTEIERMARK, WESTSTEIERMARK (south, southeast, west Styria).

Südburgenland r w Small south BURGENLAND wine region. V.gd BLAUFRÄNKISCH wines. Best: KRUTZLER, Schiefer, Wachter-Wiesler.

Süd-Oststeiermark SE Styria w (r) STYRIAN region with excellent v'yds. Best producers: NEUMEISTER, WINKLER-HERMADEN.

Südsteiermark S Styria w Best STYRIA region; popular whites (MORILLON, MUSKATELLER, WELSCHRIESLING and Sauv Bl). Best: GROSS, Jaunegg, LACKNER-TINNACHER, E & W POLZ, Potzinger Sabathi, W SATTLER, Skoff, M TEMENT, Wohlmuth.

Tegernseerhof w WACHAU producer, newly invigorated and producing v. interesting RIES and GRÜNER VELTLINER.

Tement, Manfred w ★★★★ 03 04 05 06 07 08 Renowned south STYRIA estate with esp fine Sauv Bl and MORILLON from Zieregg site. International-style wines, modern reds.

Thermenregion r w dr sw Wine/hot-springs region, south of VIENNA. Indigenous grapes (eg. ZIERFANDLER, ROTGIPFLER), historically one of the most important regions for reds (esp ST LAURENT) from Baden, GUMPOLDSKIRCHEN, Tattendorf, Traiskirchen areas. Producers: Alphart, Biegler, Fischer, JOHANNESHOF REINISCH, Schafler, Spätrot-Gebelshuber, STADLMANN, ZIERER.

Traisental 700 ha just south of Krems on Danube. Dry whites can be similar to WACHAU in style, not usually in quality. Top producers: Huber, NEUMAYER.

Triebaumer, Ernst r (w) dr sw ★★★★ 01 02 03 04 05 06 07 08 Important RUST producer, BLAUFRÄNKISCH (inc the legendary Mariental), Cab Sauv/Merlot blend. V.gd AUSBRUCH.

Uhudler Local south BURGENLAND specialty. Wine made directly from American rootstocks, with a foxy, strawberry taste.

Umathum, Josef r w dr sw ★★★ V.gd and thoughtful NEUSIEDLERSEE producer. V.gd reds, inc Pinot N, ST LAURENT; gd whites.

Velich Neusiedlersee w sw ★★★★ A searching, intellectual producer. Excellent burgundian-style Tiglat Chard (99 00 01 02 03 06) with fine barrel-ageing. Some of top sweet wines in the SEEWINKEL.

Vienna w (r) Wine region in suburbs. Mostly simple wines, served to tourists in HEURIGEN. Quality producers on the rise: CHRIST, MAYER AM PFARRPLATZ, F WIENINGER, Zahel.

Vinea Wachau WACHAU appellation started by winemakers in 1983 with three categories of dry wine: STEINFEDER, FEDERSPIEL and the powerful SMARAGD.

Wachau w World-renowned Danube region, home to some of Austria's best wines. Top: Alzinger, J DONABAUM, Freie Weingärtner Wachau, F HIRTZBERGER, HÖGL,

J JAMEK, E KNOLL, Lagler, NIKOLAIHOF, FX PICHLER, R PICHLER, F PRAGER, Schmelz, WESS.

Wachau, Domäne w (r) ★ 01 02 06 07 08 Important growers' co-op in Dürnstein. V.gd GRÜNER VELTLINER and RIES.

Wagram w (r) Wine region just west of VIENNA, inc KLOSTERNEUBURG. Mainly whites, esp GRÜNER VELTLINER. Best: EHMOSER, Fritsch, Stift Klosterneuburg, Leth, B OTT, Wimmer-Czerny, R Zimmermann.

Weingut Stadt Krems ★ Co-op steered by Fritz Miesbauer, reliable and increasingly gd. Miesbauer also vinifies for Stift Göttweig.

Weinrieder w sw WEINVIERTEL grower with expressive GRÜNER VELTLINER and RIES.

Weinviertel ("Wine Quarter") w (r) Largest Austrian wine region, between Danube and Czech border. First to adopt DAC appellation system. Largely simple qualities but increasingly striving for quality and regional character. Refreshing whites, esp from Poysdorf, Retz. Best: Bauer, J Diem, GRAF HARDEGG, Gruber, PFAFFL, Schwarzböck, WEINRIEDER, Zull.

Weissburgunder (Pinot Blanc) Ubiquitous: gd dry wines and PRÄDIKATS. Esp J BECK, Fischer, GROSS, G HEINRICH, F HIRTZBERGER, LACKNER-TINNACHER, E & W POLZ, M TEMENT.

Welschriesling White grape, not related to RIES, grown in all wine regions: simple, fragrant, dry wines for everyday drinking.

Weninger, Franz r (w) ★★★ Top MITTELBURGENLAND (Horitschon) estate, with *fine reds, esp BLAUFRÄNKISCH*, Dürrau and Merlot.

Wenzel r w sw ★★★ V.gd AUSBRUCH. Junior Michael makes ambitious and increasingly fine reds. Father Robert pioneered the FURMINT revival in RUST.

Wess w ★ Gd WACHAU winemaker, vinifying bought-in grapes, some from famous v'yds.

Weststeiermark W Styria p Small wine region specializing in SCHILCHER. Best: Klug, Lukas, DOMAINE MÜLLER, Reiterer, Strohmeier.

Wien See VIENNA.

Wieninger, Fritz r w ★★ 01 02 03 04 05 06 07 08 V.gd VIENNA-Stammersdorf grower with HEURIGE: CHARD, BLAUER BURGUNDER, esp gd GRÜNER VELTLINER, RIES.

Winkler-Hermaden r w sw ★★★ Outstanding and individual southeast STYRIAN producer, gd Traminer and MORILLON, also one of the region's few v.gd reds, the ZWEIGELT-based Olivin.

Winzer Krems Large KREMSTAL co-op with 1,300 growers. Esp GRÜNER VELTLINER.

Zierer r w THERMENREGION producer, esp fine ROTGIPFLER.

Zierfandler (Spätrot) White variety almost exclusive to THERMENREGION. Often blended with ROTGIPFLER. Best: Biegler, Spaetrot, STADLMANN, ZIERER.

Zweigelt See BLAUER ZWEIGELT.

England & Wales

Sparkling wine is the focus now, and plantings continue unabated, with another 200+ hectares planted in 2009, bringing the total up to around 1,350–1,400 ha. The new vines are mainly Champagne varieties: Pinot Noir, Chardonnay and Pinot Meunier now account for 40 per cent of the total UK vineyard area. The only still wine variety showing increases in planting is Bacchus, which consumers seem to like.

Astley Worcestershire ★★ Wines continue to win awards and medals. Late Harvest 07 v.gd.

Biddenden Kent Established in 1969 so one of the UK's oldest vineyards. Spicy Ortega 08 dry and Ortega 08 med-dry both worth trying. Also makes v.gd cider and apple juice.

Breaky Bottom E Sussex Sparkling wines well worth trying. Cuvée Brian Jordan 05.

Brightwell Oxon Up-and-coming producer. Try: Oxford Rosé 08.

Camel Valley Cornwall ★★★ Lindo *père et fils* (Bob and Sam) continue to improve. Pinot Rosé 06 sparkling, White Pinot 07 sparkling, Rosé 08 and Atlantic 08 all excellent.

Chapel Down Kent ★★★ Still the UK's largest producer. NV Brut best value UK sparkling wine. Classy Pinot Reserve 04 sparkling very good, also Pinot Blanc 07 and Bacchus 07. V.gd visitor facilities, inc excellent restaurant.

Coates & Seely Hampshire Still a twinkle in its makers' eyes, but look out for this sparkler in 2011. Seely is the Englishman who runs AXA wines Millésimes, owner of Bordeaux's Pichon-Longueville *et al*.

Davenport Kent/Sussex Organic Limney Estate 05 sparkling and Horsmonden 07 dry white well worth trying.

Denbies Surrey ★★ No longer the UK's largest v'yd. Wines continue to improve. Greenfields 02 sparkling, oaky Hillside Chardonnay 06 and Juniper Hill 07 well worth trying. V.gd visitor facilities..

Gusbourne Kent Large new sparkling producer. Classic Blend 06 and Blanc de Blancs 06 excellent.

Hush Heath Estate Kent Balfour Brut Rosé 06 excellent.

Jenkyn Place Hampshire Newcomer with v.gd first release: Jenkyn Place 06.

Nyetimber W Sussex ★★★ Recent plantings have brought total up to 142 ha, making this the largest UK v'yd. Blanc de Blancs 92 and 98, Classic Cuvée 01 and 03 v.gd. Harvested almost 1,000 tonnes in 2009 and planning huge new winery for 2012.

Parva Farm Monmouthshire, Wales One of the v. few Welsh v'yds to produce interesting wines. Bwthyn Rhosyn 07 worth trying.

RidgeView E Sussex ★★★ Great quality, consistency and gd value keep this winery at the top of UK producers. Bloomsbury 06, Cavendish 06, Grosvenor 06 and Knightsbridge 06 all v.gd.

Sharpham Devon ★★ Gd range of wines (and also great cheeses). Barrel-Fermented 07 and very fruity Bacchus 07 best wines.

Stanlake Park Berkshire ★★ Large range of wines of above-average quality, although not quite as good as previously. Fumé 07 and Hinton Grove 07 best wines. Sparkling Rosé also good.

Three Choirs Glos ★★ 07 Large range of gd-value wines, plus v.gd visitor facilities, hotel and restaurant. Med-dry Siegerrebe 07 and Willow Brook 08 best wines.

Central & Southeast Europe

More heavily shaded areas are the wine-growing regions

HUNGARY

Of all the countries of Eastern Europe, Hungary seems to be the one most successfully combining modernization with individuality. And so it should be, given its wealth of indigenous grapes. Furmint is as good as almost any vine on the planet, and is being made into some really wild, fiery wines of huge character. Hárslevelü is another vine to watch. Whites can be superbly exciting, reds perhaps a pace or two behind but still very good. Tokáji proliferates and should be explored by anyone keen on sweet and not-so-sweet wine. As the wines become more available abroad, so the labels will become more intelligible.

Alana-Tokaj New promising young producer with great v'yds.

Alföld Hungary's Great Plain makes mostly everyday wine from three districts: Hajós-Baja (Brillant Holding, Sümegi), Csongrád (Somodi), Kunság (Frittmann).

Árvay Family Winery 08 Established in 2008 after the talented János Árvay split with former partner Sauska. Gd dry Muscat so far.

Ászár-Neszmély w dr ★→★★ Region in northwest Hungary near the Danube, mainly white grapes. HILLTOP is leading winery.

Aszú Botrytis-shrivelled grapes and the sweet wine made from them in TOKAJ. The wine is graded in sweetness, from 3 PUTTONYOS up.

Aszú Essencia Tokaj sw ★★★ 93 96' 99' 00' 02 03' 05' 06' (07') (08') Second sweetest TOKÁJI quality. 7 PUTTONYOS+; should be superb amber elixir.

Badacsony w dr sw ★★→★★★ Wine district on north shore of Lake BALATON, on slopes of extinct volcano. The basalt soil can give rich, highly flavoured white wines; esp well-made Ries and SZÜRKEBARÁT; Pinot N also promising. Look for SZEREMLEY and Villa Tolnay.

Balaton Europe's largest freshwater lake. Wines from BADACSONY and BALATONFURED-CSOPAK on north shore. Wines from BALATONBOGLÁR on south.

Balatonboglár r w dr ★★→★★★ Name of wine district and also a progressive winery owned by Henkell & Söhnlein on south shore of Lake BALATON. Gd-value whites (Chard, Pinot Gr, Muscat). Top producers: GARAMVÁRI, KONYÁRI, Légli.

Balatonfured-Csopak r w dr ★★ District on north shore of Lake BALATON. Mainly whites, esp OLASZRIZLING, Chard. Best producers: Feind, Jasdi, Figula.

Barta New producer since 2008. Highest v'yd in TOKAJ. Dry FURMINT impressive.

Béres w dr sw ★★→★★★ New and immaculate TOKAJ producer.

Bikavér r ★→★★★ 03 05 06 07 Literally "Bull's Blood" with past reputation for ordinary quality. Now being revived as flagship blended red. Produced by law only in SZEKSZÁRD and EGER. Egri Bikavér gained protected origin status from 2004. Must be blend of at least three varieties; usually includes KÉKFRANKOS, and in SZEKSZÁRD sometimes KADARKA. Reserve level requires min of four varieties, obligatory tasting and restricted yield. Best producers for Egri Bikavér: Bolyki, Gróf Buttler, TIBOR GÁL, Kaló, Pók Tamás, ST ANDREA, Thummerer.

Bock, József r dr ★→★★★ Leading family winemaker in VILLÁNY. Hearty reds, varietal and blends. Best wines are Cab Fr-based Capella Cuvée 00 03' 06' and Syrah 03' 05' 06' and juicy, brisk Portugieser 07 08.

Bodrogkeresztúr Village in TOKAJ region with several up-and-coming estates, inc DERESZLA, Füleky, Tokajbor Bene, TINON, Tokáji Nobilis.

Bor "Wine": *vörös* is red; *fehér* is white; *edes* is sweet, *száraz* is dry.

Bussay, Dr w dr ★★ 05 06 07 Part-time doctor and impressive winemaker SW of Lake BALATON. Intense Pinot Gr, OLASZRIZLING and Ries.

Csányi r ★→★★ Major investment in VILLÁNY. Chateau Teleki range is best.

Degenfeld, Gróf w dr sw ★★ 00 03 05 06 Large TOKAJ estate with luxury hotel. Range of styles from dry to ASZÚ, inc Fortissimo late harvest and Andante botrytis *cuvée*. New winemaker from 09 should raise quality.

Demeter, Zoltan ★★★ V.gd dry and ASZÚ wines from own v'yds. Don't confuse with Demeter in Eger (also v.gd).

Dereszla w dr sw ★★★ 50-ha TOKAJ estate owned by D'Aulan family from Champagne. V.gd ASZÚ, inc ASZÚ ESSENCIA and *flor*-matured dry SZAMORODNI. Also superb dry Kabar 07'.

Districtus Hungaricus Controllatus (DHC) Term adopted for wines with specific protected designation of origin (PDO). VILLÁNY was first region to use. Symbol is a local crocus and DHC on label.

Disznókö w dr sw ★★→★★★★ 96' 97 99' 00' 03' 05 06 (07') (08') Important TOKAJ estate, owned by French company AXA. Wines of great finesse and expressiveness. Single-v'yd Kapi 6 Puttonyos Aszú 99' is notable.

Dobogó ★★→★★★ 99' 00' 03' 05 06 (07) Fine small TOKAJ estate. V gd ASZÚ. Also late-harvest Mylitta, Mylitta Álma (modern take on ASZÚ ESENCIA) 05' 06' 07' and increasingly gd dry FURMINT 05 06' 07' 08. Pinot N since 2007.

Eger r w dr ★→★★★ Best-known red wine centre of north Hungary. BIKAVÉR most famous wine, but increasingly recognized for Cab Fr, Pinot N and Syrah. Whites include LEÁNYKA, OLASZRIZLING, Chard, Pinot Bl. Top producers: Bolynki, Grof Buttler, DEMETER, TIBOR GÁL, Gundel, Kaló, ST ANDREA, Thummerer, .

Essencia (or Eszencia) ★★★★ 93 96 99 03 (06) Heart of TOKÁJI: thick, syrupy, luscious, aromatic juice that trickles from trodden ASZÚ grapes. V. low alcohol; sugar can be over 900g/l. Reputed to have miraculous medicinal properties.

Etyek-Buda Wine region near Budapest. Some gd crisp varietal whites, esp Chard, Sauv Bl, Pinot Gr, and IRSAI OLIVÉR. Leading producers: Etyeki Kúria, NYAKAS (Budai label), György Villa (owned by TÖRLEY).

Ezerjó Literally "thousand blessings". Hungarian local grape variety with sharp acids. Frittmann and MAURUS are making more exciting versions.

Furmint The classic grape of TOKAJ, with great flavour, acidity and potential for both great dry and sweet wines. Also grown in SOMLÓ.

Garamvári r w dr sp ★→★★ Family owned v'yd and St Donatus winery. Also owns *Chateau Vincent*, Hungary's top bottle-fermented sparkling wine.

Gere, Attila r ★★→★★★★ Highly reputed family winemaker in VILLÁNY with gd, forward-looking reds, esp rich Solus Merlot 02 03' 06', intense Kopar Cuvée 00 03' 04 06'. New top wine Grand Vin de Villány 03'.

Hárslevelü "Linden-leaved" grape variety widely grown. Gd in SOMLÓ and important as second grape of TOKAJ. Gentle, mellow wine; peach aroma.

Hétszölö w dr sw ★★→★★★ Noble first-growth 55-ha TOKAJ estate bought in 2009 by Michel Rebier, owner of Ch Cos d'Estournel. Investment should raise standards.

Hilltop Neszmély r w dr sw ★ Winery in ÁSZÁR-NESZMÉLY makes gd international-style wines, inc Riverview and Woodcutters White from Cserszegi Füszeres. Premium range best.

Irsai Olivér Local white cross of two table varieties making aromatic, Muscat-like wine for drinking young. Try NYAKAS, GARAMVÁRI.

Kadarka Traditional red grape with light colour and distinct spicy character, being revived esp in SZEKSZÁRD where regarded as essential element of BIKAVÉR. Known as Gamza in Bulgaria.

Kékfrankos Hungarian for Blaufränkisch. Most widely planted red variety. Gd light or full-bodied reds.

Kéknyelü "Blue stalk". High-flavoured, low-yielding white grape needing a cross-pollinator. Makes best and most structured wine of BADACSONY. Try SZEREMLEY.

Királyudvar w dr sw ★★★ 99' 00' 01 02 03' 05 06' (07). Fine TOKAJ winery in old royal cellars at Tarcal, owned by Anthony Hwang. Wines include dry and late-harvest FURMINT 05 06 07, Cuvée Ilona (early bottled ASZÚ), 03' 07', stunning Cuvée Patricia 06 and 6 PUTTONYOS Lapis Aszú 99' 00' 02' 03' 05 06 (07).

Konyári r w dr ★★→★★★ Father-and-son team making high-quality red and white from own estate at BALATONBOGLÁR, esp Loliense r and w, and Sessio Merlot and v.gd Pava blend. Also own new Ikon winery for better-value varietals.

Kreinbacher w dr ★→★★ 05 06 07 (08) Major investment; is focusing on local grapes and blends. Good Somlói Cuvée 2007.

Leányka "Little girl". White grape from Transylvania known as Feteascӑ Albӑ. Attractive, aromatic, light dry wine. Királyleányka or Feteascӑ Regalӑ is a cross of Feteascӑ Albӑ with Grasӑ of Cotnari.

Mád Old commercial centre of the TOKAJ region with top v'yds and circle of Mád producers. Growers include ALANA-TOKAJ, BARTA, OROSZ GABOR, ÁRVAY, Demetervin, Gundel, ROYAL TOKAJI, SZEPSY, Tokaj Classic.

Malatinszky r w dr ★★★ Immaculate winery making characterful unfiltered Kúria Cab Fr 03' 04 06' 07, Cab Sauv 03' 04 06' 07. Gd Kékfrankos Rosé 07 08, Pinot Bleu 07, Siklosi Chard 05 06 07. New single-v'yd, blended red Kövesföld 06 07'.

Mátra w (r) ★→★★ District in foothills of Mátra range. Promising dry SZÜRKEBARÁT (Pinot Gr), Chard, MUSKOTÁLY, Sauv Bl. Producers worth a mention include drummer-turned-winemaker Gabor Karner, Szöke Mátyás and co-operative Szölöskert (Nagyrede and Spice Trail labels). Also Nemeth Cellars (owner of ALANA-TOKAJ).

Maurus Winery w dr ★★ Young winemaker Ákos Kamocsay Jr is setting out to revitalize sleepy MÓR. EZERJÓ, After Press Chard, Ries, Tramini show promise.

Megyer, Château w dr sw ★★→★★★ TOKAJ estate bought by Jean-Louis Laborde of Château Clinet in Pomerol. Also owns CHÁTEAU PAJZOS. Megyer is lighter wine from cooler north of region. Quality improving, esp dry FURMINT 06 07 08, Aszú 6 Puttonyos 93 99 00 03' 05 06' (07) (08). Appealing dry Muscat.

> **PDO and DHC**
> In Hungary there are currently 23 general Protected Designations of Origin
> (PDOs) and 12 specific PDOs. Hungary's own term, Districtus Hungaricus
> Controllatus (DHC), will increasingly appear for specific PDOs while others
> will become Protected Geographical Indications (PGIs).

Mézes Mály In Tarcal. Historically one of the best v'yds of TOKAJ.

Mór N Hungary w ★→★★ Region famous for fresh, dry EZERJÓ. Now also Ries and TRAMINI. Look for MAURUS WINERY.

Muskotály Muscat; usually Ottonel, except TOKAJ where Sárga Muskotály is yellow Muscat or Muscat Lunel. A little goes into the TOKÁJI blend. V. occasionally makes a v.gd ASZÚ wine solo; try KIRÁLYUDVAR's Cuvée Patricia.

Nyakas w dr ★★ Winery in Etyek Budai noted for well-made, fresh varietal whites under Budai label. V.gd Sauv Bl, Pinot Gr, IRSAI OLIVÉR and Chard.

Olaszrizling Hungarian name for the Italian Ries or Welschriesling.

Orosz Gábor w dr sw ★★→★★ 00 03 05 06 08 17 ha, mostly first-class TOKAJ v'yds. Best dry wines are single-vy'd FURMINT and HÁRSLEVELÜ (06 08), plus ASZÚ sold under owner's name. Bodvin is cheaper second label.

Oremus w dr sw ★★→★★★★ 99' 00' 02 03' 05 06' (07) (08) Ancient TOKAJ v'yd of founding Rakóczi family, owned by Spain's Vega Sicilia. First-rate ASZÚ and v.gd dry FURMINT Mandolás.

Pajzos, Château w dr sw ★★→★★★ 93 99 00 02 03' 05 06' (07) (08) Bordeaux-owned TOKAJ estate with some fine ASZÚ. See MEGYER.

Pannonhalma r w dr ★★ Region in north. Recent joint venture has revived historic Pannonhalma Abbey winery and v'yds dating back to AD 996. TRAMINI, Ries do well and v.gd value. Attractive white blend Tricollis and young Pinot N.

Patricius w dr sw ★★→★★★ 00' 02 03 05 06' (07) (08) New quality TOKAJ estate (2000). V.gd dry FURMINT and ASZÚ. 4 Puttonyos is unusual, with lovely balance.

Pécs w (r) ★→★★ Newly renamed wine district in southern Hungary, around the city of Pécs. Known for whites, inc local Cirfandl. Pinot N is promising if Ebner Borhaz's latest 07 is a guide.

Pendits Winery w sw ★★→★★★ TOKAJ estate certified organic from 2008 and working on biodynamic lines (using horses and not machines), run by Márta Wille-Baumkauff and her sons. Luscious ASZÚ ESSENCIA 00 03, Botrytis *Selection 01*. Attractive Szello Cuvée 06 07 and crunchy Dry Muscat 08.

Puttonyos Measure of sweetness in TOKÁJI ASZÚ. A *puttony* is a 25-kg measure, traditionally a hod of grapes. The number of *putts* per barrel (136 litres) of dry base wine or must determines the final richness of the wine, from 3 *putts* to 6 (3 putts = 60g of sugar per litre, 4 = 90g, 5 = 120g, 6 = 150g, 7 = 180g). See also ASZÚ ESSENCIA and ESSENCIA.

Royal Tokaji Wine Co Pioneer foreign joint venture at MÁD in 1989. 81 ha, mainly first- or second-growth. First wines 90 91 (esp) 93 led renaissance of TOKAJ. 96 99 00 03 06 (07) (08) to follow. (I am a co-founder.) Also well-made dry FURMINT and v.gd-value late-harvest Áts Cuvee 06 07 08. New winery built 2009.

Sauska ★★→★★★ 06 07 (08) New immaculate winery in VILLÁNY. Also eponymous winery (former casino) in TOKAJ (formerly ÁRVAY). Finely crafted examples of KADARKA, KÉKFRANKOS, Cab Fr and impressive red blends.

Siklós City of southern Hungary; part of VILLÁNY-SIKLÓS. Best-known for whites, esp HÁRSLEVELÜ and ripe, fruity Chard. Plantings of promising reds, esp Cab Fr.

Somló w ★★→★★★ Isolated but dramatic area on slopes of extinct volcano famous for its mineral-rich whites. Traditionally wines fermented and aged in barrel; leading producers inc Fekete, Györgykovács, Hollovar, while TORNAI and KREINBACHER now lead the way with more modern and exciting versions of local grapes: Juhfark ("sheep's tail"), OLÁSZRIZLING, FURMINT and HÁRSLEVELÜ.

Sopron W Hungary r ★★→★★★ Historic enclave south of Neusiedlersee (see Austria). Traditionally known for lighter reds from KÉKFRANKOS but showing promise for more full-bodied reds, plus Cab Sauv, Syrah, Pinot N. Top producer WENINGER, also look for Luka, Pfneiszl, Ráspi, Taschner.

St Andrea r w dr ★★ 05 06 07 (08) One of the most important producers in EGER. Model for modern high-quality BIKAVÉR (Merengö, Aldas). Gd white blends Napbor, Orokke plus Pinot N and KÉKFRANKOS.

Szamorodni Literally "as it was born"; describes TOKÁJI not sorted in the v'yd. Dry or (fairly) sweet, depending on proportion of ASZÚ grapes present. In vintage TOKAJ ASZÚ yrs, sweet style can offer ASZÚ character at less cost. The best dry versions are *flor*-aged; try TINON or DERESZLA.

Szekszárd r ★★→★★★ District in south Hungary; some of country's top reds from KÉKFRANKOS, Cab Sauv, Cab Fr and Merlot. Also KADARKA being revived and BIKAVÉR. Look for: Dúzsi, Heimann, Sebestyén, Szent Gaál, Takler, Vesztergombi, Vida, Dom Grof Zichy.

Szepsy, István w dr sw ★★★★ 99' 00' 02 03' 05 06 07 (08) Impeccable small production of long-ageing TOKÁJI ASZÚ from own winery in MÁD. Recent releases of *excellent single-v'yd dry wines from Furmint* and HÁRSLEVELÜ 05 06' 07, and new sweet SZAMORODNI from 03 06. Same family name as the man who created the ASZÚ method in 17th century.

Szeremley, Huba r w dr sw ★★→★★★ Leader in BADACSONY. Ries, *Szürkebarát*, KÉKNYELÜ, sweet Zeus are modern models. Promising Pinot N since 03.

Szürkebarát Literally "Grey Monk": Pinot Gr. Widely planted and produces high-quality dry wines and inexpensive Italian lookalikes, esp around BALATON.

Tibor Gál r w dr ★★ Winery in EGER founded by the late Tibor Gál, who made his name as winemaker at Ornellaia. Look for single-v'yd bottlings of Pinot N and v.gd dry Viognier. Son working hard to improve wines.

Tiffán, Ede ★★ VILLÁNY grower: full-bodied, oaked reds.

Tinon, Samuel ★★→★★★ r dr sw Frenchman from Ste Croix du Mont, in TOKAJ since 1991. Distinctive and v.gd TOKÁJI ASZÚ with v. long maceration and barrel-ageing. Cellars at BODROGKERESZTÚR. Also superb flor-aged SZAMORODNI.

Tokaj/Tokaji w dr sw ★★→★★★ Tokaj is the town; Tokáji is the wine, Tokay the old French and English name. Appellation covers 5,967 ha. See ESSENCIA, FURMINT, PUTTONYOS, SZAMORODNI. Also dry table wine of character.

Tokaj Trading House State-owned TOKAJ company, buying grapes from over 2,000 small growers plus 55 ha own vines, inc the fine Szarvas v'yd. Also called Kereskedöház, or Crown Estates. Quality is underperforming.

Tolna Declared separate region from SZEKSZÁRD in 1997. Largest single estate is Antinori-owned Bátaapáti with 155 ha. Good TRAMINI, Chard, blended reds. German-owned Danubiana based here though most of its v'yds are at MÁTRA.

Törley r w dr ★→★★ Large company (was Hungarovin): sound international varietals (Chard, Cab Sauv, Merlot), also *cuve close*, transfer and classic sparkling (the one to try). Owned by German sekt specialist Henkell & Söhnlein. Chapel Hill is well-made, gd-value commercial brand, György-Villa and Kemendy for better selections.

Tornai w dr ★★→★★★ 06 07 08 Largest producer in this region. Family-owned, making v.gd, complex, intense dry whites (Juhfark, HÁRSLEVELÜ, OLASZRIZLING and FURMINT). Top Selection wines notable.

Tramini Gewurz.

Villány-Siklós (S Pannonia) Southern wine region with two main towns. Villány makes mostly red, often good-quality Bordeaux styles. Siklós makes mostly white. High-quality producers: BOCK, CSÁNYI, ATTILA GERE, Tamas Gere, Heumann, MALATINSZKY, Polgár, SAUSKA, TIFFÁN, Wunderlich, VYLYAN.

Vylyan r w dr ★★→★★★ 03' 04 06' 07 (08) Run by the dynamic Monika

Debreczeni. 130 ha with local and international varieties. Burgundian consultant's influence shows in stylish Pinot N. *Duennium Cuvée* (Cab Fr, Cab Sauv, Merlot and Zweigelt) is flagship red.

Weninger r ★★★ Standard-setting winery in Balf, SOPRON, run by Austrian Franz Weninger Jr. Biodynamic since 2006. Single-v'yd *Spern Steiner Kékfrankos* 04' 06 one of best in country. Syrah, Pinot N and red blends also impressive.

Weninger Gere r ★★★ Austro-Hungarian joint venture since 1992 between Franz Weninger Sr and ATTILA GERE. Cab Fr Selection excellent 00' 02 03' 04' 06, gd-value Cuvée Phoenix 04 06', Rosé 08.

Zéta A cross of Bouvier and FURMINT used by some in ASZÚ production.

BULGARIA

Most new wineries (and some older ones) now have their own vineyards, which has led to much improved quality. The 2009 vintage was mixed, good in parts. The global economic crisis has badly affected many traditional export markets, notably Russia, so winemakers face a tough year.

Assenovgrad r ★→★★ MAVRUD and RUBIN specialists. MAVRUD 04 07.

Belvedere Group Owns KATARZYNA, ORIACHOVITZA and VINIMPEX brands.

Bessa Valley r ★★★ Stephan von Neipperg (Canon la Gaffelière, Bordeaux) and K-H Hauptmann's exciting winery near Pazardjik. Enira and Enira Reserve 06. The only quality Bulgarian wine readily available in UK – at Waitrose.

Blueridge r w ★→★★ Large DOMAINE BOYAR winery. Gd Chard and Cab Sauv.

Castra Rubra r ★★ New winery of TELISH in south. Michel Rolland advising. Try the Via Diagonalis and Pendar 07.

Chateau de Val r ★★ Small producer of distinctive top-end wines. Grand Claret 03. Award-winning new white, Cuvée Trophy 07.

Damianitsa r ★★→★★★ Winery specializing in MELNIK grape. V.gd Redark Merlot 04; Uniqato and No Man's Land labels consistent quality.

Dimiat Native white grape. Gd examples from BLUERIDGE and POMORIE.

Domaine Boyar Main exporter to UK, own v'yds and wineries. Best-known producer in Bulgaria. Award-winning Solitaire Merlot Vintage 06. Solitaire range extended with Pinot N, Cab Franc and Grand Cépage.

Dragomir r ★★ Promising new winery near Plovdiv. Cab Sauv/Merlot blands such as Karizma 07.

Gamza Red grape (Kadarka of Hungary) with potential, mainly from Danube region. Novo Selo is specialist.

Karnobat ★★ r w Winery to watch. Chateau Karnobat Merlot 08 and Muscat-Traminer 08 recommended.

Katarzyna ★★ Promising quality from new cellar in southeast. Look for Question Mark 07, Mezzek Merlot 07.

Khan Krum ★Gd whites, esp Chard and TRAMINER.

Korten ★★ Boutique cellar of DOMAINE BOYAR. Traditional styles.

Leventa ★★ Small new winery in Russe with particularly gd whites, esp TRAMINER. 06 Chard and 05 Merlot Grand Selections recommended.

Logodaj ★→★★ Winery at Blagoevgrad. Soetto Cab Fr 05. Nobile Rubin 06. Value.

Mavrud Considered the best indigenous red variety, v. popular at home. Age-worthy, dark, plummy wines only grown in the Plovdiv area.

Maxxima ★ r (w) Full-bodied reds esp Cab Sauv, Merlot and MAVRUD. Private Reserve 03 is recommended.

Melnik Southwest village and highly prized indigenous grape variety grown throughout Struma Valley. Dense, full-bodied reds for ageing.

Miroglio, Edoardo r w ★★ Italian investor with own v'yds. Merlot Elenovo 06,

Miroglio, Edoardo r w ★★ Italian investor with own v'yds. Merlot Elenovo 06, Chard 06, Sauv Bl 07 and Pinot N 06 recommended. Producer of Bulgaria's best sparkling wine: Miroglio Brut Metodo Classico 05.

Misket Indigenous grape, mildly aromatic. The basis for most country whites. Sungurlare and Karlovo in the Valley of the Roses are specialists.

Oriachovitza r ★★ Winery owned by Belvedere. Gd Reserve Cab Sauv 04. Richly fruity reds at their best after 4–5 yrs.

Pamid Light, soft, everyday red in southeast and northwest.

Pomorie w (r) ★ Black Sea winery. Try Chard and DIMIAT 08.

Rubin Bulgarian cross (Nebbiolo x Syrah); gd in blends, but gaining favour in single-varietal niche wines.

Sakar Southeast area with some of Bulgaria's best Merlot. Domaine Sakar Merlot and Pinot N 05 recommended.

Santa Sarah r w ★★ Premium wine brand for fine Cab Sauv, Merlot. Privat (Cab Sauv/MAVRUD blend) 06 is outstanding. Bin 41 Merlot 06. Also gd whites.

Shumen r w ★ New World-style reds and esp whites from Black Sea-region winery. Good TRAMINER, popular on home market.

Slaviantsi ★ Gd varietal whites.

Sliven, Vini r (w) ★ Thracian Valley winery for Merlot, MISKET and Chard.

Targovishte w ★ Winery in east. Quality Chard, Sauv Bl and TRAMINER.

Telish r ★★ Innovative winery in north. Cab Sauv 06 and Merlot 06. Gd value.

Terra Tangra r w ★★→★★★ Winery in southeast near Harmanli fulfilling early promise, own v'yds in a gd area. Impressive wines, widely recommended. Try the Cab Sauv and Merlot Grand Reserves 06, Roto 06 and Cuvée 06.

Todoroff r (w) ★→★★ Thracian-region, high-profile (25 ha): Cab Sauv, MAVRUD, Merlot.

Traminer Fine whites with hints of spice. Most popular white in Bulgaria.

Valley Vintners ★★ Pioneer terroir wine Sensum 03 is excellent. Recommend Dux 03. Le Cubiste Cab Sauv 03.

Villa Lyubimets ★→★★ V'yds in southeast nr Greek-Turkish borders. Mainly reds. Villa Hissar is sister white label. Syrah 06 is worth a try.

Vinimpex A major exporter of Bulgarian wines.

Yambol r w ★ Winery in Thracian plain, specializing in Cab Sauv and Merlot.

SLOVENIA

A star of central Europe for its dramatic scenery, great terroirs and a raft of exciting and improving winemakers. There's an east-west divide, with the east near Austria producing zesty whites to rival New Zealand, while the west is notable for full, rich whites and serious reds.

Batic ★★ Organic-oriented wine-grower in VIPAVA. Try Bonissimus 07, Zarija 06' 07 and Rosso 05.

Bjana ★★ Gd BRDA producer. Aged sparklers are much respected locally.

Blazic ★★★ BRDA producer with a sense of place. Top whites, esp complex REBULA and SAUVIGNONASSE. .

Brda (Goriska) District in PRIMORJE. Centre of quality with many gd producers, inc BJANA, BLAZIC, Četrtič, EDI SIMCIC, Erzetič, JAKONCIC, Kabaj, Klinec, Kristancic, MOVIA, Prinčič, SIMCIC, SCUREK, VINSKA KLET GORISKA BRDA, Zanut.

Cotar ★★ Leading producer from KRAS. Hazy white blend Dražna and Vitovska are made with long skin contact. Also TERAN and Terra Rossa. Reds need keeping.

Curin-Prapotnik ★★ Legendary pioneer of private wine-growing from early 1970s onward. PREDIKATS are world-class ★★★★. Also brand PRA-Vino. 99' 04' 05' 06'.

Cvicek Locally popular traditional pink blend of POSAVJE. Low alcohol, high acid. Usually based on local Zametovka. Try Bajnof.

value whites, esp Sauv Bl and Furmint. Premium line, inc renowned RENSKI RIZLING "M", 04' 06' 07 08, is mostly from single v'yds. V.gd MODRI PINOT 06' 07 08 .

Istenič ★★→★★★ NV Barbara and Miha are gd value, while Gourmet vintage range is often Slovenia's best.

Jakončič ★★★ V.gd BRDA producer with elegant whites and reds. Top wines: white 04' 05' 06'; red 04' 05' 06 blend Carolina.

Jeruzalem Ormož ★★ Well-known co-op near dramatic hilltop town of Jeruzalem producing crisp whites DYA, esp SIPON (Furmint), Sauv Bl, RENSKI RIZLING (Ries) and great-value blend Terase.

Joannes ★★ Winery near Maribor. Pioneer in dry wines, esp Ries 04' 05' 06' 07 and Chard 05 06 07.

Kogl ★★★ Hilltop winery near Ormož, dating back to 16th century. Whites among Slovenia's best, either varietal (Mea Culpa) or Duo, Trio, Quartet blends. Premium blends (r/w) Magna Domenica. Delicate PREDIKATS. Repays ageing.

Kras Small, famous district in PRIMORJE. Best-known for TERAN but trend is toward whites, esp MALVAZIJA. Look for ČOTAR, Jazbec, Lisjak Boris, RENČEL.

Kupljen ★★ Dry wine pioneer near Jeruzalem known for RENSKI RIZLING, Sauv Bl, SIVI PINOT, Chard, Pinot N. Great for ageing, consistent.

Laški Rizling Welschriesling. Most-planted variety, but rarely made as a varietal.

Ledeno vino Icewine. Getting rare but made almost every yr. Can be sublime.

Ljutomer Ormož ★→★★★ Famous wine subdistrict in PODRAVJE, known for crisp, delicate white varieties and top botrytis, has still more to deliver. See ČURIN, JERUZALEM ORMOŽ, KOGL, Krainz, Krajnc, KUPLJEN, VERUS.

Macerated whites Recently v. popular. Whites produced with long maceration for several days at higher temperatures. There is hardly an important producer in PRIMORJE not using this technique at least in part.

Malvazija Slightly bitter yet generous flavour, which goes v. well with seafood. Malvazija by VINAKOPER is gd value. Also v.gd from Pucer z Vrha, Montemoro, SANTOMAS, Rojac, Bordon, Korenika and Moškon. In recent yrs successfully grown in BRDA and KRAS.

Marof ★★ New winery in Prekmurje raising the potential of the district. DYA white, oak-aged line Breg and single-v'yd line Cru.

Mlečnik ★★★ Disciple of Italy's Joško Gravner from VIPAVA.

Modra Frankinja ★→★★★ Austria's Blaufränkisch. Traditionally best in POSAVJE, but DVERI-PAX and PTUJSKA KLET are overtaking.

Modra Pinot (Pinot N) Slovenia's best red? Some are fine and age-worthy.

Movia ★★★ High-profile biodynamic winery run by charismatic showman Aleš Kristančič. Winemaking is extreme, but excellent results, esp Veliko Belo (w) 96' 99' 00' 01' 02 03' 04' 05 and Veliko Rdeče (r) 93 96' 97' 00' 01' 02 and released mature. V. gd varietals esp MODRI PINOT 02' 03' 04. Lunar (REBULA) 05' 06' 07 08 and sparkling Puro are out of the ordinary style. Age well. Vikmarija label for lighter wines.

Penina Quality sparkling wine made by either *charmat* or traditional method. Lots of styles available. Look for RADGONSKE GORICE (biggest), ISTENČ (biggest private), BJANA (most fashionable), Medot, MOVIA.

Podravje Region in the northeast. Recent comeback with aromatic whites and increasingly fine reds, mostly Pinot N and MODRA FRANKINJA.

Posavje Conservative wine region in the southeast. Producers: ISTENČ, PRUS, ŠTURM.

Predikat Wines made from botrytis-affected grapes. Expensive. Pozna Trgatev is Spätlese, Izbor is Auslese, Jagodni Izbor is Beerenauslese, Suhi Jagodni Izbor is Trockenbeerenauslese (TBA), while LEDENO VINO is Icewine. Try to find some!

Primorje Region in the southwest from the Adriatic to BRDA. Currently most forward-looking Slovenian wine region for both reds and whites. Aka Primorska.

Prus Small producer from the Bela Krajina district in POSAVJE. His delicate and complex PREDIKATS and Icewines are ★★★★.

Ptujska Klet ★★→★★★ Winery in Ptuj producing gd, international-style white. Brand Pullus since 2007. Sauv Bl is regularly v.gd, esp "G", and lovely Laški Rizling TBA 08'.

Radgonske Gorice ★ Well-known co-op producing best-selling Slovenian sparkler Srebrna ("silver") PENINA, classic-method Zlata ("golden") PENINA, and legendary *demi-sec* Traminec with black label.

Rebula Traditional white variety of BRDA. Can be exceptional. Varietal or with Chard for top blends. AKA Ribolla Gialla in Italy.

Refošk ★ A local strain of Refosco (not as Italy). Prone to being thin and high-acid. Producers like SANTOMAS, ROJAC, Steras show what can be done with low yields.

Renčel ★★★ Remarkable producer from KRAS (tiny quantities, experiments).

Renski Rizling Ries. Floral, fruity, or minerally (ageing potential). Best: Ducal, DVERI-PAX, JERUZALEM ORMOŽ, JOANNES, Krajnc, KUPLJEN, MAROF, VALDHUBER, VERUS.

Rojac ★★ High-quality organic producer. Try Renero 05 as new take on REFOŠK. Also Stari d'Or blends 05 06 and Malvazija 08.

Rumeni Muskat Yellow Muscat, or Muscat Blanc à Petits Grains.

Santomas ★★★ SLOVENSKA ISTRA. French consultant is helping to produce some of the country's best REFOŠK and REFOŠK-Cab Sauv blends. Antonius 03 04 (06), Grande Cuvée 03 04 05.

Sauvignonasse Aka Tocai Friulano, mostly in BRDA. Popular locally and in Italy.

Ščurek ★★→★★★ V. reliable BRDA producer. DYA varieties Chard, REBULA, Tokáji, Sauv Bl, Cab Fr. V. particular red and white blends, Stara Brajda 05 06 07. Also premium red blend Up 04 05, unusual rare Pikolit 05 06.

Simčič, Edi ★★★ BRDA producer. Best: white blend Triton Lex, Kozana (single-v'yd Chard); red blend Duet Lex 02 03' 04' 06 and v. expensive top-class Kolos 03' 04.

Simčič, Marjan ★★★★ Excellent BRDA producer. Gd varietal whites, esp SIVI PINOT, SAUVIGNONASSE, REBULA. Chard and Sauv Bl Selekcija impress and age well. Teodor Belo (w) 00 02 03 04 06 and Merlot-based Teodor Rdeče 00 02 03 04 (06) red are superb and MODRI PINOT is elegant (03' 04' 06' 07). V.gd single-v'yd range called Opoka from 2006. Sweet Leonardo is great 03 04.

Sipon Aka Furmint. Up-and-coming dry, crisp and delicate white. See VERUS, KUPLJEN, Ducal, Püklavec, Miro, Krainz, JERUZALEM ORMOŽ. Excellent for botrytis.

Sivi Pinot Pinot Grigio. Increasingly fine, fruity, with much more character and body than in neighbouring Fruili Venezia-Giulia. Fine aromatics in PODRAVJE.

Slovenska Istra Coastal district in PRIMORJE, known for REFOŠK and constantly improving MALVAZIJA. SANTOMAS and VINAKOPER lead.

Štajerska Slovenija New and important wine district since 2006 that encompasses practically whole PODRAVJE region.

Steyer ★★ Top name from RADGONSKE GORICE. Best-known for Traminec in all possible forms and styles. Sweet Vaneja 03 impresses.

Šturm ★★ Long-established, yet lone star of the Bela Krajina district in POSAVJE. Many PREDIKATS are outstanding.

Sutor ★★★ Excellent producer from VIPAVA. Look for MODRI PINOT 06' 07' and Chard 04' 05' 06' 07' , white blend Burja 06' 07' and Merlot 03 06'.

Teran ★ REFOŠK from KRAS. Dark, high-acidity red, v. popular locally.

Tilia ★★ Young couple from VIPAVA produce international style white and red. MODRI PINOT 04 06' is usually great. SIVI PINOT and local Zelen are gd 07 (08).

Valdhuber ★★★ Dry wine pioneers in PODRAVJE. Top (dry) Traminec; v.gd Sauv Bl.

Verus Vinogradi ★★★ 07' 08' Young team, distinctive white varietals; acclaim for maiden vintage 2007, esp with Furmint. Also v.gd Sauv Bl and Chard from 08.

Vinakoper ★★ Large company with own v'yds in SLOVENKSA ISTRA. Gd-value brand Capris line and premium Capo d'Istria Cab Sauv 99' 02 03' 06.

SLOVENIA

> AOP the Slovenian way
> Vino ZGP (Zaščitemim Geograskim Pareklem) remains the term for AOP divided into Vrnsko (top quality) and Kakovostno (quality). IGP is Dezlnovino.

Vinska Klet Gorišk Brda ★→★★★ Immensely improved big winery from BRDA. Big range, mostly varietals, often excellent value, esp Quercus whites.

Vipava Valley noted for cool breezes in PRIMORJE. Fine producers: BATIČ, Guerila, Štokelj, MLEČNIK, SUTOR, TILIA. Vipava co-op ★ has premium brand Lanthieri ★★.

Zanut ★★ Controversial, expressive Sauv Bl; single-v'yd Merlot Brjac (99 03) in BRDA.

CROATIA

Croatia's domestic demand has increased along with tourism and has contributed to eye-watering prices and little export for the best wines. Distinctive local grapes and varied terrain make it worth exploring nonetheless. The country is divided into two distinct regions: Kontinentralja Hrvatska and Primorska Hrvatska.

Babić Dark, native red from north DALMATIA, grown in stony seaside v'yds near Šibenik. Exceptional quality potential. Try Gracin.

Badel 1862 ★→★★★ Biggest wine producer, surprisingly gd. Best: Ivan Dolac (PZ Svirče), DINGAČ (PZ i Vinarija Dingač). Sweet GRAŠEVINA Duravar 07 is excellent.

Bibich ★★ Pioneering winery near Šibenik. Native Plavina, BABIČ, Lasina and Rhône grapes used for elegant reds. Sweet Ambra is figgy and rich.

Bodren Small producer with superb range of sweet wines (esp 07), inc Chateau Bezanec Chard, Sivi Pinot and Ries.

Bura ★★★ 04' 05' 06 07 Considered best DINGAČ producer. Tiny quantities.

Crljenak Almost extinct indigenous grape identified recently by DNA testing as the original Zinfandel.

Dalmatia Dalmacija. The coast of Croatia is a grower's paradise. Traditionally high in alcohol. Whites (Debit, Maraština) improving, reds improving faster.

Dingač 03' 04' 05' 06 (07) V'yd designation on PELJEŠAC's steep southern slopes. *Grand cru* for PLAVAC MALI. From partially dried grapes: robust, dry (over-) expensive red. Look for: BURA, Kiridžija, Matusko, Miličić, Radović, Skaramuča.

Enjingi, Ivan ★★→★★★ Producer of v.gd sweet botrytis and dry whites, esp v.gd Venje blend from Požega. GRAŠEVINA, esp Kasna Berba (06).

Graševina Welschriesling. Best in SLAVONIJA. Look for Adžić, Belje Enjingi, Kalazić, KRAUTHAKER, KUTJEVO, Vinarija Daruvar. From dry to top botrytis.

Grgić ★★→★★★ PLAVAC and oaky POŠIP on Pelješac Peninsula.

Hvar Beautiful island in mid-Dalmatia. Look for: Ivan Dolac, Carić Faros, Plančić, ZLATAN PLAVAC, PZ Svirče, TOMIĆ, Boskinač.

Ilocki w dr sw ★★ 06 07 V.gd sweet Traminac and weighty dry version.

Istria N Adriatic peninsula. MALVAZIJA is the main grape here. Gd also for Cab Sauv and TERAN. Look for Benvenuti, Clai, Coronica, Kozlović, Matoševič, Roxanich.

Korta Katarina ★★★ New and v. promising small producer with 6 ha. POŠIP 06 07 is excellent and v. gd PLAVAC MALI 06 07, esp Reuben's Reserve.

Krauthaker, Vlado ★★★ 06 07 08 Top producer of dry and sweet whites from KUTJEVO, esp Chard (Rosenberg), GRAŠEVINA Mitrovac and Friskova. Gd Sauv Bl.

Kutjevo Name shared by a town in SLAVONIJA, centre of GRAŠEVINA and ★★→★★★ Kutjevo Cellars. Gewurz, GRAŠEVINA and Traminec Icewine.

Malvazija Most impressive grape in ISTRIA. Malvazija Istarka, not the same as Mediterranean Malvasia. Often vinified in light, minerally style to drink young; try Arman Franc, Benvenuti, Coronica, Kozlović, Malić and Trapan. Also rich, full-bodied versions with barrel ageing: Clai, Kozlevic, Matosević and Roxanich.

Mendek Highly regarded winery near Dubrovnik serious reds. Selekcija 03 04 06.

Plavac Mali Croatia's top red grape, related to Zinfandel. Potential for high quality and ageability, though can be alcoholic and lack elegance. Producers Bakovič, BURA, Medvid, Miličič, Svirče, Matruško, Miloš Frano, Lučič, Zlatan Plenkovic, TOMIČ, KORTA KATARINA are well regarded.

Posip Best DALMATIAN white, mostly on island of Korčula.

Postup Famous v'yd designation northwest of DINGAC. Medium to full-bodied red from PLAVAC MALI. Donja Banda, Miličič, Radović are a gd call.

Prosek *Passito*-style dessert wine from DALMATIA, made from dried local grapes Bogdanuša, Maraštrina, Prč. Look for Hectorovich from TOMIČ.

Slavonija Subregion in north for white. Look out for ADZIČ, Belje, ENJINGI, KRAUTHAKER, KUTJEVO, Zdjelarevic. Famous for its oak, too.

Teran Grape also found in Slovenia. A relative of Italy's Refosco.

Tomič ★★ Cr dr sw 03 04 05 06 Owner of Bastijana winery on island of Hvar. V.gd barrique PLAVAC MALI 06 and PROSEK Hectorovich from dried grapes.

Vrhunsko vino A fairly rigorous designation for high-quality wines.

Zlatan Otok ★★★ Zlatan Plavac Grand Cru 03' 04' 05' 06 is constantly among top Croatian reds. POSIP 08 is charming; ZLATAN PLAVAC 07 approchable and appealing.

Zlatan Plavac *Grand cru* designation for PLAVAC MALI. Usually v. high alcohol.

BOSNIA & HERZEGOVINA, SERBIA, MONTENEGRO, MACEDONIA

These smaller countries have a wealth of native grapes and original styles, though inevitably international flavours are creeping in. In Bosnia & Herzegovina, look out for the herbal notes of the red Blatina and the pungent white Zilavka grapes; Serbia's WOW winery (yes, really) is forward-looking and new; Aleksandrović is another leader of the new wave. Radovanović, Rubin and Vrsac Vinogradi are also worth a look. Montenegro's vineyards are confined to the coastal strip and the basin of Lake Skadar: 13 Jul Plantaže is the biggest producer, still state-owned. In Macedonia wine accounts for 17–20 per cent of GDP, making it one of the most reliant countries in the world on wine; most is exported to Germany and elsewhere, but there's an increasing focus on quality. Promising wineries include Cekorov, Château Kamnik, Dalvina, Fonko, Pivka, Popova Kula, Skovin and Tikveš.

THE CZECH REPUBLIC & SLOVAKIA

Czech Republic

Czech wines continue to be sent abroad in droves to garner medals at international competitions, though these do not translate into exports as both wines and producers are almost totally unknown to the world's consumers, while the wines are noticeably overpriced. Luckily local drinkers remain fairly patriotic. Based on the German system, grapes are judged primarily on must-weight levels. This obsession has given rise to a fashion for semi-sweet and sweet offerings. New appellation VOC Znojmo is the first step to denominating a specific place definition rather than just variety on the wine label and has made a tentative start. NB: Blends are still looked down upon by the locals.

Bohemia 730 ha in two demarcated wine subregions: Mělnická (Mělník) and Litoměřická (Litoměřice). Some similarity to wines in neighbouring east Germany. Best in the Elbe Valley (north of Prague), notably at Mělník , Roudnice and Žernoseky. Vineyard renewal, esp in Prague (Gröbovka, Salabka and Svatováclavská), inc several small boutique wineries east of the capital: Kutná

Hora, Konárovice and Chateau Kuks. Notable producers: Bettina Lobkowicz (Mělník), Vilém Kraus III (Mělník), Lubomír Bílík–Salabka (Troja, near Prague Zoo). Kosher wines: České vinařství Chrámce. Bohemia Sekt and Soare dominate sparkling wine production

Moravia 18,700 ha in four demarcated wine subregions: Znojemská (Znojmo), Mikulovská (Mikulov), Velkopavlovická (Velké Pavlovice) and Slovácko. Vineyards situated in southeast along Austrian and Slovak borders: similar grapes. Look for: Stapleton & Springer (Bořetice), Krist (Milotice), S, Spielberg (Archlebov), Baloun (Velké Pavlovice), František Mádl (V. Bílovice), Reisten (Pavlov), Sonberk (Pouzdřany), Valihrach (Krumvíř). The established giants get stronger, as do groupings such as Collegium Vinitorum, Bonus Eventus and newcomer V8. Icing on the cake is Icewine and straw wine – highly popular and expensive. Moravia also has sparkling wine, esp the renewed Sekt label of the late Jan Petrák.

Slovak Republic

Over 17,000 ha of vineyards in six wine regions along the western and southern borders: Malokarpatská (Little Carpathians), Juhoslovenská (southern Slovakia), Nitrianska (Nitra), Stredoslovenská (central Slovakia), Východoslovenská (eastern Slovakia) and the smallest Tokajská (Tokaj) region, neighbouring Hungary's Tokaj and making wines of traditional character. Classic central European and international varieties. Nearly all consumed locally with some sold in bulk to the Czech Republic. Leading producers: Château Belá (Mužla) with Egon Müller's involvement, In Vino (Modra) – NZ ce, Malík (Modra), Mrva & Stanko (Trnava), and JJ Ostrožovič (V Tŕňa, Tokaj). For sparkling wine: JE Hubert and Pálffy Sekt.

ROMANIA

The quality of Romanian wine continues to improve as recent investments in vineyards and wineries bear fruit. This year's announcement of Antinori's joint venture in Dealu Mare district with British-owned Halewood adds support to claims of excellent soils and top sites, and promises more in the future. Overall vineyard area is still falling as small, fragmented holdings disappear, but Romania remains one of Europe's top-ten producers. Exports remain small, so you will have to visit the country to track down the most exciting wines.

Băbească Neagră Traditional "black grandmother grape" of MOLDOVA ; light body and ruby-red colour.

Banat Small wine region on western border, with two DOCS: Banat itself and Recas. Main winery is CRAMELE RECAŞ.

Burgund Mare Romanian name for Blaufränkisch (Kékfrankos in Hungary).

Carl Reh ★★ German-owned winery with 190-ha v'yd in Oprisor. V.gd reds, esp La Cetate Pinot N is best (05 06' 07 08). Val Duna is export label for gd varietal white and rosé, esp Pinot Gr. New fine red blend Fragmentarium from 07'.

Cotnari Region in northeast with v.gd botrytis conditions. Famous for over 500 yrs for medium to sweet GRASĂ, FETEASCĂ ALBĂ, TĂMÂIOASĂ and dry Frâncusă. The Tokaj of Romania.

Cotnari Winery 1,200 ha in COTNARI region. Wines range from dry to v. sweet, inc v.gd collection wines.

Cramele Odobeşti Controls 800 ha with four wineries. South African winemaker David Lockley now consulting: whites sound, reds underperform.

Cramele Recaş r w dr ★★ 06 07 08 British/Romanian firm in BANAT region. PINOT N with potential. Best: Sole Chard, La Putere red. Gd Pinot Gr, promising new Syrah from 06 07 08. Also v.gd Merlot Rosé 08 and Cuvée Uberland red blend 06. Other labels include V, Terra Dacica.

Crişana & Maramures Western region, inc DOCs of Crişana and historical Miniş (since 15th century): esp red Cadarca; crisp, white Mustoasă.

Davino Winery ★★→★★★ Premium producer with 68 ha in DEALU MARE. V.gd Dom Ceptura white 06 07 (08) and red 04 05 06 07. Alba Valahica and Purpura Valahica Fetească Neagră 06. Flagship blend is Flamboyant 03' 06'.

Dealu Mare (Dealul Mare) "The Big Hill". Important, well-situated area in southeastern Carpathian foothills. Excellent reds, esp FETEASCĂ NEAGRĂ, Cab Sauv, MERLOT, PINOT N. Whites from TĂMÂIOASĂ.

Dobrogea Black Sea region. Includes DOC regions of MURFATLAR, Badabag and Sarica Niculitel. Famous for sweet, late-harvest Chard and now for full-bodied reds.

Domeniile Tohani Winery ★ Major holding in DEALU MARE, specializing in red wines (inc FETEASCĂ NEAGRĂ, Cab Sauv, PINOT N, MERLOT) and sweet Dollette.

Domeniile Viticole Franco Române Frenchman Denis Themas set up this organic estate in DEALU MARE to make fine PINOT N. Also local red and white grapes.

Domeniile Sahateni 100-ha estate in DEALU MARE, founded in 2003. Blended red and whites under Divin label made by Aurelia Visinescu.

Domeniul Coroanei Segarcea ★ Former royal estate, southernmost winery in Oltenia. Replanted since 2004 and improved quality, esp aromatic whites, inc Muscat Frontignan Rosé, FETEASCĂ REGALĂ, Sauv Bl.

Drăgăşani Region in Olteria south of Carpathians. Traditional (white: Crâmposie Selectionată; reds: Novac, Negru de Drăgăşani) and international varieties.

Fetească Albă Romania's third-most-planted white grape with gentle Muscat aroma. Same as Hungary's Leányka.

Fetească Neagră "Black maiden grape" with potential as showpiece variety. Difficult to handle, but can give deep, full-bodied wines with character.

Fetească Regală A cross of FETEASCĂ ALBĂ with GRASĂ (gd for sparkling and recently some successful barrel-fermented versions). Most-planted white.

Grasă Local Romanian grape whose name means "fat". Prone to botrytis and v. important grape in COTNARI. Grown as Kövérszölö in Hungary's Tokaj region.

Halewood Winery r d r w sp sw ★→★★ 06 07 08 09 British-owned company with new focus on regional v'yds and improving quality, esp Hyperion and Cherry Tree brands. New single-v'yd bottlings of Romania's first Viognier are v.gd. Also sparkling at Azuga Cellar.

Iordana High acid, low alcohol local white grown in TRANSYLVANIA for sparkling wines.

Jidvei ★ Requipped winery in subregion of the same name in TRANSYLVANIA (TÂRNAVE). Whites: FETEASCĂ, ITALIAN RIES, Sauv Bl, Traminer and sparkling.

Lacrima lui Ovidiu "Ovid's Tear": sweet fortified wine aged for many yrs in oak barrels until amber coloured, from MURFATLAR.

Merlot Romania's most widely planted red variety.

Moldova (Moldavia) Western part of former Romanian province (eastern part became Republic of Moldova). Largest wine region, lying northeast of Carpathians. DOC areas include Bohotin, COTNARI, Dealu Bujorului, Huşi, Iaşi, Odobeşti, Coteşti, Nicoreşti.

Muntenia and Oltenia Hills Major wine region covering the DOC areas of DEALU MARE, Dealurile Olteniei, DRĂGĂŞANI, PIETROASA, Sâmbureşti, Stefaneşti.

Murfatlar Area with v'yds in DOBROGEA near Black Sea; v.gd Chard, Pinot Gr and Cab Sauv. Subregions are Cernavoda and Megidia.

Murfatlar Winery ★→★★ Largest bottled-wine producer. V.gd labels Trei Hectare (FETEASCĂ NEAGRĂ, Cab Sauv, Chard) and Ferma Nouă (MERLOT, Sauv Bl).

Pietroasa Area in DEALU MARE for sweet whites, esp TĂMÂIOASĂ ROMÂNEASCĂ.

Pinot Noir Grown for over 100 yrs, originally as sparkling base. Newer plantings of French clones show promise.

Prince Stirbey w r dr sw ★★ 08 20-ha estate in DRĂGĂŞANI returned to Austrian-Romanian noble family (Kripp-Costinescu). V.gd dry whites, esp local Crâmposie Selectionată 07 08, FETEASCĂ REGALĂ and TĂMÂIOASĂ ROMÂNEASCĂ and rosé. Has successfully revived local red varieties, esp v.gd Novac and Negru de Drăgăşani 06.

Riesling, Italian Widely planted Welschriesling, sold locally as Ries.

SERVE r w dr ★★→★★★ 03' 06' 07 08 Owned by Corsican Count Guy de Poix, basd in DEALU MARE. Terra Romana range is excellent, esp Cuvée Charlotte 03' 06' and Cuvée Amaury white.

Tămâioasă Românească White "frankincense" grape, with exotic aroma and taste belonging to Muscat family. Often makes fine botrytis wines in COTNARI and PIETROASA.

Transylvania Cool mountain plateau in centre of Romania. V'yds often steep and mostly producing white wines with gd acidity from FETEASCĂ ALBA, FETEASCĂ REGALĂ, Muscat, Traminer, ITALIAN RIES. Subregions include Târnave, Alba-Iulia, Lechinta, Aiud and Apold.

Valea Călugărească "Valley of the Monks". Part of DEALU MARE, site of research winery.

Vanju Mare Warm region in southwest noted for full-bodied reds.

Vinarte Winery ★★→★★★ 01 03 05 06 07 Italian investment covering three estates: Villa Zorilor in DEALU MARE, Castel Bolovanu in DRĂGĂŞANI, Terase Danubiane in VANJU MARE. Best are Soare Cabernet, Prince Matei Merlot and Swallowtail FETEASCĂ NEAGRĂ.

Vincon Vrancea Winery r w dr sw ★ One of Romania's largest producers with 2,150 ha in Vrancea, plus DOBROGEA and DEALU MARE.

Vinia r w dr sw ★ One of Romania's largest wineries at Iaşi. Major producer of COTNARI wines. Also whites and light reds.

Vinterra Dutch/Romanian venture reviving FETEASCĂ NEAGRĂ; also makes sound PINOT N, MERLOT. Black Peak is brand name.

Vitis Metamorphosis r ★★ 07 New high-profile joint venture between Italy's historic Antinori family and British-owned Halewood. 100 ha in DEALU MARE chosen for quality potential. First release is 07 Cantus Primus Cab Sauv.

WineRo New premium estate in Dolorogea owned by Stephan von Niepperg of Bordeaux's Canon-la-Gaffelière, with Dr Hauptmann and Marc Dworkin. The same threesome own/run Bulgaria's Bessa Valley.

MALTA

The introduction of new Demoninazzjoni ta' Origini Kontrollata, or DOK, regulations, enforceable from the 2008 vintage, bans *chaptalization* and brings vy'd, winemaking and labelling practices into line with the EU. The traditional, indigenous grapes are w Girgentina and r Gellewza, now being joined by international varieties in the island's 800 ha of vineyard. Antinori-backed Meridiana remains the driving force of the region, producing excellent Maltese Isis and Mistral Chards, Astarte Vermentino, Melquart Cab Sauv/Merlot, Nexus Merlot, *outstanding Bel Syrah* and premium Celsius Cab Sauv Reserve from island vines. Volume producers of note are Delicata, Marsovin and Camilleri.

Greece

The Greeks love foreign grapes, and they especially love French ones. However, foreigners love Greek varieties, and Greek winemakers understand that the key to international success lies in local vines. Realizing their potential in the vineyard will keep growers busy for the next 20 years easily.

Aghiorghitiko NEMEA's red grape, now planted almost everywhere, even in the north. Extemely versatile, from soft and charming to dense and age-worthy.

Aivalis ★★★ Boutique NEMEA producer: extracted style. Top (and pricey) wine is "4", from 120+-yr-old vines. Merlot is less successful.

Alpha Estate ★★★ Impressive estate in cool-climate Amindeo. Excellent Merlot/Syrah/XINOMAVRO blend, pungent Sauv Bl, unfiltered XINOMAVRO from ungrafted vines. Top wine: Alpha 1 that demands ageing. **★★★★** soon?

Antonopoulos ★★★ PATRAS-based winery, with top-class MANTINIA, crisp Adoli Ghis, Lafon-(Burgundy)-like Anax Chard, and Cab-based Nea Dris (stunning 04 and 06). Top wine: violet-scented Vertzami/Cab Fr.

Argatia ★★→★★★ Small KTIMA, just outside NAOUSSA, crafting tiny quantities of excellent XINOMAVRO, quite modern in style.

Arghyros ★★→★★★ Top SANTORINI producer with exemplary but expensive VINSANTO aged 20 yrs in cask (**★★★★**). Exciting KTIMA white, a critically acclaimed oak-aged Vareli white and fragrant (dry) Aidani. Try the rare red MAVROTRAGANO.

Assyrtiko One of the v. best white grapes of the Mediterranean, balancing power, minerality, extract and high acid. Built to age.

Avantis ★★★ Boutique winery in Evia with (red) v'yds in Boetia. Dense Syrah, Aghios Chronos Syrah/Viognier, pungent Sauv Bl and rich MALAGOUSIA. Top wine: elegant single-v'yd Avantis Collection Syrah **03 04** 05 06 07.

Biblia Chora ★★★ Polished New-World-style wines. Highly sought-after Sauv Bl/ASSYRTIKO. Floral Syrah Rosé. Ovilos white 08 pushed Greek oaked whites to a new level.

Boutari, J & Son ★→★★★ Producers in NAOUSSA. Excellent-value wines, esp *Grande Reserve Naoussa*, popular MOSCHOFILERO. Top Santorini Kalisti Reserve, single-v'yd Skalani from CRETE. Try the sweet red Liatiko.

Cair Large co-op winery in RHODES specializing in sparkling (esp rosé) but Pathos still range is v.gd value and v. drinkable.

Cambas, Andrew ★ Large-volume brand owned by BOUTARI.

Carras, Domaine ★→★★ Estate at Sithonia, Halkidiki, with its own OPAP (Côtes de Meliton). Chateau Carras **01** 03 04 05. Underperforming.

Cava Legal term for cask-aged still white and red table wines, eg. Cava Amethystos Kosta Lazaridi, Cava Hatzimihali.

Cephalonia (Kephalonia) Ionian island: excellent, floral white Robola, emerging styles of sweet Muscat, MAVRODAPHNE.

Crete Quality improves led by Ekonomou, Lyrarakis, Douloufakis, MANOUSSAKIS.

Dougos ★★→★★★ From the Olympus area, producing interesting Rhône blends, top Methymon range, esp opulent, dry, late harvest red Opsimo. New RAPSANI.

Driopi ★★★ New venture of TSELEPOS in high NEMEA. Initial vintages are serious (esp single-v'yd KTIMA) and of the high-octane style. Tavel-like Driopi rosé.

Emery ★→★★ Historic RHODES producer, specializing in local varieties. Brands Villaré, Grand Rosé. V.gd-value Rhodos Athiri. Sweet Efreni Muscat.

Feggites ★★ New winery in Drama, from ex-winemaker of NICO LAZARIDI. Fine range, excellent oak. Sauv Bl Deka.

Gaia ★★★ Top-quality NEMEA-based producer and winery on SANTORINI. Fun Notios label. New World-like AGHIORGHITIKO. Thought-provoking but top-class dry white Thalassitis Santorini and *wild-ferment Assyrtiko*. Top wine Gaia Estate (97 98 99 00 01 03 04 05 06 07). Anatolikos sweet NEMEA and dazzling Gaia S red (AGHIORGHITIKO with a touch of Syrah).

Gentilini Cephalonia ★★→★★★ Exciting whites inc *v.gd Robola*. New Unique Red, Serious Syrah and Selection Robola are top.

Georgakopoulos Central Greece ★★ Full-throttle, New World-style reds, *blanc de noir* Cab Sauv and rich, unoaked Chard. Producer to watch.

Gerovassiliou ★★★ Perfectionist miniature estate near Salonika. Benchmark ASSYRTIKO/MALAGOUSIA, smooth Syrah/Merlot blend, age-worthy, Burgundian in style Chard. Herby, red Avaton 03 from rare indigenous varieties. Top wine: Syrah (01 02 03 04 05). For many, the quality leader.

Greek Wine Cellars New company name for KOURTAKIS.

Goumenissa (OPAP) ★→★★ XINOMAVRO and Negoska oaked red from Macedonia. Esp Aidarinis, BOUTARI (esp Filiria), Ligas and Tatsis Bros.

Hatzidakis ★★★ Low-tech but high-class producer, redefining SANTORINI appellation, esp with *cuvées* No. 15 and 17. Stunning range across the board. Try the excellent Nihteri. Collio meets Aegean Sea.

Hatzimichalis, Domaine ★→★★★ Large v'yds and merchant in Atalanti. Huge range. Greek and French varieties, many bottlings labelled after their v'yd names. Top red Rahes Galanou Merlot/Cab Fr.

Helios, Domaine New umbrella name and new owners for SEMELI, Nassiakos and Orinos Helios wines. Move towards more modern pitch.

Katogi-Strofilia ★★→★★★ V'yds and wineries in Attica, Peloponnese and east Epirus. Greek varieties but also Chard, Cab Sauv, Traminer and even Pinot N. Katogi was the first premium Greek wine. Top wine: Ktima Averoff.

Katsaros ★★★ Small organic winery of v.gd standard on Mt Olympus. KTIMA red, a Cab Sauv/Merlot, has staying power. Chard gets better with each vintage. New Merlot.

Kir-Yanni ★★→★★★ V'yds in NAOUSSA and at Amindeo. Vibrant white Samaropetra; complex and age-worthy Dyo Elies red; NAOUSSA Ramnista turning towards more supple approach, making way for XINOMAVRO/Syrah blend Diaporos.

Kourtakis, D ★★ Merchant: *mild Retsina* and gd NEMEA. See GREEK WINE CELLARS.

Ktima Estate, farm. Term not exclusive to wine.

Lazaridis, Domaine Kostas ★★★ V'yds and wineries in Drama and Kapandriti (near Athens and sold under the Oenotria Land label). Quality Amethystos label (white, red, rosé). Top wine: unfiltered red CAVA Amethystos (97 98 99 00 01 02 03 04). First Greek consultancy of Bordeaux's Michel Rolland.

Lazaridi, Nico ★★→★★★ Spectacular post-modernist winery and v'yds in Drama, Kavala and Mykonos. Gd Château Nico Lazaridi (white, rosé and red). Top wine: Magiko Vouno white, red. Ultra-premium range under Perpetuus brand.

Lemnos (OPAP) Aegean island: mainly co-op fortified dessert wines, delicious, lemony Muscat of Alexandria.

Lyrarakis ★★→★★★ V.gd producer from CRETE. Whites from the rare Plyto and Dafni varieties, as well as a deep, complex blend of Syrah and Kotsifali. Top red: Grande Cuvée.

Magel ★★ Up-and-coming KTIMA in uncharted territory, in Kastoria, west Macedonia. Dressed-to-kill, vibrant wines, mainly from Bordeaux varieties.

Malagousia Rediscovered perfumed white grape, stunning in the hands of AVANTIS, GEROVASSILIOU and MATSA.

Manoussakis ★★★ Impressive newcomer from CRETE, with Rhône-inspired blends. Delectable range under Nostos brand, led by Roussanne and Syrah.

Mantinia (OPAP) w High, central Peloponnese region. Fresh, crisp, utterly charming *Moschofilero*.

Matsa, Château ★★→★★★ Historic and prestigious small estate in Attica, owned now by BOUTARI. MALAGOUSIA is a leading example.

Mavrodaphne (OPE) r sw "Black laurel", and red grape. Cask-aged port-style/*recioto*-like, concentrated red; fortified. Specialty of PATRAS, north Peloponnese. Dry versions (eg. ANTONOPOULOS) are increasing, with much promise.

Mavrotragano Almost extinct but now-revived red grape of SANTORINI. Top quality. Try SIGALAS, HATZIDAKIS, ARGHYROS.

Mediterra (ex-Creta-Olympias) ★★ V.gd Cretan producer. Value Nea Ghi range, spicy white Xerolithia, red Mirabelo. Interesting Pirorago 04 Syrah/Cab Sauv/Kotsifali blend. Fantastic and v.gd-value Silenius range.

Mercouri ★★★ Peloponnese family estate. V.gd Refosco, delicious RODITIS. Age-worthy CAVA. Classy Refosco dal Penducolo red and stunning sweet Belvedere Malvasia.

Mezzo Sweet wine produced in SANTORINI from sun-dried grapes, lighter and less sweet than VINSANTO. Some dispute over style – some producers (eg. SIGALAS) use the term for wine made from the red Mandilaria variety, while others (eg. ARGHYROS) use the same white varieties as VINSANTO.

Mitravelas ★★→★★★ Outstanding new entry in NEMEA, promising great things. GAIA-influenced.

Moraitis ★★ Small quality producer on the island of Paros. V.gd smoky (white) Monemvasia, (red) tannic Moraitis Reserve.

Moschofilero Pink-skinned, rose-scented, high-quality, high-acid, low-alcohol grape variety.

Naoussa (OPAP) r High-quality region for XINOMAVRO. One of two Greek regions where a *cru* notion may soon develop, since soil patterns are so complex.

Nemea (OPAP) r Region in east Peloponnese producing dark, spicy AGHIORGHITIKO wines. Recent investment has moved it into higher gear. High Nemea merits its own appellation. Koutsi is front-runner for *cru* status (see GAIA, HELIOS and DRIOPI).

Nemeion A new KTIMA in NEMEA, setting new pricing standards (esp Igemon) for the appellation, with wines to match. Owned by Vassiliou, an Attika producer.

Oenoforos ★★ Gd Peloponnese producer with high v'yds. Extremely elegant RODITIS Asprolithi. Also delicate white Lagorthi, nutty Chard (Burgundian, limited release, magnum only), and delicate Mikros Vorias reds and whites. .

OPAP "Appellation of Origin of Higher Quality". In theory, equivalent to French VDQS, but in practice where many gd appellations and wines belong.

OPE "Appellation of Origin Controlled". In theory equivalent to French *appellation contrôlée* but mainly reserved for Muscat and MAVRODAPHNE.

Papaïoannou ★★→★★★ If NEMEA were Burgundy, Papaioannou would be Jayer. Classy reds (inc Pinot N and Petit Verdot); flavourful whites. A wonderful flight of NEMEAS: Ktima Papaioannou, Palea Klimata (old vines), Microklima (a micro-single v'yd) and top-end Terroir (a super-strict, 200%-new-oaked selection).

Patras (OPAP) w White wine (based on RODITIS) and wine town facing the Ionian Sea. Home of MAVRODAPHNE. Rio-Patras (OPE) sweet Muscat.

Pavlidis ★★★ Ambitious new v'yds and winery at Kokkinogia near Drama. Gd ASSYRTIKO/Sauv Bl, v.gd ASSYRTIKO. Excellent Syrah and Tempranillo. KTIMA red recently switched from Bordeaux blend to AGHIORGHITIKO/Syrah in a masterful move. At the top tier of Drama.

Pyrgakis ★★→★★★ Highly experimental KTIMA, fully capitalizing on the highest parts of NEMEA OPAP. Try the new Petit Verdot.

Rapsani Interesting oaked red from Mt Olympus. Rasping until rescued by TSANTALIS, but new producers, like Liappis and DOUGOS, are moving in.

Retsina Attica specialty white with Aleppo pine resin added. Domestic consumption waning, but holds well in the north.

Rhodes Easternmost island and OPAP for red and white. Home to creamy (dry) Athiri white grape. Top wines include CAIR (co-op) Rodos 2400 and Emery's Villare. Also some sparkling.

Roditis White grape grown all over Greece. Gd when yields are low. Asprolithi is top example.

Samos w sw Island near Turkey famed for sweet, golden Muscat. Esp (fortified) Anthemis, (sun-dried) Nectar. Rare old bottlings can be ★★★★, such as the hard-to-find 75.

Santo ★★ The all-important co-op of SANTORINI. Vibrant portfolio, with excellent VINSANTOS.

Santorini Volcanic island north of CRETE and OPAP for w, dr, sw. Luscious VINSANTO and MEZZO, mineral-laden, bone-dry white from fine ASSYRTIKO. Oaked examples can also be v.gd. Top producers include GAIA, HATZIDAKIS, SIGALAS, SANTO. Try ageing everything. Possibly the cheapest great whites around.

Semeli ★★→★★★ Estates near Athens and NEMEA and a new winery in MANTINIA under the Nassiakos name. Value Orinos Helios (white and red) and convincing, top-end Grande Reserve, released after 4 yrs. See HELIOS.

Sigalas ★★★ Top SANTORINI estate producing leading oaked Santorini Bareli. Stylish VINSANTO. Also rare red, Mourvèdre-like Mavrotragano.

Skouras ★★→★★★ Innovative Peloponnese wines. First to use screwcaps on Chard Dum Vinum Sperum with most of white range following suit. Interesting Synoro (Cab Fr-dominated). Top wines: Grande Cuvée Nemea, Megas Oeros.

Spiropoulos, Domaine ★★ Organic producer in MANTINIA and NEMEA. Oaky, red Porfyros (AGHIORGHITIKO, Cab Sauv, Merlot). Sparkling Odi Panos has potential. Firm single v'yd Astala Mantinia.

Tetramythos ★★ Exploring the possibilities of cool-climate parts of Peloponnese, a new and promising venture. The winery was burned in the great summer fires of 2007, but slowly returns to top form. Excellent Sauv Bl.

TO "Regional Wine", French VDP equivalent. Most exciting Greek wine category.

Tsantalis ★→★★★ Merchant and v'yds at Agios Pavlos, Thrace and other areas. Gd red Metoxi, Rapsani Res and Grande Res, gd-value organic Cab Sauv, excellent Avaton and cult Kormilitsa.

Tselepos ★★★ Top-quality MANTINIA producer and Greece's best Gewurz. Other wines: fresh, oaky Chard, v.gd Cab Sauv/Merlot, single v'yd Avlotopi Cab Sauv. Top wine: single v'yd Kokinomylos Merlot. See DRIOPI.

Vinsanto Sweet wine style produced in SANTORINI, from sun-dried ASSYRTIKO and Aidani. Require long ageing, both in oak and bottle. The best and oldest Vinsantos are ★★★★ and practically indestructible. See also MEZZO.

Voyatzi Ktima ★★ Small estate near Kozani. Aromatic white, classy, elegant red.

Xinomavro The tastiest of indigenous red grapes (name means "acidic-black"). Grown in the cooler north, it is the basis for NAOUSSA RAPSANI, GOUMENISSA, Amindeo. High ageing and quality potential: Greece's answer to Nebbiolo.

Zafeirakis ★★→★★★ Small KTIMA in Tyrnavos, central Greece, uncharted territory for quality wine-growing. Fastidious winemaker and a much anticipated Limniona red, the first bottling of a v. promising and rare variety.

Zitsa Mountainous Epirus AC. Delicate Debina white, still, or sparkling. Best from Glinavos.

North Africa & Eastern Mediterranean

NORTH AFRICA

The golden days of North Africa left with the French, long ago. Since then, wine has struggled against growing religious pressure. (Consumption in Morocco is one litre of wine per head per year.) However, foreign investors are again investing in North African wine – though Bernard Magrez of Bordeaux is now losing interest in Algeria – and some wines merit attention. The vineyards are in coastal regions north of the Atlas Mountains that straddle Morocco (Mor), Algeria (Alg) and Tunisia (Tun). There are many old-vine vineyards of Carignan, Cinsault and Grenache. Syrah is best of the newer varieties. Best wines are red or *vin gris*.

Castel Frères Mor r p ★ Owners of Sahari, Meknes and Boulaouane facilities. Gd-value brands like Bonassia, El Baraka, Halana, Larroque and Mayole.
Celliers de Meknes Mor r p w ★→★★★ Dominates Moroccan market. Modern facility Château Roselane. Les Coteaux de Atlas is top of range. New fizz.
Ceptunes Tun r w ★ Promising winery using classic varieties.
Dom Neferis Tun r p w ★→★★ Calastrasi joint venture. Selian Carignan best.
Dom de St Augustin Alg r ★★ One-off blockbuster by Depardieu/Magrez.
Kurubis Tun r w sp ★ Producers of traditional-method sparkling wine.
Les Deux Domaines Mor r ★★→★★★ Depardieu and Bernard Magrez joint venture. Magrez Kahina and Depardieu Lumière are powerful Syrah/Grenache blends.
Sahara Vineyards Egypt w ★ Project by big producer, Gianaclis, to upgrade wines.
Thalvin Mor rpw★→★★ Gd whites. Warm, spicy Syrah with Alan Graillot.
Val d'Argan Mor r p ★ Organic grown v'y'ds near Essaouira on west coast.
Vignerons de Carthage Tun r p w ★ Best from UCCV co-op: Clipea Chard, Kelibia dry Muscat and Magon Elissa reds. Encouraging foreign partners.
Vins d'Algerie r ★ OCNC marketing company. Top blend: Cuvée du President. Wines named after regions: Mascara, Medea and Tlemcen.
Volubilia Mor r p w Promising new joint venture with Dom de la Zouina.

EASTERN MEDITERRANEAN

This is the region which gave wine culture to the world, 2,000 years before the vine reached France and Italy. Lebanon, with French influence, and Israel, with New World technology, have progressed no end in the last ten years and are producing some high-quality reds. War and violence make this a difficult area for wine-growers, so the courage of Israeli and Lebanese winemakers should be encouraged – better to make wine than war. Turkey missed the quality revolution that has taken place in the Levant, but it has no less potential and numerous indigenous varieties.

Cyprus

Cyprus has a lot going for it as a wine-producing country. It is phylloxera-free with ancient vines, several unique grapes and a sunny, dry, mountain climate, meaning little need for spraying. Until Cyprus joined the EU, its wine industry was dominated by the Big Four and reliant on bulk exports and cheap fortified wines. Today, the industry has been reinvented, with smaller growers showing what the island is capable of while the Big Four have also changed direction and switched production to the hills to improve quality.

Ayia Mavri ★★ Lovely sweet Muscats from semi-dried Muscat of Alexandria. Attractive Grenache rosé.

Commandaria A sweet, deliberately oxidized wine made from sun-dried XYNISTERI and MAVRO. The greatest Cypriot wine, almost certainly the wine with the longest heritage in the world. (The poet Hesiod wrote of its ancestor in BCE 800.) Produced in hills north of Limassol.

ETKO r w ★ One of former Big Four, but much reduced in size. Improved quality from Olympus winery in hills. Produces St Nicholas Commandaria.

Hadjiantonas ★★ Spotless new winery owned by pilot, making v.gd Chard.

KEO★ Second-largest producer; of mixed quality. St John is COMMANDARIA brand. Best wines from Mallia Estate (Ktima Keo) and Heritage label for local grapes.

Kyperounda r w dr ★★ 05 06' 07' (08) Probably Europe's highest v'yd at 1,450 m. White Petritis from barrel-aged Xynisteri is island's best example and keeps well. Reds, esp Andessitis, also gd.

Lefkada Rediscovered indigenous black grape variety. Higher quality than MAVRO. Usually blended as tannins can be aggressive.

Maratheftiko Deep-coloured local grape with potential as high-quality signature red. Tricky to grow well, but getting better as winemakers learn.

Mavro The black grape of Cyprus. Easier to cultivate than MARATHEFTIKO, but only moderate quality. Best for rosé.

SODAP r w dr ★ Grower-owned co-op and island's largest producer. New winery at Stroumbi village in hills has transformed quality, esp whites. Gd value. Look for Island Vines, Mountain Vines and Kamanterena labels.

Tsiakkas r w dr ★→★★ Banker turned winemaker with help from VLASSIDES. Makes v.gd fresh, zesty whites, esp Sauv Bl, XYNISTERI and Chard.

Vasa ★★ 03 05 06' 07' (08) Small but immaculate winery. Best example of the MARATHEFTIKO so far. V.gd Chard and St Tinon red blend. VLASSIDES consults.

Vlassides ★★→★★★ 03' 04 06' 07' (08) Davis-trained owner Sophocles Vlassides crafts some of the island's best wines in a tiny village winery. Shiraz Reserve is a real star and shows the potential of Cyprus for exciting wines. Also v.gd Cab Sauv and MARATHEFTIKO.

Xynisteri Cyprus's most planted white grape. Can be dull and is usually drunk young but when grown at altitude makes fresh, appealing, minerally whites. KYPEROUNDA's Petritis is best. Also try TSIAKKAS, VLASSIDES, ZAMBARTAS, Kolios, Aes Ambelis, K&K Vasilikon.

Zambartas ★★ 07' (08) Father and Australian-trained son run new winery making exciting Cab Franc/LEFKADA rosé, v.gd Shiraz/LEFKADA red and attractive XYNISTERI/Sem.

Israel

Modern Israeli wine was built on French roots, with investment from a Rothschild, cuttings from Château Lafite and experts from Bordeaux. But it was not until Californian expertise was imported in the 1980s, followed more recently by influences from Australia, that international-class wines began to be made. Recently, scores of small wineries have opened and there are numerous young winemakers with international experience leading a drive for quality in what has become a young, dynamic wine industry. The best growing regions are the higher-altitude, cooler-climate Upper Galilee, Golan Heights and Judean Hills, near Jerusalem, but (typical of the Israelis) they also have vineyards in the desert.

Agur r ★→★★ Characterful boutique. Well-integrated Kessem Bordeaux blend.

Alexander r(w) ★→★★ Cab Sauv is incredibly oaky, but well-made.

Avidan r(w) ★→★★ Cab Sauv/Petite Sirah blend is best. Grenache of interest.

Barkan-Segal r w ★★ Israel's second-largest winery. Barkan Altitude Cabs are high-quality. New Carignan. Gd-value reds at every price point. Single-v'yd Segal Argaman of interest. Owned by Israel's largest brewery.

Bazelet ha Golan Golan r ★ Approachable Cab Sauv, in lighter style of late.

Binyamina r w ★→★★ Big investments by new owner. The Cave blend is a step up.

Carmel r w sp ★★→★★★ Founded in 1882 by a Rothschild. Strong v'yd presence in Upper Galilee. Elegant Limited Edition (03' 04 05 07'). Smoky, tarry Kayoumi Cab Sauv. Excellent Old-vine Carignan and Petite Sirah. Luscious late-harvest Gewurz. Appellation and Private Collection labels gd value.

Château Golan Golan r (w) ★★→★★★ Extravagant winery experimenting with Mediterranean varieties. Intense, jammy Eliad. Flavourful Syrah.

Chillag r ★→★★ Israel's most prominent female winemaker. Elegant Merlot.

Clos de Gat Judean Hills r w ★★★ Classy estate with big, blowsy wines. The spicy, powerful Sycra Syrah 04' 06 and buttery Chard are superb.

Dalton Upper Galilee r w ★→★★ Aromatic, wild-yeast Viognier. Huge, ripe Zin.

Domaine du Castel Judean Hills r w ★★★★ Family estate in Jerusalem mountains. Consistently top performer with critics. Characterful, supple Grand Vin (00' 03 04' 05 06' 07. Petit Castel great value. Outstanding "C" Blanc du Castel.

Ella Valley Judean Hills r w ★★ V.gd Chard. Cab Fr showing finesse.

Flam r (w) ★★→★★★ Family winery. Fine Cab Sauv, tight Merlot, earthy, herbal Syrah Cab. Classico gd value. Crisp, refreshing unoaked white.

Galil Mtn Upper Galilee r w ★★→★★★ Yiron and Meron red blends are firm and elegant. Opulent Viognier-based Avivim. Owned by GALIL HEIGHTS.

Golan Heights Golan r w sp ★★★ Now a large winery producing 6m bottles. Best wines under Yarden label. Cab Sauv consistently gd. Spicy Ortal v'yd Syrah. Rare Bordeaux blend Katzrin 96 00' 03 04'. Superb Heights Wine dessert and Blanc de Blancs sparkling. Other labels: Gamla and Golan.

> ### Grapes of the moment
> It is curious that no indigenous varieties exist in Israel, when there are so many in nearby Cyprus and Turkey. However, Israel's varietal menu is not entirely standard: Cab Franc looks interesting, and there are some v.gd, low-yield, old-vine Carignans of real character. Petite Sirah seems ideal for the climate, yielding deep, full-bodied wines. Petit Verdot is also proving useful, and often more important than Merlot in Bordeaux-style blends.

Margalit r ★★★ Father-and-son team making wines in a more elegant style, in particular Bordeaux blend. Enigma (05' 06 07). and *Special Reserve*.

Mony r w ★ Israeli Arab making kosher wine at a monastery. Fresh Colombard.

Pelter r w (sp) ★★→★★★ Flavourful, chewy Shiraz and promising Cab Fr.

Recanati r w ★★ Aromatic Sauv Bl. Quality, New World Special Reserve.

Saslove r (w) ★★ Father and daughter making wines in new Upper Galilee winery. Reds are a complex avalanche of fruit and spice.

Sea Horse r (w) ★→★★ Idiosyncratic *garagiste*. Superb, rare old-vine Chenin Bl.

Tabor Galilee r w →★★ Growing fast. Lively wines. Aromatic Sauv Bl.

Teperberg r w ★ Efrat reborn. Meritage has sweet fruit, medium body.

Tishbi r w ★ Deep Bordeaux blend from Sde Boker in desert, best yet.

Tulip r (w) ★★ Winery workers are people with special needs. Excellent Shiraz blend and Syrah Reserve. Powerful wines, but great value.

Tzora r w ★★ Misty Hills is high-quality red with ageing potential.

Vitkin r w ★★ Steely, floral, dry Ries and honeyed dessert wine from same grape. Black, plummy Petite Sirah. Specialist in unusual, unfashionable varieties.

Yarden See GOLAN HEIGHTS.

Yatir Judean Hills r (w) ★★★→★★★★ Outstanding Yatir Forest 01 02 03' 04 05' 06.

Rich, velvety, concentrated. Well-balanced Yatir blend and Cab Sauv with mouthfilling flavour. Minerally Sauv Bl. Fragrant Viognier. Owned by CARMEL.

Zion r (w) ★ Ninth-generation family winery making gd-value reds.

Lebanon

Lebanon was a one-winery country for many years, holding on to the coat-tails of Chateau Musar. Since the civil war, a number of new wineries have started up, supplemented in the last year or two with some producing hand-crafted wines. Once, all serious wine production was solely in the Bekaa Valley. Today, interesting new vineyards are springing up in other parts of Lebanon.

Château Belle-Vue r ★→★★ New *garagiste*. La Renaissance is top-notch red.

Château Ka r w ★ Basic range promising, esp the white from Chard, Sauv, Sem.

Chateau Kefraya r w ★★→★★★ Spicy, minerally *Comte de M* (00' 01 02) from Cab, Syrah and Mourvèdre. Fruity, easy-drinking Les Bretèches. Quality dessert wine.

Chateau Ksara r w ★★→★★★ 150 yrs old but still progressive. Excellent-value wines Reserve du Couvent has mouthfilling flavour. Top of range Troisième Millénaire 02 03' 04 05. Le Souverain of interest – from Cab Sauv and Arinarnoa.

Château Marsyas r Grand launch of new winery. Definitely one to watch.

Chateau Musar r (w) ★★★ Unique, long-lasting Cab Sauv/Cinsault/Carignan red (95' 96' 98 99 00' 01 02). Legendary to some (the 1979 is still splendid); past its best to others. Hochar red is fruitier. Oaky white from indigenous Obaideh and Merwah.

Chateau Nakad r w ★ Chateau des Coteaux red is spicy and oaky from this traditional winery.

Clos St Thomas r w ★★ Deep but silky red wines. Les Emirs great value.

Domaine de Baal r w Very promising new winery with organic v'yd.

Domaine des Tourelles r w ★→★★ Old winery reborn. Elegant Marquis des Beys.

Domaine Wardy r w ★→★★ New-World-style Private Selection. Crisp, fresh whites.

Heritage r w ★ Easy-drinking, fruity wines like Le Fleuron and Nouveau.

Karam ★→★★ Promising boutique from Jezzine, south Lebanon. Cloud 9 gd value.

Kouroum r w ★ Sept Cépages is an interesting blend of seven varieties.

Massaya r w ★★ Silver Selection red is a complex Rhône-style blend showing sun and spice of Lebanon. Classic series with screwtop represents great value.

Turkey

Turkey could make good wine, but has as yet failed to excite. Yet imported international expertise, clever blending of indigenous varieties with international ones and a desire to improve are producing some interesting results. Main developments are in the Marmara region.

Bogazkere Tannic, indigenous red variety. Produces full-bodied wines.

Büyülübag r (w) ★★ Hope for the future. New boutique winery. Good Cab Sauv.

Buzbag A blend of Turkey's most famous red-wine grapes from E. Anatolia.

Corvus r w ★→★★★ Boutique winery on Bozcaada island. Corpus is powerful.

Doluca r w ★→★★ Large winery. Karma label blends local and classic varieties.

Kavaklidere r w sp ★→★★ Large winery in Ankara. Turkish variety specialists.

Kayra r w ★→★★ Reincarnation of state enterprise Tekel. Promising Shiraz.

Kocabag r w ★ Large winery based in Cappadocia. Owned by KAVAKLIDERE.

Narince White variety. Can produce fresh, fruity wines.

Okuzgozu Soft, fruity local red variety. Often blended with BOGAZKERE.

Sarafin r w ★→★★ Good Cab Sauv and Sauv Bl. Brand owned by DOLUCA.

Asia & Old Russian Empire

ASIA

China China will one day become the biggest wine-consuming market in the world, but what is less certain is the current size of its own vineyard, and how much imported wine is blended with Chinese. Around 220 producers make some 700 m litres of wine, with large brands such as Dynasty, China Great Wall and Changyu Pioneer accounting for 40 per cent of the industry. About a third of China's wine comes from the Yantai Penglai area in Shandong province, a coastal area south of Beijing, but vineyards are spread across China. Nearly 90 per cent of wine consumption in China is red wine, and imported wines now make up 15 per cent of the market. A lot of foreign investment from Europe, the USA and Australia has allowed technology and expertise to develop, although the overall quality of Chinese wines is still low. Of course the outside world is largely unaware of Chinese wines, as the vast majority are consumed inside China. Look out for Catai and Grace Vineyard.

India A small wine industry is beginning to flourish here, fostered by a middle class (over 300 million strong) that wants the trappings of Western success. There is clear evidence that quality wine can be made, particularly in Nashik, near Mumbai, and at Karnataka, south of Goa. There are about 50 wineries, mostly in the Maharashtra region (where Nashik is located). They account for 1,200 ha and bottle around 6.2 m litres. Cabernet Sauvignon, Merlot, Syrah and Pinot Noir are used for reds; Chenin Blanc, Sauvignon Blanc, Chardonnay and Riesling for whites. The red/white split is about 50:50. The most notable names are Chateau Indage, Grover Vineyards and Sula Vineyards, creating wines of strong varietal character. Sparkling wine has long been creditable.

Japan Although wine has been made in Japan since 1875, most is consumed domestically and the market is dominated by imports. Wine awareness has increased markedly in recent years with a whole new generation of single, worldly and financially confident younger patrons who are exploring wine to the detriment of sake. A dynamic winemaking industry is developing, particularly in the horticultural prefectures (regions) of Yamanashi and Hokkaido, with input from some serious international heavyweights such as Denis Dubourdieu and Bernard Magrez (both of Bordeaux).

Good wine is being made in Japan despite a climate of high humidity and consistent rainfall during the growing season, and fertile yet acidic soils. The search for new regions continues but seems to be hampered by poor spring conditions. The indigenous Koshu grape is Japan's point of difference. It is *vinifera* and its history dates back many hundreds of years, making lightly aromatic whites – most being perfectly pleasant but unremarkable. The first international gold medal was awarded to the 2008 Grace Wines Koshu in 2009. Other local wines are mostly from hybrid varieties: Muscat Bailey A, Black Queen and Yama Sauvignon. Chardonnay, Cabernet Sauvignon and Merlot are minor varieties in small microclimates.

It is impossible to know whether these traditional varieties are authentic: local laws allow up to 95% imported wine must to be blended with a small fraction of local wine and still be called "Wine of Japan". The industry is dominated by the large brewery companies Mercian, Sapporo and Suntory, but there are nearly 250 producers in all. A number of these currently lack consistency, but look for Grace Wines, Katsunuma Winery, Obuse and Takahata Wines.

OLD RUSSIAN EMPIRE

Ex-Soviet wine-producing countries are increasingly going their own way. The image of genuine Russian wine is slowly improving inside the country; local producers benefited from the crisis by offering better value. Ukraine and Moldova rely for export on Russia. Georgia is modernizing and learning to produce quality styles which can be marketed abroad: some are very attractive. There has been some investment and help from international consultants in all countries – basic quality has improved, but there are no outstanding wines yet.

Georgia Wine has been made for over 7,000 years; ancient methods such as fermentation in clay vats (*kwevris*) still exist, but are gradually being supplanted by modern methods. There are around 500 indigenous grape varieties, the most popular being red Saperavi (gd wines are intense and structured) and white Rkatsiteli (lively, refreshing). Wine is made in five defined areas, total vineyards are approximately 50,000 ha, 70% is produced in Kakheti (southeast). Big producers include Tbilvino, Telavi Wine Cellar, Teliani Veli, Shumi, Askaneli. First small premium producers emerging: Glakhuna), Khetsuriani. Foreign investors have developed, among others, GWS (Pernod Ricard), Vinoterra and Pheasant's Tears.

Moldova Winemaking is the main agricultural activity, but gd natural and climatic conditions haven't been used to full advantage. European grapes are widely used, with gd results for Chard, Sauv Bl, Pinot Gr, Merlot, Cab Sauv. Quality leaders: Acorex Wine Holding (Sauv Bl, Traminer, Pinot N, Merlot, Cab Sauv), Vinaria Bostavan (Negru and Rosu de Purcari), Château Vartely (Traminer, Merlot), Dionysos Mereni (Carlevana Res range, late-harvest and Icewine Ries), DK Intertrade (Chard, Pinot Gr, Pinot Bl, Sauv Bl), Vinaria Purcari (Negru de Purcari), Lion Gri (sparkling, Sauv Bl, Merlot), Cricova (sparkling). There is plenty of historical evidence of the country's high potential.

Russia There are 65,000 ha of v'yds in the southwest of the country. The Krasnodar, Dagestan and Stavropol regions lead in production. European and local cold-resistant varieties are grown. Most wine is still of basic quality, made in off-dry or semi-sweet styles and often anonymously blended with cheap imported bulk. There are signs of a new quality movement. Along with the pioneering Château le Grand Vostock (Cuvée Karsov, Chêne Royal), premium wines are now made by Fanagoria, esp Cru Lermont range (gd Sauv Bl, Aligoté, interesting Pinot N), Russkaya Loza (Premier), Myskhako, Vina Vedernikoff (Russian grape varieties), Abrau-Durso (sparkling).

Ukraine The Odessa region dominates in grape-growing and in wine production, but Crimea has better quality potential, yet to be realized in full. Traditionally the best wines were modelled on sherry, port and Madeira – and Champagne – historic producers such as Massandra, Magarach and Solnechnaya Dolina have kept great cellars. Gd examples of fortified styles are made by Massandra, Koktebel, Dionis. Novy Svet, and Artyomovsk Winery produce traditional-method sparkling wines. Inkerman is known for dry wines. New names to watch: Veles (Kolonist), Gouliev Wines.

North America

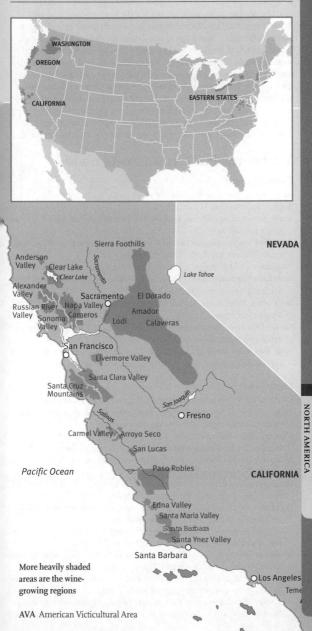

More heavily shaded
areas are the wine-
growing regions

AVA American Victicultural Area

CALIFORNIA

After France, Italy and Spain, California is the world's fourth-largest wine producing region. The state produces some 95 per cent of all US wine. Two of every three bottles of wine sold in the US come from California. There is wine from the Mexican border in the south almost to the Oregon border in the north, from foggy vineyards near the Pacific Ocean to the inland foothills of the Sierra Nevada. Each region has distinctive soils and weather patterns that influence the flavour profile of the wines and also play a role in what varieties of grape are grown. If your palate is getting tired of the concentrated power and assertive structure of a Napa Valley Cabernet Sauvignon, pop open a bottle of silky Central Coast Pinot Noir as a refresher. Or for something completely different, reach for a bottle of minerally Albariño from Lodi in the state's Central Valley. They're all robust up-front wines, as Americans like them, but no one can say they don't have variety.

The principal Californian vineyard areas

Central Coast

An umbrella region stretching from San Francisco Bay south almost to Los Angeles. Important sub-AVAs include:

Arroyo Seco Monterey County. Excellent Ries both dry and late-harvest, citrussy Chard and Cab Sauv.

Edna Valley San Luis Obispo County. Cool winds whip through a gap in the coastal range off Morro Bay. Excellent minerally Chard.

Paso Robles San Luis Obispo County. Known for Zin, Syrah and Rhône varieties.

Santa Lucia Highlands Monterey County. AVA above the Salinas Valley. Excellent Syrah and Ries; outstanding Pinot N.

Santa Maria Valley Santa Barbara County. Outstanding Pinot N, good Chard, Viognier and Syrah.

Sta Rita Hills Santa Barbara County. For legal reasons calls itself Sta rather than Santa. Very good Pinot N.

Santa Ynez Valley Santa Barbara County. Like Santa Maria but warmer inland regions. Rhône grapes, Pinot N, Chard in cool areas. Sauv Bl a good bet.

North Coast

Lake, Mendocino, Napa, Sonoma counties, all north of San Francisco Bay. Ranges from v. cool climate near the bay and the coast to very warm interior regions. Soils vary from volcanic to sandy loam. Includes the following:

Alexander Valley Sonoma County. Fairly warm AVA bordering Russian River. Excellent Cab Sauv in a ripe, juicy style. Gd Sauv Bl near the river.

Anderson Valley Mendocino County. Cool valley opening to the Pacific. Outstanding sparkling wine, very good Gewurz and Pinot N.

Carneros Napa and Sonoma counties. Cool and foggy region bordering San Francisco Bay. Top site for Pinot N and Chard. Very good sparkling wine.

Dry Creek Valley Sonoma County. Relatively warm region offering distinctive Zin and Sauv Bl, with Cab Sauv a winner on rocky hillsides.

Lake County Warm to hot mountainous region centred on Clear Lake. Good Zin, Sauv Bl near the lake and lush, fruity Cab Sauv on cooler hillsides.

Mendocino County Large region north of Sonoma County with a wide range of growing regions from hot interior valleys to cooler regions near the coast.

Mount Veeder Napa County. High-altitude AVA (vineyards planted up to 730 m) best-known for concentrated Cab Sauv and rich Chard.

Napa Valley Napa's vineyard land has become the most expensive outside Europe. Great diversity of soil, climate and topography in such a small area can produce a wide range of wines, especially the red Bordeaux varieties. Wines have achieved international acclaim, and are priced to match.

Oakville Napa County. Located in mid-valley, the heart of Cab Sauv country.

Redwood Valley Mendocino County. Warm interior region. Good basic Cab Sauv, excellent Zin, everyday Chard and Sauv Bl.

Russian River Valley Sonoma County. Very cool, often fog-bound until noon. Outstanding Pinot N, Zin and Cab Sauv on hillside vineyards. Green Valley is a small, super-cool AVA located within the Russian River AVA.

Rutherford Napa County. Rivals Oakville as Cab Sauv heartland. Long-lived reds from hillside vineyards.

St Helena V.gd Cab Sauv with elegant fruit and a silky mouthfeel; good Sauv Bl.

Sonoma Coast Sonoma. Very cool climate, very poor soils. New plantings of Pinot N show great promise.

Sonoma Valley Varied growing regions produce everything from Chard to Zin. Sub-AVA Sonoma Mountain good for powerful Cab Sauv.

Spring Mountain Napa County. Very good Cab Sauv with pockets of delicious Sauv Bl at lower elevations, plus good Ries.

Stags Leap Napa County. East of Napa River, distinctive Cab Sauv and Merlot.

Bay Area

Urban sprawl has wiped out most of the vineyards that once surrounded San Francisco Bay, although there is still good Cab Sauv and Sauv Bl in the Livermore AVA, east of the bay, and small amounts of outstanding Cab Sauv and Pinot N from Santa Cruz County, south of the bay.

Central Valley

About 60 per cent of California's vineyards are in this huge region that runs north to south for several hundred miles. Now shedding its image as a low-quality producer, as valley growers realize they must go for quality to keep up. Lodi region in particular turning up very good Zin, Sauv Bl and Rhône, Spanish varieties.

Sierra Foothills

Vines were first planted here during Gold Rush in the 1850s. Best regions include:

Amador County Warm region famous for old Zin vineyards producing jammy, intense wines, as well as crisp Sauv Bl.

El Dorado Good Zin, lean Cab Sauv, bright Sauv Bl.

Fiddletown Amador County. High-elevation vineyards produce a more understated, elegant Zin than much of Amador.

Shenandoah Valley Amador County. Powerful Zins and some increasingly well-regarded Syrah.

Recent vintages

Its size and wide range of microclimates make it impossible to produce a one-size-fits-all vintage report for California. Its climate is not as consistent as its "land of sunshine" reputation suggests. Although grapes ripen regularly, they are often subject to spring frosts, sometimes a wet harvest time and (too often) drought. The following vintage assessment relies most heavily on evaluation of Cab Sauv from North Coast regions. For Chard, the best vintages are: 05 07 08.

2009 A superb growing season throughout the state with ample winter and spring rainfall in most areas to assure even growth. Temperatures were moderate with only a few heat spikes near harvest. Both red and white wines showing good balance and ageing potential.

2008 September heat led to an early harvest, with most grapes picked two to three weeks earlier than normal. There is also concern that acid levels are low and in some areas the grapes may not have reached physiological ripeness. Uneven quality.

2007 Early bud-break and a fairly mild summer growing season with a burst of heat in August followed by a cool September seemed to set the stage for a textbook-perfect harvest; then came rains in late September and October, so results were mixed, especially for Cab Sauv on the North Coast.

2006 Wines, esp Pinot N and Chard, looking good. Cab Sauv improving with age. Overall, above-average.

2004 After sorting out this vintage some of the early promise has faded. Wines likely to be for short-term consumption.

2004 Grapes ripened quickly with uneven quality. At best average.

2003 A difficult year all around. Overall, spotty.

2002 The growing season was cool, leading to an average-sized crop with superior quality and showing well with age.

2001 Excellent quality with Cab Sauv. Drink in the next year or two.

2000 Biggest harvest on record. Okay quality.

Abreu Vineyards Napa ★★★ 03 05 06 Massive Cab Sauv that's worth waiting for.

Acacia Carneros ★★★ (Pinot N) 04 05 06 CARNEROS pioneer in Chard and Pinot N, always reliable, recently emphasizing single-v'yd wines. Luscious Viognier.

Alban V'yds Edna Valley ★★→★★★ Got into the Rhône game early. Excellent Viognier. Grenache, Roussanne and Marsanne also top-rated.

Alma Rosa Sta Rita Hills ★★★ Richard Sanford, a master Pinot N wine whizz at SANFORD and Benedict Winery, is making lovely Pinot N and Chard from organic v'yds at his new winery. Also v.gd Pinot Gr and Vin Gris from Pinot N.

Altamura Vineyards Napa ★★★ 00 01 02 03 04 05 06 Cab Sauv is one of NAPA's best, with a firm structure and deep flavours; also a gd Sangiovese.

Amador Foothills Winery Amador ★★→★★★ Top Zin and a bright, zingy Sauv Bl.

Andrew Murray Santa Barbara ★★★ It's Rhônes around the clock here. Outstanding Viognier and Roussanne among the whites and a solid Syrah.

Araujo Napa ★★★ 99 00 02 03 04 05 06 Powerful but never over-the-top cult Cab Sauv made from historic Eisele v'yd.

Arthur Earl Santa Barbara ★★★ Artisan bottlings of mostly Rhône varietals, splashing out with an occasional Italian. Quality steadily improving.

Au Bon Climat Santa Barbara ★★★→★★★★ Owner Jim Clendenen listens to his private drummer: ultra-toasty Chard, flavourful Pinot N, light-hearted Pinot Bl. Vita Nova label for Bordeaux varieties, Podere Olivos for Italianates. See QUPÉ.

Babcock Vineyards Santa Barbara ★★★ V.gd Pinot N, Chard and Sauv Bl from cool climate v. near the Pacific in SANTA YNEZ VALLEY. New Grand Cuvée Pinot N has moved quality up a notch.

Balletto Russian River Valley ★★★ Look for outstanding estate Chard and single-v'yd Pinot N. Also a cheerful dry rosé of Pinot N and a v.gd Pinot Gr.

Beaulieu Vineyard Napa ★★→★★★ 00 03 05 06 Not the jewel it was when André Tchelistcheff was setting the style for NAPA Cab Sauv half a century ago, but still worth looking out for, esp the Georges de Latour Private Reserve Cab Sauv. Decent budget wines under the Beaulieu Coastal label.

Bell Wine Cellars Napa ★★ Understated Cab Sauv. Bordeaux blend "Claret" also gd.

Benessere Napa ★★★ Sangiovese and Syrah worth a try. New Super Tuscan-style blend called Phenomenon is outstanding.

Benovia Sonoma ★★→★★★ Silky and balanced Chard from RUSSIAN RIVER VALLEY and SONOMA COAST. The cool-climate coast bottling has a rich, creamy centre that is pure yummy.

Benziger Family Winery Sonoma ★★★ A leader in biodynamic movement. V.gd Cab Sauv, Merlot, Sauv Bl.

Beringer Blass (Foster's Group) Napa ★→★★★ (Cab) **99 00 01 03** A NAPA classic. Single-v'yd Cab Sauv Reserves can sometimes be over-the-top, but otherwise worthy of ageing. Velvety, powerful Howell Mountain Merlot one of the best. Look for Founder's Estate bargain line from NORTH COAST and CENTRAL COAST grapes. Also owns CHÂTEAU ST JEAN ★★→★★★, ETUDE, Meridian ★, ST CLEMENT ★★★, STAGS' LEAP WINERY ★ and Taz, a brawny ★★ Pinot from Santa Barbara.

Boeger El Dorado ★★→★★★ First EL DORADO winery after Prohibition. Mostly estate wines. Attractive Merlot, Barbera, Zin and Meritage. More understated than many in SIERRA FOOTHILLS and always reliable.

Bogle Vineyards Yolo ★★ Major grower in the Sacramento Delta, the Bogle family makes an attractive line of consistently gd and affordable wines.

Bokisch Lodi ★★→★★★ The focus is on Spanish varieties at this family estate. Garnacha, Albariño and Tempranillo show gd varietal character. Tempranillo esp impressive.

Bonny Doon Santa Cruz Mts ★★★ Original Rhône Ranger Randall Grahm has slashed production, selling off his budget brands to concentrate on single-v'yd biodynamic wines with v.gd results.

Bonterra See FETZER.

Bouchaine Vineyards Napa, Carneros ★★→★★★ Look for Chard and juicy but serious single-v'yd Pinot N.

Bronco Wine Company San Joaquin Founded by Fred Franzia, the nephew of ERNEST GALLO. Franzia sources inexpensive CENTRAL VALLEY grapes for his well-known Charles Shaw Two Buck Chuck brand. Franzia also fields several other labels, inc Napa Creek and Napa Ridge. Quality is not the point: Franzia is selling wine as a popular beverage.

Buena Vista Napa, Carneros ★★★ Historic winery now focuses on wines from CARNEROS estate. Wines from Ramal v'yd showing v. well, esp Pinot N and Chard.

Burgess Cellars Napa ★★★ (Cab) **00 01 02 03 05** Cab Sauv from Howell Mountain grapes is splendid, sleek and powerful while remaining balanced.

Cain Cellars Napa ★★★ **00 01 03 05** One of NAPA's jewels, with consistent bottlings of Cain Five, a supple and elegant red wine based on Cab Sauv and its four Bordeaux cousins, from SPRING MTN grapes.

Cakebread Napa ★★★→★★★★ (Cab) **01 02 03 05 06** Quality improving with each vintage, esp the Cab Sauv, which shows great balance and harmony.

Calera San Benito ★★★★ Josh Jensen fell in love with Pinot N while at Oxford, and still is. He makes three supple and fine Pinot Ns named after v'yd blocks in the dry hills of San Benito, inland from Monterey: Reed, Seleck and Jensen; also intense, flowery Viognier.

Caymus Napa ★★★→★★★★★ **97 99 00 01 06** The Special Selection Cab Sauv is consistently one of California's most formidable: rich, intense, slow to mature. Also a regular bottling, balanced and a little lighter. Gd Chard from Mer Soleil in Monterey, inc an unoaked Chard called Silver.

Ceago Vinegarden Lake ★★→★★★ Jim Fetzer, well settled into his biodynamic ranch on Clear Lake in LAKE COUNTY, produces v.gd Sauv Bl and Cab Sauv.

Ceja Vineyards Napa ★★→★★★ Established 1999, one of few California wineries owned by former Mexican v'yd workers. Cab Sauv, CARNEROS Chard top the list.

Cesar Toxqui Cellars Mendocino ★★ Toxqui came north from Mexico when he was 16, and landed his first job at FETZER V'YDS. He makes a tiny amount of Pinot N from NORTH COAST organic grapes. The wine is superb: well worth the search.

Chalk Hill Sonoma ★★→★★★ Cab Sauv with ageing potential; buttery Chard.

Chalone Monterey ★★★ Historic mountain estate above the Salinas Valley in Monterey. Marvellous flinty Chard and rich, intense Pinot N.

Chappellet Napa ★★★ An age-worthy Cab Sauv, *esp Signature label*. Pleasing Chard; gd Cab Fr, Merlot. Chenin Bl is one of the best.

Charles Krug Napa ★★→★★★ Historically important winery; wines on an upward trend under third generation of (the other) Mondavi family. New focus on red Bordeaux styles showing gd results.

Château Montelena Napa ★★★→★★★★ (Chard) 05 07 (Cab) 99 00 01 03 05 06 Historic NAPA winery offers that rare thing in California: an age-worthy Chard. The estate Cab Sauv is also capable of extended ageing.

Château St Jean Sonoma ★★→★★★ Pioneered single-v'yd Chard in California under Richard Arrowood in the 1970s, still outstanding; gd Sauv Bl. Cinq Cépages, made from the five Bordeaux varieties, can be ★★★★ quality. Sonoma County Cab Sauv and Chard are gd budget buys.

Chimney Rock Napa ★★★→★★★★ (Cab) 97 99 STAGS LEAP AVA producer of elegant, sometimes understated Cab Sauv capable of long ageing.

Christopher Creek Sonoma ★★→★★★ The estate Petite Sirah from RUSSIAN RIVER VALLEY grapes revived faith in the variety. Also worth a glass are the lean and brambly Cab Sauv and a honeyed Viognier.

Claiborne & Churchill Santa Barbara ★★★ The accent here is Alsace with a consistently top-rated Ries, v.gd Pinot Gr and Gewurz.

Clavo Cellars Paso Robles ★★→★★★ Veteran grower Neil Roberts' venture into winemaking is a grand success. Collusion, his Bordeaux red blend, is a deeply flavoured, powerful wine with a touch of finesse. The Syrah is v.gd, as is the Zin.

Clos du Bois Sonoma ★★→★★★ Large-scale SONOMA producer of quaffable everyday wines, with the exception of a single-v'yd Cab Sauv (Briarcrest) and Calcaire Chard, which can be v.gd.

Clos du Val Napa ★★→★★★ Consistently elegant Cab Sauvs that are among the best ageing candidates in the state. *Chard is a delight* and a Scm/Sauv Bl blend called Ariadne is a charmer.

Clos Pegase Napa ★★→★★★ Is it a winery or a museum? Sometimes hard to tell, but at best a sleek Cab Sauv from v'yds near Calistoga, and a minerally Chard from CARNEROS grapes.

Cobb Wines Sonoma ★★→★★★ Father-son team makes excellent Pinot N from SONOMA COAST v'yds. The Coastlands V'yd bottling is three-star quality, with bright fruit and true varietal character.

Conn Creek Napa ★★★ V.gd Cab Sauv sourced from several NAPA VALLEY v'yds; elegant wines with gd structure and long ageing potential.

Constellation ★→★★★★ Owns wineries in California, NY, Washington State, Canada, Chile, Australia and NZ. Produces 90 million cases annually, selling more than any other wine company in the world. Once a bottom-feeder, now going for the top. Bought ROBERT MONDAVI at end of 2004 and also owns FRANCISCAN V'YD, Estancia, Mount Veeder, RAVENSWOOD, Simi, among others.

The Petite Sirah comeback

Petite Sirah has been grown for more than a century in California, often misidentified as Syrah early on. It is, of course, the grape known as "Durif" in France. In the past the wines were often not handled properly, resulting in heavy, awkward bottlings. In the past few years there has been a revival of interest in the grape, leading to a leap in quality. At its best Petite Sirah is a powerful wine with an intriguing underlying base of coffee and chocolate with a range of dark fruit. Top California producers include BOGLE V'YDS, CHRISTOPHER CREEK, FOPPIANO, PARDUCCI, PEDRONCELLI and STAGS' LEAP.

Corison Napa ★★★★ 95 96 97 99 00 01 02 05 06 07 Cathy Corison is a treasure of a winemaker. While many in NAPA VALLEY follow the $iren call of overextracted, powerhouse wines delivering big numbers from critics but no satisfaction in the glass, Corison continues to make flavoursome, *age-worthy Cab Sauv*.

Cornerstone Cellars Napa, Howell Mtn ★★★ 00 01 02 03 05 Consulting winemaker Celia Mayzcek makes impressive Cab Sauv from mountain v'yds with a focus on harmony and balance. Also look for Stepping Stone label featuring small lots of wine from select NAPA VALLEY v'yds.

Cosentino Napa ★★→★★★★ Irrepressible winemaker-owner Mitch Cosentino always full tilt. Results sometimes odd, sometimes brilliant, never dull. Cab Sauv always worth a look; Chard can be v.gd.

Cuvaison Napa ★★★ (Cab) 00 01 02 05 Gd to sometimes v.gd Chard, Merlot, Syrah from CARNEROS. Impressive Cab Sauv from MOUNT VEEDER.

Dalla Valle Napa ★★★→★★★★★ 00 01 03 05 06 Hillside estate with a cult following for Maya, a Cab Sauv-based, deeply extracted wine that is slow to develop.

David Arthur Vineyards Napa ★★ Classic NAPA VALLEY Cab Sauv balanced and bright on the palate; also gd Sauv Bl.

David Bruce Santa Cruz Mts ★★★ Legendary mountain estate is still on top of the game with powerful, long-lasting Chard and superb Pinot N.

Davis Bynum Sonoma ★★★ Bynum pioneered often superb single-v'yd Pinot N in the RUSSIAN RIVER VALLEY. Chard is lean and minerally with a silky mouthfeel. Winery now owned by Rodney Strong V'yds.

Dehlinger Sonoma ★★★★ (Pinot) 06 07 08 Outstanding Pinot N from estate RUSSIAN RIVER VALLEY v'yd. Also gd Chard and Syrah.

Del Carlo Dry Creek Valley ★★→★★★ New winery from the Teldeschi family, long-time growers in DRY CREEK VALLEY. Terrific Zin from century-old vines; Cab Sauv has intense black cherry and blueberry fruit with the structure to age 8–10 yrs.

Delicato Vineyards San Joaquin ★→★★ One-time CENTRAL VALLEY jug producer has moved upscale with purchase of Monterey v'yds and several new bottlings from Lodi. Watch this brand for gd quality at everyday price.

De Loach Vineyards Sonoma ★★ Owned by Boisset Wines US, De Loach offers gd to *v.gd single-v'yd Chard*, Pinot N and Zin from mostly RUSSIAN RIVER VALLEY sites at a reasonable price.

Derbrès Sonoma ★★★ Elegant, nuanced Chard and Pinot N from cool-climate v'yds in CARNEROS and RUSSIAN RIVER VALLEY. The Pinot N is aromatic with gd acidity; Chard is balanced with a rich, full mouthfeel and a touch of spice.

Diamond Creek Napa ★★★★ 91 94 95 99 00 01 03 06 Austere, stunning cult Cabs from hilly v'yd near Calistoga go by names of v'yd blocks: Gravelly Meadow, Volcanic Hill, Red Block Terrace. Wines age beautifully. One of Napa's jewels.

Domaine Carneros Carneros ★★★ Showy US outpost of Taittinger in NAPA VALLEY, Domaine Carneros echoes austere style of its parent in Champagne (see France), but with a delicious dollop of California fruit. Vintage Blanc de Blancs v.gd. La Rêve the luxury *cuvée*. Still Pinot N and Chard also impressive.

Domaine Chandon Napa ★★→★★★★ NAPA VALLEY branch of Champagne house. Look for the NV reserve called Etoile, esp the rosé.

Dominus Estate Napa ★★★★ 97 99 01 02 05 06 Christian Moueix of Pomerol produces red Bordeaux blend that is slow to open but ages beautifully.

C Donatiello Sonoma ★★→★★★★ Newcomer producing gd Chard and Pinot N from selected v'yds. Floodgate Pinot N esp attractive.

Dry Creek Vineyard Sonoma ★★ Sauv (Fumé) Bl set standard for California for decades. Still impressive. Pleasing Chenin Bl; gd Zin.

Duckhorn Vineyards Napa ★★★→★★★★★ Known for dark, tannic, almost plummy-ripe, single-v'yd Merlots (esp Three Palms) and Cab Sauv-based blend Howell Mountain. New winery in ANDERSON VALLEY for Golden Eye Pinot N in a robust style more akin to Cab Sauv than Pinot. Makes a Zin/Cab Sauv blend in Paraduxx, a second NAPA VALLEY winery.

Dunn Vineyards Napa ★★★★ 91 95 97 99 01 03 06 Owner Randy Dunn makes superb and *intense Cab Sauv* from Howell Mountain, which ages magnificently;

milder bottling from valley floor. One of a few NAPA VALLEY winemakers to resist the stampede to jammy, lush wines to curry wine critics' favour.

Dutcher Crossing Dry Creek Valley ★★ Fairly complex Cab Sauv with a splash of Syrah shows bright fruit and a long finish, marred by a little heat from high alcohol. Decant.

Dutton-Goldfield Western Sonoma County ★★★ Winemaker–grower duo crafting outstanding Pinot N and Chard from top cool-climate sites; rapidly being recognized as modern California classics.

Edmunds St John ★★→★★★ Steve Edmunds and wife Cornelia St John are dedicated to Rhône varieties. From leased space in Berkeley they make outstanding wines chosen from a jumble of California v'yds. The line-up changes from vintage to vintage but is always worth a look, esp the treatment of Grenache.

Edna Valley Vineyard San Luis Obispo ★★★ Much improved in past few vintages; v.gd Chard, crisp and fruity, *lovely Sauv Bl*, impressive Syrah.

Ehlers Estate Napa St Helena ★★★ This 19th-century winery has been revived by Jean Leducq, a French entrepreneur and philanthropist. The v'yds are certified organic and biodynamic. The new wines are outstanding, esp an elegant Cab Sauv and a delicious Sauv Bl.

Elke Vineyards Anderson Valley ★★→★★★ A newcomer producing elegant and silky Pinot N in the Diamond Series and a starter Pinot N with forward fruit under Mary Elke label.

Etude Napa See BERINGER BLASS.

Failla Napa ★★→★★★ Winery on the Silverado Trail in NAPA VALLEY gaining a reputation for SONOMA COAST and RUSSIAN RIVER VALLEY Pinot N and Chard.

Far Niente Napa ★★★ (Cab) oo 01 03 05 Opulence is the goal in both Cab Sauv and Chard from luxury NAPA VALLEY estate. Can go over-the-top.

Ferrari-Carano Sonoma ★★→★★★ Wines from this showcase estate in DRY CREEK VALLEY have been erratic in recent yrs. Cab Sauv is slow to open. Merlot is reliable and sometimes v.gd. The owners recently bought Lazy Creek winery in MENDOCINO, offering a promising old-vine Pinot N and a gd Gewurz.

Fetzer Vineyards Mendocino ★★→★★★ A leader in the organic/sustainable-viticulture movement, Fetzer has produced consistent-value wines from least expensive range (Sundial, Valley Oaks) to brilliant Reserve wines. Also owns BONTERRA v'yds (all organic grapes) where *Roussanne and Marsanne are stars*.

Ficklin Vineyards Madera, Central Valley ★★★ Lush and delicious port-style dessert wines made from the classic Portuguese varieties.

Firestone Santa Ynez Valley ★★ Pioneering producer offers an excellent Sauv Bl and a lively off-dry Ries.

Flora Springs Wine Co Napa ★★★ Best are the two Meritage wines, red Trilogy and white Soliloquy, made from v'yds above valley floor. Juicy Merlot worth a look.

Flowers V'yd & Winery Sonoma ★★★ Intense, terroir-driven Pinot N and Chard from v. cool-climate vines only a few miles from the Pacific. Flowers has won early critical acclaim and is clearly a winery to watch.

Foppiano Sonoma ★★→★★★ One of the grand old families in California wine. You can count on the Zin every time but look esp for Petite Sirah, better known as "petty sir" among the California rearguard.

Forman Vineyard Napa ★★★★ 99 oo 01 03 05 Winemaker who found fame at STERLING in the 1970s now makes his own v.gd Cab Sauv and Chard from mountain v'yds.

Franciscan Vineyard Napa ★★★ Quality has been maintained under CONSTELLATION ownership, esp the top-of-the-line wines such as the graceful red Magnificat and the Cuvée Sauvage Chard. Gd budget wines under Estancia label.

Freeman Russian River Valley ★★★ Freeman has developed a cult following with outstanding cool-climate Pinot N (Akiko's Cuvée from SONOMA COAST) and RUSSIAN RIVER VALLEY Pinot N.

Freemark Abbey Napa ★★★→★★★★ Historic and currently underrated but consistent producer of *stylish Cab Sauv to age*. Single-v'yd Sycamore and Bosché bottlings often reach ★★★★.

Frog's Leap Napa ★★★→★★★★ 99 00 01 02 03 Small winery, as charming as its name (and T-shirts) suggests. Lean, *minerally Sauv Bl*, toasty Chard, spicy Zin. Supple and delicious Merlot, Cab Sauv. Converting to organic and biodynamic with recent wines showing more depth and intensity. Not a coincidence.

Gallo, E & J San Joaquin ★→★★ With a history of cheap jug wines, California's biggest winery is an easy target for wine snobs. In the long view, Gallo has done more to open up the American palate to wine than any other winery. Gallo's 1960s Hearty Burgundy was a groundbreaking popular wine. It still does the basic commodity wines, but it has also created an imposing line of regional varieties, such as Anapauma, Marcellina, Turning Leaf and more, all wines of modest quality perhaps but predictable and affordable.

Gallo Sonoma Sonoma ★★→★★★★ DRY CREEK VALLEY winery bottles several wines from Sonoma, NORTH COAST. Cab Sauv can be v.gd, esp the single-v'yd. Chard also better than average. Other wines made in SONOMA worth a try include Frei Brothers and McMurray, esp Pinot Gr.

Gary Farrell Sonoma ★★★→★★★★ Well established with some of the best Pinot N and Chard from the RUSSIAN RIVER VALLEY over the yrs. Also look for Zin, Chard and a v.gd Sauv Bl. Encounter, a new red Bordeaux blend, is v.gd.

Geyser Peak Sonoma ★★→★★★ A sometimes underrated producer of toasty Chard, powerful Cab Sauv, juicy Shiraz. A recent focus on Sauv Bl is welcome.

Gloria Ferrer Sonoma, Carneros ★★★ Built by Spain's Freixenet for sparkling wine, now producing spicy Chard and bright, silky Pinot N and other varietals, all from CARNEROS fruit. Bubbly quality remains high.

Grace Family Vineyard Napa ★★★★ 99 00 01 03 05 06 Stunning Cab Sauv. Shaped for long ageing. One of the few cult wines that may actually be worth the price.

Greenwood Ridge Mendocino ★★→★★★ Winery well above the floor of ANDERSON VALLEY offers engaging off-dry, perfumed Ries. Reds, esp Cab Sauv and Pinot N, also v.gd. Zin from SONOMA grapes.

Grgich Hills Cellars Napa ★★★→★★★★ Solid NAPA VALLEY producer of supple Chard (that can age); balanced, elegant Cab Sauv; jammy, ripe Zin from SONOMA grapes and gd Sauv Bl in minerally style.

Groth Vineyards Napa ★★★★ 97 99 00 01 05 06 OAKVILLE estate Cab Sauv has been four-star for a decade, with big, wraparound flavours made for ageing.

Hall Napa ★★★→★★★★ Kathryn Hall's family has been growing wine grapes in MENDOCINO for almost four decades. She bought historic Bergfeld winery in Napa in 2005; the new winery was designed by architect Frank Gehry. There is a stunning Diamond Mountain District Cab Sauv (★★★★) and a v.gd ST HELENA Bergfeld Cab Sauv. The Sauv Bl is delicious and minerally .

Handley Cellars Mendocino ★★★ Winemaker Mila Handley makes excellent ANDERSON VALLEY Chard, Gewurz, Pinot N. V.gd DRY CREEK VALLEY Sauv Bl and Chard from family vines in SONOMA COUNTY; small amount of intense sparkling.

Hanna Winery Sonoma ★★★ Has been reaching for four-star status for yrs. Recent vintages of Cab Sauv and well-made Sauv Bl are excellent.

Hanzell Sonoma ★★★★ (Chard) 05 06 07 (Pinot N) **01 02** 03 05 Pioneer (1950) small producer of outstanding terroir-driven Chard *and Pinot N* from estate vines. Always gd; quality level has risen sharply in the past few yrs. Deserves to be ranked with the best of California.

Harlan Estate Napa ★★★★ 97 99 00 01 03 Concentrated, sleek, cult Cab Sauv from small estate commanding luxury prices.

Harney Lane Winery Lodi ★ Rising star from Lodi, CENTRAL VALLEY. Best is the Lizzie James Old-Vine Zin; also look out for the Tempranillo and a delicious Albariño.

> **Bargain bottles**
> An often overlooked strength of California is the wealth of palatable (if
> not always distinctive) wines for the mass market. Everyday wines from
> producers such as BRONCO WINE COMPANY, CONSTELLATION, E & J GALLO and
> THE WINE GROUP are available everywhere in bottle and box for under $5 a
> bottle – a gd price for entry-level drinkers or wine consumers on a budget.

Harrison Clarke Santa Ynez Valley ★★ All about Syrah and Grenache. Estate Syrah is worth seeking out and the Grenache has rich flavour profile and mouthfeel.

Hartford Court Sonoma ★★★ Part of KENDALL-JACKSON's Artisans & Estates group showing v.gd single-v'yd Pinot Ns, tight coastal-grown Chard and wonderful old-vine RUSSIAN RIVER VALLEY Zins.

HdV Wines Carneros ★★★ *Complex and layered Chard* with a minerally edge from grower Larry Hyde's v'yd in conjunction with Aubert de Villaine of Domaine de la Romanée-Conti (see France).

Heitz Cellar Napa ★★★→★★★★ 99 00 01 03 05 History-making, deeply flavoured, minty Cab Sauv from Martha's V'yd. Bella Oaks and newer Trailside V'yd rival but can't match Martha. Some feel quality has slipped in recent vintages.

Heller Estate Carmel Valley ★★ *Gd organic Cab Sauv* and a charming Chenin Bl.

Hess Collection, The Napa ★★→★★★ Owner and art collector Donald Hess uses winery visiting area as a museum. Cab Sauv from MOUNT VEEDER v'yds step up to new quality level; Chard crisp and bright; Hess Select label v.gd value.

Hobbs, Paul ★★★ Sonoma Hobbs divides his time between Argentina and California. His RUSSIAN RIVER VALLEY Pinot N is lush and silky; the Chard, also from Russian River, is creamy with a gd bit of oak. The NAPA VALLEY Cab Sauv is supple with hints of bitter chocolate; gd structure.

Honig Napa ★★★ Big jump in quality after switching to organic farming. V.gd Cab Sauv in classic NAPA VALLEY style and seriously delicious Sauv Bl lead the parade.

Iron Horse Vineyards Sonoma ★★★→★★★★ RUSSIAN RIVER VALLEY family estate producing gd bubbly. Chard from RUSSIAN RIVER VALLEY is v.gd and an above-average Cab Sauv from ALEXANDER VALLEY v'yds.

Ironstone Lodi & Calaveras County ★→★★ Long-time growers with a destination winery in SIERRA FOOTHILLS making honestly priced and easy-drinking wines from mostly CENTRAL VALLEY grapes. Verdelho from Lodi is superb.

Jade Mountain Napa ★★→★★★ V.gd Rhône-style wines, esp Syrah, Mourvèdre.

Jessie's Grove Lodi ★★ Old Zin vines work well for farming family's venture.

Jordan Sonoma ★★★★ (Cab) 98 99 00 01 02 05 Winemaker Rob Davis makes consistently balanced and elegant wines from ALEXANDER VALLEY estate. The Cab Sauv tastes like an homage to Bordeaux. And it lasts. Minerally Chard is made in a Burgundian style.

Jorian Hill Santa Ynez Valley ★★★ Outstanding Rhône-inspired wines from organically farmed hillside v'yds. Beespoke is a powerful yet elegant Grenache/Syrah blend; Viognier is brilliant.

Joseph Phelps Napa ★★★★ (Insignia) 97 99 00 01 03 05 06 A true Napa "first growth"; Phelps Cab Sauv, esp the Insignia and Backus bottlings, are always near the top.

Joseph Swan Sonoma ★★★ Long-time RUSSIAN RIVER VALLEY producer of intense Zin and classy Pinot N capable of ageing in the 10-yr range.

J Vineyards Sonoma ★★★ A creamy, rich Brut sparkling wine is one of state's best. Also look for v.gd Pinot N and Pinot Gr from RUSSIAN RIVER VALLEY v'yds.

Joyce Vineyards Carmel Valley ★★ Artisan producer of unfined, unfiltered wines of gd varietal character. Cab Sauv is flirting with ★★★. Merlot v.gd.

Justin Central Coast ★★★→★★★★ Splendid proprietary red wine blends, all with gd structure and ageing potential. Top of the line is Isosceles, a Bordeaux blend

CALIFORNIA | Har–Mal | 241

with layers of fruit; Savant is a bold and spicy blend of Syrah and Cab Sauv from biodynamic v'yds. Also try the Justification, as well as an elegant Cab Sauv Reserve.

Kendall-Jackson Sonoma ★★→★★★ Legendary market-driven Chard, Cab Sauv. Even more noteworthy for the development of a diversity of wineries under the umbrella of Kendall-Jackson's Artisans & Estates (see HARTFORD COURT, STONESTREET).

Kent Rasmussen Winery Carneros ★★★ Crisp, lingering Chard and delicious Pinot N. Ramsay is an alternative label for small production lots.

Kenwood Vineyards Sonoma ★★→★★★ (Jack London Cab) 00 01 03 05 Single-v'yd Jack London Cab Sauv, Zin (several) the high points of a consistent line. Sauv Bl is reliable value.

Kistler Vineyards Sonoma ★★★ Still chasing the Burgundian model of single-v'yd Pinot N, most from RUSSIAN RIVER VALLEY, with mixed success. Chards can be v. toasty, buttery and over-the-top, though they have a loyal following.

Korbel Sonoma ★★ Largest US producer of *méthode champenoise* with focus on fruit flavours. Gd picnic wines.

Kunde Estate Sonoma ★★★ Solid SONOMA VALLEY producer and noted grower with an elegant, understated Chard, flavourful Sauv Bl, peachy Viognier and silky Merlot. All estate-bottled.

La Jota Howell Mtn, Napa ★★★ Long-lived Cab Sauv and Merlot from hillside v'yds. Cab Fr v.gd recently with a spicy richness and a long, complex finish.

Lamborn Howell Mtn, Napa ★★★ V'yd planted on historic 19th-century site. Big, juicy Zin, Cab Sauv coming along for this cult winery.

Lane Tanner Santa Barbara ★★★ Owner-winemaker makes v. personal and superb single-v'yd Pinot N (Bien Nacido, Sierra Madre Plateau) reflecting terroir with a quiet, understated elegance.

Lang & Reed Napa ★★★ Specialist focusing on delicious Loire-style Cab Fr.

Laurel Glen Sonoma ★★★★ 95 97 99 00 01 03 05 06 Floral and long-lived Cab Sauv from steep v'yd on Sonoma Mountain. Mid-priced Counterpoint label is gd quality at a reasonable price; budget Reds label offers exceptional value.

Lava Cap El Dorado ★★ Zin is outstanding but Petite Sirah from Grand Hill v'yd is winning a lot of fans with its well-balanced structure and fine fruit.

Lockwood Monterey ★→★★ South Salinas Valley v'yd. Gd value in Chard, Sauv Bl.

Lohr, J Central Coast ★★→★★★ Large winery with extensive v'yds; v.gd PASO ROBLES Cab Sauv Seven Oaks. Recent series of Meritage-style reds best yet. Commodity line is Cypress.

Long Meadow Napa ★★★ Elegant, silky Cab Sauv better with each vintage. Lively *Graves-style Sauv Bl* a winner as well. V'yd is organically farmed.

Louis M Martini Napa ★★→★★★ Long, history-making, age-worthy Cab Sauv, Zin. On down-slide for several yrs. Now on the way back after purchase by GALLO in 2002. Recent bottlings of Cab Sauv showing v. well, esp Monte Rosso and ALEXANDER VALLEY bottlings.

Luli Santa Lucia Highlands ★★ The Pisoni family grows outstanding Chard. It has joined with master sommelier Sara Floyd to produce a Chard gem with a touch of tropical fruit and peaches. Take this little number on your next picnic.

L'Uvaggio Napa ★★→★★★ Former ROBERT MONDAVI winemaker Jim Moore specializes in Italian varieties. An outstanding Barbera leads the way; also look for Vermentino from Lodi and a rosé from Barbera. Can't go wrong here.

MacPhail Sonoma ★★★ Pinot N specialist offering intense wines from select v'yds on the SONOMA COAST and in ANDERSON VALLEY. Wines are silky and luscious with wraparound flavours.

Malibu Vineyards Central Coast ★★ Vines in Malibu? Better believe it. Cab Fr one of California's best. Also v.gd Syrah and Sangiovese.

Marcassin Sonoma Coast Cult queen Helen Turley's own tiny label. Worth so much at auction that few ever drink it. Concentrated Chard and dense Pinot N. Chard so densely concentrated that those who do taste it never forget.

Marimar Torres Estate Sonoma ★★★★ (Chard) 05 06 08 (Pinot N) 01 02 03 05 06 Several bottlings of Chard and Pinot N from Don Miguel estate v'yd in Green Valley. The Chard is complex and sometimes rather edgy, with gd ageing potential. Acero Don Miguel Chard is unoaked and *a lovely expression of Chard fruit*. Pinot N from the Doña Margarita v'yd, only a few miles from the ocean, is intense and surprisingly rich for young vines. V'yds now farmed organically and moving towards biodynamics.

Markham Napa ★★★ Underrated producer of elegant Merlot and solid Cab Sauv.

Martinelli Russian River Valley ★★★ Family growers from fog-shrouded western hills of Sonoma, famous for old-vine Jackass Hill V'yd Zin.

Mayacamas Vineyards Napa ★★★ Pioneer boutique v'yd with rich Chard and firm (but no longer steel hard) *Cab Sauv, capable of long ageing*. Also a gd Sauv Bl.

Melville Vineyards Sta Rita Hills ★★→★★★ The winning wines here are the estate Chard and Pinot N. Both excellent expressions of varietal character, with layers of fruit nicely balanced by a lively acidity.

Merry Edwards Russian River Valley ★★★★ Superstar consultant has planted her own Pinot N v'yd in RUSSIAN RIVER VALLEY district and buys in grapes. Her Pinot N is "must drink". Also lovely, true-to-varietal Sauv Bl.

Merryvale Napa ★★★ Best at Cab Sauv and Merlot, which have elegant balance and supple finish. Sauv Bl can be v.gd.

Mettler FamilyVineyards Lodi ★★ Long-time growers now producing a sleek and tangy Cab Sauv and a powerful Petite Sirah.

Milano Mendocino ★★ Small producer of Zin, Cab Sauv, worth seeking out. New Hopland Cuvée, a blend of Cab Sauv and Pinot N is ★★★★ all the way.

Miner Family Vineyards Napa ★★★ Powerful and potentially long-ageing reds based on Cab Sauv are the star turn here. Look esp for the Icon bottling, a blend of Bordeaux varieties. The family also owns OAKVILLE RANCH.

Mitchell Katz Livermore Valley ★★→★★★ An upcoming winery in LIVERMORE VALLEY. Makes v.gd Cab Sauv and a blockbuster Petite Sirah. Watch for more.

Monticello Vineyards Napa ★★★ 99 01 03 05 Top Cab Sauv and Chard under Corley label, basic line under Monticello.

Morgan Monterey ★★★★ Top-end single-v'yd Pinot Ns and Chards from SANTA LUCIA HIGHLANDS v'yds. Esp fine, unoaked Chard Metallico. Estate Double L v'yd farmed organically. New Rhônish entry Côtes du Crows is charming.

Moshin V'yds Sonoma ★★→★★★ The RUSSIAN RIVER VALLEY Chard is the go-to wine here. Creamy and rich mouthfeel with just a whiff of oak and a long finish that echoes through the palate. The Sauv Bl and Pinot N also worth a look.

Mumm Napa Valley Napa ★★→★★★ Stylish bubbly, esp *delicious Blanc de Noirs* and a rich, complex DVX single-v'yd fizz to age a few yrs in the bottle.

Murphy-Goode Sonoma ★★ Sauv Bl, Zin are tops. Tin Roof (screwcap) line offers refreshing Sauv Bl and Chard *sans* oak.

Nalle Sonoma ★★★★ Doug Nalle makes lovely Zins from DRY CREEK VALLEY fruit; juicy and delicious young but will also mature gracefully.

Napa Wine Company Napa ★★★ Largest organic grape-grower in NAPA VALLEY sells most of the fruit and operates a custom-crush facility for several small premium producers. Offers v.gd Cab Sauv under own label.

Navarro V'yds Mendocino ★★★→★★★★ Modern ANDERSON VALLEY pioneer producing Ries and Gewurz ranking with the best of the New World. Also Pinot N in two styles, homage to Burgundy from ANDERSON VALLEY grapes, plus a brisk and juicy bottling from bought-in grapes.

Newton V'yds Napa ★★★→★★★★ (Icon) 03 05 06 SPRING MTN estate produces three tiers of wines: Icon, a Bordeaux blend; The Puzzle, site-specific bottlings of Cab Sauv, Merlot and Chard, and the fruit-forward Red Label. Supple and elegant expressions of mtn v'yds. Gd ageing potential.

Nickel & Nickel Napa ★★★ Specialist in exceptional terroir-driven single-v'yd Cab Sauv from NAPA VALLEY and SONOMA.

Niebaum-Coppola Estate Napa ★★★ (Rubicon) "Godfather" Francis Ford Coppola has proven he is as serious about making wine as making movies. Rubicon, a Bordeaux blend, is best on the list, although it can be too jammy in some vintages; Edizione Pennino concentrates on delightfully old-fashioned Zin.

Novy Family Wines Sonoma ★★→★★★ This no-frills winery is tucked away in a warehouse in Santa Rosa, proving that you do not need to a showcase château to make gd wine. Current favourites: a Rhônish Syrah from SANTA LUCIA HIGHLANDS grapes and a lovely RUSSIAN RIVER VALLEY Viognier. Under the Sidura label they make v.gd single v'yd Pinot N from both California and Oregon.

Oakville Ranch Napa ★★★ This estate on the Silverado Trail (owned by the MINER FAMILY) produces consistently gd wines, esp a creamy Chard.

Ojai Santa Barbara ★★★ Former AU BON CLIMAT partner Adam Tolmach makes range of v.gd wines, esp Syrah and other Rhônes from CENTRAL COAST v'yds.

Opus One Napa ★★★ With a lot of in-and-out yrs at Opus, the wines rarely lived up to the hype for this red Bordeaux blend. The past few vintages, beginning with 2004, are showing well with the wines harmonious and balanced.

Pahlmeyer Napa ★★★ Producer of tannic Cab Sauv and more supple Merlot.

Paloma Vineyard Spring Mtn ★★→★★★ Merlot specialist from high-elevation v'yds on mostly lava-based soils. The wines have a gd structure with layers of fruit and hints of chocolate. Drink now or let them age a decade.

Paradigm Napa ★★★ Westside OAKVILLE v'yd with a fine Merlot and a bright, supple Cab Sauv.

Parducci Mendocino ★★ The True Grit Petite Sirah is a gd example of why this orphan variety is getting new respect and attention in California.

Patianna Vineyards Russian River Valley ★★★ Biodynamic v'yds farmed by Patty FETZER. Also sources grapes from organic v'yds in MENDOCINO. Lovely Sauv Bl and v.gd Syrah are main strengths.

Paul Dolan Mendocino ★★★ Pioneer of organic and biodynamic farming when he was winemaker at FETZER, Dolan's own brand offers outstanding Zin, Syrah, Cab Sauv, Chard and Sauv Bl from organic, biodynamic NORTH COAST v'yds.

Pedroncelli Sonoma ★★ Old hand in DRY CREEK VALLEY producing bright, elbow-bending Zin, Cab Sauv and a solid Chard.

Pellegrini Family Vineyards Sonoma ★★ Long-time producer (established in 1933) of gd-value wines is revitalized with a series of bottlings from the RUSSIAN RIVER VALLEY and ALEXANDER VALLEY. Milestone, a Bordeaux blend, is esp gd; also a pleasing Olivet Lane Estate Pinot N.

Peltier Station Lodi ★★→★★★ The Schatz family has been growing wine grapes in Lodi for over 50 yrs. Now making its own wines, and the results are gd to outstanding. Look esp for the refreshing Viognier and a yummy Zin.

Periano Lodi ★★ Gd example of the new look of Lodi wines. Esp Barbera, brilliant Viognier and v.gd Chard.

Perry Creek El Dorado ★★→★★★ An extraordinary Syrah and above-average Cab Sauv from high-elevation vines.

Peter Michael Winery Sonoma ★★★→★★★★ Complex Chard from Howell Mtn in a powerful style, and a more supple ALEXANDER VALLEY bottling. Cab Sauv on the tight side.

Philips, R H Yolo, Dunnigan Hills ★→★★ The only winery in the Dunnigan Hills AVA makes a wide range of wines. Excellent job with Rhône varieties under the EXP label and gd-value Toasted Head Chard.

Philip Togni V'yds Napa ★★★→★★★★ 00 01 03 05 Veteran NAPA VALLEY winemaker makes v. *fine long-lasting Cab Sauv* from SPRING MOUNTAIN.

Pine Ridge Napa ★★★ Tannic and concentrated Cab Sauvs from several NAPA VALLEY AVAs. The just off-dry Chenin Bl is a treat.

Preston Dry Creek Valley, Sonoma ★★★ Lou Preston is a demanding terroirist, making DRY CREEK VALLEY icons such as Zin and fruity, marvellous Barbera. His Sauv Bl is delicious as well as several gd Rhône varietals.

Pride Mountain Spring Mtn ★★★ Well known for Bordeaux blends, Pride has moved into the front for Merlot bottlings. There is typical mountain fruit, dominated by black cherry and a touch of chocolate. Wines are built for age.

Provenance Napa ★★★ Lovely, elegant and supple Cab Sauv from heart of NAPA VALLEY estate. Winemaker Tom Rinaldi also makes superb Hewitt V'yd Cab Sauv. Don't overlook the crisp Rutherford Sauv Bl.

Quady Winery San Joaquin ★★→★★★ Imaginative Madera Muscat dessert wines include famed orangey Essensia, rose-petal-flavoured Elysium and Moscato d'Asti-like Electra. A recent addition, Vya Vermouth, is an excellent apéritif.

Quintessa Napa ★★★→★★★★ Homage-to-Bordeaux blend, from a biodynamic estate on the Silverado Trail, developed by the Huneeus family of Chile. The wines show great finesse and balance, improving with each vintage.

Quivira Sonoma ★★★ Focus on classic and v. drinkable DRY CREEK VALLEY Zin; also a range of delicious Rhône varietals. V'yds farmed biodynamically.

Qupé Santa Barbara ★★★ Never-a-dull-moment cellar-mate of AU BON CLIMAT. *Marsanne*, Pinot Bl, Syrah are all well worth trying.

Radio-Coteau Sonoma ★★★ V.gd Pinot N with a little Syrah from cool-climate v'yds on the SONOMA COAST. There's a lot to like: Sonoma Coast La Neblina Pinot N leads the charge. It has enough structure to keep for 5–8 yrs but tastes good young.

Rafanelli, A Sonoma ★★★→★★★★ Extraordinary Dry Creek Valley Zin from this family estate. The Zin will age, but it's so delightful when young, why bother?

Ramey Wine Cellars Russian River Valley ★★★→★★★★ V.gd single-v'yd Cab Sauv from NAPA VALLEY, and rich and complex Chard from cooler v'yds, esp the Hudson V'yd Napa Valley-Carneros. Don't pass on the intense and complex SONOMA COAST Syrah.

Ravenswood Sonoma ★★★ Joel Peterson pioneered single-v'yd Zin. Later added a budget line of Sonoma and Vintners Reserve Zin and Merlot. Now owned by CONSTELLATION, but quality appears to be holding.

Raymond V'yds and Cellar Napa ★★★ 99 00 01 03 05 Balanced and understated Cab Sauv from family v'yds with potential for long-term ageing, esp The Generations blend.

Ridge Santa Cruz Mts ★★★★ (Cab) 95 96 99 00 01 03 05 Founder and wine master Paul Draper continues to work his magic here. Supple and harmonious *Montebello Cab Sauv* from estate is superb. Also outstanding single-v'yd Zin from SONOMA, NAPA VALLEY, SIERRA FOOTHILLS and PASO ROBLES. Most Zin has gd ageing potential. *Outstanding Chard* from wild-yeast fermentation often overlooked.

Robert Craig Vineyard Napa ★★ Cab Sauv with gd structure, attractive spice and fruit. Long, balanced finish. The Affinity blend is tops.

Robert Keenan Winery Napa ★★★ Winery on SPRING MTN: supple, restrained Cab Sauv, Merlot; also Chard.

Robert Mondavi Napa ★→★★★★ Brilliant innovator, bought in 2004 by CONSTELLATION, has wine at all price/quality ranges. At the top are the NAPA VALLEY Reserves, NAPA VALLEY appellation series (eg. Carneros Chard, Oakville Cab Sauv, etc.), NAPA VALLEY (basic production). At the low end are various CENTRAL COAST wines and Robert Mondavi-Woodbridge from Lodi. While the v. top wines may be holding their quality level, mid-ranges seem to be slipping.

Rochioli Vineyards & Winery Sonoma ★★★→★★★★ Long-time RUSSIAN RIVER VALLEY grower sells most fruit to other top Pinot N producers, but holds back enough to make lovely complex Pinot N under his own label, esp the Special Cuvée Pinot N. Also v.gd Sauv Bl.

Roederer Estate Mendocino ★★★★ ANDERSON VALLEY branch of Champagne house. Supple, elegant house style. Easily one of the top three sparklers in California and hands-down the best rosé. Luxury *cuvée* L'Ermitage is superb.

Rosenblum Cellars San Francisco Bay ★★→★★★ Makes a wide range of Zins and Rhône varietals from v'yds up and down the state. Quality varies but always well above average.

Saddleback Cellars Napa ★★★→★★★★ 01 05 06 Owner-winemaker Nils Venge is a legend in NAPA VALLEY. Lush Zin and long-lived Cab Sauv. In some vintages he makes a super Sauv Bl.

St Clement Napa ★★★→★★★★ 99 00 01 03 05 06 Long-time NAPA VALLEY producer has a new life under BERINGER BLASS ownership, with a turn towards terroir-based wines. Supple, long-lived Oroppas, a Cab Sauv-based blend, is the go-to wine here. Merlot and Chard also outstanding.

St Francis Sonoma ★★★ 00 01 03 05 06 Deep and concentrated Cab Sauv from single v'yds. Look for the Wild Oak V'yd Chard finished with a nod to Burgundy. The old-vine Zin is super.

St Rose Winery Sonoma ★★ Limited production but worth seeking out for its single wine, a RUSSIAN RIVER VALLEY Pinot N from Nunes V'yd. Layers of dark fruit balance with a pleasing earthiness; should age nicely for 4–6 yrs.

Saintsbury Carneros ★★★→★★★★ Outstanding Pinot N, denser than most from CARNEROS and can take a few yrs of bottle age. Chard full-flavoured, nicely balanced. Garnet Pinot N, made from younger vines, is a light-hearted quaff.

St-Supéry Napa ★★→★★★★ Sleek and graceful Merlot; Cab Sauv can be outstanding, as is red Meritage. *Sauv Bl one of best in state.* Sources some grapes from warmer Pope Valley east of NAPA VALLEY. French-owned (Skalli).

Sanford Santa Barbara ★★ Founder Richard Sanford was one of the first to plant Pinot N in Santa Barbara, but wines have hit a rough patch under new owners.

Santa Cruz Mountain Vineyard Santa Cruz ★★→★★★ Produces wines of strong varietal character from estate grapes, inc v.gd Pinot N and an exceptional Cab Sauv – big, concentrated, age-worthy.

Sattui, V Napa ★★ King of direct-only sales (ie. winery door or mail order). Wines made in a rustic, drink-now style. Reds are best, esp Cab Sauv, Zin.

Sbragia Sonoma ★★★ Ed Sbragia, long-time winemaker at BERINGER BLASS, has established his own family winery in DRY CREEK VALLEY. A splendid selection of single-v'yd Cab Sauv and Merlot shows him at top form. Wines show classic California character, concentrated but not over-the-top. Also a v.gd Sauv Bl from estate vines.

Schramsberg Napa ★★★★ Sparkling wine that stands the test of time. The first to make a true *méthode champenoise* in the state in commercial quantity. Reserve is splendid; Blanc de Noirs outstanding. Luxury *cuvée* J Schram is America's Krug. Mirabelle is second label for palate-pleasing bubbly. Now making a *v.gd Cab Sauv*, J Davies, from mountain estate vines.

Screaming Eagle Napa ★★★★ Small lots of cult Cab Sauv at luxury prices for those who like that kind of thing.

Sebastiani Sonoma ★ Former jug-wine king has tried to go upscale with v'yd wines with limited critical success.

Seghesio Sonoma ★★★ Respected family winery has a double focus: Italian varietals and Zin. *The Zins are superb*, drinkable when young, taking on new depth with age. The Italians are a cut above most California efforts in that line, esp Barbera and Sangiovese.

Selby Sonoma ★★ Susie Selby left her MBA corporate track in Texas for the lure of California wine. She's clearly having too much fun, with more than a dozen different wines in her portfolio. Head straight for the RUSSIAN RIVER VALLEY Chard but have a few sips of a v.gd SONOMA COUNTY Merlot as well.

Selene Napa ★★★→★★★★ Mia Klein makes rich, concentrated Bordeaux-varietal wines. Hyde V'yd Sauv Bl is super; Chester V'yd red blend a must.

Sequana Sonoma ★★→★★★ Pinot N-only venture established by California veterans Tom Selfridge and James MacPhail (who also has his own label). Three wines, two from the RUSSIAN RIVER VALLEY and one from SANTA LUCIA HIGHLANDS in Monterey. All feature a silky complexity and intensity.

Sequoia Grove Napa ★★★ Estate Cab Sauvs are intense and long-lived with the trend clearly upwards. Chard is balanced and has ageing potential most yrs.

Shafer Vineyards Napa ★★★→★★★★ (Cab Sauv) 97 99 00 01 02 03 05 (Merlot) 03 05 Top marks for deep yet supple Cab Sauv, esp the Hillside Select, and Merlot, which is capable of several yrs of bottle ageing.

Signorello Napa ★★★ Concentrated and rich Cab Sauv, complex, full-bodied Chard with sometimes unresolved oak tannins. Syrah is always worth a look, as are single-v'yd Pinots N from CARNEROS. Looking better with each vintage.

Silverado Vineyards Napa ★★★→★★★★ 99 00 01 03 05 06 Showy hilltop STAGS LEAP district winery offering supple Cab Sauv, lean and minerally Chard and distinctive Sangiovese.

Silver Oak Napa/Sonoma ★★★→★★★★ Separate wineries in NAPA and ALEXANDER VALLEYS make Cab Sauv only. NAPA VALLEY wines can be super-concentrated but they have a loyal following. ALEXANDER VALLEY a bit more supple.

Sinskey Vineyards Napa ★★★ Chard with a gd acidic bite and luscious Pinot N are the highlights of this reliable CARNEROS estate.

Smith-Madrone Napa ★★ High up on SPRING MOUNTAIN, the Smith brothers make *one of the state's best Ries* in an aromatic, off-dry style. V'yds are dry-farmed.

Sonoma-Cutrer Vineyards Sonoma ★★→★★★ Big step up for this Chard specialist with the 2004 and 2005 vintages, esp the SONOMA COAST bottling, flinty and hard-edge Chard with real bite, and the Les Pierres v'yd.

Spottswoode St Helena, Napa ★★★★ 97 99 00 01 03 05 06 *Outstanding Cab Sauv* from estate v'yd is long-lasting, balanced and harmonious. Another California "first growth". Brilliant Sauv Bl is a bonus.

Spring Mountain Vineyard Napa ★★★→★★★★ Historic mtn estate on a winning path; excellent Cab Sauv with gd structure and depth, and outstanding Sauv Bl.

Staglin Family Vineyard Napa ★★★ 99 00 01 03 05 Elegant Cab Sauv from Rutherford Bench.

Stag's Leap Wine Cellars Napa ★★★★ 97 99 00 01 03 05 Celebrated for silky, seductive Cab Sauvs (SLV, Fay, top-of-line Cask 23) and Merlots. Gd Chard is often overlooked. Holding the line for balance and harmony against the onslaught of over-the-top, super-concentrated NAPA VALLEY Cabs. Now owned by partnership of Piero Antinori (see Italy) and CHATEAU STE MICHELLE in Washington State.

Stags' Leap Winery Napa See BERINGER BLASS.

Steele Wines Lake ★★→★★★★ Jed Steele is a genius at sourcing v'yds for a series of single-v'yd wines under main label and a second label called Shooting Star. Chard can get a little oaky, but Pinot N and some specialty wines, such as Washington State Aligoté, are outstanding.

Sterling Napa ★★→★★★ NAPA VALLEY estate making Chard and understated single-v'yd Cab Sauv. Has never seemed to fulfil potential, despite gd v'yd sources.

Stonestreet Sonoma ★★★ One of the stars of Jess Jackson's Artisans & Estates stable. The ALEXANDER VALLEY Cab Sauv is a brawny but balanced wine with layers of flavours; Chard can get too buttery but worth a look.

> **Napa Cabs with balance**
>
> My thanks for this list go to Eric Asimov of *The New York Times*,
> who tastes far more Napa Cabernets than I do. But we have similar
> tastes: Chateau Montelena, Clark-Claudon Vineyards, CLOS DU VAL,
> Continuum, CORISON, DOMINUS ESTATE, Dyer, FORMAN VINEYARD,
> FROG'S LEAP, GRGICH HILLS, HDV WINES, HEITZ CELLAR, J. Davies,
> Joseph Carr, Kongsgaard, MAYACAMAS VINEYARDS, M by Michael MONDAVI,
> Rubicon Estate, Seps Estate, SMITH-MADRONE, SPOTTSWOODE, Tom Eddy
> Wines, TREFETHEN FAMILY VINEYARDS, TRUCHARD VINEYARDS and
> White Rock Vineyards

Stony Hill Napa ★★★★ (Chard) 91 95 97 99 00 01 03 05 06 Amazing hillside Chard for past 50 yrs, made in an elegant "homage to Chablis" style. Most wine sold from mailing list. Wines are v. long-lived.

Storrs Winery Santa Cruz Mts ★★→★★★ Top-rated Chard from mtn v'yds leads the way. A lovely and quaffable Grenache from CENTRAL COAST grapes.

Sutter Home Napa ★→★★ Famous for white Zin and rustic AMADOR red Zin. New upscale Signature Series and Trinchero Family Estates a step up, esp Cab Sauv.

Swanson Napa ★★→★★★ Outstanding Merlot and balanced and bright Alexis Cab Sauv get top marks. Also v.gd Pinot Grigio.

Tablas Creek Paso Robles ★★★ Joint venture between owners of Château de Beaucastel (see France) and importer Robert Hass. V'yd based on cuttings from Châteauneuf v'yds. Côtes de Tablas red and white are amazingly gd, as is the Tablas Creek Esprit. These are *must-drink wines for Rhônistas*.

Talbott, R Monterey ★★★ Chard from single v'yds in Monterey is the name of the game, with the famed Sleepy Hollow v'yd in the SANTA LUCIA HIGHLANDS at the heart. Approach is Burgundian.

Thomas Fogarty Santa Cruz Mts ★★→★★★ Go here for a rich, complex Chard that ages fairly well. Also gd Pinot N from estate v'yds and a delightful Gewurz from Monterey grapes.

Titus Vineyards Napa ★★★ Family estate on the Silverado Trail making v.gd Cab Sauv, an outstanding spicy Zin and Cab Fr.

Trefethen Family Vineyards Napa ★★★ Historic family winery with record for consistency and durability. Gd off-dry Ries, balanced Chard for ageing. Cab Sauv shows increasing complexity, esp top-of-the-line Halo.

Trenza San Luis Obispo ★★→★★★ Dedicated to Spanish varieties, this new winery is off to a terrific start with a red and a white blend and a rosé, all gd. The Trenza Blanco, a blend of Albariño and white Grenache, is a real treat.

Tres Sabores Rutherford ★★★ Newcomer making three different Zins all from the same RUTHERFORD organically farmed hillside v'yds. Wines are consistently balanced and elegant, emphasizing different elements of the v'yd.

Tricycle Wine Company Lake ★★ A newcomer showing great promise from the Obsidian Ridge V'yd in the Red Hills AVA of LAKE COUNTY. Cab Sauv is classic California with ripe blackberry fruit and gd structure. Keep an eye on this one.

Truchard Carneros ★★★→★★★★ Merlot in CARNEROS? For sure. From the warmer north end of Carneros comes one of the flavourful, firmly built Merlots that give the AVA identity. Cab Sauv and Syrah even better, and the tangy, lemony Chard is a must-drink. New bottlings of Tempranillo outstanding, as is a Roussanne.

Valley of the Moon Sonoma ★→★★ Reliable and gd-value elbow-benders, occasionally rising to two stars, such as the current Pinot Bl.

Viader Estate Napa ★★★★ 97 99 00 01 03 05 06 A blend of Cab Sauv and Cab Fr from Howell Mtn hillside estate. Powerful wines, yet balanced and elegant in best yrs. This is a classic NAPA VALLEY mtn red. Ages well. Also look for new series of small-lot bottlings, inc Syrah, Tempranillo.

Volker Eisele Family Estate Napa ★★★→★★★★ 97 99 00 01 03 05 Sleek, luscious blend of Cab Sauv and Cab Fr from the little-known Chiles Valley AVA. Also look for a spicy Sauv Bl.

Wente Vineyards Livermore and Monterey ★★→★★★ Historic specialist in whites, *esp Livermore Sauv Bl* and Sem. New range of single-v'yd Chard has moved the quality bar higher.

Whitehall Lane Napa ★★→★★★ New releases have revived this ST HELENA winery, esp the elegant and balanced Cab Sauv and a zippy Sauv Bl.

Williams Selyem Sonoma ★★★ Intense, smoky RUSSIAN RIVER VALLEY Pinot N, esp Rochioli V'yds and Allen V'yd. Now reaching to SONOMA COAST, MENDOCINO for grapes. Cultish favourite can sometimes lose its balance and fall.

Willowbrook Sonoma ★★★ Single-v'yd Pinot N; wines are stylish and elegant, with bright, opening fruit and deep flavours in the middle and finish. To watch.

Wilson Vineyards Sonoma ★★→★★★★ Newcomer with an eye for Zin. The estate old-vine Ellie's V'yd is outstanding – classic DRY CREEK VALLEY Zin. The impressive Reserve Zin has a rich, brambly mouthfeel.

Wine Group, The Central Valley The third-largest producer of wine in the world, by volume, after E & J GALLO and CONSTELLATION, offers mostly bargain wines, such as Glen Ellen, Almaden and Inglenook, as well as bag-in-box bargains such as Franzia. The wine is drinkable, for the most part, and certainly helps balance out grape supply and demand in California and around the world.

Zaca Mesa Santa Barbara ★★→★★★★ Now turning away from Chard and Pinot N to concentrate on estate Rhône grapes (esp Viognier) and blends (Cuvée Z).

Zahtila Vineyards Napa ★★★ Newcomer in north NAPA VALLEY. Elegant, inviting Cab Sauv and intense Zin (one from Oat Hill estate v'yd near Calistoga). Also makes DRY CREEK VALLEY and RUSSIAN RIVER VALLEY Zins from SONOMA COUNTY. To watch.

THE PACIFIC NORTHWEST

Can we stop talking about the "potential" of Pacific Northwest wines? The wines coming from Oregon and Washington are world-class, right now. Oregon Pinot Noir has more than fulfilled its early promise. In this edition four Pinot producers have moved up to a four-star rating. The news is much the same in Washington, with scores of top-ranked Cabernets and other Bordeaux reds. The best wines of both regions capture the splendid fruit of the Pacific Northwest, balanced with bright acidity, leading to balanced and elegant wines, many with good ageing potential.

Recent vintages

Any general discussion of vintages is difficult because of the wide variation in climate over the area and the jumble of microclimates in small regions.

2009 It was a hot growing season for both Oregon and Washington. Harvest was early, with the red wines in particular showing good fruit.

2008 A cool spring led to a late harvest. The typical autumn rain pattern was late to develop and wine-growers are optimistic about the future of the young wines, some calling it the best vintage of the decade. In Oregon the Pinot N looked especially promising. In Washington and Idaho the harvest was up from 2007 and grapes were in near-perfect condition.

2007 Not an easy vintage across the Northwest; rain and even some hail during harvest caused problems but, as always, those growers and wineries that paid attention will get it right.

2006 The century is young, but when talk turns to vintage of the century, this is it so far for Oregon. Incredible quality across the board. Washington and Idaho reporting similar quality.

2005 This is turning out to be an amazing vintage, if the winery paid attention. Oregon Pinot N, Washington Cab Sauv, Merlot, could be exceptional.

Oregon

Abacela V'yds Umpqua Valley ★★★ V.gd Tempranillo, Dolcetto, Cab Fr. Syrah a treat.

Adelsheim Vineyard Yamhill County ★★★→★★★★ 04 05 06 07 Oregon Pinot N veteran remains on top of the game with elegant Pinot N. New Dijon clone Chard, Ries, top Pinots Gr and Bl: clean, bracing.

Amalie Robert Estate Willamette ★★★ Promising new estate winery with a minerally, terroir-driven Pinot N and luscious Chard.

Amity Willamette ★★→★★★ Pioneer in Oregon with exceptional Ries and Pinot Bl. The Pinot often rises to ★★★.

Anam Cara Cellars Willamette ★★★ An extraordinary Chehalm Mts Reserve Pinot N, rich and deeply concentrated. Elegant estate Pinot N and delicious estate Ries.

Andrew Rich (Tabula Rasa) Willamette ★★→★★★ Ex-California winemaker. Small lots of artisan wines, inc a supple Pinot N and exceptional Syrah.

Anne Amie Willamette ★★★ Outstanding Winemaker's Selection Pinot N, balanced and harmonious; v.gd Pinot Gr as well.

Antica Terra Willamette ★★→★★★ Now owned by four partners, inc ex-California winemaker Maggie Harrison (Sin Qua Non). The Pinot N, made from Amity Hills fruit, is California-meets-Oregon, with rich, deep flavours.

Archery Summit Williamette ★★★ Powerful Pinot N bottlings from several v'yds in the Red Hills AVA; made in a bold style that has won a loyal following.

Argyle Yamhill County ★★→★★★★ V.gd Ries and v. fine Pinot N lead the way; also *bargain bubbly*. Winery founded by Aussie superstar winemaker Brian Croser.

Beaux Frères Yamhill County ★★★ Pinot N has more concentration than most Oregon offerings. Part-owned by critic Robert Parker.

Benton Lane Willamette ★★ A delicious Pinot N, balanced and harmonious. Also v.gd Pinot Gr. If you are lucky enough to find the rosé of Pinot N, grab it.

Bethel Heights Willamette ★★→★★★ 04 05 Deftly made estate Pinot N. *Chard one of best in state*; gd Pinot Bl, Pinot Gr.

Brick House Yamhill County ★★★ 01 02 Huge estate Pinot N. Dark and brooding; Estate Select a leaner, more balanced version.

Brooks Willamette ★★★ Established only a decade ago, Brooks is making its name with superb organic/biodynamic Ries and Pinot N. The wines are elegant with long, echoing flavours and are v.gd value as well. Seek these out.

Carabella Willamette ★★ Dijon Clone 76 Chard is outstanding, with a silky mouthfeel and just a touch of oak.

Chehalem Yamhill County ★★→★★★ Outstanding Chard with ageing potential, as well as a new drink-me-now, no-oak Chard. V.gd Ries, Pinot Gr.

Coehlo Winery Willamette ★★ Pinot N-only producer is off to a gd start with an aromatic, lively wine that shows promise for the future.

Cooper Mtn Willamette ★★★→★★★★ Complex Pinot N and a rich, intense Chard capable of some bottle-age. Certified biodynamic v'yds.

Domaine Danielle Laurent Yamhill-Carlton ★★★ New producer of gd to v.gd single-v'yd Pinot N and other varieties, inc Syrah. The Pinot N, esp the Soléna label bottling, is superb.

Domaine Drouhin Willamette ★★★→★★★★ 03 04 05 06 *Outstanding Pinot N* silky and elegant, improving with each vintage. Chard also a winner.

Domaine Serene Willamette ★★★★ 02 04 05 06 Burgundian approach to single-v'yd Pinot N is usually well ahead of the pack. Bottled unfiltered.

Elk Cove V'yds Willamette ★★→★★★ V.g Ries, inc late-harvest. Top Pinot N.

Erath V'yds Yamhill County ★★★→★★★★ Oregon pioneer, founded 1968. V.gd Chard, Pinot Gr, Gewurz, Pinot Bl. Pinots and Ries age well.

Evesham Wood Willamette ★★★ Small family winery with fine Pinot N, Pinot Gr and dry Gewurz. Pinot N leaping ahead in recent vintages. Organic.

Eyrie Vineyards Willamette ★★★ Chard and Pinot Gr: rich yet crisp. All wines age.

Foris Vineyards Rouge Valley ★★ A lovely Pinot Bl and a classic red-cherry Pinot N top the list. One of the best in the south of the state.

Four Graces Willamette ★★→★★★ The great strength here is an exceptional estate Pinot N offering bright, lively fruit and gd mouthfeel.

Freja Willamette ★★★ Only estate-grown Pinot N. Wines are silky on the palate but with an underlying power, clearly in homage to Burgundy.

Henry Estate Umpqua Valley ★★ In this warmer section of Oregon, Henry Estate makes a solid Cab Sauv and a gd Merlot. Also look for a v.gd dry Gewurz.

Ken Wright Cellars Yamhill County ★★★ 02 05 06 Highly regarded Pinot N and a v.gd Chard from single v'yds.

King Estate South Willamette ★★★→★★★★ 03 04 05 06 07 One of Oregon's largest wineries. Organic. Lovely, constantly improving Pinot N, outstanding Chard.

Lachini Vineyards ★★★ Upcoming producer of outstanding Pinot N and v.gd Pinot Gr. Biodynamic. New wines from v'yds in Washington's Red Mtn AVA, a Bordeaux blend and a bold Cab Sauv. Has recently planted Ries and Albariño.

Lange Winery Yamhill County ★★→★★★ Rich and silky Pinot N, backed by a v.gd Pinot Gr and excellent Chard.

Monk's Gate Willamette ★★★ Small-production Pinot N is complex and rich while maintaining balance and harmony. Worth looking for.

Montinore Willamette ★★ Estate Pinot N is the flagship but save room for a spicy and inviting Pinot Gr. Borealis, a blend of Müller-Thurgau, Gewurz and Pinot Gr, is a delightful off-dry apéritif.

Oak Knoll Willamette ★★ Pinot is the big story at this popular winery, with intense but balanced bottlings. Also a v.gd off-dry Ries.

Panther Creek Willamette ★★ Pinot N from several v'yds is concentrated, built to age; new is a delicious unoaked Chard.

Patricia Green Cellars Yamhill County ★★★→★★★★ Exciting single-v'yd Pinot N is the heart of the story here. Wines vary in style from light, racy Pinot to bolder, concentrated, but all worth a look.

Penner-Ash Yamhill County ★★★★ REX HILL winemaker Lynn Penner-Ash and her husband are making intense, rich Pinot N from up to a half-dozen v'yds in a bolder style than many in Oregon. Also a v.gd Viognier.

Ponzi Vineyards Willamette ★★★→★★★★ 03 05 06 Long-established with consistently *outstanding Pinot N* and v.gd Pinot Gr and Chard.

Resonance Yamhill Carlton ★★ Kevin and Carla Chambers now out with their own complex and delicious Pinot N made from organic and biodynamic grapes.

Retour Wines Willamette ★★★ Terroir-driven old-vine Pinot N is stunning with touches of earthy spice and anise. Keep an eye on Retour.

Rex Hill Willamette ★★★→★★★★ Excellent Pinot N, Pinot Gr and Chard from several north Willamette v'yds. Reserve wines can hit ★★★★.

RoxyAnn Rouge River ★★ Southern Oregon producer of an esp gd Viognier and excellent Pinot Gr. Claret red blend is a pleasing quaff.

Sokol Blosser Willamette ★★★→★★★★ Superb wines throughout with an esp v.gd Pinot N, Chard and Gewurz, balanced and harmonious. Syrah is a treat.

Soter Yamhill-Carlton ★★★ Tony Soter has moved his winemaking skills from California to Oregon and he got it right with first release, *Mineral Springs Vineyard Pinot N*: a superb wine, balanced and harmonious with a long, lyrical finish. He recently followed up with a North County Pinot N, elegant and sleek.

Stoller Estate Dundee Hills ★★★ The SV Estate Pinot N is a balanced, elegant wine with supple fruit, the JV Estate Pinot N is riper with softer tannins. Also a gd Chard from estate grapes.

Torii Mor Yamhill Co ★★★ V.gd single-v'yd Pinot N bottlings and superior Pinot Gr.

Tyee Wine Cellars Willamette ★★ Artisan producer of v.gd Pinot N, Pinot Gr and tasty Gewurz.

Van Duzer Winery Willamette ★★→★★★ Bright, fruity Pinot N, delicious Pinot Gr, from hillside v'yds in a v. cool part of Willamette Valley. Steadily improving.

Willakenzie Estate Yamhill County ★★★ Specialist in small lots of Pinot N, Pinot Gr, Pinot Bl and Pinot Meunier with a minuscule amount of Gamay Noir. Wines can be outstanding and are always worth a look.

Willamette Valley V'yds Willamette ★★→★★★ Gd Ries, Chard and v.gd Pinot N. New clonal selection Chard raises the quality bar.

Washington & Idaho

Abeja Walla Walla ★★→★★★ Abeja first made a name for Cab Sauv and Chard, but the Syrah has been attracting attention recently. It shows the same balance and harmony as the Cab Sauv, with a spicy edge and lingering finish.

Alexandria Nicole Cellars Columbia Valley ★★→★★★ Artisan estate in the Horse Heaven Hills AVA makes a number of wines, inc Bordeaux varietals, but once more it is the Syrah that draws rave reviews.

Andrew Will Puget Sound ★★★★ 97 00 01 02 05 07 Owner Chris Camarda sources Bordeaux varietals, making balanced single-v'yd reds: balanced, elegant, tremendous ageing potential.

Arbor Crest Spokane, Washington ★★ The top draw here is the Chard, followed closely by a floral Sauv Bl.

Badger Mtn Columbia Valley ★★→★★★ Washington's first organic v'yd, producing gd Cab Sauv and Chard. Also a new line of "no sulfites" organic wines.

Barnard Griffin Columbia Valley ★★→★★★ Well-made Merlot, Chard (esp barrel-fermented), Sem, Sauv Bl. Top Syrah and Viognier.

Basel Cellars Walla Walla ★★★ Newcomer sweeps the board with gd Bordeaux varieties and a fine Syrah. Look esp for Merriment, a Bordeaux blend.

Bergevin Lane Walla Walla ★★ Gd beginning for another new Washington winery with Syrah out in front.

Brian Carter Cellars Woodinville, Washington ★★→★★★ Limited production of gd to v.gd blends, inc a white blend of aromatic varietals, a Sangiovese-based Super Tuscan, two Bordeaux blends and Byzance, a ★★★ Rhône blend.

Bunnell Cellars Columbia Valley ★★★ Rhône rules at this estate winery. Top marks for a series of single v'yd Syrahs, a v.gd Viognier and a new Grenache.

Buty Walla Walla ★★★ The focus is on Bordeaux blends and the results have been outstanding. A recent favorite is the Champoux V'yd Horse Heaven Hills Cab Sauv/Cab Fr blend. There is lovely fruit behind a perfumed nose, with a long, elegant finish.

Cadaretta Walla Walla ★★★ This newcomer opened with a terrific pair of wines, SDS, a blend of Sauv Bl and Sem, and a silky Syrah that will have you reaching for a second glass. Expect even better things as the estate v'yds mature.

Cayuse Walla Walla ★★→★★★ Several bottlings of gd to v.gd Syrah and an outstanding Bordeaux blend have buyers calling. Biodynamic grapes.

Charles Smith Wines Walla Walla ★ Ex-rock band manager Smith has gained a cult following for jammy, concentrated Syrah and Syrah blends from mostly Columbia Valley Ries. Also bottles under the K-Wine label. Get it? K-Syrah.

Chateau Ste Michelle Woodinville, Washington ★★→★★★★ Washington's largest winery; also owns COLUMBIA CREST, Northstar (top Merlot), Domaine Ste Michelle and SNOQUALMIE, among others. Major v'yd holdings, first-rate equipment and skilled winemakers keep wide range of varieties in front ranks. V.gd v'yd-designated Cab Sauv, Merlot and Chard. Links with Loosen (see Germany) and Antinori (see Italy).

Chinook Wines Yakima Valley, Washington ★★★ 01 02 03 06 07 Elegant Merlot and Cab Sauv; outstanding Cab Fr and a delicious Cab Fr rosé.

Columbia Crest Columbia Valley ★★→★★★ Cab Sauv, Merlot, Syrah and Sauv Bl are gd-value favourites.

Columbia Winery Woodinville, Washington ★★★ Pioneer and still a leader, with balanced, stylish, understated single-v'yd wines. *Marvellous Syrah*.

DeLille Cellars Woodinville, Washington ★★★→★★★★ 00 01 02 03 05 A Bordeaux specialist producing v.gd to excellent wines. New addition is Syrah, Doyenne.

Di Stefano Woodinville, Washington ★★→★★★ Best bet is Bordeaux red, inc a v.gd, elegant Cab Sauv and an elegant Cab Fr; also a bright and juicy Syrah.

Dunham Cellars Walla Walla ★★→★★★ Artisan producer focusing on long-lived Cab Sauv and superb Syrah and a v.gd Chard.

Forgeron Walla Walla ★★ New producer making small lots of single-v'yd wines; v.gd Syrah in a juicy style and notable Roussanne and Pinot Gr.

Glacial Lake Missoula (GLM) Wine Company Yakima Valley ★★★ Keep an eye on GLM – the name comes from a huge lake formed by glacial melt at the end of the last ice age. Deluge, a blend of Cab Sauv and Cab Fr, is superb. It has structure for ageing with complex layers of fruit and a long, wraparound finish.

Glen Fiona Walla Walla ★★→★★★ Syrah blends from Rhône specialist, esp Syrah/Cinsault/Counoise *cuvée*.

Hedges Cellars Yakima Valley, Washington ★★★→★★★★ V. fine Bordeaux reds from Red Mtn AVA. Fumé is a delicious and popular blend of Chard and Sauv Bl.

Hogue Cellars, The Yakima Valley, Washington ★→★★ Large, reliable producer known for excellent, gd-value wines, esp Ries, Chard, Merlot, Cab Sauv.

Hyatt Vineyards Yakima Valley, Washington ★★→★★★ Stylish Merlot is among the state's best. Seek Black Muscat Icewine when conditions are right.

Indian Creek Idaho ★→★★★ Top wine is Pinot N, plus a v.gd Ries and gd Cab Sauv.

Kiona Vineyards Yakima Valley, Washington ★★ Solid wines from Red Mtn AVA, esp Cab Sauv; gd value and quality.

Lake Chelan Winery Columbia Valley ★★ A promising new winery with range of wines, inc gd Cab Sauv, an attractive Syrah and a floral Ries.

L'Ecole No 41 Walla Walla ★★★→★★★★ (Merlot) 02 04 05 06 Blockbuster but balanced reds (Merlot, Cab Sauv and super Meritage blend) with forward, age-worthy fruit. Gd barrel-fermented Sem.

Leonetti Walla Walla ★★★→★★★★ One of Washington's cult wineries, Leonetti's bold Cab Sauv is a gd match for the v. fine Merlot, one of Washington's stars.

Long Shadows Columbia Valley ★★★→★★★★ Former CHATEAU STE MICHELLE CEO Allen Shoup brought together leading international winemakers to make wines from Washington grapes. Can't go wrong with any of them but look for *Poet's Leap Ries* by Armin Diel (Germany), Feather, a Cab Sauv made by Randy Dunn (California) and Sequel, a glorious Syrah made by John Duval (Australia).

McCrea Puget Sound ★★★ A Rhône pioneer making small lots of gd to v. fine Viognier, Syrah and Grenache, even a rare varietal bottling of Counoise.

Milbrandt Vineyards ★★→★★★ Long-time growers with more than 650 ha of vines

---

Look north for Cab bargains

If you are looking for gd value in top-quality Cab Sauv, Washington State is an ideal hunting ground. While many Napa Cab bottles top $100, there are dozens of Washington Cabs of at least equal quality selling for under $50, some at well under that price. Three examples: COLUMBIA WINERY's Red Willow V'yd Cab at around $30; an astonishingly gd L'ECOLE NO 41 Walla Walla Valley Cab in the $40 range, and CHATEAU STE MICHELLE's Ethos Cab, also at $40.

No more Riesling roulette

The extraordinary versatility of Ries is both a blessing and a curse. Ries is the fastest-growing white wine in the USA, yet many consumers think of it only as a sweet wine. Most labels do little to indicate whether the Ries is sweet, dry, semi-sweet or bone-dry. The International Riesling Foundation was created to clarify some of the confusion. Based in New York's Finger Lakes region, this private not-for-profit association has developed a Ries Tasting Profile that enables consumers to pin down specific wines via a simple standardized graph on the bottle's back label. An increasing number of wineries worldwide, from Alsace to New Zealand, are signing on to this campaign – which can only be good news for consumers.

---

in eastern Washington, the Milbrandt brothers are now producing their own wine. The Legacy Evergreen Chard is a winner, with crisp minerality; also look for Traditions bottlings, esp the Syrah.

Nicolas Cole Cellars Columbia Valley ★★→★★★ Limited bottlings of balanced and elegant Bordeaux-style reds and Rhônes that will age.

Nota Bene Cellars Puget Sound ★★→★★★ Amazing red wines from Bordeaux varietals sourced in Red Mtn AVA and other top Washington v'yds. Wines are built to last. Worth seeking out.

Owen Roe Washington ★★→★★★ Look for the Yakima Valley Chard and Ries; reds, esp Bordeaux varieties, from Columbia Valley are v.gd. Gd-value wines under the O'Reilly label with a v.gd Pinot Gr.

Pacific Rim Washington ★★→★★★ Randall Grahm first made Pacific Rim Ries at his California winery BONNY DOON in 1992. The wine became so popular that he built a winery in Washington in 2006, which is now in full production. There are several Ries. Both the dry and sweet versions are super. Also *gd single-v'yd Ries*. Don't overlook the Chenin Bl.

Quilceda Creek Puget Sound ★★★→★★★★★ 01 03 04 05 Expertly crafted *Columbia Valley Cab Sauv*. Wines are beautifully balanced to age.

Reininger Walla Walla ★★→★★★ Small producer of gd Merlot and v. fine Syrah. Helix label features wines from throughout the state; esp gd Syrah.

Robert Karl Columbia Valley ★★→★★★ Spokane-based winery making small lots of single-v'yd wines from the Horse Heaven Hills AVA in the Columbia Valley. Both the Merlot and Cab Sauv can hit ★★★.

Ste Chapelle Snake River Valley, Idaho ★★ Pleasant, forward Chard, Cab Sauv, Merlot and Syrah. Also v.gd Ries and Gewurz in dry Alsace style. Attractive sparkling wine. Chateau Series label features gd-value wines.

Sandhill Winery Columbia Valley ★★★ Estate-only wines from the Red Mtn AVA. Outstanding Cab Sauv and Merlot and a v.gd Pinot Gr. Cinnamon Teal Red Table Wine is a local favourite.

Saviah Cellars Walla Walla ★★→★★★ V.gd Bordeaux blends from small family winery; outstanding Syrah.

Sawtooth Cellars Idaho ★★ Gd Cab Sauv with latest Syrah and Viognier v.gd. Recently added an excellent Roussanne.

Seven Hills Walla Walla ★★→★★★ Known for balanced, elegant Cab Sauv and Merlot. Ciel du Cheval Bordeaux blend v.gd. Pinot Gr from Oregon grapes well received.

Snoqualmie Vineyards Columbia Valley ★★→★★★ Always a reliable producer of Cab Sauv and Merlot, among others. Quality has gone up with the introduction of the Naked bottlings, made from organically grown grapes. The luscious Naked Ries is an instant classic.

Three Rivers Winery Walla Walla ★★ A "destination" winery producing a wide range of wines. Look esp for the bold Syrah and v. drinkable Grenache.

Woodward Canyon Walla Walla ★★★→★★★★ (Cab) 01 02 03 04 05 06 The winery
has set the standard for *Washington Cab Sauv* and Merlot for almost 30 yrs. Often
overlooked, the Chard is also excellent.

EAST OF THE ROCKIES

Overall, this is an exciting wine time east of the Rockies. All states are
growing in both number of wineries and quality of the wines. In most
regions the quality of the wine industry has been a bit of an aberration in
an otherwise gloomy economy, in part because off-premise sales continue
to increase, but mostly due to the ever-expanding number of oeno-tourists.
In New York State approximately five million visited wineries in the past
year. Every state has seen an explosion of growth, from Virginia (up from
141 to 157 wineries) to Ohio (121 to 135). North Carolina saw ten new
wineries open. More than 33 wineries opened in New York in the past two
years, with the strongest growth in non-traditional wine regions – the
Thousand Islands, the Champlain region and even New York City all have
wineries now. In New York State, top Rieslings from the Finger Lakes are
now challenging the world's best, while Long Island's Merlot, Syrah and
Cabernets Sauvignon and Franc are gaining recognition. Virginia is making
some notable Viognier as well as impressive Cabernet Franc and Petit Verdot,
along with Syrah and other Rhône grapes. New York is the nation's third-largest
grape-growing state (after California and Washington).

Recent vintages

While it's difficult to generalize about such a vast region, 2007 was generally an
exceptional vintage for most of the eastern states. 2008 was above average in some
areas, average in others. 2009 saw smaller crops due to a cold, rainy spring, but
overall quality looks good.

Anthony Road Finger Lakes, NY ★★★ 07 08 09 Fine Ries; Pinot Gr, Cab Fr-
Lemberger, late-harvest Vignoles.

Barboursville Virginia ★★★ 07' 08 09 Oldest of the state's modern-era wineries
(founded 1976), owned by the Zonin family (see Italy). Excellent Chard, Cab Fr,
Barbera, Nebbiolo, Pinot Gr and *Malvasia*. Elegant inn and restaurant.

Bedell Long Island, NY ★★ 07 08 09 Owned by co-founder of New Line Cinema
(and producer of *Lord of the Rings* trilogy). Outstanding small-batch series of
varietally labelled wines, inc Chard, Gewurz and Cab Fr.

Breaux Virginia ★→★★ 08' 09 V'yd an hour from Washington DC. Gd Chard,
Merlot.

Chamard Connecticut ★→★★ One of Connecticut's best wineries. AVA
Southeastern New England.

Channing Daughters ★★ 08 09 LONG ISLAND's innovative South Fork estate, with
excellent eclectic white blends and uncommon varietals (Tocai Friulano).

Château LaFayette Reneau Finger Lakes, NY ★★★ 07 08 09 Stylish Chard, Ries and
top-notch Cab Sauv. Stunning lakeside setting.

Chrysalis Virginia ★★★Top Viognier, v.gd Petit Manseng, Albariño and Norton.

Clinton Vineyards Hudson River, NY ★→★★ 09 Clean, gd, dry Seyval. Exceptional
sparkling, also fine cassis, wild black raspberry and peach wines.

Debonné Vineyards Lake Erie, Ohio ★→★★ 08 09 Largest OHIO estate winery.
Chard, Ries, Pinot Gr and some hybrids: Chambourcin and Vidal.

Ferrante Winery Harpersfield, Ohio Venerable estate (since 1937) with fine Chard,
Cab Sauv, Ries and superb Icewine.

Finger Lakes Beautiful upstate New York region, with over 100 wineries source of most of state's wines. Top wineries: ANTHONY ROAD, CHATEAU LAFAYETTE RENEAU, DR. KONSTANTIN FRANK, FOX RUN, HERON HILL, KING FERRY, Lakewood, LAMOREAUX LANDING, Ravines, RED NEWT, STANDING STONE, Swedish Hill and Wiemer.

Firelands Lake Erie, Ohio ★→★★Cab Sauv, Gewurz, Pinot Gr. Notable Icewine.

Fox Run Finger Lakes, NY ★★ 08 09 Some of region's best Chard, Gewurz, Ries and Pinot N. Plus a gd café for lunch or light refreshment.

Frank, Dr Konstantin (Vinifera Wine Cellars) Finger Lakes, NY ★★★ 07 08 09 Continues to set the pace for serious winemaking. The late Dr F was a pioneer in growing European vines in the FINGER LAKES. *Excellent Ries*, Gewurz; gd Chard, Cab Sauv and Pinot N. Also v.gd Château Frank sparkling.

Glen Manor V'yds ★→★★ VIRGINIA winery with gd Sauv Bl and Bordeaux varietals.

Hamptons, The (aka **South Fork**) LONG ISLAND AVA. The top winery is moneyed WÖLFFER ESTATE. Showcase Duck Walk owns 52 ha of vines, CHANNING DAUGHTERS produces masterful blends.

Hermann J Wiemer Finger Lakes, NY ★→★★ 07 08 09 Established by creative German-born former owner/winemaker. Outstanding Ries; v.gd Chard. Winemaker Fred Merwarth recently took over operations from eponymous founder.

Heron Hill Finger Lakes, NY ★★ Great Ries and dessert wines.

Horton Virginia ★★ 07 08 09 Established early 1990s. Gd Viognier, Mourvèdre, Cab Fr, Norton.

Hudson River Region America's oldest wine-growing district (35 producers) and New York's first AVA. Straddles the river, two hours' drive north of Manhattan.

Jefferson Virginia ★★ 07 08 Near Thomas Jefferson's Monticello estate. Fine Pinot Gr, Viognier, Chard, Petit Verdot, Merlot, Bordeaux blend.

Keswick Virginia ★★ 07 08 Elegant Chard, v.gd Viognier, Touriga/Cab-based blend.

King Family Vineyards ★★ Excellent VIRGINIA estate (Viognier, Cab Fr, Bordeaux blends).

King Ferry Finger Lakes, NY ★★ 08 09 Label is Treleaven. Gd Ries, stylish Chards.

Kluge Virginia ★★ 07 08 Showplace moneyed estate, ambitious wines include Viognier, gd brut sparkling and Bordeaux blend.

Lake Erie Largest grape-growing district in the eastern US; 10,117 ha along shore of Lake Erie, includes portions of New York, PENNSYLVANIA and OHIO. Also name of a tri-state AVA: New York has 16 wineries, PENNSYLVANIA's ten and OHIO's 45.

Lamoureaux Landing Finger Lakes, NY ★★ 08 09 Among *NY's best Chard*, Ries and Cab Fr from striking Greek Revival winery.

Lenz Long Island, NY ★★ 07 08 09 Classy winery of NORTH FORK AVA. Fine *austere Chard in the Chablis mode* as well as rich, barrel-fermented one; also notable Gewurz, Merlot and sparkling wine.

Linden Virginia ★★★ 08 09 Impressive VIRGINIA producer in mts 100-km west of Washington DC. Notable Sauv Bl, Cab Fr, Petit Verdot, Bordeaux-style "claret".

Long Island, New York In 1973 there was one v'yd on Long Island; today there are 62 wineries, most of them on the NORTH FORK (three AVAs: LONG ISLAND, NORTH FORK and THE HAMPTONS), all *vinifera*. Merlot dominates Cab Fr; top notch in gd vintages. The younger generation of wineries includes Comtesse Thérèse, Martha Clara, Raphael, Shinn Estate, Sherwood House. Up-and-coming: Bouké, Clovis Point, Roanoke, Sparkling Pointe.

Maryland Has more than 42 wineries with more on the way. Black Ankle, Sugarloaf and Elk Run are surging ahead with two terrific recent vintages. Woodhall also excelled with two fine vintages of Barbera – which may yet prove to be the region's signature grape.

Michael Shaps/Virginia Wineworks ★★★ 08 09 Burgundy-trained vintner turns out fine Viognier, Chard, Petit Verdot under Michael Shaps label.

Michigan Impressive Ries and Gewurz, gd Pinot N, and Cab Fr are emerging; 70 wineries using Michigan grapes and four AVAs (750 ha grapes, two-thirds of them *vinifera*). Best include Bel Lago, Black Star, Bowers Harbor, Brys, Château

Grand Traverse, Fenn Valley, Peninsula Cellars (esp dry Gewurz), Tabor Hill and Mawby (outstanding sparkling). Up-and-coming: Domaine Berrien, Chateau Fontaine, Cherry Creek, 45 North, Left Foot Charley, Longview, 2 Lads.

Millbrook Hudson River, NY ★★ 08 09 Chards modelled on Burgundy; Cab Fr can be delicious.

North Carolina Look for Chard, Viognier, Cab Fr. 90 wineries, inc Childress, Duplin (for Muscadine), Hanover Park, Iron Gate, Laurel Gray, McRitchie, Old North State, RagApple, RayLen, Raffaldini, Rockhouse, Shelton. Biltmore is most visited winery in the US.

North Fork Long Island AVA. New York AVA (two hours' drive from Manhattan) with 49 wineries. Top producers include: Bedell, Jamesport, Lieb, LENZ, PALMER, PAUMANOK, PELLEGRINI, PINDAR, Raphael.

Ohio 135 wineries, five AVAs, inc LAKE ERIE. Some exceptional Pinot Gr, Ries, Pinot N, Icewine. Grand River Valley emerging as a prime viticultural district with top producers Harpersfield, DEBONNÉ, FERRANTE and St Joseph.

Palmer Long Island, NY ★★08 09 Superior NORTH FORK producer; byword in Darwinian metropolitan market. Tasty Chard, Sauv Bl, Chinon-like Cab Fr.

Paumanok Long Island, NY ★★★08 09 NORTH FORK winery; impressive Ries, Chard, Merlot, Cab Sauv; v.gd Chenin Bl; late-harvest botrytized Sauv Bl.

Pellegrini Long Island, NY ★★★ 08 09 An enchantingly designed winery on NORTH FORK. Opulent Merlot, stylish Chard, Bordeaux-like *Cab Sauv*.

Pennsylvania 120 wineries, with quality rapidly rising. Leading estates: Chaddsford (esp Chambourcin, a Barbera/Sangiovese blend and a Cab/Sangiovese blend), Allegro (worthy Chard, Cab Sauv, Merlot), Pinnacle Ridge (sparkling and Chambourcin), Manatawny Creek (noteworthy Cabs Fr and Sauv, and Bordeaux-style blend), Waltz (Cabs and Merlot) and LAKE ERIE's Mazza for Vidal Icewine.

Pindar Vineyards Long Island, NY ★★ 08 09 116-ha operation at NORTH FORK. Range of blends and popular varietals, inc Chard, Merlot, sparkling, v.gd Bordeaux-style red blend Mythology Meritage. Visits.

Pollack Virginia One of the state's most promising young wineries: Chard, Cab Fr, Bordeaux blend, Viognier.

Red Newt Finger Lakes, NY ★★ 08 09 Turns out top Chard, Ries and some of the best reds in NY, esp Cab Fr, Merlot and Bordeaux-inspired red blend.

Sakonnet Little Compton, Rhode Island ★ 08 09 Largest New England winery. Gd Chard and Vidal Blanc.

Standing Stone Finger Lakes, NY ★★ 07 08 09 One of the region's finest wineries with v.gd Ries, Gewurz and Bordeaux-type blend.

Tomasello New Jersey ★→★★ Gd Chambourcin, Cab Sauv and Petit Verdot.

Unionville Vineyards New Jersey ★→★★ Nice Chard and gd Bordeaux-style red.

Valhalla Virginia ★★ 08 09 V'yd at 600 m atop a granite mountain yields spicy Sangiovese, and gd red blend of all five Bordeaux grapes.

Veritas Virginia ★★ 08 09 Excellent Petit Manseng, Cab Fr.

Villa Appalaccia Virginia ★★ 08 09 Italian-inspired winery in the Blue Ridge Mountains with quality Primitivo, Sangiovese, Malvasia, Pinot Gr.

Virginia With 157 bonded wineries and six AVAs, Virginia is turning out some of the most sophisticated wines in the east. The modern winemaking era now encompasses virtually every part of the state, some less than an hour's drive from Washington DC.

Wagner Vineyards Finger Lakes, NY ★→★★ 08 09 Chard, dry and sweet Ries, Bordeaux blend and Icewine. Also has microbrewery and restaurant.

Westport Rivers Southeast New England ★★ 09 Massachusetts house established in 1989. Gd Chard and elegant sparkling.

Whitehall Virginia ★★★ 08 09 A handsome estate near historic Charlottesville.

Outstanding Viognier, noteworthy Pinot Gr, lush Petit Manseng, top Chard, Cab Fr, Touriga Nacional and Cab Sauv blend.

Wölffer Estate Long Island, NY ★★★ 08 09 Fine Chard, vibrant rosé and gd Merlot from talented German-born winemaker.

Southeast & central states

Missouri Continues to expand, with 92 producers in three AVAs: **Augusta**, **Hermann**, and **Ozark Highlands**. Best wines are Seyval Blanc, Vidal, Vignoles (sweet and dry versions) and Chambourcin. The Unversity of Missouri has a new experimental winery to test techniques and grape varieties. **Stone Hill** in Hermann produces v.gd Chardonel (a frost-hardy hybrid of Seyval Blanc and Chard), Norton and gd Seyval Blanc and Vidal Blanc. **Hermannhof** is also drawing notice for Vignoles, Chardonel and Norton. Also notable: **St James** for Vignoles, Seyval, Norton; **Mount Pleasant** in Augusta for rich port-style and Norton; **Adam Puchta** for gd port-style wines and Norton, Vignoles, Vidal Blanc; **Augusta Winery** for Chambourcin, Chardonel, Icewine; **Les Bourgeois**: gd Syrah, Norton, Chardonel, Montelle, v.gd Cynthiana and Chambourcin.

Georgia There are now over a dozen wineries here. Look for: **Three Sisters** (Dahlonega), **Habersham V'yds** and **Chateau Elan** (Braselton), which features Southern splendour with v'yds, wine and a resort.

Wisconsin Best is Wollersheim, specializing in variations of Maréchel Foch. Prairie Fumé (Seyval Bl) is a commercial success.

THE SOUTHWEST

Texas maintains its ranking as fifth in the United States in grape and wine production. Arizona, with one winery in 1980, now has over 40. Southwest wineries are expanding offerings with varied styles and vines. New Mexico is experimenting with more than 35 varieties such as Refosco, Tempranillo and Petit Verdot. Drought and hail have limited grape quantity but quality remains high. Colorado makes rich, full-bodied wines from *vinifera*; Oklahoma includes hybrids, native American grapes and local fruits, leaning to the sweet side. Arizona may be the most exciting state of the region, with Hollywood filmmaker Sam Pillsbury and Oregon winemaker Dick Erath both in. Expanding varieties while employing vineyard practices such as organic, biodynamic and solar techniques, Arizona is poised for dramatic growth.

Texas

Alamosa Texas Hill Country Gd white blends, esp Scissortail with Marsanne.

Becker Vineyards Stonewall ★★ V.gd Cab Sauv, Viognier, Cab Fr, Malbec.

Brennan Vineyards Comanche Excellent Viognier, Cab Sauv, v.gd Syrah.

La Bodega A winery in Dallas-Fort Worth airport. V.gd Merlot, Cab Sauv.

Driftwood Vineyards Texas Hill Country ★ V.gd Muscat Canelli, Viognier, Merlot Rosé.

Fairhaven Vineyards Hawkins Focus on French/American and American hybrids. To watch.

Fall Creek Texas Hill Country V.gd Meritus (red blend), gd Viognier, Cab Sauv.

Flat Creek Texas Hill Country Gd Pinot N, Pinot Bl and Sangiovese.

Haak Winery Galveston County ★ V.gd Malbec, Blanc du Bois; excellent Madeira.

Kiepersol Estates Vineyards Tyler Excellent Sangiovese, Syrah, Cab Sauv.

Light Catcher Lake Worth V.gd Cab Sauv, Orange Muscat, Merlot Rosé.

Llano Estacado Near Lubbock ★★ The pioneer with v.gd Chard, Cab Sauv, Merlot.

McPherson Cellars ★ Lubbock Created to honour Dr. Clinton McPherson, a Texas wine pioneer, with excellent Cab Sauv, Sangiovese, Viognier and Syrah.

Messina Hof Wine Cellars Bryan ★★ Excellent Ries, Cab Sauv, Meritage (red), Shiraz and surprising sparkling wines flavoured with raspberry and almond. Winemaker Paul Bonarrigo continues to charm with his red beret.

Val Verde Del Rio A 4th-generation tradition. V.gd Chard, Pinot Grigio, Merlot.

Wichita Falls Vineyards and Winery Iowa Park Gd Moscato, Sangiovese and Wichita Red (blend).

Zin Valle Anthony V.gd Rising Star Brut (sparkling); gd Pinot N, Gewurz.

Colorado, etc.

Colorado Balistreri V'ds: V.gd Merlot, Zin. **Black Bridge:** V.gd Pinot N, Ries. **Carlson Cellars:** ★★ Excellent Ries; v.gd Lemberger, fruit wines, esp cherry served with melted chocolate. **Creekside Cellars:** Gd Chard, Cab Fr. **Garfield Estates:** V.gd Sauv Bl, Cab Fr. **Grande River:** V.gd Syrah, Meritage (white). **Graystone:** Only port-style wines, all v.gd, esp "ruby". **Plum Creek:** ★★V.gd Cab Sauv, Ries, Sauv Bl. **Guy Drew:** Excellent Syrah, v.gd Petit Verdot, Cab Fr. **Snowy Peaks Winery:** V.gd Gewurz, Cab Sauv. **Two Rivers Winery:** V.gd Cab Sauv, Ries, "ruby" port-style. **Winery at Holy Cross:** ★ Excellent Cab Sauv, Syrah. V.gd Ries, Merlot, Cab Fr. **Whitewater Hill:** Gd Cab Fr, Gewurz.

New Mexico Black Mesa: ★★ V.gd Cab Sauv, Black Beauty (dessert wine with chocolate), Chard, Dolcetto. **Casa Rondeña:** ★ V.gd Viognier, Meritage (red). **Gruet:** ★★ Excellent sparkling; v.gd Chard. **La Chiripada:** ★→★★ V.gd Ries, Chard, port-style wine. **Ponderosa Valley:** ★ V.gd late-harvest Ries and blends. **Matheson Wine Co:** V.gd Chard. **Southwest Wines:** under winemaker Florent Lescombes gd variety of wines, esp Muscat Canelli and Shiraz. **Luna Rossa:** ★→★★ V.gd Italian-style wines, esp Nebbiolo, Sangiovese.

Arizona Alcantara V'yds: Gd Sauv Bl, Pinot Gr, Nebbiolo. **Callaghan V'yds:** ★★ Excellent Syrah, Cab Sauv, blends. **Dos Cabezas:** ★ V.gd Cab Sauv, Sangiovese. **Colibri:** Gd Viognier, Roussanne, Syrah. **Granite Creek:** Organic. V.gd late-harvest Zin. **Echo Canyon:** Gd Syrah, Triad. **Keeling Schaefer V'yds:** Gd Grenache, Syrah. **Lightning Ridge Cellars:** New winery with gd Muscat. **Pillsbury Wine Company:** V.gd Pinot Gr, red blends, esp Roan Red. Filmmaker Sam Pillsbury may add a Hollywood touch. **Sonoita:** Gd Sirah, Colombard, Cab Sauv.

Oklahoma Deer Creek Edmond: Gd Muscat Canelli. **Greenfield V'yd** Chandler: Gd Merlot, Sauv Bl. **Stone Bluff Cellars** Haskell: Gd Vignoles, Cynthiana, Chardonel. **Oak Hills Winery** Chelsea: V.gd Catawba, Chambourcin, Seyval Bl, Traminette. **Tres Suenos** Luther: Gd Merlot, Cynthiana. **Stable Ridge** Stroud: V.gd Chenin Blanc, Jeremiah Red (blend).

Nevada Churchill V'yds: Located in Lahontan Valley. Gd Ries, Chard. **Pahrump Valley:** Near Las Vegas: Gd Symphony, Zin.

Canada

The last 20 years have seen Canada emerge as an international player, with *vinifera* vines being planted in preference to the old hybrids, though both Ontario and British Columbia are definitely cool-climate regions. BC's Okanagan Valley grows a broad spectrum of varieties in a continental climate: look for Prospect Winery, Road 13, Sandhill and Thornhaven. Ontario has four VQA wine-growing regions, including the Niagara Peninsula, Canada's largest viticultural area. Promising young wineries include Foreign Affair, Norman Hardie, Ravine, Wayne Gretzky Estate. And Icewine? Still the star, and you can't get much cooler than that.

British Columbia

Cedar Creek ★→★★★ Outstanding Chard, Pinot N, Meritage and Syrah.

Inniskillin Okanagan ★★★ 06 07 08 Excellent Viognier, Icewine and Ries.

Jackson-Triggs Okanagan Estate ★★★ 06 07 08 V.gd Cab Sauv, Meritage, Shiraz.

Lake Breeze Gd Chard, Gewurz.

Mission Hill ★→★★★★ 06 07 08 Acclaimed Chard, Syrah and flagship Oculus. *Al fresco* dining, high culinary standards.

Nk'Mip ★★ Look for Chard, Merlot.

Osoyoos Larose fine Bordeaux blend red.

Quails' Gate ★★ Chard, Optima, Pinot N and Old Vines Foch.

Sumac Ridge ★★ 02 04 05 06 07 Gewurz, sparkling Stellar's Jay among region's best.

Tantalus ★★★ Excellent Ries.

Wild Goose ★★ Noteworthy Ries, Gewurz.

Ontario

13th Street Winery ★★★ Small producer of 100% hand-picked, old-vine Gamay, Chard. Excellent range of traditional-method sparkling wines.

Cave Spring Cellars ★★→★★★ Benchmark Ries, sophisticated Chard from old vines, exceptional late-harvest and Icewines.

Creekside Estate ★→★★★ Broad range of Bordeaux-style reds, Chard and Syrah.

Flat Rock Cellars ★★→★★★ Consistently excellent Ries, Pinot N.

Henry of Pelham ★★★ Respected family-owned winery with elegant Chard and Ries; Bordeaux -style reds, distinctive Baco Noir, Icewine.

Hillebrand Estates ★→★★★ Large producer of gd sparkling, excellent Ries under Thirty Bench label. Part of Andrew Peller Ltd, Canada's second-largest winery.

Inniskillin ★★★ Spearheaded birth of modern Ontario wine industry. Skilful Burgundy-style Chards, Pinot N, Bordeaux-style red; Icewine specialist.

Jackson-Triggs ★★★ State-of-art winery, Ries, Chard and Bordeaux-style reds.

Le Clos Jordanne ★★★★ Best-of-class Pinot N and Chard from organic v'yds.

Malivoire ★★→★★★ Small, innovative, gravity-flow winery with v.gd Pinot N, Chard and Gamay. Some organic.

Stratus ★★★ High-tech winery, flagship white and red multi-varietal blends; excellent Icewine.

Tawse ★★★ Gravity-flow winery with much-admired Chard, Pinot N and Cab Fr.

Vincor International ★→★★ Owned by CONSTELLATION (see California). Wineries include JACKSON-TRIGGS, INNISKILLIN, and LE CLOS JORDANNE, and NK'MIP and OSOYOOS LAROSE in British Columbia.

Vineland Estates ★★★ Beautiful country estate with 1st-class restaurant. Good Ries, Icewine and Bordeaux-style reds.

Vintners Quality Alliance (VQA) Provincially controlled appellation body guaranteeing 100% regional grapes; strict rules concerning grape production/winemaking.

South America

More heavily shaded areas are the wine-growing regions

Recent vintages

Vintages do differ but not as much as in Europe. Whites are almost without exception at their best within two years of vintage, reds within three years. The most ambitious reds (Chilean Cabernet-based wines and Syrah, Argentine Cabernets and Malbecs) will last for a decade or more but whether they improve beyond their fifth year is debatable (although the top 2007 Chilean reds have great potential). Also, recent improvements mean that wines from a lesser vintage today outperform those from earlier, more favourable years.

CHILE

The word on many people's lips in Chile at the moment is "sustainability". The aim is to show that one of the world's most exciting sources of wine also cares about the environment. The South Africans tried this but are now quiet on the subject. Maybe the Chileans should take note, as there's plenty more to talk about in this dynamic country, eg. new vineyard developments along the coast: coastal Casablanca, for Syrah and Sauvignon Blanc, and Paredones, where the Colchagua Valley meets the ocean. Further south, there are now vines in Chilean Patagonia; while many feel that this cool, wet region is a step too far, others point out that, if global warming takes hold, that could change.

In established regions, large estates that were once seen as single homogenous entities are now viewed as an agglomeration of smaller sites, and the result is healthier, riper grapes. Winemakers may try to extract too much flavour, but in general, higher-end Chilean wines now offer growing complexity to complement the intensity that was already there. Cabernet Sauvignon remains the most widely planted grape, but Syrah and Pinot Noir are *the* hot red varieties, with Carmenère in close pursuit. There's a buzz around Carignan and Grenache, with new plantings and the resurrection of some ancient, abandoned vineyards. Riesling and Gewurztraminer from Bío-Bío can be excellent, but most successful are minerally Sauvignon Blanc and Chardonnay from Casablanca and San Antonio.

Aconcagua Northernmost quality region, inc CASABLANCA, Panquehue, SAN ANTONIO.

Almaviva ★★★ Expensive but classy, claret-style MAIPO red – a joint venture between CONCHA Y TORO and Baron Philippe de Rothschild.

Altaïr ★★→★★★ Ambitious joint venture between Château Dassault (St-Emilion) and SAN PEDRO DE YACOHUYA. Pascal Chatonnet of B'x is consultant; *grand vin* (mostly Cab Sauv, Carmenère) complex, earthy. Second wine: Sideral, earlier drinking.

Anakena Cachapoal ★→★★ Solid range. Flagship wines under ONA label include punchy Syrah, single-v'yd bottlings and reserve Chard also gd. Look for Viognier and ONA Pinot N.

Antiyal ★★→★★★ Alvaro Espinoza's own estate, making fine, complex red from biodynamically grown Cab Sauv, Syrah, Carmenère. Second wine: Kuyen.

Apaltagua ★★→★★★ Carmenère specialist drawing on old-vine fruit from Apalta (Colchagua). Grial is rich, herbal flagship wine.

Aquitania, Viña ★★→★★★ Chilean/French joint venture involving Paul Pontallier and Bruno Prats from Bordeaux (Paul Bruno was old label), making v.gd Lazuli Cab Sauv (MAIPO) and Sol de Sol Chard from Malleco.

Arboleda, Viña ★★→★★★ Part of the ERRÁZURIZ/CALITERRA stable, with whites from Leyda and CASABLANCA and reds from ACONCAGUA, inc polished Cab Sauv/ Merlot/Carmenère blend Seña and excellent varietal Carmenère.

Bío-Bío Promising southern region. Potential for gd whites and Pinot N.

Botalcura ★★→★★★ Curicó venture with French winemaker Philippe Debrus. Grand Reserve Cab Fr and red blend Cayao are the stars; promising Nebbiolo, too.

Caliterra ★→★★ Sister winery of ERRÁZURIZ. Chard and Sauv Bl improving (more CASABLANCA grapes), reds becoming less one-dimensional, esp Tributo range and new flagship red Cenit.

Carmen, Viña ★★→★★★ MAIPO winery, organic pioneer; same ownership as SANTA RITA. Ripe, fresh Casablanca Chard Special Reserve; top late-harvest MAIPO Sem. Reds even better: RAPEL Merlot, MAIPO Petite Sirah, Gold Reserve Cab Sauv.

Carta Vieja ★→★★ Long-established MAULE winery, better for reds but Chard Gran Reserva is gd.

Casablanca Cool-climate region between Santiago and coast. Little water: drip irrigation essential. Top-class Chard, Sauv Bl; promising Merlot, Pinot N.

Casablanca, Viña ★→★★ RAPEL and MAIPO fruit used for some reds; but better wines – Merlot, Sauv Bl, Chard, Gewurz – from CASABLANCA. Also look for super-*cuvée* Neblus and new Nimbus Estate varietals.

Casa Lapostolle ★★→★★★★ Impressive French-owned, Michel Rolland-inspired winery. Gd across the board, with new Sem highlight of the whites and Borobo red blend, Cuvée Alexandre Merlot and Syrah and Carmènere-based Clos Apalta pick of the reds. Classic range now renamed Casa, and look for lower-alcohol, more elegant whites from 2008.

Casa Marín ★★★ Dynamic white specialist, v.gd Gewurz and superb Sauv Bl. Syrah and Pinot N promising.

Casa Rivas Maipo ★★ Part of group that includes TARAPACÁ, VIÑA MAR, Missiones de Rengo. Best: Sappy Sauv Bl; gentle, citrussy Chard Reserve; blackcurrant-pastille-y Cab Sauv; generously fruity Maria Pinto Syrah/Cab Sauv Reserve.

Casas del Bosque ★→★★ CASABLANCA winery; using Cachapoal Cab Sauv for elegant range, inc juicy, underrated Sauv Bl, svelte Pinot N and peppery Syrah Reserve.

Casa Silva ★★ Colchagua estate, now with v'yds in the coastal zone of Paredones. Solid range topped by silky, complex Altura red and Quinta Generación Red and White. Also commendable Doña Dominga range; Carmenère is v.gd.

Casas del Toqui ★→★★★ RAPEL venture by Médoc Château Larose-Trintaudon under the Las Casas del Toqui and Viña Alamosa labels. Silky top-end Leyenda red blend and Prestige Cab Sauv.

Chocalan, Viña ★★ MAIPO winery for gentle, friendly reds, inc fragrant Gran Reserva Malbec. Also new range of Malvilla whites from SAN ANTONIO.

Concha y Toro ★→★★★ Mammoth, quality-minded operation. Best: subtle Amelia Chard (CASABLANCA); *grippy Don Melchor Cab Sauv*; Terrunyo; Winemaker Lot single-v'yd range; and complex Carmin de Peumo (Carmenère). Marqués de Casa Concha, Trio, Explorer, Casillero del Diablo (now shifting to cooler-climate grapes) offer v.gd value. Maycas del Limarí is new winery in the north (gd Chard); owns Fairtrade producer Viña Los Robles and recently acquired Palo Alto. See also Baron Philippe de Rothschild, CONO SUR, TRIVENTO (Argentina).

Cono Sur Chimbarongo, Colchagua ★★→★★★ V.gd Pinot N, headed by Ocio. Other top releases appear as 20 Barrels selection; new innovations under Visión label (BÍO-BÍO Ries is superb). Also *dense, fruity Cab Sauv*, delicious Viognier, rose-petal Gewurz, impressive new Syrah. Style is aimed at drinkability, not muscle. Second label: Isla Negra; owned by CONCHA Y TORO.

Córpora ★→★★★ Major company with v'yds in various regions, inc over 700 ha in BÍO-BÍO, and brands Gracia de Chile, Porta, Agustinos (good, peppery Grand Reserve Malbec) and Veranda, formerly a joint venture with Boisset of Burgundy, and now making v'gd Pinot N – Millerandage is top *cuvée*.

Cousiño Macul ★★→★★★ MAIPO producer now relocated to Buin. Now more modern in style, but better? Reliable Antiguas Reserve Cab Sauv; zesty Sauvignon Gris; new top-of-the-range label Lota. Cab Sauv rosé v. refreshing.

Edwards, Luís Felipe ★★ Colchagua winery, now with v'yds in Leyda. Citrus-like Chard, silky Reserve Cab Sauv. Shiraz and plump Doña Bernarda are specialties.

Emiliana ★→★★★ Organic/biodynamic specialist involving Alvaro Espinoza (see ANTIYAL, GEO WINES). Complex, Syrah-heavy "G" and Coyam show almost Mediterranean-style wildness; cheaper Adobe and Novas ranges v.gd for affordable complexity.

Errázuriz ★→★★★ Main winery in ACONCAGUA, v'yds mostly in warm Panquehue district, but also new cooler coastal site, plus another property in CASABLANCA. Complex *Wild Ferment Chard*, brooding La Cumbre Syrah; complex Don Maximiano Cab Sauv; new KAI Carmenère. See also ARBOLEDA, CALITERRA, VIÑEDO CHADWICK.

Falernia, Viña ★★ Winery in far north Elqui Valley, v'yds cooled by sea breezes range from 350–2,000 m in altitude, suitable for several varieties; Rhône-like Syrah, fragrant Carmenère and tangy Sauv Bl most successful so far. Labels include Alta Tierra and Mayu.

Fournier, Bodegas O ★★ Promising new venture for one of Argentina's top producers, already v'gd Leyda Sauv Bl and Centauri Red blend (MAULE).

Garcés Silva, Viña Leyda ★★→★★★ Exciting SAN ANTONIO bodega making excellent, full-bodied Sauv Bl and commendable Pinot N and Chard under Amayna label.

Geo Wines Umbrella under which Alvaro Espinoza makes wines for several new wineries. Look for earthy Chono San Lorenzo MAIPO red blend and tangy Quintay BÍO-BÍO Ries.

Hacienda Araucano ★★→★★★ François Lurton's Chilean enterprise. Complex Gran Araucano Sauv Bl (CASABLANCA), refined Carmenère/Cab Sauv blend Clos de Lolol, heady Alka Carmenère. New Humo Blanco Pinot N could prove better.

Haras de Pirque ★★→★★★ Pirque (MAIPO) estate. Smoky Sauv Bl, stylish Chard, dense Cab Sauv/Merlot. Top wine Albis (Cab Sauv/Carmenère) is solid, smoky red made in joint venture with Antinori (see Italy).

Kingston ★★ Exciting CASABLANCA newcomer specializing in Syrah, Pinot N and Sauv Bl.

Koyle ★→★★ The UNDURRAGA family's new winery, making solid Syrah and Cab Sauv.

Leyda, Viña ★★→★★★ SAN ANTONIO pioneers producing elegant Chard (Lot 5 Wild Yeasts is the pick), lush Pinot N (esp Lot 21 *cuvée* and lively rosé), tangy Garuma Sauv Bl. Now under same ownership as TABALÍ.

Limarí Northerly, high-altitude region, so quite chilly (for Chile); already impressing with Syrah and Chard.

Loma Larga ★★→★★★ New CASABLANCA venture impressing with Sauv Bl, Pinot N, Cab Fr and Syrah. V. classy wines.

Maipo Famous wine region close to Santiago. Chile's best Cab Sauvs often come from higher, eastern subregions such as Pirque and Puente Alto.

Mar, Viña CASABLANCA ★→★★ Bordeaux-style reds are a little scrawny, but Pinot N, Sauv Bl and Chard all show Casablanca at its best. See CASA RIVAS.

de Martino Maipo ★★→★★★ Ambitious Carmenère pioneer; one of west MAIPO's best wineries, esp for Cab Sauv Gran Familia, single v'yd (inc two Bush Vine *cuvées*) and Legado range.

Matetic SAN ANTONIO ★★★ Decent Pinot N and Chard from exciting winery. Stars are fragrant, *zesty Sauv Bl* and spicy, berry EQ Syrah. Second label: Corralillo.

Maule Southernmost region in Valle Central. Claro, Loncomilla, Tutuven valleys.

Montes ★★→★★★★ Highlights of a first-class range are Alpha Cab Sauv, Bordeaux-blend Montes Alpha M, *Folly Syrah from Apalta* and Purple Angel: Carmenère at its most intense. Also promising new Leyda Sauv Bl and Pinot N. Experiments with v. high-density plantings – 15,000 vines/ha! – in Marchihue.

MontGras ★★→★★★ State-of-the-art Colchagua winery with fine limited-edition wines, inc Syrah and Zin. High-class flagships Ninquén Cab Sauv and Antu Ninquén Syrah. Gd-value organic Soleus, gentle but fine Intriga (MAIPO) Cab Sauv and excellent Amaral (Leyda) whites.

Morandé ★★ Gd-value range, inc César, Cinsault, Bouschet, Carignan. Edición Limitada range, inc a spicy Syrah/Cab Sauv, inky Malbec; top wine is Cab Sauv-based House of Morandé.

Neyen ★★★ New project in Apalta for Patrick Valette of St-Emilion, making intense old-vine Carmenère/Cab Sauv blend.

Odfjell ★→★★★ MAIPO-based red specialist. Top wines: Odfjell (04 Carmenère, 05 Carignan) and Aliara (a blend); other ranges Orzada and entry-level Armador.

Pérez Cruz, Viña ★★★ MAIPO winery with Alvaro Espinoza (ANTIYAL) in charge of winemaking. Fresh, spicy Syrah, aromatic Cot, stylish Quelen, Liguai red blends.

Polkura ★★ Syrah specialist making rich but restrained wine in Colchagua's Marchihue district.

Quebrada de Macul, Viña ★★→★★★ Ambitious winery making gd Chard and v.gd Domus Aurea Cab Sauv; sister Cabs Stella Aurea and Peñalolen also tasty.

Rapel Central quality region divided into Colchagua and Cachapoal valleys. Great "Merlot" (much is still actually Carmenère). Watch for subregion Marchihue.

La Rosa, Viña ★★ Reliable RAPEL Chard, Merlot and Cab Sauv under La Palma, La Capitana and Cornellana labels. Don Reca reds are the stars, plus Ossa Sixth Generation red blend.

San Antonio Coastal region west of Santiago benefiting from sea breezes; v. promising for whites, Syrah and Pinot N. Leyda is a subzone.

San Pedro ★→★★★ Massive Curicó-based producer. 35 South (35 Sur) for affordable varietals; Castillo de Molina a step up. Best are 1865 reds and elegant Cabo de Hornos. Under same ownership as ALTAÏR, VIÑA MAR, Missiones de Rengo, Santa Helena, TARAPACÁ.

Santa Alicia ★→★★★ MAIPO red specialist. Best wines: firm but juicy Millantu Cab Sauv-based flagship wine, and lithe but structured Anke Blend 1 (Cab Fr/ Petit Verdot).

Santa Carolina, Viña ★★→★★★ Historic bodega. Quality ladder goes varietal, Reserva, Barrica Selection, Reserva de Familia and new VSC Cab Sauv/ Syrah/Petit Verdot blends. Syrah and Carmenère gd at all levels.

Santa Ema ★→★★ Gd-value range from a winery based in MAIPO but working with grapes from several regions. Top wines are two Peumo (Cachapoal) reds, Carmenère-based Rivalta and Cab-based Catalina.

Santa Mónica ★→★★ Rancagua (RAPEL) winery; the best label is Tierra del Sol. Ries, Sem and Merlot under Santa Mónica label also gd.

Santa Rita ★★→★★★★ Quality-conscious MAIPO bodega, now working with Aussie Brian Croser. Best: *Casa Real Cab Sauv*; but Pehuén (Carmenère), Triple C (Cab Sauv/Cab Fr/Carmenère) and Floresta range nearly as gd.

Seña See VIÑA ARBOLEDA.

Tabalí Limarí ★★ Winery partly owned by SAN PEDRO, making refined Chard and earthy, peppery Syrah. Look out for fine newcomers Viognier and Pinot N.

Tamaya, Viña Casa ★★ New LIMARÍ winery already on the ball with Graves-like Winemaker's Selection Sauv Bl, and gd Reserve Carmenère and Syrah.

Tarapacá, Viña ★★ MAIPO winery improved after investment, but inconsistent. Now part of the VSPT group with SAN PEDRO.

TerraMater ★→★★ Wines from all over Valle Central, inc v.gd Altum Cab Sauv.

Terra Noble ★→★★ Talca winery specializing in grassy Sauv Bl and light, peppery Merlot. Range now includes v.gd, spicy Carmenère Gran Reserve.

Torres, Miguel ★★→★★★★ Fresh whites and gd reds, esp sturdy *Manso de Velasco* single-v'yd Cab Sauv and Cariñena-based Cordillera. Conde de Superunda is rare top *cuvée*, also new organic range Tormenta. See also Spain.

Undurraga ★→★★★ Historic MAIPO estate, now impressing under new ownership. Best wines are LIMARÍ Syrah and the Sauv Bls from Leyda and CASABLANCA under the TH (Terroir Hunter) label; also lively Brut Royal Chard/Pinot N sparkler and peachy Late Harvest Sem.

Valdivieso ★→★★★ Major producer impressing in recent yrs with Reserve and single-v'yd range from top terroirs around Chile (Leyda Chard esp gd), NV red blend Caballo Loco and wonderfully spicy new Carignan-based Éclat.

Vascos, Los ★→★★★ Lafite-Rothschild venture moving from Bordeaux wannabe to more successful yet still elegant style. Top: Le Dix and Grande Réserve.

Ventisquero, Viña ★→★★★ Ambitious winery, whose labels include Chilano and Yali; top wines are two Apalta reds: rich but fragrant Pangea Syrah and Carmenère/Syrah blend Vertice. Promising new Herú CASABLANCA Pinot N.

Veramonte ★★ Whites from CASABLANCA fruit, red from Valle Central grapes – all gd. Top wine: Primus red blend.

Villard ★★ Sophisticated wines made by French-born Thierry Villard. Gd MAIPO reds, esp heady Merlot, Equis Cab Sauv and CASABLANCA whites.

Viñedo Chadwick Maipo ★★★ Stylish Cab Sauv improving with each vintage from v'yd owned by Eduardo Chadwick, chairman of ERRÁZURIZ.

Viu Manent ★→★★ Emerging Colchagua winery. Dense, fragrant Viu 1 tops range; Secreto Malbec and Viognier also v.gd. Late-harvest Sem top notch.

Von Siebenthal ★★★ Small (in Chilean terms) Swiss-owned ACONCAGUA winery. V.gd Carabantes Syrah, elegant Montelig blend, fine-boned Toknar Petit Verdot and conocentrated but v. pricey Carmenère-based Tatay de Cristóbal.

ARGENTINA

Argentina's evolution from a nation of winemakers to a nation of wine-growers continues – from the growing number of single-vineyard bottlings, usually of old-vine Malbec, to the exploration of cooler, higher regions, where the aim is to make wines that combine ripeness with perfume and freshness. There are still too many wines that aim to impress rather than satisfy – at most bodegas, the fresh, appetizing entry-level wines are more successful than the overstated icon wines in their heavy bottles. Malbec continues to win friends and attract wine lovers to other treasures – high-altitude Salta Torrontés, Rio Negro Pinot Noir, San Juan Shiraz. Cabernet Sauvignon from Mendoza terroirs can be a match for Malbec.

Achaval Ferrer Mendoza ★★★ Super-concentrated Altamira, Bella Vista and Mirador single-v'yd Malbecs and Quimera Malbec/Cab/Merlot blends.

Alta Vista ★→★★★ French-owned MENDOZA venture. Dense, spicy *Alto* (Malbec/Cab) and trio of single-v'yd Malbecs excellent. Also fresh, zesty Torrontés. Sister winery Navarrita makes fine Winemaker's Selection Malbec.

Altocedro ★★→★★★ Malbec and Tempranillo are the trump cards for this La Consulta (Valle de Uco) winery – the two are blended for the top wine Desnudos.

Altos las Hormigas ★★★ Italian-owned Malbec specialist, wines made by consultant Alberto Antonini (ex-Italy's Antinori). Best: Viña las Hormigas Reserva.

La Anita, Finca ★★→★★★ MENDOZA estate making high-class reds, esp Syrah, Malbec and new Varúa Merlot. Intriguing whites, inc Sem and Tocai Friulano.

Antucura ★★★ Valle de Uco bodega with beautifully balanced, spicy Cab Sauv/Merlot blend. Second label: Calvulcura.

Argento ★→★★ CATENA offshoot making gd commercial wine under the Libertad, Malambo and Argento labels.

Bianchi, Valentin ★ San Rafael red specialist. Enzo Bianchi (Cab Sauv/Merlot/Malbec) is excellent flagship. Gd-value Elsa's V'yd, inc meaty Barbera. Pithy Sauv Bl; also decent sparkling.

Bressia ★★→★★★ Tiny new winery already on form with classy Malbec-dominated Profundo from Agrelo and Conjuro Malbec from Tupungato.

Cabernet de los Andes ★★ Promising organic (and partly biodynamic) Catamarca estate with big, fragrant, balanced reds under Vicien and Tizac labels.

Canale, Bodegas Humberto ★★ Premier RÍO NEGRO winery known for its Sauv Bl and Pinot N, but Merlot and Malbec (esp Black River label) are the stars.

CarinaE ★★ New winery in Cruz de Piedra: rich, fragrant, elegant reds are the forte.

Catena Zapata, Bodega ★★→★★★★ Consistently gd range rises from Alamos through Catena and Catena Alta to flagship Nicolas Catena Zapata and Malbec Argentino, plus occasional single-v'yd Malbecs. Also joint venture with the Rothschilds of Lafite: seriously classy *Caro* and younger Amancaya; see ARGENTO; LUCA/TIKAL/TAHUAN/ALMA NEGRA.

Chacra ★★★ Superb RÍO NEGRO Pinot N from bodega owned by Piero Incisa della Rocchetta of Sassicaia (see Italy). Wines made by the team at NOEMIA.

Chakana ★★ Agrelo winery to watch for joyful Malbec, Cab Sauv, Syrah, Bonarda.

Chandon, Bodegas ★→★★ Makers of Baron B and M Chandon sparkling under Moët & Chandon supervision; promising Pinot N/Chard blend. See TERRAZAS DE LOS ANDES.

Clos de los Siete ★★ Reliable, plump Vistaflores (Valle de Uco) blend of Merlot, Malbec, Syrah and Cab Sauv, with Michel Rolland overseeing winemaking (see MONTEVIEJO, VAL DE FLORES).

Cobos, Viña ★★→★★★★ Ultra-rich, ultra-ripe (too ripe?) reds from Californian Paul Hobbs with the best using fruit from the Marchiori v'yd. Bramare and Felino are 2nd and 3rd tiers. Look, too, for the Marchiori & Barraud wines from two of the Cobos winemaking team.

Colomé, Bodega ★★→★★★ SALTA bodega owned by California's Hess Collection. Pure, intense, biodynamic Malbec-based reds, lively Torrontés, smoky Tannat.

Decero, Finca ★★→★★★ Lush yet elegant reds, inc a fine Petit Verdot, from the Remolinos v'yd in Agrelo.

Desierto, Bodega del ★→★★ Pioneering winery in La Pampa; promising wines under 25/5 and Desierto Pampa labels.

Dominio del Plata ★→★★★ Two ex-CATENA winemakers produce superior wines under the Crios, Susana Balbo, BenMarco, Anubis and Budini labels. Nosotros is bold Malbec/Cab Sauv flagship. BenMarco Expresivo also v.gd.

Doña Paula ★ Luján de Cuyo estate owned by SANTA RITA (see Chile). Elegant, structured Malbec; modern fleshy Cab Sauv; tangy Los Cardos Sauv Bl; exotic new Naked Grape Viognier.

Etchart ★★→★★★ Reds gd, topped by plummy Cafayate Cab Sauv. Torrontés also one of the best, with intriguing late-harvest Tardío.

Fabre Montmayou ★★ French-owned operation, aka Domaine Vistalba, with v'yds in Luján de Cuyo (MENDOZA) and RÍO NEGRO (sometimes labelled Infinitus); reds with a French accent esp good. Second label Phebus; also gd-value Viñalba wines on some export markets.

Familia Schroeder ★★ NEUQUÉN estate impressing with reds and whites. V.gd Saurus Select range, inc sappy Sauv Bl, earthy Merlot and fragrant Malbec.

Familia Zuccardi ★→★★★ Dynamic MENDOZA estate producing gd-value Santa Julia range, led by new blend Magna, better Q label (impressive Malbec, Merlot, Tempranillo), and deep yet elegant Zeta (Malbec/Tempranillo).

Fin del Mundo, Bodega del ★★ First winery in the province of NEUQUÉN; Malbec a specialty; top wine Special Blend is Merlot/Malbec/Cab Sauv.

Flichman, Finca ★★ Owned by Sogrape (see Portugal), impressing with Syrah. Best: Dedicado blend (mostly Cab Sauv/Syrah). Paisaje de Tupungato (Bordeaux blend), Paisaje de Barrancas (Syrah-based) v.gd.

Foster, Enrique ★★ MENDOZA Malbec specialist, all excellent from young, fragrant Ique to powerful Edición Limitada and Terruño single-v'yd wines.

Kaikén ★★→★★★ MENDOZA venture for Aurelio Montes (see Chile) making user-friendly range topped by Ultra Cab Sauv and Malbec.

Luca/Tikal/Tahuan/Alma Negra ★★★ Classy boutique wineries owned by Nicolas CATENA's children Laura (Luca) and Ernesto (Tikal/Tahuan/Alma Negra). Winemaker Luis Reginato also makes excellent La Posta del Viñatero range.

Luigi Bosca ★★→★★★ Small MENDOZA bodega with three tiers of quality: Finca La Linda, Luigi Bosca Res and a top level that includes esp gd Finca Los Nobles Malbec/Verdot and Cab Sauv/Bouchet, plus impressive Gala blends.

Lurton, Bodegas François ★→★★★ Juicy Piedra Negra Malbec and complex, earthy Chacayes (Malbec) head range; Flor de Torrontés more serious than most, also sweet but fresh Pasitea Torrontés/Pinot Grigio and slightly oaky white blend Corte Friulano.

Masi Tupungato ★★→★★★ MENDOZA enterprise for the well-known Valpolicella producer (see Italy). Passo Doble is fine *ripasso*-style Malbec/Corvina/ Merlot blend; Corbec is even better Amarone lookalike (Corvina/Malbec).

Melipal ★ Top-class Malbec from old Agrelo v'yds; gd-value second label Ikella.

Mendel ★★★ Former TERRAZAS DE LOS ANDES winemaker Roberta de la Mota makes plummy Malbec and graceful Unus blend from old Luján de Cuyo vines.

Mendoza Most important province for wine (over 70% of plantings). Best subregions: Agrelo, Valle de Uco (includes Tupungato), Luján de Cuyo, Maipú.

Michel Torino ★★ Rapidly improving organic Cafayate enterprise; Don David Malbec, Cab Sauv and Syrah v.gd. Altimus is rather oaky flagship.

Monteviejo ★★→★★★★ One of the v'yds of CLOS DE LOS SIETE, now with top-class range of reds headed by wonderfully textured Monteviejo blend (Malbec/Merlot/Cab Sauv/Syrah); Lindaflor Malbec also v.gd.

Las Moras, Finca ★★ SAN JUAN bodega with chunky Tannat, chewy Malbec Reserva and plump, fragrant Malbec/Bonarda blend Mora Negra.

Neuquén Patagonian region to watch: huge developments since 2000.

Nieto Senetiner, Bodegas ★★ Luján de Cuyo-based bodega. Quality rises from *tasty entry-level Santa Isabel* through Reserva to top-of-range Cadus reds.

Noemia ★★★→★★★★ Old-vine RÍO NEGRO Malbec from Hans Vinding-Diers and Noemi Cinzano. J Alberto and A Lisa new second labels.

Norton, Bodega ★→★★★ Austrian-owned old bodega. Gd whites; v.gd reds, esp Malbec, v.gd-value Privada (Merlot/Cab Sauv/Malbec), lush, complex Perdriel (Malbec/Merlot/Cab Sauv) and new Malbec-based Gernot Langes icon.

O Fournier ★→★★★ Spanish-owned Valle de Uco bodega. Urban v.gd entry-level range; then come B Crux and Alfa Crux, both fine Tempranillo/Merlot/Malbec blends. Also fragrant but rare Syrah. Now producing Chilean wines, too.

Peñaflor ★→★★★ Argentina's biggest wine company. Labels include Andean V'yds and finer TRAPICHE, FINCA LAS MORAS, Santa Ana and MICHEL TORINO.

Poesia ★★→★★★★ Exciting Luján de Cuyo producer under same ownership as Clos l'Eglise of Bordeaux; stylish Poesia (Cab Sauv/Malbec), chunkier but fine Clos des Andes (Malbec) and juicy Pasodoble Malbec/Syrah/Cab Sauv blend.

Porvenir de los Andes, El ★★ Cafayate estate with classy Laborum reds, inc fine, smoky Tannat. Amauta blends also gd. Watch out, too, for Camino del Inca, a new venture making Tannat-based Quipu.

Pulenta, Carlos ★★ Vistalba bodega, basic range is Tomero, upper tier has fine trio of Malbec-based reds, Vistalba Corte A, B and C.

Pulenta Estate ★★→★★★★ Luján de Cuyo winery. Gd Sauv Bl and v.gd reds. Best: Gran Corte (Cab Sauv/Malbec/Merlot/Petit Verdot), Cab Fr and Malbec.

Renacer ★★→★★★★ Old-vine Malbec specialist, Renacer (mostly Malbec) is flagship, but most interesting wine is Enamore – an Amarone-style red made with help from Allegrini (see Italy).

Riglos ★★ New bodega; intense, powerful, oak-infused reds from Tupungato fruit.

La Riojana ★→★★ Dynamic La Rioja company, currently the world's largest Fairtrade wine producer. *Raza Ltd Edition Malbec* is top wine, but quality and value at all levels.

Río Negro Patagonia's oldest wine region, gd for Pinot N and Malbec.

Rosell-Boher ★★ Sparkling wine specialist, using Chard and Pinot N from high-altitude Tupungato sites to rich yet never too boisterous effect .

Ruca Malen ★★→★★★★ Promising red wine specialist with v'yds in Luján de Cuyo and the Uco Valley. Top range is Kinien, tender, floral Malbec and svelte, aromatic Don Raúl blend.

Salentein, Bodegas ★★ MENDOZA red specialist. Highlights are Primus Pinot N and Malbec, and Numina (Malbec/Merlot). Finca El Portillo gd for cheaper wines; also Bodegas Callia in SAN JUAN, where Shiraz is the focus.

Salta Northerly province with some of the world's highest v'yds. Subregion Cafayate renowned for Torrontés.

San Juan Second-largest wine region, home to promising Shiraz and Tannat.

San Pedro de Yacochuya ★★★ SALTA collaboration between Michel Rolland (see France) and the ETCHART family. Ripe but fragrant Torrontés; dense, earthy Malbec; and powerful, stunning Yacochuya Malbec from oldest vines.

Soluna ★★ Ambitious new Fairtrade project making Malbec in Luján de Cuyo; top wine: fleshy Primus.

Sophenia, Finca Tupungato bodega. Advice from Michel Rolland (see France). Malbec and Cab Sauv shine; gd Altosur entry-level range; top Synthesis.

Tapiz ★★ Luján de Cuyo-based bodega, punchy Sauv Bl, v'gd red range topped by serious Reserva Selección de Barricas (Cab Sauv/Malbec/Merlot).

Terrazas de los Andes ★★→★★★ CHANDON enterprise. Three ranges: entry-level Terrazas (juicy Cab Sauv is the star), mid-price Reserva, and top-of-the-tree Afincado, inc v.gd Tardio Petit Manseng. Joint venture with Château Cheval Blanc of Bordeaux making superb *Cheval des Andes* blend.

Toso, Pascual ★★→★★★ Californian Paul Hobbs heads a team making gd-value, tasty range, inc ripe but finely structured Magdalena Toso (mostly Malbec) and Malbec/Cab Sauv single v'yd Finca Pedregal.

Trapiche ★★→★★★ PEÑAFLOR premium label increasingly potent under head winemaker Daniel Pi. Trio of single-v'yd Malbecs and new Manos Malbec shine out; red blend Iscay is gd but pricey. Better value under the Oak Cask, Fond de Cave, Briquel (promising new Cab Fr) and Medalla labels.

Trivento ★→★★ Owned by CONCHA Y TORO of Chile, making gd-value range, with Viognier standing out; also under Otra Vida label.

Val de Flores ★★★ Another Michel Rolland-driven enterprise close to CLOS DE LOS SIETE for compelling yet elegant (and biodynamic) old-vine Malbec.

Viña 1924 de Angeles ★★★ New Luján de Cuyo winery whose forte is old-vine Malbec. Top wine Gran Malbec.

Weinert, Bodegas ★→★★ Potentially fine reds, esp Cavas de Weinert blend (Cab Sauv/Merlot/Malbec), are occasionally spoiled by extended ageing in old oak. MENDOZA-based, but with Argentina's most southerly v'yd in Chubut.

OTHER SOUTH AMERICAN WINES

Bolivia Most of Bolivia is too hot and humid for vines, but some decent Syrah, Cab and Malbec are emerging from high-altitude v'yds in the southern province of Tarija, just over the border from SALTA in Argentina. Pick of the small number of wineries are La Concepción, Kohlberg, Magnus, Aranjuez and Campos de Solana.

Brazil Brazil is coming of age as a serious wine-consuming and -producing country, and now has a raft of quite interesting wines, and a new national research body can only be good. Most wine comes from the Vale dos Vinhedos in the southern province of Rio Grande do Sul. With improved viticulture, the wineries are overcoming issues with humidity, and already there are several impressive reds (look out for Merlot and, surprisingly, Teroldego and Nebbiolo) and some decent sparklers. Further north, continuous harvesting is possible in some equatorial v'yds. Producers to watch out for are Salton, Lidio Carraro, Pizzato, Dom Cândido, Amadeu (for the Geisse sparklers), Casa Valduga and the pioneering Miolo, with Aurora and Rio Sol providing gd value. Most unusual wine? The Perico Winery in Santa Catarina is working on a Cab Sauv Ice Wine.

Peru Lima's first wine bar is now open. Viña Tacama exports some pleasant wines, esp the Gran Vino Blanco; also Cab Sauv and classic-method sparkling. Chincha, Moquegua and Tacha regions are making progress, but phylloxera is a serious problem.

Uruguay If Argentina re-invented Malbec in the modern world, Uruguay has done the same for Tannat. Tannat here is beautifully balanced and ripe, and often blended with Merlot and Cab Sauv). Viognier also does well. The key is a maritime climate in much of the country. Pisano wines are stylish and fine. Juanicó is equally impressive, with flagship red blend Preludio and joint venture with Bernard Magrez of Château Pape Clément to produce Gran Casa Magrez de Uruguay. Bouza is focused, elegant. Others: Ariano, Bruzzone & Sciutto, Carrau/Castel Pujol, Casa Filguera, Castillo Viejo, De Lucca, Los Cerros de San Juan, Dante Irurtia, Marichal, Pizzorno, Stagnari and Traversa.

Australia

More heavily shaded areas are the
wine-growing regions

en years ago the Australian wine industry was rampant. In the past
year there have been calls for it to contract by 30 per cent. The Aussie
wine boom has not stopped; it has collapsed. The pain of the past five
years – drought, oversupply of grapes and wines, bush fires and, to a lesser
extent, frost – has led to an industry-wide rethink. Too many Australian
wineries are not viable in either the short or the long term. Too much
precious water has been poured on too many unwanted vines. Too many
brands have been created and too few warning signs heeded. It's not just
that Australia (like so many other countries and regions) cannot sell all the
wine it produces (current estimates suggest this is between 20–40 million
cases annually), it struggles to fetch an appropriate price for the wine it
does sell. It's not a fair situation but it is an enduring concern. Can
Australia convince the world to take its fine, elegant cool-climate wines
seriously? They deserve to be. Making matters worse, domestically, is the
Sauvignon Blanc boom of New Zealand. The cash cow of the Australian
wine industry has recently been thrashed by the fruity wines of the Kiwis.
For the first time in Australian history, the top-selling wines domestically
are not the home-grown products but imports (New Zealand savvy).

AUSTRALIA

Recent vintages

New South Wales (NSW)

2009 Excellent vintage all over although reds better than whites. Both rain and heat caused some damage but Mudgee, Cowra, Hilltops and the Canberra District producers excited by the results.

2008 Another record early start with good whites; torrential rain then destroyed virtually all Hunter reds. Canberra reds outstanding. Coonawarra stands out.

2007 The earliest vintage ever recorded for all regions; full flavour across white and red wines. Peak Hunter red vintage.

2006 A burst of extreme heat around Christmas in some regions did no real damage. Time kind to reds.

2005 A very good to exceptional year across almost all districts, especially the Hunter, Mudgee and Orange.

2004 Hunter Valley suffered; other regions good to very good outcomes.

2003 Continued drought broken by heavy rain in January/February meant variable outcomes.

2002 Heavy February rain caused problems in most areas. Riverina outstanding.

Victoria (Vic)

2009 Characterized by tragic bush fire. Extreme heat, drought, fire and related smoke taint. Yarra Valley worst (but not uniformly) affected. Beechworth, Goulburn Valley, Grampians, King Valley, Pyrenees, Mornington Peninsula and Sunbury reds of good, concentrated quality.

2008 Started one day later than 2007 but finished one week earlier. Reds excellent in Grampians, Mornington Peninsula, Yarra Valley.

2007 Broke the record for the earliest vintage; frost and bush-fire smoke taint hit some regions hard.

2006 One of the earliest and most compressed vintages on record; paradoxically fruit flavour came even earlier. A charmed year.

2005 Rain up to end of February was followed by a freakish three-month Indian summer, giving superb fruit.

2004 Near-perfect weather throughout ripened generous yields.

2003 Overall, fared better than other states, except for bush-fire-ravaged Alpine Valleys. Hot vintage.

2002 Extremely cool weather led to tiny yields, but wines of high quality. Sweet-sour reds.

South Australia (SA)

2009 Low yields; hot vintage. Dire predictions for the state's whites but Clare Valley and Eden Valley Ries both look very good as young wines. Adelaide Hills very good for both whites and reds. Coonawarra reds excellent. McLaren Vale and Barossa Valley generally very good for Shiraz.

2008 The very early start in February turned out to create a curate's egg: excellent wines picked prior to March 6, non-fortified "ports" for those picked after the record heatwave. Very high alcohols.

2007 Devastating frosts hit the Limestone Coast repeatedly. A dry, warm vintage favoured red wines across the board. Good at best.

2006 A great Cab year; for other reds those picked before Easter rains did best. Here, too, flavour ripeness came early.

2005 Clare Valley, Coonawarra, Wrattonbully and Langhorne Creek did best in what was a large but high-quality vintage with reds to the fore.

2004 Excellent summer/autumn weather helped to offset large crops (big bunches/berries); heavy crop-thinning needed. Barossa Valley Shiraz excellent.

2003 A curate's egg. The good: Limestone Coast and Clare Ries (yet again); the bad: rain-split Shiraz.

2002 Very cool weather led to much reduced yields in the south and to a great Riverland vintage in both yield and quality. Fine Ries again.

Western Australia (WA)

2009 Low yields but excellent quality. Mild summer. Particularly good year for Margaret River (whites and reds) and Pemberton (whites). Margaret River so often experiences polar-opposite conditions to the regions of the eastern states. Here so again.

2008 The best vintage for many years across all regions and all varieties; normal harvest dates.

2007 A warm quickfire vintage made white quality variable; fine reds.

2006 Complete opposite to Eastern Australia; a cool, wet and late vintage – searing whites, highly dubious reds.

2005 Heavy rain spoiled what would have been the vintage of a generation for Cab and Shiraz in the south; whites uniformly excellent.

2004 More of the same; mild weather, long autumn. Good flavours, some lacking intensity.

2003 An in-between year with ill-timed rainfall nipping greatness in the bud.

2002 Best since 1984 in Swan District. In the south, quality is variable.

Adelaide Hills SA Best Sauv Bl region: cool 450-m sites in Mount Lofty ranges.

Alkoomi Mount Barker, WA r w ★★→★★★ (Ries) 01 02' 04 05' 07' 08 (Cab Sauv) 01' 02' 04 05' 07 A veteran of 35 yrs making fine Ries and long-lived reds.

All Saints Rutherglen, Vic r w br ★★ Historic producer making creditable table wines; great fortifieds.

Alpine Valleys Vic Geographically similar to KING VALLEY. Similar use of grapes.

Angove's SA r w (br) ★→★★ Long-established MURRAY VALLEY family business. Gd-value range of white and red wines.

Annie's Lane Clare V, SA r w ★★→★★★ Part of FWE. Consistently gd, boldly flavoured wines; flagship Copper Trail excellent, esp Ries and Shiraz.

Arrivo Adelaide Hill, SA r Arrivo has arrived. Long-maceration Nebbiolo. Dry, sophisticated, sexy rosé. Minute quantities.

Ashbrook Estate Margaret R, WA r w ★★★ Minimum of fuss; consistently makes 8,000 cases of exemplary Sem, Chard, Sauv Bl, Verdelho and Cab Sauv.

Ashton Hills Adelaide Hills, SA r w (sp) ★★★ Fine, racy, long-lived Ries and compelling Pinot N crafted by Stephen George from 25-yr-old v'yds.

Bailey's NE Vic r w br ★★ Rich Shiraz and magnificent dessert Muscat (★★★★) and "Tokay". Part of FWE but now for sale.

Balgownie Estate Bendigo and Yarra V, Vic r w ★ Rejuvenated producer of v. well-balanced wines, esp Cab Sauv, now with separate YARRA VALLEY arm.

Balnaves of Coonawarra SA r w ★★★ Grape-grower since 1975; winery since 1996. V.gd Chard; excellent supple, medium-bodied Shiraz, Merlot, Cab Sauv.

Bannockburn Geelong r w ★★★ (Chard) 00 02' 03 04 05' 06 (Pinot N) 02' 03' 04' 05' 06 07 Intense, complex Chard and Pinot N produced using Burgundian techniques. Winemaker Michael Glover is a whizz.

Banrock Station Riverland, SA r w ★→★★★ Almost 1,600-ha property on Murray River, 243-ha v'yd, owned by HARDYS. Impressive budget wines.

Barossa Valley SA Australia's most important winery (but not v'yd) area; grapes from diverse sources make diverse wines. Local specialties: v. old-vine Shiraz, Mourvèdre and Grenache.

AUSTRALIA

NB Vintages in colour are those you should choose first for drinking in 2011.

Bass Phillip Gippsland, Vic r ★★★→★★★★ (Pinot N) 99' 02' 03 04 05' 06' 07' Tiny amounts of stylish, eagerly sought-after Pinot N in three quality grades; v. Burgundian in style though quality can be erratic (to say the least).

Bay of Fires North Tasmania r w sp ★★★ Pipers River outpost of CONSTELLATION empire. Produces stylish table wines and Arras super-*cuvée* sparkler.

Beechworth Vic Trendy region; CASTAGNA and GIACONDA are best-known wineries.

Beggars' Belief 50/50 blend of Chard and high-toast Zimbabwean oak now losing market share.

Bellarmine Wines Pemberton, WA w (r) ★★★ German Schumacher family is long-distance owner of this 20-ha v'yd: (*inter alia*) startling Mosel-like Ries at various sweetness/alcohol levels, at low prices.

Bendigo Vic Widespread region with 34 small v'yds. Some v.gd quality: BALGOWNIE ESTATE, Passing Clouds, PONDALOWIE, Turner's Crossing and Water Wheel.

Best's Grampians, Vic r w ★★→★★★ (Shiraz) 97' 01' 03' 04' 05' 06 Conservative old family winery; *v.gd mid-weight reds*. Thomson Family Shiraz from 120-yr-old vines is superb.

Big Rivers Zone NSW and Vic The continuation of South Australia's Riverland, inc the Murray Darling, Perricoota and Swan Hill regions.

Bindi Macedon, Vic r w ★★★→★★★★ (Pinot N) 04' 06' 08' Ultra-fastidious, terroir-driven maker of outstanding, long-lived Pinot N and Chard.

Blue Pyrenees Pyrenees, Vic r w sp ★★ 180 ha of mature v'yds are being better utilized than before across a broad range of wines.

Boireann Granite Belt Queensland r ★★→★★★ Consistently the best producer of red wines in Queensland (in tiny quantities).

Botobolar Mudgee, NSW r w ★★ Marvellously eccentric little organic winery.

Brand's of Coonawarra Coonawarra, SA r w ★★ 91' 94 96 98' 02' 03 05' 07 Owned by MCWILLIAM'S. Super-premium Stentiford's Reserve Shiraz (100-yr-old vines) and *Patron's Reserve Cab Sauv* are tops.

Bremerton Langhorne Creek, SA r w ★★ Well-priced red wines with silky-soft mouth-feel and stacks of flavour. Brand is thriving since sisters Lucy and Rebecca Willson, who are definitely doing it for themselves, took over the family winery.

Brokenwood Hunter V, NSW r w ★★★ (ILR Reserve Sem) 03' 05' (07') (Graveyard Shiraz) 93' 97' 98' 00' 02' 03' 05' 07' and Cricket Pitch Sem/Sauv Bl fuel sales.

Brookland Valley Margaret River, WA r w ★★★ Superbly sited winery (with a restaurant) doing great things, esp with Sauv Bl. Owned by CWA.

Brown Brothers King V, Vic r w br dr sw sp ★→★★★ (Noble Ries) 99' 00 02' 04 05 Old family firm with new ideas. Wide range of delicate, varietal wines, many from cool mountain districts, inc Chard and Ries. *Dry white Muscat is outstanding*. Cab Sauv blend is best red. Extensive Prosecco plantings.

Buller Rutherglen, Vic br ★★★★ Rated for superb Rare Liqueur Muscat and the newly minted name TOPAQUE (replacing "Tokay").

By Farr/Farr Rising Geelong, Vic r w ★★★ Father Gary and son Nick's own, after departure from BANNOCKBURN. Chard and Pinot N can be minor masterpieces.

Campbells Rutherglen, Vic r br (w) ★★ Smooth ripe reds and unusually elegant; Merchant Prince Rare Muscat and Isabella Rare Topaque (★★★★).

Canberra District NSW Both quality and quantity on the increase; altitude-dependent, site selection important. CLONAKILLA best known.

Capel Vale Geographe, WA r w ★★→★★★ 165-ha estate. V'yds across four regions and 13 varieties make every post a winner.

Cape Mentelle Margaret R, WA r w ★★★ Robust Cab Sauv gd, Chard even better; also Zin and v. popular Sauv Bl/Sem. Owned by LVMH Veuve Clicquot.

Capercaillie Hunter V, NSW r w ★★→★★★ Sudden death of owner Alasdair Sutherland hasn't changed winning formula of supplementing local grapes with purchases from elsewhere, inc MCLAREN VALE, ORANGE etc.

Carlei Estate Yarra V, Vic r w ★★ Winemaker Sergio Carlei sources Pinot N and Chard from cool regions to make wines of character. Largely biodynamic.

Casella Riverina, NSW r w ★The (Yellow Tail) phenomenon has swept all before it with multimillion-case sales in US. Like Fanta: soft and sweet. High Aussie dollar a threat.

Castagna Beechworth, Vic r ★★★ (Syrah) 01' 02' 04' 05' 06 Julian Castagna; as much a chef as a winemaker. Deserved leader of the biodynamic brigade. Shiraz/Viognier and Sangiovese/Shiraz blends v.gd.

Centennial V'yds Southern Highlands, NSW r w ★★ Sources its best grapes from ORANGE, but winemaking skills and a large chequebook are there.

Central Ranges Zone NSW Encompasses MUDGEE, ORANGE and Cowra regions, expanding in high-altitude, moderately cool to warm climates.

Chalkers Crossing Hilltops, NSW r w ★★→★★★ Beautifully balanced cool-climate wines made by French-trained Celine Rousseau; esp Shiraz.

Chambers Rosewood Northeast Vic br (r w) ★★→★★★ Viewed with MORRIS as the greatest maker of sticky TOPAQUE and Muscat. Less successful table wines.

Chapel Hill McLaren Vale, SA r T The darling of modern-day MCLAREN VALE has risen once more. Went through a flat patch from the late 1990s until 2005, but operating again at high revs.

Charles Melton Barossa, SA r w (sp) ★★★ Tiny winery with bold, luscious reds, esp Nine Popes, an old-vine Grenache/Shiraz blend.

Clarendon Hills McLaren Vale, SA r ★★★ Deeply structured reds from small parcels of contract grapes around hills above MCLAREN VALE.

Clare Valley SA Small high-quality area 145 km north of Adelaide. Best for Ries; also Shiraz and Cab Sauv.

Clonakilla Canberra District, NSW r w ★★★ (Shiraz) 01' 03' 05' 06' 07' 08 *Deserved leader of the Shiraz/Viognier brigade*. Ries and other wines also v.gd. May well be Australia's best auction performer.

Coldstream Hills Yarra V, Vic r w (sp) ★★★ (Chard) 02' 03 04' 05' 06' 07 (Pinot N) 92' 96' 02' 04' 06' Established in 1985 by wine critic James Halliday. Delicious Pinot N to drink young, and *Reserve to age*. V.gd Chard (esp Reserve), fruity Cab Sauv, Merlot. Part of FWE.

Constellation Wines Australia (CWA) Name for all wines/wineries previously under HARDYS brand. Like FWE seeking to shed regional wineries and v'yds.

Coonawarra SA Southernmost v'yds of state: home to most of Australia's best Cab Sauv; successful Chard, Ries and Shiraz.

Coriole McLaren Vale, SA r w ★★→★★★ (Lloyd Reserve Shiraz) 91' 96' 98' 02' 04' 06' To watch, esp for old-vine Shiraz Lloyd Reserve.

Craiglee Macedon, Vic r ★★★ (Shiraz) 96' 97' 98' 00' 02' 04' 05 06' Re-creation of famous 19th-century estate. Fragrant, peppery Shiraz, Chard.

Crawford River Henty, Vic r w ★★★ John Thomson consistently produces some of Australia's best Ries from this ultra-cool region.

Cullen Wines Margaret R, WA r w ★★★★ (Chard) 00' 02' 04' 05' 07 (08') (Cab Sauv/ Merlot) 94' 95' 98' 04' 05' 07' Vanya Cullen makes strongly structured *substantial but subtle Sem/Sauv Bl*, bold Chard and outstanding Cab/Merlot.

Cumulus Orange, NSW r w ★★ By far the largest v'yd owner and producer in the region. Variable quality.

Dalwhinnie Pyrenees, Vic r w ★★★ (Chard) 04' 05' 06' (Shiraz) 99' 00 02 04' 05' 06' 07 Rich Chard and Shiraz. Cab Sauv best in PYRENEES.

d'Arenberg McLaren Vale, SA r w (br sp sw) ★★→★★★ Old firm with new lease of life; sumptuous Shiraz and Grenache, lots of varieties and wacky labels.

Words within entries marked like this *Alter Ego de Palmer* indicate wines especially enjoyed by Hugh Johnson over the past 12 months (mid 09–10).

AUSTRALIA

Deakin Estate Murray Darling r w ★ Part of KATNOOK group, producing large volumes of v. decent varietal table wines. V. low-alcohol Moscato.

De Bortoli Griffith, NSW r w dr sw (br) ★→★★★ (Noble Sem) Irrigation-area winery. Standard red and white but v.gd sweet, botrytized, Sauternes-style Noble Sem.

De Bortoli Yarra V, Vic r w ★★★ (Chard) 02' 04 05' 06' 07 08' (Shiraz) 02' 04' 05' 06' (07) 08' YARRA VALLEY'S largest producer. Main label is v.gd; second label Gulf Station and third label Windy Peak v.gd value. Flying.

Devil's Lair Margaret R, WA r w ★★★ Opulently concentrated Chard and Cab Sauv/Merlot. Fifth Leg is fast-growing trendy second label. Part of FWE.

Diamond Valley Yarra V, Vic r w ★★ (Pinot N) 02' 04' 05' 06' V.gd Pinot N in significant quantities; others gd, esp Chard.

Domaine A South Tasmania r w ★★★ Swiss owners/winemakers Peter and Ruth Althaus are perfectionists; v.gd Sauv Bl (Fumé Blanc) and Cab Sauv.

Domaine Chandon Yarra V, Vic sp (r w) ★★★ Gd sparkling wine, grapes from cooler wine regions. Owned by Moët & Chandon. Well-known in UK as GREEN POINT.

Eden Road r Ambitious new producer making wines from EDEN VALLEY, Hilltops, TUMBARUMBA and CANBERRA DISTRICT regions. V.gd Shiraz. Won Australia's most prominent wine award, the Jimmy Watson Trophy, in 2009.

Eden Valley SA Hilly region home to HENSCHKE and PEWSEY VALE; Ries and Shiraz of v. high quality.

Elderton Barossa, SA r w (br sp) ★★ Old vines; rich, oaked Cab Sauv and Shiraz.

Eldridge Estate Mornington Pen, Vic ★★ Winemaker David Lloyd would drive you mad with his fastidious experimentation. Pinot N and Chard are worth the fuss.

Evans & Tate Margaret R, WA r w ★★→★★★ In October 2007, the brand was finally acquired (from receivers) by a syndicate headed by MCWILLIAM'S. Wine quality has remained remarkably stable during extended financial woes.

Ferngrove V'yds Great Southern, WA r w ★★★ Cattle farmer Murray Burton's syndicate has established 223 ha since 1997; great Ries, Malbec.

Freycinet Tasmania r w (sp) ★★★ (Pinot N) 96' 00' 02' 05' 06' 07 East coast winery producing voluptuous, rich Pinot N and gd Chard.

Fosters Wine Estates (FWE) Official name of the merged Beringer Blass and SOUTHCORP wine groups. Dozens of brands in Australia (which use contract grapes, contract wineries, contract staff) that come and go like mushrooms after rain, but has embarked on a brand weight-loss programme.

Gapsted Wines Alpine V, Vic r w Large winery that crushes grapes for 50 growers; own-label okay.

Geelong Vic Once-famous area destroyed by phylloxera, re-established in the mid-1960s. V. cool, dry climate. Names include BANNOCKBURN, BY FARR, Curlewis, LETHBRIDGE, Paradise IV, SCOTCHMANS HILL.

Gemtree V'yds McLaren Vale, SA r (w) ★★→★★★ Top-class Shiraz alongside Tempranillo and other exotica, linked by quality. Largely biodynamic.

Geoff Merrill McLaren Vale, SA r w ★★ Ebullient maker of Geoff Merrill and Mt Hurtle. Wine: mixed. TAHBILK owns 50%. Wine report mixed.

Geoff Weaver Adelaide Hills, SA r w ★★★ An 8-ha estate at Lenswood. V. fine Sauv Bl, Chard, Ries and Cab Sauv/Merlot blend.

Giaconda Beechworth, Vic r w ★★★ (Chard) 96' 00' 02' 04' 05' 06' (Shiraz) 02' 04' 06' In the mid-1980s Rick Kinzbrunner did that rare thing: walked up a steep, stony hill and came down a champion wine producer. Now contends with LEEUWIN ESTATE for the mantle of Australia's best Chard. Pinot N less successful. Oaked Roussanne gd. Funkified Shiraz the rising star.

Glaetzer Wines Barossa, SA r ★★★ Hyper-rich, unfiltered, v. ripe old-vine Shiraz led by iconic Amon-Ra. V.gd examples of high-octane style admired by US critics.

Goulburn Valley Vic V. old (TAHBILK) and relatively new (MITCHELTON) wineries in temperate mid-Victoria region. Full-bodied table wines.

Grampians Vic Region previously known as Great Western. Temperate region in central west of state. High quality, esp Shiraz and sparkling Shiraz.

Granite Belt Queensland High-altitude, (relatively) cool region just north of Queensland/NSW border. Esp spicy Shiraz and rich Sem.

Granite Hills Macedon, Vic r w ★★ 30-yr-old family v'yd and winery has regained original class with fine, elegant Ries and spicy Shiraz.

Grant Burge Barossa, SA r w (br sw sp) ★★ 400,000 cases of silky-smooth reds and whites from the best grapes of Burge's large v'yd holdings.

Great Southern WA Remote cool area; FERNGROVE and Goundrey are the largest wineries. Albany, Denmark, Frankland River, Mount Barker and Porongurup are official subregions. First-class Ries and Shiraz.

Greenstone V'yd Heathcote, Vic r ★★ A partnership between David Gleave MW (London), Alberto Antonini (Italy) and Australian viticulturist Mark Walpole; great Shiraz, gd Sangiovese.

Green Point See DOMAINE CHANDON.

Grosset Clare, SA r w ★★★→★★★★ (Ries) 00' 02' 03 06' 07' (Gaia) 90' 91' 96' 98' 99 02' 04' 05' 06 09 Fastidious winemaker. Foremost Australian Ries, lovely Chard, Pinot N and *exceptional Gaia Cab Sauv/Merlot* from dry v'yd in Watervale and Polish Hill subregions.

Hanging Rock Macedon, Vic r w sp ★→★★★ (Heathcote Shiraz) 00' 01' 02' 04' 06' Has successfully moved upmarket with sparkling Macedon and Heathcote Shiraz; bread and butter comes from contract winemaking.

Hardys r w sp (sw) ★★→★★★★ (Eileen Chard) 01' 02' 04' 05 06' (Eileen Shiraz) 70' 96' 98' 02' 04' 06' Historic company blending wines from several areas. Best are Eileen Hardy and recent Heritage Reserve Blend (HRB) series seeking synergy from classy components. Part of CWA.

Heathcote Vic The 500-million-yr-old, blood-red Cambrian soil has seemingly unlimited potential to produce reds, esp Shiraz, of the highest quality.

Heggies Eden V, SA r w dr (sw) ★★ V'yd at 500 m owned by S SMITH & SONS, like PEWSEY VALE with v.gd Ries, but gd Viognier and Chard, too.

Henschke Eden V, SA r w ★★★★ (Shiraz) 58' 84' 86' 90' 91' 96' 98' 01 02' 04' 06' (Cab Sauv) 86' 88 90' 96' 98 99' 02' 04' 06' A 120-yr-old family business, perhaps Australia's best, known for delectable Hill of Grace (Shiraz), v.gd Cab Sauv and red blends, and value whites, *inc long-ageing Ries*. Lenswood v'yds in ADELAIDE HILLS add excitement. Fervent opponent of corks for reds, too.

Hewitson SE Aus r (w) ★★★ Much-travelled winemaker Dean Hewitson's virtual winery sourcing parcels of v. old vines, making wines in rented space.

Hollick Coonawarra, SA r w (sp) ★★→★★★ Has expanded estate v'yds, most recently in WRATTONBULLY. Cab Sauv, Shiraz and Merlot. Top-class restaurant.

Hope Estate Lower Hunter V, NSW ★★ Snapped up Rothbury Estate Winery from FWE; also owns Virgin Hills and Western Austalia v'yds.

Houghton Swan V, WA r w ★→★★★ The most famous old winery of Western Australia. Soft, ripe Supreme is top-selling, age-worthy white; *a national classic*. Also excellent Cab Sauv, Verdelho, Shiraz, etc. sourced from MARGARET RIVER and GREAT SOUTHERN. Part of CWA.

Howard Park Mount Barker and Margaret R, WA r w ★★★ (Ries) 97' 99' 02' 04 05' 07' 08 (Cab Sauv) 88' 94' 96' 99' 01' 05' 07' (Chard) 01' 02' 04 05' 07' Scented Ries, Chard; spicy Cab Sauv. Second label: MadFish Bay is excellent value.

Hunter Valley NSW Great name in NSW. Broad, soft, earthy Shiraz and gentle Sem that live for 30 yrs. Cab Sauv not important; Chard is.

Islander Estate, The Kangaroo Island, SA r w ★★★ New, full-scale development by Jacques Lurton of Bordeaux, planned as likely retirement venture. Grenache, Malbec, Cab Sauv/Shiraz/Viognier all v.gd.

Jacob's Creek (Orlando) Barossa, SA r w sp (br sw) ★→★★★ Great pioneering company, now owned by Pernod Ricard. Almost totally focused on three tiers of Jacob's Creek wines, covering all varieties and prices.

Jasper Hill Heathcote, Vic r w ★★→★★★ (Shiraz) 85' 96' 97' 98' 99' 02' 04' 06' Emily's Paddock Shiraz/Cab Fr blend and Georgia's Paddock Shiraz from dry-land estate are intense, long-lived and much admired.

Jim Barry Clare V, SA r w ★★→★★★ Some great v'yds provide gd Ries, McCrae Wood Shiraz, and richly robed and oaked The Armagh Shiraz.

John Duval Wines Barossa, SA r ★★★ The eponymous business of former chief red winemaker for PENFOLDS (and Grange), making delicious reds that are supple and smooth, yet amply structured.

Kaesler Barossa, SA r (w) ★★→★★★ Old Bastard Shiraz outranks Old Vine Shiraz. Wine in the glass generally gd, too (in heroic style), though alcohol levels too high for me.

Katnook Estate Coonawarra, SA r w (w sw sp) ★★★ (Odyssey Cab Sauv) 91' 92' 94' 96' 97' 98' 00 01' 02' 05' Excellent pricey icons Odyssey and Prodigy Shiraz. Lavishly oaked.

Keith Tulloch Hunter V, NSW r w ★★★ Ex-Rothbury winemaker fastidiously crafting elegant yet complex Sem, Shiraz, etc.

Killkanoon Clare V, SA ★★→★★★ r w Ries and Shiraz have been awesome performers in shows over past yrs. In Sept 2007, acquired National Trust-ranked SEPPELTSFIELD. Luscious, beautifully crafted reds.

Kingston Estate SE Aus ★→★★ Kaleidoscopic array of varietal wines from all over the place, consistency and value providing the glue.

King Valley Vic Altitude between 155 m and 860 m has massive impact on varieties and styles. 29 wineries headed by BROWN BROS and PIZZINI, and important supplier to many others.

Knappstein Wines Clare V, SA r w ★★→★★★ Reliable Ries, Cab Sauv/Merlot, Shiraz and Cab Sauv. Owned by LION NATHAN.

Kooyong Mornington Pen, Vic ★★★ Pinot N and Chard of power and structure. Single-v'yd wines. Winemaker Sandro Moselle is a force to be reckoned with.

Lake Breeze Langhorne Creek, SA r (w) ★★ Long-term grape-growers turned winemakers, producing succulently smooth Shiraz and Cab Sauv.

Lake's Folly Hunter V, NSW r w ★★★★ (Chard) 97' 99' 00' 01' 04' 05' 07' (Cab Sauv) 69' 89' 93 97' 98' 03' 05' 07' Founded by Max Lake, pioneer of HUNTER VALLEY Cab Sauv. New owners since 2000. Now Chard usually better than Cab Sauv.

Langmeil Barossa, SA r w ★★★ Owns oldest block of Shiraz (planted in 1843) in world plus other old v'yds, making opulent Shiraz without excessive alcohol.

Larry Cherubino Wines Frankland R, WA r w ★★ Ex-HARDYS wunderkind winemaker now putting runs on the board under his own name. Sauv Bl and Shiraz are causing the main excitement. Spicy, specific, thoughtful styles.

Lazy Ballerina McLaren Vale, SA r Run by (young) viticulturist James Hook, who enjoys thumbing his nose at the big companies. Calls his winery newsletter *Wine Fight Club*. Rich, tannic, textured Shiraz; excellent value.

Leasingham Clare V, SA r w ★★ Once-important brand with v.gd Ries, Shiraz, Cab Sauv and Cab Sauv/Malbec blend. Various labels, inc individual v'yds.

Leeuwin Estate Margaret R, WA r w ★★★★ (Chard) 85' 87' 92' 97' 99' 01' 02' 04' 05' 06 07' Leading Western Australia estate. Superb, age-worthy Art Series Chard. Sauv Bl, Ries and Cab Sauv also gd.

Leo Buring Barossa, SA w ★★★ 79' 84' 91' 94 98 02' 04 05' 06' Part of FWE. Now exclusively Ries producer; Leonay top label, ages superbly. Screwcapped.

Lethbridge Geelong, Vic w r ★★ Stylish small-run producer of Chard, Shiraz and Pinot N. Darling in the making.

Limestone Coast Zone SA Important zone, inc Bordertown, COONAWARRA, Mount Benson, Mount Gambier, PADTHAWAY, Robe and WRATTONBULLY.

Lindemans r w ★→★★ One of the oldest firms, now owned by FWE. Low-price Bin range (esp Bin 65 Chard) now its main focus, a far cry from former glory. Lindemans Coonawarra reds still gd.

Lion Nathan New Zealand brewery; owns KNAPPSTEIN, MITCHELTON, PETALUMA, ST HALLET, Smithbrook, STONIER and TATACHILLA.

Macedon and **Sunbury** Vic Adjacent regions, Macedon higher elevation, Sunbury near Melbourne airport. CRAIGLEE, GRANITE HILLS, HANGING ROCK.

Main Ridge Estate Mornington Pen, Vic r w Rich, age-worthy Chard and Pinot N. Peninsula pioneer Nat White boasts that the region has now made all of its mistakes "because I made them all".

Majella Coonawarra, SA r (w) ★★★→★★★★ Rising to the top of COONAWARRA cream. The Malleea is outstanding Cab Sauv/Shiraz super-premium red. Shiraz and Cab Sauv also v.gd.

Margaret River WA Temperate coastal area south of Perth, with superbly elegant wines. Australia's most vibrant tourist wine (and surfing) region.

McLaren Vale SA Historic region on southern outskirts of Adelaide. Big, alcoholic, flavoursome reds have great appeal to US, but CORIOLE, HARDYS, WIRRA WIRRA and others show flavour can be gained without sacrificing elegance.

McWilliam's Yarra V, Vic; Coonawarra SA; Margaret River, WA r w (br sw) ★★→★★★ Still family-owned (Gallo lurking with 10% of shares) but has reinvented itself with some flair, often overdelivering. *Elizabeth Sem* the darling of Sydney, cheaper Hanwood blends in many parts of the world. Elizabeth and Lovedale Sem so consistent and age-worthy that vintages irrelevant.

Meerea Park Hunter V, NSW r w Brothers Garth and Rhys Eather have taken nearly 20 yrs to be an overnight success. Bright-flavoured Sem, Chard, Shiraz.

Mike Press Wines Adelaide Hills, SA r w Tiny production, extreme value. Shiraz, Cab Sauv, Chard. No one knows how he does it, but a lot of folks would like to.

Mitchell Clare V, SA r w ★★→★★★ (Ries) 00' 01' 04 05' 06' 07 Small family winery for excellent Cab Sauv and *firmly structured dry Ries*, screwcap since 2000.

Mitchelton Goulburn V, Vic r w (w sw) ★★ Reliable producer of Ries, Shiraz, Cab Sauv at several price points, plus specialty of *Marsanne* and Roussanne.

Mitolo McLaren Vale; Barossa, SA r ★★★ One of the best "virtual wineries" (ie. contract v'yds, wineries, winemaker), paying top dollar for top-quality Shiraz and Cab Sauv; Ben GLAETZER winemaker. Heroic but (virtually) irresistible wines.

Moorilla Estate Tasmania r w (sp) ★★★ Near Hobart on Derwent River: v.gd Ries and Chard; Pinot N gd. Superb restaurant and world-class art gallery.

Moorooduc Estate Mornington Pen, Vic r w ★★★ Stylish and sophisticated (wild yeast, etc.) producer of top-flight Chard and Pinot N. Influential.

Moppity V'yds Hilltops, NSW r w Making a name for its Reserve Shiraz/Viognier (Hilltops) and Chard (TUMBARUMBA). Name to watch.

Mornington Peninsula Vic Exciting wines in cool coastal area 40 km south of Melbourne; 1,000 ha. Many high-quality boutique wineries.

Morris NE Vic br (r w) ★★→★★★★ Old winery at RUTHERGLEN for some of Australia's greatest dessert Muscats and "Tokays".

Moss Wood Margaret R, WA r w ★★★★ (Cab Sauv) 80' 85 90' 91' 04' 05' 07' To many, the best MARGARET RIVER winery (11.7 ha). Sem, Cab Sauv, Chard, all with rich fruit flavours. Cab Sauv smoother than a baby's bottom.

Mount Horrocks Clare V, SA r w ★★★→★★★★ Finest dry Ries and sweet Cordon Cut Ries; *Chard best in region*. Related to GROSSET.

Mount Langi Ghiran Grampians, Vic r w ★★★ (Shiraz) 89' 93' 96' 03' 05' 06' (08) Esp for superb, rich, peppery, Rhône-like Shiraz, one of Australia's best cool-climate versions. Sister of YERING STATION.

Mount Mary Yarra V, Vic r w ★★★★ (Pinot N) 97' 99 00' 02' 05' 06' (Quintet) 84' 86' 88' 90' 92' 96' 98' 02' 04' 06 The late Dr John Middleton made tiny amounts of suave Chard, vivid Pinot N and (best of all) Cab Sauv blend: Australia's most Bordeaux-like "claret". All age impeccably. His family goes on.

Mudgee NSW Long-established region northwest of Sydney. Big reds, surprisingly fine Sem and full Chard. Struggled to gain traction of late.

Murdock Coonawarra, SA r ★★★ Long-term grower now making classic Cab Sauv.

Murray Valley SA, Vic, NSW Vast irrigated v'yds. Now at the epicentre of the drought/climate-change firestorm.

Ngeringa Adelaide Hills, SA r Excellent, v. perfumed, biodynamic Pinot N. Family history in the cosmetics industry. In the first blush of a long wine journey.

Ninth Island See PIPERS BROOK.

O'Leary Walker Wines Clare V, SA r w ★★★ Two whizz-kids have midlife crisis and leave Beringer Blass to do their own thing – v. well.

Orange NSW Cool-climate, high-elevation region: lively Chard, Merlot, Shiraz.

Padthaway SA Large area developed as overspill of COONAWARRA. Cool climate; gd Chard and excellent Shiraz (Orlando).

Pannell, SC McLaren Vale, SA r ★★★ Ex-HARDYS chief winemaker Steve Pannell now with eponymous label. Gd Shiraz and Grenache-based wines.

Paringa Estate Mornington Pen, Vic r w ★★★★ Maker of quite spectacular Chard, Pinot N and Shiraz, winning innumerable trophies.

Parker Estate Coonawarra, SA r ★★★ Small estate making v.gd Cab Sauv, esp Terra Rossa First Growth. Sister of YERING STATION since 2004.

Paxton McLaren Vale, SA r Significant v'yd holder. Largely organic/biodynamic. Ripe but elegant Shiraz and Grenache. Driven by humble ambition.

Pemberton WA Region between MARGARET RIVER and GREAT SOUTHERN; initial enthusiasm for Pinot N replaced by Ries, Chard, Merlot, Shiraz.

Penfolds Originally Adelaide, now everywhere r w (br sp) ★★→★★★★ (Grange) 52' 53' 55' 60' 62' 63' 66' 71' 76' 78' 83' 86' 90' 94' 96' 98' 99' 02' 04' (05', 06') (Cab Sauv Bin 707) 64' 66' 76' 86' 90' 91' 96' 98' 02' 04' (06') Consistently Australia's best red wine company, if you can decode its labels. Its Grange (was called Hermitage) is deservedly ★★★★. Yattarna Chard was released in 1998. Bin 707 Cab Sauv not far behind.

Penley Estate Coonawarra, SA r w ★★ Rich, textured, fruit-and-oak Cab Sauv; Shiraz/Cab Sauv blend; Chard.

Perth Hills WA Fledgling area 30 km east of Perth with a larger number of growers on mild hillside sites. Millbrook and Western Range best.

Petaluma Adelaide Hills, SA r w sp ★★★ (Ries) 04' 05' 06' (Chard) 01' 03' 04' 05 06' 07 (Cab Sauv Coonawarra) 79' 90' 91' 95' 98' 03' 05' 06' Created by the fearsome intellect and energy of Brian Croser. Red wines richer from 1988 on. Fell prey to LION NATHAN in 2002.

Peter Lehmann Wines Barossa, SA r w (w br sw sp) ★★★ Defender of BAROSSA VALLEY faith; fought off Allied-Domecq by marriage with Swiss Hess group. Consistently well-priced wines in substantial quantities. Try Stonewell Shiraz and outstanding Reserve Bin Sem and Ries with 5 yrs' age.

Pewsey Vale Adelaide Hills, SA w ★★★→★★★★ Glorious Ries, esp The Contours, released with screwcap, five yrs' bottle-age and multiple trophies.

Pierro Margaret R, WA r w ★★★ (Chard) 96' 99' 00' 01' 02' 03 05' (06) Highly rated producer of expensive, tangy Sem/Sauv Bl and v.gd barrel-fermented Chard.

Pipers Brook Tasmania r w sp ★★★ (Ries) 99' 00' 01' 02' 04' 06' 07 (Chard) 00' 02' 05' 06 07' Cool-area pioneer; v.gd Ries, Pinot N, *restrained Chard and sparkling* from Tamar Valley. Second label: Ninth Island. Owned by Belgian Kreglinger family, owners of Vieux-Château-Certan (see Châteaux of Bordeaux).

Pirramimma McLaren Vale, SA r w ★★ Century-old family business with large v'yds moving with the times; snappy new packaging, the wines not forgotten.

Pizzini King Valley, Vic r (Nebbiolo) 98' 02' **04** Leads the charge towards Italian varieties in Australia. Nebbiolo and Sangiovese, and blends. V'yds by Fred Pizzini, winemaking by son Joel Pizzini, marketing by daughter Natalie Pizzini. Eh, it's the family.

Plantagenet Mount Barker, WA r w (sp) ★★★ (r) 95 98' 01' 03 04' 05' 07' The region's elder statesman: wide range of varieties, esp rich Chard, Shiraz and vibrant, potent Cab Sauv.

Pondalowie Bendigo, Vic r ★★ Flying winemakers with exciting Shiraz/Viognier/Tempranillo in various combinations.

Primo Estate SA r w dr (w sw) ★★★ Joe Grilli's many successes include v.gd MCLAREN VALE cherry, spicy Shiraz/Sangiovese, tangy Colombard and potent Joseph Cab Sauv/Merlot.

Pyrenees Vic Central Victoria region producing rich, often minty reds.

Redheads MacLaren V, SA r ★★ Tiny "studio" for super-concentrated reds.

Richmond Grove Barossa, SA r w ★→★★★ Offers v.gd Ries at bargain prices; other wines are okay. Owned by Orlando Wyndham.

Riverina NSW Large-volume irrigated zone centred on Griffith. Its water supply will be better than the Murray Darling over next few yrs.

Robert Oatley Wines Mudgee, NSW r w Robert Oatley created ROSEMOUNT ESTATE, back when it was gd. Ambition burns anew. Initial releases weren't quite there but they are fast improving. Shiraz v.gd.

Rockford Barossa, SA r w sp ★★→★★★★ Small producer from old, low-yielding v'yds; reds best, also iconic sparkling Black Shiraz.

Rosemount Estate Upper Hunter V, NSW; McLaren Vale, Coonawarra, SA r w A major presence in production terms but a shadow of its former self quality-wise. Top end missing in action.

Rutherglen and **Glenrowan** Vic Two of four regions in the northeast Victoria zone, justly famous for weighty reds and magnificent fortified dessert wines.

St Hallett Barossa, SA r w ★★★ (Old Block) 86' 90' 91' 98 99' 01 02' 04 05' (06') Old Block Shiraz the star; rest of range is smooth, stylish. LION NATHAN-owned.

St Sheila's SA p sw sp 36 22 38 Full-bodied fizzer. Ripper grog, too.

Saltram Barossa, SA r w ★★→★★★ Mamre Brook (Shiraz, Cab Sauv, Chard) and No 1 Shiraz are leaders. An FWE brand.

Samuel's Gorge McLaren Vale, SA r Justin McNamee has hair like Sideshow Bob (*The Simpsons*) but is making Shiraz and Tempranillo of precision and place.

Sandalford Swan V, WA r w (br) ★→★★ Fine old winery with contrasting styles of red and white single-grape wines from SWAN VALLEY and MARGARET RIVER areas.

Savaterre Beechworth, Vic r w (Pinot N) 02 04' 06' Tough run of seasons (03 07 09) but a v.gd producer of Chard and Pinot N. Close-planted vines. Biodynamic practices. Winery a room of owner/winemaker Keppell Smith's house.

Scotchmans Hill Geelong, Vic r w ★★ Makes significant quantities of stylish Pinot N, gd Chard and spicy Shiraz.

Seppelt Bendigo, Grampians, Henty, Vic r w br sp (w sw) ★★★ (St Peter's Shiraz) 71' 85 86' 91' 96 97' 99' 04' 05' 06 (08) Now a specialist table wine producer for FWE with a v. impressive array of region-specific Ries, Chard, Shiraz and Cab Sauv.

Seppeltsfield Barossa, SA National Trust Heritage Winery purchased by KILLKANOON shareholders in 2007 and being restored to full working order. Priceless stocks of fortified wines in barrels dating back to 1878.

Setanta Wines Adelaide Hills, SA r w ★★★ The Sullivan family, first-generation Australians originally from Ireland, produces wonderful Ries, Chard, Sauv Bl, Shiraz and Cab Sauv with Irish mythology labels of striking design.

Sevenhill Clare V, SA r w (br) ★★ Owned by the Jesuitical Manresa Society since 1851. Consistently gd wine; Shiraz and Ries can be outstanding.

Seville Estate Yarra V, Vic r w ★★★ (Shiraz) 94 97' 99' 02' 04' 05' 06' (08) Ownership changes have not affected quality of Chard, Shiraz, Pinot N.

Shadowfax Geelong, Vic r w ★★→★★★ Stylish winery, part of Werribee Park; also hotel based on 1880s mansion. V.gd Chard, Pinot N, Shiraz.

Shaw & Smith Adelaide Hills, SA w (r) ★★★ Founded by Martin Shaw and Australia's first MW, Michael Hill-Smith. Crisp Sauv Bl, complex barrel-fermented M3 Chard and, of course, Shiraz.

Shelmerdine V'yds Heathcote, Yarra V, Vic r w ★★→★★★ Well-known family with v. elegant wines from estate in the YARRA VALLEY and HEATHCOTE.

Sirromet Queensland Coast r w ★★ A striking (100-ha) 100,000-case winery. Wines from 100-plus ha of estate v'yds in GRANITE BELT can be okay.

Smith, S & Sons (alias Yalumba) Barossa, SA r w br sp (w sw) ★★→★★★ Big, old family firm with considerable verve. *Full spectrum of high-quality wines*, inc HEGGIES, PEWSEY VALE and YALUMBA. Angas Brut, a gd-value sparkling wine, and Oxford Landing varietals are now world brands. In outstanding form.

South Burnett Queensland's second region: 15 wineries and more births (and some deaths) imminent, symptomatic of southeast corner of the state.

South Coast NSW Zone Includes Shoalhaven Coast and Southern Highlands.

Southcorp The former giant of the industry; now part of FWE. Owns LINDEMANS, PENFOLDS, ROSEMOUNT ESTATE, Seaview, SEPPELT, WYNNS and many others.

Southern NSW Zone inc CANBERRA, Gundagai, Hilltops, TUMBARUMBA.

Spinifex Barossa V, SA r ★★★ Small, high-quality producer of complex Shiraz and Grenache blends. Nothing over-the-top here. In the past 2 yrs it has pulled clearly ahead of the pack of new Aussie producers.

Stanton & Killeen Rutherglen, Vic r br ★★★ The sudden and untimely death of Chris Killeen in 2007 was a major blow to this fine producer of fortified and dry red wines but his children are carrying on as the 4th generation.

Stefano Lubiana South Tasmania r w sp ★★→★★★ Beautiful v'yds on the banks of the Derwent River 20 minutes from Hobart. V.gd Pinot N, sparkling and Chard.

Stella Bella Margaret R, WA r w ★★★ Labels and names shouldn't obscure quality commitment. Try Cab Sauv, Sem/Sauv Bl, Chard, Shiraz, Sangiovese/Cab Sauv.

Stonier Wines Mornington Pen, Vic r w ★★★ (Chard) 02 03' 04' 05 06' 07 (Pinot N) 00' 02' 04' 05 06' 07 (08) Consistently v.gd; Reserves notable for their elegance. Owned by LION NATHAN.

Sunbury see MACEDON.

Swan Valley WA Located 20 minutes north of Perth. Birthplace of wine in the west. Hot climate makes strong, low-acid wines; being rejuvenated for wine tourism.

Tahbilk Goulburn V, Vic r w ★★→★★★ (Marsanne) 74' 82' 92' 97' 99' 01' 03' 05' 06' 07' (Shiraz) 68' 71' 76' 86 98' 02 04' 05 06' Beautiful historic family estate: long-ageing reds, also Ries and *Marsanne*. Reserve Cab Sauv outstanding; value for money rich. Rare 1860 Vines Shiraz, too.

Taltarni Pyrenees, Vic r w (sp) Shiraz and Cab Sauv in best shape for yrs.

Tamar Ridge North Tasmania r w (sp) ★★→★★★ Public-company ownership, Dr Richard Smart as viticulturist, Dr Andrew Pirie as CEO/chief winemaker and 230-plus ha of vines make this a major player in TASMANIA. 75,000 cases.

Tapanappa SA r ★★★ New WRATTONBULLY collaboration between Brian Croser, Bollinger and J-M Cazes of Pauillac. To watch. Cab Sauv blend, Shiraz, Merlot. *Surprising Pinot N* from Fleurieu peninsula.

Tarrawarra Yarra V, Vic r w ★★★ (Chard) 02' 04' 05' 06' (Pinot N) 00' 01 02' 04' 05' 06' 08' Has moved from idiosyncratic to elegant, mainstream Chard and Pinot N. Tin Cows is the second label.

Tasmania Production continues to surge but still small. Outstanding sparkling Pinot N and Ries in cool climate, Chard, Sauv Bl and PINOT GR v.gd cool-climate styles, all in great demand.

Tatachilla McLaren Vale, SA r w ★★ Significant production of nice whites and v.gd reds. Acquired by LION NATHAN in 2002.

Taylors Wines Clare V, SA r w ★★ Large-scale production led by Ries, Shiraz, Cab Sauv. Exports under Wakefield Wines brand (trademark issues with Taylor's of Oporto) with much success.

Ten Minutes by Tractor Mornington Pen, Vic r w ★★★ Amusing name and sophisticated packaging rapidly growing under owner Martin Spedding. Sauv Bl, Chard, Pinot N are all v.gd.

Teusner Barossa V, SA r ★★ Old vines, clever winemaking, pure fruit flavours. Leads a BAROSSA VALLEY trend towards "more wood, no good". All about the grapes.

T'Gallant Mornington Pen, Vic w (r) Improbable name and avant-garde labels for Australia's best-known Pinot Gr producer. Quixotic acquisition by FWE.

Topaque Iconic fortified Australian (Rutherglen) wine Tokay gains a new name: Topaque. Don't confuse with topic. Name change the result of EU negotiations.

Torbreck Barossa, SA ★★★ r (w) The most stylish of the cult wineries beloved of the US; focus on old-vine Rhône varieties led by Shiraz. Rich, sweet, high alcohol.

Torzi Matthews Eden V, SA r Rich, stylish Shiraz. Lower-priced wines generally better. Torzi Schist Rock Shiraz difficult to say, politely, after a glass or two.

Trentham Estate Murray Darling (r) w ★★ 60,000 cases of family-grown and made, sensibly priced wines from "boutique" winery on Murray River; is building diversified portfolio from distinguished Victoria regions.

Tumbarumba Cool-climate NSW region nestled in the Australian Alps. Sites between 500 m and 800 m above sea level. Chard the star. Mandatory to add "cha-cha-cha" after saying "Tumbarumba".

Turkey Flat Barossa, SA r p ★★★ Fine producer of rosé, Grenache and Shiraz from core of 150-yr-old v'yd. Top stuff; controlled alcohol and oak (and price).

Two Hands Barossa, SA r ★★ Cult winery with top Shiraz from PADTHAWAY, MCLAREN VALE, Langhorne Creek, BAROSSA VALLEY and HEATHCOTE stuffed full of alcohol, rich fruit, oak and the kitchen sink.

Tyrrell's Hunter V, NSW r w ★★★★ (Sem) 99' 00' 01' 05' 07' (Vat 47 Chard) 00' 02 04 05' 07' Australia's greatest maker of Sem, Vat 1 now joined with a series of individual v'yd or subregional wines, one or more of which will stand out in any given vintage, hence the unusual vintage ratings for the Sems. Vat 47, too, continues to defy the climatic odds, albeit in a different style to LAKE'S FOLLY. Excellent old-vine 4 Acres Shiraz, too.

Upper Hunter NSW Established in early 1960s; irrigated vines (mainly whites), lighter and quicker developing than Lower Hunter's.

Vasse Felix Margaret R, WA r w ★★★ (Cab Sauv) 97 98 99' 01 04' 05' 07 With CULLEN, pioneer of MARGARET RIVER. Elegant Cab Sauv for mid-weight balance.

Voyager Estate Margaret R, WA r w ★★★ 35,000 cases of estate-grown, rich, powerful Sem, Sauv Bl, Chard, Cab Sauv/Merlot. New star of MARGARET RIVER.

Wendouree Clare V, SA r ★★★★ Treasured maker (tiny quantities) of powerful and concentrated reds, based on Shiraz, Cab Sauv, Mourvèdre and Malbec. Immensely long-lived, so much so that any wine less than 20 yrs old is unlikely to have reached maturity.

Prosecco heads south

The Italians don't like it but the Aussies are moving into Prosecco – with gusto. Over the past five years KING VALLEY producers BROWN BROTHERS, Dal Zotto, Sam Miranda and Chrismont have all planted Prosecco vines at altitude and produced Prosecco sparkling wines in the past yr. A proprietary bottle is in the pipeline. Prosecco is a grape variety, not a place. As a result, the Italian wine industry has moved to change the name of the grape to Glera, to protect Prosecco as a regional wine style. What the wines are actually called when they land in the UK will be interesting.

West Cape Howe Denmark, WA r w ★★ The minnow that swallowed the whale in 2009 when it purchased 7,700-tonne Goundrey winery and 237 ha of estate v'yds. V.gd Shiraz and Cab Sauv blends.

Willow Creek Mornington Pen, Vic r w ★★★ Impressive producer of Chard and Pinot N in particular. Ex-STONIER winemaker Geraldine McFaul recently took the helm.

Wilson Vinyard Clare V, SA r w ★★ Stylish Ries from CLARE VALLEY and adjoining Polish Hill River; Hand Plunge Shiraz and Cab Sauv often of gd quality.

Wirra Wirra McLaren Vale, SA r w (w sw sp) ★★★ (RSW Shiraz) 98' 99' 02' 04' 05' 06' (Cab Sauv) 97' 98' 01' 02' 04' 05' 06' High-quality wines making a big impact. RSW Shiraz has edged in front of Cab Sauv; both superb. The Angelus Cab Sauv now Dead Ringer in export markets.

Wolf Blass Barossa, SA r w (br sw sp) ★★★ (Cab Sauv blend) 90' 91' 96' 98' 02' 04' 05 06' Now swallowed up by FWE. Not the player it once was.

Woodlands Margaret R, WA r (w) ★★★→★★★★ 7 ha of 30+-yr-old Cab Sauv among top v'yds in region, plus younger but still v.gd plantings of other Bordeaux reds. Family owned; single-barrel Rés du Cave releases are on their own.

Wrattonbully SA Important grape-growing region in LIMESTONE COAST ZONE for 30 yrs; profile lifted by recent arrival of TAPANAPPA.

Wynns Coonawarra, SA r w ★★★ (Shiraz) 55' 63 86' 90' 91' 94' 96' 98 99' 02 04' 05' 06 (Cab Sauv) 57' 60' 82' 85' 86' 90' 91' 94' 96' 98' 00 02 04' 05' 06 07 Foster's-owned COONAWARRA classic. Ries, Chard, Shiraz and *Cab Sauv* are all v.gd, esp *John Riddoch Cab Sauv* and Michael Shiraz. In top form.

Yabby Lake Mornington Pen, Vic r w Joint venture between movie magnate Robert Kirby, Larry McKenna (ex-Martinborough) and Tod Dexter. Quality on the up.

Yalumba See S SMITH & SONS.

Yarra Burn Yarra V, Vic r w sp ★★→★★★ Estate making Sem, Sauv Bl, Chard, sparkling Pinot N/Chard/Pinot Meunier. Acquired by HARDYS in 1995. Bastard Hill Chard and Pinot N legitimate flag-bearers.

Yarra Valley Vic Historic area near Melbourne. Growing emphasis on v. successful Pinot N, Chard, Shiraz and sparkling. The 2007 discovery of phylloxera could pose challenges down the track.

Yarra Yarra Yarra V, Vic r w ★★★ Recently increased to 7 ha, giving greater access to fine Sem/Sauv Bl and Cab Sauv, each in classic Bordeaux style.

Yarra Yering Yarra V, Vic r w ★★★→★★★★ (Dry Reds) 80' 81' 82' 83 84 85' 90' 91' 93' 94 97' 99' 00 01 02' 04' 05' 06' (08) Best-known Lilydale boutique winery. Esp racy, powerful Pinot N; deep, herby Cab Sauv (Dry Red No 1); Shiraz (Dry Red No 2). Luscious, daring flavours in red and white. Much-admired founder/owner Bailey Carrodus died in 2008. Acquired in 2009 by KAESLER.

Yellow Tail See CASELLA.

Yeringberg Yarra V, Vic r w ★★★ (Marsanne) 91' 92 94' 95 97 98 00 02' 04 05 06' (Cab Sauv) 77' 80 81' 84' 88' 90 97' 98 00' 02 04 05' 06' Dreamlike historic estate still in the hands of founding family. Makes small quantities of v. high-quality Marsanne, Roussanne, Chard, Cab Sauv and Pinot N.

Yering Station/Yarrabank Yarra V, Vic r w sp ★★ On site of Victoria's first v'yd; replanted after 80-yr gap. Extraordinary joint venture: Yering Station table wines (Reserve Chard, Pinot N, Shiraz, Viognier); Yarrabank (esp fine sparkling wines for Champagne Devaux).

Zema Estate Coonawarra, SA r ★★ One of the last bastions of hand-pruning in COONAWARRA; silkily powerful, disarmingly straightforward reds.

NB Vintages in colour are those you should choose first for drinking in 2011.

New Zealand

More heavily shaded areas are the
wine-growing regions

Sauvignon Blanc still rules in New Zealand: well over half of all New
Zealand wine is not just Sauvignon Blanc, but Sauvignon Blanc from
one region: Marlborough. In Australia, Oyster Bay Marlborough Sauvignon
Blanc is the most popular white wine of all, beating all home-grown whites,
to the consternation of the Australians. (The price-cutting that helped to put
it there doesn't please producers of Australian Sauvignon, either.) Nobilo
has recently topped the Sauvignon Blanc sales charts in the USA.

But after two decades of relentless growth, there's an air of caution
in the NZ wine industry. Between 2000 and 2009, the country's area
of bearing vineyards tripled, its production soared from less than
seven million cases to more than 22 million, and 300 new wineries
opened for business. Exports expanded at an exhilarating rate, from
NZ$125 million to NZ$1 billion, but still not fast enough to keep pace
with the surging output. The bumper 2008 crop, a 39 per cent leap
on the previous record, was followed by an equally large 2009 vintage.

A recent major concern is a trend to bulk wine exports, cannibalizing
the sale of bottled wine and threatening to undermine New Zealand's
super-premium reputation and prices. Pinot Noir from Central Otago
is suddenly everywhere, with most producers launching increasingly
affordable second- and third-tier labels. Hawke's Bay reds, both
Cabernet/Merlot blends and Syrahs, are winning international acclaim
and offer good value.

Recent vintages

2009 Another large crop. A favourably dry autumn produced aromatic, intense
and zingy Marlborough Sauv Bl and concentrated, ripe Hawke's Bay reds.
Central Otago frosty and cool, with variable Pinot N.

2008 Heaviest-yielding vintage of the decade. A warm growing season and
heavy autumn rains in Marlborough led to many wines of below-average

quality; growers who picked early fared best. Regular autumn rainfall also caused variable quality in Hawke's Bay.

2007 Notably dry autumn yielded excellent wines in Hawke's Bay and Gisborne, and punchy, ripe, slightly lower-alcohol Marlborough Sauvignon Bl.

2006 In the North Island some reds were caught by autumn rains. Average to good Marlborough Sauvignon Bl; some lack pungency.

Akarua Central Otago ★★ Respected producer with powerful, concentrated Cadence Pinot N, crisp, citrus, slightly nutty Chard and full-bodied, dry, spicy Pinot Gr. Supple, charming 2nd-tier Pinot N labelled Gullies.

Allan Scott Marlborough ★★ V.gd Ries (from vines up to 30 yrs old), elegant, fruit-focused Chard, tropical fruit-flavoured Sauv Bl; sturdy, spicy Pinot N.

Alpha Domus Hawke's Bay ★★ Gd Chard and concentrated reds, esp savoury Merlot-based The Navigator, and notably dark, rich Cab Sauv-based The Aviator. Top wines labelled AD.

Amisfield Central Otago ★★ Impressive, fleshy, smooth Pinot Gr; tense, minerally Ries (dry and sw); and floral, complex Pinot N. Lake Hayes is lower-tier label.

Astrolabe Marlborough ★★ Label part-owned by WHITEHAVEN winemaker Simon Waghorn. Strikingly intense, harmonious Sauv Bl. Awatere Valley Sauv Bl is more herbaceous.

Ata Rangi Martinborough ★★★ Small but highly respected winery. *Outstanding Pinot N* (05 06' 07 08 09) is one of NZ's greatest, and v.gd young-vine Crimson Pinot N. Rich, concentrated Craighall Chard and Lismore Pinot Gr.

Auckland Largest city in NZ. Henderson, Huapai, Kumeu, Matakana, Clevedon, Waiheke Island districts – pricey, variable but often classy Bordeaux-style reds, rich, earthy Syrah and ripe, rounded Chard – nearby.

Awatere Valley Marlborough Fast-expanding subregion, slightly cooler and drier than the larger WAIRAU VALLEY, with racy, herbaceous, minerally Sauv Bl and scented, slightly leafy Pinot N.

Babich Henderson (Auckland) ★★–★★★★ Mid-size family firm, established 1916; quality, value. AUCKLAND, HAWKE'S BAY, MARLBOROUGH v'yds. Refined, slow-maturing Irongate Chard (06 07'); elegant Irongate Cab/Merlot/Cab Fr (single v'yd). Ripe, dry Marlborough Sauv Bl is big seller. Mid-tier Winemaker's Reserve.

Bald Hills Central Otago ★★ Bannockburn v'yd with crisp, dryish Pinot Gr; floral, slightly sweet Ries and generous, savoury Pinot N.

Bilancia Hawke's Bay ★★ Small producer of classy Syrah (inc brilliant hill-grown La Collina) and rich Viognier, Pinot Gr.

Blackenbrook Nelson ★★ Small winery with perfumed, rich Gewurz, Pinot Gr, Ries; punchy Sauv Bl; sturdy, generous Pinot N. St Jacques is second label.

Borthwick Wairarapa ★★ Lively, tropical-fruit-flavoured Sauv Bl; rich, dryish Ries; peachy, toasty Chard and *gd Pinot N*.

Brancott V'yds ★–★★★★ Brand used by PERNOD RICARD NZ in US.

Brightwater Nelson ★★ Impressive whites, esp crisp, flavour-packed Ries and Sauv Bl. Top wines labelled Lord Rutherford.

Brookfields Hawke's Bay ★★ Excellent "gold label" Cab Sauv/Merlot; gd Chard, Pinot Gr, Gewurz and Syrah.

Cable Bay Waiheke Island ★★ Mid-sized producer with tight, refined Waiheke Chard and spicy, savoury Five Hills red; subtle, finely textured Marlborough Sauv Bl. Second label is Culley.

Canterbury NZ's 4th-largest wine region; most of its top v'yds are in warm, sheltered Waipara district. Long, dry summers favour Pinot N, Ries.

Carrick Central Otago ★★ Bannockburn winery with flinty, flavourful whites (Pinot Gr, Sauv Bl, Chard, Ries) and densely packed Pinot N, built to last. Second-tier Unravelled Pinot N is also sturdy and rich.

Central Otago (r) 07 08 (w) 08 Fast-expanding cool, mountainous region (now NZ's 5th-largest) in southern South Island. Scented, crisp Ries and Pinot Gr; Pinot N perfumed and silky, with intense character.

Chard Farm Central Otago ★★ Fresh, *vibrant Ries*, Pinot Gr and perfumed, graceful, supple Pinot N. Also light, smooth Rabbit Ranch Pinot N.

Cheviot Hills Promising new subregion in the South Island, north of Waipara in North Canterbury, pioneered by Mt Beautiful.

Church Road Hawke's Bay ★★→★★★ PERNOD RICARD NZ winery. Rich, refined Chard and elegant, *distinctly Bordeaux-like Merlot/Cab Sauv*. Top Reserve wines; prestige claret-style red TOM (02'). New mid-priced Cuve range is superb quality and value. Magnificent new TOM Chard (06').

Churton Marlborough ★★ Subtle, complex, finely textured Sauv Bl; fragrant, spicy, v. harmonious Pinot N.

Clayridge Marlborough ★★ Distinctive wines showing complexity and strong personality. Excalibur range (top, more oak-influenced), inc refined, rich, silky Pinot N.

Clearview Hawke's Bay ★★→★★★ Burly, lush, super-charged Reserve Chard; dark, rich Reserve Cab Fr, Enigma (Merlot-based), Old Olive Block (Cab Sauv blend).

Clifford Bay Marlborough ★★ AWATERE VALLEY producer. Scented, intense Sauv Bl is best. Now linked to VAVASOUR.

Clos Henri Marlborough ★★→★★★ Established by Henri Bourgeois (see France). First vintage 2003. Deliciously weighty, rounded Sauv Bl and vibrant, supple Pinot N. Second label: Bel Echo.

Cloudy Bay Marlborough ★★★ Large-volume Sauv Bl (dry, finely textured), Chard (robust, complex, crisp) and Pinot N (floral, supple) are v.gd. Pelorus vintage-dated sparkling toasty, rich. Rarer Gewurz, Late Harvest Ries and Te Koko (oak-aged Sauv Bl) now the finest wines. Owned by LVMH.

Constellation New Zealand Auckland ★→★★ NZ's 2nd-largest wine company, previously Nobilo Wine Group, now owned by Constellation Brands. Nobilo Marlborough Sauv Bl is solid, sharply priced. Superior varietals labelled Nobilo Icon; v.gd Drylands Sauv Bl. See KIM CRAWFORD, MONKEY BAY, SELAKS.

Cooper's Creek Auckland ★★ Excellent Swamp Reserve Chard; v.gd Sauv Bl, Ries; Merlot, top-value Viognier; debut Grüner Veltliner 2008 (NZ's first). SV (Select V'yd) range is mid-tier.

Corbans Auckland ★→★★★ PERNOD RICARD NZ brand. Best: Cottage Block; Private Bin. Quality from basic to outstanding (esp Cottage Block Hawke's Bay Chard).

Craggy Range Hawke's Bay ★★→★★★ Mid-sized winery with v'yds in MARTINBOROUGH and HAWKE'S BAY. Restrained Sauv Bl, *stylish Chard*, Pinot N; strikingly dense, ripe, firm Merlot and Syrah (esp majestic Le Sol) from GIMBLETT GRAVELS. Cheaper regional blends labelled Wild Rock.

Delegat's Auckland ★★ Large, fast-expanding company, still mostly family-owned. V'yds and other big wineries in HAWKE'S BAY and MARLBOROUGH. Reserve Chard and Cab Sauv/Merlot offer v.gd quality and value. Hugely successful OYSTER BAY brand.

Delta Marlborough ★★ Promising young producer with substantial, graceful Pinot N. Top label: Hatter's Hill.

Destiny Bay Waiheke Island ★★★ Expatriate Americans produce expensive Bordeaux-style reds: lush, brambly and silky. Part of Specialist Winegrowers of NZ: five top-end companies.

Deutz Auckland ★★★ Champagne company gives name to fine sparkling from MARLBOROUGH by PERNOD RICARD NZ. NV: lively, yeasty, intense. Vintage Blanc de Blancs: finely focused, citrusy, piercing. Rosé: crisp, yeasty, strawberryish.

Dog Point Marlborough ★★ Grape-grower Ivan Sutherland and winemaker James Healy (both ex-CLOUDY BAY) produce unusually complex, finely textured, oak-aged Sauv Bl (Section 94), Chard and *Pinot N*. Also limey, smooth, unoaked Sauv Bl.

Dry River Martinborough ★★★ Tiny winery, now American-owned. Penetrating, long-lived Chard, Ries, Pinot Gr, Gewurz and notably ripe, powerful, slowly evolving Pinot N (03' **05 06'** 07).

Escarpment Martinborough ★★ Sturdy, Alsace-like Pinot Gr and complex, concentrated Pinot N from Larry McKenna, ex-MARTINBOROUGH V'YD. Top label: Kupe. Single-v'yd reds launched from 2006.

Esk Valley Hawke's Bay ★★→★★★ Owned by VILLA MARIA. Some of NZ's most voluptuous Merlot-based reds (esp Winemakers – formerly Reserve – label 06' 07'), excellent Merlot/Malbec rosé (NZ's best), satisfying Chards, Chenin Bl and Sauv Bl.

Fairhall Downs Marlborough ★★ Single-v'yd wines from elevated site. Weighty, dry Pinot Gr, intense, racy Sauv Bl and perfumed, smooth Pinot N.

Felton Road Central Otago ★★★ Star winery in warm Bannockburn area. Bold, supple, graceful Pinot N Block 3 and 5, and light, intense Ries outstanding; excellent Chard and regular Pinot N.

Fiddler's Green Waipara ★★ Flavourful, crisp, cool-climate Chard, Ries, Sauv Bl; vibrant, Pinot N. New Glasnevin brand includes scented, rich Pinot Gr.

Forrest Marlborough ★★ Mid-size winery; easy-drinking Chard, gd Sauv Bl and Ries; gorgeous botrytized Ries; flavour-crammed Hawke's Bay Newton/ Forrest Cornerstone (Bordeaux red blend). Distinguished flagship range John Forrest Collection. Popular low-alcohol Ries under The Doctors' label.

Foxes Island Marlborough ★★ Small producer of rich, smooth Chard, finely textured Sauv Bl and elegant, supple Pinot N. Gd, large-volume Sauv Bl and Pinot N under Seven Terraces brand.

Framingham Marlborough ★★ Owned by Sogrape (see Portugal). Superb aromatic whites, notably intense, *zesty Ries* and lush, slightly sweet Pinot Gr, Gewurz. Subtle, dry Sauv Bl. Scented, silky Pinot N.

Fromm Marlborough ★★★ Swiss-founded, focusing initially on powerful tannic but now more charming red wines. Sturdy, long-lived Pinot N, esp under Fromm V'yd and *Clayvin V'yd* labels. Also unusually stylish Clayvin Chard. Earlier-drinking La Strada range also v.gd, inc deliciously fruity, supple Syrah.

Gibbston Valley Central Otago ★★ Pioneer winery with popular restaurant. Greatest strength is Pinot N, esp rich, complex CENTRAL OTAGO regional blend and robust, exuberantly fruity Reserve (**06**). Racy local whites, esp zingy, flavour-packed, medium-dry Ries.

Giesen Canterbury ★ German family winery. Gd, slightly honeyed Ries; bulk of production is average-quality MARLBOROUGH Sauv Bl.

Gimblett Gravels Hawke's Bay Defined area with v. free-draining soils, noted for rich, ripe Bordeaux-style reds and Syrah. Best of both are world-class.

Gisborne (r) 07' 09' (w) 07' 09' NZ's 3rd-largest region. Abundant sunshine and rain, with fertile soils. Key strength is Chard (typically deliciously fragrant, ripe and soft in its youth). Gd Gewurz and Viognier; Merlot more variable.

Gladstone Wairarapa ★→★★ Tropical fruit-flavoured Sauv Bl and dry, weighty Pinot Gr under top label, Gladstone; 12,000 Miles is lower-priced brand.

Goldwater Waiheke Island ★★→★★★ Region's pioneer Cab Sauv/Merlot Goldie (05') has Médoc-like finesse. Also full-flavoured, finely balanced Chard and ripe, non-herbaceous Sauv Bl from MARLBOROUGH. Now American-owned.

Gravitas Marlborough ★★ Solid Chard (Reserve and Unoaked), subtle, sustained Sauv Bl and graceful, flowing Pinot N. Second label: Wandering Piano.

Greenhough Nelson ★★→★★★ One of region's top producers, with immaculate and deep-flavoured Ries, Sauv Bl, Chard, Pinot N. Top label: Hope V'yd.

Greystone Waipara ★★ Stylish, aromatic Riesl, Gewurz, Pinot Gr; promising Pinot N.

Greywacke Marlborough ★★ New label of Kevin Judd, ex-CLOUDY BAY. First 2009 Sauv Bl is tight, elegant, lingering.

Grove Mill Marlborough ★★ Attractive whites, inc vibrant Chard; excellent Ries, Sauv and slightly sweet Pinot Gr. Reds less enjoyable. Gd lower-tier Sanctuary brand. First winery to earn carboNZero certification.

Hans Herzog Marlborough ★★★ Established by Swiss immigrants. Power-packed, classy Merlot/Cab Sauv, Montepulciano, Pinot N, Chard, Viognier and Pinot Gr; fleshy, rich Sauv Bl. Sold under Hans brand in Europe and US.

Hawke's Bay (r) 05' 05 06 07' 09' (w) 07 NZ's 2nd-largest region. Long history of winemaking in sunny, warm climate; shingly and heavier soils. Full, rich Merlot and Cab Sauv-based reds in gd vintages; Syrah a fast-rising star; powerful Chard; rounded Sauv Bl; NZ's best Viognier.

Highfield Marlborough ★★ Japanese-owned with quality Ries, Chard, Sauv Bl and Pinot N. Elstree sparkling variable lately; can be almost Champagne-like.

Huia Marlborough ★★ Mouthfilling, subtle wines that age well, inc savoury, rounded Chard, sturdy, dryish Pinot Gr and perfumed, well-spiced Gewurz.

Hunter's Marlborough ★★→★★★ Pioneering winery (since 1982) with intense, immaculate, dry Sauv Bl. *Fine, delicate Chard.* Excellent sparkling (MiruMiru), Ries, Gewurz; light, elegant Pinot N.

Isabel Estate Marlborough ★→★★ Family estate with formerly outstanding Pinot N, Sauv Bl and Chard, but lately less exciting.

Jackson Estate Marlborough ★★ Rich, ripe, full-flavoured Sauv Bl, attractive, fruit-driven Chard and sweet-fruited, supple Pinot N (much improved since 2005, esp top-tier Gum Emperor Pinot N).

Johanneshof Marlborough ★→★★ Small, low-profile winery with outstandingly perfumed, lush Gewurz. Other wines more variable.

Julicher Martinborough ★★ Small, consistently excellent producer of scented, tangy, dry Ries and generous, complex Pinot N. (99 Rows is 2nd tier and gd value.)

Karikari Northland ★★ NZ's northernmost v'yd and winery, US-owned. Rich, ripe Bordeaux-style reds, Pinotage, Syrah. Robust, creamy-smooth Chard.

Kemblefield Hawke's Bay ★→★★ US-owned. Mid-tier The Distinction range includes ripely herbal, oak-aged Sauv Bl; soft, peppery Gewurz; fleshy, lush Chard.

Kim Crawford Hawke's Bay ★★ Now part of US-based CONSTELLATION empire. Easy-drinking wines, inc rich, oaky Gisborne Chard and scented, strong-flavoured Marlborough Sauv Bl. Top range labelled SP (Small Parcel).

Kumeu River Auckland ★★→★★★ Rich, refined Kumeu Estate Chard (07 08') single-v'yd Mate's V'yd Chard even more opulent. Two new single-v'yd Chards in 2006. Weighty, floral Pinot Gr; tropical-fruit-flavoured, dry MARLBOROUGH Sauv Bl. Second label: Kumeu River Village.

Lake Chalice Marlborough ★★ Small producer with vibrant, creamy Chard and incisive, slightly sweet Ries; v.gd-quality Sauv Bl. Platinum premium label.

Lawson's Dry Hills Marlborough ★★→★★★ Weighty wines with intense flavours. Unusually complex Sauv Bl and *opulent Gewurz*; gd Pinot Gr and Ries.

Plentiful Pinot

Pinot N yields NZ's most sought-after reds, esp from CENTRAL OTAGO, where it accounts for more than 75% of all vines. In 2008 the region's 100-plus wineries produced more than 500,000 cases of Pinot N. Some was snapped up by wineries based further north, eager to add Central Otago Pinot Noir to their export portfolio; some was sold unbranded on the domestic market at NZ$14.95 (under £7). When made from young or heavily cropped vines, with little or no oak, these are drink-young reds, offering a Beaujolais-like simplicity and charm.

Lincoln Auckland ★→★★ Long-established family winery. New export brand: Distant Land (includes smooth, easy HAWKE'S BAY Sauv Bl and high-flavoured MARLBOROUGH Sauv Bl).

Lindauer See PERNOD RICARD NZ.

Mahi Marlborough ★★ Stylish, complex, mostly single-v'yd wines from Brian Bicknell, ex-SERESIN winemaker. Finely textured Sauv Bl, Chard and Pinot N.

Margrain Martinborough ★★ Small winery with firm, concentrated Chard, Ries, Pinot Gr, Gewurz and Pinot N, all of which reward bottle-ageing.

Marlborough (r) 07 09' (w) 09' NZ's largest region (more than half of all plantings). Warm days and cold nights give aromatic, crisp whites. Intense Sauv Bl, from sharp, green capsicum to ripe tropical fruit. Fresh, limey Ries (inc recent wave of low-alcohol wines); v. promising Pinot Gr and Gewurz; Chard leaner, more appley than HAWKE'S BAY. High-quality sparkling and botrytized Ries. Pinot N underrated, top examples among NZ's finest.

Martinborough (r) 07 08' 09 (w) 08' 09 Small, high-quality area in south WAIRARAPA (foot of North Island). Warm summers, dry autumns, gravelly soils. Success with white grapes but renowned for sturdy, rich, long-lived Pinot N.

Martinborough V'yd Martinborough ★★★ Distinguished small winery; one of NZ's *top Pinot N* (06' 07'). Rich, biscuity Chard and intense Ries. Also single-v'yd Burnt Spur and drink-young Te Tera ranges (top-value Pinot N).

Matakana Estate Auckland ★→★★ Largest producer in Matakana district. Powerful, complex Chard, rich, dry Pinot Gr and spicy, earthy Syrah. Often plain but improving lower-tier Goldridge range.

Matariki Hawke's Bay ★★ Stylish white and red, large v'yds in stony Gimblett Road. Rich Sauv Bl; tight, concentrated Chard; robust Quintology red blend. Reserve is top range; Aspire is for everyday drinking.

Matua Valley Auckland ★→★★ Producer of NZ's first Sauv Bl in 1974. Now owned by Foster's Group, with v'yds in four regions. Top range Ararimu, inc fat, savoury Chard and dark, rich Merlot. Many attractive GISBORNE (esp Judd Chard), HAWKE'S BAY and MARLBOROUGH wines. Shingle Peak Sauv Bl top value.

Mills Reef Bay of Plenty ★★→★★★ The Preston family produces impressive wines from HAWKE'S BAY grapes. Top Elspeth range includes dense, rich Bordeaux-style reds and Syrah. Reserve range reds also impressive and outstanding value.

Millton Gisborne ★★→★★★★ Region's top small winery: wines certified organic. Hill-grown single-v'yd Clos de Ste Anne range (Chard, Viognier, Syrah, Pinot N) is v. concentrated and full of personality. *Rich, long-lived Chenin Bl* is NZ's finest (honeyed in wetter vintages; tight, pure and long-lived in drier yrs).

Mission Hawke's Bay ★→★★ NZ's oldest wine producer, established 1851, still run by Catholic Society of Mary. Solid varietals: creamy-smooth Chard is esp gd value. Reserve range includes gd Bordeaux-style reds, Syrah and Chard. Top label: Jewelstone (v. classy, concentrated Chard).

Monkey Bay ★ CONSTELLATION NZ brand, modestly priced and v. popular in US. Easy-drinking, dryish Chard; gently sweet Sauv Bl; light Pinot Gr; leafy, slightly sweet Cab/Merlot; fresh, fruity Merlot.

Montana Auckland ★→★★★ A key brand of PERNOD RICARD NZ. Top wines are Letter Series (eg. "B" Brancott Sauv Bl). Showcase Series is 2nd tier, followed by Reserve. Big-selling varietals include peachy Gisborne Unoaked Chard, crisp, grassy Marlborough Sauv Bl and floral, smooth South Island Pinot N. "Icon" project aims to take Sauvignon Bl to another level.

Morton Estate Bay of Plenty ★→★★ Mid-size producer with v'yds in HAWKE'S BAY and MARLBOROUGH. Refined Black Label Chard. White Label Chard and Premium Brut v.gd and top value. Reds less exciting.

Mount Riley Marlborough ★→★★ Fast-growing. Easy-drinking Chard; punchy Sauv Bl; dark, flavoursome Merlot/Malbec. Top range is Seventeen Valley.

Sauv Bl; dark, flavoursome Merlot/Malbec. Top range is Seventeen Valley.

Mt Difficulty Central Otago ★★ Quality producer in relatively hot Bannockburn area. Best-known for v. refined, intense Pinot N (Roaring Meg is for early consumption; Single V'yd Pipeclay Terrace is dense, lasting). Classy whites (Ries, Pinot Gr).

Muddy Water Waipara ★★ Small, high-quality producer with beautifully intense Ries, minerally Chard and savoury, subtle Pinot N (esp Slowhand).

Mud House Canterbury ★★ Large, fast-expanding WAIPARA-based winery. Brands include Mud House (top range is Swan), Hay Maker (lower tier), Waipara Hills. Punchy, vibrant, herbaceous Marlborough Sauv Bl; intense, racy Waipara Ries.

Nautilus Marlborough ★★ Small range of distributors Négociants (NZ), owned by S Smith & Sons (see Australia). Top wines include stylish, finely balanced Sauv Bl, savoury Pinot N and fragrant, classy sparkler. Lower tier: Twin Islands. Mid-tier: Opawa Pinot N – floral, supple, charming.

Nelson (r) 07 09 (w) 09 Small, steadily expanding region west of MARLBOROUGH; climate wetter but equally sunny. Clay soils of Upper Moutere hills and silty Waimea plains. Strengths in aromatic whites, esp Ries, Sauv Bl, Pinot Gr, Gewurz; also gd Chard and Pinot N.

Neudorf Nelson ★★★ A top smallish winery. Powerful yet elegant *Moutere Chard* (06 07) is one of NZ's greatest; superb, v. savoury Moutere Pinot N. Sauv Bl and Ries also top-flight.

Ngatarawa Hawke's Bay ★★→★★★ Mid-sized. Top Alwyn range, inc powerful Chard and dark, generous Merlot/Cab. Mid-range Glazebrook also excellent.

Nga Waka Martinborough ★★ Steely whites of high quality. Outstanding bone-dry Sauv Bl; piercingly flavoured Ries; robust, savoury Chard. Pinot N scented and supple. Three Paddles is 2nd tier; gd value.

Nobilo See CONSTELLATION NZ.

Obsidian Waiheke Island ★★ V. stylish Bordeaux blend, Viognier and Chard under top brand Obsidian. Gd-value Waiheke reds (inc Syrah and Montepulciano) under 2nd-tier Weeping Sands label.

Olssens Central Otago ★★ Consistently attractive Pinot N, from first Bannockburn v'yd. Softly seductive, rich Jackson Barry Pinot N is mid-tier; top wine is bold Slapjack Creek Reserve Pinot N.

Omaka Springs Marlborough ★→★★ Punchy, herbaceous Sauv Bl (esp Falveys), solid Ries, Chard and leafy reds.

Oyster Bay Marlborough ★★ From DELEGAT'S, this huge-selling brand now exceeds 1.5 million cases. Vibrant, elegant, fruit-driven wines, mostly from Sauv Bl, Chard and Pinot N.

Palliser Martinborough ★★→★★★ One of the area's largest and best wineries. Superb-tropical fruit-flavoured Sauv Bl, excellent Chard, Ries, Pinot N. Top wines: Palliser Estate. Lower tier: Pencarrow (not always MARTINBOROUGH).

Paritua Hawke's Bay ★→★★ Fast-expanding American-owned producer. Stone Paddock brand for lower-tier blends; top wines, labelled Paritua, include refined, creamy, nutty Chard and excellent Bordeaux-style reds since 2007.

Pask, C J Hawke's Bay ★★ Mid-size winery, extensive v'yds in GIMBLETT GRAVELS. Gd Chard. Cab Sauv, Syrah and Merlot-based reds now consistently impressive and fine value. Top wines labelled Declaration.

Passage Rock Waiheke Island ★★ Powerful, densely coloured, opulent Syrah, esp Reserve.

Pegasus Bay Waipara ★★★ Small but distinguished range: notably taut, cool-climate Chard; *complex, oaked Sauv Bl*/Sem; rich, zingy, medium Ries. Merlot-based reds are region's finest. Pinot N lush and silky (esp old-vine Prima Donna). Second label: Main Divide.

Peregrine Central Otago ★★ Crisp, cool-climate Ries, Pinot Gr, Gewurz and

Pernod Ricard New Zealand Auckland ★→★★★ NZ wine giant, formerly called MONTANA. Wineries in AUCKLAND, GISBORNE, HAWKE'S BAY and MARLBOROUGH. Extensive co-owned v'yds for MARLBOROUGH whites, inc top-value Montana Sauv Bl (Reserve range esp gd). Strength in sparkling, inc DEUTZ, and huge volume, moderately yeasty, fine-value Lindauer. Elegant CHURCH ROAD reds and quality Chard. Other key brands: CORBANS, Saints, STONELEIGH. Triplebank offers intense, racy AWATERE VALLEY wines; Camshorn is gd Waipara Ries and Pinot N. New chief winemaker in 2010: Patrick Materman.

Providence Auckland ★★★ Rare Merlot and Cabernet Fr-based red from Matakana district. Perfumed, lush and silky; v. high-priced.

Puriri Hills Auckland ★★ Silky, seductive Merlot-based reds from Clevedon. Reserve is esp rich and plump, with more new oak.

Quartz Reef Central Otago ★★ Quality producer with weighty, flinty Pinot Gr; rich Pinot N; yeasty, lingering, *Champagne-like sparkler* (vintage esp gd).

Rimu Grove Nelson ★★ Small American-owned coastal v'yd. Concentrated, minerally Chard and Pinot Gr; rich, spicy Pinot N. Bronte range has drink-young charm.

Rippon V'yd Central Otago ★★ Stunning v'yd on shores of Lake Wanaka. Fine-scented, fruity Pinot N (Jeunesse from younger vines) and slowly evolving whites, inc steely, appley Ries.

Rockburn Central Otago ★★ Crisp, racy Chard, Pinot Gr, Gewurz, Ries, Sauv Bl. Fragrant, supple, rich Pinot N is best and an emerging star.

Sacred Hill Hawke's Bay ★★→★★★ Mid-size producer, partly Chinese-owned. Distinguished Riflemans Chard (powerful but refined, from cool, elevated site) and dark, rich Brokenstone Merlot. Punchy Marlborough V'yds Sauv Bl. Other brands: Gunn Estate (lush Skeetfield Chard), Wild South (MARLBOROUGH range), *Helmsman* (Gimblett Gravels).

Saint Clair Marlborough ★★→★★★ Fast-growing, export-led producer with substantial v'yds. Acclaimed Sauv Bl, fragrant Ries, easy Chard and plummy, early drinking Merlot. Rich Reserve Chard, Merlot, Pinot N. Exceedingly intense Wairau Reserve Sauv Bl. Bewildering array of 2nd-tier Pioneer Block wines (inc seven Sauv Bls). Vicar's Choice is lower tier, gd value.

St Helena Canterbury ★ The region's oldest winery, founded near Christchurch in 1978. Low profile in NZ, but exports crisp MARLBOROUGH Sauv Bl in bulk.

Seifried Estate Nelson ★★ Region's biggest winery. Known initially for Ries and Gewurz; now also producing gd-value, often excellent Sauv Bl and Chard. Best wines: Winemakers Collection. Old Coach Road is 3rd tier. Plain reds.

Selaks Marlborough ★→★★★ Now a brand of CONSTELLATION NZ. Moderately priced, fruit-driven MARLBOROUGH Sauv Bl, Ries, Chard under Premium Selection label are its traditional strengths; reds are plain but improving. Top: Founders Reserve. Emerging mid-tier, Winemaker's Favourite, offers great quality/value.

Seresin Marlborough ★★→★★★ Established by NZ film producer Michael Seresin. V. stylish, concentrated Sauv Bl, Chard, Pinots N and Gr, Ries; 2nd tier: Momo (gd quality/value). Overall, complex, finely textured wines.

Sherwood Waipara ★→★★ Family-owned firm with three brands – Clearwater (Waipara), Sherwood (Waipara or MARLBOROUGH) and Stratum (cheap).

Sileni Hawke's Bay ★★ Architecturally striking winery with extensive v'yds and classy Chard, Merlot and Marlborough Sauv Bl. Top wines: rare EV (Exceptional Vintage), then a range with individual names, followed by Cellar Selection. Rich, smooth MARLBOROUGH Sauv Bl (esp The Straits).

Southbank Hawke's Bay ★→★★★Creamy, rich Hawke's Bay Chard and penetrating Marlborough Sauv Bl are best. Other brands: Crossroads (HAWKE'S BAY) and The Crossings (MARLBOROUGH).

Spy Valley Marlborough ★★→★★★ High-achieving company with extensive v'yds.

Spy Valley Marlborough ★★→★★★ High-achieving company with extensive v'yds. Sauv Bl, Chard, Ries, Gewurz, Pinot Gr and Pinot N are all v.gd and priced right. Superb top selection: Envoy (inc rich yet subtle Chard and Mosel-like Ries).

Staete Landt Marlborough ★★ Dutch immigrants, producing v. refined Chard, Sauv Bl and Pinot Gr, and graceful, supple Pinot N.

Stonecroft Hawke's Bay ★★→★★★ Small winery. NZ's first serious Syrah (since 1989), more Rhône than Oz. Outstanding Chard, v. rich Old Vine Gewurz.

Stoneleigh ★★ Owned by PERNOD RICARD NZ. Impressive MARLBOROUGH whites (inc punchy, tropical-fruit Sauv Bl, refined, medium-dry Ries and creamy-smooth Chard) and Pinot N, esp Rapaura Series.

Stonyridge Waiheke Island ★★★ Boutique winery. Famous for exceptional Bordeaux-style red, Larose (00' **04' 05'** 06 07 08' 09). Also powerful, dense Rhône-style blend Pilgrim and super-charged Luna Negra Malbec. Second label: Fallen Angel.

Tasman Bay Nelson ★→★★★ Best-known for creamy-smooth Chard. Solid, gently oaked Sauv Bl and light Pinot N.

Te Awa Hawke's Bay ★★ US-owned estate v'yd. Classy Chard and nutty, leathery Boundary (Merlot-based blend). NZ's best Pinotage: dense, brambly, earthy. Now linked to DRY RIVER.

Te Kairanga Martinborough ★→★★ One of district's largest wineries; chequered history. Now headed by part-owner Peter Hubscher (former boss at MONTANA). Strategy is to focus on MARTINBOROUGH for only Pinot N, with other varieties drawn from elsewhere. Moderately complex Estate Pinot N is gd value.

Te Mata Hawke's Bay ★★★→★★★★ Prestigious, long-established winery. Fine, powerful Elston Chard; super-stylish Coleraine (Merlot/Cab Sauv/Cab Fr blend) (98' 00 **02 04** 05' 06' 07'). Syrah among NZ's finest. Woodthorpe range for early drinking (v.gd Chard, Sauv Bl, Viognier, Gamay Noir, *Merlot/Cab*, Syrah/Viognier).

Te Motu Waiheke Island ★★ Top wine of Waiheke V'yds. Concentrated, mellow Cabernet/Merlot, sold when well matured. Second label: Dunleavy.

TerraVin Marlborough ★★ Weighty, dry, tropical-fruit-flavoured Sauv Bl, but real focus is rich, firmly structured, complex Pinot N, esp Hillside Reserve.

Te Whau Waiheke Island ★★→★★★ Tiny winery/restaurant. Beautifully ripe, long Chard and savoury, earthy, complex red, The Point (Bordeaux blend). Now also good Syrah.

The Ned Marlborough ★★ Latest venture of Brent Marris, ex-WITHER HILLS. Full-flavoured, vibrant Sauv Bl and berryish, supple Pinot N.

Tohu ★→★★ Maori-owned venture with extensive v'yds. Punchy, racy Sauv Bl (Mugwi is esp powerful), moderately complex Pinot N, both from MARLBOROUGH; full-flavoured Gisborne Chard; scented, weighty NELSON Pinot Gr.

Torlesse Waipara ★→★★ Small, gd-value CANTERBURY producer of fresh, flinty Ries and firm, toasty, citrus Chard. Mid-weight Pinot N. Top range: Omihi Road.

Trinity Hill Hawke's Bay ★★→★★★ Innovative winery with firm, concentrated reds (Bordeaux-style The Gimblett is rich, refined) and top-flight Gimblett Gravels Chard. Exceptional Homage Syrah – scented, muscular, dense. V. promising Tempranillo. Scented, soft, rich Pinot Gr and Viognier among NZ's best.

Two Paddocks Central Otago ★★ Actor Sam Neill produces several Pinot Ns, inc Picnic (drink-young style), First Paddock (leafy), Last Chance (warm, savoury).

Unison Hawke's Bay ★★→★★★ Red specialist with dark, spicy, flavour-crammed blends of Merlot, Cab Sauv, Syrah. Selection label is oak-aged the longest. Also fragrant, fleshy, flavour-rich Syrah. New owners since 2008.

Vavasour Marlborough ★★ Based in AWATERE VALLEY. Immaculate, intense Chard and Sauv Bl; promising Pinot N and Pinot Gr. Vavasour Awatere Valley is top label; Vavasour Redwood Pass and Dashwood are regional blends (aromatic,

Vidal Hawke's Bay ★★→★★★ Part of VILLA MARIA. Distinguished Reserve Chard and Reserve Merlot/Cab Sauv. Mid-priced Merlot/Cab Sauv is gd value. Top Syrahs (Reserve and Soler) outstanding. Excellent MARLBOROUGH Sauv Bl, Ries and Pinot N.

Villa Maria Auckland ★★→★★★ NZ's largest family-owned wine company, VIDAL and ESK VALLEY. Top ranges: Reserve (express regional character) and Single V'yd (reflect individual sites); Cellar Selection: mid-tier (less oak) is often v.gd; 3rd-tier Private Bin wines can be excellent and gd value (esp Ries, Sauv Bl, Gewurz, Pinot Gr, Pinot N). Brilliant track record in competitions. Thornbury brand: rich, soft Merlot and perfumed, supple Pinot N.

Vinoptima Gisborne ★★→★★★ Small Gewurz specialist, owned by Nick Nobilo (ex-NOBILO wines). Top vintages (06') are full of power and personality. Also gorgeous Noble Late Harvest.

Voss Martinborough ★★ Small, respected producer of Pinot N (perfumed, weighty, silky); Chard (lush, creamy smooth).

Waimea Nelson ★★ One of region's top and best-value producers. Punchy, ripe, dry Sauv Bl, rich, softly textured Pinot Gr, gd Ries (Classic is honeyed, medium style). Top range: Bolitho SV. Spinyback range: DYA.

Waipara Hills Canterbury ★★ Now a brand of MUD HOUSE. Intense, ripe, racy MARLBOROUGH Sauv Bl, top-flight Waipara Ries. Equinox: top range.

Waipara Springs Canterbury ★★ Small producer of lively, cool-climate Ries, Sauv Bl and Chard; impressive top range: Premo (inc finely fragrant, concentrated Pinot N).

Wairarapa NZ's 6th-largest wine region. Includes East Taratahi and Gladstone. See MARTINBOROUGH. Coolest in North Island: strength in whites and Pinot N.

Wairau River Marlborough ★★ Intense, racy Sauv Bl; full-bodied, well-rounded Pinot Gr; perfumed, softly mouthfilling Gewurz. Home Block is top label.

Wairau Valley MARLBOROUGH's largest subregion, with most of the region's v'yds and wineries Sauv Bl grown on the stony, silty plains; Pinot N on the clay-based hills.

Waitaki Valley New region in North Otago. Promising Pinot N, Pinot Gr and Ries.

Wellington Capital city and official name of region; includes WAIRARAPA, Te Horo, MARTINBOROUGH.

Whitehaven Marlborough ★→★★ Scented, v. pure and harmonious Sauv Bl is best; other whites and Pinot N: sound, easy drinking. Gallo (see California) is part-owner. Second label: Mansion House Bay.

Winegrowers of Ara Marlborough ★★ Huge v'yd, devoted to Sauv Bl and Pinot N. Top wines labelled Resolute; Composite also v.gd. Dry, minerally wines, full of interest. New 3rd-tier Pathway wines gd value.

Wither Hills Marlborough ★★→★★★ Large producer, owned since 2002 by Lion Nathan. Popular, crisp, gooseberry/lime Sauv Bl. Rich Chard and Pinot N; latest vintages less oak-influenced. Outstandingly intense Single V'yd Sauv Bl and Pinot N since 2007. Other brands: Shepherds Ridge, Two Tracks.

Wooing Tree Central Otago ★★ Young producer at Cromwell. Rich Pinot N (Beetle Juice Pinot N less new oak).

Woollaston Nelson ★→★★ Producer of Pinot N, Sauv Bl, Pinot Gr and Ries, under Woollaston and Tussock brands. Ries and Pinot Gr best.

Yealands Marlborough ★→★★ Privately owned v'yd, one of NZ's biggest, in AWATERE VALLEY. First vintage 2008. Top wines labelled Estate; 2nd tier is Peter Yealands. Estate Sauv Bl: punchy, herbaceous. Now using miniature sheep (yes, really) to crop the grass between the rows . Regular sheep eat the grapes, apparently. And guinea pigs proved unviable – easy prey for the local hawks.

South Africa

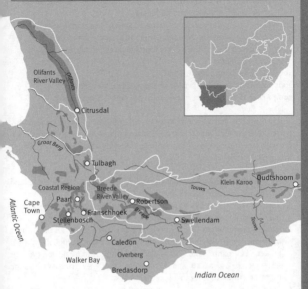

Along with a very large and visible marketing platform in the shape of FIFA World Cup 2010, South Africa's wine-growers have been handed the dual challenge of convincing football fans and their entourages to pay return visits in 2011 and beyond, and to convert hoopla-assisted first-time samplings of South African wines into regular purchases.

Disincentives to revisit Cape Town and the winelands include economic factors, safety and security issues, and their relative remoteness. But there are also many – hopefully irresistible – inducements to make the return trip: newly upgraded facilities and infrastructure, glorious beaches and mountains, a lively restaurant scene, and increasingly sophisticated and varied cellar-door experiences amid some of the finest scenery in winedom.

Turning trial tastings of wine into a habit will require local growers to see off spirited competition from both the New and Old worlds. Despite a stronger currency, South Africa still offers remarkable value for money: a younger, unfettered winemaking generation is in ascendance and its influence is felt in, among others, a new wave of Mediterranean-style reds and Chenin Blanc blends; flowering of varietal Pinot Noir; revival of traditional varieties such as Clairette Blanche and Cinsault; strengthening of successful categories such as Sauvignon Blanc and Méthode Cap Classique sparkling; and new vineyard developments in some of the highest and coolest sites, auguring well for the future. For now, the billion-rand question is: will the morning after the World Cup bring an expensive hangover or a new round of toasts and celebrations?

Recent vintages

2009 South Africa's 350th harvest and, serendipitously, one of its best. Stellar
whites and most reds; standout Merlot.

2008 One of the more challenging harvests in recent years but also one of the
coolest, yielding ripe but elegant wines with lower-than-usual alcohol.

2007 Dry, largely disease-free. Sturdy whites for keeping; soft, easy reds for
earlier drinking.

2006 The 5th sound vintage in a row.

2005 Small, thick-skinned berries; concentrated reds for keeping.

2004 Above-average quality. Intense reds, especially Shiraz, Pinotage.

Vineyard practices and cellar techniques are improving each vintage: a producer's
reputation is usually a better guide to wine quality than the vintage. South Africa
generally experiences warm to hot summers. Most dry whites are best drunk
within two to three years.

Adoro Wines St'bosch r w ★★★ Sophisticated, food-friendly red/white blends and
SAUV BL from multiple coastal sites.

Alto Estate St'bosch r ★★→★★★ Historic DISTELL co-owned property on Helderberg
mtn slopes. Age-worthy CAB SAUV (00 01' 02 03 04 05 06 07).

Anthonij Rupert Wines Franschhoek r w ★★→★★★ Total revamp under
billionaire owner Johann Rupert. Impressive four-tier portfolio (Anthonij
Rupert, L'Ormarins and Terra del Capo) from immaculate v'yds in
FRANSCHHOEK, SWARTLAND and Villiersdorp. Plus new single-v'yd range
(PINOTAGE, CHENIN BL) from 50- to 80-yr-old vines.

Anwilka St'bosch r ★★→★★★ Partnership between KLEIN CONSTANTIA and
Bordeaux's Bruno Prats and Hubert de Boüard. Flagship is Anwilka
(SHIRAZ/CAB SAUV 05 06 07 08); second wine is Ugaba.

Asara Estate St'bosch r (p) w (br sw) ★★→★★★ Five-star hotel and winery; off-beat
range includes Amarone-style PINOTAGE/SHIRAZ and white CAB SAUV.

Ashbourne See HAMILTON RUSSELL.

Ataraxia Walker Bay r w ★★★ Kevin Grant, ex-HAMILTON RUSSELL, flying solo to rave
reviews. Penetrating, minerally CHARD among South Africa's best.

L'Avenir V'yds St'bosch r (p) w (sw sp) ★★→★★★ Historic focus on PINOTAGE and
CHENIN BL continues under owner Michel Laroche of Chablis. Portfolio now
features lightly wooded Grand Vin Chenin Bl and MCC Brut Rosé in Icon range.
French ownership (Michel Laroche/Jeanjean), with bottling at three different
quality levels.

Avondale Bio-LOGIC & Organic Wines Paarl r (p) w (sw sp) ★→★★★ Pioneering
family farm, now 100% organic, refocusing extensive range on CHENIN BL,
Rhône-style reds and MCC.

Axe Hill Calitzdorp br ★★→★★★★ Outstanding tiny port-style specialist.
Restrainedly opulent Cape Vintage (Touriga Nacional/Tinta Barroca/Souzão
00' 01 02' 03' 04 05' 06); solera-aged Dry White Port from CHENIN BL.

Backsberg Estate Cellars Paarl r (p) w (br s/sw sp) ★★→★★★ Social media-savvy
enterprise with 20-plus labels in five ranges. New MCC in KOSHER range one of
South Africa's first.

Bamboes Bay Tiny (5 ha) maritime WARD in OLIFANTS RIVER region. Fryer's Cove
first and still only winery, known for pyrotechnic SAUV BL.

Beaumont Wines Walker Bay r (p) w (br sw) ★★→★★★ Rustic family home to
characterful CHENIN BL, PINOTAGE, Mourvèdre and Bordeaux red Ariane.

NB Vintages in colour are those you should choose first for drinking in 2011.

Bellingham r (p) w ★→★★★ Revivified DGB brand led by flamboyant Bernard Series; above-average Legends Collection; easy-drinkers in Fusion and Blends ranges.

Beyerskloof St'bosch r (p w br sp) ★→★★★ Top grower/producer of PINOTAGE in Cape: 12 versions of grape on offer, inc various CAPE BLENDS. Only Bordeaux-style Field Blend (00 01 02 03' 04 05) is Pinotage-free.

Biodynamic Anthroposophic mode of wine-growing practised by a small handful of local producers. Best is Reyneke Wines. See also ORGANIC.

Boekenhoutskloof Winery Franschhoek r (p w sw) ★★→★★★★ Consistently excellent grower/producer specializing in unfiltered, native-yeast ferments. Spicy Syrah (01' 02' 03 04' 05 06' 07); intense, minerally CAB SAUV (01' 02' 03 04' 05 06' 07'). Also fine *Sem*, Mediterranean-style red The Chocolate Block and gd-value labels Porcupine Ridge and Wolftrap.

Boland Kelder Paarl r (p) w (br sw s/sw) ★→★★★ Large (24,500 tonnes), enterprising winery with two-dozen labels in five ranges, including new "terroir" label Boland Private Cellar.

Bon Courage Estate Robertson r (p) w (br) sw sp ★★→★★★ Extensive range led by improving Inkará reds, stylish MCC and pair of outstanding desserts.

Boplaas Family V'yds Calitzdorp r (p) w br (sp) ★→★★★ Best known for port styles (esp Vintage Reserve 99' 01 03 04' 05' 06' 07' and Cape Tawny). New Cool Bay (unfortified) range from ocean-facing vines.

Boschendal Wines Paarl r (p) w sp ★★→★★★ Famous old estate showing new elan under DGB ownership. Calling cards: SHIRAZ, CAB SAUV, SAUV BL and Bordeaux/Shiraz Grand Reserve. Revived emphasis on MCC.

Bot River See WALKER BAY.

Bouchard Finlayson Hemel-en-Aarde r w ★★→★★★★ V. fine PINOT N grower. Galpin Peak (01 02' 03 04 05 07 08), barrel selection Tête de Cuvée (99 01' 03' 05' 07) and Unfiltered Limited Edition (07). Impressive CHARD, SAUV BL and exotic red blend Hannibal.

Breedekloof Large (12,300 ha) inland district in Breede River Valley region producing mainly bulk wine for distilling and the merchant trade. Notable exceptions: Avondrood, Bergsig, Deetlefs, Mtn Oaks, Du Preez and Merwida.

Buitenverwachting Constantia r (p) w (sw sp) ★★→★★★ Classy family-owned v'yds, cellar and restaurant; *standout Sauv Bl*, Cab Fr and yin-yang Bordeaux blends: restrained Christine (00 01' 02 03 04 06) and exuberant new Rough Diamond (06).

Cabernet Sauvignon Ubiquitous but truly at home on the slopes around ST'BOSCH. Top names: DE TRAFFORD, EDGEBASTON, KANONKOP, NEIL ELLIS, LE RICHE, RUSTENBERG, Stark-Condé, THELEMA, VERGELEGEN, WATERFORD ESTATE, Blue Creek; elsewhere: BOEKENHOUTSKLOOF, CEDERBERG PRIVATE CELLAR.

Cabrière Franschhoek (r p w br) sp ★★→★★★ Reliable NV MCC sparkling under Pierre Jourdan label (Brut Sauvage, Blanc de Blancs). Fine PINOT N in some yrs.

Calitzdorp District in KLEIN KAROO region, climatically similar to the Douro and known for port styles. Best: AXE HILL, BOPLAAS, DE KRANS, Peter Bayly.

Camberley Wines St'bosch r (br sp) ★★→★★★ Family-run red specialist: fine SHIRAZ; impressive Bordeaux blend Philosopher's Stone; massive, plummy PINOTAGE.

Capaia Estate Philadelphia r (w) ★★→★★★ German-owned winery employing top French and Austrian advisers for pair of Bordeaux blends and SAUV BL.

Cape Agulhas See ELIM.

Cape blend Usually a red blend with proportion of PINOTAGE. Top exponents include BEYERSKLOOF, GRAHAM BECK, GRANGEHURST, KAAPZICHT ESTATE, MEINERT, RAKA, REMHOOGTE.

Cape Chamonix Wine Farm Franschhoek r w (sp) ★★→★★★ Rising star. V.gd PINOT N, CHARD, SAUV BL, Chard MCC; and Bordeaux blend Troika.

Cape Point Tiny (30 ha) Atlantic-cooled district on southern tip of the Cape Peninsula. Mainly white varieties. Viticulturally challenging but rising to great heights in the cellars of CAPE POINT V'YDS, the area's first and only winery.

Cape Point V'yds Cape Point (r) w ★★→★★★★ One of South Africa's most exciting producers. Complex SAUV BL/SEM blend Isliedh, racy CHARD and thrilling SAUV BL, inc new gd-value Splattered Toad label, helping to save endangered amphibians.

Cape Winemakers Guild (CWG) Stages a benchmarking annual auction of limited, premium bottlings by 37 of South Africa's top growers.

Cederberg WARD in craggy Cederberg mountain range. 61 ha, mainly red varieties, among the highest in South Africa. Sole producer is CEDERBERG PRIVATE CELLAR.

Cederberg Private Cellar Cederberg r w (sp) ★★→★★★ Combines high-altitude minerality with intense flavour in SHIRAZ, CAB SAUV, SAUV BL, SEM, CHENIN BL and new oaked CHARD MCC.

Chardonnay Styles from cool and lean to warm and fleshy, with a more sensitive use of oak. ATARAXIA, CAPE CHAMONIX, GLEN CARLOU, HAMILTON RUSSELL, HARTENBERG, NEWTON JOHNSON, PAUL CLUVER, RUSTENBERG, THELEMA, UVA MIRA, VERGELEGEN, WATERFORD, THE WINERY OF GOOD HOPE, BOUCHARD FINLAYSON, JORDAN, SPRINGFIELD, DE WETSHOF, the last four also offer v.gd unwooded versions.

Chenin Blanc Many styles, from unwooded to heavily oaked off-dry. Brands worth trying: BEAUMONT, CEDERBERG, De Morgenzon, JEAN DANEEL, KEN FORRESTER, Old Vines, Post House, RAATS, RIJK'S, RUDERA, SPICE ROUTE, SPIER, Springfontein, Teddy Hall.

Coastal Large (32,000 ha) region, inc sea-influenced districts of CAPE POINT, DARLING, Tygerberg, ST'BOSCH, SWARTLAND and landlocked PAARL and TULBAGH.

The Company of Wine People r (p) w (sw sp) ★→★★★ 2.5-million-case-a-yr ST'BOSCH operation with 40-plus labels in a dozen tiers. Best is Kumkani; also well-priced easy-drinkers in Arniston Bay, Versus and Welmoed lines.

Constantia South Africa's original fine-wine-growing area; home of the famous sweet Muscat-based wines of the 18th and 19th centuries, revived in recent yrs by GROOT and KLEIN CONSTANTIA. Other leading names: BUITENVERWACHTING, Constantia Glen, CONSTANTIA UITSIG, Eagles' Nest, STEENBERG.

Constantia Uitsig Constantia (r) w (br sp) ★★★ Premium v'yds and tourist destination, partly black-owned. Mainly white wines and MCC, all excellent.

Dalla Cia Wine & Spirit Company St'bosch r w ★★→★★★ Italian-owned and -toned wine cellar, *grappa*-style distillery and restaurant. Varietal CAB SAUV has joined Bordeaux blend Giorgio; lightly oaked CHARD; SAUV BL.

Danie de Wet See DE WETSHOF.

Darling Coastal district (2,700 ha) around eponymous west coast town; best v'yds in hilly Groenekloof WARD. Top producers: Cloof, GROOTE POST and Ormonde. Much of fruit transported out of appellation for other labels.

David Frost Estate Paarl r (p w) ★→★★★ South African golfing legend's increasingly respected small range of reds partnered by gd-value Signature Series.

De Grendel Wines Durbanville r (p) w (sp) ★★★ Cool sites facing Table Bay on Sir David Graaff's hillside property yield brisk, layered reds, whites and MCC.

De Krans Calitzdorp r (p) w br (sw) ★→★★★ Old family-run Karoo v'yds make rich, impressive port styles (esp Vintage Reserve 99 01 02 03' 04' 05' 06' 07). Tasty, gd-value SHIRAZ and SAUV BL under cool-climate-sourced Garden Route label.

Delaire Graff Estate St'bosch r (p) w (sw) ★★★ Spectacular eyrie on Helshoogte Pass, owned by international jeweller Laurence Graff. New-look line-up includes SHIRAZ and coastal SAUV BL.

Delheim St'bosch r (p) w (sw s/sw) ★★→★★★ Eco-minded family winery. Acclaimed Vera Cruz Shiraz; plummy Grand Reserve CAB SAUV (00 01 03 04' 05 06 07).

> **Pinotage 2.0**
> First vinified exactly 70 yrs ago, Pinotage hasn't quite set the wine world
> alight with its strawberry-and-smoke flavour, but a new generation of
> bottlings, inspired by (of all things) coffee, just might change all that.
> PAARL estate DIEMERSFONTEIN was first, with a vinification accentuating
> the espresso character present in the fruit. Easily recognized and
> appealing, the style has since gone mainstream and "coffee Pinotage"
> is now made by, among others, KWV with Café Culture, BOLAND KELDER
> with tongue-twister Cappupinoccinotage and Val de Vie with cleverly
> packaged Barista. Meanwhile, growers of other varieties are jumping
> in with variations on the theme, including chocolate-toned Tinta Barroca
> and a red blend appropriately named Pepper Pot. What's next? A wine
> that mimics the famously spicy local salsa chakalaka? Actually, that's
> already on the market...

De Toren Private Cellar St'bosch r ★★★ Consistently fine, flavourful Bordeaux
blend Fusion V (01 02 03' 04 05' 06' 07) and earlier-maturing MERLOT-based
blend "Z".

De Trafford Wines St'bosch r w (sw) ★★★★ Exceptional boutique grower with
international reputation for bold but elegant wines. Brilliant Bordeaux/SHIRAZ
blend Elevation 393 (00 01 03' 04 05 06 07); CAB SAUV (00 01 03' 04 05 06 07).
New Sijnn brand showcases promising young maritime v'yds.

DeWaal Wines r (w) ★★→★★★ HQ at Uiterwyk, now more visitor-friendly family
farm near ST'BOSCH. PINOTAGE a forte: old-vines Top of the Hill among South
Africa's best.

De Wetshof Estate Robertson (r p) w (br sw) ★★ Famed CHARD pioneer under newly
revamped De Wetshof branding. Danie de Wet label features promising PINOT N.

DGB Well-established Wellington-based producer/wholesaler; brands include
BELLINGHAM, BOSCHENDAL, Brampton and Douglas Green.

Diemersdal Estate Durbanville r (p) w (sw) ★★→★★★ Family firm with dynamic
younger generation specializing in red blends, CHARD and SAUV BL. Exciting
west coast joint venture, Sir Lambert Sauv Bl.

Diemersfontein Wines Wellington r (w) ★★→★★★ Noted for full-throttle styling,
esp PINOTAGE; new MCC for empowerment brand Thokozani.

Distell South Africa's biggest drinks company, headquartered in ST'BOSCH. Owns
many brands, spanning quality scales. Also interests in various top ST'BOSCH
wineries, inc ALTO and STELLENZICHT, and in empowerment brand Tukulu.

Dornier Wines St'bosch r (p) w (sw) ★★→★★★ Architectural showpiece in a sylvan
setting. Stylish Red and White flagships under Donatus label.

Durbanville Cool, hilly WARD (1,500 ha) known for pungent, characteristically
"dusty" SAUV BL, and for MERLOT. Altydgedacht, Bloemendal, DE GRENDEL,
DIEMERSDAL, DURBANVILLE HILLS, Hillcrest and NITIDA CELLARS worth seeking out.

Durbanville Hills Durbanville r w ★★→★★★ Serially awarded maritime-cooled
v'yds co-owned by DISTELL. Best are single-v'yd and Rhinofields Reserve ranges.

Edgebaston St'bosch r w ★★→★★★ Finlayson family (GLEN CARLOU fame). V.gd GS
CAB SAUV (05 '06 07); new Berry Box mid-level red joins fast-selling Pepper Pot.

Elgin Cool upland WARD east of Cape Town; burgeoning corps of vintners;
winemakers Ross Gower and Catherine Marshall and viticulturist Paul
Wallace with eponymous labels; PAUL CLUVER, Oak Valley, Iona, Almenkerk,
Shannon and Elgin Vintners.

Elim Sea-breezy WARD (150 ha) in southernmost district, Cape Agulhas. Mainly
SAUV BL and SHIRAZ. Aromatic, elegant wines from The Berrio, Black
Oystercatcher, Land's End/Hidden Valley, Lomond, Strandveld and Zoetendal.

Ernie Els Wines St'bosch r ★★→★★★★ South African golfer's joint venture with Jean Engelbrecht (RUST EN VREDE). Rich, aromatic Bordeaux blend Ernie Els (01 02' 03 04' 05 06) among Cape's priciest wines. Also new Bordeaux/SHIRAZ blend Big Easy, honouring Els's famously effortless swing. V.gd GUARDIAN PEAK range.

Estate Wine Official term for wines grown, made and bottled on "units registered for the production of estate wine". Not a quality designation.

Fairview Paarl r (p) w (sw s/sw) ★★→★★★★ Dynamic, export-savvy, innovative proprietor Charles Back. Under Fairview label, a top range of single-v'yd and "terroir-specific" wines, plus kaleidoscope of blends and varietals. Also successful with Goats do Roam – taunting, gimmicky labels that usually overdeliver. "Goat" theme continues with new easy-drinking La Capra range, from young vines. See also SPICE ROUTE.

FirstCape V'yds r w ★→★★ Major South African export success. Joint venture of NEWTON JOHNSON, Brand Phoenix in the UK, and five local co-ops; HQ at Simondium near PAARL. V.gd price/quality in eight ranges, inc new Cape Bay collection.

Flagstone Winery Somerset West r w (br) ★★→★★★★ Owned by Constellation. Two dozen cheerfully idiosyncratic labels. Best: Mary Le Bow Bordeaux/SHIRAZ. Dark Horse Shiraz; Longitude red blend; Free Run SAUV BL. Fish Hoek brand is joint venture with SWARTLAND's Riebeek Cellars.

Franschhoek French Huguenot-founded WARD in Paarl district. 1,200 ha, mainly SAUV BL, CAB SAUV and SHIRAZ. Many wineries (and restaurants), inc ANTHONIJ RUPERT, BOEKENHOUTSKLOOF, CABRIÈRE, CAPE CHAMONIX, GRAHAM BECK, LA MOTTE, Môreson, SOLMS-DELTA, Stony Brook and newcomer Maison.

Fleur du Cap r w (sw) ★★→★★★ DISTELL premium label; includes v.gd Unfiltered Collection, plush Bordeaux blend Laszlo and racy botrytis SEM.

The Foundry St'bosch r w ★★★ MEERLUST winemaker Chris Williams, buying in site-specific parcels for outstanding Syrah, Viognier and new Grenache Blanc.

Glen Carlou Paarl r (p) w (sw) ★★→★★★ First-rate winery, v'yds, fine-art gallery and restaurant, owned by Donald Hess. Standout, spicy Syrah (02 03 04' 05 06); *fine Bordeaux blend Grand Classique* (00 01 02 03 04 05 06').

Glenelly St'bosch Launched with the 08 vintage, this is the new venture of May-Eliane de Lencquesaing, who used to own Château Pichon Lalande in Bordeaux; aim is not to impose Bordeaux ideas.

Graham Beck Wines Robertson/Franschhoek r (p) w sp (br sw) ★★→★★★ Top-rank properties of mining tycoon Graham Beck, making *classy MCC sparkling*, varietal and blended reds/whites, inc power-packed new Bowed Head and Gamekeeper's Reserve CHENIN BLS.

Grangehurst Winery St'bosch r (p) ★★→★★★ Small, top red and, latterly, rosé specialist. CAPE BLEND Nikela (98 99 00 01 02 03), v.gd PINOTAGE (97 98 99 01 02 03') etc. released when ready to drink.

Groot Constantia Constantia r (p) w (br sw sp) ★★→★★★ Showy wines befitting a showcase winery and tourist destination. Best in Gouverneurs range. Grand Constance revives tradition of Muscat desserts.

Groote Post V'yds Darling r w (sw sp) ★★→★★★ Ocean-facing property of the Pentz family. V.gd CHARD and SAUV BL Reserve, juicy PINOT N..

Guardian Peak See ERNIE ELS.

Hamilton Russell V'yds (HRV) Walker Bay r w ★★★★ Burgundian-style specialist estate at Hermanus. Fine PINOT N (01' 03' 04 05 06 07 08); *classy Chard*. Gd SAUV BL, PINOTAGE and white blend under Southern Right and Ashbourne labels.

Hartenberg Estate St'bosch r w ★★★★ Cape front-ranker. Trio of outstanding SHIRAZ: always serious Shiraz (01 02 03 04' 05 06), flagship single-site The Stork (03 04' 05' 06) and Gravel Hill; fine MERLOT and CHARD.

Hemel-en-Aarde Trio of cool-climate WARDS in WALKER BAY district (Hemel-en-Aarde Valley, Upper Hemel-en-Aarde, Hemel-en-Aarde Ridge), producing some of South Africa's finest PINOT N, CHARD and SAUV BL. BOUCHARD FINLAYSON, ATARAXIA, NEWTON JOHNSON and HAMILTON RUSSELL are top names.

J C le Roux St'bosch sp ★★ South Africa's largest sparkling wine house, DISTELL-owned. Best are PINOT N, Scintilla (CHARD/ PINOT N), and PINOT N Rosé, all MCC.

Jean Daneel Wines Napier r w (br sp) ★★★ Outstanding Signature Series, esp *Chenin Bl*, CAB SAUV/MERLOT/SHIRAZ, CHARD MCC sparkling.

Jordan Estate St'bosch r (p) w ★★→★★★ Consistency, quality and value, from entry-level Bradgate and Chameleon lines to immaculate CWG Auction bottlings. Flagship CHARD Nine Yards; Bordeaux blend Cobblers Hill (00 01 03 04' 05' 06); CAB SAUV; MERLOT; SAUV BL; RIES botrytis dessert.

J P Bredell Wines St'bosch r (w) br ★★→★★★ Best known for port styles, esp plush Cape Vintage Reserve (97' 98' 00 01' 03') and Late Bottled Vintage.

Kaapzicht Estate St'bosch r (p) w (br sw) ★★→★★★ Family run red wine specialist. Concentrated Vision CAPE BLEND (01' 02'03' 04 05' 06) and PINOTAGE under Steytler banner.

Kanonkop Estate St'bosch r ★★→★★★★ Grand local status past three decades, mainly with oak-polished PINOTAGE (01 02 03' 04 05 06 07) and, with a fanatical following, Bordeaux blend Paul Sauer (01 02 03 04' 05 06'), plus CAB SAUV. Second label is CAPE BLEND Kadette.

Kanu Wines St'bosch r (p) w (sw) ★★→★★★ Reputation for barrel-aged CHENIN BL; also v. gd Bordeaux red Keystone, SHIRAZ, and botrytis CHENIN BL Kia-Ora.

Ken Forrester Wines St'bosch r w (sw) ★★→★★★★ Vintner/restaurateur Ken Forrester and wine-grower Martin MEINERT collaboration. Benchmark CHENIN BL in Ken Forrester range; also *outstanding off-dry FMC version*. Sumptuous botrytis CHENIN BL named "T".

Klein Constantia Estate Constantia r (p) w sw (sp) ★★→★★★ Luscious (non-botrytis) Vin de Constance (00' 01 02' 04 05 06) convincingly re-creates legendary 18th-century Muscat dessert. Current line-up also includes elegant Marlbrook blends, age-worthy RIES, classy SAUV BL and earlier-ready KC range. See also ANWILKA.

Kleine Zalze Wines St'bosch r (p) w ★★→★★★ CAB SAUV and SHIRAZ head v.gd Family Reserve and V'yd Selection reds; oaked and (despite recent controversy) CHENIN BL.

Klein Karoo Inland semi-arid region with 2,800 ha under vine. Best quality in CALITZDORP district and Tradouw WARD. Cool, high-altitude WARDS of Outeniqua and Upper Langkloof show potential.

Kosher Small but growing category. BACKSBERG, Hill & Dale/STELLENZICHT, Kleine Draken, Rose Garden, Tempel.

Krone (w sw) sp ★★★ Fine, elegant *brut* MCC, inc Borealis, Rosé and *prestige cuvée* Nicolas Charles Krone, from CHARD/PINOT N, by Twee Jonge Gezellen Estate.

Kumala r (p) w ★ Hugely successful Constellation-owned export label undergoing quality boost under aegis of Bruce Jack, founder of sister brand FLAGSTONE.

KWV Paarl r (p) w br (s/sw sp) ★→★★★ Formerly the national wine co-op and controlling body, today a listed, partly black-owned group. Top ranges are Cathedral Cellar, Laborie, Reserve and Mentors; also vast range of reds, whites, sparkling, port styles and fortified desserts.

Lamberts Bay Recent standalone west coast WARD (20 ha) close by Atlantic. Mostly SAUV BL; Sir Lambert, local joint venture with DIEMERSDAL, a cracker.

Lourensford St'bosch r (p) w (sw) ★★→★★★ Sibling to Lanzerac, rejuvenated and refocused on SHIRAZ, CAB SAUV, SAUV BL and Viognier. Best in Lourensford range. Eden Crest and River Garden are entry-level labels.

Lower Orange Standalone inland "super WARD" (12,300 ha) following contours of the Gariep (Orange) River; hot, dry, dependent on irrigation; overwhelmingly white wine territory; major winery is Oranjerivier Wine Cellars.

Meerlust Estate St'bosch r w ★★★★ Prestigious v'yds and cellar, probably South Africa's best-known quality red label. Hallmark elegance and restraint in flagship Rubicon (**99 00 01' 03' 04 05**), one of Cape's first Bordeaux blends; also excellent MERLOT, CAB SAUV, CHARD and PINOT N.

Meinert Wines St'bosch r (w) ★★→★★★ Small-scale producer/consultant Martin Meinert makes two fine blends, Devon Crest (Bordeaux) and Synchronicity (Bordeaux/PINOTAGE), CAB SAUV and MERLOT from Devon Valley v'yds; SAUV BL from ELGIN fruit.

Merlot Temperamental and site-specific, thus seldom rises to great heights. Amani, Bein, Eikendal, HARTENBERG, JORDAN, Laibach, MEERLUST, QUOIN ROCK, RAKA, STEENBERG, THELEMA and VEENWOUDEN are consistent performers.

Méthode Cap Classique (MCC) South African term for classic-method sparkling wine. Ambeloui, BON COURAGE, BOSCHENDAL, CABRIÈRE, Colmant, CONSTANTIA UITSIG, GRAHAM BECK, JC LE ROUX, KLEIN CONSTANTIA, KRONE, Silverthorn, SIMONSIG, *Tanzanite*, VILLIERA and WELTEVREDE have real style.

Morgenhof Estate St'bosch r (p) w (br s/sw) ★→★★★ Old property (1692) revitalized by Anne Cointreau (of Cognac/liqueur family). Bordeaux red The Morgenhof Estate and CHENIN BL. Gd everyday Fantail range.

Morgenster Estate St'bosch r (p) ★★→★★★ Immaculate Italian-owned wine and olive farm, Pierre Lurton of Cheval Blanc consulting. Classically styled Bordeaux blend Morgenster (**00 01 03 04 05' 06'**); second label Lourens River Valley. Expanded Italian Collection has style and character.

La Motte Franschhoek r w ★★→★★★ Increasingly ORGANIC venture by the Ruperts, a leading Cape wine family. Fine, distinctive SHIRAZ/Viognier. SAUV BL and Shiraz/Grenache in flagship Pierneef range. Also excellent Bordeaux-style red Millennium, stylish SHIRAZ.

Lanzerac St'bosch r (p) w ★★ Venerable property (inc luxury hotel) long associated with PINOTAGE (1st vintage 1959). Sister farm to Lourensford.

Mulderbosch V'yds St'bosch r (p) w (sw) ★★→★★★ Individualistic offerings, inc SAUV BL, just-dry and botrytis; wood-fermented CHARD; new old-vines CHENIN BL Small Change; Bordeaux-style red blend Faithful Hound.

Mvemve Raats St'bosch r ★★★ Partnership between Mzokhona Mvemve, first university-qualified black winemaker, and Bruwer RAATS. Complex Bordeaux blend De Compostella. Promising Sagila range, by Mvemve alone.

Nederburg Wines Paarl r (p) w sw s/sw sp ★→★★★ Among South Africa's biggest (one million-plus cases per annum) and best-known brands, owned by DISTELL. V.gd new Ingenuity Red (05 06) and White (07' 08'); excellent Manor House label; reliable Winemaster's Reserves, inc enduring Edelrood and Baronne reds. Also inexpensive quaffers, still and sparkling. Small quantities of v.gd Private Bins for annual Nederburg Auction, inc CHENIN BL botrytis Edelkeur (**02 03' 04' 05 06 07' 08**).

Neethlingshof Estate St'bosch r w sw ★★ Tourist magnet co-owned by DISTELL. Best in flagship Short Story Collection (esp botrytis RIES); v.gd floral Gewurz.

Neil Ellis Wines St'bosch r w ★★★ Veteran winemaker Neil Ellis sources cooler-climate parcels for site expression. Top V'yd Selection CAB SAUV (**99 00' 01 03 04' 05 06 07**), Syrah, SAUV BL and new PINOTAGE and Grenache Noir.

Newton Johnson Wines Upper Hemel-en-Aarde r w ★★→★★★ Cellar and restaurant with breathtaking view. One of few v.gd Cape PINOT N; *outstanding Chard; intense Sauv Bl*; peppery SHIRAZ/Mourvèdre. See also FIRSTCAPE.

Nitida Cellars Durbanville r w (sp) ★★→★★★ Expanding v.gd range from sea-cooled v'yds; fresh, vital SAUV BL, SEM and Bordeaux-style white blend Coronata.

Olifants River West coast region. Warm valley floors, conducive to ORGANIC cultivation, and cooler, fine-wine-favouring sites in the mtn WARD of Piekenierskloof, and, near the Atlantic, BAMBOES BAY and Koekenaap.

Organic Quality variable but producers with track records include AVONDALE, Bon Cap, Laibach, Mtn Oaks, Stellar, Tukulu, Tulbagh Mtn V'yds, Upland and Waverley. Lazanou one to watch. See also BIODYNAMIC.

L'Ormarins See ANTHONIJ RUPERT.

Outeniqua See KLEIN KAROO.

Overgaauw Estate St'bosch r (p) w (br) ★★→★★★ Van Velden family team, now led by scion David. Dependable, classic-style Bordeaux blend Tria Corda; CAB SAUV; Cape's only bottling of Sylvaner. Everyday fare in Shepherd's Cottage line.

Paarl Town and demarcated wine district about 50 km northeast of Cape Town. 16,000 ha. Diverse styles and approaches; best results with Mediterranean varieties (r and w), CAB SAUV. Leading producers: AVONDALE, BACKSBERG, BOLAND KELDER, BOSCHENDAL, DIEMERSFONTEIN, FAIRVIEW, GLEN CARLOU, KWV, NEDERBURG, PLAISIR DE MERLE, RUPERT & ROTHSCHILD, Schalk Burger, VEENWOUDEN, VILAFONTÉ.

Paul Cluver Wines Elgin r w sw ★★★ Appellation's leading winery, on scenic De Rust estate; convincing PINOT N, esp new Seven Flags reserve; elegant CHARD, always gorgeous Gewurz and botrytis RIES (03' 04 05' 06' 07 08').

Pinotage South Africa's "own" red grape in sympathetic hands is accessible, harmonious, even profound. Try ASHBOURNE, L'AVENIR, BEYERSKLOOF, DEWAAL, DIEMERSFONTEIN, FAIRVIEW, GROOT CONSTANTIA, KANONKOP, Perdeberg, Scali, SIMONSIG, Springfontein.

Pinot Noir Inspires a passion inversely proportionate to its less than 1% share of the national v'yd. BOUCHARD FINLAYSON, CAPE CHAMONIX, Catherine Marshall, Crystallum, Creation, DE TRAFFORD, GLEN CARLOU, HAMILTON RUSSELL, MEERLUST, NEWTON JOHNSON, Oak Valley, PAUL CLUVER, Shannon, VRIESENHOF.

Plaisir de Merle Paarl r w ★★★ Imposing DISTELL-owned cellar and v'yds. Much-improved range headlined by outstanding Cab Fr (03' 04 05 06 07).

Pongrácz sp ★★ DISTELL-owned MCC brand; vintaged Desiderius and popular NV Pongrácz.

Quoin Rock Winery St'bosch r w (sp sw) ★★→★★★ Classically styled wines, some featuring grapes from Cape Agulhas own v'yds. Syrah, MERLOT, white flagship Oculus, SAUV BL The Nicobar and new CHARD/PINOT N MCC. Second label is Glenhurst.

Raats Family Wines St'bosch r w ★★→★★★ Acclaimed, minerally Cab Fr, and two pure-fruited CHENIN BL, oaked and unoaked, both worth keeping a few yrs.

Raka Klein River r w ★★→★★★ Powerful, personality-packed wines, inc Biography Shiraz, Figurehead CAPE BLEND, MERLOT and SAUV BL.

Remhoogte Estate St'bosch r (w) ★★→★★★ Boustred family partnered by international consultant Michel Rolland; best known for trio of CAPE BLENDS.

Le Riche Wines St'bosch r (w) ★★★ Fine CAB SAUV-based boutique wines, hand-crafted by respected Etienne le Riche and family.

Riesling Steadily diminishing area under vine (to just 0.2% of total) but BUITENVERWACHTING, DE WETSHOF, GROOTE POST, Jack & Knox, HARTENBERG, KLEIN CONSTANTIA, NEDERBURG, NITIDA, PAUL CLUVER and THELEMA keep the faith.

Rijk's Tulbagh r w ★★→★★★ Depth, intensity are hallmarks of this operation, now vinifying/marketing both as "Estate" (focused on SHIRAZ) and "Private Cellar" (varietal and blended reds/whites, notably CAB SAUV, Shiraz, PINOTAGE, CHENIN BL).

Robertson District Low-rainfall inland valley; 13,400 ha; lime soils; historically gd CHARD, dessert styles (notably Muscat); more recently SAUV BL, SHIRAZ, CAB SAUV; proliferation of family-run boutiques (best include Quando, Arendsig); condusive climate for ORGANIC production (eg. Bon Cap). Major cellars: BON COURAGE, DE WETSHOF, GRAHAM BECK, Rietvallei, ROBERTSON WINERY, Rooiberg, SPRINGFIELD, WELTEVREDE, Zandvliet.

Robertson Winery Robertson r (p) w (br sw) s/sw ★→★★ Gd value from co-op-scale winery. Best is No.1 Constitution Rd SHIRAZ; also v.gd V'yd Selection.

Rudera Wines St'bosch r w (sw) ★★★ Hailed for consistently excellent CHENIN BL (dry/semi-dry and botrytis), CAB SAUV, Syrah. Second label: Lula.

Rupert & Rothschild Vignerons r w ★★★ Top v'yds, cellar near PAARL. Joint-owned by the Rothschilds and the Ruperts, two old French and South African wine families. Impressive Bordeaux blend Baron Edmond (98 00 01 03' 04 05); CHARD Baroness Nadine is a deep-flavoured classic.

Rustenberg Wines St'bosch r w (sw) ★★★★ Prestigious family winery. Flagship is single-v'yd *Cab Sauv Peter Barlow* (99' 01' 03 04 05 06). Outstanding Bordeaux blend John X Merriman; savoury Syrah; single-v'yd CHARD called Five Soldiers. Second label Brampton recently sold to DGB.

Rust en Vrede Estate St'bosch r ★★★ Strong, individual offering features pricey single-v'yd Syrah and limited-release SHIRAZ/CAB SAUV blend "1694". Critically acclaimed restaurant.

Sadie Family Swartland r w ★★★★ Organically grown, traditionally made Columella (SHIRAZ/Mourvèdre) (01 02' 03 04 05' 06 07') a Cape benchmark. Complex, intriguing CHENIN BL-based white Palladius. Star winemaker Eben Sadie also grows the rated Sequillo Red and White with Cape Wine Master Cornel Spies.

Saronsberg Cellar Tulbagh r (p) w (br sw sp) ★★→★★★ Growing following for Rhône varieties and blends, inc SHIRAZ and Viognier-seasoned Full Circle. Unfrivolous entry-level Provenance range.

Sauvignon Blanc South Africa's white grape *du jour* comes in a multitude of styles, from racy and herbaceous to sedate and tropical. Some names to watch for: Black Oystercatcher, Constantia Glen, Bloemendal, FLAGSTONE, Hermanuspietersfontein, Iona, SPRINGFIELD, STEENBERG, TOKARA.

Saxenburg St'bosch r (p) w (sp sw) ★★→★★★ Swiss-owned v'yds, winery and restaurant. Roundly oaked reds, SAUV BL and CHARD in high-end Private Collection; flagship SHIRAZ Select (98 00 01 02 03' 05').

Semillon Enjoying renewed interest in blends, but BOEKENHOUTSKLOOF, CONSTANTIA UITSIG, Eikendal, FAIRVIEW, Landau du Val, NITIDA, RIJK'S, STEENBERG and STELLENZICHT still offer varietal bottlings worth sampling.

Shiraz Wins plaudits solo and in blends. Top varietal bottlings (sometimes as "Syrah"): BOEKENHOUTSKLOOF, BON COURAGE, CEDERBERG, DE TRAFFORD, FAIRVIEW, GLEN CARLOU, GRAHAM BECK, HARTENBERG, Haskell, Luddite, QUOIN ROCK, SARONSBERG, SIMONSIG, STELLENZICHT, WATERFORD.

Signal Hill Cape Town r (p) w sw ★★→★★★ French flair in lively range; widely sourced grapes, inc tiny parcels in/around Cape Town city centre.

Simonsig Estate St'bosch r w (sw s/sw) sp ★★→★★★ Consistency and value among hallmarks of Malan family winery. Extensive but serious top end, inc decorated Merindol Syrah (01 02' 03 04 05 06), Red Hill Pinotage (01 02 03' 04 05 06 07'). First (30 yrs ago) with an *MCC*, *Kaapse Vonkel*.

Solms-Delta Franschhoek r (p) w (sp) ★★→★★★ Delightfully different wines; Amarone-style SHIRAZ Africana, sophisticated dry rosé Lekkerwijn, scented RIES blend Koloni, Cape Jazz series *pétillant* SHIRAZ, rosé and white.

Southern Right See HAMILTON RUSSELL.

Spice Route Winery Swartland r w ★★→★★★ Cellar owned by Charles Back (FAIRVIEW); Rhône-style reds, esp spicy Chakalaka blend; also scented Viognier. Non-Rhône offerings include v.gd old-vines CHENIN BL and classy PINOTAGE.

Spier St'bosch r (p) w (sw) ★★→★★★ A serious player (one-million-plus cases per annum), notably Spier and Savanha, each with tiers of quality. New flagship is CAPE BLEND Frans K Smit.

Springfield Estate Robertson r w ★★★ Cult wines, traditionally vinified, oozing personality. *Méthode ancienne* CHARD; unwooded Wild Yeast CHARD; SAUV BL labelled Special Cuvée and Life from Stone.

Stables Estate, The r (p) w (br) ★→★★★ KwaZulu-Natal's first registered wine estate, family-run; mix of KwaZulu-Natal and Western Cape grapes.

Steenberg V'yds Constantia r w (sp) ★★★→★★★★ Top winery and v'yds, known for arresting SAUV BL and SAUV BL/SEM blends. Reds include fine Nebbiolo.

Stellenbosch (St'bosch) Oak-shaded university town and demarcated wine district 50 km east of Cape Town. Heart of the wine industry – the Napa of the Cape. Many top estates, esp for reds, tucked into mountain valleys and foothills; extensive wine routes and increasing number of fine restaurants.

Stellenzicht V'yds St'bosch r w ★★→★★★ DISTELL co-owned winery and v'yds; excellent, sturdy Syrah, v.gd barrelled Sem Reserve; also vinifies stand-alone Hill & Dale easy-drinkers.

Swartland Undulating warm-climate district in COASTAL region; 12,000 ha, mainly shy-bearing, unirrigated bush vines producing concentrated, hearty wines. AA Badenhorst/Secateurs, Allesverloren, DeanDavid, Kloovenburg, Lammershoek, Mullineux, SADIE FAMILY, SPICE ROUTE.

Thandi Wines St'bosch r w ★→★★★ Newly stand-alone black-empowerment venture providing shareholding/land ownership for over 240 farm-worker families. Best: CAB SAUV, PINOT N, CHARD.

Thelema Mtn V'yds St'bosch r w (br s/sw) ★★★→★★★★ Pioneer of South Africa's modern wine revival. Top labels: *Cab Sauv* (00' 03 04 05 06 07); The Mint Cab Sauv (05 06' 07); Merlot Reserve; Shiraz; Chard; Sauv Bl. Enlarged Sutherland range in ELGIN includes new Viognier.

Tokara St'bosch r (p) w (sw) ★★★ Showcase cellar and v'yds. Best: CAB SAUV-based red and SAUV BL/SEM white; elegant CHARD and SAUV BL, one each from young ELGIN vines. *Entry-level range Zondernaam* puts many top-tier labels to shame. Gd restaurant. Winemaker Miles Mossop's own eponymous label shows pedigree.

Tulbagh Inland district historically associated with white wine and bubbly, now also known for beefy reds, some sweeter styles and ORGANIC. 1,200 ha. KRONE, RIJK'S, SARONSBERG, Tulbagh Mtn V'yds, Waverley.

Twee Jonge Gezellen See KRONE.

Uva Mira V'yds St'bosch r w ★★→★★★ Lofty Helderberg sites yielding v.gd CHARD, Bordeaux/SHIRAZ Red Blend, Syrah and SAUV BL.

Veenwouden Private Cellar Paarl r (w) ★★→★★★ Range recently revamped but MERLOT, Bordeaux-style red Classic and CHARD remain first choices.

Vergelegen Somerset West r w (sw) ★★→★★★★ To many, still the top South African winery. A great mansion, immaculate v'yds and wines, serially awarded cellar door. Flagship is powerful, luxury-priced "V" (01' 03 04 05 06) (single-v'yd CAB SAUV); Bordeaux blend Vergelegen red is lower-keyed but still sumptuous. "White" is *minerally, oak-fermented* SEM *blend*.

Vilafonté Paarl r ★★★ California's Zelma Long (ex-Simi) and Phil Freese (ex-Mondavi viticulturalist) partnering WARWICK's Mike Ratcliffe. Two acclaimed Bordeaux blends: firmly structured Series C, earlier accessible Series M.

Villiera Wines St'bosch r w sp (br sw) ★★→★★★ Grier family v'yds and winery with excellent quality/value range. Cream of crop: Bordeaux red Monro; Bush Vine SAUV BL; Traditional CHENIN BL; five MCC bubblies (inc sulphur-free Brut Natural). Boutique-scale Domaine Grier near Perpignan.

Vriesenhof V'yds St'bosch r w (br) ★★→★★★ Three ranges, vinified by veteran Jan Coetzee; best are Bordeaux blends Kallista and Talana Hill Royale, PINOTAGE-based Enthopio.

Walker Bay Small (800 ha), fast-developing and highly reputed district, with sub-appellations HEMEL-EN-AARDE, Bot River and Sunday's Glen. PINOT N, SHIRAZ,

CHARD and SAUV BL are standouts; some top producers: ATARAXIA, BEAUMONT, BOUCHARD FINLAYSON, Creation, HAMILTON RUSSELL, Hermanuspietersfontein, La Vierge, Luddite, RAKA, Springfontein.

Ward Geographically the smallest of the four main WINE OF ORIGIN demarcations (largest is Geographical Unit, followed by Region and District).

Warwick Estate St'bosch r w ★★→★★★ Steered by dynamic Ratcliffe family (scion Mike also partner VILAFONTÉ). Fine Bordeaux reds *Trilogy (aka Estate Reserve)* and The First Lady; PINOTAGE blend Three Cape Ladies; new Syrah.

Waterford Estate St'bosch r (p) w (sw sp) ★★→★★★ Outstanding v'yds and visitor-friendly hewn-stone cellar. SHIRAZ (01 02' 03 04 05 06 07) is Cape classic; minerally CAB SAUV (01 02 03' 04 05 06) and CHARD. Superb CAB SAUV-based flagship, The Jem, among South Africa's priciest wines.

Weltevrede Estate Robertson r w (br sw sp) ★★→★★★ Well-crafted CHARD, SAUV BL and Syrah emphasizing diverse soils. Expanded Philip Jonker Brut MCC range.

Wine of Origin South Africa's "AC" but without French crop yield, etc. restrictions. Certifies vintage, variety, area of origin. See also WARD.

The Winery of Good Hope St'bosch r w (sw) ★★→★★★ Australian-French-South African joint venture. Flagship range is Radford Dale with promising new Freedom PINOT N. First-rate CAB SAUV and CHENIN BL in Vinum and Land of Hope ranges.

Zorgvliet Wines St'bosch r (p) w ★★→★★★ Vinous arm of lifestyle group Zorgvliet Portfolio. 20+ labels in three ranges, topped by pricey Bordeaux red Richelle.

The reinvention of
Spain

Making waves: architect Santiago Calatrava's winery for Isios, in Rioja

This is the new Spain. It has wineries that don't look much like buildings, never mind like normal wineries. It has food that bears no relationship to the dishes on which most of us dine nightly. It has grape varieties so old and so nearly extinct that nurseries have been propagating them from perhaps a couple of surviving plants – and one so new that it has been propagated from a single freak branch.

The vinous Spain of today is a very different place to the vinous Spain of even 20 years ago. For some while now it has been common to describe Spain as reinventing itself, and the description sometimes involved more aspiration than reality. But now it's fact. In Rioja, the most traditional of Spanish regions, where even the new-wave wines were not always quite as shockingly modern as they were touted, a middle way has emerged that confidently blends tradition with modernity in a style that is thoroughly Riojan. Terroir is the focus of every winemaker's attention, and white wines, in a country that never really took them seriously, are suddenly not just serious international contenders, but serious contenders with a properly Spanish slant.

Spain's learning curve, on the journey from tradition to a brand-new identity, has taken it down the odd tangent – overoaking, overextraction – but these are all part of the process. The Spanish wines that are emerging now show increasing deftness and sleekness, but personality, too: they are not being submerged in a global rent-a-style of ripeness and alcohol. For consumers, it's a whole new country.

Tempranillo
Spain's secret weapon

Tempranillo is the great red grape of Spain. It is grown almost everywhere in the country, and makes every conceivable quality, from the lightest of jug wines to the most complex of cellar-worthy offerings. Tempranillo is one of the things that makes Spanish wine different from all others (though other countries, inevitably, are experimenting with it), and Spain is probably where it first appeared.

How do we know this? Well, one gauge of the antiquity of a vine is the number of clones to be found in its birthplace. In Spain, 552 different clones of Tempranillo have been counted; that represents a good few hundred years of chance mutation. And it is probably Spain, and probably Rioja, where it originated, spreading from there to anywhere needing a grape that can deal with heat and drought.

Tempranillo, in fact, can deal with most things and still produce liquid that is recognizably wine. But if you want good Tempranillo you have to be fussy. In particular, you have to keep the yields down: the problem with Rioja, in the 1970s and 1980s, was that it got lazy about yields and started producing weak, pallid wines that could not stand up to the long oak-ageing that was traditional. Cut the yields and you get flavour, colour and vigour.

If you want more than that – if you want complexity, aroma, the fascination of fine wine – then you must look to climate. Where do Spain's most elegant, complex Tempranillos come from?

A grape that is always recognizably itself...

From the upland vineyards of Rioja, where the climate is coolest. Or from the north-facing vineyards of Vega Sicilia in Ribera del Duero. The warmer the climate, the chunkier Tempranillo will tend to be. Over in Toro, where it's hotter again, the wines can be very chunky indeed, and some winemakers resort to frightening amounts of new oak to curb the rustic tannins. They're gradually feeling their way towards more balanced wines, but it's a challenge.

However, it's not only climate that accounts for Tempranillo's protean nature. Soil plays its part – and Spain has very varied soils. Ribera del Duero alone has 31 distinct soil types, and these detailed differences are a godsend to anyone with the energy to exploit them.

What we should beware of, however, is the old chestnut that there are different clones of Tempranillo in different regions, and that it is this that gives each wine its character. This is tosh. Tempranillo has many local names – Tinta de Toro, Tinto Fino, Cencibel, Ull de Llebre, Ojo de Liebra, Tinta del País, Tinto Madrid and Tinto de la Rioja. But instead of having just one special clone, Toro has at least half a dozen. The "unique" Tinto Fino of Ribera del Duero is usually ten or 12 commercial clones, mostly obtained from nurseries in Rioja. None is particularly local. The clonal differences within each region are likely to be greater than the differences between regions. Tempranillo is adaptable: take the same clone, plant it in different places, and it will adapt differently. The truth is, as so often happens, far more interesting and subtle than the myth.

...yet adapts to different places

Whites
The next big thing

The Spanish have never really rated white wine. Wine, to be considered real wine, proper wine, had to be red. Spain always had plenty of white vines – more of the dull Airén grape than anywhere else in the world, not that anyone else was competing – but much of it got blended with a dash of something opaquely black to make a cheap bar drink. If you wanted decent white you headed for sherry, or for white Rioja (which too often veered between oaky and insipid), or, more recently, for aromatic Albariño or Rueda.

And now? Now white wines are the most fashionable thing around. Ancient white vines are being rediscovered and propagated; Spain is discovering that, after all, she has a talent for whites of flavour and depth. The region of Valdeorras in the northwest has shot to fame with Godello, a grape which, thanks to the region's slate and granite soils, makes wines of richness and character: think lime cordial, herbs and apricots. In Priorat, down in Catalunya, Terra Alta and Montsant, Garnacha Blanca (normally a rather dull, workaday grape) responds well to the warm, dry conditions and is being bottled on its own; and the exotic, apricot-scented Albariño, now being planted on poorer soils, has more complexity and is starting to live up to its hype.

Old varieties? How about Albillo, unctuous and minerally on granite soils; exotic Albarín from Tierra de León, and acidic, mineral Hondarribi Zuri from the Basque country? Majorca has fleshy Prensal Blanc, and there is even Tempranillo Blanca, propagated from a single branch of red Tempranillo that happened to mutate to white. Some of these wines are only just beginning to appear. But in five years' time we'll all be drinking them.

All that's missing is a glass of chilled white

Cult wines
Role models or fashion victims?

What does the phrase "cult wine" mean to you? Are they wines you would seize from a sinking ship and take to your desert island? Or, if you found a stash of them and nothing else on said desert island, would you prefer to abandon yourself to the sharks? They tend to be divisive because they are extreme. They have the reputation of being enormously rich, big and oaky, and there can be an element of truth in this. They also have the reputation of being very expensive and available in tiny quantities, and there's usually quite a lot of truth in this. But cult status is really about attention to detail: taking the most fastidious care in both vineyard and winery, and being content with nothing but the very best. That may well result in wines that are lush, concentrated and opulent beyond everyday needs; and they are made by winemakers who seek out exceptional but unknown terroirs and lavish all their talent on them. They are the pioneers of wine, leading whole regions out of mediocrity.

Take Toro, for example. It's a region of immense potential, with a clutch of cult wines: Termanthia, Campo Eliseo, Gran Elias Mora, San Román. Whether or not you can afford to drink them, or want to, they are showing how to master the rough, rustic tannins of the region and produce something (almost) elegant. Priorat is another region for cult-wine hunting, with Finca Dofí, Clos Erasmus, Clos Mogador, Clos de l'Obac; nobody had heard of Priorat until these wines came along. Bierzo, too, with Villa de Corullón: Bierzo is one of the newest regions to hit the headlines, because winemakers are now taking it seriously. Ribera del Duero came to prominence the same way, with such wines as Pingus. One could go on and on.

It's easy to caricature such wines; they do tend to be on the weighty side. But are they in fact caricatures? It's true that they tend to be so massive that when it comes to choosing something to drink, one might well go a notch or two lower and choose a lesser wine from the same stable: same skill, less challenge. But wine needs extremes if it is to advance. These wines show what Spain is capable of, and they challenge everyone else to do better – at every level.

Spain is fortunate in having such a wealth of amazing but underexploited land that winemakers can search until they find something remarkable. Of course, not all will stand the test of time: some will disappear, some will become classics. In the meantime Spain has some of the most imaginative winemakers of their generation tramping over its hills, examining its soil and measuring its rainfall. For us as wine lovers, it's all gain.

From the roots up

The rise and rise of terroir

It is a scientifically proven fact that winemakers, as infants, do not utter the word "mama" as their first word. What they say is "fruit". Soon after that comes the phrase "ripe tannins". And then, as they get older and more experienced, they attempt something much more difficult: they say "ter – terr – terroir!" And then they've got a task on their hands. Because to make wines that have oodles of fruit and ripe tannins is relatively easy; making wines that reflect their terroir, because such wines are almost impossible to define (though less difficult to recognise), is trickier.

First of all, what *is* terroir? The usual definition is that it comprises the soil, climate, and exposure to the sun that makes each vineyard different. It's a contentious subject because it's difficult to define and even more difficult to prove: but winemakers love it.

Now Spain is focusing on terroir; and suddenly the country is benefiting from its years in the doldrums – years when only a handful of regions made fine wines, and the rest made wines for local consumption or blending. It has old vines, which nobody bothered to replace because it probably wasn't worthwhile: a third of the vines in Toro are over 80 years old. It's the most mountainous country in Europe, which means steep slopes and rocky soils – both potentially good for quality. It has a climate of hot summers and cold winters, and often of hot days and cold nights. (Again, this is good.) It also has a wealth of indigenous

Vineyards in Priorat, which has some of the most distinctive terroir in Spain

vines, which were almost submerged under a flood of Tempranillo and Garnacha. Add some adventurous winemakers and you have a very interesting mix indeed.

It's in the newer regions that terroir is really catching people's imaginations. Bierzo has hillsides of clay or slate so steep that only a horse can work them. Winemaker Amancio Fernández is demonstrating the effect of each type on the Mencía grape. (There's more silkiness from clay, apparently.)

Bierzo is a perfect spot for the terroir-obsessed winemaker: old vines are found in a patchwork of tiny plots, all of them different. Ribera Sacra, on the banks of the Duero, has slate terraces planted by the Romans – and by medieval Cistercian monks, who generally had an eye for a good vineyard site. In Arribes del Duero there are high slopes and terraces, with alluvial fans of granite and slate soil. On the other side of the country, Priorat and its subzone Montsant have steep slopes of shallow *licorella* soil, and a harsh climate that produces rugged, concentrated wines.

These days Spaniards differentiate between two styles of wine: there are *vinos de autor*, or winemaker wines, and *vinos de terroir*. The latter require the winemaker to step back and let the terroir speak (assuming it has anything to say: not all terroirs do). And letting the terroir speak instead of you is another big step to take.

Modernity or tradition
The battle for Spain's tastebuds

Surely Spain has, on every gastronomic count, opted for modernity? This is the country of El Bulli and food reinvented to the point where it is unrecognizable, where intense flavours have unexpected textures and temperatures, like friable, flaky, freeze-dried pineapple chips, or crunchy beetroot "coral" with beet juice, or baby cuttlefish with pesto "ravioli" that burst in the mouth.

But it is also a country that treasures its traditions, where *jamón Ibérico* is properly valued and where local dishes and seasonal produce – the vegetable stews of Rioja, the seafood of the coast – are neither submerged in an international tide of burgers and weak coffee, nor shipped off to some other, more appreciative nation. In spite of decades of mass tourism, Spanish food away from the *costas* has retained its soul.

Look at its wines, and the same pattern emerges. Wine quality was in danger some decades ago, as overproduction and the desire for vast quantities of cheap and cheerful plonk threatened the integrity of great names like Rioja and sherry. Spain has had its share of crises, and the journey out of them has been neither even nor smooth. Its winemakers have sometimes regarded new oak and lots of extraction as a panacea; its consumers have sometimes fallen for the lure of muscle and power over subtlety and balance. But these are phases: they're a sort of adolescence that winemakers must go through. Consumers, too. But now the world is moving away from massive oaking, and Spain is moving with us.

Not that bodybuilder wines were ever ubiquitous in Spain. Rioja is the most traditional of Spanish table wine regions; and Rioja faced a problem no other region had. Consumers brought up on faded, ultra-mature reds released only after long ageing in old barrels liked that taste. A younger generation, though, liked darker, more fruit-driven wines. How to reconcile the two? And how to get younger drinkers on board without antagonizing the older ones? The answer was ingenious. Traditional Rioja still exists, but has been updated slowly and subtly. Barrels are renewed more often and wines are bottled earlier, so that aficionados of the old style have been weaned unnoticeably onto slightly more fruit and slightly more vigour. And at the same time, new ranges have been introduced, of new-wave wines full of dark fruit and lush tannins. Even Vega Sicilia, the most Riojan of Ribera del Dueros, is not the same as it was – though still clearly with the same sense of place.

Elsewhere, where tradition weighs less heavily, international grape varieties have made inroads (they're even permitted in Rioja now). But that is balanced by a new focus on almost extinct varieties being coaxed back to commercial life: Maturana Tinta, Maturana Parda and Maturano; Monastel (not the same as Monastrell) and white Turrentés (not the same as Torrontés). There is Prieto Picuda, Bobal, Sumoll, Paraleta, Callet, Trepat and Moristel; Juan García, Rufete and Bruñal. Some of these are already being bottled as varietals; others are useful blending grapes. Modernity of the most confident sort often involves a return to tradition.

Spanish food has kept its identity; Spanish wines are rediscovering theirs

Sherry

Teaching old dogs old tricks

Things don't change much in the sherry country. In the lands between and around Jerez, Puerto de Santa María and Sanlúcar, right down in the south of Spain, sherry goes on being made and aged as it has been for a long time. Go in search of news stories and you'll be faced instead by the silence of bodegas in which sherry butts, darkened and warped by time, snooze their way to maturity. You breathe essence of sherry in these bodegas, pungent and pure. You did 100 years ago, and you do today. The smell, and the sight, don't change. So, what makes sherry newsworthy? Simply that we are coming, at last, to appreciate the astonishing stocks of old wines in the region. And the producers are raiding their bodegas to reveal to us new facets of these old wines. Everything new in sherry that is worth having is old.

VOS or VORS (see p. 186) are the letters to look for on the label; these are the designations for exceptionally old wines of very high quality. Or there's the newer idea of vintage sherry. Lustau started its experiments with these in 1985, and leaves selected butts to age for 15–18 years before bottling. It still isn't certain about how such wines will age after that – sherry is not a wine that can be hurried – or, in this case, predicted. Fine sherry has a habit of defying expectations. Old dry Oloroso might be seen as

Ageing gracefully: barrels in Osborne's bodega in Puerta de Santa María

361
Solera 2ª B
Bajamar
1 DE 1

winter wine, complex and comforting, but Hidalgo does a bone-dry 1986 Oloroso which, if you can find it, is one of the most austere, and finest, wines you will ever drink. Think of Chaucer's description of sack as "searching"; this wine is as searching and accurate as a laser.

Such wines are not for everyday drinking, but good fino or manzanilla is very much so, and amazingly cheap for the quality. These are as young as fine sherry gets, which means they're released at about the same age that New World Sauvignon Blanc lies down and dies. Other wines change faster than sherry because their life cycle is so brief in comparison: if you want to produce a new style of sherry next year, you should have started some years ago; maybe a generation ago.

But while it can take a generation to produce a great sherry, it can take just a moment to ruin one. Put some inferior wine into a solera and you taste the effects for years after. To make great sherry takes rigorous attention to quality, even when nothing appears to be happening; the annual dramas that punctuate the year of the table wine producer – the price hikes, the vintages of the century – just don't happen in sherry. There's nothing to write about, really. Unless you happen to be interested in some of the most complex and challenging wines in the world.

Key people

Who's who in the new Spain

PETER SISSECK

Why would you call a wine Pingus? Simple: it was winemaker
Peter Sisseck's childhood nickname. Sisseck is Danish by birth,
and arrived in Ribera del Duero in 1990. In due course he
bought some vineyards for himself – parcels of very old vines
on great terroir – called the property Dominio de Pingus and
in 1995 made his first vintage. He was a star almost instantly,
and the wine, now less overtly oaky than it was (some of the
wine used to get 200% new oak) but still super-concentrated,
has a global following. He says he didn't set out to be *garagiste*,
but simply wanted to make the best wine possible; quantities
are tiny, however, and prices high.

CARLOS FALCO

The Marqués de Griñon was one of the first to unleash
modern winemaking technology on Spain, and he did it on
land given to an ancestor by Don Pedro I after the siege of
Toledo. The wines from Dominio de Valdepusa, near Toledo,
have a DO created specially for them and are mostly from
non-Spanish vines like Cabernet, Syrah and Petit Verdot, but
taste utterly Spanish. Water stress in the vineyards is judged
by measuring the daily expansion and contraction of the vine
trunks: the technique was developed by Boeing for measuring
metal fatigue. Innovatory and perfectionist, his importance
has been in producing very good wine on a reasonably large
scale: more challenging, in many ways, than producing a tiny
amount of something wildly expensive.

MIGUEL TORRES

Miguel Torres, heir to the Torres company in Penedès, started
his career in his autocratic father's shadow and made his mark
by researching old and forgotten vine varieties. He started
making wine in Chile in 1979, but it is his achievement in
keeping his Spanish wines at the top of the quality tree for over

30 years, and tasting better than ever, that earns him a place
in any list of great Spanish wine names. His father made
Torres famous; Miguel has made it an institution. Torres
wines from Priorat, Ribera del Duero and Rioja have been
added to the range, and the next generation is already working
in the company.

RENÉ BARBIER
René Barbier was a pioneer of Priorat, someone who (as far
back as 1979) saw potential in this dry, hot, mountainous
region with its *licorella* schist soil. He planted vines at Clos
Mogador in Gratallops, and in the early days shared facilities
with other like-minded winemakers: Carlos Pastrana of Clos
de l'Obac, José Luis Pérez Verdú of Clos Martinet and, later,
Dafné Glorian of Clos Erasmus and Alvaro Palacios of Clos
Dofí. Barbier's aim has always been to express the essence of
the Priorat terroir through wines of power and muscle, ultra-
richness and weight: cult wines by any standards.

ALEJANDRO FERNÁNDEZ
The creator of Pesquera, Alejandro Fernández started the
resurgence of Ribera del Duero. He established himself there
in 1972, and it was a bottle of 1982 Pesquera that caused Robert
Parker to label it the Château Pétrus of Spain. That might or
might not have been an apt comparison, but it did bring the
wine and the region to worldwide attention. Ribera del Duero
became DO in 1982, and it was immediately clear to everybody
that there was now an alternative to the (then somewhat
unreliable) Vega Sicilia – what's more, an alternative in the
modern idiom that showed the way forward for the region.

JUAN CARLOS SANCHA
He could be known as Señor Obscure Grape Variety – or
alternatively, Señor Organic. Bodegas Viña Ijalba in Rioja,

A little learning...

A few technical words

The jargon of laboratory analysis is often seen on back-labels. It creeps menacingly into newspapers and magazines. What does it mean? This hard-edged wine-talk, unsympathetic as it is to most lovers of wine, is very briefly explained below.

Alcohol content (mainly ethyl alcohol) is expressed in per cent by volume of the total liquid. (Also known as "degrees".) Table wines are usually between 12.5° and 14.5°, though up to 16° is increasingly seen.

Acidity is both fixed and volatile. Fixed acidity consists principally of tartaric, malic and citric acids, all found in the grape, and lactic and succinic acids, produced during fermentation. Volatile acidity consists mainly of acetic acid, which is rapidly formed by bacteria in the presence of oxygen. A small amount of volatile acidity is inevitable and even attractive. With a larger amount the wine becomes "pricked"– to use the Shakespearian term. It turns to vinegar. Acidity may be natural, in warm regions it may also be added.

Total acidity is fixed and volatile acidity combined. As a rule of thumb, for a well-balanced wine it should be in the region of one gram per thousand for each 10° Oechsle (see above).

Barriques Vital to modern wine, either in ageing and/or for fermenting in barrels (the newer the barrel the stronger the influence) or from the addition of oak chips or – at worst – oak essence. Newcomers to wine can easily be beguiled by the vanilla-like scent and flavour into thinking they have bought something luxurious rather than something cosmetically flavoured. But barrels are expensive; real ones are only used for wines with the inherent quality to benefit long-term. French oak is classic and most expensive. American oak has a strong vanilla flavour.

Malolactic fermentation is often referred to as a secondary fermentation, and can occur naturally or be induced. The process involves converting tart malic acid into softer lactic acid. Unrelated to alcoholic fermentation, the "malo" can add complexity and flavour to both red and white wines. In hotter climates where natural acidity may be low canny operators avoid it.

Micro-oxygenation is a widely used technique that allows the wine controlled contact with oxygen during maturation. This mimics the effect of barrel-ageing, reduces the need for racking, and helps to stabilize the wine.

pH is a measure of the strength of the acidity: the lower the figure the more acid. Wine usually ranges from pH 2.8 to 3.8. High pH can be a problem in hot climates. Lower pH gives better colour, helps stop bacterial spoilage and allows more of the SO_2 to be free and active as a preservative.

Residual sugar is that left after fermentation has finished or been stopped, measured in grams per litre. A dry wine has virtually none.

Sulphur dioxide (SO_2) is added to prevent oxidation and other accidents in winemaking. Some of it combines with sugars etc and is "bound". Only the "free" SO_2 is effective as a preservative. Total SO_2 is controlled by law according to the level of residual sugar: the more sugar, the more SO_2 is needed.

Tannins are the focus of attention for red-winemakers intent on producing softer, more approachable wines. Later picking, and picking by tannin ripeness rather than sugar levels gives riper, silkier tannins.

Toast refers to the burning of the inside of the barrel. "High toast" gives the wine caramel-like flavours.